Lecture Notes in Computer Science 9144

Commenced Publication in 1973
Founding and Former Series Editors:
Gerhard Goos, Juris Hartmanis, and Jan van Leeuwen

More information about this series at http://www.springer.com/series/7410

Ernest Foo · Douglas Stebila (Eds.)

Information Security and Privacy

20th Australasian Conference, ACISP 2015
Brisbane, QLD, Australia, June 29 – July 1, 2015
Proceedings

 Springer

Editors
Ernest Foo
Queensland University of Technology
Brisbane, QLD
Australia

Douglas Stebila
Queensland University of Technology
Brisbane, QLD
Australia

ISSN 0302-9743   ISSN 1611-3349 (electronic)
Lecture Notes in Computer Science
ISBN 978-3-319-19961-0   ISBN 978-3-319-19962-7 (eBook)
DOI 10.1007/978-3-319-19962-7

Library of Congress Control Number: 2015940421

LNCS Sublibrary: SL4 – Security and Cryptology

Printed on acid-free paper

Springer International Publishing AG Switzerland is part of Springer Science+Business Media (www.springer.com)

Preface

This volume contains the papers presented at ACISP 2015: the 20th Australasian Conference on Information Security and Privacy held from June 29 to July 1, 2015, in Brisbane, Australia. The conference was hosted by the Institute for Future Environments at the Queensland University of Technology, who provided the wonderful facilities and material support. The local Organizing Committee was led by the ACISP 2015 general chair, Josef Pieprzyk, with administration led by Cindy Mayes. We appreciate the support of Ed Dawson and Seyit Camtepe in the conference organization. We made use of the excellent EasyChair submission and reviewing software.

There were 112 submissions. Each submission was allocated to three Program Committee members and each paper received on average 2.9 reviews. The committee decided to accept 28 papers. Accepted papers came from 13 countries with the largest proportions coming from Australia (6), Japan (6), India (5), China (4), and Germany (2). Other authors are from Belgium, Canada, France, Luxembourg, The Netherlands, New Zealand, Singapore, and the USA. We would like to extend our sincere thanks to all authors who submitted papers to ACISP 2015.

The program also included three excellent and informative invited talks. One of these was from an eminent cryptography researcher and the other two were from highly experienced security practitioners: Professor Colin Boyd, from the Norwegian University of Science and Technology (NTNU); Jason Smith, from CERT Australia; and Simon Pope, from the Microsoft Security Response Center.

We would like to thank the team of experts who made up the Program Committee. Their names are listed overleaf. The Program Committee was assisted by an even larger team of people who reviewed papers in their area of expertise. The list of these reviewers is also included. Finally, we would like to thank Springer for their help with the production of these conference proceedings and their commitment to the ACISP conference for the last 20 years. We look forward to many more years of ACISP.

June 2015

Ernest Foo
Douglas Stebila

Organization

Program Committee

Joonsang Baek	Khalifa University of Science, Technology and Research, UAE
Paulo Barreto	University of São Paulo, Brazil
Alex Biryukov	University of Luxembourg, Luxembourg
Colin Boyd	Norwegian University of Science and Technology (NTNU), Norway
Xavier Boyen	Queensland University of Technology, Australia
Jean Camp	Indiana University, USA
Kim-Kwang Raymond Choo	University of South Australia, Australia
K.P. Chow	University of Hong Kong, SAR China
Craig Costello	Microsoft Research
Cas Cremers	University of Oxford, UK
Marc Fischlin	Technical University of Darmstadt, Germany
Ernest Foo	Queensland University of Technology, Australia
Praveen Gauravaram	Queensland University of Technology, Australia
Joanne L. Hall	Queensland University of Technology, Australia
Jiankun Hu	University of New South Wales at ADFA, Australia
Tancrède Lepoint	CryptoExperts
Sachin Lodha	Tata Consultancy Services
Mark Manulis	University of Surrey, UK
Atsuko Miyaji	Japan Advanced Institute of Science and Technology, Japan
Yi Mu	University of Wollongong, Australia
C. Pandu Rangan	Indian Institute of Technology, Madras, India
Udaya Parampalli	University of Melbourne, Australia
Rei Safavi-Naini	University of Calgary, Canada
Palash Sarkar	Indian Statistical Institute, India
Jennifer Seberry	University of Wollongong, Australia
Leonie Simpson	Queensland University of Technology, Australia
Douglas Stebila	Queensland University of Technology, Australia
Suriadi Suriadi	Massey University, New Zealand
Willy Susilo	University of Wollongong, Australia
Tsuyoshi Takagi	Kyushu University, Japan
Berkant Ustaoglu	NTT Information Sharing Platform Laboratories
Vijay Varadharajan	Macquarie University, Australia
Kan Yasuda	NTT Secure Platform Laboratories
Jianying Zhou	Institute for Infocomm Research, Singapore

Additional Reviewers

Abdelraheem, Mohamed
Ahmed
Aditya, Riza
Alkhzaimi, Hoda
Aoki, Kazumaro
Bagheri, Nasour
Baignères, Thomas
Bouzefrane, Samia
Bringer, Julien
Chalamala, Srinivas
Chen, Jiageng
Cheng, Shu
D'Orazio, Christian
Damavandinejadmonfared,
Sepehr
Dawson, Ed
Delerablée, Cécile
Derbez, Patrick
Deva Selvi, Sharmila
Dilruba, Raushan
Dong, Xinshu
Dong, Zheng
Dowling, Benjamin
Dunkelman, Orr
Emmadi, Nitesh
Fan, Jia
Fehr, Victoria
Futa, Yuichi
Gagliardoni, Tommaso
Garratt, Luke
Guo, Fuchun

Han, Jinguang
Henricksen, Matt
Hitchens, Michael
Hou, Shuhui
Huang, Kun
Huang, Qiong
Jhawar, Mahavir Jhawar
Jindal, Arun
Kamara, Seny
Karande, Shirish
Khovratovich, Dmitry
Kojima, Tetsuya
Kumari, Rashmi
Laarhoven, Thijs
Liang, Kaitai
Lin, Fuchun
Liu, Joseph
Liu, Zhenhua
Longa, Patrick
Lopez-Alt, Adriana
Luykx, Atul
Manjunath, R. Sumesh
Marson, Giorgia Azzurra
Min, Byungho
Mittelbach, Arno
Mouha, Nick
Naehrig, Michael
Narumanchi, Harika
Neves, Samuel
Nikova, Svetla
Ohtake, Go

Omote, Kazumasa
Perrin, Léo Paul
Poettering, Bertram
Pustogarov, Ivan
Radke, Kenneth
Roy, Sujoy Sinha
Sadeghian, Saeed
Sasaki, Yu
Shull, Adam
Simplicio Jr, Marcos
Soltani Panah, Arezou
Su, Chunhua
Syed, Habeeb
Tanaka, Satoru
Teske-Wilson, Edlyn
Todo, Yosuke
Tupakula, Uday
Tupsamudre, Harshal
Udovenko, Aleksei
Velichkov, Vesselin
Wang, Pengwei
Wu, Wei
Xu, Jia
Xu, Rui
Yang, Guomin
Yasuda, Masaya
Yasuda, Takanori
Zhang, Hui
Zhang, Mingwu
Zhou, Lan

Contents

Privacy Protocols

Symmetric Constructions

Homomorphic Encryption and Obfuscation

Symmetric Cryptanalysis

Weak-Key and Related-Key Analysis of Hash-Counter-Hash Tweakable Enciphering Schemes

Zhelei Sun[1,2,3], Peng Wang[1,2(✉)], and Liting Zhang[4]

[1] State Key Laboratory of Information Security, Institute of Information Engineering, Chinese Academy of Sciences, Beijing 100093, China
{zhlsun,wp}@is.ac.cn
[2] Data Assurance and Communication Security Research Center, Chinese Academy of Sciences, Beijing 100093, China
[3] University of Chinese Academy of Sciences, Beijing, China
[4] Institute of Software, Chinese Academy of Sciences, Beijing, People's Republic of China
zhangliting@is.iscas.ac.cn

Abstract. We analyze three tweakable enciphering schemes (TES) XCB, HCTR and HCH, which all consist of polynomial evaluation hash function as their first and third layers and CTR mode in the middle. The weak keys of polynomial evaluation hash in message authentication code and authenticated encryption have been thoroughly analyzed, but have never applied in TES. We point out that XCB, HCTR and HCH (and two variations of HCH: HCHp and HCHfp) can not resist distinguishing attack, key-recovery attack and plaintext-recovery attack once the weak key is recognized. We also analyze the security of related-key attacks against these schemes, showing that HCTR, HCHp and HCHfp suffer related-key attack and XCB and HCH can resist related-key attack under the assumption that the underlying block cipher resists related-key attack.

Keywords: Universal hash function · Tweakable enciphering scheme · Weak keys · Related-key attack

1 Introduction

XCB [1], HCTR [2] and HCH [3] are three tweakable enciphering schemes (TES) following the hash-counter-hash approach. Tweakable enciphering schemes are generalized block ciphers with extra input of tweaks and more variable block lengths. It takes as input a key K, a tweak (or associated data) T and a plaintext P, and outputs a ciphertext C. We write it as

$$\widetilde{E}_K^T(P) = C,$$

where the lengths of P and C are the same and for any K and T the transformation $\widetilde{E}_K^T(\cdot)$ is a permutation. TES is specially suitable for disk sector encryption

© Springer International Publishing Switzerland 2015
E. Foo and D. Stebila (Eds.): ACISP 2015, LNCS 9144, pp. 3–19, 2015.
DOI: 10.1007/978-3-319-19962-7_1

(where the sector number can be regarded as the "tweak") [4] and other length-preserving encryptions. TES can also be turned into an authenticated encryption scheme like AEZ [5], Deoxys, Joltik, and KIASU proposed in CAESAR [6]. AEZ is built on EME [7], which is a TES constructed by two layers of ECB encryption and a mix layer in between. Deoxys, Joltik, and KIASU are direct TES designs which can resist related-key attack and have variable size key and tweak. In addition to this XCB has been included in the IEEE Security in Storage Working Group for wide-block encryption for shared storage media [4]. HCTR is the most efficient scheme in hardware among existing TESes so far [8].

The constructions of XCB, HCTR and HCH all consist of universal hash function as their first and third layer and CTR mode in the middle. The universal hash function [9] is a polynomial in which the variables are the key of the function and the coefficients are made up of message blocks such as $h_H(M) = \sum M_i H^i$ where H is the key and M_i is a message block. This kind of universal hash function is called polynomial evaluation hash in literature, which has been widely used to construct message authentication code (MAC) [10–12], authenticated encryption (AE), TES [1–3] and other cryptographic schemes. CTR uses the block cipher to generate the key stream used in the message encryption: $e_K(S_i)$, $i = 1, 2, \cdots$, where K is the key of block cipher and S_i is the number generated by a counter.

XCB is one of first constructions of the hash-counter-hash type. HCTR is constructed based on XCB with less block cipher invocations than XCB. HCH is similar to the structure of HCTR with a goal of obtaining a quadratic bound while maintaining the efficiency of HCTR, although HCTR later was proved to also have quadratic bound but not previous cubic bound [13]. There are two variations of HCH: HCHp and HCHfp. HCHp is designed to utilize pre-computation by using a separate hash key. HCHfp works for fixed length messages, which can also utilize pre-computation and further reduces one block cipher invocation. All three schemes are proved to be secure in the sense that they are indistinguishable from a family of independent random permutations labeled by tweaks if the underlying block cipher is a pseudorandom permutation (PRP).

WEAK-KEY. In recent years, a serial research focused on the weak keys of the polynomial evaluation hash function in MAC and AE, trying to find more classes of weak keys, which can be applied to forgery and key-recovery attacks once weak keys are detected. Handschuh et al. [14] pointed out that 0 is the weak key of the polynomial evaluation hash in MAC. Saarinen's work [15] showed other weak key classes for GHASH besides 0 and applied these weak keys in forgery attack against GCM. Then Gordon et al. promoted this work [16], analyzed the underlying algebraic structure of the polynomial evaluation hash, which provided a more general attack on GHASH and expanded the number of weak keys. Bo Zhu et al. [17] improved forgery attacks against MAC based on polynomial evaluation hash and put forward that all non-singleton subsets of keys are weak keys. We notice that the weak-key analysis has never been applied in TES.

RELATED-KEY. Related-key attacks were firstly introduced by Biham and Knudsen for block ciphers in [18,19], and they can be turned into key-recovery attacks [20] or distinguishing attacks [21], the security against related-key attack has become a basic and mandatory requirement for block ciphers. Bellare and Kohn [22] firstly gave a theoretical related-key security model for block ciphers, and Bhattacharyya and Roy presented related-key security analysis also applied to encryption schemes, MACs [23] and other cryptographic objects. TESes are generalized block ciphers, therefore it is natural to consider the related-key security of TES. But as far as know, few related-key analysis has been presented on TES.

In this paper, we analyze XCB, HCTR and HCH from the above two aspects. We show that XCB, HCTR and HCH suffer the trouble of weak keys of polynomial evaluation hash, which leads to distinguishing attack, key-recovery attack and plaintext-recovery attack once weak keys are detected. Meanwhile we show that XCB and HCH can resist related-key attack under the assumption that the underlying block cipher resists related-key attack; HCTR, HCHp and HCHfp cannot resist related-key attack, which turns into distinguishing attack with two queries.

The paper is organized as follows. Section 2 gives the notations throughout the paper, a brief description of universal hash function, the security of block cipher and TES, and weak keys in MAC and AE based on polynomial evaluation hash. Sections 4, 5 and 6 present the analyses of XCB, HCTR and HCH from the two aspects: related-key and weak-key respectively and section 6 concludes the full paper at last.

2 Preliminaries

2.1 Notations

Let $\{0,1\}^n$ denote the set of all strings of length n. Let $\{0,1\}^*$ be the set of all bit strings. For a string $X \in \{0,1\}^*$, $len(X)$ denotes the bit-length of string X. Let 0^w and 1^w denote strings of w zeros and w ones respectively, where w is a nonnegative integer. $|\mathcal{D}|$ means the number of members of set $\mathcal{D}$. If $X, Y \in \{0,1\}^*$, $X\|Y$ is their concatenation. For a finite set $\mathcal{D}$, if d is uniformly chosen from $\mathcal{D}$ we write $d \xleftarrow{\$} \mathcal{D}$. Throughout this paper the block cipher, and operations of finite field are done over blocks and the block length is fixed as w bits.

2.2 Universal Hash Function

Universal hash functions are widely used in the design of cryptographic schemes. Almost universal [9] and almost xor universal [24] hash functions are defined as follows.

Definition 1. $h : \mathcal{K} \times \mathcal{D} \to \mathcal{R}$ is ϵ-almost-universal if for all $M, M' \in \mathcal{D}$ and $M \neq M'$,

$$\Pr_{H \in \mathcal{K}}[h_H(M) = h_H(M')] \leq \epsilon.$$

Definition 2. $h : \mathcal{K} \times \mathcal{D} \to \mathcal{R}$ *is ϵ-almost-xor-universal if for all M, $M' \in \mathcal{D}$,
$M \neq M'$, $c \in \mathcal{R}$,*

$$\Pr_{H \in \mathcal{K}}[h_H(M) \oplus h_H(M') = c] \leq \epsilon.$$

Clearly, if h is ϵ-AXU, it is also ϵ-AU, for ϵ-AU is a special case of ϵ-AXU where
$c = 0$.

Polynomial Evaluation Hash. Polynomial evaluation hash is one of the
method to realize ϵ-AXU (or ϵ-AU) function, for $H \in \{0,1\}^n$, $M = M_1 \cdots M_m \in$
$\{0,1\}^{mn}$, $M_i \in \{0,1\}^n$, $1 \leq i \leq m$, we define,

$$h_H(M) = \sum_{i=1}^{m} M_i H^{i-1}.$$

Clearly, it is $(m-1)/2^n$-AU. $H \cdot h_H(M) = H \cdot \sum_{i=1}^{m} M_i H^{i-1} = \sum_{i=1}^{m} M_i H^i$ is
$m/2^n$-AXU.

2.3   Block Cipher and Tweakable Enciphering Scheme Security

We consider the pseudorandom permutation (PRP) [25] security of blook cipher
as the indistinguishability between it and an ideal "random permutation" π,
chosen randomly from the set of permutations over $\{0,1\}^w$,

$$\pi \xleftarrow{\$} \mathrm{Perm}(w),$$

under chosen plaintext attack (CPA). The strong pseudorandom permutation
(SPRP) security is similar with PRP except that the block cipher is under the
chosen ciphertext attack (CCA).

We can similarly utilize the above descriptions to define tweakable PRP
(TPRP) [26], strong tweakable TPRP (STPRP) security of tweakable enciphering scheme (TES) [27] as the indistinguishability between it and an "tweakable
random permutation" $\tilde{\pi}$ (a family of independent random permutations labeled
by the tweak T. For each T, we let $\tilde{\pi}^T \leftarrow \mathrm{Perm}(w)$, where $\tilde{\pi}^T$ is a randomly
chosen permutation labeled by T) under CPA and CCA respectively.

While considering the security under related-key attacks (RKA), the adversary can apply related-key transformations ϕ to change the key and observe the
output under the modified keys [22]. Here we only consider the transformation
that exclusive-or (xor) differences on key K (one of the most common way):
$\oplus_\Delta(K) = K \oplus \Delta$.

We consider the PRP secure against RKA (PRP-RKA) [22] and SPRP secure
against RKA (SPRP-RKA) of block cipher as the indistinguishability between
it on the target key as well as on some related-keys and a family of random
permutations labeled by the target key as well as on some related-keys under
CPA and CCA respectively. For each K, we let $\pi_K \leftarrow \mathrm{Perm}(w)$, where π_K is a
randomly chosen permutation labeled by K.

We consider the TPRP secure against RKA (TPRP-RKA) and STPRP secure against RKA (STPRP-RKA) of TES as the indistinguishability between it on the target key as well as on some related-keys and a family of tweakable random permutations labeled by the target key as well as on some related-keys under CPA and CCA respectively. For each tuple (T, K), we let $\widetilde{\pi}_K^T \leftarrow \text{Perm}(w)$ where $\widetilde{\pi}_K^T$ is a randomly chosen permutation labeled by (T, K).

More specifically, the advantage function of the adversary is defined as:

$$Adv_{Object}^{Type}(A) = \Pr[A^{Real} \Rightarrow 1] - \Pr[A^{Ideal} \Rightarrow 1],$$

where $Type$ is one of the above PRP, SPRP, TPRP, STPRP, PRP-RKA, SPRP-RKA, TPRP-RKA, or STPRP-RKA, $Object$ is the block cipher or TES, $Real$ is the real oracle and $Ideal$ is the ideal oracle. As to SPRP, STPRP, SPRP-RKA, STPRP-RKA, the objects and oracles are listed as following:

$Type$	$Object$	$Real$	$Ideal$
SPRP	E	$E_K(\cdot), E_K^{-1}(\cdot)$	$\pi(\cdot), \pi^{-1}(\cdot)$
STPRP	$\widetilde{E}$	$\widetilde{E}_K^{(\cdot)}(\cdot), \widetilde{E}_K^{-1(\cdot)}(\cdot)$	$\widetilde{\pi}^{(\cdot)}(\cdot), \widetilde{\pi}^{-1(\cdot)}(\cdot)$
SPRP-RKA	E	$E_{K\oplus(\cdot)}(\cdot), E_{K\oplus(\cdot)}^{-1}(\cdot)$	$\pi_{K\oplus(\cdot)}(\cdot), \pi_{K\oplus(\cdot)}^{-1}(\cdot)$
STPRP	$\widetilde{E}$	$\widetilde{E}_{K\oplus(\cdot)}^{(\cdot)}(\cdot), \widetilde{E}_{K\oplus(\cdot)}^{-1(\cdot)}(\cdot)$	$\widetilde{\pi}_{K\oplus(\cdot)}^{(\cdot)}(\cdot), \widetilde{\pi}_{K\oplus(\cdot)}^{-1(\cdot)}(\cdot)$

2.4   Weak Keys in MAC and AE Based on Polynomial Evaluation Hash

In recent years, a lot of works have been proposed to analyze the weak keys of polynomial evaluation hash in MAC and AE. How to find, detect and utilize the weak keys is a serial of problems in weak-key analysis.

The Definition of Weak Keys. In 2008, Handschuh and Preneel [14] gave the following definition of weak keys :

> a class of keys is called a weak key class if for the members of that class the algorithm behaves in an unexpected way and if it is easy to detect whether a particular unknown key belongs to this class. For a MAC algorithm, the unexpected behavior can be that the forgery probability for this key is substantially larger than average. Moreover, if a weak key class is of size C, one requires that identifying that a key belongs to this class requires testing fewer than C keys by exhaustive search and fewer than C verification queries.

According to this definition, a lot of work have been proposed which analyzed the security of MAC and AE based on polynomial evaluation hash, especially for GCM. Handschuh and Preneel regarded 0 as the only weak key for all polynomial-evaluation-hash based schemes. However, Markku-Juhani et al. [15] showed that there exist wider classes of weak keys besides 0 for GCM. Later,

Gordon Procter et al. expanded the number of weak keys and showed that almost every subset of the keyspace is a weak key class [16] in GCM. $\mathcal{D}$ is composed of GCM authentication keys, then

$\mathcal{D}$ is a weak key class for GCM, if $0 \in \mathcal{D}$ and $|\mathcal{D}| \geq 2$, or $|\mathcal{D}| \geq 3$.

Then Bo Zhu et al. [17] gave a further definition of weak keys which can be described as follows:

$\mathcal{D}$ is a weak key class for GCM, if $|\mathcal{D}| \geq 2$.

Utilize the Weak Keys to Analyze the Security of GCM. $\mathcal{D} = \{H_1, H_2, \cdots, H_r\}$ where H_i is chosen from $\{0, 1\}^w$ for $1 \leq i \leq r$, $r \geq 2$. According to the previous discussion [16,17], $\mathcal{D}$ is a weak key class for authentication key of GCM. Next we show how to analyze the security of GCM if the unknown authentication key H falls into $\mathcal{D} \cup 0$. Similar methods will be used in the following analyses. We construct a polynomial $q(x) = x \prod\limits_{i=1}^{r} (x \oplus H_i) = \sum\limits_{i=1}^{r+1} q_i x^i$, where q_i is the coefficient of x^i. Let $Q = q_1 \| q_2 \| \cdots \| q_{r+1}$. Assume $H \in \mathcal{D} \cup 0$ (or we say $q(x)$ is valid for H and $q(H) = 0$), then a successful forgery will occur, implying a collision of polynomial evaluation hash,

$$h_H(C) = h_H(C) \oplus q(H) = h_H(C \oplus Q),$$

where we xor coefficients of $q(x)$'s terms with C. The probability of a successful GCM forgery is directly related to the choice of D: $\frac{\#\text{roots of } q(x)}{2^w}$. Once we find a valid $q(x)$ for H, we say H is recognized as weak key. Furthermore we can utilize the valid $q(x)$ to make more forgery attacks and even recover H [16,17]. Meanwhile, we adopt the method in [16] to avoid the effect brought by modifying the length information when $q(x)$ has a high degree: if $q(H) = 0$, then $aq(H) = 0$ for any $a \in \{0, 1\}^w$, then

$$h_H(C) = h_H(C) \oplus aq(H) = h_H(C \oplus aQ),$$

where $aQ = aq_1 \| aq_2 \| \cdots$. So we can choose a differential between the original message and the forged message at the location of length information to avoid the effect brought by modifying the length information. Else, we set $q(x) = xq(x)$ to avoid modifying the length block. The two methods will be applied appropriately to analysis below by default.

3   Analysis of XCB

XCB is an STPRP under the assumption that the underlying block cipher is an SPRP [28].[1]

---

[1] Here we only discuss the initial version of XCB. The standardized version [28] is a little different from the initial one that there is only one single hash key. In addition to this, the inputs to the hash function and the plaintexts are arranged differently from the initial version. Even so, the analysis on the initial version applies to the standardized one.

3.1   Definition of XCB

XCB is comprised of a block cipher $\mathbf{e}$ ($\mathbf{d}$ is the inverse function of $\mathbf{e}$), a polynomial evaluation hash function $\mathbf{h}$, and a CTR function $\mathbf{c}$, where $\mathbf{c}$ is similar to the one presented in introduction. XCB drives five sub-keys $(K_0, K_1, K_2, K_3, K_4)$ from the master key by the encryption of five constants. Three of them (K_0, K_2, K_4) are used as the keys of the underlying block cipher, the rest two keys (K_1, K_3) are used as the keys of polynomial evaluation hash:

$$K_0 \leftarrow \mathbf{e}_K(0^w), K_1 \leftarrow \mathbf{e}_K(0^{w-1}\|1), K_2 \leftarrow \mathbf{e}_K(0^{w-2}\|1\|0),$$

$$K_3 \leftarrow \mathbf{e}_K(0^{w-2}\|1^2), K_4 \leftarrow \mathbf{e}_K(0^{w-3}\|1\|0^2).$$

Polynomial Evaluation Hash. $\mathbf{h}_H(A, C) : \{0,1\}^w \times \{0,1\}^m \times \{0,1\}^n \rightarrow \{0,1\}^w$, where $m = len(A) \in [w, 2^{39}]$, $n = len(C) \in [0, 2^{39}]$. $len(A) = w(p-1) + m_1$, $len(C) = w(q-1) + n_1$ for $1 \le m_1, n_1 \le w$. Partition A and C into $A_1\|A_2\|\cdots\|A_p$ and $C_1\|C_2\|\cdots\|C_q$ respectively, where $len(A_i) = w$ for $1 \le i \le p - 1$, $len(C_i) = w$ for $1 \le i \le q - 1$,

$$B_i = \begin{cases} A_i & \text{for } 1 \le i \le p-1, \\ A_i\|0^{w-m_1} & \text{for } i = p, \\ C_i & \text{for } p+1 \le i \le p+q-1, \\ C_i\|0^{w-n_1} & \text{for } i = p+q, \\ len(A)\|len(C) & \text{for } i = p+q+1, \end{cases}$$

the computation is defined as

$$\sum_{i=1}^{p+q+1} B_i H^{p+q+2-i}.$$

The encryption process and decryption process of XCB are written as $XCB.Enc_K^T(M)$ and $XCB.Dec_K^T(C)$ respectively. See more in Appendix A.

3.2   Weak-Key Analysis of XCB

We show that if the sub-key K_1 or K_3 for polynomial evaluation hash $\mathbf{h}$ is identified as a weak key, we can utilize the similar method used in GCM to analyze XCB. Contrary to creating a successful forgery in GCM, here we create same key streams generated by the CTR mode $\mathbf{c}$. Moreover, the identification of weak keys lead to more powerful attacks: distinguishing attack, key-recovery attack and plaintext-recovery attack against XCB more than forgery attack.

Identify Weak Key. For XCB, $\mathcal{D}$ is a weak key class if $0 \in \mathcal{D}$ and $|\mathcal{D}| \ge 2$, or $|\mathcal{D}| > 2$. For we cannot full control the output of $\mathbf{e}_{K_0}(A)$, we can only consider the collision of universal evaluation hash which has no constant term. If $\mathcal{D}$ contains 0, we only need to set $q(x) = \prod_{L \in \mathcal{D}} (x \oplus L)$, which requires at least one query. Else if $0 \notin \mathcal{D}$, we need to set $q(x) = x \prod_{L \in \mathcal{D}} (x \oplus L)$. We first test whether $H \in \mathcal{D} \cup 0$, which needs at least one query. Then consider whether $H = 0$. The whole process needs at least two queries.

We choose such a $\mathcal{D} = \{H_1, H_2, \cdots, H_r\}$ meeting the requirement, where H_i is chosen from $\{0,1\}^w$ for $1 \le i \le r$. We will show how to test whether $K_1 \in \mathcal{D} \cup 0$ (the case for K_3 is similar to the one for K_1).

Assume (A, B, T, G, E) obtained by querying the encryption process (see Figure 1). Firstly, we construct a polynomial $q(x) = x \prod_{i=1}^{r} (x \oplus H_i) = \sum_{i=1}^{r+1} q_i x^i$, where $Q = q_1 \| q_2 \cdots \| q_{r+1}$. We set $A' = A$, $(B', T') = (B, T) \oplus Q$, which means xor coefficients of $q(x)$'s terms with the message $B \| T$. Then send (A', B', T') to the encryption oracle and get a new ciphertext (G', E'). Considering the hash-counter-hash construction of XCB, we will obtain the same key streams: $B \oplus E = B' \oplus E'$ if $q(K_1) = 0$. This holds because:

$$\mathbf{h}_{K_1}(B, T) = \mathbf{h}_{K_1}(B, T) \oplus q(K_1) = \mathbf{h}_{K_1}((B, T) \oplus Q) = \mathbf{h}_{K_1}(B', T'),$$

$$A = A' \Rightarrow C = C'.$$

Then $O = O'$, which are the initial counter values of the CTR mode $\mathbf{c}$. Clearly the key streams $\mathbf{c}$ generates are the same.

The identification goes as follows:

1. Obtain a tuple (A, B, T, G, E) by querying the encryption process as illustrated in Figure 1;
2. Construct $q(x) = x \prod_{i=1}^{r} (x \oplus H_i)$;
3. Perform an encryption querying for $(A, (B, T) \oplus Q)$, if we observe the same key streams $(B \oplus E = B' \oplus E')$, we identify the key K_1 as a weak key, which is a root of $q(x)$ and a member of $\mathcal{D} \cup 0$.

Owing to the hash-counter-hash construction of XCB, once observing the same key streams, $q(x)$ is valid for K_1. Then we can utilize $q(x)$ to attack XCB.

Distinguishing Attack Against XCB. Once that K_1 or K_3 is recognized as weak key, we can make a distinguishing attack against XCB. Assume $q(x)$ is valid for K_1. We query two tuples (A, B, T) and $(A, (B, T) \oplus Q)$, then $B \oplus E = B' \oplus E'$, which can be used to distinguish XCB from tweakable random permutation. The case is same to K_3 for the symmetry of the structure of XCB.

Plaintext-Recovery Attack Against XCB. We can utilize the decryption querying of XCB to recover plaintext if we have a valid $q(x)$ for K_1 or K_3.

For obtaining the plaintext of the ciphertext (G^*, E^*) with the tweak T^*, we firstly try to recover part of the plaintext, where $q(x)$ is valid only for K_3. We set $G' = G^*$ and $(E', T') = (E^*, T^*) \oplus Q$. Send (G', E') with T' to the decryption oracle, obtain the plaintext (A', B'). Obviously we get:

$$B^* \oplus E^* = B' \oplus E'.$$

This can be proved as follows. From line 18 in Algorithm 1 we can see that $F^* = F'$. Along with $q(x)$ is valid for K_3, then $\mathbf{h}_{K_3}(E^*, T^*) = \mathbf{h}_{K_3}(E', T')$, leading to $O^* = O'$. Clearly the key streams $\mathbf{c}$ generates are the same.

Furthermore, we could recover all the plaintext under the special restriction to $q(x)$, for example, $q(x) = I(x) \cdot J(x)$, where K_1 is the root of polynomial $I(x)$ and K_3 is the root of polynomial $J(x)$, then, we will obtain the output:

$$A^* = A',$$
$$B^* \oplus E^* = B' \oplus E'.$$

As $q(x)$ is also valid for K_1, $\mathbf{h}_{K_1}(B^*, T^*) = \mathbf{h}_{K_1}(B', T')$, along with the result that $O^* = O'$, we would obtain the output:

$$C^* = C' \Rightarrow A^* = A'.$$

Key-Recovery Attack Against XCB. Once we find a valid $q(x)$ for K_1, namely $K_1 \in \mathcal{D} \cup 0$, we can utilize binary tree search to determine the value of K_1. Divide $\mathcal{D} = \{H_1, H_2, \cdots, H_r\}$ into two parts: $\{H_1, H_2, \cdots, H_j\}$ and $\{H_{j+1}, H_2, \cdots, H_r\}$ (where $j = \lceil \frac{i}{2} \rceil$). Construct two polynomials $x \prod_{t=j+1}^{r} (x \oplus H_t)$ and $x \prod_{t=1}^{j} (x \oplus H_t)$. Apply them to the process of identifying weak key respectively. $K_1 = 0$ if both are valid for K_1. Otherwise, keep the successful one, and repeat above steps $log_2 r$ times, until find the exact key value. Then we recover the key K_1 of XCB. Owing to the structure symmetry, we can recover K_3 similar to K_1.

From above analysis, we conclude that once the key K_1 or K_3 of XCB are recognized as weak keys, namely, we successfully find a valid polynomial for the key K_1 or K_3, we can make distinguishing attack, key-recovery attack and plaintext-recovery attack against XCB.

3.3   Related-Key Analysis of XCB

We show that XCB can resist related-key attacks if the underlying block cipher $\mathbf{e}$ is an SPRP-RKA. Assume that $\oplus_\Delta(K)$ is the related-key transformation to map K to $K \oplus \Delta$, and that there are t different values $\Delta_1, \cdots, \Delta_t$ used in the related-key transformation when the adversary query the encryption or decryption oracle. For each Δ_i $(1 \leq i \leq t)$, the sub-keys are generated like this:

$$K_0^{\Delta_i} \leftarrow \mathbf{e}_{K \oplus \Delta_i}(0^w), K_1^{\Delta_i} \leftarrow \mathbf{e}_{K \oplus \Delta_i}(0^{w-1}\|1), K_2^{\Delta_i} \leftarrow \mathbf{e}_{K \oplus \Delta_i}(0^{w-2}\|1\|0),$$
$$K_3^{\Delta_i} \leftarrow \mathbf{e}_{K \oplus \Delta_i}(0^{w-2}\|1^2), K_4^{\Delta_i} \leftarrow \mathbf{e}_{K \oplus \Delta_i}(0^{w-3}\|1\|0^2),$$

where $K_j^{\Delta_i}$ means the jth sub-key $(1 \leq i \leq t)$. For $\mathbf{e}$ is an SPRP-RKA, then each $\mathbf{e}_{K \oplus \Delta_i}$ is an independent SPRP, which result in:

$(K_0^{\Delta_i}, K_1^{\Delta_i}, K_2^{\Delta_i}, K_3^{\Delta_i}, K_4^{\Delta_i})$ is independent for $1 \leq i \leq t$, and each one of them is indistinguishable from the output of random permutation, which is uniformly random.

Therefore each XCB decided by $(K_0^{\Delta_i}, K_1^{\Delta_i}, K_2^{\Delta_i}, K_3^{\Delta_i}, K_4^{\Delta_i})$ is not only an STPRP [1,28,29], but also independent. All in all, XCB is an STPRP-RKA.

4 Analysis of HCTR

HCTR is an STPRP under the assumption that the underlying block cipher is an SPRP [2].

4.1 Definition of HCTR

HCTR is similar to the structure of XCB, hence we use the same notations to describe it. HCTR is comprised of a block cipher $\mathbf{e}$ ($\mathbf{d}$ is the inverse function of $\mathbf{e}$), a polynomial evaluation hash function $\mathbf{h}$, and a CTR function $\mathbf{c}$ (similar to the CTR function in XCB). Different from XCB, HCTR has two master keys: K and H, where K is for block cipher $\mathbf{e}$ and H is for polynomial evaluation hash function $\mathbf{h}$.

Polynomial Hash Function. $\mathbf{h}_H(X) : \{0,1\}^w \times \{0,1\}^* \rightarrow \{0,1\}^w$, $len(X) = w(p-1)+q$ for $1 \le q \le w$. Partition X into $X_1\|X_2\|\cdots\|X_p$, where $len(X_i) = w$ for $1 \le i \le p-1$, 0^{w-q} are appended at the end of X to complete the block,

$$\mathbf{h}_H(X) = \begin{cases} H, & \text{if } X \text{ is an empty string,} \\ X_1 H^{p+1} \oplus \cdots \oplus (X_p\|0^{w-q})H^2 \oplus len(X)H, & \text{else.} \end{cases}$$

HCTR is described into two parts: the encryption process $HCTR.$ $Enc_{K,H}^T(M)$ and the decryption part $HCTR.Dec_{K,H}^T(M)$, where $K \in \{0,1\}^k$ and $H \in \{0,1\}^w$. See more in Appendix A.

4.2 Weak-Key Analysis of HCTR

In consequence of the hash-counter-hash structure, HCTR suffers the same problems as XCB. According to the previous discussion, $\mathcal{D}$ is a weak key class for HCTR if $|\mathcal{D}| \ge 2$ [17]. We can take similar distinguishing attack and key-recovery attack against HCTR. In addition, the same universal hash key H for the two layer polynomial evaluation hashes unlike XCB results in a more simple plaintext-recovery attack than that in XCB.

For obtaining the plaintext of the ciphertext (E^*, D^*) with tweak T^*. We set $E' = E^*$ and $(D',T') = (D^*,T^*) \oplus Q$. Send (E',D') with T' to the decryption oracle as illustrated in Figure 2, where $q(x)$ is valid for the hash key H, and obtain the plaintext (A', B'). We get the following equations:

$$A^* = A', B^* \oplus D^* = B' \oplus D'.$$

This can be proved as follows. From line 16 in Algorithm 2, we can know that $O^* = O'$ and $C^* = C'$ for $E' = E^*$ and $q(x)$ is valid for H. Clearly the key streams CTR mode generates are the same for $S^* = S'$. So $B^* \oplus D^* = B' \oplus D'$. Also $A^* = A'$ for $q(x)$ is valid for H.

4.3   Related-Key Analysis of HCTR

HCTR can not resist related-key attack. We can distinguish HCTR from a tweak-able random permutation under the related-key attack within two queries. Next we present the related-key analysis of HCTR in two different cases.

Case 1: B is an Empty String and $0 < len(T) \leq w$. Let A and A' be two messages to be encrypted by H and $H' = H \oplus \Delta$ with the same T respectively. Let $A' = A \oplus T'\Delta^2 \oplus len(T)\Delta$, where $T' = T\|0^{w-len(T)}$. The ciphertexts are E and E' respectively.

Then, we get:

$$
\begin{aligned}
C' &= A' \oplus \mathbf{h}_{H'}(T) \\
&= A \oplus T'\Delta^2 \oplus len(T)\Delta \oplus T'H'^2 \oplus len(T)H' \\
&= A \oplus T'\Delta^2 \oplus len(T)\Delta \oplus T'(H \oplus \Delta)^2 \oplus len(T)(H \oplus \Delta) \\
&= A \oplus T'H^2 \oplus len(T)H \\
&= A \oplus \mathbf{h}_H(T) \\
&= C.
\end{aligned}
$$

In a similar way, $E \oplus E' = T'\Delta^2 \oplus len(T)\Delta$.

In our attack, $T'\Delta^2 \oplus len(T)\Delta$ is a constant value we choose. We see that the ciphertext of A has a specific relationship with the ciphertext of A' under the encryption keys H and H' respectively, which is a successful related-key distinguishing attack against HCTR.

In addition to this, we can conduct a plaintext-recovery attack using the related key. Assume that the plaintext of E with T is needed under the key H, where D is an empty string. Send $E' = E \oplus T'\Delta^2 \oplus len(T)\Delta$ with T to the decryption oracle under $H'(= H \oplus \Delta)$ and obtain the plaintext,

$$
A = A' \oplus T'\Delta^2 \oplus len(T)\Delta.
$$

Case 2: T is an Empty String and $0 < len(B) \leq w$. Similar to case 1, we choose M and M' to be the two messages encrypted by H and $H' = H \oplus \Delta$ respectively, where $M = (A, B)$ and $M' = (A', B') = (A \oplus (B\|0^{w-len(B)})\Delta^2 \oplus len(B)\Delta, B)$. (E, D) and (E', D') are the corresponding ciphertexts. Then, we draw a conclusion as follows:

$$
E \oplus E' = (D\|0^{w-len(B)})\Delta^2 \oplus len(B)\Delta,
$$

$$
D = D'.
$$

In our attack, $(B\|0^{w-len(B)})\Delta^2 \oplus len(B)\Delta$ is a constant value that we choose. Moreover, $(D\|0^{w-len(B)})\Delta^2 \oplus len(B)\Delta$ is also a deterministic value after the encryption of M. We see that the ciphertext of M has a specific relationship with the ciphertext of M' under the encryption keys H and $H' = H \oplus \Delta$ respectively, which is a successful related-key distinguishing attack against HCTR.

This time, we can also conduct a plaintext-recovery under the related-key attack. Assume that the plaintext of (E, D) (where $0 < len(D) \leq w$) under key H is needed. Then we send $(E', D') = (E \oplus (D \| 0^{w-len(D)}) \Delta^2 \oplus len(D) \Delta, D)$ under the key $H' = H \oplus \Delta$ to the decryption oracle, and get the plaintext (A', B'):

$$A = A' \oplus (B \| 0^{w-len(B)}) \Delta^2 \oplus len(B) \Delta,$$

$$B = B'.$$

5   Analysis of HCH

HCH [3] is another TES similar to HCTR. More specifically, HCH has an extra block cipher call $\mathbf{e}$ before the CTR mode $\mathbf{c}$ and derive the keys of universal hash function by using master key encrypting two values like XCB does, T is the tweak, l is the message length in bits:

$$R \leftarrow \mathbf{e}_K(T), \ Q \leftarrow \mathbf{e}_K(R \oplus l).$$

The polynomial evaluation hash function in HCH is defined as follows,

$$\mathbf{h}_{R,Q}(X_1 \| X_2 \| \cdots \| X_p) = Q \oplus X_1 R^p \oplus X_2 R^{p-1} \oplus \cdots \oplus X_{p-1} R^2 \oplus X_p R.$$

See more in Appendix A. There are two variations of HCH: HCHp and HCHfp. HCHp is designed to utilize pre-computation by using a separate hash key. HCHfp works for fixed length messages, which can also utilize pre-computation and further reduce one block cipher invocation. All three schemes are proved to be secure in the sense that they are indistinguishable from a family of independent random permutations labeled by tweaks if the underlying block cipher is a pseudorandom permutation (PRP).

Owing to the hash-counter-hash structure similar to HCTR, HCH, HCHp and HCHfp, suffer distinguishing attack, key-recovery attack, plaintext-recovery attack when the key R of polynomial evaluation hash is recognized as weak key. According to the previous discussion, $\mathcal{D}$ is a weak key class for HCH if $|\mathcal{D}| \geq 2$ [17].

HCHp and HCHfp can not resist related-key attack for the similar reason with HCTR. However HCH can resist related-key attack if the underlying block cipher $\mathbf{e}_K$ is an SPRP-RKA. HCH has already been proved to be an STPRP [3]. Also use $\oplus_\Delta(K)$ as a related-key transformation map K to $K \oplus \Delta$. Assume that $\oplus_\Delta(K)$ is the related-key transformation to map K to $K \oplus \Delta$, and that there are t different values $\Delta_1, \cdots, \Delta_t$ used in the related-key transformation when the adversary query the encryption or decryption oracle. For $\mathbf{e}_K$ is an SPRP-RKA, then each $\mathbf{e}_{K \oplus \Delta_i}$ ($1 \leq i \leq t$) is an independent SPRP, which results in that each HCH decided by $\mathbf{e}_{K \oplus \Delta_i}$ is an independent STPRP. So we conclude that HCH is an STPRP-RKA.

6   Conclusion

In this paper, we focus on three hash-counter-hash tweakable enciphering scheme XCB, HCTR and HCH. We point out that once the key of polynomial evaluation hash in these schemes is identified as weak key, we can make several powerful attacks on XCB, HCTR and HCH (including two variations of HCH: HCHp and HCHfp): distinguishing attack, key-recovery attack and plaintext-recovery attack. Moreover, HCTR, HCHp and HCHfp suffer related-key attack, which turns into distinguishing attack within two queries. We also show that XCB and HCH can resist related-key attack if the underlying block cipher is related-key secure.

The identification of weak key can lead to a lot of serious consequences, like forgery attack against GCM and distinguishing attack, key-recovery attack and plaintext-recovery attack presented in this paper. But the process of identification is not an easy task. The probability of a successfully identification is limited by the size of the weak-key class. Usually the probability is small enough to be ignored if the key is uniformly distributed. We stress that the weak-key analysis does not break the security bounds which have been proved, but it indeed provides us an alternative way to analyze such schemes once the key for polynomial evaluation hash is recognized as weak key.

Through the related-key analysis of XCB, HCTR and HCH, we can draw a conclusion that XCB and HCH provide two typical methods to "inherit" the related-key security of underlying block cipher, which can be extended to other schemes. 1) Sub-key generation method. XCB uses a master key to generate sub-keys by encryptions of block cipher and can be proved to be secure when the sub-keys are uniformly random. Once a related key is derived by the adversary, the related-key security of block cipher guarantee that the sub-keys are random and independent, which lead to an independent scheme with new sub-keys. This method can turn any secure multiple-key scheme into related-key secure one. For example if we generate the two key in HCTR using a master key K as $K' = E_K(0^w)$ and $H = E_K(1^w)$, HCTR is also a related-key secure TES. 2) Identical one key method. HCH is an one-key scheme and the key is also the key of underlying block cipher. HCH can be proved to be secure when the underlying block cipher is secure. Once a related key is derived by the adversary, the related-key security of block cipher guarantee that different related key corresponds to a new independent PRP, which also leads to an independent scheme. This applies to some TESes like EME [7], PEP [30], HEH [31], HMCH [32], HOH [32], some AEes like GCM [33], OCB [34], some MACes like PMAC [35] and OMAC [36].

Acknowledgments. The authors would like to thank the anonymous reviewers for their helpful comments and suggestions. The work of this paper is supported by the National Key Basic Research Program of China (2014CB340603), the National Natural Science Foundation of China (Grants 61272477, 61472415, 61272476), the Strategic Priority Research Program of Chinese Academy of Sciences under Grant XDA06010702.

References

1. McGrew, D.A., Fluhrer, S.R.: The extended codebook (XCB) mode of operation. IACR Cryptology ePrint Archive **2004**, 278 (2004)
2. Wang, P., Feng, D., Wu, W.: HCTR: a variable-input-length enciphering mode. In: Feng, D., Lin, D., Yung, M. (eds.) CISC 2005. LNCS, vol. 3822, pp. 175–188. Springer, Heidelberg (2005)
3. Chakraborty, D., Sarkar, P.: HCH: a new tweakable enciphering scheme using the hash-encrypt-hash approach. In: Barua, R., Lange, T. (eds.) INDOCRYPT 2006. LNCS, vol. 4329, pp. 287–302. Springer, Heidelberg (2006)
4. IEEE Std 1619.2-2010. IEEE standard for wide-block encryption for shared storage media. IEEE Computer Society (2011)
5. Hoang, V.T., Krovetz, T., Rogaway, P.: Robust authenticated-encryption: AEZ and the problem that it solves. IACR Cryptology ePrint Archive **2014**, 793 (2014)
6. CAESAR: Competition for authenticated encryption: Security, applicability, and robustness. http://competitions.cr.yp.to/caesar.html
7. Halevi, S., Rogaway, P.: A parallelizable enciphering mode. In: Okamoto, T. (ed.) CT-RSA 2004. LNCS, vol. 2964, pp. 292–304. Springer, Heidelberg (2004)
8. Mancillas-López, C., Chakraborty, D., Rodríguez-Henríquez, F.: Efficient implementations of some tweakable enciphering schemes in reconfigurable hardware. In: Srinathan, K., Rangan, C.P., Yung, M. (eds.) INDOCRYPT 2007. LNCS, vol. 4859, pp. 414–424. Springer, Heidelberg (2007)
9. Carter, L., Wegman, M.N.: Universal classes of hash functions. J. Comput. Syst. Sci. **18**(2), 143–154 (1979)
10. Brassard, G.: On computationally secure authentication tags requiring short secret shared keys. In: Chaum, D., Rivest, R.L., Sherman, A.T. (eds.) Advances in Cryptology: Proceedings of CRYPTO 1982, pp. 79–86. Plenum Press, New York (1982)
11. Wegman, M.N., Carter, L.: New hash functions and their use in authentication and set equality. J. Comput. Syst. Sci. **22**(3), 265–279 (1981)
12. McGrew, D.A., Viega, J.: The galois/counter mode of operation (GCM) (2004)
13. Chakraborty, D., Nandi, M.: An improved security bound for HCTR. In: Nyberg, K. (ed.) FSE 2008. LNCS, vol. 5086, pp. 289–302. Springer, Heidelberg (2008)
14. Handschuh, H., Preneel, B.: Key-recovery attacks on universal hash function based MAC algorithms. In: Wagner, D. (ed.) CRYPTO 2008. LNCS, vol. 5157, pp. 144–161. Springer, Heidelberg (2008)
15. Saarinen, M.-J.O.: Cycling attacks on GCM, GHASH and other polynomial MACs and hashes. In: Canteaut, A. (ed.) FSE 2012. LNCS, vol. 7549, pp. 216–225. Springer, Heidelberg (2012)
16. Procter, G., Cid, C.: On weak keys and forgery attacks against polynomial-based MAC schemes. In: Moriai, S. (ed.) FSE 2013. LNCS, vol. 8424, pp. 287–304. Springer, Heidelberg (2014)
17. Zhu, B., Tan, Y., Gong, G.: Revisiting MAC forgeries, weak keys and provable security of galois/counter mode of operation. In: Abdalla, M., Nita-Rotaru, C., Dahab, R. (eds.) CANS 2013. LNCS, vol. 8257, pp. 20–38. Springer, Heidelberg (2013)
18. Biham, E.: New types of cryptanalytic attacks using related keys. J. Cryptology **7**(4), 229–246 (1994)
19. Knudsen, L.R.: Cryptanalysis of LOKI91. In: Zheng, Y., Seberry, J. (eds.) AUSCRYPT 1992. LNCS, vol. 718, pp. 196–208. Springer, Heidelberg (1993)

20. Biham, E., Dunkelman, O., Keller, N.: Related-key boomerang and rectangle attacks. In: Cramer, R. (ed.) EUROCRYPT 2005. LNCS, vol. 3494, pp. 507–525. Springer, Heidelberg (2005)
21. Biryukov, A., Dunkelman, O., Keller, N., Khovratovich, D., Shamir, A.: Key recovery attacks of practical complexity on AES-256 variants with up to 10 rounds. In: Gilbert, H. (ed.) EUROCRYPT 2010. LNCS, vol. 6110, pp. 299–319. Springer, Heidelberg (2010)
22. Bellare, M., Kohno, T.: A theoretical treatment of related-key attacks: RKA-PRPs, RKA-PRFs, and applications. In: Biham, E. (ed.) EUROCRYPT 2003. LNCS, vol. 2656, pp. 491–506. Springer, Heidelberg (2003)
23. Bhattacharyya, R., Roy, A.: Secure message authentication against related-key attack. In: Moriai, S. (ed.) FSE 2013. LNCS, vol. 8424, pp. 305–324. Springer, Heidelberg (2014)
24. Krawczyk, H.: LFSR-based hashing and authentication. In: Desmedt, Y.G. (ed.) CRYPTO 1994. LNCS, vol. 839, pp. 129–139. Springer, Heidelberg (1994)
25. Bellare, M., Desai, A., Jokipii, E., Rogaway, P.: A concrete security treatment of symmetric encryption. In: 38th Annual Symposium on Foundations of Computer Science, FOCS 1997, pp. 394–403. IEEE Computer Society, Miami Beach, 19–22 October 1997
26. Liskov, M., Rivest, R.L., Wagner, D.: Tweakable block ciphers. J. Cryptology 24(3), 588–613 (2011)
27. Halevi, S., Rogaway, P.: A tweakable enciphering mode. In: Boneh, D. (ed.) CRYPTO 2003. LNCS, vol. 2729, pp. 482–499. Springer, Heidelberg (2003)
28. Chakraborty, D., Hernandez-Jimenez, V., Sarkar, P.: Another look at XCB. IACR Cryptology ePrint Archive 2013, 823 (2013)
29. McGrew, D.A., Fluhrer, S.R.: The security of the extended codebook (XCB) mode of operation. IACR Cryptology ePrint Archive 2007, 298 (2007)
30. Chakraborty, D., Sarkar, P.: A new mode of encryption providing a tweakable strong pseudo-random permutation. In: Robshaw, M. (ed.) FSE 2006. LNCS, vol. 4047, pp. 293–309. Springer, Heidelberg (2006)
31. Sarkar, P.: Improving upon the TET mode of operation. In: Nam, K.-H., Rhee, G. (eds.) ICISC 2007. LNCS, vol. 4817, pp. 180–192. Springer, Heidelberg (2007)
32. Sarkar, P.: Efficient tweakable enciphering schemes from (block-wise) universal hash functions. IEEE Transactions on Information Theory 55(10), 4749–4760 (2009)
33. McGrew, D.A., Viega, J.: The security and performance of the galois/counter mode (GCM) of operation. In: Canteaut, A., Viswanathan, K. (eds.) INDOCRYPT 2004. LNCS, vol. 3348, pp. 343–355. Springer, Heidelberg (2004)
34. Rogaway, P., Bellare, M., Black, J.: OCB: A block-cipher mode of operation for efficient authenticated encryption. ACM Trans. Inf. Syst. Secur. 6(3), 365–403 (2003)
35. Rogaway, P.: Efficient instantiations of tweakable blockciphers and refinements to modes OCB and PMAC. In: Lee, P.J. (ed.) ASIACRYPT 2004. LNCS, vol. 3329, pp. 16–31. Springer, Heidelberg (2004)
36. Iwata, T., Kurosawa, K.: OMAC: one-key CBC MAC. In: Johansson, T. (ed.) FSE 2003. LNCS, vol. 2887, pp. 129–153. Springer, Heidelberg (2003)

A   Illustrations of XCB, HCTR and HCH

The following illustrations show XCB, HCTR and HCH.

Algorithm 1. XCB

1: **procedure** $XCB.Enc_K^T(M)$
2:　　Partition M into $M[1] \cdots M[m]$
3:　　$K_0 \leftarrow \mathbf{e}_K(0^w)$
4:　　$K_1 \leftarrow \mathbf{e}_K(0^{w-1}\|1)$
5:　　$K_2 \leftarrow \mathbf{e}_K(0^{w-2}\|1\|0)$
6:　　$K_3 \leftarrow \mathbf{e}_K(0^{w-2}\|1^2)$
7:　　$K_4 \leftarrow \mathbf{e}_K(0^{w-3}\|1\|0^2)$
8:　　$A \leftarrow M[1]$
9:　　$B \leftarrow M[2] \cdots M[m]$
10:　　$C \leftarrow \mathbf{e}_{K_0}(A)$
11:　　$O \leftarrow C \oplus \mathbf{h}_{K_1}(B,T)$
12:　　$E \leftarrow B \oplus \mathbf{c}_{K_2}(O)$
13:　　$F \leftarrow O \oplus \mathbf{h}_{K_3}(E,T)$
14:　　$G \leftarrow \mathbf{d}_{K_4}(F)$
15:　　**return** $G\|E$
16: **end procedure**

17: **procedure** $XCB.Dec_K^T(C)$
18:　　Partition C into $C[1] \cdots C[c]$
19:　　$K_0 \leftarrow \mathbf{e}_K(0^w)$
20:　　$K_1 \leftarrow \mathbf{e}_K(0^{w-1}\|1)$
21:　　$K_2 \leftarrow \mathbf{e}_K(0^{w-2}\|1\|0)$
22:　　$K_3 \leftarrow \mathbf{e}_K(0^{w-2}\|1^2)$
23:　　$K_4 \leftarrow \mathbf{e}_K(0^{w-3}\|1\|0^2)$
24:　　$G \leftarrow C[1]$
25:　　$E \leftarrow C[2] \cdots C[c]$
26:　　$F \leftarrow \mathbf{e}_{K_4}(G)$
27:　　$O \leftarrow F \oplus \mathbf{h}_{K_3}(E,T)$
28:　　$B \leftarrow E \oplus \mathbf{c}_{K_2}(O)$
29:　　$C \leftarrow O \oplus \mathbf{h}_{K_1}(B,T)$
30:　　$A \leftarrow \mathbf{d}_{K_0}(C)$
31:　　**return** $A\|B$
32: **end procedure**

Algorithm 2. HCTR

1: **procedure** $HCTR.Enc_{K,H}^T(M)$
2:　　Partition M into $M[1] \cdots M[m]$
3:　　$A \leftarrow M[1]$
4:　　$B \leftarrow M[2] \cdots M[m]$
5:　　$C \leftarrow A \oplus \mathbf{h}_H(B\|T)$
6:　　$O \leftarrow \mathbf{e}_K(C)$
7:　　$S \leftarrow C \oplus O$
8:　　$D \leftarrow \mathbf{c}_K(S) \oplus B$
9:　　$E \leftarrow O \oplus \mathbf{h}_H(D\|T)$
10:　　**return** $E\|D$
11: **end procedure**

12: **procedure** $HCTR.Dec_{K,H}^T(C)$
13:　　Partition C into $C[1] \cdots C[c]$
14:　　$E \leftarrow C[1]$
15:　　$D \leftarrow C[2] \cdots C[c]$
16:　　$O \leftarrow E \oplus \mathbf{h}_H(D\|T)$
17:　　$C \leftarrow \mathbf{d}_K(O)$
18:　　$S \leftarrow C \oplus O$
19:　　$B \leftarrow D \oplus \mathbf{c}_K(S)$
20:　　$A \leftarrow C \oplus \mathbf{h}_H(B\|T)$
21:　　**return** $A\|B$
22: **end procedure**

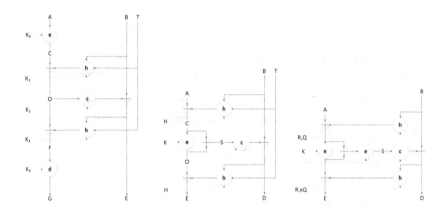

Fig. 1. XCB   **Fig. 2.** HCTR   **Fig. 3.** HCH(xQ = $xQ(x)$mod $\tau(x)$, $\tau(x)$ is an irreducible polynomial of degree w)

Cryptanalysis of Reduced-Round Whirlwind

Bingke Ma[1,2,3]($\boxtimes$), Bao Li[1,2], Ronglin Hao[1,2,4], and Xiaoqian Li[1,2,3]

[1] State Key Laboratory of Information Security, Institute of Information
Engineering, Chinese Academy of Sciences, Beijing 100093, China
{bkma,lb,xqli}@is.ac.cn

[2] Data Assurance and Communication Security Research Center,
Chinese Academy of Sciences, Beijing 100093, China

[3] University of Chinese Academy of Sciences, Beijing, China

[4] Department of Electronic Engineering and Information Science,
University of Science and Technology of China, Hefei 230027, China
haorl@mail.ustc.edu.cn

Abstract. The Whirlwind hash function, which outputs a 512-bit
digest, was designed by Barreto *et al.* and published by *Design, Codes
and Cryptography* in 2010. In this paper, we provide a thorough cryptanalysis on Whirlwind. Firstly, we focus on security properties at the
hash function level by presenting (second) preimage, collision and distinguishing attacks on reduced-round Whirlwind. In order to launch
the preimage attack, we have to slightly tweak the original Meet-in-
the-Middle preimage attack framework on AES-like compression functions by partially fixing the values of the state. Based on this slightly
tweaked framework, we are able to construct several new and interesting
preimage attacks on reduced-round Whirlpool and AES hashing modes
as well. Secondly, we investigate security properties of the reduced-round
components of Whirlwind, including semi-free-start and free-start (near)
collision attacks on the compression function, and a limited-birthday distinguisher on the inner permutation. As far as we know, our results are
currently the best cryptanalysis on Whirlwind.

Keywords: Cryptanalysis · Hash function · Whirlwind · Whirlpool ·
AES · PGV

1 Introduction

Cryptographic hash functions are widely acknowledged as the Swiss Army Knife
of modern cryptography thanks to its versatility and numerous applications.
A secure hash function should at least preserve three basic security properties,
namely, collision resistance, preimage resistance and second preimage resistance.
Several other security properties are also concerned, such as the limited-birthday
distinguisher on hash functions [11].

This work was supported by the National High Technology Research and Development Program of China (863 Program, No.2013AA014002) and the National Natural
Science Foundation of China (No.61379137).

© Springer International Publishing Switzerland 2015
E. Foo and D. Stebila (Eds.): ACISP 2015, LNCS 9144, pp. 20–38, 2015.
DOI: 10.1007/978-3-319-19962-7_2

In order to hash an input message, many state-of-the-art hash functions divide the message into many blocks and process each block iteratively with the inner components. The Merkle-Damgård construction [8,23] is one of the most classical constructions following this principle, and the underlying component which processes the message block in the Merkle-Damgård construction is called the compression function. Security properties of the compression function often have great impacts on the hash function, thus cryptanalysis of the compression function is important and meaningful. For the compression function, there are security notions such as semi-free-start (near) collision, free-start (near) collision [1] and (pseudo) preimage. Most of the compression functions used in practice are constructed with cryptographic permutations adopting proper modes of operation such as the PGV modes [26]. Security evaluations of the underlying permutation are quite necessary and helpful in order to know the potential weaknesses, the security margins which are crucial especially in the design of new primitives and the validity of the security proofs. A noted example is the limited-birthday distinguisher on permutations [9] which has been applied to many symmetric primitives, including [9,12,13], to name but a few.

The Whirlwind hash function [5] was designed by Barreto *et al.* and published by *Design, Codes and Cryptography* in 2010. It takes messages up to 2^{256} bits as inputs and outputs a 512-bit digest. At the high level construction, Whirlwind adopts a Merkle-Damgård construction with a final output transformation. At the compression function level, it employs an AES-like [7,24] design embedded in a Davies-Meyer-like mode. The state of the compression function can be seen as an 8×8 array of 16-bit elements, while the left (resp. right) half of the input state array is the 512-bit chaining value (resp. message block). Besides the high level structure of Whirlwind, it has some unique underlying components, *i.e.*, the interesting 16-bit SBox and the linear layer which are friendly to both software and hardware implementations. Actually some of its novelty design philosophies have influences on several recent works, *e.g.*, its linear layer design based on the strategy of subfield construction has been further investigated in [1] and [15]. Although Whirlwind contributes many heuristic and inspiring ideas to the design of symmetric cryptographic primitives, its concrete security properties are less evaluated in literature. Besides the analyses provided by the designers at the compression function level in [5], Riham *et al.* recently presented second preimage attacks on 5 and 6 rounds of Whirlwind [2].

Our Contributions. We present a thorough cryptanalysis on Whirlwind. Firstly, we focus on security properties at the hash function level by presenting several attacks on reduced-round versions of the 12-round Whirlwind hash function, including improved second preimage attack reduced to 6 rounds, the preimage attack reduced to 4 rounds, the collision attack reduced to 5 rounds,

---

[1] A semi-free-start collision attack aims to find two distinct messages (M, M') and an identical chaining value h_0 satisfying $CF(h_0, M) = CF(h_0, M')$. A free-start collision attack searches for two messages (M, M') and two chaining values (h_0, h'_0) satisfying $CF(h_0, M) = CF(h'_0, M')$, and $h_0 = h'_0$ and $M_0 = M'_0$ do not hold concurrently.

and the limited-birthday distinguisher reduced to 6 rounds. Secondly, security properties of the reduced-round inner components of Whirlwind are evaluated. More precisely, we launch semi-free-start collision and free-start near collision attacks on 6-round and 7-round Whirlwind compression function, and build a multiple limited-birthday distinguisher [14] on the inner permutation reduced to 9 rounds. Our attacks show that Whirlwind offers a quite comfortable security margin with respect to existing attacks. The results are summarized in Table 1.

In order to launch the preimage attacks on 4-round Whirlwind, we need to slightly tweak the original Meet-in-the-Middle preimage attack framework on AES-like compression functions by partially fixing the values of the state. Although this small tweak is rather simple, it has several further applications. For instance, we present two new preimage attacks on 5 and 6 rounds of Whirlpool [6,10], which significantly reduce the preimage lengths compared with previous attacks [29] (though our attacks require higher time complexities). We also show the first preimage attacks on several PGV hashing modes instantiated with 6-round AES at the hash function level.

Table 1. Summary of results on Whirlwind †

Target	Attack Type	Rounds	Time	Memory	Ideal	Reference
Hash Function (12 rounds)	Preimage	4	2^{496} 2^{497}	2^{255} 2^{208}	2^{512}	Section 3
	Second Preimage	5	2^{449}	2^{128}	2^{512}	[2]
		6	2^{505}	2^{112}	2^{512}	[2]
		6	2^{497}	2^{128}	2^{512}	Section 3
	Collision	5	2^{240}	2^{128}	2^{256}	Section 4
		4	2^{128}	2^{128}		Full Version [19]
	LBD Distinguisher ◇	6	2^{353}	2^{160}	2^{449}	Full Version [19]
Compression Function (12 rounds)	SFS. Near Collision ♡	5.5	2^{176}	2^{32}	2^{224}	[5]
	SFS. Collision ♡	4.5	2^{64}	2^{32}	2^{256}	[5]
		6	2^{128}	2^{128}	2^{256}	Full Version [19]
	FS. Near Collision ♣	7	2^{224}	2^{128}	2^{448}	Full Version [19]
Inner Permutation (12 rounds)	MLBD Distinguisher ♠	9	2^{730}	2^{128}	2^{763}	Full Version [19]

† : We do not consider the attacks starting from a middle round.
◇: Limited-birthday distinguisher on the hash function.
♡: Semi-free-start (near) collision on the compression function.
♣: Free-start near collision (896 colliding bits out of 1024 bits) on the compression function with no truncation.
♠: Multiple limited-birthday distinguisher on the permutation.

Structure. The remainder of this paper is organized as follows: Section 2 provides a brief description of the Whirlwind hash function, and the techniques utilized in this paper. We present the (second) preimage attacks and the collision attacks on reduced-round Whirlwind in Section 3 and Section 4 respectively. Section 5 concludes and summarizes the paper. Due to the space limit, we will report the additional analyses on reduced-round Whirlwind and its components, as well as the slightly tweaked Meet-in-the-Middle preimage attack framework on AES-like compression functions without truncation and its applications on Whirlpool and AES hashing modes in the full version of this paper [19].

2 Preliminaries

2.1 The Whirlwind Hash Function

The Whirlwind hash function takes any message up to 2^{256} bits as input, and outputs a 512-bit digest. It adopts the Merkle-Damgård construction with an output transformation, and the padding algorithm of Whirlwind is MD-strengthening with a 256-bit length padding L.

The compression function of Whirlwind is an AES-like design and has a 1024-bit state which can be represented by an 8×8 array of 16-bit elements. As depicted in Fig. 1, the compression function CF takes a 512-bit chaining value h^t and a 512-bit message block M^t as inputs, and performs the round function 12 times to derive the 512-bit output chaining value h^{t+1}, namely, $h^{t+1} = CF(h^t, M^t)$. Each round function consists of four maps, which are as follows:

- **SubBytes(γ):** process each cell of the state with the 16-bit SBox.
- **MixRows(θ):** multiply each row of the state array by a matrix.
- **Transposition(τ):** transpose the k-th column to be the k-th row for $k = 0, 1, 2, ..., 7$, *i.e.*, transposition of the state array.
- **AddRoundConstant(σ^r):** XOR the 1024-bit constant of the r-th round to the state array.

The designers also provide an alternative understanding for the concatenation of θ and τ, namely, $\tau \circ \theta$ as:

- θ_R: multiply each row of the state array by a matrix in even rounds.
- θ_C: multiply each column of the state array by a matrix in odd rounds.

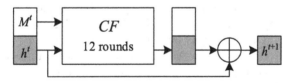

Fig. 1. The compression function of Whirlwind

For the remainder of this paper, we will adopt this alternative understanding of the round function. Now we give detailed algorithm of the compression function CF.

1. Initialize the state array S^0 with the input chaining value h^t and the input message block M^t:

$$\begin{cases} S^0_{i,j} = h^t_{i,j} \\ S^0_{i+4,j} = M^t_{i,j} \end{cases}, \text{ for } 0 \leq i < 4,\ 0 \leq j < 8.$$

2. Apply 12 iterations of the round function to the initial state S^0, and derive the final state S^{12}:

$$S^{k+1} = \begin{cases} (\sigma^k \circ \theta_R \circ \gamma)(S^k), & k \text{ is even,} \\ (\sigma^k \circ \theta_C \circ \gamma)(S^k), & k \text{ is odd,} \end{cases} \quad \text{for } 0 \leq k < 12.$$

3. Truncate the final state S^{12} and perform the feed-forward to derive the output chaining value h^{t+1}:

$$h_{i,j}^{t+1} = h_{i,j}^t \oplus S_{i,j}^{12}, \text{ for } 0 \leq i < 4, \ 0 \leq j < 8.$$

After all message blocks have been processed with the compression function iteratively, the output transformation is performed to avoid trivial length extension attacks. Suppose the output chaining value of the last message block is h^{LAST}, then the final 512-bit digest h^X is computed as:

$$h^X = CF(h^{\text{LAST}}, 0),$$

with the message block equal to the 8×4 null matrix.

2.2 The Meet-in-the-Middle Preimage Attack

The Meet-in-the-Middle (MitM) preimage attack was first introduced by Aoki and Sasaki in their preimage attacks against MD4 and 63-step MD5 [4]. The basic idea of this technique, which is known as *splice-and-cut*, aims to divide the target cipher into two sub-ciphers which can be computed independently. Due to the feed-forward operations in hash functions, the MitM attack can then be applied. Several advanced techniques to further improve the basic attack are developed, such as partial matching [4], partial fixing [4], initial structure [28], indirect partial matching [3], bicliques [16] and differential MitM attack [17].

In [27], Sasaki proposed the first MitM preimage attack on AES-like compression functions. Two main techniques were presented, namely, initial structure in an AES-like compression function and indirect partial matching through an MixColumn layer. This work was later improved by Wu *et al.* in [30]. Thanks to the delicate descriptions of the MitM preimage attack framework on AES-like compression functions presented in [30], the chunk separations can be easily represented by introducing several essential integer parameters, and the best attack parameters can be easily derived through an exhaustive search. In [29], Sasaki *et al.* introduced the guess-and-determine approach to extend the basic attack by one more round.

2.3 The Rebound Attack and the SuperSBox Technique

The rebound attack was first introduced by Mendel *et al.* in their attacks against reduced-round Whirlpool and Grøstl [20]. It aims to find a pair of inputs satisfying some unique properties for some specific (truncated) differential characteristics faster than the ideal case. There are two main procedures of the rebound attack, namely, the inbound phase and the outbound phase. Let $\mathcal{C}$ and $\mathcal{D}$ denote the certain non-full-active differential forms (normally with very few active cells) in the inbound phase, and $\mathcal{F}$ denote the full-active differential form, then the differentials in the inbound phase of the basic rebound attack can be denoted as $\mathcal{C} \rightarrow \mathcal{F} \leftarrow \mathcal{D}$. The available freedom degrees are used to connect these middle rounds with relatively small amount of computations using the match-in-the-middle technique. In the outbound phase, solutions from the inbound phase are propagated both forwards and backwards to connect the differentials in both directions.

The SuperSBox technique for the rebound attack was independently introduced in [9,18]. This technique exploits the fact that the non-linear layers between two rounds, $i.e.$, SB, SR, MC, AC, SB can be computed for each column independently. Therefore, by constructing the look-up tables for each individual column, the SuperSBox technique is able to cover one more full-active state in the inbound phase, namely, $\mathcal{C} \rightarrow \mathcal{F} \leftrightarrow \mathcal{F} \leftarrow \mathcal{D}$. The look-up tables built are hence called the SuperSBoxes.

3   (Second) Preimage Attacks on Reduced-Round Whirlwind

Firstly, we present the second preimage attack on 6-round Whirlwind with the aid of the plain MitM preimage attack on AES-like compression functions. Then the preimage attack on 4-round Whirlwind is illustrated. The whole preimage attack consists of four steps. In some steps of the attack partial values of the initial state are fixed, and the plain MitM preimage attack framework on AES-like compression functions cannot be directly applied under this scenario. Fortunately, we slightly tweak the original attack framework by partially fixing the values of the state, and make the preimage attack feasible. Despite the simplicity of this small tweak, its effectiveness are further stated with several new and interesting preimage attacks on reduced-round Whirlpool and AES hashing modes.

3.1   Second Preimage Attack on 6-Round Whirlwind

Before describing all attacks, we stress that a single compression function computation (resp. the state bit size of the compression function) is used as the basic unit of time (resp. memory) throughout this paper. The second preimage attack on 6-round Whirlwind is less complex and more traditional. As depicted in Fig. 2, suppose we expect to find a second preimage of $M_1||M_2||...||M_s$, the attack procedures can be divided into two phases. In the first phase, we find sufficient pseudo preimages and derive a set of h'_{t+1}s for a chaining value in the middle h_{t+2}. In the second phase, we launch the traditional MitM method [22, Fact9.99] to convert the pseudo preimages into a second preimage. More precisely, we choose random values of M_t to compute a set of h_{t+1}s from h_t, and search for a match of h_{t+1} in the set of h'_{t+1}s. A second preimage is successfully constructed if a match is derived.

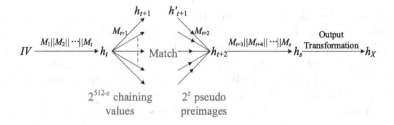

Fig. 2. Second preimage attack on 6-round `Whirlwind`

The main task lies in the first phase where sufficient pseudo preimages have to be generated. This can be done by utilizing the MitM preimage attack framework on `AES`-like compression functions which have been extensively investigated in [27,29,30]. Without loss of generality, we introduce the plain attack framework with the MitM preimage attack on 6-round `Whirlwind` compression function, and Fig. 3 depicts the basic chunk separation of this attack. Before more details are illustrated, we define several notations which are used throughout this paper.

n Bit size of the digest.
N_c Bit size of the cell.
N_t Number of columns (or rows) in the state.
b Number of blue columns (or rows) in the initial structure, and
r Number of red columns (or rows) in the initial structure.
c Number of constant cells in each column (or row) corresponding to the red column (or row) in the initial structure.
g Number of guessed rows (or columns, in purple) in the backward (or forward) computation.
D_b Freedom degrees of the blue chunk in bits.
D_r Freedom degrees of the red chunk in bits.
D_g Bit size of the guessed cells.
D_m Bit size of the match point.
T Time complexity of the attack.
M Memory requirement of the attack.

The attack procedures of the first phase can be further divided into five steps which are elaborated as follows, and the interested readers are referred to [27,29,30] for more detailed descriptions.

Step 1. Initial Structure. The purpose of the initial structure is to use several consecutive rounds as the starting point and divide the target cipher into two sub-ciphers which can be independently computed. For this purpose, as shown in Fig. 3, we choose random values for the constants (in grey) which are used in the linear transformations between states #1 ↔ #2, and states #3 ↔ #4. Following the linear relations of the θ_C and θ_R operations, compute the values in the initial structure for the forward chunk (in blue) which has D_b freedom degrees and the backward chunk (in red) which has D_r freedom degrees. After this step, the compression function is divided into two independent chunks thanks to the initial structure.

Step 2. Forward Computation. For all the blue and grey cells at state #4, the forward chunk can be computed forwards independently until state #5.

Step 3. Backward Computation. For all the red cells at #1, the backward chunk can be computed backwards independently until state #7. In order to proceed the backward computation by one more round, the guess-and-determine strategy is applied at state #6 by guessing the value of g rows.

Step 4. Indirect-Partial-Matching through the MixRow Layer. We have partial information of the red and blue cells from both directions, and linear relations of the θ_C operation can be further exploited at the match point to perform the indirect-partial-matching between states #5 ↔ #7.

Step 5. Recheck. Check whether the guessed cells of the partial match derived in step 4 are guessed correctly. If so, check whether the partial match is also a full match. Repeat the above steps 1-5 until a preimage is found.

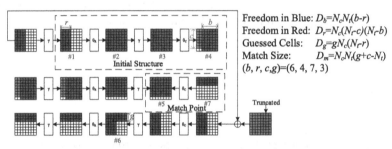

Freedom in Blue: $D_b = N_c N_t(b-r)$
Freedom in Red: $D_r = N_c(N_t-c)(N_t-b)$
Guessed Cells: $D_g = g N_c(N_t-r)$
Match Size: $D_m = N_c N_t(g+c-N_t)$
$(b, r, c, g) = (6, 4, 7, 3)$

Fig. 3. Chunk separation for the 6-round pseudo preimage attack

Deriving the Attack Parameters. As studied in [29,30], the attack parameters, *e.g.*, (D_b, D_r, D_g, D_m) can be easily represented with several predefined integer parameters (b, r, c, g) as shown in Fig. 3. The attack complexities can be denoted as follows:

$$T = 2^n(2^{-D_r} + 2^{D_g-D_b} + 2^{D_g-D_m}),$$
$$M = min\{2^{D_r+D_g}, 2^{D_b}\}. \tag{1}$$

We can derive the optimal attack parameters by enumerating all possible values of (b, r, c, g).

Complexity Analysis. Fig. 3 gives the optimal chunk separation for the pseudo preimage attack on the compression function, and it requires 2^{480} time and 2^{128} memory. In order to balance the overall complexities, we generate 2^{16} pseudo preimages in the first phase. In the second phase of the attack, we compute 2^{496} h_{t+1}s, and find a match with the pseudo preimages generated in the first phase with a high probability. Finally, it would require 2^{497} time and 2^{128} memory to launch a second preimage attack on 6-round Whirlwind.

3.2 Overview of the 4-Round Preimage Attack

Due to the strong impacts introduced by the truncation operation and the partially fixed state of Whirlwind (especially by the output transformation), our preimage attack can only work up to 4 rounds. The gap between the attacked rounds of preimage and second preimage attacks demonstrates that the adoptions of the truncation operation and the partially fixed state do strengthen Whirlwind in terms of preimage resistance.

Before describing the details, we give a brief overview of the 4-round preimage attack. As depicted in Fig. 4, the three-block preimage attack on 4-round Whirlwind consists of four steps. In the first step, the attack is carried out on the output transformation, and the given challenge digest h_X is inverted. In the second step, we invert the chaining value h_3, and derive the value of the last message block M_3 which contains the padding part. In the third step, we generate several pseudo preimages h'_1, and sufficient values for the second last message block M_2 are obtained simultaneously. In the last step, the traditional MitM method [22, Fact9.99] which converts pseudo preimages in to a preimage is launched, and we expect to find a match between h_1s and h'_1s. If all steps succeed, the three-block message $M_1\|M_2\|M_3$ is a preimage for 4-round Whirlwind.

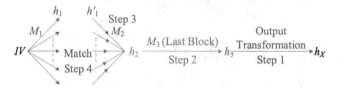

Fig. 4. Overview of the preimage attack on 4-round Whirlwind

3.3 The Slightly Tweaked MitM Preimage Attack on AES-like Compression Functions

The main bottlenecks of the preimage attack lie in step 1 and step 2 where partial values of the initial states are already fixed before launching the attack. More precisely, in step 1 the rightmost 4 columns of the state are fixed to 0 in the output transformation. As in step 2, since the preimage we try to build consists of 3 blocks, and the last block contains 255 message bits and 257 padding bits according to the MD-strengthening padding algorithm, the rightmost 2 columns of the state are fixed to the value $512 + 512 + 255 = 1279$. The plain MitM preimage attack framework on AES-like compression functions described in Section 3.1 seems inapplicable in this scenario. Luckily, we can apply a small and simple tweak which partially fixes the values of the state, and thus make the original attack framework feasible.

The Tweaked Attack Framework with Truncation. There are two main differences in the tweaked attack framework compared to the plain framework, namely, the partially fixed input state before the first round and the truncation operation carried after the last round. Also notice that the first and the last rounds are connected by the feed-forward operation, thus the initial structure in the tweaked framework needs to be located carefully between the first and the last rounds. Without loss of generality, we use the attack on 4-round Whirlwind compression function as an instance to elaborate the tweaked framework, and

Fig. 5 depicts the basic chunk separation of this attack. Following the definitions in Section 3.1, several additional notations need to be specified before providing more details. Since the half truncation is performed in Whirlwind, we will describe the slightly tweaked attack framework under the setting that the output chaining value is truncated in the following part.

tr Number of columns (or rows) truncated in the output chaining value.

fi Number of columns (or rows) fixed in the initial state before the attack.

b_1 Number of blue columns (or rows) with partial freedom degrees in the initial structure.

b_2 Number of blue columns (or rows) with full freedom degrees in the initial structure, we have $b = b_1 + b_2$.

D_{b_1} Freedom degrees of the blue chunk with partial freedom degrees in bits.

D_{b_2} Freedom degrees of the blue chunk with full freedom degrees in bits, we have $D_b = D_{b_1} + D_{b_2}$.

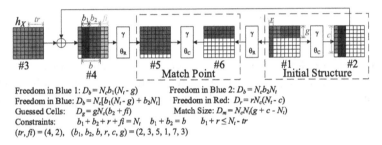

Fig. 5. The tweaked MitM preimage attack framework with truncation

For the sake of simplicity, we only consider the cases where full columns (or rows) are fixed (resp. truncated) in the initial state (resp. the output chaining value). Given a specific attack target, the values of (fi, tr) are prefixed before the attack, and the values of (b_1, b_2, r, c, g) can be chosen by the attacker in order to derive optimal attacks. The attack procedures are as follows:

Step 1. Initialization. Set the fi yellow columns in the initial state to the prefixed values, and denote the target digest as h_X.

Step 2. Initial Structure. Randomly choose values for the constants which are denoted in grey in the initial structure. According to the prefixed values in step 1 and the chosen constants in step 2, compute all values for the blue and red cells in the initial structure. After this step, the compression function is divided into two independent chunks.

Step 3. Backward Computation. In order to perform the backward computation, we have to apply the guess-and-determine strategy by guessing g rows which are denoted in purple at state #1. For all values of the red and guessed purple cells, compute backwards to the matching point at state #6 and store all partial matching values in a sorted table TL (e.g. hash table).

Step 4. Forward Computation. The blue cells in the forward computation can be further classified into two categories. For the b_1 columns, their values are constrained by the constant values in the initial structure, and there are overall $2^{D_{b_1}}$ values for these blue cells. Due to the truncation, we have to ensure $r + b_1 \leq N_t - tr$. For the b_2 columns, they can take all $2^{D_{b_2}}$ possible values of these blue cells. Combining these two categories, the freedom degrees in the blue cells are $2^{D_b} = 2^{D_{b_1} + D_{b_2}}$. For all values of the blue cells, compute forwards to the matching point at state #5.

Step 5. Indirect-Partial-Matching. Check whether the partial matching values derived in step 4 is also in the table TL built in step 3.

Step 6. Recheck. Check whether the guessed cells of the partial match derived in step 5 are guessed correctly. If so, check whether the partial match is also a full match. Repeat the above steps 2-6 until a preimage is found.

Complexity Analysis. Note that we can also swap the orders of step 3 and step 4, and the selection depends on which step requires less memory. Similar to the plain framework described in Section 3.1, the complexities of the tweaked attack are as follows:

$$T = 2^n (2^{-D_r} + 2^{D_g - D_b} + 2^{D_g - D_m}),$$
$$M = min\{2^{D_r + D_g}, 2^{D_b}\}.$$

We do not provide detailed deductions, but it is convenient to check that the quartet (D_b, D_r, D_g, D_m) can be represented with the integer variables defined as given in Fig. 5. The optimal attack parameters can be easily achieved by an exhaustive search for all valid values of (b_1, b_2, r, c, g) with a prefixed (fi, tr).

3.4 Details of the 4-Round Preimage Attack

Step 1. In this step, we need to invert the output transformation and derive the chaining value h_3. Since the right half of the input state #1 is fixed to 0, and the right half of the output state #2 is truncated, we have to utilize the tweaked MitM preimage attack framework with truncation under the parameters $(fi, tr) = (4, 4)$. As shown in Fig. 6, we derive the optimal chunk separation with parameters $(b_1, b_2, r, c, g) = (3, 0, 1, 7, 3)$ after an exhaustive search. Finally, it requires 2^{496} time and 2^{208} memory to invert the output transformation of 4-round Whirlwind. Note that since we need to match a 512-bit target digest, but there are only 2^{512} freedom degrees in the input chaining value h_3, step 1 will succeed with probability $1 - e^{-1}$.

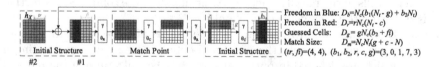

Freedom in Blue: $D_b = N_c(b_1(N_t - g) + b_2 N_t)$
Freedom in Red: $D_r = r N_c(N_t - c)$
Guessed Cells: $D_g = g N_c(b_2 + fi)$
Match Size: $D_m = N_c N_t(g + c - N)$
$(tr, fi) = (4, 4)$, $(b_1, b_2, r, c, g) = (3, 0, 1, 7, 3)$

Initial Structure   Match Point   Initial Structure
#2   #1

Fig. 6. Step 1. Invert the output transformation

Step 2. In this step, given the value of h_3, we have to invert the compression function in order to derive the input chaining value h_2 and the last message block M_3 which contains the padding part. Since we aim to build a three-block preimage, according to the MD-strengthening padding algorithm, the last 257 bits of M_3 are fixed to the padding value. Consequently, the 2 rightmost columns of the initial state are prefixed as denoted with yellow in Fig. 7. Note that since the 256-th bit of M_3 has to be '1' due to the padding, we lose one bit freedom degree of the blue chunks. We utilize the tweaked MitM preimage attack framework with truncation under the parameters $(fi, tr) = (2, 4)$, and exhaustively search for all valid values of (b_1, b_2, r, c, g). The chunk separation with $(b_1, b_2, r, c, g) = (0, 2, 4, 7, 3)$ as shown in Fig. 7 is the best result achieved. As a result, step 2 requires 2^{449} time and 2^{255} memory. Since step 2 requires much less computations than step 1, one can also carry out step 2 with parameters $(b_1, b_2, r, c, g) = (3, 2, 1, 7, 3)$ to minimize the memory requirement. The corresponding complexities are $(T, M) = (2^{496}, 2^{208})$.

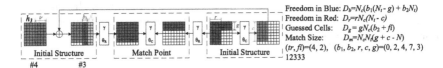

Fig. 7. Step 2. Derive the last message block

Step 3. In this step, given the value of h_2, we have to invert the compression function in order to derive the value of the second message block M_2 and the input chaining value h_1. The only constraint of this step is the final truncation, thus the traditional MitM preimage attack can be launched. We omit these details. As depicted in Fig. 8, with parameters $(b, r, c) = (5, 3, 4)$, the attack is optimized with complexities $(T, M) = (2^{320}, 2^{192})$. Since we will perform the traditional MitM procedure [22, Fact9.99] to convert the pseudo preimages into a preimage in step 4, we have to generate and store multiple say 2^x pairs of (h_1, M_2), which require 2^{320+x} time and 2^x memory.

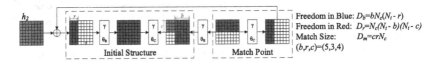

Fig. 8. Step 3. Generate sufficient values for the second last message block

Step 4. In this step, we launch the traditional MitM method to connect the values of h'_1 generated in step 3. More precisely, we choose random values of M_1 and compute the corresponding output chaining values h_1, then match it with the values of h'_1 generated in step 3. After choosing 2^{512-x} distinct values of M_1, we expect to find a match and finally derive a preimage of 4-round Whirlwind. Since each h_1 can be checked on the fly, the memory requirement for step 4 is negligible. We choose $x = 96$ to minimize the overall time complexity for step 3 and step 4 which is $2^{512-96} + 2^{320+96} = 2^{417}$.

Complexity Analysis. Now to sum up, the time complexity is dominated by step 1, and the memory requirement is dominated by step 2. Finally, the complexities for the 4-round preimage attack are $(T, M) = (2^{496}, 2^{255})$. One can also minimize the memory requirement by adopting the alternative attack parameters provided in step 2, which results in complexities of $(T, M) = (2^{497}, 2^{208})$.

4   Collision Attacks on Reduced-Round Whirlwind

This section presents the collision attack on 4- and 5-round Whirlwind hash function. Due to the Davies-Meyer-like mode of Whirlwind, it is feasible to launch semi-free-start or free-start collision attacks on the reduced-round compression function with the rebound attack, but deriving a collision attack at the hash function level seems difficult. Fortunately, with the aid of the multi-block strategy, we are able to launch collision attacks on 4 and 5 rounds of the Whirlwind hash function. We only describe the 5-round attack, and the 4-round attack is reported in the full version of this paper [19].

4.1   Overview of the 5-Round Collision Attack

The previous collision attacks on Grindahl [25] and Grøstl [21] generate colliding messages which contain several consecutive message blocks. The general strategy in these attacks is after introducing the differences into the chaining values, the differences are gradually cancelled with the posterior message blocks, and eventually lead to collisions by eliminating the differences in the output chaining values. Our attack is based on a similar multi-step process which gradually introduces, restricts and finally cancels the differences. As shown in Fig. 9, the overall attack consists of three steps and outputs a 3-block colliding pair, and each step targets on a certain message block.

Before providing more detailed descriptions of the collision attack, it is necessary to specify several notations used. As depicted in Fig. 9, we use $\Delta St = St \oplus St'$ to denote the difference between two states St and St'. LEFT(St) and RIGHT(St) denote the left half and the right half of the state St respectively. Also note that in the figures of the collision attacks, active (resp. inactive) cells are denoted in grey (resp. white). The red cells correspond to the input message blocks which can be freely controlled by the attacker, and the green cells in the output chaining value of the compression function are truncated. The overall collision attack consists of three steps, and the collision pair has three blocks, i.e., $(M_1||M_2||M_3, M_1||M_2'||M_3')$.

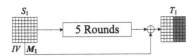

Step 1. Generate sufficient chaining values LEFT(T_1)

Step 2. Generate the second message block pair (M_2, M_2')

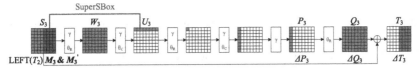

Step 3. Generate the third message block pair (M_3, M_3')

Fig. 9. Collision attack on 5-round Whirlwind

Step 1. Provide the freedom degrees. The purpose of the first step is to provide sufficient freedom degrees for the subsequent two steps. We randomly choose the values of the first message block M_1 and compute the output chaining values LEFT(T_1).

Step 2. Introduce the input differences and restrict the outpu differences. We introduce the input differences by choosing different values for the second message block, *i.e.*, (M_2, M_2'), such that the difference of the output chaining values for the second compression function call, namely, LEFT(ΔT_2), satisfies that LEFT(ΔT_2) = LEFT(ΔQ_2), where $\Delta Q_2 = \theta_R(\Delta P_2)$ and the difference of P_2 only lies in the first column.

Step 3. Cancel the output differences. We need to generate the message block pair (M_3, M_3'), such that the output difference of the permutation for the third compression function call, namely, LEFT(ΔQ_3), satisfies that $\Delta Q_3 = \theta_R(\Delta P_3)$, where the difference of P_3 only lies in the first column. It is clear that the values of ΔQ_2 and ΔQ_3 are in the same subspace thanks to their unique differential forms, and moreover, if $\Delta P_2 = \Delta P_3$ is satisfied, we can directly deduct that $\Delta Q_2 = \Delta Q_3$ due to the linear properties of θ_R. Consequently, the output difference of the third compression function call, namely, LEFT(ΔT_3) will be 0, since we have LEFT(ΔT_3) = LEFT(ΔT_2) $\oplus$ LEFT(ΔQ_3) = LEFT(ΔQ_2) $\oplus$ LEFT(ΔQ_3) due to the feed-forward operation. Finally, appending any identical message blocks which satisfy padding to ($M_1 || M_2 || M_3, M_1 || M_2' || M_3'$) will lead to a collision on the hash function.

4.2   Impacts of the Partially Fixed States

As shown in Fig. 9, partial values of the input states are fixed in the last two steps of the attack. More precisely, the left half of S_2 is fixed to LEFT(T_1) in the second step of the attack, and the left half of the paired values S_3 are fixed to LEFT(T_2) and LEFT(T_2') in the last step of the attack. Since the SuperSBox technique is utilized at the input states of the last two steps, it is essential to discuss the impacts brought by the partially fixed states.

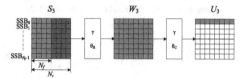

Fig. 10. Illustrations of the tweaked SuperSBox technique with partially fixed states

Without loss of generality, we use the inbound phase of step 3 which connects S_3 and U_3 as an instance to discuss a similar and generalized problem as depicted in Fig. 10. Suppose that both the differences and the values of the N_f grey columns in S_3 are fixed, and the differences and the values of the $N_t - N_f$ remaining red columns in S_3 can be freely chosen. According to the SuperSBox technique, the three layers $\gamma \rightarrow \theta_R \rightarrow \gamma$ can be seen as N_t parallel row-wise SuperSBoxes, namely, $SSB_0, SSB_1, ..., SSB_{N_t-1}$. Regarding some of the definitions in Section 3.1, the exact attack steps of the tweaked SuperSBox technique with partially fixed states are as follows:

1. From the forward direction, for every difference of the red cells in SSB_0, we enumerate all $2^{N_c(N_t-N_f)}$ possible values conforming to this difference, and compute the corresponding values and differences in $\gamma(W_3)$. We save them in a sorted table. Since we can enumerate all $2^{N_c(N_t-N_f)}$ differences in SSB_0, so the lookup table of SSB_0 has at most $2^{2N_c(N_t-N_f)}$ entries. For the remaining $N_t - 1$ SuperSBoxes, the procedures are similar.

2. From the backward direction, we select a random difference of U_3, and compute it backwards to get the value of $\theta_C^{-1}(\Delta U_3)$. We match this difference with the N_t SuperSBox tables built in step 1. Since a N_cN_t-bit difference needs to be matched for each SuperSBox, two different cases need to be considered:

   Case 1. The number of entries in each table is insufficient to derive a N_cN_t-bit match, namely, $2N_c(N_t - N_f) < N_cN_t$ (equivalent to $2N_f > N_t$). In this case, we have to compute $2^{N_cN_t-2N_c(N_t-N_f)} = 2^{N_c(2N_f-N_t)}$ differences of $\theta_C^{-1}(\Delta U_3)$ to derive a match for a single SuperSBox. Consequently, in order to derive a match for all N_t SuperSBoxes simultaneously, we have to choose $2^{N_cN_t(2N_f-N_t)}$ different values of $\theta_C^{-1}(\Delta U_3)$. Since there are overall $2^{N_cN_t}$ possible differences of U_3, if $N_cN_t < N_cN_t(2N_f - N_t)$ which is equivalent to $2N_f > N_t + 1$, we are not able to derive a match for all the SuperSBoxes at the same time.

   Case 2. The number of entries in each table is sufficient to derive a match, namely, $2N_c(N_t - N_f) \geq N_cN_t$ (equivalent to $2N_f \leq N_t$). In this case, instead enumerating all differences and values of the red cells in each row of S_3, we only need to select suffiecient say 2^X differences of the red cells, and exhaust all $2^{X+N_c(N_t-N_f)}$ corresponding values for each

SuperSBox. We choose $X + N_c(N_t - N_f) = N_cN_t$ (equivalent to $X = N_cN_f$), because we only need to match a N_cN_t-bit difference for each SuperSBox. It requires $2^{N_cN_t}$ time and memory to generate and store the N_t SuperSBoxes tables. Given a specific difference $\theta_C^{-1}(\Delta U_3)$, we expect to get a match for each of the N_t SuperSBoxes simultaneously, thus derive a solution for the inbound phase. After exhausting all $2^{N_cN_t}$ differences of U_3, we expect to get $2^{N_cN_t}$ solutions for the inbound phase with $2^{N_cN_t}$ time and memory. Since there are overall $2^{2N_cN_t(N_t-N_f)}$ differences and corresponding values of the red cells S_3, and N_t active cells in U_3, we can generate at most $2^{2N_cN_t(N_t-N_f)-N_cN_t(N_t-1)} = 2^{N_cN_t(N_t-2N_f+1)}$ solutions for the inbound phase.

To summarize the above analysis, if $2N_f \leq N_t$, we can generate $2^{N_cN_t}$ solutions for the inbound phase with $2^{N_cN_t}$ time and memory, and at most $2^{N_cN_t(N_t-2N_f+1)}$ solutions can be generated for the inbound phase. Otherwise if $2N_f > N_t$, the attack would be infeasible due to the lack of freedom degrees.

4.3   Details of the Collision Attack

For Whirlwind, $N_c = 16, N_t = 8, N_f = 4$ which satisfies the condition discussed in Section 4.2, and the SuperSBox technique can be adapted. We illustrate the detailed procedures of the 5-round collision attack as shown in Fig. 9.

Step 1. From the specified IV, we choose a random value for the first message block M_1, and compute its output chaining value which is LEFT(T_1) due to the truncation.

Step 2. From LEFT(T_1), we utilize the SuperSBox technique by exploiting the freedom degrees in both the values and the differences of M_2 in the inbound phase (in red). We get 2^{128} solutions for the inbound phase with 2^{128} time and 2^{128} memory. Based on the analysis in Section 4.2, the overall number of solutions for the inbound phase is 2^{128}. The probability of the outbound phase (in blue) is $2^{-16\times7} = 2^{-112}$, thus we expect to get 2^{16} pairs of (M_2, M_2').

Step 3. From a specific pair of LEFT(T_2) and LEFT(T_2') which is generated in step 2, we utilize the SuperSBox technique by exploiting the freedom degrees in both the values and the differences of M_3 in the inbound phase (in red). We get 2^{128} solutions for the inbound phase with 2^{128} time and 2^{128} memory. The probability of the outbound phase (in blue) is $2^{-16\times7} = 2^{-112}$, and we need to guarantee $\Delta P_3 = \Delta P_2$ which happens with probability $2^{-16\times8} = 2^{-128}$ in order to eliminate the difference. So we need 2^{240} solutions from the inbound phase of step 3, and the freedom degrees seem insufficient. By choosing 2^{96} different values of M_1 in step 1, and combining the 2^{16} solutions (LEFT(T_2), LEFT(T_2')) generated in step 2 for each value of M_1, the overall number of solutions reaches $2^{96+16+128} = 2^{240}$, and we expect to derive a collision.

Complexity Analysis. As illustrated above, it requires 2^{240} compression function computations to generate a collision for 5-round `Whirlwind`. The memory requirement is 2^{128} due to the SuperSBox technique.

5   Conclusion

We provide a thorough security analysis of `Whirlwind`. Firstly, we focus on security properties at the hash function level, and present 6-round second preimage, 4-round preimage, 5-round collision and 6-round distinguishing attacks out of the 12-round hash function. Then we investigate security properties of the `Whirlwind` components with several reduced-round attacks on the compression function and the underlying permutation.

Moreover, we show how to generate preimages with significantly reduced lengths for reduced-round versions of `Whirlpool`, and also present the first preimage attacks at the hash function level for several PGV modes instantiated with 6-round `AES`.

Acknowledgments. We would like to thank the anonymous reviewers of ACISP 2015 for their valuable comments and suggestions.

References

1. Albrecht, M.R., Driessen, B., Kavun, E.B., Leander, G., Paar, C., Yalçın, T.: Block ciphers – focus on the linear layer (feat. PRIDE). In: Garay, J.A., Gennaro, R. (eds.) CRYPTO 2014, Part I. LNCS, vol. 8616, pp. 57–76. Springer, Heidelberg (2014)
2. AlTawy, R., Youssef, A.: Second preimage analysis of whirlwind. In: Lin, D., Yung, M., Zhou, J. (eds.) Inscrypt 2014. LNCS, vol. 8957, pp. 311–328. Springer, Switzerland (2015)
3. Aoki, K., Guo, J., Matusiewicz, K., Sasaki, Y., Wang, L.: Preimages for step-reduced SHA-2. In: Matsui, M. (ed.) ASIACRYPT 2009. LNCS, vol. 5912, pp. 578–597. Springer, Heidelberg (2009)
4. Aoki, K., Sasaki, Y.: Preimage attacks on one-block MD4, 63-step MD5 and more. In: Avanzi, R.M., Keliher, L., Sica, F. (eds.) SAC 2008. LNCS, vol. 5381, pp. 103–119. Springer, Heidelberg (2009)
5. Barreto, P., Nikov, V., Nikova, S., Rijmen, V., Tischhauser, E.: Whirlwind: a new cryptographic hash function. In: Designs, Codes and Cryptography, vol. 56, pp. 141–162. Springer, US (2010)
6. Barreto, P., Rijmen, V.: The Whirlpool Hashing Function. Submitted to NESSIE (2000). http://www.larc.usp.br/pbarreto/WhirlpoolPage.html
7. Daemen, J., Rijmen, V.: The Design of Rijndael: AES - the Advanced Encryption Standard. Springer, Heidelberg (2002)
8. Damgård, I.B.: A design principle for hash functions. In: Brassard, G. (ed.) CRYPTO 1989. LNCS, vol. 435, pp. 416–427. Springer, Heidelberg (1990)
9. Gilbert, H., Peyrin, T.: Super-sbox cryptanalysis: improved attacks for AES-like permutations. In: Hong, S., Iwata, T. (eds.) FSE 2010. LNCS, vol. 6147, pp. 365–383. Springer, Heidelberg (2010)

10. International Organization for Standardization: ISO/IEC 10118–1:2004: Information technology - Security techniques - Hash-functions - Part 3: Dedicated hash-functions (2004)
11. Iwamoto, M., Peyrin, T., Sasaki, Y.: Limited-birthday distinguishers for hash functions. In: Sako, K., Sarkar, P. (eds.) ASIACRYPT 2013, Part II. LNCS, vol. 8270, pp. 504–523. Springer, Heidelberg (2013)
12. Jean, J., Naya-Plasencia, M., Peyrin, T.: Improved rebound attack on the finalist grøstl. In: Canteaut, A. (ed.) FSE 2012. LNCS, vol. 7549, pp. 110–126. Springer, Heidelberg (2012)
13. Jean, J., Naya-Plasencia, M., Peyrin, T.: improved cryptanalysis of AES-like permutations. In: J. Cryptology, pp. 1–27. Springer, US (2013)
14. Jean, J., Naya-Plasencia, M., Peyrin, T.: Multiple limited-birthday distinguishers and applications. In: Lange, T., Lauter, K., Lisoněk, P. (eds.) SAC 2013. LNCS, vol. 8282, pp. 533–550. Springer, Heidelberg (2014)
15. Khoo, K., Peyrin, T., Poschmann, A.Y., Yap, H.: FOAM: searching for hardware-optimal SPN structures and components with a fair comparison. In: Batina, L., Robshaw, M. (eds.) CHES 2014. LNCS, vol. 8731, pp. 433–450. Springer, Heidelberg (2014). http://eprint.iacr.org/2014/530
16. Khovratovich, D., Rechberger, C., Savelieva, A.: Bicliques for preimages: attacks on skein-512 and the SHA-2 family. In: Canteaut, A. (ed.) FSE 2012. LNCS, vol. 7549, pp. 244–263. Springer, Heidelberg (2012)
17. Knellwolf, S., Khovratovich, D.: New preimage attacks against reduced SHA-1. In: Safavi-Naini, R., Canetti, R. (eds.) CRYPTO 2012. LNCS, vol. 7417, pp. 367–383. Springer, Heidelberg (2012)
18. Lamberger, M., Mendel, F., Rechberger, C., Rijmen, V., Schläffer, M.: Rebound distinguishers: results on the full whirlpool compression function. In: Matsui, M. (ed.) ASIACRYPT 2009. LNCS, vol. 5912, pp. 126–143. Springer, Heidelberg (2009)
19. Ma, B., Li, B., Hao, R., Li, X.: Cryptanalysis of Reduced-Round Whirlwind. Cryptology ePrint Archive (2015)
20. Mendel, F., Rechberger, C., Schläffer, M., Thomsen, S.S.: The rebound attack: cryptanalysis of reduced whirlpool and grøstl. In: Dunkelman, O. (ed.) FSE 2009. LNCS, vol. 5665, pp. 260–276. Springer, Heidelberg (2009)
21. Mendel, F., Rijmen, V., Schläffer, M.: Collision attack on 5 rounds of grøstl. In: Cid, C., Rechberger, C. (eds.) FSE 2014. LNCS, vol. 8540, pp. 509–521. Springer, Heidelberg (2015)
22. Menezes, A.J., Van Oorschot, P.C., Vanstone, S.A.: Handbook of Applied Cryptography. CRC Press (2010)
23. Merkle, R.C.: One way hash functions and DES. In: Brassard, G. (ed.) CRYPTO 1989. LNCS, vol. 435, pp. 428–446. Springer, Heidelberg (1990)
24. National Institute of Standards and Technology (NIST): FIPS-197: Advanced Encryption Standard. Federal Information Processing Standards Publication 197, U.S. Department of Commerce, November 2001. http://csrc.nist.gov/publications/fips/fips197/fips-197.pdf
25. Peyrin, T.: Cryptanalysis of grindahl. In: Kurosawa, K. (ed.) ASIACRYPT 2007. LNCS, vol. 4833, pp. 551–567. Springer, Heidelberg (2007)
26. Preneel, B., Govaerts, R., Vandewalle, J.: Hash functions based on block ciphers: a synthetic approach. In: Stinson, D.R. (ed.) CRYPTO 1993. LNCS, vol. 773, pp. 368–378. Springer, Heidelberg (1994)
27. Sasaki, Y.: Meet-in-the-middle preimage attacks on AES hashing modes and an application to whirlpool. In: Joux, A. (ed.) FSE 2011. LNCS, vol. 6733, pp. 378–396. Springer, Heidelberg (2011)

28. Sasaki, Y., Aoki, K.: Finding preimages in full MD5 faster than exhaustive search. In: Joux, A. (ed.) EUROCRYPT 2009. LNCS, vol. 5479, pp. 134–152. Springer, Heidelberg (2009)
29. Sasaki, Y., Wang, L., Wu, S., Wu, W.: Investigating fundamental security requirements on whirlpool: improved preimage and collision attacks. In: Wang, X., Sako, K. (eds.) ASIACRYPT 2012. LNCS, vol. 7658, pp. 562–579. Springer, Heidelberg (2012)
30. Wu, S., Feng, D., Wu, W., Guo, J., Dong, L., Zou, J.: (Pseudo) Preimage attack on round-reduced grøstl hash function and others. In: Canteaut, A. (ed.) FSE 2012. LNCS, vol. 7549, pp. 127–145. Springer, Heidelberg (2012)

Improving the Biclique Cryptanalysis of AES

Biaoshuai Tao$^{(\boxtimes)}$ and Hongjun Wu$^{(\boxtimes)}$

Nanyang Technological University, Singapore, Republic of Singapore
taob0001@e.ntu.edu.sg, wuhj@ntu.edu.sg

Abstract. Biclique attack is currently the only key-recovery attack on the full AES with a single key. Bogdanov *et al.* applied it to all the three versions of AES by constructing bicliques with size $2^8 \times 2^8$ and reducing the number of S-boxes computed in the matching phase. Their results were improved later by better selections of differential characteristics in the biclique construction. In this paper, we improve the biclique attack by increasing the biclique size to $2^{16} \times 2^8$ and $2^{16} \times 2^{16}$. We have a biclique attack on each of the following AES versions:
- AES-128 with time complexity $2^{126.13}$ and data complexity 2^{56},
- AES-128 with time complexity $2^{126.01}$ and data complexity 2^{72},
- AES-192 with time complexity $2^{189.91}$ and data complexity 2^{48}, and
- AES-256 with time complexity $2^{254.27}$ and data complexity 2^{40}.

Our results have the best time complexities among all the existing key-recovery attacks with data less than the entire code book.

Keywords: AES · Biclique attack · Large biclique

1 Introduction

Rijndael was selected as the Advanced Encryption Standard (AES) in 2001 [13]. AES is widely used today since it is strong in security and efficient in both software and hardware. AES was designed to resist differential, linear cryptanalysis and square attacks. The best impossible differential attack (first introduced in [2]) can break 7-round AES-128 [22], and the best square attack can break 8-round AES-192 [14]. The recent meet-in-the-middle (MITM) attack can break 9-round AES-192 and AES-256 [20]. The related-key attacks are powerful against AES [3–6,15,17], but the related-key attacks have limited impact on the security of AES when the secret keys in AES are generated securely.

The first key-recovery attack on the full AES with single key is the *biclique attack* [9]. Biclique attack on AES is faster than brute force by a factor of three to four. Biclique attack can be considered as an enhanced version of the meet-in-the-middle (MITM) attack. It was first introduced in the preimage attacks against hash functions Skein and SHA-2 [19]. After being applied to AES, the biclique attack was applied to attack other block ciphers, such as ARIA [1,11], Hight [16], IDEA [18], Piccolo [23], SQUARE [21], Twine [12].

Although the idea in [9] is revolutionary, both the time complexities and the data complexities of the attacks in [9] have room for improvement by better

© Springer International Publishing Switzerland 2015
E. Foo and D. Stebila (Eds.): ACISP 2015, LNCS 9144, pp. 39–56, 2015.
DOI: 10.1007/978-3-319-19962-7_3

selections of differential characteristics in the biclique construction. This has been illustrated in [1, 7, 8].

The independent-biclique paradigm can be further improved in time complexity by the *sieve-in-the-middle* (SIM) technique [10], a clever way to further speed up the matching computation by precomputing and storing the possible transitions for the middle superbox in a table of size 2^{32}, but with the extra cost of accessing large lookup tables is introduced.

In this paper, we improve the independent-biclique paradigm in [9] by using larger bicliques. We improve the time complexities for all the three AES versions. We also obtain improvements in data complexity for AES-128. Our results are summarized in Table 1 with comparison to the previous results. Among all the existing attacks which have data complexities that are less than 2^{128}, our results have minimum time complexities. Notice that our results can be naturally combined with sieve-in-the-middle (SIM) technique as shown in Table 1, which is further discussed in Sect. 7.

Table 1. Summary of our results

algorithm	data	computation without SIM	memory in bytes	computation with SIM	memory in bytes	reference
	2^{88}	$2^{126.21}$	$2^{14.32}$	-	-	[9]
	2^4	$2^{126.89}$	$2^{14.32}$	-	-	[8]
AES-128	2^{72}	$2^{126.72}$	$2^{14.32}$	-	-	[1]
previous results	-	-	-	$2^{126.01}$ ($2^{125.69}$)[1]	2^{64}	[10]
	2	$2^{126.67}$	$2^{14.32}$	$2^{126.59}$	2^{64}	[7][2]
	2^{64}	$2^{126.16}$	$2^{14.32}$	$2^{126.01}$	2^{64}	[7]
AES-128	2^{56}	$2^{126.13}$	$2^{22.07}$	$2^{125.99}$	2^{64}	Sect. 4
our results	2^{72}	$2^{126.01}$	$2^{26.14}$	$2^{125.87}$	2^{64}	Appendix A
	2^{80}	$2^{190.16}$ ($2^{189.74}$)[3]	$2^{14.39}$	-	-	[9]
AES-192	2^{48}	$2^{190.28}$	$2^{14.39}$	-	-	[1]
previous results	-	-	-	$2^{190.04}$	2^{64}	[10]
	2	$2^{190.9}$	$2^{14.39}$	$2^{190.83}$	2^{64}	[7]
	2^{48}	$2^{190.16}$	$2^{14.39}$	$2^{190.05}$	2^{64}	[7]
AES-192 our results	2^{48}	$2^{189.91}$	$2^{22.27}$	$2^{189.76}$	2^{64}	Appendix B
	2^{40}	$2^{254.58}$ ($2^{254.42}$)[4]	$2^{14.54}$	-	-	[9]
AES-256	2^{64}	$2^{254.53}$	$2^{14.54}$	-	-	[1]
previous results	-	-	-	$2^{254.51}$	2^{64}	[10]
	3	2^{255}	$2^{14.54}$	$2^{254.94}$	2^{64}	[7]
	2^{40}	$2^{254.31}$	$2^{14.54}$	$2^{254.24}$	2^{64}	[7]
AES-256 our results	2^{40}	$2^{254.27}$	$2^{22.61}$	$2^{254.18}$	2^{64}	Appendix B

[1] Our analysis shows that the time complexity to be $2^{126.01}$ instead of $2^{125.69}$ claimed in [10], based on the same criteria used in Sect. 4.5.

[2] The results with data complexity 2^{128} in [7] are not shown here, as we do not discuss the attack with entire code book in this paper.

[3] The accurate result is $2^{190.16}$ instead of $2^{189.74}$ originally claimed, as already corrected in [1].

[4] The accurate result is $2^{254.58}$ instead of $2^{254.42}$ originally claimed, as already corrected in [7].

This paper is organized as follows. The biclique attack on AES is introduced in Sect. 2. Section 3 gives an overview of our biclique attack on AES. Our detailed biclique attack on AES-128 is given in Sect. 4. Section 5 gives comparisons with our results to the previous ones. We verify our results in Sect. 6, and combine our results to the sieve-in-the-middle technique in Sect. 7. Section 8 concludes the paper.

2   The Biclique Attack

In this section, we give the general description of the biclique attack against block ciphers.

2.1   The Biclique

Consider a block cipher e which maps plaintext P to ciphertext C. Assume that the cipher can be decomposed as $e = g_2 \circ f \circ g_1$:

$$e : P \xrightarrow{g_1} S \xrightarrow{f} T \xrightarrow{g_2} C.$$

Consider 2^{d_1} intermediate states $\{S_i : i = 0, 1, \ldots, 2^{d_1} - 1\}$, 2^{d_2} intermediate states $\{T_j : j = 0, 1, \ldots, 2^{d_2} - 1\}$ and $2^{d_1 + d_2}$ keys $\{K[i,j]\}$. The 3-tuple $(\{S_i\}, \{T_j\}, \{K[i,j]\})$ is called a *biclique*, if $S_i \xrightarrow[f]{K[i,j]} T_j$ for all $i \in \{0, 1, \ldots, 2^{d_1} - 1\}$ and all $j \in \{0, 1, \ldots, 2^{d_2} - 1\}$. Here $K[i,j]$ maps the state S_i to the state T_j by the subcipher f.

In most of the attacks against AES as well as ours, bicliques are constructed "at the end", in which case g_2 is the identity map and $\{T_j\}$ becomes ciphertexts set $\{C_j\}$. Correspondingly, the biclique takes the form $(\{S_i\}, \{C_j\}, \{K[i,j]\})$. Bicliques "in the middle" are also considered in [7]. However, attacks based on such bicliques usually require extremely high data complexities, as the differences in $\{T_j\}$ will propagate to ciphertexts (refer to [7] for examples in AES).

Define the *length* of a biclique be the number of rounds covered by f, and the *size* be $2^{d_1} \times 2^{d_2}$. In the original attack [9] and most of the subsequent improvements, bicliques of size $2^8 \times 2^8$ are constructed in all the three versions of AES. In [7], bicliques of size $2^{16} \times 1$, i.e. stars, are also considered. The attack with stars only requires minimal data, but the time complexity becomes higher (refer to Table 1, the rows with data complexities 2 or 3). In our attack, the size of bicliques is enlarged to $2^{16} \times 2^8$, and even to $2^{16} \times 2^{16}$ for AES-128.

2.2   Outline of the Biclique Attack

As mentioned in the last section, we focus on the attack with g_2 being the identity map in which the biclique is "at the end". In this case, the biclique attack can be sketched as follows:

1. **Partition:** Partition 2^n keys into $2^{n-(d_1+d_2)}$ sets of size $2^{d_1+d_2}$.

2. **Biclique Construction**: For each partition $\{K[i,j]\}$, construct biclique $(\{S_i\}, \{C_j\}, \{K[i,j]\})$.

3. **Oracle Decryption**: Decrypt 2^{d_2} ciphertexts $\{C_j\}$ by the oracle with the secret key to obtain the corresponding 2^{d_2} plaintexts $\{P_j\}$.

4. **Matching**: for each pair (P_j, S_i), if $P_j \xrightarrow[g_1]{K[i,j]} S_i$, $K[i,j]$ is a candidate.

In the following sections, we introduce in details how the bicliques can be constructed, and how we can reduce the time complexity for the matching step (Step 4) by using a technique called *matching with precomputation* in [9].

2.3 Constructing Bicliques from Independent Related-Key Differentials

Two biclique attack paradigms are shown in [9], long biclique and independent biclique. We will only focus on independent biclique, as long-biclique-based attack currently cannot work for full AES.

Fix a tuple $(S_0, C_0, K[0,0])$ where $K[0,0]$ maps S_0 to C_0, and we aim to fill in the other $2^{d_1} - 1$ intermediate states, $2^{d_2} - 1$ ciphertexts and $2^{d_1+d_2} - 1$ keys to get a biclique. Consider the following two sets of related-key differentials with respect to the base computation $S_0 \xrightarrow[f]{K[0,0]} C_0$:

- Δ_j-**differential**: It maps a zero input difference to an output difference Δ_j under a key difference Δ_j^K:

$$0 \xrightarrow[f]{\Delta_j^K} \Delta_j \text{ with } \Delta_0^K = 0 \text{ and } \Delta_0 = 0, \text{ where } j = 0, 1, \ldots, 2^{d_2} - 1;$$

- ∇_i-**differential**: It maps an input difference ∇_i to a zero output difference under a key difference ∇_i^K:

$$\nabla_i \xrightarrow[f]{\nabla_i^K} 0 \text{ with } \nabla_0^K = 0 \text{ and } \nabla_0 = 0, \text{ where } i = 0, 1, \ldots, 2^{d_1} - 1.$$

According to [9], if the characteristics of Δ_j-differentials do not share active nonlinear components (which are S-boxes in our case of AES) with the characteristics of ∇_i-differentials, then the tuple $(S_0, C_0, K[0,0])$ will conform to all the $2^{d_1+d_2}$ combined (Δ_j, ∇_i)-differentials:

$$\nabla_i \xrightarrow[f]{\Delta_j^K \oplus \nabla_i^K} \Delta_j \text{ for } i \in \{0, 1, \ldots, 2^{d_1} - 1\} \text{ and } j \in \{0, 1, \ldots, 2^{d_2} - 1\},$$

which means

$$S_0 \oplus \nabla_i \xrightarrow[f]{K[0,0] \oplus \Delta_j^K \oplus \nabla_i^K} C_0 \oplus \Delta_j.$$

Finally, we obtain the biclique by putting

$$S_i = S_0 \oplus \nabla_i, \qquad C_j = C_0 \oplus \Delta_j \qquad \text{and} \qquad K[i,j] = K[0,0] \oplus \Delta_j^K \oplus \nabla_i^K,$$

where we require $\Delta_j^K \neq \nabla_i^K$ whenever $i + j > 0$, as we want all the $2^{d_1+d_2}$ keys in $\{K[i,j]\}$ to be distinct.

In the attack, an attacker first finds the key group $\{K[i,j]\}$ satisfying the above independent differentials property, then computes all the C_j from S_0 by Δ_j-differentials, and all the S_i from C_0 by ∇_i-differentials. This requires at most $2^{d_1} + 2^{d_2}$ computations of f.

In the case of the independent-biclique attack against AES, the cost of constructing a biclique turns out to be low, compared to the matching part (Step 4) which requires almost $2^{d_1+d_2}$ computations of g_1. Naturally, we aim to construct bicliques as long as possible in order to reduce the number of rounds of g_1. In [9], the biclique of length 3 is constructed for AES-128, and of length 4 for AES-192 and AES-256. Unfortunately, we cannot enlarge these lengths due to the extremely fast diffusion of AES, otherwise this will yield a decent improvement in time complexity. Instead, we increase the biclique size as mentioned. This reduces the time complexity in the matching part, as will be shown later.

2.4   Matching with Precomputations

In the last step, i.e. the matching step, an attacker needs to check whether P_j is mapped to S_i by the key $K[i,j]$ through g_1. To speed up the attack, instead of matching on a full state, an attacker considers matching variable v, which can be a single byte in the case of AES:

$$P_j \xrightarrow{K[i,j]} v \xleftarrow{K[i,j]} S_i.$$

This involves $2^{d_1+d_2}$ computations for g_1. However, for fixed j and two different i_1, i_2, some parts of the states in the forward computation $P_j \xrightarrow{K[i_1,j]} v$ and $P_j \xrightarrow{K[i_2,j]} v$ are still the same, for which we only need to compute once. It is similar for $v \xleftarrow{K[i,j_1]} S_i$ and $v \xleftarrow{K[i,j_2]} S_i$ in the backward computation. The *matching with precomputation* technique, introduced in [9], makes use of this observation. It precomputes and stores those parts that are neutral to different i values in forward direction, and those parts that are neutral to different j values in backward direction. As a result, we only need to recompute those unneutral parts in the matching step, and look up from the stored precomputation for neutral parts.

3   Overview of Our Biclique Attacks on AES

We construct bicliques with sizes $2^{16} \times 2^8$ and $2^{16} \times 2^{16}$ to improve the biclique attack against AES. In this section, we give an overview of our technique.

3.1   The Bicliques in Our Attacks

In our attacks, the state sets $\{S_i\}$ are increased by a factor of 2^8:

$$(\{S_{i_1,i_2}\}, \{C_j\}, \{K[i_1,i_2,j]\}) \text{ for all } i_1, i_2, j \in \{0, 1, \dots, 2^8 - 1\},$$

where

$$S_{i_1,i_2} \xrightarrow[f]{K[i_1,i_2,j]} C_j.$$

Note that this biclique is now of size $2^{16} \times 2^8$:

$$|\{S_{i_1,i_2}\}| = 2^{16}, \qquad |\{C_j\}| = 2^8, \qquad \text{and} \qquad |K[i_1,i_2,j]| = 2^{24}.$$

To construct such a biclique, we first fix the base computation $S_{0,0} \xrightarrow[f]{K[0,0,0]} C_0$. We then look for

- Δ_j-**differentials** which maps input difference 0 to an output difference Δ_j;
- ∇_{i_1}-**differentials** and ∇_{i_2}-**differentials** which map input differences ∇_{i_1} and ∇_{i_2} respectively to the output difference 0.

To make the biclique valid, we only need to make sure that there is no common active nonlinear components, the S-boxes in the case of AES, in either pair of differential characteristics: (Δ_j, ∇_{i_1}) and (Δ_j, ∇_{i_2}). To get the actual biclique, we need 3×2^8 computations of f for each of the three differentials above.

We have also designed a second attack specifically for AES-128 which considers even larger biclique $(\{S_{i_1,i_2}\}, \{C_{j_1,j_2}\}, \{K[i_1,i_2,j_1,j_2]\})$, in which the size of the ciphertext sets $\{C_j\}$ is further increased by a factor of 2^8. Correspondingly, we look for $\Delta_{j_1}, \Delta_{j_2}, \nabla_{i_1}, \nabla_{i_2}$ differentials such that none of $(\Delta_{j_1}, \nabla_{i_1})$, $(\Delta_{j_2}, \nabla_{i_1})$, $(\Delta_{j_1}, \nabla_{i_2})$ and $(\Delta_{j_2}, \nabla_{i_2})$ shares active nonlinear components. As a result, a total of 4×2^8 computations of f is needed.

3.2   Less Parts Being Recomputed in the Matching Step

After decrypting each C_j by the oracle, we obtain 2^8 plaintexts $\{P_j\}$. In the matching step, we apply subcipher g_1 to each P_j with key $K[i_1,i_2,j]$ to check whether we could get exactly S_{i_1,i_2}. If so, $K[i_1,i_2,j]$ is proposed as a candidate. We again match only the matching variable v:

$$P_j \xrightarrow{K[i_1,i_2,j]} v \xleftarrow{K[i_1,i_2,j]} S_{i_1,i_2}.$$

In the precomputation phase, we store the following 3×2^{16} computations:

Computation 1. $P_j \xrightarrow{K[0,i_2,j]} v$ for $i_2, j \in \{0, 1, \ldots, 2^8 - 1\}$,

Computation 2. $P_j \xrightarrow{K[i_1,0,j]} v$ for $i_1, j \in \{0, 1, \ldots, 2^8 - 1\}$,

Computation 3. $v \xleftarrow{K[i_1,i_2,0]} S_{i_1,i_2}$ for $i_1, i_2 \in \{0, 1, \ldots, 2^8 - 1\}$.

Same as in Sect. 2.4, in the recomputation phase when we match P_j to S_{i_1,i_2} on v, we only need to recompute those unneutral parts. The advantage of our technique is that less parts are needed to be recomputed. In the forward computation, we only need to recompute those parts which are unneutral to *both* i_1 and i_2. In other words, we can look up from two computations (Computation

1 and Computation 2 above) for the forward recomputation, instead of only one in the original attack, which causes less parts being recomputed and thus less time complexity in recomputation phase. Since the recomputation phase is the computational bottleneck, this advantage will reduce the total time complexity.

In our second attack on AES-128 with the biclique of size $2^{16} \times 2^{16}$ taking the form $(\{S_{i_1,i_2}\}, \{C_{j_1,j_2}\}, \{K[i_1,i_2,j_1,j_2]\})$, we decrypt each C_{j_1,j_2} to get P_{j_1,j_2}. In this case, we need to store 4×2^{24} computations in the precomputation phase:

Computation 1. $P_{j_1,j_2} \xrightarrow{K[0,i_2,j_1,j_2]} v$ for $i_2, j_1, j_2 \in \{0, 1, \ldots, 2^8 - 1\}$,

Computation 2. $P_{j_1,j_2} \xrightarrow{K[i_1,0,j_1,j_2]} v$ for $i_1, j_1, j_2 \in \{0, 1, \ldots, 2^8 - 1\}$,

Computation 3. $v \xleftarrow{K[i_1,i_2,0,j_2]} S_{i_1,i_2}$ for $i_1, i_2, j_2 \in \{0, 1, \ldots, 2^8 - 1\}$,

Computation 4. $v \xleftarrow{K[i_1,i_2,j_1,0]} S_{i_1,i_2}$ for $i_1, i_2, j_1 \in \{0, 1, \ldots, 2^8 - 1\}$.

The time complexity is further reduced as we also have two different references for the backward recomputation to looked up, namely, Computation 3 and 4. However, this improvement in time complexity does have disadvantages. Besides the obviously higher cost of memory, this attack may also pay extra cost on data complexity, as the additional Δ_{j_2}-differential may corrupt the extra neutral bytes in ciphertext.

4   The Improved Biclique Attacks Against AES

In this section, we describe our biclique attack against AES-128 by using the $2^{16} \times 2^8$ biclique. The attack on AES-128 with $2^{16} \times 2^{16}$ biclique is given in Appendix A, while the attacks on AES-192 and AES-256 with $2^{16} \times 2^8$ bicliques are illustrated with figures in Appendix B. Refer to Table 1 for all the results.

In this section and the two Appendix sections, we will use $0, 1, 2, \ldots$ to denote the round keys. Bytes within a state and a round key are enumerated as follow, and byte i in state Q is denoted as Q_i.

0	4	8	12
1	5	9	13
2	6	10	14
3	7	11	15

4.1   Key Partitioning

We define the key space with respect to the round key $8 (the same as that in [9]). This definition is valid as the AES-128 key schedule bijectively maps each key to $8. The base keys $K[0,0,0]$ are all the possible 2^{104} 16-byte values with three bytes, $8_0, 8_1, 8_6$, fixed to 0, whereas the remaining 13 bytes run over all values. The keys $\{K[i_1,i_2,j]\}$ in a group are enumerated by all possible byte differences i_1, i_2 and j with respect to the base key $K[0,0,0]$. The space of the round key $8 (and hence the AES key space) is thus partitioned into 2^{104} sets of size 2^{24}.

0			
0			
	0		

i_1	i_1		
i_2	i_2		
	j		

4.2   3-round Biclique of Size $2^{16} \times 2^8$

In the next step, we construct a 3-round biclique by following the steps in Sect. 3. Figure 1 illustrates the $\Delta_j, \nabla_{i_1}, \nabla_{i_2}$ differentials, from which we can easily verify that (Δ_j, ∇_{i_1}) and (Δ_j, ∇_{i_2}) shares no common active S-box.

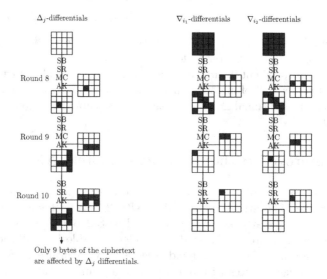

Fig. 1. All the $\Delta_j, \nabla_{i_1}, \nabla_{i_2}$ differentials: AES-128

4.3   Computing Round Keys

Now for each round key $K[i_1, i_2, j]$ of round 8, we calculate its corresponding round keys \$0, \$1, ..., \$7. At the first glance, it requires 2^{24} operations of the AES key schedule. However, the calculation can be speed up with the precomputation technique introduced earlier. We will apply this technique only on the first column of each round key, as the rest three columns require only xor operations to be computed which has negligible time complexity.

In the precomputation phase, we compute all the 8 round keys for the following:

- $K[0, i_2, j]$ for all $i_2, j \in \{0, 1, ..., 2^8 - 1\}$;
- $K[i_1, 0, j]$ for all $i_1, j \in \{0, 1, ..., 2^8 - 1\}$.

This requires at most 2×2^{16} 8-round computations of key schedule.

In the recomputation phase when we are calculating $K[i_1, i_2, j]$ (for all the 8 round keys from \$7 all the way down to \$0), we only need cheap xor and lookup operations (no S-box operation in particular) by storing all the bytes with $*$ and the S-box substitution values of all the bytes with $\circ$ in Fig. 2.

For example, to compute the first byte of \$7, we have $\$7_0 = \$8_0 \oplus s(\$7_{13}) \oplus roundConst$, where $s(\$7_{13})$ has the same value for $K[0, i_2, j]$ and $K[i_1, i_2, j]$ and we already store the one for $K[0, i_2, j]$. For the second and the third bytes $\$7_1, \$7_2$, we look them up directly from $K[0, i_2, j]$, and we lookup from $K[i_1, 0, j]$ for the forth byte $\$7_3$. After we obtain the first column of \$7, we compute the rest 12 bytes and get the entire \$7. After we recover the full \$7, we do the same to compute \$6 and so on.

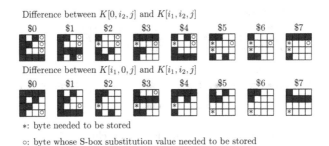

Fig. 2. Precomputation and recomputation of round keys: AES-128

4.4   Matching Over 7 Rounds

Now we check whether the secret key belongs to the key group $\{K[i_1, i_2, j]\}$. As shown in Fig. 3 and Fig. 4, we match the first byte in the state after Round 2, which is the same as [9]. So we only need to compute 4 bytes in Round 2, 1 byte in Round 3 and 4 bytes in Round 4. Additionally, benefiting from the matching with precomputation technique (Sect. 2.4), we only need to compute very few bytes in Round 1 and Round 7 in the recomputation phase. Specifically, we only need to compute 5 bytes in Round 1 (Fig. 3) and 8 bytes in Round 7 (Fig. 4).

4.5   Complexity of the Attack

Now we evaluate the time complexity, data complexity and memory complexity of our attack.

Time Complexity. Similar to the original biclique attack [9], we count the number of S-boxes computations to determine the time complexity. Note that there are 200 S-boxes in one full AES-128 (160 for encryption/decryption, 40 for key schedule). We measure the time complexity in terms of the full AES-128 operations, so the overall time complexity will be given as the total number of S-boxes in our attack divided by 200.

Difference between the forward computations of P_j using $K[i_1, i_2, j]$ and $K[0, i_2, j]$

Difference between the forward computations of P_j using $K[i_1, i_2, j]$ and $K[i_1, 0, j]$

Byte need to be recomputed (Cells with light color are not needed as we match on only 1 byte.)

Fig. 3. Forward recomputation in matching: AES-128

Difference between the backward computations of S_{i_1, i_2} using $K[i_1, i_2, j]$ and $K[i_1, i_2, 0]$

Byte need to be recomputed (Cells with light color are not needed as we match on only 1 byte.)

Fig. 4. Backward recomputation in matching: AES-128

For the search in a single key group $\{K[i_1, i_2, j]\}$, the time complexity consists of the following components:

1. C_{biclique}: The complexity of constructing the biclique. (Sect. 4.2)
2. C_{oracle}: The complexity for the decryption of each C_j by the oracle.
3. C_{keys}: The complexity of computing all the round keys for key $K[i_1, i_2, j]$ in the set $\{K[i_1, i_2, j]\}$. (Sect. 4.3)
4. C_{prec}: The complexity of precomputation phase. (Sect. 4.4)
5. C_{rec}: The complexity of recomputation phase. (Sect. 4.4)
6. C_{falsep}: The complexity generated from false positives.

The time complexity for biclique construction is merely the 3×2^8 computations of 3 rounds subcipher f which is 56 S-boxes (including 2 rounds key schedule). This complexity is given as

$$C_{\text{biclique}} = 3 \times 2^8 \times 56/200 = 2^{7.75}.$$

We need to decrypt all the 2^8 ciphertexts $\{C_j\}$:

$$C_{\text{oracle}} = 2^8.$$

The time complexity of computing all the round keys includes the precomputation phase and recomputation phase. As mentioned in Sect. 4.3, the recomputation of round keys require only xor and lookup operations, which correspond to 0 S-box operation. As for precomputation, we need to compute those 8 round keys (equivalent to 32 S-boxes) for both groups $K[0, i_2, j]$ and $K[i_1, 0, j]$, and each group is of size 2^{16}. The time complexity of round key computation is

$$C_{\text{keys}} = 2 \times 2^{16} \times 32/200 = 2^{14.36}.$$

In the precomputation phase of matching, we only need to compute one round for Computation 1, 2 and 3 in Sect. 3.2. This is because all the 16 bytes of each state become different except for Round 1 and 7 (refer to Fig. 3 and Fig. 4), so the precomputation of other rounds provides no information for the recomputation at all, which we do not need to store. Since exactly 20 S-boxes are included in a round, we have

$$C_{\text{prec}} = 3 \times 2^{16} \times 20/200 = 2^{14.26}.$$

In the recomputation state, as shown in Fig. 3 and 4, we need to recompute 9 S-boxes in the forward direction and 45 S-boxes in the backward direction. There are 54 S-boxes in total, and it is needed for each of the 2^{24} keys $\{K[i_1, i_2, j]\}$.

$$C_{\text{rec}} = 2^{24} \times 54/200 = 2^{22.11}.$$

We performed 2^{24} matchings on a single byte with 2^8 possible values, the number of false positives is approximately $2^{24-8} = 2^{16}$. We eliminate the false positives by matching them on a full 16-byte state, which require 3 rounds computation (i.e. Round 2, 3 and 4), so 48 S-boxes are needed.

$$C_{\text{falsep}} = 2^{16} \times 48/200 = 2^{13.94}.$$

Summing up all the above, we have the total time complexity:

$$2^{104}(2^{7.75} + 2^8 + 2^{14.36} + 2^{14.26} + 2^{22.11} + 2^{13.94}) = 2^{126.13}.$$

Note that with the above time complexity, the secret key of AES-128 is obtained with success rate 1.

Data Complexity. According to Fig. 1, Δ_j-differential affect only 9 bytes of the ciphertext, and all the ciphertexts have constant values at bytes $C_{0,4,7,8,10,11,15}$. Furthermore, the ciphertext bytes C_1, C_5 and C_{13} of those 9 bytes always maintain the same difference. As a result, the data complexity does not exceed $2^{(9-3+1)\times 8} = 2^{56}$.

Memory Complexity. We need to store the biclique, as well as the precomputations for both round keys and states. Note that we do not need to store all the 2^{24} sets of round keys, as it can be computed in runtime whenever needed.

For the biclique storage, we need to store 2^{16} states $\{S_{i_1, i_2}\}$ and 2^8 ciphertexts $\{C_j\}$, with size 16 bytes for each. The total memory complexity for biclique storage is $(2^8 + 2^{16}) \times 16$ bytes.

For the precomputations for round keys and states, we only store the bytes that are looked up in the recomputation stage (those neutral bytes not affected by the differential chartertistic). For the round key precomputation, as shown in Fig. 2, we need to store a total of $2^{16} \times 32$ bytes (all the $*$ and $\circ$) which includes $2^{16} \times 23$ bytes from $K[0, i_2, j]$ and $2^{16} \times 9$ bytes from $K[i_1, 0, j]$.

Similarly, for the storage of states used in the matching, we only need to store 11 bytes in the state after the SubBytes operation in Round 1, and 8 bytes in the state between Round 6 and Round 7, which is $2^{16}(11+8) = 2^{16} \times 19$ (bytes).

Finally, the total memory complexity is

$$(2^8 + 2^{16}) \times 16 + 2^{16} \times 32 + 2^{16} \times 19 = 2^{22.07} \text{ (bytes)}.$$

We used the same criteria to analyze the memory complexities for all the previous attacks as well, and obtain these data in Table 1 (the forth column).

5   Comparing with the Previous Biclique Attacks

As mentioned in Sect. 3.2, the main advantage of our technique is reducing the number of S-boxes being recomputed in the matching step. Table 2 compares the number of S-boxes needed in the recomputation, and it shows that our attack requires least S-boxes to be recomputed (with data complexity less than the full code book).

Table 2. Comparison of the numbers of S-boxes recomputed

	our results with $2^{16} \times 2^8$ bicliques	our results with $2^{16} \times 2^{16}$ bicliques	[9] (original attack)	[7] (prev. best results)
AES-128	54	50	57	55
AES-192	52	-	61	62
AES-256	83	-	101	86

It is illuminating to compare the two results for AES-128. With larger bicliques, the number of S-boxes computed can be further reduced from 54 to 50 which leads an improvement of time complexity from $2^{126.13}$ to $2^{126.01}$ (Table 1). However, by applying larger biclique, the data complexity and memory complexity increase significantly (Table 1).

6   Verification in Experiment

In our attack against all the three AES versions, the whole key space is partitioned into $2^{104}/2^{168}/2^{232}$ sets with sizes 2^{24} (or 2^{96} sets with size 2^{32} in the second attack of AES-128). We wrote a program to search the key in a single partition. The secret key is found if it was set in the searched partition. This program proves the correctness of our attack algorithm, including the validity of bicliques and the correctness of the differential characteristics. The program also counts the number of S-boxes calculated in the search of a full partition, and outputs the time complexities in terms of equivalent full AES computations. The memory complexity is also verified in the experiment by checking the memory usage of the process. We verified the attacks on all the three versions of AES, and the experimental results are even slightly better than our theoretical results.

7   Combination with the Sieve-in-the-Middle Technique

Sieve-in-the-Middle (SIM) technique by Canteaut et al. [10] is a variant of the Meet-in-the-Middle (MITM) technique. In its application to the biclique attack against AES, it can save another 5 S-boxes in recomputation during the matching step, by storing 2^{32} lookup tables of size 2^{32} bytes each. With a large increment in memory complexities, all the numbers shown in Table 2 can be reduced by 5, which results in further improvements in time complexities (see Table 1). The reader can also refer to Sect. 8 of [7] for more details.

8   Conclusion

In this paper, we improved the independent-biclique paradigm of the biclique attack [9] by increasing the biclique size. Our technique enhances the matching-with-precomputation technique in [9] by reducing the number of S-boxes being recomputed. The data complexities in the attacks against AES-128 are also reduced. Our attacks are currently the fastest with moderate data complexities.

A   Biclique Attack on AES-128 with $2^{16} \times 2^{16}$ Biclique

A.1   Key Partitioning

We again define the key space with respect to the round key $8. Fix $8_0, $8_1, 8_7 and 8_8 to 0. The keys $\{K[i_1, i_2, j_1, j_2]\}$ in a group are enumerated by all possible byte differences i_1, i_2, j_1 and j_2 with respect to the base key $K[0, 0, 0, 0]$. The AES key space is thus partitioned into the 2^{96} sets of size 2^{32}.

0	0		
0			
	0		

i_1	$i_1 \oplus j_1$		
i_2	i_2		
	j_2		

The fact that 8_8 is shared by the byte differences i_1 and j_1 does not invalidate the biclique, as this shared difference has not passed into any non-linear S-box operation (refer to Fig. 5).

A.2   3-round Biclique of Size $2^{16} \times 2^{16}$

Figure 5 illustrates the $\Delta_{j_1}, \Delta_{j_2}, \nabla_{i_1}, \nabla_{i_2}$ differentials, from which we can easily verify that each of the two Δ differentials share no active S-boxes to each of the two ∇ differentials.

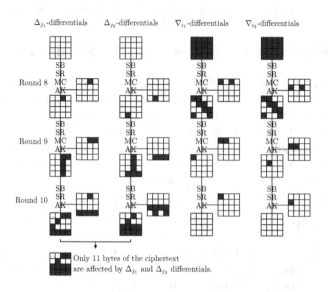

Fig. 5. All the $\Delta_{j_1}, \Delta_{j_2}, \nabla_{i_1}, \nabla_{i_2}$ differentials: AES-128

A.3   Computation of Round Keys

For each round key $K[i_1, i_2, j_1, j_2]$ of round 8, we calculate its corresponding round keys $\$0, \$1, \ldots, \$7$. In the precomputation phase, we compute and store all the 8 round keys for the following:

- $K[0, i_2, j_1, j_2]$ for all $i_2, j_1, j_2 \in \{0, 1, \ldots, 2^8 - 1\}$;
- $K[i_1, 0, j_1, j_2]$ for all $i_1, j_1, j_2 \in \{0, 1, \ldots, 2^8 - 1\}$.

This requires at most $2 \cdot 2^{24}$ 8-round computations of key schedule.

Since we are using exactly the same $\nabla_{i_1}, \nabla_{i_2}$ differential characteristics, the key differential patterns of the above two computations are the same to those in Fig. 2. For the same reason, we only need to store those marked bytes, and the recomputation of round keys require no S-box computation. The only difference is that each $*$ or $\circ$ now corresponds to 2^{24} bytes in memory, instead of 2^{16} bytes.

A.4   Matching Over 7 Rounds

Due to larger size bicliques, even less bytes need to be recomputed. We need to recompute 9 S-boxes in the forward direction and 41 S-boxes in the backward direction, which only gives us 50 in total. Refer to Fig. 6 and Fig. 7 for details.

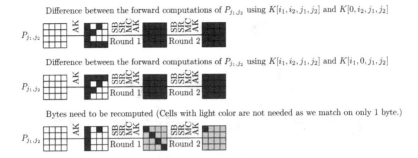

Fig. 6. Forward recomputation in matching: AES-128

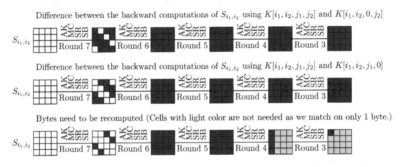

Fig. 7. Backward recomputation in matching: AES-128

A.5 Complexity of the Attack

The evaluation of time and data complexities is similar to those in Sect. 4.5, and thus are omitted here. Refer to Table 1 for the results.

Memory Complexity. Fig. 8 illustrates the bytes need to be stored in the matching phase, which suggests a total of 23×2^{24} bytes needs to be stored. Coupled with a total of 32×2^{24} bytes in the round key (those $*$ and $\circ$ in Fig. 2), it seems the total memory complexity is more than $23 \times 2^{24} + 32 \times 2^{24} = 2^{29.78}$ bytes. This complexity can be reduced if we fixed the value of j_1 first, and do the precomputation and recomputation with each fixed j_1.

To be specific, for each fixed j_1, we need to stores 7 bytes for each different value i_2, j_2 (the first row in Fig. 8), 4 bytes for each different value i_1, j_2 (the second row in Fig. 8) and 8 bytes for each different value i_1, i_2 (the last row in Fig. 8); when j_1 varies to the next value, we store the values of all those bytes again for the updated j_1 value. Thus, the memory complexity used for storing state bytes is

$$M_{\text{states}} = 7 \times 2^{16} + 4 \times 2^{16} + 4 \times 2^{24} + 8 \times 2^{16} = 2^{26.03} \text{ (bytes)}.$$

We can do the same for key bytes storage. According to Fig. 2, for each fixed j_1, we need to stores 23 bytes for each different value i_2, j_2 and 9 bytes for

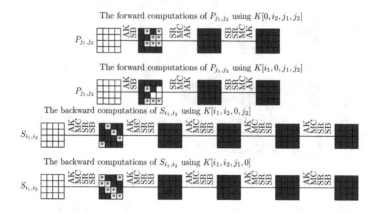

Fig. 8. Bytes to be stored in states: AES-128

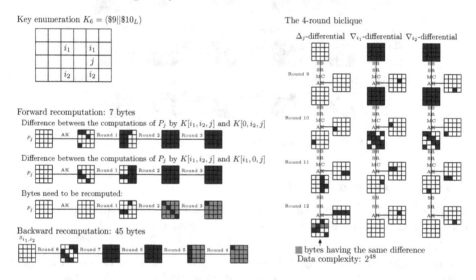

Fig. 9. Illustration for AES-192

each different value i_1, j_2, which has total memory complexity 32×2^{16}. Adding $2 \times 2^{16} \times 16$ bytes memory needed to store a biclique, we have total memory complexity to be

$$2 \times 2^{16} \times 16 + 2^{26.03} + 32 \times 2^{16} = 2^{26.11} \text{ (bytes)}.$$

B   The Improved Attacks Against AES-192 and AES-256

The attacks against AES-192 and AES-256 with $2^{16} \times 2^8$ bicliques are similar to the one for AES-128 discussed in Sect. 4. Here, we give only figures illustrations Fig. 9 and Fig. 10 showing details of key enumerations, biclique constructions

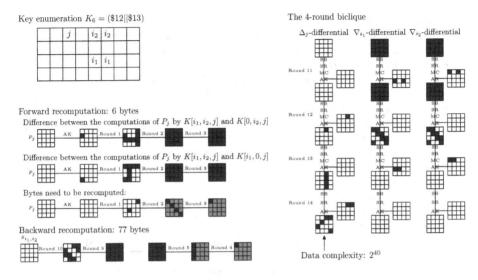

Fig. 10. Illustration for AES-256

and recomputations in both directions. Following Sect. 4, the reader can easily verify the results in Table 1 from these figures.

References

1. Abed, F., Forler, C., List, E., Lucks, S., Wenzel, J.: A framework for automated independent-biclique cryptanalysis. In: Moriai, S. (ed.) FSE 2013. LNCS, vol. 8424, pp. 561–582. Springer, Heidelberg (2014)
2. Bahrak, B., Aref, M.R.: Impossible differential attack on seven-round AES-128. Information Security, IET **2**(2), 28–32 (2008)
3. Biham, E., Dunkelman, O., Keller, N.: Related-key impossible differential attacks on 8-round AES-192. In: Pointcheval, D. (ed.) CT-RSA 2006. LNCS, vol. 3860, pp. 21–33. Springer, Heidelberg (2006)
4. Biryukov, A., Dunkelman, O., Keller, N., Khovratovich, D., Shamir, A.: Key recovery attacks of practical complexity on AES-256 variants with up to 10 rounds. In: Gilbert, H. (ed.) EUROCRYPT 2010. LNCS, vol. 6110, pp. 299–319. Springer, Heidelberg (2010)
5. Biryukov, A., Khovratovich, D.: Related-key cryptanalysis of the full AES-192 and AES-256. In: Matsui, M. (ed.) ASIACRYPT 2009. LNCS, vol. 5912, pp. 1–18. Springer, Heidelberg (2009)
6. Biryukov, A., Khovratovich, D., Nikolić, I.: Distinguisher and related-key attack on the full AES-256. In: Halevi, S. (ed.) CRYPTO 2009. LNCS, vol. 5677, pp. 231–249. Springer, Heidelberg (2009)
7. Bogdanov, A., Chang, D., Ghosh, M., Sanadhya, S.K.: Bicliques with minimal data and time complexity for AES. In: Lee, J., Kim, J. (eds.) Information Security and Cryptology-ICISC 2014. LNCS, pp. 160–174. Springer, Heidelberg (2015)

8. Bogdanov, A., Kavun, E., Paar, C., Rechberger, C., Yalcin, T.: Better than brute-force–optimized hardware architecture for efficient biclique attacks on AES-128. In: ECRYPT Workshop, SHARCS-Special Purpose Hardware for Attacking Cryptographic Systems (2012)
9. Bogdanov, A., Khovratovich, D., Rechberger, C.: Biclique cryptanalysis of the full AES. In: Lee, D.H., Wang, X. (eds.) ASIACRYPT 2011. LNCS, vol. 7073, pp. 344–371. Springer, Heidelberg (2011)
10. Canteaut, A., Naya-Plasencia, M., Vayssière, B.: Sieve-in-the-middle: improved MITM attacks. In: Canetti, R., Garay, J.A. (eds.) CRYPTO 2013, Part I. LNCS, vol. 8042, pp. 222–240. Springer, Heidelberg (2013)
11. Chen, Sz, Xu, Tm: Biclique attack of the full ARIA-256. IACR Cryptology ePrint Archive **2012**, 11 (2012)
12. Çoban, M., Karakoç, F., Boztaş, Ö.: Biclique cryptanalysis of TWINE. In: Pieprzyk, J., Sadeghi, A.-R., Manulis, M. (eds.) CANS 2012. LNCS, vol. 7712, pp. 43–55. Springer, Heidelberg (2012)
13. Daemen, J., Rijmen, V.: The design of Rijndael: AES - the advanced encryption standard. Springer Science & Business Media (2002)
14. Dunkelman, O., Keller, N., Shamir, A.: Improved single-key attacks on 8-round AES-192 and AES-256. In: Abe, M. (ed.) ASIACRYPT 2010. LNCS, vol. 6477, pp. 158–176. Springer, Heidelberg (2010)
15. Gorski, M., Lucks, S.: New related-key boomerang attacks on AES. In: Chowdhury, D.R., Rijmen, V., Das, A. (eds.) INDOCRYPT 2008. LNCS, vol. 5365, pp. 266–278. Springer, Heidelberg (2008)
16. Hong, D., Koo, B., Kwon, D.: Biclique attack on the full HIGHT. In: Kim, H. (ed.) ICISC 2011. LNCS, vol. 7259, pp. 365–374. Springer, Heidelberg (2012)
17. Jakimoski, G., Desmedt, Y.: Related-key differential cryptanalysis of 192-bit key AES variants. In: Matsui, M., Zuccherato, R.J. (eds.) SAC 2003. LNCS, vol. 3006, pp. 208–221. Springer, Heidelberg (2004)
18. Khovratovich, D., Leurent, G., Rechberger, C.: Narrow-bicliques: cryptanalysis of full IDEA. In: Pointcheval, D., Johansson, T. (eds.) EUROCRYPT 2012. LNCS, vol. 7237, pp. 392–410. Springer, Heidelberg (2012)
19. Khovratovich, D., Rechberger, C., Savelieva, A.: Bicliques for preimages: attacks on skein-512 and the SHA-2 family. In: Canteaut, A. (ed.) FSE 2012. LNCS, vol. 7549, pp. 244–263. Springer, Heidelberg (2012)
20. Li, L., Jia, K., Wang, X.: Improved single-key attacks on 9-round AES-192/256. In: Cid, C., Rechberger, C. (eds.) FSE 2014. LNCS, vol. 8540, pp. 127–146. Springer, Heidelberg (2015)
21. Mala, H.: Biclique-based cryptanalysis of the block cipher SQUARE. Information Security, IET **8**(3), 207–212 (2014)
22. Mala, H., Dakhilalian, M., Rijmen, V., Modarres-Hashemi, M.: Improved impossible differential cryptanalysis of 7-round AES-128. In: Progress in Cryptology-INDOCRYPT 2010, pp. 282–291. Springer (2010)
23. Wang, Y., Wu, W., Yu, X.: Biclique cryptanalysis of reduced-round piccolo block cipher. In: Ryan, M.D., Smyth, B., Wang, G. (eds.) ISPEC 2012. LNCS, vol. 7232, pp. 337–352. Springer, Heidelberg (2012)

Public Key Cryptography

A New General Framework for Secure Public Key Encryption with Keyword Search

Rongmao Chen[1,2]($\boxtimes$), Yi Mu[1]($\boxtimes$), Guomin Yang[1], Fuchun Guo[1], and Xiaofen Wang[1,3]

[1] Centre for Computer and Information Security Research,
School of Computing and Information Technology,
University of Wollongong, Wollongong, Australia
{rc517,ymu,gyang,fuchun}@uow.edu.au, wangxuedou@sina.com
[2] College of Computer, National University of Defense Technology,
Changsha, China
[3] Department of Computer Science and Engineering,
University of Electronic Science and Technology of China, Chengdu, China

Abstract. Public Key Encryption with Keyword Search (PEKS), introduced by Boneh et al. in *Eurocrypt'04*, allows users to search encrypted documents on an untrusted server without revealing any information. This notion is very useful in many applications and has attracted a lot of attention by the cryptographic research community. However, one limitation of all the existing PEKS schemes is that they cannot resist the Keyword Guessing Attack (KGA) launched by a malicious server. In this paper, we propose a new PEKS framework named Dual-Server Public Key Encryption with Keyword Search (DS-PEKS). This new framework can withstand all the attacks, including the KGA from the two untrusted servers, as long as they do not collude. We then present a generic construction of DS-PEKS using a new variant of the Smooth Projective Hash Functions (SPHFs), which is of independent interest.

Keywords: Dual-server public key encryption with keyword search · Smooth projective hash function

1 Introduction

To enable encrypted documents searchable on an untrusted server without revealing any information, Boneh et al. [10] introduced the notion of public key encryption with keyword search (PEKS) in Eurocrypt'04. A PEKS system has many potential applications including private databases and data mining where the users are concerned about their data privacy. In a PEKS system, a sender attaches some encrypted keywords (referred to as PEKS ciphertexts) with the encrypted data. The receiver then sends the trapdoor of a to-be-searched keyword to the server for data searching. Given the trapdoor and the PEKS ciphertext, the server can test whether the keyword underlying the PEKS ciphertxt is equal to the one selected by the receiver. If so, the server sends the matching encrypted data to the receiver.

© Springer International Publishing Switzerland 2015
E. Foo and D. Stebila (Eds.): ACISP 2015, LNCS 9144, pp. 59–76, 2015.
DOI: 10.1007/978-3-319-19962-7_4

Inside Keyword Guessing Attack. A PEKS scheme is considered secure if it reveals no information about the data to the server. To be more precise, the server can only locate the message specified by the receiver but cannot learn anything else. Nevertheless, none of the existing PEKS schemes is secure against Keyword Guessing Attack (KGA) launched by a malicious server, which is also known as inside KGA. Specifically, given a trapdoor, the adversarial server can choose a guessing keyword from the keyword space and then use the keyword to generate a PEKS ciphertext. The server then can test whether the guessing keyword is the one underlying the trapdoor. This *guessing-then-testing* procedure can be repeated until the correct keyword is found. Such a guessing attack has also been considered in many password-based systems. However, the attack can be launched more efficiently against PEKS since the keyword space is roughly the same as a normal dictionary (e.g., all the meaningful English words), which has a much smaller size than a password dictionary (e.g., all the words containing 6 alphanumeric characters).

Unfortunately, we see that the inside KGA is an inherent vulnerability of the existing PEKS framework which only involves one server. This is essentially due to the following facts.

- **Public Generation of PEKS Ciphertexts**. The generation of a PEKS ciphertext only involves public information; hence the server can generate the PEKS ciphertext for any keyword.
- **Stand-alone Testing.** The server can independently check whether a PEKS ciphertext is consistent with a trapdoor from the receiver.
- **Correctness/consistency of PEKS.** The correctness required by PEKS ensures that the test function always outputs the correct answer.

It is obvious that we should not sacrifice the correctness of PEKS; otherwise we will essentially lose the search functionality. One possible solution to overcome the problem is to disable the public generation of PEKS ciphertexts, which means the PEKS encryption performed by a sender should also take as input some secret information only known by the sender (e.g., the sender's private key). However, this solution is not practical either, since the receiver will need to embed some information of the sender (e.g., the public key) in the generation of a trapdoor. But the receiver may not be aware of the identity of the sender when performing the search, and multiple trapdoors for a keyword need to be generated for all the potential senders in the system.

Our Contributions. The contributions of this paper are two-fold. Firstly, based on the above observations, we propose to overcome the inside KGA by disallowing the stand-alone testing performed by a server. Specifically, we formally define a new PEKS framework named *Dual-Server Public Key Encryption with Keyword Search* (DS-PEKS). Secondly, we show a generic construction of DS-PEKS using a newly defined variant of *Smooth Projective Hash Function* (SPHF) which maybe of independent interest.

Overview of Techniques. The key idea of the new framework is to split the testing functionality of the PEKS system into two parts which are handled by two independent servers: *front server* and *back server*. Upon receiving a query from the receiver, the front server pre-processes the trapdoor and all the PEKS ciphertexts using its private key, and then sends some *internal testing-states* to the back server with the corresponding trapdoor and PEKS ciphertexts hidden. The back server can then decide which documents are queried by the receiver using its private key and the received internal testing-states from the front server. We show that under such a setting neither the front server nor the back server can launch the keyword guessing attack. It is worth noting that in the above process, we require that the two servers do not collude since otherwise it goes back to the one-server setting in which inside KGA cannot be prevented.

Smooth Projective Hash Function (SPHF) is originally introduced by by Cramer and Shoup [13] for construction of CCA-secure public key encryption schemes. Roughly speaking, an SPHF can be defined based on a domain $\mathcal{X}$ and an $\mathcal{NP}$ language $\mathcal{L}$, where $\mathcal{L} \subset \mathcal{X}$. The key property of SPHF is that the projection key uniquely determines the hash value of any word in the language $\mathcal{L}$ (*projective*) but gives almost no information about the hash value of any point in $\mathcal{X} \setminus \mathcal{L}$ (*smooth*). In our paper, the SPHF used is based on the hard-on-the-average $\mathcal{NP}$-language and hence is also *pseudo-random* [15]. That is, given a word $W \in \mathcal{L}$, without the corresponding witness and the secret hashing key, the distribution of its hash value is computationally indistinguishable from a uniform distribution. Our newly defined variant, named Lin-Hom SPHF, additionally requires the underlying language and the hash function to be *linear* and *homomorphic*. In a generic DS-PEKS construction, to generate the PEKS ciphertext of a keyword, the sender picks a word randomly from $\mathcal{L}$ and computes its two hash values using the witness and the public key (projection key) of the front and back servers respectively. The keyword is then concealed with these two hash values in the PEKS ciphertext. One can see that due to the *pseudo-randomness* of the SPHF, given a PEKS ciphertext, the two servers cannot learn any information about the underlying keyword individually as they do not know the witness or the private key (secret hashing key) of each other. The receiver generates the trapdoor in the same way and hence security of the trapdoor can also be guaranteed. In the pre-processing stage, the front server first removes the pseudo-random hash values in the trapdoor and the PEKS ciphertext for the back server using its private key. Due to the *linear* and *homomorphic* properties of Lin-Hom SPHF, the front server can re-randomise the *internal testing-state* to preserve the keyword privacy from the back server who can only determine whether the two keywords underlying the *internal testing-state* are the same or not. We can see that in this way, the security of DS-PEKS against inside keyword guessing attack can be obtained.

1.1   Related Work

Following Boneh et al.'s seminal work [10], Abdalla et al. [1] formalized anonymous IBE (AIBE) and presented a generic construction of searchable encryption from AIBE. They also showed how to transfer a hierarchical IBE (HIBE) scheme into a public key encryption with temporary keyword search (PETKS) where the trapdoor is only valid in a specific time interval. Waters [22] showed that the PEKS schemes based on bilinear map could be applied to build encrypted and searchable auditing logs. In order to construct a PEKS secure in the standard model, Khader [19] proposed a scheme based on the k-resilient IBE and also gave a construction supporting multiple-keyword search. The first PEKS scheme without pairings was introduced by Crescenzo and Saraswat [14]. The construction is derived from Cock's IBE scheme [12] which is not very practical.

Byun et al. [11] introduced the off-line keyword guessing attack against PEKS as keywords are chosen from a much smaller space than passwords and users usually use well-known keywords for searching documents. They also pointed out that the scheme proposed in Boneh et al. [10] was susceptible to keyword guessing attack. Inspired by the work of Byun *et al.* [11], Yau et al. [23] demonstrated that outside adversaries that capture the trapdoors sent in a public channel can reveal the encrypted keywords through off-line keyword guessing attacks and they also showed off-line keyword guessing attacks against the (SCF-)PEKS schemes in [4,5]. The first PEKS scheme secure against outside keyword guessing attacks was proposed by Rhee et al. [21]. In [20], the notion of trapdoor indistinguishability was proposed and the authors showed that trapdoor indistinguishability is a sufficient condition for preventing outside keyword-guessing attacks.

Nevertheless, all the schemes mentioned above are found to be vulnerable to keyword guessing attacks from a malicious server (i.e., inside keyword guessing attacks). Jeong et al. [17] showed a negative result that the consistency/correctness of PEKS implies insecurity to inside keyword guessing attacks in PEKS. Their result indicates that constructing secure and consistent PEKS schemes against inside keyword guessing attacks is impossible under the original framework.

1.2 Organization

In Section 2, we propose the new framework, namely DS-PEKS, and present its formal definition and security models. We then define a new variant of smooth projective hash function (SPHF), which satisfies the linear and homomorphic properties, for a special class of NP languages in Section 3. A generic construction of DS-PEKS from LH-SPHF is shown in Section 4 with formal correctness analysis and security proofs. We then give a conclusion in Section 5.

2 Dual-Server Public Key Encryption with Keyword Search

In this section, we formally define the Dual-Server Public Key Encryption with Keyword Search (DS-PEKS) and its security model.

2.1 Overview of DS-PEKS

As introduced in [10], a traditional PEKS scheme is defined by a tuple of algorithms (KeyGen, PEKS, Trapdoor, Test). The KeyGen algorithm is used for the generation of public/private key pair for the receiver. The sender runs PEKS to generate keyword ciphertexts which are attached to the data. A receiver then uses Trapdoor to generate the trapdoor for any keyword he/she wants the server to search for. Given the trapdoors, the server can run the algorithm Test to locate the data containing the keywords specified by the receiver. As shown previously, it is impossible to construct a PEKS scheme secure against keyword guessing attack from the malicious server if we follow the traditional PEKS framework due to the public generation of PEKS ciphertexts, stand-alone testing, and the correctness of PEKS. In our proposed framework, namely DS-PEKS, we disallow the stand-alone testing to obtain the security against inside keyword guessing attacks. Roughly speaking, DS-PEKS consists of (KeyGen, DS-PEKS, DS-Trapdoor, FrontTest, BackTest). To be more precise, the KeyGen algorithm generates the public/private key pairs of the front and back servers instead of that of the receiver. Moreover, the trapdoor generation algorithm DS-Trapdoor defined here is public while in the traditional PEKS definition [5,10], the algorithm Trapdoor takes as input the receiver's private key. Such a difference is due to the different structures used by the two systems. In the traditional PEKS, since there is only one server, if the trapdoor generation algorithm is public, then the server can launch an off-line guessing attack against a keyword ciphertext to recover the encrypted keyword. As a result, it is impossible to achieve the semantic security as defined in [5,10]. However, as we will show later, under the DS-PEKS framework, we can still achieve semantic security when the trapdoor generation algorithm is public. Another difference between the traditional PEKS and our proposed DS-PEKS is that the test algorithm is divided into two algorithms, FrontTest and BackTest run by two independent servers. This is essential for achieving security against the inside keyword guessing attacks.

2.2 Definition

Syntax. A DS-PEKS scheme is defined by the following algorithms.

- Setup(1^λ). Takes as input the security parameter λ, generates the system parameters P;
- KeyGen(P). Takes as input the systems parameters P, outputs the public/secret key pairs (pk_{FS}, sk_{FS}), and (pk_{BS}, sk_{BS}) for the front server, and the back server respectively;
- DS-PEKS($P, pk_{FS}, pk_{BS}, kw_1$). Takes as input P, the front server's public key pk_{FS}, the back server's public key pk_{BS} and the keyword kw_1, outputs the PEKS ciphertext CT_{kw_1} of kw_1;
- DS-Trapdoor($P, pk_{FS}, pk_{BS}, kw_2$). Takes as input P, the front server's public key pk_{FS}, the back server's public key pk_{BS} and the keyword kw_2, outputs the trapdoor T_{kw_2};
- FrontTest($P, sk_{FS}, CT_{kw_1}, T_{kw_2}$). Takes as input P, the front server's secret key sk_{FS}, the PEKS ciphertext CT_{kw_1} and the trapdoor T_{kw_2}, outputs the internal testing-state C_{ITS};

– BackTest(P, sk_{BS}, C_{ITS}). Takes as input P, the back server's secret key sk_{BS} and the internal testing-state C_{ITS}, outputs the testing result 0 or 1;

Correctness. It is required that for any keyword kw_1, kw_2, and $CT_{kw_1} \leftarrow$ DS-PEKS($P, pk_{FS}, pk_{BS}, kw_1$), $T_{kw_2} \leftarrow$ DS-Trapdoor($P, pk_{FS}, pk_{BS}, kw_2$), we have that BackTest($P, sk_{BS}, C_{ITS}) = 1$ if $kw_1 = kw_2$, otherwise 0.

2.3   Security Models

In this subsection, we formalise the security models for DS-PEKS. We define the following security models for a DS-PEKS scheme against the adversarial front and back servers, respectively. We should note that the following security models also imply the security guarantees against the outside adversaries which have less capability compared to the servers.

Adversarial Front Server. In this part, we define the security against an adversarial front server. Precisely, we introduce two games, namely semantic-security against chosen keyword attack and indistinguishability against keyword guessing attack[1] to capture the security of PEKS ciphertext and trapdoor, respectively.

Semantic-Security against Chosen Keyword Attack (SS-CKA). In the following, we define the semantic-security against chosen keyword attack which guarantees that no adversary is able to distinguish a keyword from another one given the corresponding PEKS ciphertext. That is, the PEKS ciphertext does not reveal any information about the underlying keyword to any adversary.

– Setup. The challenger runs the KeyGen(λ) algorithm to generate key pairs (pk_{FS}, sk_{FS}) and (pk_{BS}, sk_{BS}). It gives $(pk_{FS}, sk_{FS}, pk_{BS})$ to the attacker;
– Test query-I. The attacker can adaptively make the test query for any keyword and any PEKS ciphertext of its choice. The challenger returns 1 or 0 as the test result to the attacker;
– Challenge. The attacker sends the challenger two keywords kw_0, kw_1. The challenger picks $b \xleftarrow{\$} \{0, 1\}$ and generates

$$CT_{kw}^* \leftarrow \text{DS-PEKS}(P, pk_{FS}, pk_{BS}, kw_b).$$

The challenger then sends CT_{kw}^* to the attacker;
– Test query-II. The attacker can continue the test query for any keyword and any PEKS ciphertext of its choice except of the challenge keywords kw_0, kw_1. The challenger returns 1 or 0 as the test result to the attacker;
– Output. Finally, the attacker outputs its guess $b' \in \{0, 1\}$ on b and wins the game if $b = b'$.

---

[1] In this paper, we use two different terms, namely semantic security and indistinguishability, to define the security for the keyword ciphertext and the trapdoor, respectively. However, as for normal public key encryption, these two terms are equivalent.

We refer to such an adversarial front server $\mathcal{A}$ in the above game as an SS-CKA adversary and define its advantage as

$$\mathsf{Adv}^{\mathsf{SS-CKA}}_{\mathcal{FS},\mathcal{A}}(\lambda) = \Pr[b = b'] - 1/2.$$

Indistinguishability against Keyword Guessing Attack (IND-KGA). This model captures that the trapdoor reveals no information about the underlying keyword to the adversarial front server. We define the security model as follows.

- Setup. The challenger runs the KeyGen(λ) algorithm to generate key pairs (pk_{FS}, sk_{FS}) and (pk_{BS}, sk_{BS}). It gives $(pk_{FS}, sk_{FS}, pk_{BS})$ to the attacker;
- Test query-I. The attacker can adaptively make the test query for any keyword and any PEKS ciphertext of its choice. The challenger returns 1 or 0 as the test result to the attacker;
- Challenge. The attacker sends the challenger two keywords kw_0, kw_1. The challenger picks $b \xleftarrow{\$} \{0, 1\}$ and generates

$$T^*_{kw} \leftarrow \mathsf{DS\text{-}Trapdoor}(P, pk_{FS}, pk_{BS}, kw_b).$$

The challenger then sends T^*_{kw} to the attacker;
- Test query-II. The attacker can continue issue the test query for any keyword and any PEKS ciphertext of its choice except of the challenge keywords kw_0, kw_1. The challenger returns 1 or 0 as the test result to the attacker;
- Output. Finally, the attacker outputs its guess $b' \in \{0, 1\}$ on b and wins the game if $b = b'$.

We refer to such an adversarial front server $\mathcal{A}$ in the above game as an IND-KGA adversary and define its advantage as

$$\mathsf{Adv}^{\mathsf{IND-KGA}}_{\mathcal{FS},\mathcal{A}}(\lambda) = \Pr[b = b'] - 1/2.$$

Adversarial Back Server. The security models of SS-CKA and IND-KGA in terms of an adversarial back server are similar to those against an adversarial front server.

Semantic-Security against Chosen Keyword Attack. Here the game against an adversarial back server is the same as the one against an adversarial front server except that the adversary is given the private key of the back server instead of that of the front server. We omit the details here for simplicity.

We refer to the adversarial back server $\mathcal{A}$ in the SS-CKA game as an SS-CKA adversary and define its advantage as $\mathsf{Adv}^{\mathsf{SS-CKA}}_{\mathcal{BS},\mathcal{A}}(\lambda) = \Pr[b = b'] - 1/2$.

Indistinguishability against Keyword Guessing Attack. Similarly, this security model aims to capture that the trapdoor does not reveal any information to the back server and hence is the same as that against the front server except that the adversary owns the private key of the back server instead of that of the front server. Therefore, we also omit the details here.

We refer to the adversarial back server $\mathcal{A}$ in the IND-KGA game as an IND-KGA adversary and define its advantage as $\mathsf{Adv}^{\mathsf{IND-KGA}}_{\mathcal{BS},\mathcal{A}}(\lambda) = \Pr[b = b'] - 1/2$.

Indistinguishability against Keyword Guessing Attack-II (IND-KGA-II). Apart from the above two security models, we should also guarantee that the internal testing-state does not reveal any information about the keyword to the back server. We hence define another type of keyword guessing attack to capture such a requirement. The security, namely Indistinguishability against Keyword Guessing Attack-II guarantees that the back server cannot learn any information about the keywords from the internal testing-state. The security model is defined as follows.

- Setup. The challenger runs the $\mathsf{KeyGen}(\lambda)$ algorithm to generates key pairs (pk_{FS}, sk_{FS}) and (pk_{BS}, sk_{BS}). It gives $(pk_{FS}, pk_{BS}, sk_{BS})$ to the attacker.
- Challenge. The attacker sends the challenger three different keywords $kw_0, kw_1,$
  kw_2. The challenger picks $\{b_1, b_2\} \subset \{0, 1, 2\}$ randomly and computes

$$CT^*_{kw} \leftarrow \mathsf{DS\text{-}PEKS}(P, pk_{FS}, pk_{BS}, kw_{b_1}),$$
$$T^*_{kw} \leftarrow \mathsf{DS\text{-}Trapdoor}(P, pk_{FS}, pk_{BS}, kw_{b_2}),$$
$$C^*_{ITS} \leftarrow \mathsf{FrontTest}(P, sk_{FS}, CT^*_{kw}, T^*_{kw}).$$

  The challenger then sends C^*_{ITS} to the attacker.
- Output. Finally, the attacker outputs its guess on $\{b_1, b_2\}$ as $\{b'_1, b'_2\} \subset \{0, 1, 2\}$ and wins the game if $\{b'_1, b'_2\} = \{b_1, b_2\}$.

We refer to such an adversary $\mathcal{A}$ in the above two games as a IND-KGA-II adversary and define its advantage as,

$$\mathsf{Adv}^{\mathsf{IND\text{-}KGA\text{-}II}}_{BS, \mathcal{A}}(\lambda) = \Pr[\{b'_1, b'_2\} = \{b_1, b_2\}] - 1/3.$$

We should remark that in the above game, b_1 and b_2 can be equivalent. In this case, the adversary (i.e., back server) will know that the same keyword has been used in the generation of the PEKS ciphertext and the trapdoor, and the adversary's goal is to guess which keyword among the three has been used.

Based on the security models defined above, we give the following security definition for a DS-PEKS scheme.

Definition 1. We say that a DS-PEKS is secure if for any polynomial time attacker $\mathcal{A}_i$ ($i = 1, \ldots, 5$), we have that $\mathsf{Adv}^{\mathsf{SS\text{-}CKA}}_{BS, \mathcal{A}_1}(\lambda), \mathsf{Adv}^{\mathsf{SS\text{-}CKA}}_{BS, \mathcal{A}_2}(\lambda),$ $\mathsf{Adv}^{\mathsf{IND\text{-}KGA}}_{FS, \mathcal{A}_3}(\lambda)$, $\mathsf{Adv}^{\mathsf{IND\text{-}KGA}}_{BS, \mathcal{A}_4}(\lambda)$ and $\mathsf{Adv}^{\mathsf{IND\text{-}KGA\text{-}II}}_{BS, \mathcal{A}_5}(\lambda)$ are all negligible functions of the security parameter λ.

3   Smooth Projective Hash Functions

A central element of our construction for dual-server public key encryption with keyword search is *smooth projective hash function* (SPHF), a notion introduced by Cramer and Shoup [13] and extended for construction of many cryptographic primitives [2,8,15,16,18]. We start with the original definition of an SPHF.

3.1   SPHF

Syntax. An SPHF can be defined based on a domain $\mathcal{X}$ and an $\mathcal{NP}$ language $\mathcal{L}$, where $\mathcal{L}$ contains a subset of the elements of the domain $\mathcal{X}$, i.e., $\mathcal{L} \subset \mathcal{X}$. An SPHF system over a language $\mathcal{L} \subset \mathcal{X}$, onto a set $\mathcal{Y}$, is defined by the following five algorithms (SPHFSetup, HashKG, ProjKG, Hash, ProjHash):

- SPHFSetup(1^λ): generates the global parameters param and the description of an $\mathcal{NP}$ language instance $\mathcal{L}$;
- HashKG($\mathcal{L}$, param): generates a hashing key hk for $\mathcal{L}$;
- ProjKG(hk, ($\mathcal{L}$, param)): derives the projection key hp from the hashing key hk;
- Hash(hk, ($\mathcal{L}$, param), W): outputs the hash value hv $\in \mathcal{Y}$ for the word W from the hashing key hk;
- ProjHash(hp, ($\mathcal{L}$, param), W, w): outputs the hash value hv$'$ $\in \mathcal{Y}$ for the word W from the projection key hp and the witness w for the fact that $W \in \mathcal{L}$.

Property. A smooth projective hash function $\mathcal{SPHF}$ should satisfy the following properties,

- *Correctness.* If a word $W \in \mathcal{L}$ with w the witness, then for all hashing key hk and projection key hp, we have

$$\mathsf{Hash}(\mathsf{hk}, (\mathcal{L}, \mathsf{param}), W) = \mathsf{ProjHash}(\mathsf{hp}, (\mathcal{L}, \mathsf{param}), W, w).$$

- *Smoothness.* Let a point W be not in the language, i.e., $W \in \mathcal{X} \backslash \mathcal{L}$. Then the following two distributions are statistically indistinguishable :

$$\mathcal{V}_1 = \{(\mathcal{L}, \mathsf{param}, W, \mathsf{hp}, \mathsf{hv}) | \mathsf{hv} = \mathsf{Hash}(\mathsf{hk}, (\mathcal{L}, \mathsf{param}), W)\},$$

$$\mathcal{V}_2 = \{(\mathcal{L}, \mathsf{param}, W, \mathsf{hp}, \mathsf{hv}) | \mathsf{hv} \xleftarrow{\$} \mathcal{Y}\},$$

To be more precise, the quantity of $\sum_{v \in \mathcal{Y}} |\operatorname{Pr}_{\mathcal{V}_1}[\mathsf{hv} = v] - \operatorname{Pr}_{\mathcal{V}_2}[\mathsf{hv} = v]|$ is negligible.

In this paper, we require another important property of smooth projective hash functions that was introduced in [15].

- *Pseudo-Randomness.* If a word $W \in \mathcal{L}$, then without the corresponding witness w, the distribution of the hash output is computationally indistinguishable from a uniform distribution in the view of any polynomial-time adversary $\mathcal{A}$. That is, $\mathcal{A}$ can only win in the PR-game defined below with negligible probability.
  - Setup. The challenger runs SPHFSetup, HashKG, ProjKG, generates param, hk, hp, $\mathcal{L}$ and sends the adversary (param, $\mathcal{L}$, hp).
  - Challenge. The challenger picks $W \xleftarrow{\$} \mathcal{L}, b \xleftarrow{\$} \{0,1\}$ and generates

$$\mathsf{hv} = \begin{cases} \mathsf{Hash}(\mathsf{hk}, (\mathcal{L}, \mathsf{param}), W) & b = 1, \\ v \xleftarrow{\$} \mathcal{Y} & b = 0. \end{cases}$$

The challenger then sends (W, hv) to $\mathcal{A}$.

- Output. Finally, $\mathcal{A}$ outputs its guess $b' \in \{0,1\}$ on b and wins the game if $b = b'$.

We define the advantage of $\mathcal{A}$ in the above game as,

$$\mathsf{Adv}^{\mathsf{PR}}_{\mathcal{SPHF},\mathcal{A}}(\lambda) = \Pr[b = b'] - 1/2.$$

We say $\mathcal{SPHF}$ is *pseudo-random* if for any polynomial time adversary $\mathcal{A}$, we have that $\mathsf{Adv}^{\mathsf{PR}}_{\mathcal{SPHF},\mathcal{A}}(\lambda)$ is a negligible function.

3.2   Lin-Hom SPHF

In this paper, we consider a new variant of smooth projective hash function. We consider two new properties: linear and homomorphic, which are defined below. It is worth noting that Abdalla et al. [3] introduced conjunction and disjunction of languages for smooth projective hashing that were later used in the construction of blind signature [7,9], oblivious signature-based envelops [9], and authenticated key exchange protocols for algebraic languages [6]. As shown in the following, our definition for the new SPHF here is different from their work since we consider the operations on the words belonging to the same language, whereas theirs considers operations among different languages.

Let $\mathcal{SPHF}$=(SPHFSetup, HashKG, ProjKG, Hash, ProjHash) be a smooth projective hash function over the language $\mathcal{L} \subset \mathcal{X}$ onto the set $\mathcal{Y}$ and $\mathcal{W}$ be the witness space of $\mathcal{L}$. We first describe the operations on the sets $< \mathcal{L}, \mathcal{Y}, \mathcal{W} >$ as follows.

- $\odot : \mathcal{L} \times \mathcal{L} \to \mathcal{L}$. For any $W_1 \in \mathcal{L}, W_2 \in \mathcal{L}, W_1 \odot W_2 \in \mathcal{L}$;
- $\circledast : \mathcal{Y} \times \mathcal{Y} \to \mathcal{Y}$. For any $y_1 \in \mathcal{Y}, y_2 \in \mathcal{Y}, y_1 \circledast y_2 \in \mathcal{Y}$;
- $\odot, \oplus : \mathcal{W} \times \mathcal{W} \to \mathcal{W}$. For any $w_1 \in \mathcal{W}, w_2 \in \mathcal{W}, w_1 \odot w_2 \in \mathcal{W}$ and $w_1 \oplus w_2 \in \mathcal{W}$;
- $\otimes : \mathcal{W} \times \mathcal{L} \to \mathcal{L}$. For any $w \in \mathcal{W}, W \in \mathcal{L}, w \otimes W \in \mathcal{L}$;
- $\bullet : \mathcal{W} \times \mathcal{Y} \to \mathcal{Y}$. For any $w \in \mathcal{W}, y \in \mathcal{Y}, w \bullet y \in \mathcal{Y}$.

Moreover, for any element $y \in \mathcal{Y}$, we define $y \circledast y^{-1} = 1_{\mathcal{Y}}$ which is the identity element of $\mathcal{Y}$.

Our new SPHF requires the underlying language to be also *linear and homomorphic language*, which is defined below.

Definition 2 (Linear and Homomorphic Language). *A language $\mathcal{L}$ is linear and homomorphic if it satisfies the following properties.*

- *For any word $W \in \mathcal{L}$ with witness w and $\Delta w \in \mathcal{W}$, there exists a word $W^* \in \mathcal{L}$ such that $\Delta w \otimes W = W^*$ with the witness $w^* = \Delta w \odot w$.*
- *For any two words $W_1, W_2 \in \mathcal{L}$ with the witness $w_1, w_2 \in \mathcal{W}$ respectively, there exists a word $W^* \in \mathcal{L}$ such that $W_1 \odot W_2 = W^*$ with the witness $w^* = w_1 \oplus w_2$.*

We then give the definition of *Lin-Hom SPHF* as follows.

Definition 3 (Lin-Hom SPHF (LH-SPHF)). *We say $\mathcal{SPHF}$ is a Lin-Hom SPHF (LH-SPHF) if the underlying language $\mathcal{L}$ is a linear and homomorphic language and $\mathcal{SPHF}$ satisfies the following properties.*

– *For any word $W \in \mathcal{L}$ with the witness $w \in \mathcal{W}$ and $\Delta w \in \mathcal{W}$, we have*

$$\mathsf{Hash}(\mathsf{hk}, (\mathcal{L}, \mathsf{param}), \Delta w \otimes W) = \Delta w \bullet \mathsf{Hash}(\mathsf{hk}, (\mathcal{L}, \mathsf{param}), W).$$

In other words, suppose $\Delta w \otimes W = W^*$, we have,

$$\mathsf{ProjHash}(\mathsf{hp}, (\mathcal{L}, \mathsf{param}), W^*, w^*) = \Delta w \bullet \mathsf{ProjHash}(\mathsf{hp}, (\mathcal{L}, \mathsf{param}), W, w),$$

where $w^* = \Delta w \odot w$.

– *For any two words $W_1, W_2 \in \mathcal{L}$ with the witness $w_1, w_2 \in \mathcal{W}$, we have*

$$\mathsf{Hash}(\mathsf{hk}, (\mathcal{L}, \mathsf{param}), W_1 \odot W_2) =$$

$$\mathsf{Hash}(\mathsf{hk}, (\mathcal{L}, \mathsf{param}), W_1) \circledast \mathsf{Hash}(\mathsf{hk}, (\mathcal{L}, \mathsf{param}), W_2).$$

In other words, suppose $W_1 \odot W_2 = W^*$, we have,

$$\mathsf{ProjHash}(\mathsf{hp}, (\mathcal{L}, \mathsf{param}), W^*, w^*) =$$

$$\mathsf{ProjHash}(\mathsf{hp}, (\mathcal{L}, \mathsf{param}), W_1, w_1) \circledast \mathsf{ProjHash}(\mathsf{hp}, (\mathcal{L}, \mathsf{param}), W_2, w_2)$$

where $w^* = w_1 \oplus w_2$.

In this paper, we also assume that the LH-SPHF has the following property: for any $y \in \mathcal{Y}$, $W \in \mathcal{L}$ and the witness $w \in \mathcal{W}$ of W, there exists a projection key hp such that $\mathsf{ProjHash}(\mathsf{hp}, (\mathcal{L}, \mathsf{param}), W, w) = y$.

4   Generic Construction of DS-PEKS Using LH-SPHF

In this section, we show how to generically construct a Dual-Server Public Key Encryption with keyword search based on *Lin-Hom Smooth Projective Hash Functions*.

4.1   Generic Construction

Suppose $\mathcal{SPHF}$ = (SPHFSetup, HashKG, ProjKG, Hash, ProjHash) is an LH-SPHF over the language $\mathcal{L}$ onto the set $\mathcal{Y}$. Let $\mathcal{W}$ be the witness space of the language $\mathcal{L}$ and $\mathcal{KW}$ be the keyword space. Our generic construction $\mathcal{DS\text{-}PEKS}$ works as follows.

Setup(1^λ). Take as input the security parameter λ, run SPHFSetup algorithm and generate the global parameters param, the description of the language $\mathcal{L}$ and a collision-resistant hash function $\Gamma : \mathcal{KW} \to \mathcal{Y}$. Set the system parameter $P = <\mathsf{param}, \mathcal{L}, \Gamma>$.

KeyGen(P). Take as input P, run the algorithms $<$ HashKG, ProjHash $>$ to generate the public/private key pairs (pk_{FS}, sk_{FS}), (pk_{BS}, sk_{BS}) for the front server and the back server respectively.

$$pk_{FS} \leftarrow \mathsf{HashKG}(P), sk_{FS} = \mathsf{ProjKG}(P, pk_{FS}),$$

$$pk_{BS} \leftarrow \mathsf{HashKG}(P), sk_{BS} = \mathsf{ProjKG}(P, pk_{BS}).$$

DS-PEKS$(P, pk_{FS}, pk_{BS}, kw_1)$. Take as input P, pk_{FS}, pk_{BS} and the keyword kw_1, pick a word $W_1 \in \mathcal{L}$ randomly with the witness w_1 and generate the PEKS ciphertext CT_{kw_1} of kw_1 as following.

$$x_1 = \mathsf{ProjHash}(P, pk_{FS}, W_1, w_1),$$

$$y_1 = \mathsf{ProjHash}(P, pk_{BS}, W_1, w_1),$$

$$C_1 = x_1 \circledast y_1 \circledast \Gamma(kw_1).$$

Set $CT_{kw_1} = < W_1, C_1 >$ and return CT_{kw_1} as the keyword ciphertext.

DS-Trapdoor$(P, pk_{FS}, pk_{BS}, kw_2)$. Take as input P, pk_{FS}, pk_{BS} and the keyword kw_2, pick a word $W_2 \in \mathcal{L}$ randomly with the witness w_2 and generate the trapdoor T_{kw_2} of kw_2 as follows.

$$x_2 = \mathsf{ProjHash}(P, pk_{FS}, W_2, w_2),$$

$$y_2 = \mathsf{ProjHash}(P, pk_{BS}, W_2, w_2),$$

$$C_2 = x_2 \circledast y_2 \circledast \Gamma(kw_2)^{-1}.$$

Set $T_{kw_2} = < W_2, C_2 >$ and return T_{kw_2} as the trapdoor.

FrontTest$(P, sk_{FS}, CT_{kw}, T_{kw})$. Takes as input P, the front server's secret key sk_{FS}, the PEKS ciphertext $CT_{kw_1} = < W_1, C_1 >$ and the trapdoor $T_{kw_2} = < W_2, C_2 >$, pick $\Delta w \in \mathcal{W}$ randomly, generate the internal testing-state C_{ITS} as follows.

$$W = W_1 \odot W_2,$$

$$x = \mathsf{Hash}(P, sk_{FS}, W),$$

$$C = C_1 \circledast C_2 \circledast x^{-1},$$

$$W^* = \Delta w \otimes W, C^* = \Delta w \bullet C.$$

Set $C_{ITS} = < W^*, C^* >$ and return C_{ITS} as the internal testing-state.

BackTest(P, sk_{BS}, C_{ITS}). Takes as input P, the back server's secret key sk_{BS} and the internal testing-state $C_{ITS} = < W^*, C^* >$, test as follows.

$$\mathsf{Hash}(P, sk_{BS}, W^*) \overset{?}{=} C^*$$

If yes output 1, else output 0.

Correctness Analysis. One can see that the correctness of this construction is guaranteed by the important properties of the LH-SPHF. To be more precise, we give the analysis as follows.

For the algorithm FrontTest, we have

$$
\begin{aligned}
x &= \mathsf{Hash}(P, sk_{FS}, W) \\
&= \mathsf{Hash}(P, sk_{FS}, W_1 \odot W_2) \\
&= \mathsf{Hash}(P, sk_{FS}, W_1) \circledast \mathsf{Hash}(P, sk_{FS}, W_2) \\
&= \mathsf{ProjHash}(P, pk_{FS}, W_1, w_1) \circledast \mathsf{ProjHash}(P, pk_{FS}, W_2, w_2) \\
&= x_1 \circledast x_2.
\end{aligned}
$$

Therefore,

$$
\begin{aligned}
C &= C_1 \circledast C_2 \circledast x^{-1} \\
&= x_1 \circledast y_1 \circledast \Gamma(kw_1) \circledast x_2 \circledast y_2 \circledast \Gamma(kw_2)^{-1} \circledast (x_1 \circledast x_2)^{-1} \\
&= y_1 \circledast y_2 \circledast \Gamma(kw_1) \circledast \Gamma(kw_2)^{-1}.
\end{aligned}
$$

For the algorithm BackTest, we have

$$
\begin{aligned}
&\mathsf{Hash}(P, sk_{BS}, W^*) \\
&= \mathsf{Hash}(P, sk_{BS}, \Delta w \otimes W) \\
&= \Delta w \bullet \mathsf{Hash}(P, sk_{BS}, W) \\
&= \Delta w \bullet \mathsf{Hash}(P, sk_{BS}, W_1 \odot W_2). \\
&= \Delta w \bullet (\mathsf{Hash}(P, sk_{BS}, W_1) \circledast \mathsf{Hash}(P, sk_{BS}, W_2)) \\
&= \Delta w \bullet (\mathsf{ProjHash}(P, pk_{BS}, W_1, w_1) \circledast \mathsf{ProjHash}(P, pk_{BS}, W_2, w_2)) \\
&= \Delta w \bullet (y_1 \circledast y_2).
\end{aligned}
$$

It is easy to see that if $kw_1 = kw_2$, then $\mathsf{Hash}(P, sk_{BS}, W^*) = \Delta w \bullet C = C^*$. Otherwise, $\mathsf{Hash}(P, sk_{BS}, W^*) \neq C^*$ due to the collision-resistant property of the hash function Γ.

4.2   Security of $\mathcal{DS\text{-}PEKS}$

In this subsection, we analyse the security of the above generic construction.

Theorem 1. *The generic construction $\mathcal{DS\text{-}PEKS}$ is semantically secure under chosen keyword attacks.*

The above theorem can be obtained from the following two lemmas.

Lemma 1. *For any polynomial-time adversary $\mathcal{A}$, $\mathsf{Adv}_{\mathcal{FS},\mathcal{A}}^{\mathsf{SS\text{-}CKA}}(\lambda)$ is a negligible function.*

Proof. We define a sequence of games as follows.

Game0. This is the original SS-CKA game against the adversarial front server.

- Setup. The challenger runs the Setup, KeyGen to generate system parameter P, key pairs (pk_{FS}, sk_{FS}) and (pk_{BS}, sk_{BS}). It then gives adversary $\mathcal{A}$ the key pair $(P, pk_{FS}, sk_{FS}, pk_{BS})$.

- Test Query-I. The adversary makes a query on $< kw, CT >$. Suppose $CT = (W, C)$, the challenger computes the following.

$$T \leftarrow \text{DS-Trapdoor}(P, pk_{FS}, pk_{BS}, kw),$$

$$C_{ITS} \leftarrow \text{FrontTest}(P, sk_{FS}, C, T).$$

The challenger then runs the algorithm $\text{BackTest}(P, sk_{BS}, C_{ITS})$ and returns the output to the adversary.

- Challenge. $\mathcal{A}$ chooses two keywords kw_0, kw_1 and sends kw_0, kw_1 to the challenger. The challenger first picks $b \xleftarrow{\$} \{0, 1\}$, and then picks a word $W_1 \in \mathcal{L}$ randomly with the witness w_1 and generates the PEKS ciphertext CT_{kw}^* of kw_b as follows.

$$x_1 = \text{ProjHash}(P, pk_{FS}, W_1, w_1), y_1 = \text{ProjHash}(P, pk_{BS}, W_1, w_1),$$

$$C_1 = x_1 \circledast y_1 \circledast \Gamma(kw_b).$$

The challenger sets $CT_{kw}^* = < W_1, C_1 >$ as the keyword ciphertext and sends CT_{kw}^* to $\mathcal{A}$.

- Test Query-II. The procedure is the same as that in Test Query-I.
- Output. Finally, $\mathcal{A}$ outputs its guess $b' \in \{0, 1\}$ on b and wins the game if $b = b'$.

We define the advantage of $\mathcal{A}$ in Game0 as $\text{Adv}_{\mathcal{FS}, \mathcal{A}}^{\text{Game0}}(\lambda)$ and have that

$$\text{Adv}_{\mathcal{FS}, \mathcal{A}}^{\text{Game0}}(\lambda) = \text{Adv}_{\mathcal{FS}, \mathcal{A}}^{\text{SS-CKA}}(\lambda)$$

as Game0 strictly follows the SS-CKA model.

Game1. Let Game1 be the same game as Game0, except that the challenger chooses $y_1 \xleftarrow{\$} \mathcal{Y}$ instead of computing y_1 as $\text{ProjHash}(P, pk_{BS}, W_1, w_1)$. Due to the correctness and pseudo-randomness of $\mathcal{SPHF}$, that is, the distribution $\{(P, W_1, pk_{BS}, y_1)|y_1 = \text{ProjHash}(P, pk_{BS}, W_1, w_1)\}$ is computationally indistinguishable from the distribution $\{(P, W_1, pk_{BS}, y_1)|y_1 \xleftarrow{\$} \mathcal{Y}\}$, we have that

$$|\text{Adv}_{\mathcal{FS}, \mathcal{A}}^{\text{Game1}}(\lambda) - \text{Adv}_{\mathcal{FS}, \mathcal{A}}^{\text{Game0}}(\lambda)| \le \text{Adv}_{\mathcal{SPHF}, \mathcal{A}}^{\text{PR}}(\lambda).$$

Game2. Let Game2 be the same game as Game1, except that the challenger chooses $C_1 \xleftarrow{\$} \mathcal{Y}$ instead of computing $C_1 = x_1 \circledast y_1 \circledast \Gamma(kw_b)$. We can see that

$$\text{Adv}_{\mathcal{FS}, \mathcal{A}}^{\text{Game2}}(\lambda) = \text{Adv}_{\mathcal{FS}, \mathcal{A}}^{\text{Game1}}(\lambda).$$

It is easy to see that the adversary in Game2 can only win with probability $1/2$ as C_1 is independent of b. Therefore, we have that $\text{Adv}_{\mathcal{DS\text{-}PEKS}, \mathcal{A}}^{\text{Game2}}(\lambda) = 0$. Therefore, from Game0, Game1 and Game2, we have that

$$|\text{Adv}_{\mathcal{FS}, \mathcal{A}}^{\text{Game2}}(\lambda) - \text{Adv}_{\mathcal{FS}, \mathcal{A}}^{\text{SS-CKA}}(\lambda)| \le \text{Adv}_{\mathcal{SPHF}, \mathcal{A}}^{\text{PR}}(\lambda).$$

As $\text{Adv}_{\mathcal{FS}, \mathcal{A}}^{\text{Game2}}(\lambda) = 0$ and $\text{Adv}_{\mathcal{SPHF}, \mathcal{A}}^{\text{PR}}(\lambda)$ is negligible, we have that $\text{Adv}_{\mathcal{FS}, \mathcal{A}}^{\text{SS-CKA}}(\lambda)$ is also negligible, which completes the proof.

Lemma 2. *For any polynomial-time adversary $\mathcal{A}$, $\mathsf{Adv}_{BS,\mathcal{A}}^{\text{SS-CKA}}(\lambda)$ is a negligible function.*

The proof of **Lemma 2.** can be easily obtained by following the proof of **Lemma 1.**, and hence is omitted.

Theorem 2. *The generic construction $\mathcal{DS}\text{-}\mathcal{PEKS}$ is secure against keyword guessing attack.*

The above theorem can be obtained from the following lemmas.

Lemma 3. *For any polynomial-time adversary $\mathcal{A}$, $\mathsf{Adv}_{\mathcal{FS},\mathcal{A}}^{\text{IND-KGA}}(\lambda)$ is a negligible function.*

Lemma 4. *For any polynomial-time adversary $\mathcal{A}$, $\mathsf{Adv}_{BS,\mathcal{A}}^{\text{IND-KGA}}(\lambda)$ is a negligible function.*

The proofs of **Lemma 3.** and **Lemma 4.** are similar to those of **Lemma 1.** and **Lemma 2.** as the generation of a trapdoor is the same as that of a PEKS ciphertext, and the security model of IND-KGA is also similar to that of SS-CKA. Therefore, we omit the proof details here. For the security against the keyword guessing attack-II, we have the following lemma.

Lemma 5. *For any polynomial-time adversary $\mathcal{A}$, $\mathsf{Adv}_{BS,\mathcal{A}}^{\text{IND-KGA-II}}(\lambda)$ is a negligible function.*

Proof. In the IND-KGA-II game, if $b_1 = b_2$, then it is easy to see that the adversary has no advantage since the two keywords are canceled out in the internal testing-state C_{ITS}, which means C_{ITS} is independent of the keywords. In the following, we focus on the case that $b_1 \neq b_2$.

Here, we use the game-hopping technique again to prove this lemma. We define a sequence of attack games as follows.

Game0. Let the original IND-CKA game be Game0.

- Setup. The challenger runs the Setup, KeyGen to generate system parameter P, key pairs (pk_{FS}, sk_{FS}) and (pk_{BS}, sk_{BS}). It gives adversary $\mathcal{A}$ the key pairs $(P, pk_{FS}, pk_{BS}, sk_{BS})$.
- Challenge. $\mathcal{A}$ chooses challenge keywords kw_0, kw_1, kw_2 adaptively and sends them to the challenger. The challenger firstly picks $\{b_1, b_2\} \subset \{0, 1, 2\}$ randomly.

  The challenger picks two words $W_1, W_2 \in \mathcal{L}$ randomly with the witness w_1, w_2 respectively and generates the internal testing-state C_{ITS} as follows.

$$x_1 = \mathsf{ProjHash}(P, pk_{FS}, W_1, w_1), y_1 = \mathsf{ProjHash}(P, pk_{BS}, W_1, w_1),$$

$$x_2 = \mathsf{ProjHash}(P, pk_{FS}, W_2, w_2), y_2 = \mathsf{ProjHash}(P, pk_{BS}, W_2, w_2),$$

$$W = W_1 \odot W_2, x = \mathsf{Hash}(P, sk_{FS}, W),$$

$$C = x_1 \circledast x_2 \circledast y_1 \circledast y_2 \circledast x^{-1} \circledast \Gamma(kw_{b_1}) \circledast \Gamma(kw_{b_2})^{-1},$$

$$W^* = \Delta w \otimes W, C^* = \Delta w \bullet C.$$

Set $C_{ITS}^* = <W^*, C^*>$ and return C_{ITS}^* to $\mathcal{A}$.

– Output. Finally, $\mathcal{A}$ outputs its guess on $\{b_1, b_2\}$ as $\{b_1', b_2'\} \subset \{0, 1, 2\}$ and wins the game if $\{b_1', b_2'\} = \{b_1, b_2\}$.

We define the advantage of $\mathcal{A}$ in Game0 as $\mathsf{Adv}_{BS,\mathcal{A}}^{\mathsf{Game0}}(\lambda)$ and have that

$$\mathsf{Adv}_{BS,\mathcal{A}}^{\mathsf{Game0}}(\lambda) = \mathsf{Adv}_{BS,\mathcal{A}}^{\mathsf{IND\text{-}KGA\text{-}II}}(\lambda)$$

as Game0 strictly follows the IND-KGA-II model.

Game1. Let Game1 be the same game as Game0, except that the challenger chooses $y \xleftarrow{\$} \mathcal{Y}$ and computes C^* as follows.

$$C^* = (x_1 \circledast x_2 \circledast y_1 \circledast y_2 \circledast x^{-1}) \circledast y.$$

In other words, the challenger replaces the part $\Delta w \cdot (\Gamma(kw_{b_1}) \circledast \Gamma(kw_{b_2})^{-1})$ with a random chosen element $y \in \mathcal{Y}$ during the generation of C^*. We now prove that the replacement in this way can make at most a negligible difference, that is,

Claim. For any polynomial-time adversary $\mathcal{A}$,

$$|\mathsf{Adv}_{BS,\mathcal{A}}^{\mathsf{Game1}}(\lambda) - \mathsf{Adv}_{BS,\mathcal{A}}^{\mathsf{Game0}}(\lambda)| \leq \mathsf{Adv}_{\mathcal{SPHF},\mathcal{A}}^{\mathsf{PR}}(\lambda).$$

Proof. Since the language $\mathcal{L}$ is a linear and homomorphic language, we have that the witness of W^* is $w^* = \Delta w \otimes w$ where w is the witness of W. Then based on our definition of LH-SPHF there exists a projection key hp' that

$$\mathsf{ProjHash}(P, \mathsf{hp}', W, w) = \Gamma(kw_{b_1}) \circledast \Gamma(kw_{b_2})^{-1}.$$

As $\mathcal{SPHF}$ is a Lin-Hom SPHF, we have that

$$\begin{aligned}
\mathsf{ProjHash}(P, \mathsf{hp}', W^*, w^*) &= \Delta w \bullet \mathsf{ProjHash}(P, \mathsf{hp}', W, w) \\
&= \Delta w \bullet (\Gamma(kw_{b_1}) \circledast \Gamma(kw_{b_2})^{-1}).
\end{aligned}$$

Moreover, the distribution $\{(P, W^*, \mathsf{hp}', y) | y = \mathsf{ProjHash}(P, \mathsf{hp}', W^*, w^*)\}$ is computationally indistinguishable from the distribution $\{(P, W^*, \mathsf{hp}', y) | y \xleftarrow{\$} \mathcal{Y}\}$ due to the correctness and pseudo-randomness of $\mathcal{SPHF}$. Therefore, we have that

$$|\mathsf{Adv}_{BS,\mathcal{A}}^{\mathsf{Game1}}(\lambda) - \mathsf{Adv}_{BS,\mathcal{A}}^{\mathsf{Game0}}(\lambda)| \leq \mathsf{Adv}_{\mathcal{SPHF},\mathcal{A}}^{\mathsf{PR}}(\lambda).$$

Game2. Let Game2 be the same game as Game1, except that the challenger chooses $C^* \xleftarrow{\$} \mathcal{Y}$. We can see that

$$\mathsf{Adv}_{BS,\mathcal{A}}^{\mathsf{Game2}}(\lambda) = \mathsf{Adv}_{BS,\mathcal{A}}^{\mathsf{Game1}}(\lambda).$$

It is easy to see that the adversary can only win in the Game2 with probability $1/3$ as C^* is independent of b_1, b_2. Therefore, we have that $\mathsf{Adv}_{BS,\mathcal{A}}^{\mathsf{Game2}}(\lambda) = 0$.

Therefore, from Game0, Game1 and Game2, we have that

$$|\mathsf{Adv}_{BS,\mathcal{A}}^{\mathsf{Game2}}(\lambda) - \mathsf{Adv}_{BS,\mathcal{A}}^{\mathsf{IND\text{-}KGA\text{-}II}}(\lambda)| \leq \mathsf{Adv}_{\mathcal{SPHF},\mathcal{A}}^{\mathsf{PR}}(\lambda).$$

As $\mathsf{Adv}_{BS,\mathcal{A}}^{\mathsf{Game2}}(\lambda) = 0$ and $\mathsf{Adv}_{\mathcal{SPHF},\mathcal{A}}^{\mathsf{PR}}(\lambda)$ is negligible, we have that $\mathsf{Adv}_{BS,\mathcal{A}}^{\mathsf{IND\text{-}KGA\text{-}II}}(\lambda)$ is also a negligible function, which proves the lemma.

5 Conclusion

In this paper, we proposed a new framework, named Dual-Server Public Key Encryption with Keyword Search (DS-PEKS), that can prevent the inside keyword guessing attack which is an inherent vulnerability of the traditional PEKS framework. We then introduced a new Smooth Projective Hash Function (SPHF) and used it to construct a generic DS-PEKS scheme. The new variant of SPHF introduced in this paper is of independent interest.

References

1. Abdalla, M., et al.: Searchable encryption revisited: consistency properties, relation to anonymous IBE, and extensions. In: Shoup, V. (ed.) CRYPTO 2005. LNCS, vol. 3621, pp. 205–222. Springer, Heidelberg (2005)
2. Abdalla, M., Benhamouda, F., Blazy, O., Chevalier, C., Pointcheval, D.: SPHF-friendly non-interactive commitments. In: Sako, K., Sarkar, P. (eds.) ASIACRYPT 2013, Part I. LNCS, vol. 8269, pp. 214–234. Springer, Heidelberg (2013)
3. Abdalla, M., Chevalier, C., Pointcheval, D.: Smooth projective hashing for conditionally extractable commitments. In: Halevi, S. (ed.) CRYPTO 2009. LNCS, vol. 5677, pp. 671–689. Springer, Heidelberg (2009)
4. Baek, J., Safavi-Naini, R., Susilo, W.: On the integration of public key data encryption and public key encryption with keyword search. In: Katsikas, S.K., López, J., Backes, M., Gritzalis, S., Preneel, B. (eds.) ISC 2006. LNCS, vol. 4176, pp. 217–232. Springer, Heidelberg (2006)
5. Baek, J., Safavi-Naini, R., Susilo, W.: Public key encryption with keyword search revisited. In: Gervasi, O., Murgante, B., Laganà, A., Taniar, D., Mun, Y., Gavrilova, M.L. (eds.) ICCSA 2008, Part I. LNCS, vol. 5072, pp. 1249–1259. Springer, Heidelberg (2008)
6. Ben Hamouda, F., Blazy, O., Chevalier, C., Pointcheval, D., Vergnaud, D.: Efficient UC-secure authenticated key-exchange for algebraic languages. In: Kurosawa, K., Hanaoka, G. (eds.) PKC 2013. LNCS, vol. 7778, pp. 272–291. Springer, Heidelberg (2013)
7. Ben Hamouda, F., Blazy, O., Chevalier, C., Pointcheval, D., Vergnaud, D.: New smooth projective hash functions and one-round authenticated key exchange. IACR Cryptology ePrint Archive 2013, 34 (2013)
8. Benhamouda, F., Blazy, O., Chevalier, C., Pointcheval, D., Vergnaud, D.: New techniques for SPHFs and efficient one-round PAKE protocols. In: Canetti, R., Garay, J.A. (eds.) CRYPTO 2013, Part I. LNCS, vol. 8042, pp. 449–475. Springer, Heidelberg (2013)
9. Blazy, O., Pointcheval, D., Vergnaud, D.: Round-optimal privacy-preserving protocols with smooth projective hash functions. In: Cramer, R. (ed.) TCC 2012. LNCS, vol. 7194, pp. 94–111. Springer, Heidelberg (2012)
10. Boneh, D., Di Crescenzo, G., Ostrovsky, R., Persiano, G.: Public key encryption with keyword search. In: Cachin, C., Camenisch, J.L. (eds.) EUROCRYPT 2004. LNCS, vol. 3027, pp. 506–522. Springer, Heidelberg (2004)
11. Byun, J.W., Rhee, H.S., Park, H.-A., Lee, D.-H.: Off-line keyword guessing attacks on recent keyword search schemes over encrypted data. In: Jonker, W., Petković, M. (eds.) SDM 2006. LNCS, vol. 4165, pp. 75–83. Springer, Heidelberg (2006)

12. Cocks, C.: An identity based encryption scheme based on quadratic residues. In: Honary, B. (ed.) Cryptography and Coding 2001. LNCS, vol. 2260, pp. 360–363. Springer, Heidelberg (2001)

13. Cramer, R., Shoup, V.: Universal hash proofs and a paradigm for adaptive chosen ciphertext secure public-key encryption. In: Knudsen, L.R. (ed.) EUROCRYPT 2002. LNCS, vol. 2332, pp. 45–64. Springer, Heidelberg (2002)

14. Di Crescenzo, G., Saraswat, V.: Public key encryption with searchable keywords based on jacobi symbols. In: Srinathan, K., Rangan, C.P., Yung, M. (eds.) INDOCRYPT 2007. LNCS, vol. 4859, pp. 282–296. Springer, Heidelberg (2007)

15. Gennaro, R., Lindell, Y.: A framework for password-based authenticated key exchange. In: Biham, Eli (ed.) EUROCRYPT 2003. LNCS, vol. 2656, pp. 524–543. Springer, Heidelberg (2003)

16. Halevi, S., Kalai, Y.T.: Smooth projective hashing and two-message oblivious transfer. J. Cryptology $25(1)$, 158–193 (2012)

17. Jeong, I.R., Kwon, J.O., Hong, D., Lee, D.H.: Constructing PEKS schemes secure against keyword guessing attacks is possible? Computer Communications $32(2)$, 394–396 (2009)

18. Katz, J., Vaikuntanathan, V.: Round-optimal password-based authenticated key exchange. In: Ishai, Y. (ed.) TCC 2011. LNCS, vol. 6597, pp. 293–310. Springer, Heidelberg (2011)

19. Khader, D.: Public key encryption with keyword search based on K-resilient IBE. In: Gavrilova, M.L., Gervasi, O., Kumar, V., Tan, C.J.K., Taniar, D., Laganá, A., Mun, Y., Choo, H. (eds.) ICCSA 2006. LNCS, vol. 3982, pp. 298–308. Springer, Heidelberg (2006)

20. Rhee, H.S., Park, J.H., Susilo, W., Lee, D.H.: Trapdoor security in a searchable public-key encryption scheme with a designated tester. Journal of Systems and Software $83(5)$, 763–771 (2010)

21. Rhee, H.S., Susilo, W., Kim, H.: Secure searchable public key encryption scheme against keyword guessing attacks. IEICE Electronic Express $6(5)$, 237–243 (2009)

22. Waters, B.R., Balfanz, D., Durfee, G., Smetters, D.K.: Building an encrypted and searchable audit log. In: Proceedings of the Network and Distributed System Security Symposium, NDSS 2004, San Diego, California, USA (2004)

23. Yau, W.-C., Heng, S.-H., Goi, B.-M.: Off-line keyword guessing attacks on recent public key encryption with keyword search schemes. In: Rong, C., Jaatun, M.G., Sandnes, F.E., Yang, L.T., Ma, J. (eds.) ATC 2008. LNCS, vol. 5060, pp. 100–105. Springer, Heidelberg (2008)

Dynamic Threshold Public-Key Encryption with Decryption Consistency from Static Assumptions

Yusuke Sakai[1]([✉]), Keita Emura[2], Jacob C.N. Schuldt[1],
Goichiro Hanaoka[1], and Kazuo Ohta[3]

[1] National Institute of Advanced Industrial Science and Technology (AIST),
Tsukuba, Japan
yusuke.sakai@aist.go.jp
[2] National Institute of Information and Communications Technology (NICT),
Koganei, Japan
[3] The University of Electro-Communications, Chofu, Japan

Abstract. *Dynamic threshold public-key encryption* (dynamic TPKE) is a natural extension of ordinary TPKE which allows decryption servers to join the system dynamically after the system is set up, and allows the sender to dynamically choose the authorized set and the decryption threshold at the time of encryption. Currently, the only known dynamic TPKE scheme is a scheme proposed by Delerablée and Pointcheval (CRYPTO 2008). This scheme is proven to provide message confidentiality under a q-type assumption, but to achieve decryption consistency, a random oracle extension is required.

In this paper we show *conceptually simple* methods for constructing dynamic TPKE schemes with decryption consistency from only static assumptions (e.g., the decisional linear assumption in bilinear groups) without relying on random oracles. Our first construction is a purely generic construction from public-key encryption with non-interactive opening (PKENO) formalized by Damgård et al. (CT-RSA 2008). However, this construction achieves a slightly weaker notion of decryption consistency compared to the random oracle extension of the Delerablée and Pointcheval scheme, which satisfies the notion defined by Boneh, Boyen and Halevi (CT-RSA 2005). Our second construction uses a specific PKENO scheme based on the decisional linear assumption in combination with the efficient zero-knowledge proofs by Groth and Sahai. In contrast to our first construction, our second construction achieves the stronger notion of decryption consistency defined by Boneh, Boyen and Halevi.

1 Introduction

Dynamic Threshold Encryption. Threshold public-key encryption (TPKE) [4,7,9,24] is an extension of ordinary public-key encryption which distributes the secret key among several (say, n) decryption servers such that arbitrary k servers

© Springer International Publishing Switzerland 2015
E. Foo and D. Stebila (Eds.): ACISP 2015, LNCS 9144, pp. 77–92, 2015.
DOI: 10.1007/978-3-319-19962-7_5

are required to cooperate to successfully decrypt a ciphertext. This is desirable, for example, when attempting to hedge against key exposure. In this paper, we consider non-interactive TPKE schemes, which means that each decryption server is able to produce its "decryption share" without interacting with other parties, and any k decryption shares from k different servers can be combined successfully to produce the correct plaintext.

In addition to (a threshold variant of) chosen-ciphertext security, TPKE schemes are required to satisfy *decryption consistency* [3,24]. This security property requires that even if a sender and the decryption servers collude, they cannot create two different sets of k decryption shares which respectively produce different plaintexts when honestly combined. This property forces a sender to commit to the message being encrypted. More specifically, decryption consistency prevents a malicious sender from creating "equivocal" ciphertexts essentially corresponding to the encryption of two different messages, and then, at a later stage, deciding what message the ciphertext should be decrypted to by forcing a specific set of servers to participate in the decryption process.

Many TPKE schemes have the limitation that the set of authorized decryption servers (i.e. the servers allowed to participate in the decryption process) and the threshold are required to be fixed at the setup time of the scheme. In addition, decryption servers cannot join the system after the system is set up. This restricts the flexibility of these schemes, and potentially limits their applications.

To address these restrictions, Delerablée and Pointcheval [8] proposed dynamic TPKE. A dynamic TPKE scheme allows a decryption server to join the system after the setup, and furthermore allows a sender to choose the threshold k and the authorized set of servers, among which any k servers can successfully decrypt the ciphertext when they cooperate. However, their scheme is proven secure under a q-type assumption called the multi-sequence of exponent Diffie-Hellman (MSE-DDH) assumption, and the proof of decryption consistency furthermore relies on the random oracle model. In summary, *the only known dynamic TPKE with decryption consistency relies on both a q-type assumption and the random oracle model.*

Our Contribution. In this paper, we propose new dynamic TPKE schemes supporting decryption consistency without relying on random oracles or q-type assumptions. More precisely we propose two constructions of dynamic TPKE, both of which use public-key encryption with non-interactive opening (PKENO) [5] as a core component. PKENO is an extension of ordinary public-key encryption that allows the receiver to prove the validity of the decryption result without revealing the decryption key. Note that PKENO can be constructed from any group signature satisfying standard security notions [11], and thus our result also implies that *TPKE (satisfying a strong security notion) can be obtained from any group signature.* Furthermore, it is known that we can construct a PKENO scheme from the decisional linear (DLIN) or decisional bilinear Diffie-Hellman (DBDH) assumptions [12,13]. This also implies that it is possible to construct *a dynamic TPKE scheme with decryption consistency from any of these assumptions.*

Our first construction uses a PKENO scheme in a black-box manner i.e. it is a generic construction of dynamic TPKE from PKENO. More specifically, this construction converts any PKENO scheme (satisfying standard security notions) to a *dynamic* TPKE scheme with a relatively weaker notion of decryption consistency. Our construction combines the Dodis-Katz multiple encryption technique [10] and verifiable secret sharing [1,2] to ensure decryption consistency. By applying this generic construction to existing PKENO schemes such as [13] and [12], we can obtain dynamic TPKE schemes with decryption consistency which are secure under the DLIN and DBDH assumptions, respectively, without relying on random oracles. Our construction implies a ciphertext overhead proportional to n^2, where n is the number of decryption servers.

Our second construction improves upon the first construction by providing a stronger notion of decryption consistency, which is achieved by relying on a direct construction. *This is the first dynamic TPKE scheme with strong decryption consistency which is proven secure under the DLIN assumption without using random oracles.* This scheme provides decryption consistency which is similar in strength to that of the (non-dynamic) Boneh-Boyen-Halevi scheme [3]. Furthermore, it also achieves an asymptotically shorter ciphertext overhead than the first generic construction; the ciphertext overhead is proportional to the number of decryption servers n.

Our results highlight the usefulness of PKENO to construct TPKE schemes, as both of the above constructions make use of PKENO as a central building block. Note that the usability of PKENO for constructing TPKE has been conjectured by [13], although the conjecture has not been explored in detail in the literature. The subtleties in the conjecture is evidenced by the fact that neither of our two constructions are straightforward combinations of existing techniques (e.g. [10]) and PKENO, and still do not *simultaneously* achieve strong decryption consistency and the property of being a black-box construction from PKENO.

Our schemes are shown secure in a dynamic extension of the Boneh-Boyen-Halevi security model [3]. Hence, like [3], we consider a static corruption model in which the set of corrupt users are fixed in the beginning of the security game. Note that while Delerablée-Pointcheval presented an adaptive corruption model in [8], their scheme is only shown secure in a static model. It remains an open problem to construct a dynamic TPKE scheme secure in an adaptive corruption model, or a dynamic TPKE scheme with constant ciphertext size, which maintains the security properties of our constructed schemes (without relying on random oracles).

Difficulty. Our approach is to enhance the Dodis-Katz multiple encryption technique [10] to obtain the ability to detect malicious behavior of both sender and decryption servers. Using the Dodis-Katz multiple encryption technique, a TPKE scheme can be constructed from an ordinary PKE scheme. In this construction, each decryption server is assigned a key pair of a PKE scheme. To encrypt a plaintext, the sender divides the plaintext into multiple shares using a k-out-of-n secret sharing scheme, and each share is then encrypted for one of the decryption servers. Using this construction, we might easily implement a dynamic TPKE without decryption consistency, as each decryption server can generate its own key pair to join the system, and to specify the authorized set dynamically, a sender simply encrypts for the public keys of the servers that the sender wants to be authorized. More specifically, the sender will generate a ciphertext by simply dividing the plaintext into shares of a secret sharing scheme (with an appropriated threshold), and encrypting these shares one by one using each of the servers' public keys.

The problem with this approach is the difficulty of ensuring consistency among the shares. Namely, if we combine Shamir's k-out-of-n scheme with the Dodis-Katz multiple encryption, the encrypted n shares should correspond to points on a degree-$(k-1)$ polynomial, since otherwise different k shares may result in different decryption results, which will violate decryption consistency. However, ensuring this presents a problem since the shares are encrypted. In particular, some k servers only see k shares but not the other $n-k$ shares, and thus, these k servers are not able to check the consistency of the all shares. This is the reason the straightforward application of PKENO to the Dodis-Katz construction will not provide decryption consistency.

Our Technique. The first construction combines the Dodis-Katz construction with techniques from *verifiable secret sharing* [1,2], which is a classical technique in multiparty computation for providing consistency between shares. We make use of this technique in our context to ensure decryption consistency.

The second scheme is fairly simple. We use a non-interactive zero-knowledge proof to ensure consistency between the encrypted shares. This simplicity will be obtained at the cost of efficiency, or very restricted instantiation options. That is, the only known efficient instantiation of non-interactive zero-knowledge proofs is restricted to certain relations in bilinear groups (i.e. the Groth-Sahai proofs [15]). The alternative is to employ non-interactive zero-knowledge proof for general NP-languages in a non-black-box construction. While this is feasible, it will not provide efficient instantiations.

We additionally show that a black-box construction of (non-dynamic) TPKE with strong decryption consistency from any PKENO is possible. This construction uses techniques from *multiple-assignment secret sharing* [16], which was originally developed for constructing secret sharing schemes supporting general access structures. Interestingly, these techniques are also useful for ensuring decryption consistency. The basic idea of the construction is to allow any coalition of k servers to decrypt the entire ciphertext. However, this approach only allows a small number (logarithmic in the security parameter) of decryption servers. The details of this construction will be given in the full version of this paper. We remark that this black-box construction can be seen as confirmation of the conjecture by [13]. Although not formally stated, the conjecture more specifically claims that for constructing threshold PKE from PKENO, it is sufficient to simply follow the Dodis-Katz multiple encryption, replacing the ordinary PKE scheme with a PKENO scheme (supporting labels).

Related Work. Decryption consistency was formalized by Shoup and Gennaro [24]. In the same paper, they also proposed two TPKE schemes that achieve this notion. These schemes both rely on random oracles. Boneh, Boyen, and Halevi [3] proposed a non-dynamic TPKE scheme with decryption consistency which is shown secure in the standard model.

Dodis and Katz proposed the multiple encryption technique that preserves chosen-ciphertext security of the underlying encryption scheme, and apply this technique to construct a TPKE scheme [10]. They formalized several notions of message privacy. These security notions are regarding secrecy of the plaintext, rather than resilience of the decryption process against maliciously behaving sender and receivers (decryption servers), and thus are independent notions from decryption consistency. In the same paper the authors also discuss decryption robustness which is related to decryption consistency. This notion deals with a similar requirement to decryption consistency, but assumes that the ciphertext is *honestly* generated. The notion then dictates that, if some of the decryption shares are generated maliciously, it should be possible to detect these shares, and successfully obtain the correct decryption result. Our decryption consistency notion considers a different scenario. Namely, even for a maliciously generated ciphertext, the decryption result will be uniquely determined, regardless of which decryption servers participate in the decryption procedure.

Delerablée and Pointcheval [8] proposed the notion of dynamic TPKE and a concrete instantiation. One of the advantages of their scheme, especially compared with our proposed schemes, is constant-size ciphertext. However, their scheme relies on both a q-type assumption and the random oracle model for decryption consistency. In addition, the Delerablée-Pointcheval scheme can be easily extended to the identity-based setting, while our proposed scheme is only in the public-key setting. Daza et al. [6] proposed another extension of TPKE called broadcast threshold encryption. Although this notion is similar to dynamic TPKE, in their scheme decryption consistency is not addressed.

Qin et al. [22], Libert and Yung [18,19], and Gan et al. [14] proposed TPKE schemes allowing adaptive corruption. In contrast to these scheme, all other known schemes and our proposed schemes do not allow this type of corruption. Such schemes require the set of corrupted servers to be fixed at the security game, especially before the adversary obtains the public keys.

2 Definitions of Dynamic TPKE and PKENO

In the definitions and descriptions in this paper, we denote by $[n]$ the set $\{1, \ldots, n\}$ for any positive integer n. Definitions of several standard cryptographic primitives and hardness assumptions, which are used in this paper, are given in Appendix A.

2.1 Dynamic Threshold Public-Key Encryption

We now give a formal definition of dynamic TPKE. The definition basically follows the definition given by Delerablée and Pointcheval [8] with the known-secret-keys extension. However, our syntax is modified to describe the public-key setting, rather than the identity-based setting.

We define two different variants of decryption consistency, namely weak and strong decryption consistency. While the stronger notion follows the definition in [3], the weaker notion is introduced to capture the type of decryption consistency achieved by one of our proposed schemes. To be able to define this weaker notion, our definition of a TPKE scheme allows the DVerify algorithm, which verifies validity of a decryption share, to have three possible outputs, $\top_{\mathsf{valid}}$, $\top_{\mathsf{invalid}}$, and $\bot$, rather than just binary values 1 and 0.

A dynamic TPKE scheme consists of the following probabilistic polynomial-time algorithms:

$\mathsf{DSetup}(1^\lambda)$. The setup algorithm DSetup takes as input the security parameter 1^λ and outputs the public parameter pp.

$\mathsf{DKg}(pp)$. The key generation algorithm takes as input the public parameter pp, and outputs a pair (pk, sk) of the public and secret keys for a new user. We assume that the user public key pk is made publicly available.

$\mathsf{DEnc}(pp, pk_1, \ldots, pk_n, k, m)$. The encryption algorithm DEnc take as input the public parameter pp, n public keys pk_1, ..., pk_n, the threshold k, and the plaintext m to be encrypted and outputs a ciphertext C.

$\mathsf{DDec}(pp, pk, sk, C)$. The partial decryption algorithm DDec takes as input the public parameter pp, the public and secret keys of some user, and a ciphertext C and outputs the decryption share (pk, μ).

$\mathsf{DVerify}(pp, pk, C, \mu)$. The verification algorithm $\mathsf{DVerify}$ takes as input the public parameter pp, the public key pk of some user, a ciphertext C, and its decryption share μ by (the owner of) pk and outputs either $\top_{\mathsf{valid}}$, $\top_{\mathsf{invalid}}$, or $\bot$.

$\mathsf{DCombine}(pp, C, \mu_1, \ldots, \mu_k)$. The combining algorithm $\mathsf{DCombine}$ takes as input the security parameter pp, a ciphertext C and k decryption shares μ_1, ..., μ_k and outputs a plaintext m or $\bot$.

We require dynamic TPKE schemes to satisfy the following correctness conditions: for any integer n and k ($n \geq k$), any honestly generated $pp \leftarrow \mathsf{DSetup}(1^\lambda)$, and any n honestly generated users' key pair $(pk_1, sk_1) \leftarrow \mathsf{DKg}(pp)$, ..., $(pk_n, sk_n) \leftarrow \mathsf{DKg}(pp)$, it is required that

– for any plaintext m, honestly generated ciphertext $C \leftarrow \mathsf{DEnc}(pp, pk_1, \ldots, pk_n, k, m)$, and any size-$k$ subset $\{\iota_1, \ldots, \iota_k\} \subset [n]$, if one honestly computes decryption shares as $\mu_i \leftarrow \mathsf{DDec}(pp, pk_{\iota_i}, sk_{\iota_i}, C)$ ($1 \leq i \leq k$), then we have that $\mathsf{DCombine}(pp, C, \mu_1, \ldots, \mu_k) = m$, and

– for an arbitrary ciphertext C and any $1 \leq i \leq n$, if one honestly computes a decryption share $\mu \leftarrow \mathsf{DDec}(pp, pk_i, sk_i, C)$, then we have that $\mathsf{DVerify}(pp, pk, C, \mu)$ is either $\top_{\mathsf{valid}}$ or $\top_{\mathsf{invalid}}$.

We firstly describe the secrecy requirement by the following game between a challenger and an adversary (in this game N and $\tilde{N}$ respectively denote the numbers of uncorrupted and corrupted servers):

Setup. The challenger runs $pp \leftarrow \mathsf{DSetup}(1^\lambda)$. The challenger generates N public/secret keys $(pk_i, sk_i) \leftarrow \mathsf{DKg}(pp)$ for uncorrupted users and $\tilde{N}$ keys $(\tilde{pk}_i, \tilde{sk}_i) \leftarrow \mathsf{DKg}(pp)$ for corrupted users. The challenger sends $(pp, (pk_i)_{1 \le i \le N}, (\tilde{pk}_i, \tilde{sk}_i)_{i \in [1 \le i \le \tilde{N}]})$ to the adversary.

Query I. The adversary $\mathcal{A}$ is allowed to issue decryption queries of the form (pk, C) in which pk should be one of $pk_1, \ldots, pk_N$. The challenger computes the decryption share μ by running $\mathsf{DDec}(pp, pk_i, sk_i, C)$ with the corresponding secret key sk_i of $pk = pk_i$.

Challenge. The adversary $\mathcal{A}$ submits two (equal-length) plaintexts m_0 and m_1, a set of authorized users $S = \{pk_1^*, \ldots, pk_n^*\}$ which is a subset of $\{pk_1, \ldots, pk_N, \tilde{pk}_1, \ldots, \tilde{pk}_{\tilde{N}}\}$, and a threshold k. The set S should include (at most) $k - 1$ corrupted public keys. The challenger randomly chooses a bit $b \in \{0, 1\}$, computes the challenge ciphertext C^* by running $\mathsf{DEnc}(pp, pk_1^*, \ldots, pk_n^*, k, m_b)$, and sends C^* to the adversary.

Query II. The adversary again issues decryption queries, and the challenger responds as in the previous phase. In addition to the Query I phase, in this phase the adversary is not allowed to submit a query (pk, C) such that $C = C^*$.

Guess. Finally the adversary outputs a guess $b' \in \{0, 1\}$. The adversary's advantage is defined by the difference between the probability that $b = b'$ and $1/2$.

Definition 1. *A dynamic TPKE scheme is said to be* chosen-ciphertext secure *if for any probabilistic polynomial-time adversary $\mathcal{A}$ and any N and $\tilde{N} \in \mathbb{N}$, the advantage of the adversary is negligible in λ.*

We then define the decryption consistency requirement by the following game. This definition is of the "known secret keys" variant.

Setup. The challenger obtains pp by running $\mathsf{DSetup}(1^\lambda)$ and obtains $\tilde{N}$ keys $(\tilde{pk}_1, \tilde{sk}_1), \ldots, (\tilde{pk}_{\tilde{N}}, \tilde{sk}_{\tilde{N}})$ by running $(\tilde{pk}_i, \tilde{sk}_i) \leftarrow \mathsf{DKg}(pp)$ for all $1 \le i \le \tilde{N}$. The challenger sends $(pp, (\tilde{pk}_i, \tilde{sk}_i)_{1 \le i \le \tilde{N}})$ to the adversary $\mathcal{A}$.

Forge. The adversary outputs (C, S, S') in which C is a ciphertext S and S' are respectively sets of k decryption shares. The adversary wins if one of the following conditions holds:

  1. both S and S' consists of k decryption shares from k distinct servers, S and S' are not equal to each other as sets, all shares $\mu \in S \cup S'$ satisfy $\mathsf{DVerify}(pp, pk, C, \mu) = \mathsf{T}_{\text{valid}}$ where pk is the user public key of the corresponding decryption servers of μ, and $\mathsf{DCombine}(pp, C, S) \ne \mathsf{DCombine}(pp, C, S')$, or
  2. there exists $\mu, \mu' \in S \cup S'$ which are both attributed to the same decryption server, $\mathsf{DVerify}(pp, pk, C, \mu) = \mathsf{T}_{\text{valid}}$, and $\mathsf{DVerify}(pp, pk, C, \mu') = \mathsf{T}_{\text{invalid}}$, in which pk is the user public key of the decryption server of μ and μ'.

The advantage of the adversary is defined by the probability that the adversary wins.

Definition 2. *A dynamic TPKE scheme is said to have* weak decryption con-
sistency *if for any probabilistic polynomial-time adversary $\mathcal{A}$ and any $\tilde{N} \in \mathbb{N}$ the
advantage of the adversary is negligible in λ.*

We further introduce a stronger definition of decryption consistency called
strong decryption consistency. It requires the DVerify algorithm to output either
$\top_{\text{valid}}$ or $\bot$ but never output $\top_{\text{invalid}}$. The strong decryption consistency is actually equivalent to the decryption consistency defined by Boneh, Boyen, and
Halevi [3] except for the "known secret key" extension. The formal definition
is as follows.

Definition 3. *A dynamic TPKE scheme is said to have* strong decryption
consistency *if in addition to the weak decryption consistency it satisfies the
following condition: for any $(pp, (\tilde{pk}_i, \tilde{sk}_i)_{1 \le i \le \tilde{N}}))$ generated as in the Setup
phase, any ciphertext $C \in \{0,1\}^*$, and any decryption shares $\mu \in \{0,1\}^*$,
$\mathsf{DVerify}(pp, pk, C, \mu)$ outputs either $\top_{\text{valid}}$ or $\bot$.*

2.2 Public-Key Encryption with Non-interactive Opening

We define syntax and security of public-key encryption with non-interactive
opening. We require the underlying PKENO scheme to support labels (or to be
tag-based) [17,20,21,23], whose formal definition is as follows.

A public-key encryption scheme with non-interactive opening consists of the
following five algorithms.

$\mathsf{Kg}(1^\lambda)$. The key generation algorithm $\mathsf{Kg}(1^\lambda)$ takes as input a security parameter 1^λ and outputs a pair (ek, dk) of the encryption key and the decryption
key.

$\mathsf{Enc}(ek, L, m)$. The encryption algorithm $\mathsf{Enc}(ek, L, m)$ takes as input the
encryption key ek, a label L, and a plaintext m. It outputs a ciphertext
c.

$\mathsf{Dec}(dk, L, c)$. The decryption algorithm $\mathsf{Dec}(dk, L, c)$ takes as input the decryption key dk, a label L, and a ciphertext c. It outputs a plaintext m or a
special symbol $\bot$.

$\mathsf{Prove}(dk, L, c)$. The proof algorithm $\mathsf{Prove}(dk, L, c)$ takes as input the decryption key dk, a label L, and a ciphertext c. It outputs a proof π.

$\mathsf{Verify}(ek, L, c, m, \pi)$. The verification algorithm $\mathsf{Verify}(ek, L, c, m, \pi)$ takes as
input the encryption key ek, a label L, a ciphertext c, a plaintext m, and a
proof π, and outputs a bit 1 or 0, indicating the proof is respectively *valid*
or *invalid*.

As the correctness condition, the labeled PKENO scheme is required to satisfy the following conditions.

- For any $(ek, dk) \leftarrow \mathsf{Kg}(1^\lambda)$, any plaintext $m \in \{0,1\}^*$ and any label $L \in
  \{0,1\}^*$, it holds that $\mathsf{Dec}(dk, L, \mathsf{Enc}(pk, L, m)) = m$.
- For any $(ek, dk) \leftarrow \mathsf{Kg}(1^\lambda)$, any ciphertext $c \in \{0,1\}^*$, and any label $L \in
  \{0,1\}^*$, it holds that $\mathsf{Verify}(ek, L, c, \mathsf{Dec}(dk, L, c), \mathsf{Prove}(dk, L, c)) = 1$.

Notice that in the latter conditions the ciphertext c is not restricted to the legitimate output of the encryption algorithm $\mathsf{Enc}(ek, L, m)$ with some L and m, and hence $\mathsf{Dec}(dk, L, c)$ could potentially be $\perp$.

We require the labeled PKENO scheme to be *selective-label weak chosen-ciphertext secure* and *strongly committing*. Although the former requirement for PKENO schemes has not been formally stated in the literature, it is a straightforward adoption of the similar requirement for ordinary (tag-based) public-key encryption schemes formalized by Kiltz [17]. The latter requirement is originally formalized by Galindo et al. [13]. More precisely our definition is a slightly weaker variant than that of Galindo et al.[13], as our definition requires the target key pair to be generated honestly. It is also worth noting that the requirement of *proof soundness*, which is defined by Damgård et al., is implied by our definition.

The requirement of selective-label weak chosen-ciphertext security is defined by the following game between challenger and the adversary $\mathcal{A}$.

Initialize. The adversary outputs a label $L^* \in \{0, 1\}^*$, which will be used to compute the challenge ciphertext.

Setup. The challenger generates a pair (ek, dk) of encryption and decryption keys by running the key generation algorithm $(ek, dk) \leftarrow \mathsf{Kg}(1^\lambda)$. The challenger sends ek to the adversary.

Query I. The adversary issues decryption-and-proof queries (L, c) to the challenger, where $L \neq L^*$. The challenger responds with a pair (m, π) where $m \leftarrow \mathsf{Dec}(dk, L, c)$ and $\pi \leftarrow \mathsf{Prove}(dk, L, c)$. The adversary is not allowed to issue a query (c, L^*) with any c.

Challenge. The adversary submits two messages m_0 and m_1 of same length. The challenger picks a random bit $b \in \{0, 1\}$, computes a challenge ciphertext $c^* \leftarrow \mathsf{Enc}(pk, L^*, m_b)$, and sends c^* to the adversary.

Query II. The adversary again issues decryption-and-proof queries, which are responded by the challenger as in the Query I phase. The same restriction of forbidding queries with the label L^* is also applied in this phase.

Guess. Finally the adversary outputs a bit b'. The adversary's advantage is defined by $|\Pr[b = b'] - 1/2|$.

Definition 4. *A labeled PKENO scheme is said to be* selective-label weakly chosen-ciphertext secure *if for any probabilistic polynomial-time adversary $\mathcal{A}$, the advantage of the adversary in the above game is negligible in λ.*

The committing requirement is defined by the following game.

Setup. The challenger generates $(ek, dk) \leftarrow \mathsf{Kg}(1^\lambda)$ and sends (ek, dk) to the adversary.

Forge. The adversary outputs a tuple (L, c, m, π, m', π'), where $m, m' \in \{0, 1\}^* \cup \{\perp\}$. The adversary's advantage is defined by the probability that the conditions $m \neq m'$, $\mathsf{Verify}(pk, L, c, m, \pi) = 1$, and $\mathsf{Verify}(pk, L, c, m', \pi') = 1$.

Definition 5. *A labeled PKENO scheme is said to be* strongly committing *if for any probabilistic polynomial-time $\mathcal{A}$, the advantage of the adversary in the above game is negligible in λ.*

3   Generic Construction of Dynamic Threshold PKE

In this section we present the first proposed construction which combines the Dodis-Katz construction with techniques from *verifiable secret sharing* [1,2]. The difficulty is to ensure consistency among the shares. In our construction, we adopt a technique from verifiable secret sharing [1,2] to resolve this problem. In particular, the scheme will encrypt a plaintext by dividing the plaintext with a secret sharing scheme and encrypting each share. Furthermore, the shares includes redundancy for verifying consistency between the shares.

$\mathsf{DSetup}(1^\lambda)$. Generate the commitment parameter ck as $ck \leftarrow \mathsf{ComKg}(1^\lambda)$, set $pp = ck$, and output pp.

$\mathsf{DKg}(pp)$. Generate the public and secret keys (ek, dk) of the PKENO scheme by running $(ek, dk) \leftarrow \mathsf{Kg}(1^\lambda)$. Set $(pk, sk) = (ek, dk)$ and output (pk, sk).

$\mathsf{DEnc}(pp, pk_1, \ldots, pk_n, k, m)$. Let ck be pp and ek_i be pk_i for all $i \in [n]$, and proceed as follows:

- Generate a key pair $(vk_{\mathrm{sots}}, sk_{\mathrm{sots}}) \leftarrow \mathsf{SigK}(1^\lambda)$ for the one-time signature scheme.
- Choose a random bivariate polynomial $f(x, y) = \sum_{i=0}^{k-1} \sum_{j=0}^{k-1} a_{i,j} x^i y^j$ of degree $k - 1$ with $a_{0,0} = m$ and $f(i, j) = f(j, i)$ for all i and j.
- Compute commitments and their decommitments of $f(i, j)$ for $1 \leq i \leq j \leq n$ as $(c_{i,j}, r_{i,j}) \leftarrow \mathsf{Commit}(ck, f(i, j))$.
- Let $c_{j,i} = c_{i,j}$ and $r_{j,i} = r_{i,j}$ for $1 \leq i < j \leq n$.
- Compute   PKENO   ciphertext   as $C_i = \mathsf{Enc}(pk_i, vk_{\mathrm{sots}}, \langle f(i, 1), \ldots, f(i, n), r_{i,1}, \ldots, r_{i,n} \rangle)$ for $i = 1, \ldots, n$.
- $\sigma_{\mathrm{sots}} \leftarrow \mathsf{SigS}(sk_{\mathrm{sots}}, \langle k, (pk_i)_{1 \leq i \leq n}, (c_{i,j})_{1 \leq i \leq j \leq n}, (C_i)_{1 \leq i \leq n} \rangle)$.
- Output $C = (vk_{\mathrm{sots}}, k, (pk_i)_{1 \leq i \leq n}, (c_{i,j})_{1 \leq i \leq j \leq n}, (C_i)_{1 \leq i \leq n}, \sigma_{\mathrm{sots}})$.

$\mathsf{DDec}(pp, pk, sk, C)$. Parse C as $(vk_{\mathrm{sots}}, k, (pk_i)_{1 \leq i \leq n}, (c_{i,j})_{1 \leq i \leq j \leq n}, (C_i)_{1 \leq i \leq n}, \sigma_{\mathrm{sots}})$ and find i such that $pk_i = pk$. If no such i is found, output $(pk, \perp)$. Otherwise, proceed as follows.

- Output $(pk, \perp)$ if $\mathsf{SigV}(vk_{\mathrm{sots}}, \langle k, (pk_i)_{1 \leq i \leq n}, (c_{i,j})_{1 \leq i \leq j \leq n}, (C_i)_{1 \leq i \leq n} \rangle, \sigma_{\mathrm{sots}}) = 0$.
- Decrypt C_i as $\hat{m} \leftarrow \mathsf{Dec}(sk, vk_{\mathrm{sots}}, C_i)$.
- Compute a proof π as $\pi \leftarrow \mathsf{Prove}(sk, vk_{\mathrm{sots}}, C_i)$.
- Output $\mu_i = (pk, (\hat{m}, \pi))$.

$\mathsf{DVerify}(pp, vk, C, \mu)$. Parse C as $(vk_{\mathrm{sots}}, k, (pk_i)_{1 \leq i \leq n}, (c_{i,j})_{1 \leq i \leq j \leq n}, (C_i)_{1 \leq i \leq n}, \sigma_{\mathrm{sots}})$ and parse μ as $(pk, \hat{\mu})$. Find i satisfying $pk = pk_i$. If no such i exists, output $\perp$ immediately. If such i exists, run $\mathsf{SigV}(vk_{\mathrm{sots}}, \langle k, (pk_i)_{1 \leq i \leq n}, (c_{i,j})_{1 \leq i \leq j \leq n}, (C_i)_{1 \leq i \leq n} \rangle, \sigma_{\mathrm{sots}})$ to verify the one-time signature σ_{sots} and proceeds as follows.

- If the one-time signature is invalid and $\hat{\mu} = \perp$, output $\top_{\mathrm{valid}}$.
- If the one-time signature is valid, $\hat{\mu}$ is parsed as $(\hat{m}, \pi)$, and $\mathsf{Verify}(pk_i, C_i, \hat{m}, \pi) = 1$, further verify the following three conditions:
  - $\hat{m}$ is parsed as $\langle f_1, \ldots, f_n, r_1, \ldots, r_n \rangle$,
  - $\mathsf{ComVerify}(ck, c_{i,j}, f_j, r_j) = 1$ (or $\mathsf{ComVerify}(ck, c_{j,i}, f_j, r_{j,i}) = 1$ for $j < i$) for all $j \in [n]$, and

- $(f_1, \ldots, f_n)$ defines a degree-$(k-1)$ polynomial.

If all of the three conditions holds, output $\top_{\text{valid}}$. Otherwise output $\top_{\text{invalid}}$.

- If neither two conditions hold, output $\bot$.

DCombine$(pp, vk, C, \mu_1, \ldots, \mu_k)$. Parse C as $(vk_{\text{sots}}, k, (pk_i)_{1 \leq i \leq n}, (c_{i,j})_{1 \leq i \leq j \leq n},$ $(C_i)_{1 \leq i \leq n}, \sigma_{\text{sots}})$ and μ_i as $(\hat{pk}_i, \hat{\mu}_i)$ for all $1 \leq i \leq k$.

- If there is at least one μ_i that is $\bot$, output $\bot$.
- Otherwise if all $\hat{\mu}_i$ are parsed as $((f_{i,1}, \ldots, f_{i,1}, r_{i,1}, \ldots, r_{i,n}), \pi_i)$, proceed as follows:
  - find t_i satisfying $pk_{t_i} = \hat{pk}_i$ for all i,
  - interpolate $(t_1, f_{t_i, t_1}), \ldots, (t_k, f_{t_i, t_k})$ to obtain a polynomial $g_{t_i}(x)$ for all i,[1]
  - interpolate $(t_1, g_{t_1}(0)), \ldots, (t_k, g_{t_k}(0))$ to obtain a polynomial $g(y)$, and
  - output $g(0)$.

Security. Security of the above construction is as follows. The proofs appears in the full version of this paper.

Theorem 1. *The construction is chosen-ciphertext secure if the PKENO scheme is selective-label weakly chosen-ciphertext secure, the commitment scheme is (computationally) hiding, and the one-time signature scheme is strongly unforgeable.*

Theorem 2. *The construction has the weak decryption consistency if the PKENO scheme is strongly committing and that the commitment scheme is (computationally) binding.*

3.1   Instantiating the Generic Construction.

To instantiate the generic construction, we need a "labeled" PKENO scheme. Fortunately, this is relatively easy to obtain by extending existing PKENO schemes. In the full version of the paper, we provide the description and security proofs of two labeled PKENO schemes based on the decisional linear assumption and the decisional bilinear Diffie-Hellman assumption, respectively.

If we instantiate the generic construction with the PKENO scheme from the decisional linear assumption, we obtain the first dynamic TPKE scheme *from a static assumption* which achieves weak decryption consistency without relying random oracles. However, note that our generic construction of dynamic

---

[1] One might think that the DVerify algorithm, instead of the DCombine algorithm, could perform this interpolation. We still choose this, simply for following the syntax of (dynamic) threshold PKE in an exact sense. Namely, the DVerify algorithm is required to output a ternary value $\top_{\text{valid}}$, $\top_{\text{invalid}}$, or $\bot$, but is not allowed to output further additional information passed to the DCombine algorithm. If the DVerify algorithm is allowed to output some additional information, the DVerify algorithm will perform this interpolation, and will pass the result to the DCombine algorithm.

TPKE is not as efficient as the Delerablée-Pointcheval scheme or the Daza et al. scheme, as our construction has a ciphertext size proportional to the square of the number of the authorized servers, while the previous schemes have constant size ciphertexts. Furthermore, our scheme only achieves weak decryption consistency rather than the strong notion.

4   Dynamic Threshold PKE from the Decisional Linear Assumption

In this section, we propose a dynamic TPKE scheme which, in contrast to the generic scheme above, provides *strong* decryption consistency. The idea of the construction is replacing the ordinary PKE scheme in the Dodis-Katz scheme with a PKENO scheme, and using non-interactive zero-knowledge proofs (in particular Groth-Sahai proofs) to provide decryption consistency.

DSetup(1^λ). Run the parameter generation algorithm[2] $\mathcal{G}(1^\lambda)$ for the bilinear groups to set up the bilinear group parameter $(p, \mathbb{G}, \mathbb{G}_T, e, g)$. Choose a common reference string $(\boldsymbol{f}_1, \boldsymbol{f}_2, \boldsymbol{f}_3) \in (\mathbb{G}^3)^3$ for the binding setting, where $\boldsymbol{f}_1 = (f_1, 1, g)$, $\boldsymbol{f}_2 = (1, f_2, g)$, and $\boldsymbol{f}_3 = \boldsymbol{f}_1^{\zeta_1} \boldsymbol{f}_2^{\zeta_2}$ for random f_1, $f_2 \in \mathbb{G} \setminus \{1\}$ and random $\zeta_1, \zeta_2 \in \mathbb{Z}_p$. Set $pp = (p, \mathbb{G}, \mathbb{G}_T, e, g, \boldsymbol{f}_1, \boldsymbol{f}_2, \boldsymbol{f}_3)$, and output pp.

DKg(pp). Generate public and secret keys of the PKENO scheme. by choosing random $x, y \leftarrow \mathbb{Z}_p$ and random $U, V \leftarrow \mathbb{G}$ and setting $u = g^x$ and $v = g^y$. Set $pk = (u, v, U, V)$ and $sk = (x, y)$ and output (pk, sk).

DEnc($pp, pk_1, \ldots, pk_n, k, m$). Parse pk_i as (u_i, v_i, U_i, V_i) for all $i \in [n]$. Generate verification and signing keys (vk, sk) for a one-time signature scheme by running SigK(1^λ). Choose random integers $r_1, \ldots, r_n, s_1, \ldots, s_n, a_1, \ldots, a_{k-1} \leftarrow \mathbb{Z}_p$ and compute $c_{i,1} \leftarrow u_i^{r_i}$, $c_{i,2} \leftarrow v_i^{s_i}$, $c_{i,3} \leftarrow (g^{vk}U_i)^{r_i}$, $c_{i,4} \leftarrow (g^{vk}V_i)^{s_i}$, and $c_{i,5} \leftarrow g^{r_i+s_i}mg^{a_1i+a_2i^2+\cdots+a_{k-1}i^{k-1}}$ for all $i \in [n]$. Then compute a Groth-Sahai proof π^{zk} which demonstrates that the equations: $c_{i,1} = u_i^{r_i}$, $c_{i,2} = v_i^{s_i}$, and $c_{i,5} = g^{r_i}g^{s_i}(g^{i^{k-1}})^{a_{k-1}} \cdots (g^{i^2})^{a_2}(g^i)^{a_1}m$ for all $i \in [n]$ with witness $m \in \mathbb{G}$ and $r_1, \ldots, r_n, s_1, \ldots, s_n, a_1, \ldots, a_{k-1} \in \mathbb{Z}_p$. Finally compute a one-time signature σ by running SigS($sk, \langle (pk_i)_{i \in [n]}, k, (c_{i,1}, \ldots, c_{i,5})_{i \in [n]}, \pi^{\text{zk}} \rangle$) and output $C = (vk, (pk_i)_{i \in [n]}, k, (c_{i,1}, \ldots, c_{i,5})_{i \in [n]}, \pi^{\text{zk}}, \sigma)$.

DDec(pp, pk, sk, C). Parse C as $(vk, (pk_i)_{i \in [n]}, k, (c_{i,1}, \ldots, c_{i,5})_{i \in [n]}, \pi^{\text{zk}}, \sigma)$. Find $i \in [n]$ such that $pk = pk_i$ and output $(pk, \bot)$ if no such i exists. Otherwise proceed as follows. Firstly verify that the one-time signature σ is valid, the Groth-Sahai proof π^{zk} is valid, and for all $i \in [n]$ the equations $e(u_i, c_{i,3}) = e(c_{i,1}, g^{vk}U_i)$ and $e(v_i, c_{i,4}) = e(c_{i,2}, g^{vk}V_i)$ hold. If any of the above does not holds, output $(pk, \bot)$ immediately. If all of them holds, compute $\pi^{(u)} = c_{i,1}^{1/x}$, $\pi^{(v)} = c_{i,2}^{1/y}$, and $\hat{m} = c_{i,5}/\pi^{(u)}\pi^{(v)}$, and outputs $\mu = (pk, (\hat{m}, \pi^{(u)}, \pi^{(v)}))$.

---

[2] Details are given in Appendix A.2.

DVerify(pp, pk, C, μ). Parse C as $(vk, (pk_i)_{i \in [n]}, k, (c_{i,1}, \ldots, c_{i,5})_{i \in [n]}, \pi^{zk}, \sigma)$. Then verify the following conditions: no $i \in [n]$ does not satisfy $pk = pk_i$, the one-time signature σ is invalid, the Groth-Sahai proof π^{zk} is invalid, or for some $i \in [n]$ one of $e(u_i, c_{i,3}) = e(c_{i,1}, g^{vk}U_i)$ and $e(v_i, c_{i,4}) = e(c_{i,2}, g^{vk}V_i)$ does not hold. If at least one of the above does not hold and μ is parsed as $(pk, \bot)$, output $\top_{valid}$. Otherwise, if all of the above do hold, μ is parsed as $(pk, (\hat{m}, \pi^{(u)}, \pi^{(v)}))$, and the three equations $e(u, \pi^{(u)}) = e(c_{i,1}, g)$, $e(v, \pi^{(v)}) = e(c_{i,2}, g)$, and $c_{i,5} = \hat{m}\pi^{(u)}\pi^{(v)}$ hold, output $\top_{valid}$. In any other cases, output $\bot$.

DCombine$(pp, C, \mu_1, \ldots, \mu_k)$. Parse C as $(vk, (pk_i)_{i \in [n]}, k, (c_{i,1}, \ldots, c_{i,5})_{i \in [n]}, \pi^{zk}, \sigma)$. If there is at least one μ_i that is parsed as $(pk, \bot)$, output $\bot$. Otherwise, parse μ_i as $(\hat{pk}_i, (\hat{m}_i, \hat{\pi}_i^{(u)}, \hat{\pi}_i^{(v)}))$, find t_i satisfying $pk_{t_i} = \hat{pk}_i$ for all $i \in [k]$, compute $m = \hat{m}_1^{\lambda_1} \cdots \hat{m}_k^{\lambda_k}$ in which $\lambda_i = \prod_{j \in [k] \setminus \{i\}} -t_j/(t_i - t_j)$, and output m.

Security. This scheme is proven to be secure under the decisional linear assumption. Detailed proofs are given in the full version of this paper.

Theorem 3. *The scheme is chosen-ciphertext secure if the decisional linear assumption holds with respect to $\mathcal{G}$.*

Theorem 4. *The scheme satisfies strong decryption consistency.*

5   Conclusion

We presented two constructions of TPKE with decryption consistency. The first scheme is a generic construction from PKENO with weak decryption consistency. The second scheme is a direct construction providing a shorter ciphertext length than the first scheme as well as strong decryption consistency. These two schemes are the first dynamic TPKE with (weak or strong) decryption consistency which do not rely on q-type assumptions or random oracles. In the full version of the paper, we furthermore show that a generic construction of TPKE with strong decryption consistency is possible, albeit at the cost of the scheme being a non-dynamic scheme and allowing only a smaller (logarithmic) number of decryption servers.

References

1. Backes, M., Kate, A., Patra, A.: Computational verifiable secret sharing revisited. In: Lee, D.H., Wang, X. (eds.) ASIACRYPT 2011. LNCS, vol. 7073, pp. 590–609. Springer, Heidelberg (2011)
2. Ben-Or, M., Goldwasser, S., Wigderson, A.: Completeness theorems for non-cryptographic fault-tolerant distributed computation (extended abstract). In: Proceedings of the 20th Annual ACM Symposium on Theory of Computing, pp. 1–10. ACM (1988)

3. Boneh, D., Boyen, X., Halevi, S.: Chosen ciphertext secure public key threshold encryption without random oracles. In: Pointcheval, D. (ed.) CT-RSA 2006. LNCS, vol. 3860, pp. 226–243. Springer, Heidelberg (2006)
4. Canetti, R., Goldwasser, S.: An efficient *threshold* public key cryptosystem secure against adaptive chosen ciphertext attack. In: Stern, J. (ed.) EUROCRYPT 1999. LNCS, vol. 1592, pp. 90–106. Springer, Heidelberg (1999)
5. Damgård, I., Hofheinz, D., Kiltz, E., Thorbek, R.: Public-key encryption with non-interactive opening. In: Malkin, T. (ed.) CT-RSA 2008. LNCS, vol. 4964, pp. 239–255. Springer, Heidelberg (2008)
6. Daza, V., Herranz, J., Morillo, P., Ràfols, C.: CCA2-secure threshold broadcast encryption with shorter ciphertexts. In: Susilo, W., Liu, J.K., Mu, Y. (eds.) ProvSec 2007. LNCS, vol. 4784, pp. 35–50. Springer, Heidelberg (2007)
7. De Santis, A., Desmedt, Y., Frankel, Y., Yung, M.: How to share a function securely. In: Proceedings of the Twenty-sixth Annual ACM Symposium on Theory of Computing, pp. 522–533. ACM (1994)
8. Delerablée, C., Pointcheval, D.: Dynamic threshold public-key encryption. In: Wagner, D. (ed.) CRYPTO 2008. LNCS, vol. 5157, pp. 317–334. Springer, Heidelberg (2008)
9. Desmedt, Y.: Threshold cryptosystems. In: Seberry, J., Zheng, Y. (eds.) AUSCRYPT 1992. LNCS, vol. 718, pp. 1–14. Springer, Heidelberg (1993)
10. Dodis, Y., Katz, J.: Chosen-ciphertext security of multiple encryption. In: Kilian, J. (ed.) TCC 2005. LNCS, vol. 3378, pp. 188–209. Springer, Heidelberg (2005)
11. Emura, K., Hanaoka, G., Sakai, Y., Schuldt, J.C.N.: Group signature implies public-key encryption with non-interactive opening. International Journal of Information Security **13**(1), 51–62 (2014)
12. Galindo, David: Breaking and repairing damgård *et al.* public key encryption scheme with non-interactive opening. In: Fischlin, Marc (ed.) CT-RSA 2009. LNCS, vol. 5473, pp. 389–398. Springer, Heidelberg (2009)
13. Galindo, D., Libert, B., Fischlin, M., Fuchsbauer, G., Lehmann, A., Manulis, M., Schröder, D.: Public-key encryption with non-interactive opening: new constructions and stronger definitions. In: Bernstein, D.J., Lange, T. (eds.) AFRICACRYPT 2010. LNCS, vol. 6055, pp. 333–350. Springer, Heidelberg (2010)
14. Gan, Y., Wang, L., Wang, L., Pan, P., Yang, Y.: Efficient threshold public key encryption with full security based on dual pairing vector spaces. International Journal of Communication Systems **27**(12), 4059–4077 (2014)
15. Groth, J., Sahai, A.: Efficient non-interactive proof systems for bilinear groups. In: Smart, N.P. (ed.) EUROCRYPT 2008. LNCS, vol. 4965, pp. 415–432. Springer, Heidelberg (2008)
16. Ito, M., Saito, A., Nishizeki, T.: Multiple assignment scheme for sharing secret. Journal of Cryptology **6**(1), 15–20 (1993)
17. Kiltz, E.: Chosen-ciphertext security from tag-based encryption. In: Halevi, S., Rabin, T. (eds.) TCC 2006. LNCS, vol. 3876, pp. 581–600. Springer, Heidelberg (2006)
18. Libert, B., Yung, M.: Adaptively secure non-interactive threshold cryptosystems. In: Aceto, L., Henzinger, M., Sgall, J. (eds.) ICALP 2011, Part II. LNCS, vol. 6756, pp. 588–600. Springer, Heidelberg (2011)
19. Libert, B., Yung, M.: Non-interactive CCA-secure threshold cryptosystems with adaptive security: new framework and constructions. In: Cramer, R. (ed.) TCC 2012. LNCS, vol. 7194, pp. 75–93. Springer, Heidelberg (2012)

20. Lim, C.H., Lee, P.J.: Another method for attaining security against adaptively chosen ciphertext attacks. In: Stinson, D.R. (ed.) CRYPTO 1993. LNCS, vol. 773, pp. 420–434. Springer, Heidelberg (1994)
21. MacKenzie, P., Reiter, M.K., Yang, K.: Alternatives to non-malleability: definitions, constructions, and applications. In: Naor, M. (ed.) TCC 2004. LNCS, vol. 2951, pp. 171–190. Springer, Heidelberg (2004)
22. Qin, B., Wu, Q., Zhang, L., Domingo-Ferrer, J.: Threshold public-key encryption with adaptive security and short ciphertexts. In: Soriano, M., Qing, S., López, J. (eds.) ICICS 2010. LNCS, vol. 6476, pp. 62–76. Springer, Heidelberg (2010)
23. Shoup, V., Gennaro, R.: Securing threshold cryptosystems against chosen ciphertext attack. In: Nyberg, K. (ed.) EUROCRYPT 1998. LNCS, vol. 1403, pp. 1–16. Springer, Heidelberg (1998)
24. Shoup, V., Gennaro, R.: Securing threshold cryptosystems against chosen ciphertext attack. Journal of Cryptology **15**(2), 75–96 (2002)

A   Omitted Definitions and Notations

A.1   Standard Primitives

Commitment. A commitment scheme consists of the three algorithms ComKg, Commit, and ComVerify. The algorithm ComKg takes the security parameter 1^λ and outputs a parameter ck. The commitment algorithm takes as input the parameter ck and a string m, and outputs a pair (c, r), where c is the commitment string for m and r is the corresponding decommitment string. The decommitment algorithm ComVerify takes as input the security parameter 1^λ, a commitment string c, a string m, and a decommitment string r and outputs 0 or 1, indicating the decommitment is valid or invalid. It is required that for any ck output by $\mathsf{ComKg}(1^\lambda)$, any $m \in \{0,1\}^*$, and any (c,r) output by $\mathsf{Commit}(ck, m)$, it holds that $\mathsf{ComVerify}(ck, c, m, r) = 1$. As the hiding property it is required that for any probabilistic polynomial-time adversary $\mathcal{A}$ the probability $|\Pr[b \leftarrow \{0,1\}; ck \leftarrow \mathsf{ComKg}(1^\lambda); b' \leftarrow \mathcal{A}^{\mathcal{O}_b}(ck) : b = b'] - 1/2|$ is negligible in λ, where the oracle $\mathcal{O}_b$, when receives a pair (m_0, m_1) as input, runs $\mathsf{Commit}(ck, m_b)$ to obtain (c, r) and returns c. As the binding property it is required that for any probabilistic polynomial-time adversary $\mathcal{A}$ the probability $\Pr[ck \leftarrow \mathsf{ComKg}(1^\lambda); (c, m, r, m', r') \leftarrow \mathcal{A}(ck) : m \neq m' \wedge \mathsf{ComVerify}(ck, c, m, r) = 1 \wedge \mathsf{ComVerify}(ck, c, m', r') = 1]$ is negligible in λ.

One-Time Signature. A one-time signature scheme consists of the three algorithm SigK, SigS, and SigV. The algorithm SigK takes the security parameter 1^λ and generates a key pair $(vk_{\mathsf{sots}}, sk_{\mathsf{sots}})$. The algorithm SigS takes the singing key sk_{sots} and a message m and generates a one-time signature σ_{sots}. The verification algorithm SigV takes the verification key vk_{sots}, a message m, and a signature σ_{sots} and outputs a bit 1 or 0. We require as correctness the following condition: for all λ and all $m \in \{0,1\}^*$, all $(vk_{\mathsf{sots}}, sk_{\mathsf{sots}})$ generated by running $\mathsf{SigK}(1^\lambda)$, it holds that $\mathsf{SigV}(vk_{\mathsf{sots}}, m, \mathsf{SigS}(sk_{\mathsf{sots}}, m)) = 1$. We also require the one-time signature scheme to be strongly unforgeable. This property requires that for any probabilistic polynomial-time adversary $\mathcal{A}$, when given a verification key vk_{sots} generated by running the key generation algorithm $\mathsf{SigK}(1^\lambda)$ and an signature σ on arbitrary message m chosen by the adversary after seeing vk_{sots}, the adversary outputs a forgery $(m^*, \sigma^*) \neq (m, \sigma)$ which satisfies $\mathsf{SigV}(vk_{\text{sots}}, m^*, \sigma^*) = 1$ only with negligible probability.

A.2   Bilinear Groups and Hardness Assumptions

Here we introduce the bilinear groups and hardness assumptions on which our specific instantiations of PKENO are based.

The algorithm $\mathcal{G}(1^\lambda)$, which generates a parameter of bilinear group, takes the security parameter 1^λ and outputs $(p, \mathbb{G}, \mathbb{G}_T, e, g)$ where p is a prime, $\mathbb{G}$ and $\mathbb{G}_T$ are order-p groups, $e \colon \mathbb{G} \times \mathbb{G} \to \mathbb{G}_T$ is a bilinear map, and g is a generator of the group $\mathbb{G}$. We needs the following two hardness assumptions.

Definition 6. *We say that the decision bilinear Diffie-Hellman (DBDH) assumption with respect to $\mathcal{G}$ holds if for any probabilistic polynomial-time algorithm $\mathcal{A}$, it holds that* $\Pr[(p, \mathbb{G}, \mathbb{G}_T, e, g) \leftarrow \mathcal{G}(1^\lambda); \ \alpha, \beta, \gamma \leftarrow \mathbb{Z}_p : \mathcal{A}(p, \mathbb{G}, \mathbb{G}_T, e, g, g^\alpha, g^\beta, g^\gamma, e(g, g)^{\alpha\beta\gamma}) = 1] - \Pr[(p, \mathbb{G}, \mathbb{G}_T, e, g) \leftarrow \mathcal{G}(1^\lambda); \ \alpha, \beta, \gamma, \delta \leftarrow \mathbb{Z}_p : \mathcal{A}(p, \mathbb{G}, \mathbb{G}_T, e, g, g^\alpha, g^\beta, g^\gamma, e(g, g)^\delta) = 1]$ *is negligible in λ.*

Definition 7. *We say that the decisional linear assumption (DLIN) with respect to $\mathcal{G}$ holds if for any probabilistic polynomial-time algorithm $\mathcal{A}$, it holds that* $\Pr[(p, \mathbb{G}, \mathbb{G}_T, e, g) \leftarrow \mathcal{G}(1^\lambda); \ g_1, g_2, h \leftarrow \mathbb{G}; \ \alpha, \beta \leftarrow \mathbb{Z}_p : \mathcal{A}(p, \mathbb{G}, \mathbb{G}_T, e, g_1, g_2, h, g_1^\alpha, g_2^\beta, h^{\alpha+\beta}) = 1] - \Pr[(p, \mathbb{G}, \mathbb{G}_T, e, g) \leftarrow \mathcal{G}(1^\lambda); \ g_1, g_2, h \leftarrow \mathbb{G}; \ \alpha, \beta, \delta \leftarrow \mathbb{Z}_p : \mathcal{A}(p, \mathbb{G}, \mathbb{G}_T, e, g_1, g_2, h, g_1^\alpha, g_2^\beta, h^\delta) = 1]$ *is negligible in λ.*

A.3   The Groth-Sahai Proof System

Groth and Sahai presented an efficient zero-knowledge proof system for bilinear groups, which can be based on the decisional linear assumption. The proof system has two types of the common reference string, the soundness string and the witness-indistinguishability string. For both types the string consists of three vectors $\boldsymbol{f}_1$, $\boldsymbol{f}_2$, and $\boldsymbol{f}_3$ of $\mathbb{G}^3$, in which $\boldsymbol{f}_1 = (f_1, 1, g)$, $\boldsymbol{f}_2 = (1, f_2, g)$ with random $f_1, f_2 \in \mathbb{G} \setminus \{1\}$ for both types. For the soundness string, the last vector $\boldsymbol{f}_3$ is set to $\boldsymbol{f}_3 = \boldsymbol{f}_1{}^{\varsigma_1} \boldsymbol{f}_2{}^{\varsigma_2}$, whereas for the witness-indistinguishability string, it is set to $\boldsymbol{f}_3 = \boldsymbol{f}_1{}^{\varsigma_1} \boldsymbol{f}_2{}^{\varsigma_2} (1, 1, g)^{-1}$. On the soundness string, the Groth-Sahai proof system provides *perfect soundness* of the proof system, while on the witness-indistinguishability string the proof system can provide a *zero-knowledge* simulation for certain types of a statement (that include the statement that we used in this paper).

Sponge Based CCA2 Secure Asymmetric Encryption for Arbitrary Length Message

Tarun Kumar Bansal[(✉)], Donghoon Chang,
and Somitra Kumar Sanadhya

Indraprastha Institute of Information Technology, Delhi (IIIT-D),
New Delhi, India
{tarunb,donghoon,somitra}@iiitd.ac.in

Abstract. OAEP and other similar schemes proven secure in Random-Oracle Model require one or more hash functions with output size larger than those of standard hash functions. In this paper, we show that by utilizing popular Sponge constructions in OAEP framework, we can eliminate the need of such hash functions. We provide a new scheme in OAEP framework based on Sponge construction and call our scheme *Sponge based asymmetric encryption padding* (SpAEP). SpAEP is based on 2 functions: Sponge and SpongeWrap, and requires only standard output sizes proposed and standardized for Sponge functions. Our scheme is CCA2 secure for any trapdoor one-way permutation in the ideal permutation model for arbitrary length messages. Our scheme utilizes the versatile Sponge function to enhance the capability and efficiency of the OAEP framework. SpAEP with any trapdoor one-way permutation can also be used as a key encapsulation mechanism and a tag-based key encapsulation mechanism for hybrid encryption. Our scheme SpAEP utilizes the permutation model efficiently in the setting of public key encryption in a novel manner.

Keywords: OAEP · Sponge function · Public key encryption · Hybrid encryption · CCA2 security

1 Introduction

The Optimal Asymmetric Encryption Padding (OAEP), proposed by Bellare and Rogaway at Eurocrypt '94 [11], is a technique for converting the RSA trapdoor permutation into a chosen ciphertext secure system in the random oracle model (ROM). In Crypto '01, Shoup described a modification to OAEP, called OAEP+, that provably converts any trapdoor one way permutation (f) into a chosen ciphertext secure system in the random oracle model. In 2003, Phan and Pointcheval [33,34] introduced OAEP-3R which is RCCA secure ("relaxed CCA" [34] equivalent to "replayable CCA" [19]- a slightly weaker notion than general CCA2) with any trapdoor one way permutation (f) in ROM. Let "ciphertext overhead" [4] stand for the difference between the length of ciphertext and

© Springer International Publishing Switzerland 2015
E. Foo and D. Stebila (Eds.): ACISP 2015, LNCS 9144, pp. 93–106, 2015.
DOI: 10.1007/978-3-319-19962-7_6

plaintext. OAEP-3R was shown to have only t-bit ciphertext overhead, whereas OAEP and OAEP+ have $3t$-bit ciphertext overhead, where t stands for security requirement in bits[1]. In 2008, Abe, Kiltz and Okamoto [4] showed that security reduction of OAEP-3R forces ciphertext overhead to be $2t$. A new scheme called OAEP-4X was introduced in [4] which provides CCA2 security for any trapdoor one way permutation in ROM. OAEP-4X has only t-bit ciphertext overhead which was shown to be optimal (lowest achievable bound). In OAEP-4X, reduction of t-bit ciphertext overhead with respect to OAEP-3R has only limited practical application such as in a highly bandwidth constrained network. Therefore, for general applications ciphertext overhead reduction by t-bits is a less interesting case.

Number of hash functions used in OAEP is 2 and these are used in a 2 round structure. OAEP+ is also 2 round structure but uses 3 hash functions (2 hash function can run in parallel while encryption). OAEP-3R is 3 round structure that uses 3 hash functions and OAEP-4X is 4 round structure that uses 4 hash functions. Each of these schemes (OAEP, OAEP+, OAEP-3R and OAEP-4X), proven secure in ROM, requires one or more hash functions with arbitrary size output. For example, for RSA-2048 (or RSA-3072) trapdoor one-way permutation, minimum number of hash function with arbitrary size output required in OAEP, OAEP+, OAEP-3R and OAEP-4X are 1, 1, 2 and 2 respectively.

Currently, no cryptographic standard specifies an instantiation for hash function of arbitrary size. However, some instantiations are implicit in PKCS #1 v2.1 [27], because RSA-OAEP [11] is standardized. For example, RSA-OAEP requires two random hash functions G and H with small input size (less than the RSA modulus) and arbitrary size output. Both G and H are both instantiated in PKCS by the MGF1 PRNG [27]. MGF1 uses a hash function in counter mode: $\mathrm{MGF1}(x) = h(x\langle count0\rangle)||h(x\langle count1\rangle)||h(x\langle count2\rangle)||\ldots$, where h is either SHA-1 or a SHA-2. Because MGF1 is not a regular standardized hash function, we use a term "non-standard hash function" for such functions, which instantiate a hash function of arbitrary output size by utilizing standard fixed length hash functions (e.g., SHA-1, SHA-2) to generate arbitrary hash output. Similarly, in other OAEP-type schemes, instantiation of such hash functions is done by using similar "non-standard hash function".

OAEP-type schemes (OAEP, OAEP+,OAEP-3R) discussed above, work only for restricted message length (less than input size of trapdoor one-way permutation) except OAEP-4X, which works for long messages (more than input size of trapdoor one-way permutation) as well. To encrypt lengthy messages, OAEP-4X uses one extra hash function and a passively secure symmetric encryption scheme along with 4 hash functions. In OAEP-4X, the ability of handling long messages is the result of utilizing well known Tag-KEM/DEM framework [3,18]. Tag-KEM/DEM is considered a hybrid encryption scheme [3,7,21,22,24–26,31]. In hybrid paradigm, an asymmetric key encapsulation mechanism (KEM) combines with a symmetric data encapsulation mechanism (DEM). Traditionally, KEM is

---

[1] A security requirement of t-bit implies that at-least 2^t queries are required to break the scheme with probability close to 1.

a probabilistic algorithm that produces a random symmetric key and an asymmetric encryption of that key as the key encapsulation. DEM is a deterministic algorithm that takes a symmetric key, generated by KEM, and encrypts the message under that key. In Tag-KEM/DEM framework, KEM takes a feedback, referred to as the 'tag', from DEM part and then generates key encapsulation. Final ciphertext results from concatenation of key encapsulation and encryption of message. This traditional hybrid paradigm suffers from high ciphertext overhead (difference between plaintext and ciphertext length) equivalent to the size of asymmetric encryption of key.

In 2007, Bjørstad et.al. [18] introduced KEMs (RKEM and Tag-RKEM) with partial message input/recovery. These KEMs help in significant reduction of ciphertext overhead in hybrid constructions. [18] also showed that the Tag-RKEM is more space efficient than the RKEM in terms of the ciphertext overhead. For construction of RKEMs, [18] focuses over those asymmetric encryption schemes which can recover the random variable used in encryption, during the decryption, like in OAEP-type schemes. Therefore, [18] provided the use of RSA-OAEP in RKEMs as an example. OAEP-4X has also utilized the same idea proposed in [18] along with some improvement in Tag-KEM part. This signifies that the OAEP-type schemes are good candidates for constructing RKEMs and successive improvements which took place in OAEP-type schemes helped in the instantiation of the RKEMs also.

Motivation: Almost all previous public key cryptography literature dealing with OAEP-based encryption, requires a perfect random function (a Random oracle) over an arbitrary domain, whereas in practice one is given a random function or permutation over a relatively small domain: practical block-cipher, hash functions and permutations have smaller block size and fixed output length. Therefore, for generating lengthy hash output, RSA-Full Domain Hash [10, 12, 20] or the Mask Generation Function (MGF1) [27] in RSA-OAEP are currently implemented with a complex construction of fixed length hashes and counters. For m blocks input and n blocks hash output, a fixed length hash function has to run approximately $m \times n$ times. All of above mentioned schemes (OAEP, OAEP+, OAEP-3R, OAEP-4X) proven secure in ROM require one or more hash functions with output size larger than standard sizes (e.g., SHA-1, SHA-512). [28] showed that the hash function instantiation proposed in the literature for such cases are weaker than a random oracle, where hash functions are assumed to behave like random oracle in the security analysis. The "non-standard hash function" (like MGF1) are not well analyzed in literature, have complex construction of fixed length hash functions with counter and are also proven weaker than random oracle. This raises a question on the possibility of modifying the OAEP framework which does not require any "non-standard hash function" and where all the computations are performed in standardized input-output settings.

Development of schemes from OAEP to OAEP-4X shows differences in the number of rounds, depending upon calls to the hash functions used. OAEP and OAEP+ is considered as 2 round structure, OAEP-3R as 3 round and

OAEP-4X as 4 round. This naturally poses a question on the possibility of further development of the OAEP-type scheme and reduce the number of rounds.

We have seen OAEP-type construction are good candidate in hybrid encryption for constructing KEMs like in [18] and improvements in OAEP-type construction helps the RKEMs and hybrid encryption also.

Presently, major existing and proposed crypto-systems are based on standard assumptions or proven secure in random oracle model for public key cryptography. The crypto-systems based on permutations, proven secure in ideal permutation model, and using them efficiently are yet to be explored to develop new outlooks and techniques that can cross-pollinate and advance cryptography as a whole. An open problem mentioned in [3] about having a hybrid construction from different primitives like permutation, also helps us to pursue in this direction.

Interestingly, popular Sponge constructions [15], based on iterative permutation, are found to be a suitable solution of all the questions mentioned above. Sponge constructions work in standardized input-output settings [14–17] and are useful for encryption, Authentication Encryption (AE), variable length input/output and for MAC generations [5]. In a Sponge function, for m blocks input and n blocks hash output, roughly $m + n$ calls of internal primitive permutation are required. Other than that, number of permutation calls in a Sponge function [15], used as hash function, and SpongeWrap [16], a modification of Sponge function used as AE, is equal in general. Therefore, versatility of Sponge function encourages the designers to come up with more useful and efficient design. The glimpse of popularity of Sponge functions can be seen clearly in CAESAR [1] and PHC [2] competition. Therefore, it is interesting to consider a permutation based or more concretely a Sponge construction based OAEP-type scheme having a security proof in ideal permutation model which can also be utilized in hybrid encryption.

Our Contribution: In this work, we introduce a *Sponge based Asymmetric Encryption Padding* scheme (SpAEP), a novel way to use the SpongeWrap [16] and the Sponge function [15] to encrypt arbitrary length messages in Asymmetric key cryptography. Each function (SpongeWrap and Sponge) iterates a public invertible permutation as a primitive function. Permutation calls in Sponge function and in a SpongeWrap are generally the same for equal number of input-output data blocks.

– We provide new direction for constructing asymmetric key cryptographic schemes in ideal permutation model by utilizing permutations, having smaller or practical domain, in SpAEP. Almost all previous public key cryptography literature dealing with OAEP-based encryption requires hash functions (or a random function) over an arbitrary domain.
– SpAEP uses the Sponge function and the SpongeWrap in standard input-output settings, proposed for "Sponge functions" [14–17], as per security requirement. Therefore, SpAEP remove the requirement of having "non-standard hash function", which is required in OAEP, OAEP+, OAEP-3R

and OAEP-4X for generating hash output of different sizes than standard size ("non-standard output size").

– In SpAEP, both functions (Sponge function and SpongeWrap) are used in parallel during encryption to speed-up the process. Therefore, we consider SpAEP as 1 round structure in comparison to other OAEP-type schemes. By functions in parallel we refer to potential parallelism properties of Sponge functions, where output of permutation calls of Sponge function feed into permutation calls of SpongeWrap as input in pipe-lined fashion. Let Sponge function and SpongeWrap have n, $n > 0$, permutation calls respectively, then output of nth permutation of SpongeWrap is feed into $(n+1)^{th}$ permutation of SpongeWrap and partial output in n^{th} permutation of Sponge function. This means $(n+1)^{th}$ permutation of SpongeWrap and n^{th} permutation of Sponge function can be processed in parallel. However, the functions are not parallelized during decryption.

Features of SpAEP and Comparison with other OAEP-type schemes

– Although the permutation used in Sponge is invertible, we do not use this fact for our construction and provide inverse-freeness. Therefore our construction allows using permutations which are inefficient to invert but efficient in the forward direction. That is, computation time, implementation or memory efficiency of the forward direction of the permutation can be exploited by user in our design. Moreover, our design allows using a non-invertible mapping in the Sponge function.

– Conceptually, our approach is similar to the scheme *Tag-KEM with partial ciphertext recovery* [18] but in our case the message can be directly recovered. Therefore, our scheme can be used as a *Tag-KEM with partial message recovery*. (We do not pursue this line in this paper due to the space limitation). This Tag-KEM version of our scheme is similar to OAEP-4X, which trivially take us to the comparison among OAEP-4X and SpAEP and other OAEP-type schemes.

– Let f be a trapdoor one-way permutation then we denote the instantiation of our scheme with f by f-SpAEP. The f-SpAEP can process arbitrary length messages. Our scheme is CCA2 secure when used with any trapdoor one-way permutation.

– We provide a formal security proof of f-SpAEP in adaptive chosen ciphertext attack (CCA-2) notion in the ideal permutation model. Instead of directly using security proof, in ROM, of sponge construction, we prefer a dedicated proof from scratch in ideal permutation model to avoid multi-stage game problem [6,30]. Although [33] introduced an efficient scheme in ideal permutation model with full domain permutation encryption, still it remained impractical because having such big permutation size equivalent to trapdoor one-way permutation size is itself hard. Similar problem of output size occurs when a scheme requires hash output different (generally larger) than standard sizes.

In Table 1, we compare OAEP [11], OAEP+ [36], OAEP-3R [33] and OAEP-4X [4] with SpAEP. In Table 1 cipher text overhead values are taken from Table 1 [4].

OAEP, OAEP+ and OAEP-3R can only handle messages of length less than input size of trapdoor one-way permutation unlike OAEP-4X and SpAEP can handle any message size.

In Table 1, for OAEP, number of functions run in parallel during encryption is zero, both hash function run sequentially. Similarly in the case of OAEP-3R, all three hash function calls are sequential. OAEP+ uses three hash functions, out of which only two function calls can run in parallel. In OAEP-4X, for messages having size less than input size of trapdoor one-way permutation, only 4 hash function calls are required sequentially. For long messages(message size more than input size of trapdoor one-way permutation), OAEP-4X uses 5 hash functionss (H1, H2, H3, H4, G) calls and one symmetric encryption scheme (E). Initially only two hash function calls run in parallel (H1,G) then H2 and E runs parallel, and then H3 and H4 runs sequentially. Overall in OAEP-4X, for long messages, only two functions calls can run in parallel at instant. From Table 1, we can clearly see that SpAEP is a simple and efficient scheme in comparison to other schemes. Although SpAEP has t-bit extra ciphertext overhead with respect to OAEP-4X, yet as explained earlier this is a minor concern in general applications.

Table 1. Comparison of OAEP, OAEP+, OAEP-3R, SpAEP, OAEP-4X Here t is the security requirements in term of number of bits. In order to break the scheme with probability 1 number of queries required are 2^t. ℓ is input-output size of trapdoor one way permutation f.

	OAEP [11]	OAEP+ [36]	OAEP-3R [33]	OAEP-4X [4]	SpAEP
Ciphertext-overhead	$3t$	$3t$	$2t$	t	$2t$
# Function calls	2 Hash	3 Hash	3 Hash	5 Hash, 1 Symmetric Encryption (E)	1 SpongeWrap, 1 Sponge function
# Function calls Sequential or Parallel (Encryption)	Sequential	2 parallel, 1 sequential	Sequential	Mixed	Parallel
Trapdoor Perm.-f	RSA, Rabin	Any f	Any-f	Any f	Any-f
Max. Message size with f	$\ell - 3t$	$\ell - 3t$	$\ell - 2t$	Any	Any

One may argue that in OAEP based schemes, for final encryption and decryption, trapdoor one-way permutation show dominance in computation time with respect to OAEP type structure. This makes each and every scheme in-advantageous over other schemes in terms of computation efficiency. We hope this may not be the case always or in future. Recent development in lattice based cryptography [13, 29, 32] shows up that computation time of trapdoor function can reduce significantly compared to existing traditional trapdoor permutation. Therefore, it is fruitful to have OAEP type schemes that are better than existing one and compatible with latest trends.

In summary, we are proposing an asymmetric padding scheme which is more simple and efficient in terms of structure and functionality than other existing OAEP-type schemes.

2   Preliminaries

We discuss some preliminaries in this section.

Ideal Permutation: An permutation π is a bijective function on a finite domain D and finite range R with $D = R$. An ideal permutation is a permutation chosen uniformly at random from all the available permutations. Let $D = R = \{0,1\}^b$, then $\pi \leftarrow \text{Perm}(D, D)$, where $\text{Perm}(D, D)$ is the collection of all permutations on D. Mathematically, $\pi : D \rightarrow R$ is a permutation, if for every $y \in R$ there is one and only one $x \in D$ such that $\pi(x) = y$.

Trapdoor One-Way Permutations and Their Security: We recall the security notion of a trapdoor one way permutation scheme. This scheme requires a *trapdoor permutation generator*. This is a PPT algorithm $\mathcal{F}$ such that $\mathcal{F}(1^\ell)$ outputs a pair of deterministic algorithms (f, f^{-1}) specifying a permutation and its inverse on $\{0,1\}^\ell$. We associate to $\mathcal{F}$ an *evaluation time* $t_\mathcal{F}(\cdot)$: for all l, all $(f, f^{-1}) \in [\mathcal{F}(1^\ell)]$ and all $C \in \{0,1\}^\ell$, the time to compute $f(C)$ (given f and C) is $t_\mathcal{F}(\ell)$. Note that the evaluation time depends on the setting: for example on whether or not there is hardware available to compute f.

We will be interested in two attributes of a (possibly non-uniform) algorithm $\mathcal{B}$ trying to invert $\mathcal{F}(1^\ell)$-distributed permutations; namely its running time and its success probability.

Definition 1. *Let $\mathcal{F}$ be a trapdoor permutation generator. We say that f is a one-way trapdoor permutation if for any efficient adversary $\mathcal{B}$ trying to invert $\mathcal{F}$ such that*

$$Adv_\mathcal{F}^{owtp}(\mathcal{B}) = Pr[(f, f^{-1}) \leftarrow \mathcal{F}(1^\ell); y \leftarrow \{0,1\}^\ell : \mathcal{B}(f, y) = C \text{ s.t. } f(C) = y] \leq \epsilon,$$

where ϵ is negligible in ℓ.

CCA, CCA2 Security: For probabilistic public key scheme (PKE), indistinguishability is defined by the following experiment between an adversary $\mathcal{A}$ and a challenger. For schemes based on computational security, the adversary is modeled by a probabilistic polynomial time Turing machine, meaning that it must complete the game and output a guess within a polynomial number of time steps. The scheme PKE comprise $(\mathcal{G}, \mathcal{E}_{pk}, \mathcal{D}_{sk})$. Secret/Private keys (pk, sk) is the generated by $\mathcal{G}$ and s is the auxiliary information collected by $\mathcal{A}$ using oracle $\mathcal{O}_1$. $\mathcal{E}_{pk}(M)$ represents the encryption of a message M under the public key pk and $\mathcal{D}_{sk}$ represents the decryption of ciphertext y under secret key sk.

Experiment: $Exp_{PKE,\mathcal{A}}^{ind-atk-d}(\ell)$

---

1. $(\mathbf{pk,sk}) \leftarrow \mathcal{G}(1^{\ell})$; $(M_0, M_1, s) \leftarrow \mathcal{A}^{\mathcal{O}_1(\cdot)}$; $y \leftarrow \mathcal{E}_{pk}(M_d)$;
2. $d' \leftarrow \mathcal{A}^{\mathcal{O}_2(\cdot)}(M_0, M_1, y, s)$;
3. **return** d';

---

where $|M_0| = |M_1|$ and y cannot be queried to $\mathcal{O}_2$ oracle, and

atk=CCA-1 : $\mathcal{O}_1(\cdot) = \mathcal{D}_{sk}(\cdot)$ and $\mathcal{O}_2(\cdot) = \mathcal{E}_{pk}$
atk=CCA-2 : $\mathcal{O}_1(\cdot) = \mathcal{D}_{sk}(\cdot)$ and $\mathcal{O}_2(\cdot) = \mathcal{D}_{sk}(\cdot)$

The scheme is IND-CCA1/IND-CCA2 [9] secure if adversary $\mathcal{A}$ has a non-negligible advantage in winning $(d' = d)$ the above game. The definition of security we have presented here is from [35]. It is known to be equivalent to other notions, such as non-malleability [9,23] , which is called $NM\text{-}CCA\text{-}2$ in [9].

$$\Pr[Exp_{PKE,\mathcal{A}}^{ind-cca2-d}(\ell) = d \mid d \leftarrow \{0,1\}] \leq negl(\ell) + \tfrac{1}{2}.$$

3   General View of OAEP+

In this section we provide a general view[2] of the OAEP+ with f as the trapdoor one way permutation in an informal way. This helps us to elaborate the basis of the design of our scheme. This general view is shown in Figure 2, 3. It has three parts:

1. *One time Authenticated Encryption (OAE)*: This is a one time authentication encryption that uses a one time key R and generates an encoded message C and Tag T_1 of message M. Message will be padded to suitable length according to OAE.
2. *Hash*: This is a deterministic hashing algorithm. The concatenation of the outputs of OAE with a one time key R is the input of this hashing algorithm. It outputs T_2.
3. *Trapdoor one way Permutation*: This is a trapdoor one way permutation $f : \{0,1\}^{\ell} \rightarrow \{0,1\}^{\ell}$, which takes the concatenation of the outputs of OAE and *Hash* and produces the final encryption.

---

[2] This informal general view helps in understanding our scheme.

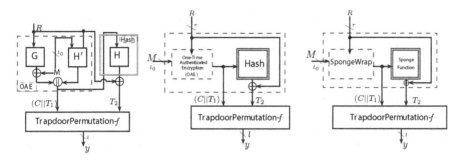

Fig. 1. OAEP+ with f **Fig. 2.** General View of   **Fig. 3.** Sponge based view of
Fig. 1   Fig. 2

Figure 1 shows OAEP+ construction with f as the trapdoor one way permutation. G, H' and H are the hash functions used in OAEP+. If we map OAEP+ on our general view then the combination of G and H' is OAE while H is the Hash part. G provides a kind of one time pad encryption (OTE) to message M, H' provides hash tag T_1 of M and H produces hash tag T_2 of OTE and tag T_1.

In this work, we provide f-SpAEP as an example of this general view where the f-SpAEP scheme uses SpongeWrap as OAE and a Sponge function as $Hash$ part with different IV.

One can view and use our scheme in hybrid encryption model and can also utilize in key/data encapsulation method. But in this paper we are more focused over sponge applicability in OAEP framework.

4   SpAEP-Sponge Based Asymmetric Encryption Padding

SpAEP is a Sponge function based construction. SpAEP iterates a fixed permutation $\pi : \{0,1\}^{b_i} \times \{0,1\}^{b_c} \rightarrow \{0,1\}^{b_i} \times \{0,1\}^{b_c}$ in a exact way to the Sponge construction and SpongeWrap [15–17].

The bit length of input and output of π, called bit rate, is $b = b_i + b_c$. The term b_i is called input rate and the term b_c is called capacity rate. The permutation π is the only underlying cryptographic primitive used by SpAEP. For using SpAEP for asymmetric key setting, one can use any trapdoor one way permutation $f : \{0,1\}^\ell \rightarrow \{0,1\}^\ell$ such as RSA. The resulting scheme is called f-SpAEP. The output of function f is $y \in \{0,1\}^\ell$ and the trapdoor of f is represented by f^{-1}. $\lfloor x \rfloor_r$ represents the first r bit of x or we can say it r-bit chop function. Similarly, $\lceil x \rceil$ represents the last r bit of x. See Figure 4 for graphical presentation.

SpAEP handles the arbitrary length message and π is fixed length permutation of input rate b_i. SpAEP uses a reversible padding function $pad(\cdot)$ to generate b_i-bit length blocks. For scheme to be compatible with f, scheme uses $pad(\cdot)$ to divided the message into two parts(M^n, M^e). First part should have minimum n-block message where each block is of b_i-bit length such that $\ell = n * b_i + 2r$, $\ell \geq b_i$ and $n \geq 1$. SpAEP process this n-block message $M^n = m_1||\ldots||m_n$ and gives output $c_1||\ldots||c_n$ which is the input of f. SpAEP process the second part of the message $M^e = m_{n+1}||\ldots||m_e$ and gives output $C_e = c_{n+1}||\ldots||c_e$. If M^e is an empty string, then C^e will also remain as empty string. SpAEP also outputs r-bit tag T_1 and T_2 which is also the input of f. Final output of the f-SpAEP will be $y||C_e$, where $y = f(C^f = c_1||\ldots||c_n||T_1||T_2)$. In case (ℓ, b_i, r) are chosen such that n is not an integer value, then $\lceil c_n \rceil_{|C^f|-\ell}$ bits removes and append to C^e to ensure $|C^f| = \ell$. Then $C^f = c_1||\ldots||\lfloor c_n \rfloor_{(b_i - (|c_{[1,n]}|-\ell))}$ and $C^e = \lceil c_n \rceil_{(|c_{[1,n]}|-\ell)}||c_{n+1}||\ldots||c_e$. In paper we will consider n as integer only which means $|C^f| = \ell$. Accordingly, Encryption : $SpAEP - E_f^\pi$ and Decryption : $SpAEP - D_{f^{-1}}^\pi$ of f-SpAEP are described in Algorithms 1 and 2 respectively.

The encryption and decryption procedures of SpAEP use forward direction of the permutation. Therefore we can have a permutation that is more efficient in forward direction than in inverse.

CCA2 Security of f-SpAEP[3]: Next we provide a formal proof of CCA2 security of f-SpAEP. As described in Section 2, the experiment of adversary $\mathcal{A}$ for f-SpAEP is the following.

Experiment: $Exp_{\mathcal{F}-SpAEP^\pi, \mathcal{A}}^{ind-cca2-d}(\ell)$

- $(\underbrace{f}_{pk}, \underbrace{f^{-1}}_{sk}) \leftarrow \mathcal{F}$;

- $(M_0, M_1, s) \leftarrow \mathcal{A}^{\pi(\cdot), SpAEP-D_{f^{-1}}^\pi(\cdot)}$;

- $y^*||C^{e*} \leftarrow SpAEP - E_f^\pi(M_d)$; $\ldots$ **one time encryption query**

- $d' \leftarrow \mathcal{A}^{\pi(\cdot), SpAEP-D_{f^{-1}}^\pi(\cdot)}(M_0, M_1, y^*||C^{e*}, s)$;

- **return** d';

where $SpAEP - D_{f^{-1}}^\pi(\cdot)$ **is decryption oracle and** $SpAEP - E_f^\pi(\cdot)$ **is encryption algorithm.**

---

[3] In this paper for security proof, f-SpAEP and $\mathcal{F}$-SpAEP$^\pi$ refer to same thing. In f-SpAEP, f and its trapdoor f^{-1} is generated by $\mathcal{F}$ like $f, f^{-1} \leftarrow \mathcal{F}$ and $\mathcal{F}$ is trapdoor permutation generator.

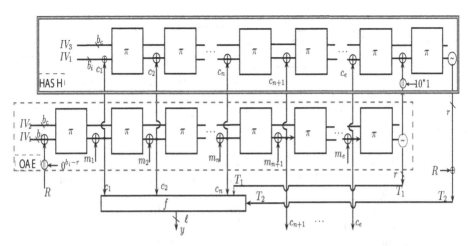

Fig. 4. SpAEP with any trapdoor one way permutation f and public invertible permutation $\pi : \{0,1\}^{b_i} \times \{0,1\}^{b_c} \leftarrow \{0,1\}^{b_i} \times \{0,1\}^{b_c}$. SpAEP accepts message M and internally OAE call $pad(M)=m_1||\dots||m_n||m_{n+1}||\dots||m_e$ such that $n = (\ell - 2r)/b_i$, $|pad(M)| \geq (\ell - 2r)$ and each message bock is of length b_i where ℓ is size of trapdoor permutation-f and $|R| = |T_1| = |T_2| = r$. The symbol $\oslash$ represents taking r-bit output from b_i-bit input. The symbol $\oplus$ represent concatenation.

Theorem 1. *The success probability of any adversary $\mathcal{A}$ for CCA2 attack in ideal permutation π on $\mathcal{F}-SpAEP^\pi$ is*

$$Pr[Exp^{ind-cca2-d}_{\mathcal{F}-SpAEP^\pi,\mathcal{A}}(\ell) = d|d \leftarrow \{0,1\}] \leq \frac{1}{2} + \frac{(q-1)q}{2^{b+1}} + \frac{q(q+1)}{2^{b_c}} + \frac{5q_D}{2^r}$$

$$+ \frac{q_{\pi_\mathcal{A}} + q_{\pi^{-1}}}{2^r} + Adv^{owtp}_f(\mathcal{B_A})$$

$$+ \frac{(q_{\pi_\mathcal{A}} + q_{\pi^{-1}})}{min(2^r, 2^{b_c})},$$

where q is the total number of (π and π^{-1}) queries, q_π and $q_{\pi^{-1}}$ are the number of π and π^{-1} queries, $q_{\pi_\mathcal{A}}$ is the number of π queries by $\mathcal{A}$, q_D is the number of decryption queries and b, b_c, r are the same as defined earlier, $\mathcal{B}$ is an adversary that finds the complete input C^f of trapdoor one way permutation f given $y \leftarrow \{0,1\}^\ell$ such that $y = f(C^f)$, without having knowledge of f^{-1}. Adversary $\mathcal{B}$ uses $\mathcal{A}$ as a subroutine internally. $Adv^{owtp}_{\mathcal{F}}(\mathcal{B_A})$ is the success advantage that a particular adversary $\mathcal{B}$ has in breaking the trapdoor one-way permutation f. The time and space requirements of $\mathcal{B}$ are related to $\mathcal{A}$ as follows:

$$Time(\mathcal{B}) = O(Time(\mathcal{A}) + (q_{\pi_\mathcal{A}} + q_{\pi^{-1}}) \cdot t_f + (q_{\pi_\mathcal{A}} + q_{\pi^{-1}} + q_D) \cdot \ell); \quad (1)$$

$$Space(\mathcal{B}) = O(Space(\mathcal{A}) + (q_{\pi_\mathcal{A}} + q_{\pi^{-1}}) \cdot \ell). \quad (2)$$

Here, t_f is the time required to compute f, and space is measured in the number of storage bits.

Proof 1. Proof can be found in full version of this paper over e-print [8].

Algorithm 1. Encryption:
$SpAEP - E_f^{\pi}(M) = y||C^e$

1 Initialization:
$IV_1 = 0^{b_i}, IV_2 = 0^{b_c}, IV_3 = IV_2 \oplus 1, w = IV_2, x = IV_1$

2 Random Nonce:
$R \leftarrow \{0,1\}^r$

3 $pad(M) = m_1||m_2||\ldots||m_e$, where $|m_i| = b_i \ \forall 1 \le i \le e$

4 $x = x \oplus R||0^{b_r-r}$

5 **for** $i = 1 \to e$ **do**

6 | $(x||w) = \pi(x||w)$

7 | $x = x \oplus m_i$

8 | $c_i = x$

9 $(x||w) = \pi(x||w); T_1 = \lfloor x \rfloor_r$

10 $x = IV_1$ and $w = IV_3$

11 **for** $i = 1 \to e$ **do**

12 | $x = x \oplus c_i$

13 | $(x||w) = \pi(x||w)$

14 $x = x \oplus T_1||0^{b_r-r}$

15 $(x||w) = \pi(x||w)$

16 $T_2 = \lfloor x \rfloor_r \oplus R$

17 $C^f = c_1||c_2||\ldots||c_n||T_1||T_2; C^e = c_{n+1}||\ldots||c_e$

18 $y = f(C^f)$

19 Return: $y||C^e$

Algorithm 2. Decryption:
$SpAEP - D_{f-1}^{\pi}(y||C^e) = M \ or \ \perp$

1 Initialization:
$IV_1 = 0^{b_i}, IV_2 = 0^{b_c}, IV_3 = IV_2 \oplus 1, w = IV_3, x = IV_1$

2 $C^f = c_1||c_2||\ldots||c_n||T_1||T_2 = f^{-1}(y); c_{n+1}||\ldots||c_e = C^e$

3 $C' = c_1||c_2||\ldots||c_n||T_1||T_2||c_{n+1}||\ldots||c_e$, where $|c_i| = b_i, |T_1| = |T_2| = r$ for $1 \le i \le e$

4 **for** $i = 1 \to e$ **do**

5 | $x = x \oplus c_i$

6 | $(x||w) = \pi(x||w)$

7 $x = x \oplus T_1||0^{b_r-r}$

8 $(x||w) = \pi(x||w); R = \lfloor x \rfloor_r \oplus T_2$

9 $x = R||0^{b_r-r}; w = IV_2$

10 **for** $i = 1 \to e$ **do**

11 | $(x||w) = \pi(x||w)$

12 | $m_i = x \oplus c_i$

13 | $x = c_i$

14 $(x||w) = \pi(x||w); T_1' = \lfloor x \rfloor_r$

15 **if** $T_1 = T_1'$ **then**

16 | **if** $\exists \ M \ s.t.$ $M = unpad(m_1||\ldots||m_e)$ **then**

17 | | Return: M

18 | **else**

19 | | Return: **Invalid**

20 **else**

21 | Invalid.

5   Conclusion

We presented a new variant, SpAEP, of OAEP using Sponge constructions that does not require hash output of arbitrary length, whereas all previous OAEP based encryption proven secure in random-oracle model require one or more hash output of arbitrary length. Versatility of Sponge construction helps us to reduce number of round function as compared to previous OAEP-type schemes (OAEP, OAEP+, OAEP-3R, OAEP-4X) and in constructing KEMs that require a PKC scheme with ability of randomness recovery. Ability of handling long messages enables the use of SpAEP with any trapdoor one-way permutation as hybrid encryption.

Acknowledgments. We thank the Cryptography Research Group (CRG) at IIIT-Delhi, India for fruitful comments and the discussion about the results of this paper. We also thank anonymous reviewers for comments, which helped to improve the paper.

References

1. Competition for Authenticated Encryption: Security, Applicability, and Robustness(CAESAR) (2014). https://competitions.cr.yp.to/caesar.html
2. Password Hashing Competition (PHC) (2014). https://password-hashing.net/index.html
3. Abe, M., Gennaro, R., Kurosawa, K.: Tag-KEM/DEM: A New Framework for Hybrid Encryption. J. Cryptology **21**(1), 97–130 (2008)
4. Abe, M., Kiltz, E., Okamoto, T.: Chosen Ciphertext Security with Optimal Ciphertext Overhead. IEICE Transactions **93–A**(1), 22–33 (2010)
5. Andreeva, E., Bilgin, B., Bogdanov, A., Luykx, A., Mennink, B., Mouha, N., Yasuda, K.: APE: authenticated permutation-based encryption for lightweight cryptography. In: Cid, C., Rechberger, C. (eds.) FSE 2014. LNCS, vol. 8540, pp. 168–186. Springer, Heidelberg (2015)
6. Baecher, P., Brzuska, C., Mittelbach, A.: Reset indifferentiability and its consequences. In: Sako, K., Sarkar, P. (eds.) ASIACRYPT 2013, Part I. LNCS, vol. 8269, pp. 154–173. Springer, Heidelberg (2013)
7. Baek, J., Susilo, W., Liu, J.K., Zhou, J.: A new variant of the cramer-shoup KEM secure against chosen ciphertext attack. In: Abdalla, M., Pointcheval, D., Fouque, P.-A., Vergnaud, D. (eds.) ACNS 2009. LNCS, vol. 5536, pp. 143–155. Springer, Heidelberg (2009)
8. Bansal, T.K., Chang, D., Sanadhaya, S.K.: Sponge based CCA2 secure asymmetric encryption for arbitrary length message. Cryptology ePrint Archive, Report 2015/330 (2015). https://eprint.iacr.org/2015/330.pdf
9. Bellare, M., Desai, A., Pointcheval, D., Rogaway, P.: Relations among notions of security for public-key encryption schemes. In: Krawczyk, H. (ed.) CRYPTO 1998. LNCS, vol. 1462, pp. 26–45. Springer, Heidelberg (1998)
10. Bellare, M.,Rogaway, P.: Random oracles are practical: a paradigm for designing efficient protocols. In: Proceedings of the 1st ACM Conference on Computer and Communications Security, CCS 1993, pp. 62–73. ACM, New York (1993)
11. Bellare, M., Rogaway, P.: Optimal asymmetric encryption. In: De Santis, A. (ed.) EUROCRYPT 1994. LNCS, vol. 950, pp. 92–111. Springer, Heidelberg (1995)
12. Bellare, M., Rogaway, P.: The exact security of digital signatures - how to sign with RSA and rabin. In: Maurer, U.M. (ed.) EUROCRYPT 1996. LNCS, vol. 1070, pp. 399–416. Springer, Heidelberg (1996)
13. Bendlin, R., Krehbiel, S., Peikert, C.: How to share a lattice trapdoor: threshold protocols for signatures and (H)IBE. In: Jacobson, M., Locasto, M., Mohassel, P., Safavi-Naini, R. (eds.) ACNS 2013. LNCS, vol. 7954, pp. 218–236. Springer, Heidelberg (2013)
14. Bertoni, G., Daemen, J., Peeters, M., Van Assche, G.: The Sponge Functions Corner. http://sponge.noekeon.org/
15. Bertoni, G., Daemen, J., Peeters, M., Van Assche, G.: Sponge functions, ECRYPT Hash Function Workshop (2007)
16. Bertoni, G., Daemen, J., Peeters, M., Van Assche, G.: Duplexing the sponge: single-pass authenticated encryption and other applications. In: Miri, A., Vaudenay, S. (eds.) SAC 2011. LNCS, vol. 7118, pp. 320–337. Springer, Heidelberg (2012)

17. Bertoni, G., Peeters, M., Daemen, J., Van Assche, G.: Permutation-based encryption, authentication and authenticated encryption. Directions in Authenticated Ciphers (2012)
18. Bjørstad, T.E., Dent, A.W., Smart, N.P.: Efficient KEMs with partial message recovery. In: Galbraith, S.D. (ed.) Cryptography and Coding 2007. LNCS, vol. 4887, pp. 233–256. Springer, Heidelberg (2007)
19. Canetti, R., Krawczyk, H., Nielsen, J.B.: Relaxing chosen-ciphertext security. In: Boneh, D. (ed.) CRYPTO 2003. LNCS, vol. 2729, pp. 565–582. Springer, Heidelberg (2003)
20. Coron, J.-S.: On the exact security of full domain hash. In: Bellare, M. (ed.) CRYPTO 2000. LNCS, vol. 1880, pp. 229–235. Springer, Heidelberg (2000)
21. Cramer, R., Shoup, V.: Design and Analysis of Practical Public-Key Encryption Schemes Secure against Adaptive Chosen Ciphertext Attack. IACR Cryptology ePrint Archive 2001, 108 (2001). http://eprint.iacr.org/2001/108
22. Dent, A.W.: A designer's guide to KEMs. In: Paterson, K.G. (ed.) Cryptography and Coding 2003. LNCS, vol. 2898, pp. 133–151. Springer, Heidelberg (2003)
23. Dolev, D., Dwork, C., Naor, M.: Non-Malleable Cryptography (Extended Abstract). In: Koutsougeras, C., Vitter, J.S. (eds.) STOC, pp. 542–552. ACM (1991)
24. Hofheinz, D., Kiltz, E.: Secure hybrid encryption from weakened key encapsulation. In: Menezes, A. (ed.) CRYPTO 2007. LNCS, vol. 4622, pp. 553–571. Springer, Heidelberg (2007)
25. Kiltz, E.: Chosen-ciphertext security from tag-based encryption. In: Halevi, S., Rabin, T. (eds.) TCC 2006. LNCS, vol. 3876, pp. 581–600. Springer, Heidelberg (2006)
26. Kurosawa, K., Desmedt, Y.: A new paradigm of hybrid encryption scheme. In: Franklin, M. (ed.) CRYPTO 2004. LNCS, vol. 3152, pp. 426–442. Springer, Heidelberg (2004)
27. RSA Laboratories. PKCS #1 v2.1: RSA cryptography standard, June 2002
28. Leurent, G., Nguyen, P.Q.: How risky is the random-oracle model? In: Halevi, S. (ed.) CRYPTO 2009. LNCS, vol. 5677, pp. 445–464. Springer, Heidelberg (2009)
29. Micciancio, D., Peikert, C.: Trapdoors for lattices: simpler, tighter, faster, smaller. In: Pointcheval, D., Johansson, T. (eds.) EUROCRYPT 2012. LNCS, vol. 7237, pp. 700–718. Springer, Heidelberg (2012)
30. Mittelbach, A.: Salvaging indifferentiability in a multi-stage setting. In: Nguyen, P.Q., Oswald, E. (eds.) EUROCRYPT 2014. LNCS, vol. 8441, pp. 603–621. Springer, Heidelberg (2014)
31. Okamoto, T.: Authenticated key exchange and key encapsulation in the standard model. In: Kurosawa, K. (ed.) ASIACRYPT 2007. LNCS, vol. 4833, pp. 474–484. Springer, Heidelberg (2007)
32. Peikert, C.: Lattice cryptography for the internet. In: Mosca, M. (ed.) PQCrypto 2014. LNCS, vol. 8772, pp. 197–219. Springer, Heidelberg (2014)
33. Phan, D.H., Pointcheval, D.: Chosen-ciphertext security without redundancy. In: Laih, C.-S. (ed.) ASIACRYPT 2003. LNCS, vol. 2894, pp. 1–18. Springer, Heidelberg (2003)
34. Phan, D.H., Pointcheval, D.: OAEP 3-round:a generic and secure asymmetric encryption padding. In: Lee, P.J. (ed.) ASIACRYPT 2004. LNCS, vol. 3329, pp. 63–77. Springer, Heidelberg (2004)
35. Rackoff, C., Simon, D.R.: Non-interactive zero-knowledge proof of knowledge and chosen ciphertext attack. In: Feigenbaum, J. (ed.) CRYPTO 1991. LNCS, vol. 576, pp. 433–444. Springer, Heidelberg (1992)
36. Shoup, V.: OAEP Reconsidered. J. Cryptology 15(4), 223–249 (2002)

Trade-Off Approaches for Leak Resistant Modular Arithmetic in RNS

Christophe Negre[1,2]([⊠]) and Guilherme Perin[3]

[1] Team DALI, Université de Perpignan, Perpignan, France
christophe.negre@univ-perp.fr
[2] LIRMM, UMR 5506, Université Montpellier 2 and CNRS, Montpellier, France
[3] Riscure, Delft, The Netherlands

Abstract. On an embedded device, an implementation of cryptographic operation, like an RSA modular exponentiation [12], can be attacked by side channel analysis. In particular, recent improvements on horizontal power analysis [3,10] render ineffective the usual counter-measures which randomize the data at the very beginning of the computations [2,4]. To counteract horizontal analysis it is necessary to randomize the computations all along the exponentiation. The leak resistant arithmetic (LRA) proposed in [1] implements modular arithmetic in residue number system (RNS) and randomizes the computations by randomly changing the RNS bases. We propose in this paper a variant of the LRA in RNS: we propose to change only one or a few moduli of the RNS basis. This reduces the cost of the randomization and makes it possible to be executed at each loop of a modular exponentiation.

Keywords: Leak resistant arithmetic · Randomization · Modular multiplication · Residue number system · RSA

1 Introduction

Nowadays, the RSA cryptosystem [12] is constantly used in e-commerce and credit card transactions. The main operation in RSA protocols is an exponentiation $x^K \bmod N$ where N is a product of two primes $N = pq$. The secret data are the two prime factors of N and the private exponent K used to decrypt or sign a message. The actual recommended size for N is around 2000-4000 bits to insure the intractability of the factorization of N. The basic approach to perform efficiently the modular exponentiation is the square-and-multiply algorithm: it scans the bits k_i of the exponent K and performs a sequence of squarings followed by a multiplication only when k_i is equal to one. Thus the cryptographic operations are quite costly since they involve a few thousands of multiplications or squarings modulo a large integer N.

A cryptographic computation performed on an embedded device can be threaten by side channel analysis. These attacks monitor power consumption or electromagnetic emanation leaked by the device to extract the secret data.

© Springer International Publishing Switzerland 2015
E. Foo and D. Stebila (Eds.): ACISP 2015, LNCS 9144, pp. 107–124, 2015.
DOI: 10.1007/978-3-319-19962-7_7

The simplest attack is the simple power analysis (SPA) [8] which applies when the power trace of a modular squaring and a modular multiplication are different. This makes it possible to read the sequence of operations on the power trace of an exponentiation and then derive the key bits of the exponent. This attack is easily overcome by using an exponentiation algorithm like the Montgomery-ladder [6] which render the sequence of operation uncorrelated to the key bits. A more powerful attack, the differential power analysis (DPA) [8], makes this counter-measure against SPA inefficient. Specifically, DPA uses a large number of traces and correlate the intermediate values with the power trace: it then track the intermediate value all along the computation and then guess the bits of the exponent. Coron in [4] has shown that the exponentiation can be protected from DPA by randomizing the exponent and by blinding the integer x. Recently the horizontal attacks presented in [3,13] require only one power trace of an exponentiation, and threaten implementations which are protected against SPA and DPA with the method of Coron [4]. The authors in [3] explains that the best approach to counteract horizontal attack is to randomize the computations all along the exponentiation.

One popular approach to randomize modular arithmetic is the leak-resistant approach presented in [1] based on residue number system (RNS). Indeed, in [1], the authors noticed that the mask induced by Montgomery modular multiplication can be randomized in RNS by permuting the moduli of the RNS bases. In this paper we investigate an alternative method to perform this permutation of bases. Our method changes only one modulus at a time. We provide formula for this kind of randomization along with the required updates of the constants involved in RNS computations. The complexity analysis shows that this approach can be advantageous for a lower level of randomization compared to [1]. In other words this provides a trade-off between efficiency and randomization.

The remainder of the paper is organized as follows. In Section 2 we review modular exponentiation methods and modular arithmetic in RNS. We then recall in Section 3 the leak resistant arithmetic in RNS of [1]. In Sections 4 and Appendix A we present our methods for randomizing the modular arithmetic in RNS. We then conclude the paper in Section 5 by a complexity comparison and some concluding remarks.

2   Review of Modular Exponentiation in RNS

2.1   Modular Exponentiation

The basic operation in RSA protocols is the modular exponentiation: given an RSA modulus N, an exponent K and a message $x \in \{0, 1, \ldots, N-1\}$, a modular exponentiation consists to compute

$$z = x^K \mod N.$$

This exponentiation can be performed efficiently with the square-and-multiply algorithm. This method scans the bits k_i of the exponent $K = (k_{\ell-1}, \ldots, k_0)_2$

from left to right and performs a sequence of squarings followed by multiplications by x if the bit $k_i = 1$ as follows:

$r \leftarrow 1$
for i **from** $\ell - 1$ **downto** 0 **do**
   $r \leftarrow r^2 \mod N$
   if $k_i = 1$ **then**
      $r \leftarrow r \times x \mod N$
   end if
end for

The complexity of this approach is, in average, ℓ squarings and $\ell/2$ multiplications.

Koche *et al.* in [8] showed that the square-and-multiply exponentiation is weak against simple power analysis. Indeed, if a squaring and a multiplication have different power traces, an eavesdropper can read on the trace of a modular exponentiation the exact sequence of squarings and multiplications, and then deduce the corresponding bits of K. It is thus recommended to perform an exponentiation using, for example, the Montgomery-ladder [6] which computes $x^K \mod N$ through a regular sequence of squarings and multiplications. This method is detailed in Algorithm 1. The regularity of the exponentiation prevents an attacker to directly read the key bits on a single trace.

Algorithm 1. Montgomery-ladder [6]

Require: $x \in \{0, \ldots, N - 1\}$ and $K = (k_{\ell-1}, \ldots, k_0)_2$
 1: $r_0 \leftarrow 1$
 2: $r_1 \leftarrow x$
 3: **for** i **from** $\ell - 1$ **downto** 0 **do**
 4:    **if** $k_i = 0$ **then**
 5:       $r_1 \leftarrow r_1 \times r_0$
 6:       $r_0 \leftarrow r_0^2$
 7:    **end if**
 8:    **if** $k_i = 1$ **then**
 9:       $r_0 \leftarrow r_0 \times r_1$
10:       $r_1 \leftarrow r_1^2$
11:    **end if**
12: **end for**
13: **return** (r_0)

Some more sophisticated attacks can threaten a naive implementation of Montgomery-ladder exponentiation. For example differential power analysis [8] makes it necessary to randomize the exponent and blind the integer x by random mask as explained in [4]. Horizontal approaches [3,13] are even more powerful since they require only a single trace to complete the attack and is effective even if the exponent K is masked and the data x is blinded. The authors in [3] propose to counteract horizontal power analysis by randomizing each multiplication and squaring using some temporary mask. In this paper we deal with the problem of randomizing modular multiplications and squarings: we will use the residue number system (RNS) to represent integers and perform efficiently modular operations.

2.2   Montgomery Multiplication in RNS

Let N be a modulus and let x, y be two integers such that $0 \leq x, y < N$. One of the most used methods to perform modular multiplication $x \times y \mod N$ is the method of Montgomery in [9]. This approach avoids Euclidean division as follows: it uses an integer A such that $A > N$ and $\gcd(A, N) = 1$ and computes $z = xyA^{-1} \mod N$ as follows:

$$
\begin{aligned}
q &\leftarrow -xyN^{-1} \mod A \\
z &\leftarrow (xy + qN)/A
\end{aligned}
\tag{1}
$$

To check the validity of the above method we notice that $(xy + qN) \mod A = 0$, this means that the division by A is exact in the computation of z and then $z = xyA^{-1} \mod N$. The integer z is almost reduced modulo N since $z = (xy + qN)/A < (N^2 + AN)/A < 2N$: if $z > N$, with a single subtraction of N we can have $z < N$. In practice the integer A is often taken as a power of 2 in order to have almost free reduction and division by A.

For a long sequence of multiplications, the use of the so-called Montgomery representation is used

$$
\widetilde{x} = (x \times A) \mod N.
\tag{2}
$$

Indeed, the Montgomery multiplication applied to $\widetilde{x}$ and $\widetilde{y}$ output $\widetilde{z} = xyA$ mod N, i.e., the Montgomery representation of the product of x and y.

Residue Number System. In [11] the authors showed that the use of residue number system (RNS) makes it possible to perform Montgomery multiplication efficiently with an alternative choice for A. Let $a_1, \ldots, a_t$ be t coprime integers. In the residue number system an integer x such that $0 \leq x < A = \prod_{i=1}^{t} a_i$ is represented by the t residues

$$
x_i = x \mod a_i \text{ for } i = 1, \ldots, t.
$$

Moreover, x can be recovered from its RNS expression using the Chinese remainder theorem (CRT) as follows

$$
x = \left(\sum_{i=1}^{t} \left[x_i \times A_i^{-1} \right]_{a_i} \times A_i \right) \mod A
\tag{3}
$$

where $A_i = \prod_{j=1, j \neq i}^{t} a_i$ and the brackets $[\,\cdot\,]_{a_i}$ denotes a reduction modulo a_i. The set $\mathcal{A} = \{a_1, \ldots, a_t\}$ is generally called an RNS basis.

Let $x = (x_1, \ldots, x_t)_\mathcal{A}$ and $y = (y_1, \ldots, y_t)_\mathcal{A}$ be two integers given in an RNS basis $\mathcal{A}$. Then, the CRT provides that an integer addition $x + y$ or multiplication $x \times y$ in RNS consists in t independent additions/multiplications modulo a_i

$$x + y = ([x_1 + y_1]_{a_1}, \ldots, [x_t + y_t]_{a_t}),$$
$$x \times y = ([x_1 \times y_1]_{a_1}, \ldots, [x_t \times y_t]_{a_t}).$$

The main advantage is that these operations can be implemented in parallel since each operation modulo a_i are independent from the others. Only comparisons and Euclidean divisions are not easy to perform in RNS and require partial reconstruction of the integers x and y.

Montgomery Multiplication in RNS. In [11] Posch and Posch notice that the Montgomery multiplication can be efficiently implemented in RNS: they use the fact that we can modify the second step of the Montgomery multiplication (1) as

$$z \leftarrow (xy + qN)A^{-1} \mod B$$

where B is an integer coprime with A and N and greater than $2N$. Furthermore, Posch and Posch propose to perform this modified version of the Montgomery multiplication in RNS. Specifically, they choose two RNS bases $\mathcal{A} = (a_1, \ldots, a_t)$ and $\mathcal{B} = (b_1, \ldots, b_t)$ such that $\gcd(a_i, b_j) = 1$ for all i, j. They perform $z = xyA^{-1} \mod N$ as it is shown in Algorithm 2: the multiplications modulo A are done in the RNS basis $\mathcal{A}$ and the operations modulo B are done in $\mathcal{B}$.

Algorithm 2. Basic-MM-RNS$(x, y, \mathcal{A}, \mathcal{B})$

Require: x, y in $\mathcal{A} \cup \mathcal{B}$
Ensure: $xyA^{-1} \mod N$ in $\mathcal{A} \cup \mathcal{B}$
1: $[q]_\mathcal{A} \leftarrow [-xyN^{-1}]_\mathcal{A}$
2: $BE_{\mathcal{A} \to \mathcal{B}}([q]_\mathcal{A})$
3: $[z]_\mathcal{B} \leftarrow [(xy + qN)A^{-1}]_\mathcal{B}$
4: $BE_{\mathcal{B} \to \mathcal{A}}([z]_\mathcal{B})$
5: **return** $(z_{\mathcal{A} \cup \mathcal{B}})$

The second and fourth steps are necessary since if we want to compute $z \leftarrow (xy + qN)A^{-1} \mod B$ in $\mathcal{B}$ we need to convert the RNS representation of q from the basis $\mathcal{A}$ to the basis $\mathcal{B}$: the base extension (BE) performs this conversion. The fourth step is also necessary to have z represented in both bases $\mathcal{A}$ and $\mathcal{B}$.

Base Extension. This is the most costly step in the RNS version of the Montgomery multiplication (Algorithm 2). We review the best known method to perform such RNS base extension. Let $x = (x_1, \ldots, x_t)_\mathcal{A}$ be the representation of an integer x in the RNS basis $\mathcal{A}$, the CRT 3 reconstructs x as follows:

$$\hat{x}_{a_i} = \left[x_{a_i} \times A_i^{-1}\right]_{a_i} \text{ for } i = 1, \ldots, t, \tag{4}$$

$$x = \left(\sum_{i=1}^{t} \hat{x}_{a_i} \times A_i\right) - \alpha A \tag{5}$$

The correcting term $-\alpha A$ corresponds to the reduction modulo A in (3). We get the RNS representation $[x]_{b_j}$ for $j = 1,\ldots,t$ of x in $\mathcal{B}$ by simply reducing modulo b_j the expression in (5):

$$
\begin{aligned}
x^*_{b_j} &= \left[\sum_{i=1}^{t} \hat{x}_{a_i} \times A_i\right]_{b_j}, \quad \text{for } j = 1,\ldots,t, \\
[x]_{b_j} &= \left[x^*_{b_j} - \alpha A\right]_{b_j} \quad \text{for } j = 1,\ldots,t.
\end{aligned}
\tag{6}
$$

We give some details on how to perform the above computations.

- *Computations of $x^*_{b_j}$.* If the constants $[A_i]_{b_j}$ are precomputed then $x^*_{b_j}$ for $j = 1,\ldots,t$ can be computed as

$$
x^*_{b_j} = \left[\sum_{i=1}^{t} \hat{x}_{a_i} \times [A_i]_{b_j}\right]_{b_j}.
$$

There is an alternative method proposed by Garner in [5] which computes $x^*_{b_j}$, but we will not use it in this paper, so we do not recall it here. The reader may refer to [5] to further details on this method.

- *Computations of α.* The base extension in (6) necessitates also to compute α. We arrange (5) as follows

$$
\sum_{i=1}^{t} \hat{x}_{a_i} \times A_i = x + \alpha A \implies \sum_{i=1}^{t} \frac{\hat{x}_{a_i}}{a_i} = \frac{x}{A} + \alpha \implies \alpha = \left\lfloor \sum_{i=1}^{t} \frac{\hat{x}_{a_i}}{a_i} \right\rfloor
\tag{7}
$$

since when $0 < x < A$ we have $0 < x/A < 1$.

The MM-RNS Algorithm. Following [7] we inject in Algorithm 2 the formulas (4), (5) and (7) corresponding to the computations of the base extensions. We obtain the Montgomery multiplication in RNS (MM-RNS) shown in Algorithm 3 after some modifications. Specifically, the base extension of q and the computation of z are merged as follows

$$
z_{b_i} \leftarrow [(s_{b_i} + \sum_{j=1}^{t} q_{a_j} A_j N - \alpha AN)A^{-1}]_{b_i} = [s_{b_i} A^{-1} + (\sum_{j=1}^{t} q_{a_j} a_j^{-1} - \alpha)N]_{b_i}.
$$

In the second base extension $BE_{\mathcal{B} \to \mathcal{A}}$ we rewrite $[B_j]_{a_i} = [b_j^{-1} B]_{a_i}$.

The complexity of each step of the MM-RNS algorithm is given in terms of the number of additions and multiplications modulo a_i or b_i. These complexities are detailed in Table 1. For the computation of α and β we assume that each a_i and b_i can be approximated by 2^w which simplifies the computations in Step 6 and Step 10 as a sequence of additions (cf. [7] for further details).

Constants Used in MM-RNS. In Algorithm 3, an important number of constants take part of the computations:

$$
\begin{aligned}
&[N^{-1}]_{\mathcal{A}}, [N]_{\mathcal{B}}, \\
&[b_j^{-1}]_{a_i}, [a_j^{-1}]_{b_i} \text{ for } i,j = 1,\ldots,t, \\
&[B]_{a_i}, [B_i^{-1}]_{b_i} \text{ for } i = 1,\ldots,t, \\
&[A^{-1}]_{b_i}, [A_i^{-1}]_{a_i} \text{ for } i = 1,\ldots,t.
\end{aligned}
\tag{8}
$$

Algorithm 3. MM-RNS($x, y, \mathcal{A}, \mathcal{B}$)

Require: x, y in $\mathcal{A} \cup \mathcal{B}$ for two RNS bases $\mathcal{A} = \{a_1, \ldots, a_t\}$ and $\mathcal{B} = \{b_1, \ldots, b_t\}$ s.t.
   $A = \prod_{i=1}^{t} a_i, B = \prod_{i=1}^{t} b_i, \gcd(A, B) = 1, 1 \leq x, y \leq N, B \geq 4N$ et $A > 2N$.
Ensure: $xyA^{-1} \bmod N$ in $\mathcal{A} \cup \mathcal{B}$
 1: **Precomputations in** $\mathcal{B}$: $[N]_\mathcal{B}, [A^{-1}]_\mathcal{B}, [b_j^{-1}]_\mathcal{B}$ for $j = 1, \ldots, t$ and $[B_i^{-1}]_{b_i}$ for
    $i = 1, \ldots, t$
 2: **Precomputations in** $\mathcal{A}$: $[N^{-1}]_\mathcal{A}$ and $[a_j^{-1}]_\mathcal{A}, [A_j^{-1}]_{a_j}$ for $j = 1, \ldots, t$ and $[B]_\mathcal{A}$
 3: $s = [x \cdot y]_{\mathcal{A} \cup \mathcal{B}}$
 4: //- - - - - - - - - base extension $\mathcal{A} \to \mathcal{B}$ - - - - - -
 5: $q_{a_i} \leftarrow [s_{a_i} \times (-N^{-1}) \times A_i^{-1}]_{a_i}$ for $i = 1$ to t
 6: $\alpha \leftarrow \lfloor \sum_{i=1}^{t} q_{a_i}/a_i \rfloor$
 7: $z_{b_i} \leftarrow [s_{b_i} A^{-1} + (\sum_{j=1}^{t} q_{a_j} a_j^{-1} - \alpha)N]_{b_i}$ for $i = 1$ to t
 8: //- - - - - - - - - base extension $\mathcal{B} \to \mathcal{A}$ - - - - - -
 9: $q_{b_i} \leftarrow [z_{b_i} \times B_i^{-1}]_{b_i}$ for $i = 1$ to t
10: $\beta \leftarrow \lfloor \sum_{i=1}^{t} q_{b_i}/b_i \rfloor$
11: $z_{a_i} \leftarrow [(\sum_{j=1}^{t} q_{b_j} b_j^{-1} - \beta)B]_{a_i}$ for $i = 1$ to t

---

Table 1. Complexity of MM-RNS

Step	#Mult.	#Add.
3	$2t$	0
5	$2t$	0
6	0	$t - 1$
7	$t(t + 2)$	$t(t + 1)$
9	t	0
10	0	$t - 1$
11	$t(t + 1)$	t^2
Total	$t(2t + 8)$	$t(2t + 3) - 2$

Only, the constants $[B^{-1}]_{a_i}, [B_i^{-1}]_{b_i}, [A]_{b_i}$ and $[A_i^{-1}]_{a_i}$ are susceptible to change and to be updated during the run of a modular exponentiation if the bases $\mathcal{A}$ and $\mathcal{B}$ are modified.

3   Leak Resistant Arithmetic in RNS

The authors in [1] notice that the use of RNS facilitates the randomization of the representation of an integer and consequently the randomization of a modular multiplication. Indeed, if a modular exponentiation $x^K \bmod N$ is computed with MM-RNS the element is set in Montgomery representation

$$\widetilde{x} = x \times A \mod N$$

and in the RNS bases $\mathcal{A}$ and $\mathcal{B}$, i.e., $[\widetilde{x}]_{\mathcal{A} \cup \mathcal{B}}$. The Montgomery representation induces a multiplicative masking of the data x by the factor A. The authors in [1] propose to randomly construct the basis $\mathcal{A}$ to get a random multiplicative mask A on the data.

Specifically, the authors in [1] propose two levels of such randomization: random initialization of the bases $\mathcal{A}$ and $\mathcal{B}$ at the very beginning of a modular exponentiation and random permutations of RNS bases $\mathcal{A}$ and $\mathcal{B}$ all along the modular exponentiation.

Random Initialization of the Bases $\mathcal{A}$ and $\mathcal{B}$ and $\widetilde{x}$. We assume that we have a set of $2t$ moduli $\mathcal{M} = \{m_1, \ldots, m_{2t}\}$. At the beginning of the computations we randomly set

$$
\begin{aligned}
\mathcal{A} &\longleftarrow \{t \text{ random distinct elements in } \mathcal{M}\} \\
\mathcal{B} &\longleftarrow \mathcal{M} \backslash \mathcal{A}
\end{aligned}
\tag{9}
$$

Note that we always have $\mathcal{A} \cup \mathcal{B} = \mathcal{M}$.

Then the input of x of the modular exponentiation algorithm is first set in the residue number system $\mathcal{M} = \mathcal{A} \cup \mathcal{B}$ by reducing x modulo each a_i and b_i

$$
[x]_{\mathcal{A} \cup \mathcal{B}} = ([x]_{a_0}, \ldots, [x]_{a_t}, [x]_{b_0}, \ldots, [x]_{b_t}).
$$

Then we need to compute the Montgomery representation $[\widetilde{x}]_{\mathcal{A} \cup \mathcal{B}}$ from $[x]_{\mathcal{A} \cup \mathcal{B}}$. The authors in [1] give a method which simplifies this computation. They assume that the RNS representation of

$$
\begin{aligned}
M \mod N &= (\textstyle\prod_{i=1}^{2t} m_i) \mod N \\
&= A \times B \mod N
\end{aligned}
$$

is precomputed. They compute $[\widetilde{x}]_{\mathcal{A} \cup \mathcal{B}}$ from $[x]_{\mathcal{A} \cup \mathcal{B}}$ by a single MM-RNS with bases $\mathcal{B}$ and $\mathcal{A}$ in reverse order:

$$
\text{MM-RNS}([x]_{\mathcal{A} \cup \mathcal{B}}, [(M \mod N)]_{\mathcal{A} \cup \mathcal{B}}, \mathcal{B}, \mathcal{A})
$$

The output of this multiplication is the expected value:

$$
[(x \times M \times B^{-1} \mod N)]_{\mathcal{A} \cup \mathcal{B}} = [(x \times A \mod N)]_{\mathcal{A} \cup \mathcal{B}} = [\widetilde{x}]_{\mathcal{A} \cup \mathcal{B}}.
$$

Random Change of the Bases $\mathcal{A}$ and $\mathcal{B}$. The authors in [1] propose to change the bases $\mathcal{A}$ and $\mathcal{B}$ during the RSA exponentiation as follows:

$$
\begin{aligned}
\mathcal{A}_{new} &\longleftarrow \{t \text{ random distinct elements in } \mathcal{M}\} \\
\mathcal{B}_{new} &\longleftarrow \mathcal{M} \backslash \mathcal{A}_{new}
\end{aligned}
\tag{10}
$$

The bases $\mathcal{A}$ and $\mathcal{B}$ change all along the exponentiation, this implies to perform the base extension (BE) in MM-RNS using the approach of Garner [5] instead of the CRT formula. Otherwise the constants A_i and B_i would have to be updated which can be expensive.

The update of the bases $\mathcal{A}$ and $\mathcal{B}$ implies to also update the Montgomery representation $\widetilde{x} = x \times A_{old} \mod N$ of x from the old bases $\mathcal{A}_{old} \cup \mathcal{B}_{old}$ to the new representation $\widetilde{x} = x \times A_{new} \mod N$ in the new bases $\mathcal{A}_{new} \cup \mathcal{B}_{new}$. The proposed approach in [1] consists in two modular multiplications (cf. Algorithm 4).

Algorithm 4. Update of $\widetilde{x}$

Require: $\widetilde{x}_{old}$ and $\mathcal{A}_{new}, \mathcal{B}_{new}, \mathcal{A}_{old}, \mathcal{B}_{old}$ and $[M \mod N]_{\mathcal{M}}$

Ensure: $\widetilde{x}_{new}$

1: $temp \leftarrow$ MM-RNS$(\widetilde{x}_{old}, (M \mod N), \mathcal{B}_{new}, \mathcal{A}_{new})$

2: $x_{new} \leftarrow$ MM-RNS$(temp, 1, \mathcal{A}_{old}, \mathcal{B}_{old})$

We can easily check the validity of Algorithm 4: Step 1 computes $temp = (xA_{old}) \times (A_{new} \times B_{new}) \times B_{new}^{-1} \mod N$ and Step 2 correctly computes $x_{new} = (xA_{old}A_{new}) \times A_{old}^{-1} \mod N = xA_{new} \mod N$ in the required RNS bases.

The main drawback of this technique is that it is a bit costly: it requires two MM-RNS multiplications to perform the change of RNS representation. Consequently, using Table 1, we deduce that the amount of computation involved in this approach is as follows

$$\#\text{Mult.} = 2t(2t + 8) \text{ and } \#\text{Add.} = 2t(2t + 3) - 4.$$

4 Random Update of the RNS Bases with a Set of Spare Moduli

In this section, our goal is to provide a cheaper variant of the leak resistant arithmetic in RNS proposed in [1] and reviewed in Section 3.

4.1 Proposed Update of the Bases and Montgomery Representation

We present a first strategy which modifies only one modulus in $\mathcal{A}$ while keeping $\mathcal{B}$ unchanged during each update of the RNS bases. We need an additional set $\mathcal{A}'$ of spare moduli where we randomly pick the new modulus for $\mathcal{A}$. We have three sets of moduli:

- The first RNS basis $\mathcal{A} = \{a_1, \ldots, a_{t+1}\}$ which is modified after each loop iteration.
- The set $\mathcal{A}' = \{a_1', \ldots, a_{t+1}'\}$ of spare moduli.
- The second RNS basis $\mathcal{B} = \{b_1, \ldots, b_{t+1}\}$ which is fixed at the beginning of the exponentiation.

The integers a_i, b_i and a_i' are all pairwise co-prime and are all of the form $2^w - \mu_i$ where w is the same for all moduli and $\mu_i < 2^{w/2}$. We will state later in Subsection 4.2 how large A and B have to be compared to N to render the proposed approach effective. But to give an insight A and B are roughly w-bits larger than N which means that the considered RNS bases contain $t + 1$ moduli.

Update of the Base $\mathcal{A}$. Updating the basis $\mathcal{A}$ is quite simple: we just swap one element of $\mathcal{A}$ with one element of $\mathcal{A}'$ as follows

- $r \leftarrow$ random in $\{1, \ldots, t, t + 1\}$

- $r' \leftarrow$ random in $\{1, \ldots, t, t+1\}$
- $a_{r,new} \leftarrow a'_{r',old}$
- $a_{r',new} \leftarrow a_{r,old}$

In the sequel we will denote $\mathcal{A}_{old}$ and $\mathcal{A}_{new}$ the base $\mathcal{A}$ before and after the update, we will use similar notation for other updated data.

Update of the Montgomery-RNS Representation. The modification of the basis requires at the same time the corresponding update of the Montgomery representation of x. Indeed we need to compute $\widetilde{x}_{new} = [(xA_{new} \mod N)]_{\mathcal{A}_{new} \cup \mathcal{B}}$ from its old Montgomery representation $\widetilde{x}_{old} = [(xA_{old} \mod N)]_{\mathcal{A}_{old} \cup \mathcal{B}}$. The following lemma establishes how to perform this update.

Lemma 1. *We consider two RNS bases $\mathcal{A}$ and $\mathcal{B}$ and let $\mathcal{A}'$ be the set of spare moduli. We consider an integer x modulo N given by its RNS-Montgomery representation $[\widetilde{x}]_{\mathcal{A} \cup \mathcal{B}} = [(x \times A \mod N)]_{\mathcal{A} \cup \mathcal{B}}$ where $A = a_1 a_2 \cdots a_{t+1}$. Let r and r' be two random integers in $\{1, \ldots, t, t+1\}$ and $\mathcal{A}_{new}$ and $\mathcal{A}'_{new}$ be the two set of moduli obtained after exchanging $a_{r,old}$ et $a'_{r',old}$. Then the new Montgomery-RNS representation of x in $\mathcal{A}_{new} \cup \mathcal{B}$ can be computed as follows:*

$$\begin{aligned} \lambda &= [-\widetilde{x}_{a_{r,old}} \times N^{-1}]_{a_{r,old}}, \\ \widetilde{x}_{new} &= [(\widetilde{x}_{old} + \lambda \times N) \times a_{r,old}^{-1} \times a_{r,new}]_{\mathcal{A}_{new} \cup \mathcal{B}} \end{aligned} \tag{11}$$

and satisfies $\widetilde{x}_{new} = (x \times A_{new}) \mod N$ given in the bases $\mathcal{A}_{new} \cup \mathcal{B}$.

Proof. We first notice that $s_1 = \widetilde{x}_{old} + \lambda N$ satisfies $s_1 \equiv \widetilde{x}_{old} \mod N$ and that

$$\begin{aligned} [s_1]_{a_{r,old}} &= [\widetilde{x}_{old} + \lambda \times N]_{a_{r,old}} \\ &= [\widetilde{x}_{old} - [\widetilde{x}]_{a_{r,old}} \times N^{-1} \times N]_{a_{r,old}} \\ &= 0. \end{aligned}$$

In other words s_1 can be divided by $a_{r,old}$ and then multiplied by $a_{r,new}$

$$\widetilde{x}_{new} = ((\widetilde{x}_{old} + \lambda N)/a_{r,old})a_{r,new}.$$

which satisfies

$$\begin{aligned} \widetilde{x}_{new} \mod N &= ((\widetilde{x}_{old} + \lambda N)/a_{r,old})a_{r,new} \mod N \\ &= xA_{old}a_{r,old}^{-1}a_{r,new} \mod N \\ &= xA_{new} \mod N \end{aligned}$$

The value of $\widetilde{x}_{new}$ is computed in the RNS basis $\mathcal{A}_{new} \cup \mathcal{B}$ by replacing the division by $a_{r,old}$ by a multiplication by $a_{r,old}^{-1}$ and by noticing that its value modulo $a_{r,new}$ is equal to 0. This leads to (11).   ∎

Update of the Constants. If we want to apply MM-RNS (Algorithm 3) after the update of the basis $\mathcal{A}$ and the Montgomery-RNS representation of x, we need also to update the constants involved in Algorithm 3. The constants considered are the one listed in (8) along with the following additional set of constants associated to the set of moduli $\mathcal{A}'$:

$$[-N^{-1}]_{a_i'} \; i = 1,\ldots,t+1,$$
$$[A^{-1}]_{a_i'}, [B]_{a_i'} \; i = 1,\ldots,t+1,$$
$$[b_j^{-1}]_{a_i'}, [a_j'^{-1}]_{b_i} \; i,j = 1,\ldots,t+1,$$
$$[a_j^{-1}]_{a_i'}, [a_j'^{-1}]_{a_i} \; i,j = 1,\ldots,t+1.$$

These constants are updated as follows:

- *Constant* $-N^{-1}$. The constants $[-N^{-1}]_{a_i}$ only changes when $i = r$ and $[-N^{-1}]_{a_i'}$ only change when $i = r'$. Then this update consists only in a single swap
$$swap([-N^{-1}]_{a_r}, [-N^{-1}]_{a_{r'}'}).$$

- *Constant* N. The constants $[N]_{b_i}, i = 1, \ldots, t+1$ do not change when the base $\mathcal{A}$ is updated.

- *Constants* A_i^{-1} *and* A^{-1}. The constants $[A_i^{-1}]_{a_i}$ and $[A^{-1}]_{a_i'}$ and $[A^{-1}]_{b_i}$ are updated as follows:

$$[A_i^{-1}]_{a_i} \leftarrow [[A_i^{-1}]_{a_i} \times a_{r,new}^{-1} \times a_{r,old}]_{a_i} \text{ for } i \neq r,$$
$$[A^{-1}]_{a_i'} \leftarrow [[A^{-1}]_{a_i'} \times a_{r,new}^{-1} \times a_{r,old}]_{a_i'} \text{ for } i \neq r',$$
$$[A^{-1}]_{b_i} \leftarrow [[A^{-1}]_{b_i} \times a_{r,new}^{-1} \times a_{r,old}]_{b_i} \text{ for } i \neq r',$$

and the two remaining special cases are:

$$[A_r^{-1}]_{a_{r,new}} \leftarrow [[A^{-1}]_{a_{r',old}'} \times a_{r,old}]_{a_{r',old}'} \quad \text{(Note that } a_{r',old}' = a_{r,new}),$$
$$[A^{-1}]_{a_{r',new}'} \leftarrow [[A_r^{-1}]_{a_{r,old}} \times a_{r,new}^{-1}]_{a_{r,old}} \quad \text{(Note that } a_{r,old} = a_{r',new}').$$

- *Constants* $[B_i^{-1}]_{b_i}, [B]_{a_i}$ *and* $[B]_{a_i'}$. The constants $[B_i]_{b_i}$ and $[B]_{a_i}$ for $i \neq r$ and $[B]_{a_i'}$ for $i \neq r'$ are not affected by the modification on $\mathcal{A}$. The only required modification is the following swap

$$\text{swap}([B]_{a_r}, [B]_{a_{r'}'}).$$

- *Constants* $[b_j^{-1}]_{a_i}, [b_j^{-1}]_{a_i'}, [a_j^{-1}]_{a_i}, [a_j^{-1}]_{a_i'}, [a_j'^{-1}]_{a_i},$ *and* $[a_j'^{-1}]_{a_i'}$. The constants which evolve are the ones corresponding to a_r and $a_{r'}'$ and require only swaps:

$$\text{swap}([b_j^{-1}]_{a_r}, [b_j^{-1}]_{a_{r'}'}) \quad \text{for } j = 1,\ldots,t+1,$$
$$\text{swap}([a_r^{-1}]_{b_j}, [a_{r'}'^{-1}]_{b_j}) \quad \text{for } j = 1,\ldots,t+1,$$
$$\text{swap}([a_j^{-1}]_{a_r}, [a_j^{-1}]_{a_{r'}'}) \quad \text{for } j = 1,\ldots,t+1 \text{ and } j \neq r,$$
$$\text{swap}([a_j'^{-1}]_{a_r}, [a_j'^{-1}]_{a_{r'}'}) \quad \text{for } j = 1,\ldots,t+1 \text{ and } j \neq r'.$$

Complexity of the Updates. We evaluate the complexity of the above random change of the basis $\mathcal{A}$: the update of $\tilde{x}$ and the update of the constants. We do not consider swap operations since they do not require any computations. The cost of the update of the Montgomery representation $\tilde{x}$ of x contributes to $6t + 4$ multiplications and $2t + 1$ additions and the contribution of the update of the constants is equal to $6t + 2$ multiplications.

Table 2. Complexity of the updates when using a set of spare moduli

Operation	#Mult.	#Add.
Updates of $\widetilde{x}$	$6t + 4$	$2t + 1$
Updates of the constants	$6t + 2$	0

4.2   Proposed Randomized Montgomery-Ladder and Its Validity

We present the modified version of the Montgomery-ladder: compared to the original Montgomery-ladder (Algorithm 1), this version inserts an update of the RNS bases and related constants along with an update of the data at the beginning of the loop iteration. This approach is shown in Algorithm 5. For the sake of simplicity, conversions between RNS and regular integer representation are skipped.

Algorithm 5. Randomized-Montgomery-ladder

Require: $x \in \{0, \dots, N - 1\}$ and $K = (k_{\ell-1}, \dots, k_0)_2$, three RNS bases $\mathcal{A}, \mathcal{A}', \mathcal{B}$
1: $\widetilde{r_0} \leftarrow [\widetilde{1}]_{\mathcal{A} \cup \mathcal{B}}$
2: $\widetilde{r_1} \leftarrow [\widetilde{x}]_{\mathcal{A} \cup \mathcal{B}}$
3: **for** i **from** $\ell - 1$ **downto** 0 **do**
4:      UpdateBases$(\mathcal{A}, \mathcal{A}')$
5:      UpdateMontRep$(\widetilde{r_0})$
6:      UpdateMontRep$(\widetilde{r_1})$
7:      **if** $k_i = 0$ **then**
8:          $\widetilde{r_1} \leftarrow$ MM-RNS$(\widetilde{r_1}, \widetilde{r_0})$
9:          $\widetilde{r_0} \leftarrow$ MM-RNS$(\widetilde{r_0}, \widetilde{r_0})$
10:     **end if**
11:     **if** $k_i = 1$ **then**
12:         $\widetilde{r_0} \leftarrow$ MM-RNS$(\widetilde{r_1}, \widetilde{r_0})$
13:         $\widetilde{r_1} \leftarrow$ MM-RNS$(\widetilde{r_1}, \widetilde{r_1})$
14:     **end if**
15: **end for**
16: **return** (r_0)

Now, we establish that the above algorithm correctly outputs the expected result $x^K \bmod N$. Indeed, during the execution of the algorithm an overflow could occur: some data could become larger than A or B. To show that no overflow occurs we first establish the growing factor produced by an update of the Montgomery representation.

Lemma 2. *Let $\mathcal{A}_{old}, \mathcal{A}'_{old}, \mathcal{B}_{old}, \mathcal{A}_{new}, \mathcal{A}'_{new}$ and $\mathcal{B}_{new}$ be the new and the old RNS bases. Let $a_{i_{max}, old}$ the largest modulus in $\mathcal{A}_{old}$ and $a_{i_{max}, new}$ the largest modulus in $\mathcal{A}_{new}$. Assume that $\widetilde{x}_{old} < N a_{i_{max}, old}$ and let a_r and $a'_{r'}$ be the two moduli swapped in $\mathcal{A}$ and $\mathcal{A}'$. Then we have*

$$\widetilde{x}_{new} < 4 N a_{i_{max}, new}$$

Proof. From Lemma 1 we have the following expression of $\tilde{x}_{new}$

$$\tilde{x}_{new} = ((\tilde{x}_{old} + \lambda N)/a_r) \times a'_{r'}. \tag{12}$$

We then notice that $\lambda < a_{i_{max},old}$. We use the fact that $\tilde{x}_{old} < Na_{i_{max},old}$ and we expand the product in (12), this gives:

$$\begin{aligned}
\tilde{x}_{new} &< (Na_{i_{max},old} + a_{i_{max},old}N) \times \frac{1}{a_r} \times a'_{r'} \\
&\le 2N \times \frac{a_{i_{max},old}}{a_r} \times a'_{r'}.
\end{aligned} \tag{13}$$

We then use that $a_i = 2^w - \mu_i$ with $0 \le \mu_i < 2^{w/2}$, which implies that for any i, j

$$\begin{aligned}
0 < \frac{a_i}{a_j} &= \frac{2^w - \mu_i}{2^w - \mu_j} = \frac{2^w - \mu_j + \mu_j - \mu_i}{2^w - \mu_j} = 1 + \frac{\mu_j - \mu_i}{2^w - \mu_j} \\
&< 1 + \frac{2^{w/2}}{2^w - \mu_j} < 2.
\end{aligned}$$

In particular for $i = i_{max}$ and $j = r$ we have $0 < \frac{a_{i_{max},old}}{a_r} < 2$. We use this to arrange (13) as follows:

$$\tilde{x}_{new} < 4Na'_{r'} \le 4Na_{i_{max},new}.$$

∎

Knowing the growing factor induced by the update of the Montgomery representation helps us to state a sufficient condition to prevent an overflow in Algorithm 5.

Lemma 3. *Let A_{min} be the product of the t smallest moduli in $\mathcal{A} \cup \mathcal{A}'$. Let $a_{i_{max}}$ be the largest modulus of $\mathcal{A}$. If N satisfies*

$$N < \frac{A_{min}}{32} \tag{14}$$

and if $\mathcal{B}$ is larger than any $\mathcal{A}$ then the following assertions hold:

i) The data $\tilde{r}_0$ and $\tilde{r}_1$ in Algorithm 5 are $< Na_{i_{max}}$ at the end of each loop.
ii) Algorithm 5 correctly computes $r_0 = x^K \mod N$.

Proof.   i) Let us prove that an update of the base $\mathcal{A}$ followed by a modular multiplication with MM-RNS keeps the data in the interval $[0, Na_{i_{max}}]$. We consider $\tilde{x}_{old} < Na_{i_{max},old}$ and $\tilde{y}_{old} < Na_{i_{max},old}$. Then, from Lemma 2, we know that the updates on $\tilde{x}_{old}$ and $\tilde{y}_{old}$ provide:

$$\tilde{x}_{new} < 4Na_{i_{max},new} \text{ and } \tilde{y}_{new} < 4Na_{i_{max},new}.$$

If we execute an MM-RNS algorithm with inputs $\tilde{x}_{new}, \tilde{y}_{new}$ and bases $\mathcal{A}_{new}$ and $\mathcal{B}$ we obtain a z satisfying

$$\begin{aligned}
z &= (\tilde{x}_{new} \times \tilde{y}_{new} + qN)/A_{new} \\
&< (16N^2 a_{i_{max},new}^2 + A_{new}N)/A_{new} \\
&< N(\frac{16N}{A_{new}/a_{i_{max},new}} \times a_{i_{max},new} + 1)
\end{aligned}$$

Now, since $\frac{A_{new}}{a_{i_{max},new}}$ is the product of t moduli of $\mathcal{A} \cup \mathcal{A}'$ it satisfies $A_{min} \leq \frac{A_{new}}{a_{i_{max},new}}$. Then using (14) we obtain that

$$\frac{32N}{A_{new}/a_{i_{max},new}} \times \frac{a_{i_{max},new}}{2} < \frac{a_{i_{max},new}}{2}$$

and consequently $z < a_{i_{max},new}N$, as required.

ii) At the beginning of each loop $\widetilde{r}_0$ and $\widetilde{r}_1$ are in $[0, Na_{i_{max}}]$ then, from i), they are in $[0, Na_{i_{max}}]$ at the end of the loop. Consequently all the computations in the algorithm are done without overflow and which then correctly outputs $r_0 = x^K \mod N$. ∎

5   Complexity Comparison and Conclusion

In Appendix A we present a variant of the proposed randomization. This variant avoids the use of the set of spare moduli $\mathcal{A}'$: the modified modulus in $\mathcal{A}$ is randomly picked in $\mathcal{B}$. The complexity of the update of the RNS bases $\mathcal{A}, \mathcal{B}$ and the update of the Montgomery representation are sightly larger compared to the approach of Section 4, but the memory requirement is reduced and the number of moduli is also reduced.

In Table 3 we report the complexity of the randomization in the Montgomery-ladder exponentiation for the two following cases:

1. *Only one modulus is modified in the basis $\mathcal{A}$.* In this case, for each loop turn, the proposed approach in Section 4 and Appendix A requires an update of the constant and an update of $\widetilde{r}_0$ and $\widetilde{r}_1$ as shown in Algorithm 5.

2. *s moduli are modified in $\mathcal{A}$.* At each loop turn, we perform s consecutive updates of the RNS bases $\mathcal{A}, \mathcal{A}'$ and the data following the strategy of Section 4: this requires s updates of the constants and s updates of $\widetilde{r}_0$ and $\widetilde{r}_1$. In this case, since an update of $\widetilde{r}_i$ multiply by 4 (cf. Lemma 2) at the end of the s the two data $\widetilde{r}_0$ and $\widetilde{r}_1$ are multiplied by 4^s. This requires to expand the three bases $\mathcal{A}, \mathcal{A}'$ and $\mathcal{B}$ with an additional modulus assuming that $2 \times 4^{2s} < 2^w$ in order to prevent an overflow in Algorithm 5. The resulting complexity of this randomization is given in Table 3.

For comparison purpose we provide in Table 3 the complexity when the randomization of [1] is performed at each loop turn in a Montgomery ladder. The complexity can be easily deduced from the complexity results of Section 3.

The above complexities show that we get a cheaper randomization by changing only one modulus, at a cost of a lower level of randomization. We can increase this level by changing more than one modulus at each loop turn, resulting in a trade-off between randomization and complexity. For the average randomization of $s = t/2$ moduli changed per loop turn, our method requires $6t^2 + O(t)$ multiplications and $2t^2 + 3t$ additions: this is better than the complexity of [1]. Another advantage of our technique is that it works in the cox-rower architecture [7] which is the most popular architecture for RNS implementation.

Table 3. Cost of the randomization in one loop iteration of randomized Montgomery-ladder

Randomization	Method	# Mul.	# Add.	Memory
1 modulus per loop	Section 4	$18t + 10$	$4t + 2$	$8t^2 + 24t + 18$
1 modulus per loop	Appendix A	$24t + 26$	$4t + 4$	$8t^2 + 19t + 20$
s moduli per loop	$s\times$ Section 4	$s(12t + 20) + 6t + 8$	$s(4t + 6)$	$8t^2 + 42t + 52$
$t/2$ moduli per loop (in average)	[1]	$8t^2 + 32t$	$8t^2 + 12t - 4$	$8t^2$

Acknowledgments. This work was partly supported by PAVOIS ANR 12 BS02 002 02. Part of this work was initiated when G. Perin was doing his PhD thesis at the LIRMM.

References

1. Bajard, J.-C., Imbert, L., Liardet, P.-Y., Teglia, Y.: Leak resistant arithmetic. In: Joye, M., Quisquater, J.-J. (eds.) CHES 2004. LNCS, vol. 3156, pp. 62–75. Springer, Heidelberg (2004)
2. Ciet, M., Joye, M.: (Virtually) free randomization techniques for elliptic curve cryptography. In: Qing, S., Gollmann, D., Zhou, J. (eds.) ICICS 2003. LNCS, vol. 2836, pp. 348–359. Springer, Heidelberg (2003)
3. Clavier, C., Feix, B., Gagnerot, G., Roussellet, M., Verneuil, V.: Horizontal correlation analysis on exponentiation. In: Soriano, M., Qing, S., López, J. (eds.) ICICS 2010. LNCS, vol. 6476, pp. 46–61. Springer, Heidelberg (2010)
4. Coron, J.-S.: Resistance against differential power analysis for elliptic curve cryptosystems. In: Koç, Ç.K., Paar, C. (eds.) CHES 1999. LNCS, vol. 1717, pp. 292–302. Springer, Heidelberg (1999)
5. Garner, H.L.: The Residue Number System. IRE Trans. on Elctronic Computers **8**, 140–147 (1959)
6. Joye, M., Yen, S.-M.: The Montgomery Powering Ladder. In: Kaliski, B.S., Koç, K., Paar, C. (eds.) Cryptographic Hardware and Embedded Systems - CHES 2002. LNCS, vol. 2523, pp. 291–302. Springer, Heidelberg (2003)
7. Kawamura, S., Koike, M., Sano, F., Shimbo, A.: Cox-rower architecture for fast parallel montgomery multiplication. In: Preneel, B. (ed.) EUROCRYPT 2000. LNCS, vol. 1807, pp. 523–538. Springer, Heidelberg (2000)
8. Kocher, P.C., Jaffe, J., Jun, B.: Differential power analysis. In: Wiener, M. (ed.) CRYPTO 1999. LNCS, vol. 1666, pp. 388–397. Springer, Heidelberg (1999)
9. Montgomery, P.: Modular Multiplication Without Trial Division. Math. Computation, 519–521 (1985)
10. Perin, G., Imbert, L., Torres, L., Maurine, P.: Attacking randomized exponentiations using unsupervised learning. In: Prouff, E. (ed.) COSADE 2014. LNCS, vol. 8622, pp. 144–160. Springer, Heidelberg (2014)
11. Posch, K.C., Posch, R.: Modulo Reduction in Residue Number Systems. IEEE Trans. Parallel Distrib. Syst. **6**(5), 449–454 (1995)
12. Rivest, R.L., Shamir, A., Adleman, L.: A Method for Obtaining Digital Signatures and Public-Key Cryptosystems. Communications of the ACM **21**, 120–126 (1978)

13. Walter, C.D.: Sliding windows succumbs to big mac attack. In: Koç, Ç.K., Naccache, D., Paar, C. (eds.) CHES 2001. LNCS, vol. 2162, pp. 286–299. Springer, Heidelberg (2001)

A   Random Update of the Basis without a Set of Spare Moduli

In this appendix we present a second approach for a low cost update of the RNS basis $\mathcal{A}$. We still want to modify the basis $\mathcal{A}$ by changing only one modulus. But we do not use a set of spare moduli $\mathcal{A}'$. The proposed approach exchanges a random modulus picked in $\mathcal{A}$ with a random modulus picked in $\mathcal{B}$. Additionally to the two RNS bases $\mathcal{A}$ and $\mathcal{B}$ we will need an additional modulus c:

- $\mathcal{A} = \{a_1, \ldots, a_{t+1}\}$,
- $\mathcal{B} = \{b_1, \ldots, b_{t+1}\}$,
- and an additional modulus $\{c\}$.

We use the following slightly modified version of the Basic-MM-RNS algorithm (Algorithm 2):

Require: x, y in $\mathcal{A} \cup \mathcal{B}$
Ensure: $xyA^{-1} \mod N$ in $\mathcal{A} \cup \{c\} \cup \mathcal{B}$
    $[q]_\mathcal{A} \leftarrow [-xyN^{-1}]_\mathcal{A}$
    $BE_{\mathcal{A} \to \mathcal{B}}([q]_\mathcal{A})$
    $[z]_\mathcal{B} \leftarrow [(xy + qN)A^{-1}]_\mathcal{B}$
    $BE_{\mathcal{B} \to \mathcal{A} \cup \{c\}}([z]_\mathcal{B})$ // modified operation
    return $(z_{\mathcal{A} \cup \mathcal{B}})$

Only the last step is modified: we compute z in $\mathcal{A} \cup \{c\}$ instead of $\mathcal{A}$. This can be performed by modifying the last step of Algorithm 3 as follows

$$[z]_{\mathcal{A} \cup \{c\}} \leftarrow [(\sum_{j=1}^{t} q_{b_j} b_j^{-1} - \beta)B]_{\mathcal{A} \cup \{c\}}.$$

The random update of the bases $\mathcal{A}, \{c\}$ and $\mathcal{B}$ is performed as follows:

$$
\begin{aligned}
r &\leftarrow \text{ random in } \{1, \ldots, t+1\}, \\
r' &\leftarrow \text{ random in } \{1, \ldots, t+1\}, \\
a_{r,new} &\leftarrow b_{r',old}, \\
b_{r',new} &\leftarrow c_{old}, \\
c_{new} &\leftarrow a_{r,old}.
\end{aligned}
\tag{15}
$$

Update of the Montgomery representation. The update of the bases $\mathcal{A}, \{c\}$ and $\mathcal{B}$ requires also to update the representation of $\tilde{x}_{old} = xA_{old} \mod N$ given in $\mathcal{A}_{old} \cup \{c_{old}\} \cup \mathcal{B}_{old}$ to the new value $\tilde{x}_{new} = xA_{new} \mod N$ in $\mathcal{A}_{new} \cup \mathcal{B}_{new}$. The following lemma establishes how to perform this update.

Lemma 4. *We consider two RNS bases $\mathcal{A}$ and $\mathcal{B}$ and an additional modulus $\{c\}$ which are updated as specified in (15). We consider an integer x given by its Montgomery representation $\widetilde{x}_{old} = xA_{old} \mod N$ in $\mathcal{A}_{old} \cup \{c_{old}\} \cup \mathcal{B}_{old}$. We obtain $\widetilde{x}_{new}$ by first performing*

$$
\begin{aligned}
x_{a_i,new} &\leftarrow x_{a_i,old}, \text{ for } i \neq r, \\
x_{a_r,new} &\leftarrow x_{b_{r'},old}, \\
x_{b_i,new} &\leftarrow x_{b_i,old}, \text{ for } i \neq r', \\
x_{b_{r'},new} &\leftarrow x_{c,old}, \\
x_{c,new} &\leftarrow x_{a_r,old}.
\end{aligned}
\tag{16}
$$

and then computes

$$
\begin{aligned}
\lambda &= [-[\widetilde{x}_{old}]_{a_{r,old}} \times N^{-1}]_{a_{r,old}}, \\
\widetilde{x}_{new} &= [(\widetilde{x}_{old} + \lambda \times N) \times a_{r,old}^{-1} \times a_{r,new}]_{\mathcal{A}_{new} \cup \mathcal{B}}.
\end{aligned}
\tag{17}
$$

Proof. The first set of operations in (16) re-expresses $\widetilde{x}_{old}$ in $\mathcal{A}_{new} \cup \mathcal{B}_{new}$ by permuting the coefficients of $\widetilde{x}_{old}$ based on the update of the bases in (15). The second set of operations (17) consists to first compute $s_1 = \widetilde{x}_{old} + \lambda N$ which satisfies $s_1 \equiv \widetilde{x}_{old} \mod N$ and

$$
\begin{aligned}
[s_1]_{a_{r,old}} &= [\widetilde{x}_{old} + \lambda \times N]_{a_{r,old}} \\
&= [\widetilde{x}_{old} - [\widetilde{x}]_{a_{r,old}} \times N^{-1} \times N]_{a_{r,old}} \\
&= 0.
\end{aligned}
$$

Then the operation $((\widetilde{x}_{old} + \lambda N)/a_{r,old}) \times a_{r,new}$ involves an exact division by $a_{r,old}$ and a multiplication by $a_{r,new}$ and produces $x \times A_{new}$ modulo N. Since $a_{r,old}$ is invertible in $\mathcal{A}_{new} \cup \mathcal{B}_{new}$ we replace the division by a multiplication with the inverse $a_{r,old}^{-1}$ in $\mathcal{A}_{new} \cup \mathcal{B}_{new}$ and a multiplication by $a_{r,new}$ which leads to (17). ∎

Update of the constants. In order to apply the MM-RNS algorithm after the update of the bases $\mathcal{A} \cup \{c\} \cup \mathcal{B}$ and of $[\widetilde{x}]_{\mathcal{A} \cup \mathcal{B}}$ we need to also update the constants involved in Algorithm 3. These constants are listed in (8), but we need to consider also the following additional set of constants relative to the modulus c:

$$
\begin{aligned}
&[a_i^{-1}]_c, [b_i^{-1}]_c \text{ for } i = 1, \ldots, t+1, \\
&[c^{-1}]_{a_i}, [c^{-1}]_{b_i} \text{ for } i = 1, \ldots, t+1, \\
&[N]_c, [N^{-1}]_c, [A]_c, [A^{-1}]_c, [B]_c, [B^{-1}]_c.
\end{aligned}
$$

Moreover since a modulus in $\mathcal{A}$ is susceptible to become a modulus in $\mathcal{B}$ and reciprocally, we need to also maintain the following constants:

$$
\begin{aligned}
&[A]_{b_i}, [A^{-1}]_{b_i} \text{ for } i = 1, \ldots, t+1, \\
&[B]_{a_i}, [B^{-1}]_{a_i} \text{ for } i = 1, \ldots, t+1.
\end{aligned}
$$

The proposed updates of the constants are listed below:

- *Constants* $N, N^{-1}, a_i^{-1}, b_i^{-1}, c^{-1}$. The update of the constants only consists in permutation, and does not require any computation.

- *Constants A^{-1} and A_i^{-1}.* We update these constants as follows:

$$[A^{-1}]_{\mathcal{B}_{new}} \leftarrow [A_{old}^{-1} \times a_{r,old} \times a_{r,new}^{-1}]_{\mathcal{B}_{new}},$$
$$[A^{-1}]_{c_{new}} \leftarrow [[A_{r,old}^{-1}]_{a_{r,old}} \times a_{r,new}^{-1}]_{c_{new}} (\text{ since } c_{new} = a_{r,old}),$$
$$[A_j^{-1}]_{a_j} \leftarrow [[A_j^{-1}]_{a_j} \times a_{r,new}^{-1} \times a_{r,old}]_{a_j} \text{ for } j \neq r,$$
$$[A_r^{-1}]_{a_{r,new}} \leftarrow [[A_{old}^{-1}]_{b_{r',old}} \times a_{r,old}]_{a_{r,new}} (\text{ since } b_{r',old} = a_{r,new}).$$

- *Constants B and B_i.* The updates work as follows:

$$[B_{new}]_{a_i} \leftarrow [B_{old} \times b_{r',old}^{-1} \times b_{r',new}]_{a_i} \text{ for } i \neq r,$$
$$[B_{new}]_{a_{r,new}} \leftarrow [[B_{r',old}]_{b_{r',old}} \times b_{r',new}]_{a_{r,new}} (\text{ since } a_{r,new} = b_{r',old}),$$
$$[B_{new}]_{c_{new}} \leftarrow [[B_{old}]_{a_{r,old}} \times b_{r',old}^{-1} \times b_{r',new}]_{c_{new}} (\text{ since } c_{new} = a_{r,old}),$$
$$[B_{j,new}]_{b_j} \leftarrow [[B_j]_{b_j} \times b_{r',old}^{-1} \times b_{r',new}]_{b_j} \text{ for } j \neq r',$$
$$[B_{r',new}]_{b_{r',new}} \leftarrow [[B_{old}]_{c_{old}} \times b_{r',old}^{-1}]_{b_{r',new}} (\text{ since } c_{old} = b_{r',new}).$$

- *Constants B^{-1} and B_i^{-1}.* We update these constants as follows:

$$[B_{new}^{-1}]_{a_i} \leftarrow [B_{old}^{-1} \times b_{r',old} \times b_{r',new}^{-1}]_{a_i}, \text{ for } i \neq r$$
$$[B_{new}^{-1}]_{a_{r,new}} \leftarrow [[B_{r',old}^{-1}]_{b_{r'}} \times b_{r',new}^{-1}]_{a_{r,new}}, (\text{ since } a_{r,new} = b_{r',old}),$$
$$[B_{new}^{-1}]_{c_{new}} \leftarrow [[B_{old}^{-1}]_{a_{r,old}} \times b_{r',old} \times b_{r',new}^{-1}]_{c_{new}}, (\text{ since } c_{new} = a_{r,old}),$$
$$[B_{j,new}^{-1}]_{b_j} \leftarrow [[B_j^{-1}]_{b_j} \times b_{r',old} \times b_{r',new}^{-1}]_{b_j}, \text{ for } j \neq r',$$
$$[B_{r',new}^{-1}]_{b_{r',new}} \leftarrow [[B_{old}^{-1}]_{c_{old}} \times b_{r',old}]_{b_{r',new}} (\text{ since } c_{old} = b_{r',new}).$$

The complexity of the update of the Montgomery representation (Lemma 4) and the updates of the constants can be directly deduced from the above formulas. Theses complexities are given in the table below.

Operation	#Mult.	#Add.
Updates of $\widetilde{x}$	$6t + 7$	$2t + 2$
Updates of the constants	$12t + 12$	0

Identity-Based Encryption

Towards Forward Security Properties
for PEKS and IBE

Qiang Tang$^{(\boxtimes)}$

SnT, University of Luxembourg 6, rue Richard Coudenhove-Kalergi,
L-1359 Walferdange, Luxembourg
qiang.tang@uni.lu

Abstract. In cryptography, forward secrecy is a well-known property for key agreement protocols. It ensures that a session key will remain private even if one of the long-term secret keys is compromised in the future. In this paper, we investigate some forward security properties for Public-key Encryption with Keyword Search (PEKS) schemes, which allow a client to store encrypted data and delegate search operations to a server. The proposed properties guarantee that the client's privacy is protected to the maximum extent even if his private key is compromised in the future. Motivated by the generic transformation from anonymous Identity-Based Encryption (IBE) to PEKS, we correspondingly propose some forward security properties for IBE, in which case we assume the attacker learns the master secret key. We then study several existing PEKS and IBE schemes, including a PEKS scheme by Nishioka, an IBE scheme by Boneh, Raghunathan and Segev, and an IBE scheme by Arriaga, Tang and Ryan. Our analysis indicates that the proposed forward security properties can be achieved by some of these schemes if the attacker is RO-non-adaptive (the attacker does not define its distributions based on the random oracle). Finally, we propose the concept of correlated-input indistinguishable hash function and show how to extend the Boyen-Waters anonymous IBE scheme to achieve the forward security properties against adaptive attackers.

1 Introduction

In the seminal work [8], Boneh et al. proposed the concept of Public-key Encryption with Keyword Search (PEKS) and formulated it as a cryptographic primitive with four algorithms (KeyGen, Encrypt, TrapGen, Test). PEKS is a two-party (i.e. client-server) primitive aiming at protecting a client's, say Alice's, privacy in the following *encrypted email routing scenario*. Alice runs the KeyGen algorithm to generate a key pair (PK, SK) and publishes PK. When any user, say Bob, sends an email to Alice, he can generate a tag Encrypt(x, PK) for a keyword x and attach it to the email (the email should be encrypted independently and the detail is omitted here). In the view of the email server, it has a list of emails indexed by Encrypt(x_1, PK), Encrypt(x_2, PK), $\cdots$ respectively. If Alice wants to retrieve those emails indexed with a keyword y, she sends a trapdoor TrapGen(y, SK) to the email server, which can then run an algorithm Test on the input (TrapGen(y, SK), Encrypt(x_i, PK)) for every $i \geq 1$ to see whether $y = x_i$.

© Springer International Publishing Switzerland 2015
E. Foo and D. Stebila (Eds.): ACISP 2015, LNCS 9144, pp. 127–144, 2015.
DOI: 10.1007/978-3-319-19962-7_8

1.1 Problem Statement

With a PEKS scheme implemented, the server receives a list of tags from message senders and a list of trapdoors from the client. As a result of the desired search functionality, the server can try to match any tag with any trapdoor. Therefore, the server can categorize the possessed tags and trapdoors into three scenarios.

- Scenario 1: the tags, which do not match any trapdoor. The seminal work [8] and all follow-ups have considered the privacy of keywords in this scenario. It is worth noting that most of these papers only consider this property.

- Scenario 2: the tags and trapdoors, which match at least one trapdoor or tag. In [9] and its full version [10], Boneh, Raghunathan and Segev defined (enhanced) function privacy properties for the keywords in this scenario. It is worth noting that the property for PEKS is not explicitly defined in [9,10], but it is implied by their discussions (in fact, they use it to motivate the property definitions for IBE).

- Scenario 3: the trapdoors, which do not match any tag. In [4], Arriaga, Tang, and Ryan defined search pattern privacy properties which captures the privacy of keywords in this scenario.

It is clear that the above scenarios are mutually independent and their security properties will not be comparable (as already indicated in [4]). *As such, a PEKS scheme should provide maximal protection for the keywords in all three scenarios.* Unfortunately, the security properties defined in [4,9] are rather weak and do not capture realistic threats. In the enhanced function privacy definition from [9], there is a min-entropy restriction on the distribution of keywords. It basically requires that if the keyword in a trapdoor $\mathsf{TrapGen}(y_i, SK)$ is different from those in $\mathsf{TrapGen}(y_1, SK)$, $\cdots$, $\mathsf{TrapGen}(y_{i-1}, SK)$, then it should be infeasible to guess y_i given $y_1, \cdots, y_{i-1}$. This restriction seems artificial and unrealistic. Taking the encrypted email routing scenario as an example, at a certain time period, the client may submit queries about a certain topic (e.g. work, family, or friends) and the keywords in the trapdoors might be highly correlated. This implies that, if some keywords are disclosed, it might be easy for the attacker to infer others. In the search pattern privacy property definition from [4], the distribution of keywords in the trapdoors is assumed to be uniform. This restriction is clearly unrealistic. Taking the encrypted email routing scenario as an example, it reasonable to expect the client to submit more queries with high-priority keywords such as "urgent" than low-priority ones such as "ordinary", which implies that the keywords are not uniformly distributed.

Furthermore, it is possible that the client's private key may get compromised at some point. If this happens, the client may still want the privacy of keywords in the tags and trapdoors to be preserved. This is similar to the forward secrecy requirement in key agreement protocols [19,22]. However, no literature work has touched upon this property for PEKS.

1.2   Our Contribution

In this paper, we first introduce two new forward security properties for PEKS. One is forward-secure function privacy, which aims at protecting the privacy of keywords in Scenario 2. The other is forward-secure trapdoor unlinkability, which aims at protecting the privacy of keywords in Scenario 3. These two properties are much stronger than those from [9] and [4], in the sense that we not only allow the attacker to compromise the long-term secret key but also give it more flexibility to define the keyword distribution in the attack games. We analyse a PEKS scheme by Nishioka [28] and show that it only achieves our properties against RO-non-adaptive attackers (which can not choose the keyword distributions based on the random oracle).

We then introduce two new forward security properties for IBE, namely msk-forward-secure function privacy and msk-forward-secure key unlinkability, and they are augmented variants of those from [9] and [4] respectively. Naturally, the new properties directly lead to those forward security properties for PEKS as a result of the generic transformation proposed in [1]. We analyse the $\mathcal{IBE}_{\text{DLIN2}}$ scheme by Boneh et al. [10], and show that it does not achieve the msk-forward-secure function privacy property. We also analyse an IBE scheme by Arriaga et al. [4], and show that it achieves our properties against RO-non-adaptive attackers. These msk-forward security properties are different from the existing forward security notions, see Section 7.

Finally, we introduce the concept of correlated-input indistinguishable hash function, which can be regarded as an enhanced variant of the correlated-input secure hash functions proposed by Goyal, O'Neil, and Rao [21]. By pre-processing the identities with such a hash function, an IBE scheme automatically achieves the msk-forward-secure function privacy property against adaptive attackers. In contrast to the "extract-augment-combine" approach from [9], there is no need to tweak the encryption and decryption algorithms of the underlying IBE scheme. We then take Boyen-Waters anonymous IBE scheme [13] as an example, and extend it with composite order bilinear groups to achieve msk-forward-secure key unlinkability.

The proofs for lemmas and theorems appear in the report [32].

1.3   Organization

The rest of this paper is organized as follows. In Section 2, we present preliminaries on notation and hardness assumptions. In Section 3, we present an enhanced security model for PEKS with a focus on the forward security properties, and analyse the Nishioka scheme. In Section 4, we propose some forward security properties for IBE. In Section 5, we analyse an IBE scheme by Boneh et al. and an IBE scheme by Arriaga et al.. In Section 6, we introduce the concept of correlated-input indistinguishable hash function and extend the Boyen-Waters scheme. In Section 7, we review some related work. In Section 8, we conclude the paper.

2 Preliminary

2.1 Notation

- $x\|y$ means the concatenation of x and y, P.P.T. stands for probabilistic polynomial time.
- $x \xleftarrow{\$} \mathcal{A}^{\mathcal{O}_1, \mathcal{O}_2, \cdots}(m_1, m_2, \cdots)$ means that x is the output of the algorithm $\mathcal{A}$ which runs with the input $m_1, m_2, \cdots$ and has access to oracles $\mathcal{O}_1, \mathcal{O}_2, \cdots$.
- When X is a set, $x \xleftarrow{\$} X$ means that x is chosen from X uniformly at random, and $|X|$ means the size of X. When $\mathbb{D}$ is a distribution on the set X, $x \xleftarrow{\mathbb{D}} X$ means that x is a value sampled from X according to $\mathbb{D}$.
- We use bold letter, such as $\boldsymbol{X}$, to denote a vector or matrix. Given a vector $\boldsymbol{X}$, we use $\boldsymbol{X}^{(i)}$ to denote the i-th element in the vector. When g is a group element, we use $g^{\boldsymbol{X}}$ to denote a new vector or matrix, whose elements are exponentiations of the corresponding elements in $\boldsymbol{X}$. For two vectors (or matrices) $\boldsymbol{Y}$ and $\boldsymbol{Z}$ whose elements are from a group, we use $\boldsymbol{Y} \otimes \boldsymbol{Z}$ to denote the new vector (or matrix) after pairwise group operations.
- A function $P(\lambda) : \mathbb{Z} \to \mathbb{R}$ is said to be negligible with respect to λ if, for every polynomial $f(\lambda)$, there exists an integer N_f such that $P(\lambda) < \frac{1}{f(\lambda)}$ for all $\lambda \geq N_f$. When $P(\lambda)$ is negligible, then we say $1 - P(\lambda)$ is overwhelming.
- A random variable V has min-entropy λ, namely $H_\infty(V) = \lambda$, if $\max_v \Pr[V = v] = 2^{-\lambda}$, or equivalently $\lambda = -\log \max_v \Pr[V = v]$. If V has min-entropy at least λ, then V is a λ source. Given two random variables V and W, the conditional min-entropy of V with respect to W is defined to be $\min_w H_\infty(V|W = w)$, or equivalently $-\log \max_{v,w} \Pr[V = v|W = w]$.

2.2 Pairing Over Composite-Order Groups

A composite-order bilinear group generator is an algorithm $\mathcal{G}_C^{(pq)}$ that takes as input a security parameter λ and outputs $\Gamma = (p, q, \mathbb{G}, \mathbb{G}_T, \hat{e}, g_p, g_q)$ where:

- $\mathbb{G}$ and $\mathbb{G}_T$ are groups of order $n = pq$, where p and q are primes, with efficiently computable group laws.
- g_p is a randomly-chosen generator of the subgroup $\mathbb{G}_p$ of order p, and g_q is a randomly-chosen generator of the subgroup $\mathbb{G}_q$ of order q.
- $\hat{e}$ is an efficiently-computable bilinear pairing $\hat{e} : \mathbb{G} \times \mathbb{G} \to \mathbb{G}_T$, i.e., a map satisfying the following properties for $g \neq 1 \in \mathbb{G}$:
  - Bilinearity: $\hat{e}(g^a, g^b) = \hat{e}(g, g)^{ab}$ for all $a, b \in \mathbb{Z}_{pq}$;
  - Non-degeneracy: $\hat{e}(g, g) \neq 1$.

Instead of setting the order of $\mathbb{G}$ to be the product of two primes (i.e. pq), we can set the order to be the product of multiple primes, e.g. [25, 26, 28]. In [28] and recapped in Section 3.2, the generator $\mathcal{G}_C^{(pqw)}$ generates $\mathbb{G}$ with the order of three primes (i.e. pqw).

Let $\Gamma = (p, q, \mathbb{G}, \mathbb{G}_T, \hat{e}, g_p, g_q)$ be the output by $\mathcal{G}_C{}^{(pq)}(\lambda)$, and $\Gamma^* = (pq, \mathbb{G}, \mathbb{G}_T, \hat{e}, g_p, g_q)$. We say the Composite-DDH assumption [4] holds if, for every P.P.T. attacker $\mathcal{A}$, its advantage $|\Pr[b' = b] - \frac{1}{2}|$ is negligible in the game, defined in Fig. 1.

1. $\Gamma = (p, q, \mathbb{G}, \mathbb{G}_T, \hat{e}, g_p, g_q) \xleftarrow{\$} \mathcal{G}_C{}^{(pq)}(\lambda)$
2. $a_1, a_2, b_1, b_2, b_3, r \xleftarrow{\$} \mathbb{Z}_{pq}$
3. $\Gamma^* = (pq, \mathbb{G}, \mathbb{G}_T, \hat{e}, g_p, g_q)$
4. $X_0 = (\Gamma^*, g_p^{a_1} \cdot g_q^{b_1}, g_p^{a_2} \cdot g_q^{b_2}, g_p^{a_1 a_2} \cdot g_q^{b_3})$
   $X_1 = (\Gamma^*, g_p^{a_1} \cdot g_q^{b_1}, g_p^{a_2} \cdot g_q^{b_2}, g_p^{r} \cdot g_q^{b_3})$
5. $b \xleftarrow{\$} \{0, 1\}$
6. $b' \xleftarrow{\$} \mathcal{A}(X_b)$

---

1. $\Gamma = (p, q, \mathbb{G}, \mathbb{G}_T, \hat{e}, g_p, g_q) \xleftarrow{\$} \mathcal{G}_C{}^{(pq)}(\lambda)$
2. $a_1, a_2, a_3, b_1, b_2, b_3, b_4, r \xleftarrow{\$} \mathbb{Z}_{pq}$
3. $\Gamma^* = (pq, \mathbb{G}, \mathbb{G}_T, \hat{e}, g_p, g_q)$
4. $X_0 = (\Gamma^*, g_p^{a_1} \cdot g_q^{b_1}, g_p^{a_2} \cdot g_q^{b_2}, g_p^{a_1 a_3} \cdot g_q^{b_3}, g_p^{a_2 a_3} \cdot g_q^{b_4})$
   $X_1 = (\Gamma^*, g_p^{a_1} \cdot g_q^{b_1}, g_p^{a_2} \cdot g_q^{b_2}, g_p^{a_1 a_3} \cdot g_q^{b_3}, g_p^{r} \cdot g_q^{b_4})$
5. $b \xleftarrow{\$} \{0, 1\}$
6. $b' \xleftarrow{\$} \mathcal{A}(X_b)$

Fig. 1. Composite-DDH assumption   **Fig. 2.** Weak Composite-DDH assumption

We say the Weak Composite-DDH assumption holds if, for every P.P.T. attacker $\mathcal{A}$, its advantage $|\Pr[b' = b] - \frac{1}{2}|$ is negligible in the game, defined in Fig. 2. Both assumptions are strictly weaker than the C3DH assumption by Boneh and Waters [12] because the attacker is given strictly more information in the C3DH attack game.

2.3   New Assumptions

In [15], Canetti proposed the DDH-II assumption which differs from the standard DDH assumption in that one exponent is chosen from a *wide spread* distribution instead of a uniform one. Damgård, Hazay and, Zottarel [18] showed that this assumption holds in the generic group model, and stated that it is a useful tool in leakage resilient cryptography.

Next, we introduce a new assumption for bilinear groups. The philosophy is similar to the case of Composite-DDH: although it is trivial to solve DDH-II problem in bilinear groups, adding an additional layer of randomization makes it difficult even with the help of the bilinear map. Formally, we say the Composite-DDH-II assumption holds if, for every P.P.T. attacker $\mathcal{A}$, its advantage $|\Pr[b' = b] - \frac{1}{2}|$ is negligible in the game, defined in Fig. 3. In the game, the distribution $\mathbb{D}$ from the attacker should guarantee that a_1 has min-entropy not smaller than λ, i.e. a_1 is *wide spread* according to Canetti [15]. Further, we say the Correlated Composite-DDH-II assumption holds if, for every P.P.T. attacker $\mathcal{A}$, its advantage $|\Pr[b' = b] - \frac{1}{2}|$ is negligible in the game, defined in Fig. 4. In the game, the distribution $\mathbb{D}$ from the attacker should guarantee that a_i for any $1 \leq i \leq L$ has min-entropy not smaller than λ. Compared to the Composite-DDH-II assumption, on one hand the values $g_p^{a_1}, \cdots, g_p^{a_L}$ are not given to the attacker (not even in the randomized form), but on the other hand the attacker is given multiple incomplete DH pairs.

1. $\Gamma = (p, q, \mathbb{G}, \mathbb{G}_T, \hat{e}, g, g_p, g_q) \xleftarrow{\$} \mathcal{G}_C^{(pq)}(\lambda)$
2. $\Gamma^* = (pq, \mathbb{G}, \mathbb{G}_T, \hat{e}, g, g_p, g_q)$
3. $\mathbb{D} \xleftarrow{\$} \mathcal{A}(\Gamma^*)$
4. $a_1 \xleftarrow{\mathbb{D}} \mathbb{Z}_p$
5. $b_1, s_1, s_2, s_3, r \xleftarrow{\$} \mathbb{Z}_{pq}$
6. $X_0 = (\Gamma^*, g_p^{a_1} \cdot g_q^{s_1}, g_p^{b_1} \cdot g_q^{s_2}, g_p^{a_1 b_1} \cdot g_q^{s_3})$
   $X_1 = (\Gamma^*, g_p^{a_1} \cdot g_q^{s_1}, g_p^{b_1} \cdot g_q^{s_2}, g_p^{r} \cdot g_q^{s_3})$
7. $b \xleftarrow{\$} \{0, 1\}$
8. $b' \xleftarrow{\$} \mathcal{A}(X_b, \mathbb{D})$

1. $\Gamma = (p, q, \mathbb{G}, \mathbb{G}_T, \hat{e}, g, g_p, g_q) \xleftarrow{\$} \mathcal{G}_C^{(pq)}(\lambda)$
2. $\Gamma^* = (pq, \mathbb{G}, \mathbb{G}_T, \hat{e}, g, g_p, g_q)$
3. $\mathbb{D} \xleftarrow{\$} \mathcal{A}(\Gamma^*)$
4. $(a_1, \cdots, a_L) \xleftarrow{\mathbb{D}} \mathbb{Z}_p^L$
5. $b_1, \cdots b_L, r_1, \cdots, r_L, s_1, \cdots, s_L,$
   $t_1, \cdots, t_L \xleftarrow{\$} \mathbb{Z}_{pq}$
6. $X_0 = (\Gamma^*, g_p^{b_1} \cdot g_q^{s_1}, g_p^{a_1 b_1} \cdot g_q^{t_1}, \cdots, g_p^{b_L} \cdot g_q^{s_L}, g_p^{a_L b_L} \cdot g_q^{t_L})$
   $X_1 = (\Gamma^*, g_p^{b_1} \cdot g_q^{s_1}, g_p^{r_1} \cdot g_q^{t_1}, \cdots, g_p^{b_L} \cdot g_q^{s_L}, g_p^{r_L} \cdot g_q^{t_L})$
7. $b \xleftarrow{\$} \{0, 1\}$
8. $b' \xleftarrow{\$} \mathcal{A}(X_b, \mathbb{D})$

Fig. 3. Composite-DDH-II assumption

Fig. 4. Correlated Composite-DDH-II assumption

As to the two new assumptions, it is not clear how to reduce one to the other. Nevertheless, we have the following lemma.

Lemma 1. *Suppose any P.P.T. attacker has at most the advantage ϵ in the Composite-DDH-II assumption. Then, any P.P.T. attacker has at most the advantage $L \cdot \epsilon$ in the Correlated Composite-DDH-II assumption in the following two scenarios.*

1. $a_1, a_2, \cdots, a_L$ *are independent according to* $\mathbb{D}$.
2. $a_1 = a_2 = \cdots = a_L$ *according to* $\mathbb{D}$.

3 Forward Security Properties for PEKS

A PEKS scheme involves a client, a server, and senders which can be any entity. Let λ be the security parameter, a PEKS scheme has the following algorithms.

- KeyGen(λ): Run by the client, this probabilistic algorithm outputs a public/private key pair (PK, SK), where PK should define a message space $\mathcal{W}$.
- Encrypt(x, PK): Run by a sender, this probabilistic algorithm outputs a ciphertext (or, tag) C_x for a message (or, keyword) $x \in \mathcal{W}$.
- TrapGen(y, SK): Run by the client, this probabilistic algorithm generates a trapdoor T_y for the message $y \in \mathcal{W}$.
- Test(C_x, T_y, PK): Run by the server, this deterministic algorithm returns 1 if $x = y$ and 0 otherwise.

Boneh et al. [8] defined ciphertext privacy property for PEKS, and Abdala et al. [1] defined computational consistency property. Next, we present the new forward security properties.

3.1 Forward Security Properties for PEKS

The forward-secure trapdoor unlinkability says that any P.P.T. attacker cannot determine the links among trapdoors as long as the underlying keywords are sampled according to distributions with min-entropy not smaller than λ. This property is an augmented variant of the strong search pattern privacy property from [4] in two aspects. (1) The attacker is given SK in the attack game, and this brings in the forward security flavor; (2) The attacker can adaptively specify the keyword distributions based on the public parameters, while the challenger samples the keywords uniformly from the keyword space in [4].

Definition 1. *A PEKS scheme achieves forward-secure trapdoor unlinkability if any P.P.T. attacker $\mathcal{A}$'s advantage $|Pr[b' = b] - \frac{1}{2}|$ is negligible in the game shown in Fig. 5. In the game, $\mathbb{D}_0$ is the joint distribution of L (dependent) λ-source random variables, while $\mathbb{D}_1$ defines L independent random variables with uniform distribution. Chosen by the attacker, the integer L is a polynomial in λ.*

1. $(PK, SK) \xleftarrow{\$} \mathsf{KeyGen}(\lambda)$
2. $(\mathbb{D}_0, \mathbb{D}_1, L, state) \xleftarrow{\$} \mathcal{A}^{\mathsf{TrapGen}}(PK)$
3. $b \xleftarrow{\$} \{0,1\}$, $\boldsymbol{x}_b \xleftarrow{\mathbb{D}_b} \mathcal{W}^L$, $\boldsymbol{T}_b = $ $\mathsf{TrapGen}(\boldsymbol{x}_b, SK)$
4. $b' \xleftarrow{\$} \mathcal{A}(\boxed{SK}, state, \boldsymbol{T}_b)$

1. $(PK, SK) \xleftarrow{\$} \mathsf{KeyGen}(\lambda)$
2. $(\mathbb{D}_0, \mathbb{D}_1, L, state) \xleftarrow{\$} \mathcal{A}^{\mathsf{TrapGen}}(PK)$
3. $b \xleftarrow{\$} \{0,1\}$, $\boldsymbol{x}_b \xleftarrow{\mathbb{D}_b} \mathcal{W}^L$, $\boldsymbol{T}_b = $ $\mathsf{TrapGen}(\boldsymbol{x}_b, SK)$, $\boldsymbol{C}_b = \mathsf{Encrypt}(\boldsymbol{x}_b, PK)$
4. $b' \xleftarrow{\$} \mathcal{A}^{\mathsf{TrapGen}, \mathsf{Encrypt}}(\boxed{SK}, state, \boldsymbol{T}_b, \boldsymbol{C}_b)$

Fig. 5. Forward-Secure Trapdoor Unlinkability

Fig. 6. Forward-Secure Function Privacy

We use $\mathsf{TrapGen}(\boldsymbol{x}_b, SK)$ to denote $(\mathsf{TrapGen}(\boldsymbol{x}_b^{(1)}, SK), \cdots, \mathsf{TrapGen}(\boldsymbol{x}_b^{(L)}, SK))$ in Fig. 5. Such notation is also used in Fig. 6 and definitions in Section 4.1.

The forward-secure function privacy property says that any P.P.T. attacker cannot determine the links among (tag, trapdoor) pairs, as long as the underlying keywords are sampled according to distributions with min-entropy not smaller than λ. This property is an augmented variant of the enhanced function privacy property from [9] in two aspects. (1) The attacker is given SK in the attack game, and this brings in the forward security flavor; (2) We get rid of the restriction in the enhanced function privacy property definition from [9], namely the conditional min-entropy of $\boldsymbol{x}_0^{(i)}$ given $\boldsymbol{x}_0^{(1)}, \cdots, \boldsymbol{x}_0^{(i-1)}$ is required to be at least λ, for all $2 \leq i \leq L$.

Definition 2. *A PEKS scheme achieves forward-secure function privacy if any P.P.T. attacker $\mathcal{A}$'s advantage $|Pr[b' = b] - \frac{1}{2}|$ is negligible in the game shown in Fig. 6. In the game, $\mathbb{D}_0$ and $\mathbb{D}_1$ are defined in the same way as in Definition 1, but with the following restriction: for $\boldsymbol{x}_0 = (\boldsymbol{x}_0^{(1)}, \boldsymbol{x}_0^{(2)}, \cdots, \boldsymbol{x}_0^{(L)}) \xleftarrow{\mathbb{D}_0} \mathcal{W}^L$ and any $1 \leq i \neq j \leq L$, the probability $Pr[\boldsymbol{x}_0^{(i)} = \boldsymbol{x}_0^{(j)}]$ is negligible.*

In practice, the client may submit search queries for the same keyword multiple times. However, the "Real-or-Random" definition approach does not allow us to *straightforwardly* capture this given that the attacker gets access to (tag, trapdoor) pairs. If we allow the sampled keywords to be equal according to $\mathbb{D}_0$, then an attacker can win the game trivially (by cross testing the trapdoors and the ciphertexts) because $\mathbb{D}_1$ samples the keywords uniformly at random. To bridge the gap, we give the attacker access to TrapGen and Encrypt oracles in Step 4 of the above game, to capture the fact that the attacker can access multiple trapdoors and tags for the same keywords. In a TrapGen oracle query, the attacker has an index $1 \leq i \leq L$ as input and receives $\mathsf{TrapGen}(\boldsymbol{x}_b^{(i)}, SK)$. In an Encrypt oracle query, the attacker has an index $1 \leq j \leq L$ as input and receives $\mathsf{Encrypt}(\boldsymbol{x}_b^{(j)}, PK)$.

3.2 Analysis of Nishioka Scheme

In [28], Nishioka modeled trapdoor unlinkability for a very restricted setting: the attacker is non-adaptive, the unlinkability is only for two trapdoors, and the model seems to be selective since the challenge keywords are chosen before the generation of other parameters (in the SPP experiment). We found a minor inconsistency in the original Nishioka scheme (referred to as Instance 3 in [28]), namely r_1 is defined to be $r_1 \xleftarrow{\$} \mathbb{Z}_p$ for the TrapGen algorithm but p is not included in the SK. There are two ways to get rid of this inconsistency. One is to include p in SK. This will make the scheme fail to achieve the forward-secure trapdoor unlinkability property even against RO-non-adaptive attackers. The other is to set $r_1 \xleftarrow{\$} \mathbb{Z}_{pqw}$, and the scheme works in the same way as in the case of $r_1 \xleftarrow{\$} \mathbb{Z}_p$. This leads to the description in Fig. 7.

KeyGen(λ)	TrapGen(y, SK)
$(p, q, w, \mathbb{G}, \mathbb{G}_T, \hat{e}, g_p, g_q, g_w) \xleftarrow{\$} \mathcal{G}_C^{(pqw)}(\lambda)$	$\boxed{r_1 \xleftarrow{\$} \mathbb{Z}_{pqw}}$
$g_q^\dagger \xleftarrow{\$} \mathbb{G}_q, g = g_p \cdot g_q^\dagger$	$g_w', g_w'' \xleftarrow{\$} \mathbb{G}_w$
$\mathcal{W} = \{0,1\}^*, \mathsf{H} : \{0,1\}^* \to \mathbb{G}_p$	$T_1 = g_p^{r_1} \cdot g_w'$
$PK = (pqw, \mathbb{G}, \mathbb{G}_T, \hat{e}, g_q, g_w, g, \mathcal{W}, \mathsf{H})$	$T_2 = \mathsf{H}(y)^{r_1} \cdot g_w''$
$SK = (PK, g_p)$	$T_y = (T_1, T_2)$
Encrypt(x, PK)	Test(C_x, T_y, PK)
$r_2 \xleftarrow{\$} \mathbb{Z}_{pqw}, g_q', g_q'' \xleftarrow{\$} \mathbb{G}_q$	if $\hat{e}(T_1, C_2) = \hat{e}(T_2, C_1)$, output 1
$C_1 = g^{r_2} \cdot g_q', C_2 = \mathsf{H}(x)^{r_2} \cdot g_q'', C_x = (C_1, C_2)$	otherwise, output 0

Fig. 7. Nishioka Scheme (with modification)

In Definition 1 and 2, we assume the attacker to be fully adaptive in the sense that it can choose the distribution $\mathbb{D}_0$ based on everything. An immediate relaxation on these definitions is to make the attacker *RO-non-adaptive*, which means that the attacker can choose the distribution $\mathbb{D}_0$ based on everything except for the random oracle (i.e. the hash function). In practice, the keywords in search queries might be related to the system parameters in some manner, but it is hard to imagine a scenario where the keywords would depend on the behavior of a random function. Following Theorem 6.1 from [10], based on the fact that the keywords are hashed in both the TrapGen and Encrypt algorithms, the scheme trivially achieves the forward-secure function privacy property in the random oracle model against RO-non-adaptive atatckers. However, it is not trivial for the forward-secure trapdoor unlinkability property, due to the fact that the attacker can let $\mathbb{D}_0$ output identical keywords and exploit this in the attack. We have the following theorem.

Theorem 1. *The scheme in Fig. 7 achieves the forward-secure trapdoor unlinkability property against RO-non-adaptive attackers based on the Weak Composite-DDH assumption in the random oracle model.*

Note that the Weak Composite-DDH assumption defined in Fig. 2 is for bilinear composite-order group of the order pq, in the above theorem we assume this assumption holds for any composite-order subgroup (i.e. $\mathbb{G}_{pq}$, $\mathbb{G}_{pw}$ and $\mathbb{G}_{qw}$) of the bilinear group $\mathbb{G}$ with the order pqw.

4   IBE and Its Security Properties

An IBE scheme is specified by four algorithms (Setup, Extract, Enc, Dec), defined in Fig. 8. Let the message space be $\mathcal{M}$ and the identity space be $\mathcal{I}$. The generic transformation from IBE to PEKS, proposed in [1], works as in Fig. 9. Note that the message space $\mathcal{W}$ of the resulted PEKS scheme is the public-key space $\mathcal{I}$ of the IBE scheme.

1. $(Msk, params) = $ Setup(λ)	1. $\boxed{\text{KeyGen}(\lambda)} = $ Setup(λ)
2. $sk_{id} = $ Extract(Msk, id)	2. $\boxed{\text{Encrypt}(x, PK)} = (m, \text{Enc}(m, x))$, for $m \xleftarrow{\$} \mathcal{M}$
3. $C = $ Enc(m, id)	3. $\boxed{\text{TrapGen}(y, SK)} = $ Extract(Msk, y)
4. Dec$(C, sk_{id}) = m$ or $\bot$	4. $\boxed{\text{Test}(C_x, T_y, PK)} = 1$ iff $m = $ Dec$($Enc$(m, x), T_y)$

Fig. 8. IBE   **Fig. 9.** Resulted PEKS

The standard IND-CPA and anonymity properties for IBE can be found in [1], and we define two new forward security properties for IBE in the next subsection. Under our definitions, the generic transformation leads to the the following property mapping. The reductions between properties are straightforward, so that we skip them here.

PEKS Properties	IBE Properties
computational consistency	IND-CPA
ciphertext privacy	anonymity
forward-secure trapdoor unlinkability	msk-forward-secure key unlinkability
forward-secure function privacy	msk-forward-secure function privacy

4.1   Forward Security Properties of IBE

The following msk-forward-secure key unlinkability property says that any P.P.T. attacker cannot determine the links among private keys if the underlying identities are sampled according to distributions with min-entropy not smaller than λ, even with the knowledge of the master secret key. This property is an augmented variant of the strong key unlinkability property from [4], where the augmentation lies in two aspects. (1) The attacker is given Msk in the attack game, and this gives the forward security flavor; (2) The attacker is allowed to adaptively choose the identity distribution $\mathbb{D}_0$ based on the public parameters, while the challenger samples the identities uniformly at random (according to certain patterns defined by the attacker) from the identity space in [4].

Definition 3. *An IBE scheme achieves* msk-*forward-secure key unlinkability if any P.P.T. attacker $\mathcal{A}$'s advantage $|Pr[b' = b] - \frac{1}{2}|$ is negligible in the game shown in Fig. 10. In the game, $\mathbb{D}_0$ is the joint distribution of L (dependent) λ-source random variables, while $\mathbb{D}_1$ defines L independent random variables with uniform distribution. Chosen by the attacker, the integer L is a polynomial in λ.*

$$
\begin{array}{|l|}
\hline
1.\ (Msk, params) \xleftarrow{\$} \mathsf{Setup}(\lambda) \\[4pt]
2.\ (\mathbb{D}_0, \mathbb{D}_1, L, state) \xleftarrow{\$} \\
\quad \mathcal{A}^{\mathsf{Extract}}(params) \\[4pt]
3.\ b \xleftarrow{\$} \{0,1\},\ \boldsymbol{id}_b \xleftarrow{\mathbb{D}_b} \mathcal{I}^L,\ \boldsymbol{sk}_b = \\
\quad \mathsf{Extract}(Msk, \boldsymbol{id}_b) \\[4pt]
4.\ b' \xleftarrow{\$} \mathcal{A}(\boxed{Msk}, state, \boldsymbol{sk}_b) \\
\hline
\end{array}
\qquad
\begin{array}{|l|}
\hline
1.\ (PK, SK) \xleftarrow{\$} \mathsf{Setup}(\lambda) \\[4pt]
2.\ (\mathbb{D}_0, \mathbb{D}_1, L, state) \xleftarrow{\$} \mathcal{A}^{\mathsf{Extract}}(params) \\[4pt]
3.\ b \xleftarrow{\$} \{0,1\},\ \boldsymbol{id}_b \xleftarrow{\mathbb{D}_b} \mathcal{I}^L,\ \boldsymbol{sk}_b = \\
\quad \mathsf{Extract}(Msk, \boldsymbol{id}_b), \\
\quad \boldsymbol{m}_b \xleftarrow{\$} \mathcal{M}^L,\ \boldsymbol{C}_b = \mathsf{Enc}(\boldsymbol{m}_b, \boldsymbol{id}_b) \\[4pt]
4.\ b' \xleftarrow{\$} \mathcal{A}^{\mathsf{Extract},\mathsf{Enc}}(\boxed{Msk}, state, \boldsymbol{sk}_b, \boldsymbol{C}_b) \\
\hline
\end{array}
$$

Fig. 10.   msk-Forward-Secure   Key   Unlinkability

Fig. 11.   msk-Forward-Secure   Function Privacy

The following msk-forward-secure function privacy property says that any P.P.T. attacker cannot determine the links among (private key, ciphertext) pairs if the underlying identities are sampled according to distributions with min-entropy not smaller than λ, even with the knowledge of the master secret key. This property is an augmented variant of the enhanced function privacy property from [9], where the augmentation lies in two aspects. (1) The attacker is given Msk in the attack game, and this gives the forward security flavor; (2) We get rid of this restriction in the enhanced function privacy property definition from [9], namely the conditional min-entropy of $\boldsymbol{id}_0^{(i)}$ given $\boldsymbol{id}_0^{(1)}, \cdots, \boldsymbol{id}_0^{(i-1)}$ is required to be at least λ, for all $2 \leq i \leq L$.

Definition 4. *An IBE scheme achieves* msk-*forward-secure function privacy if any P.P.T. attacker $\mathcal{A}$'s advantage $|Pr[b' = b] - \frac{1}{2}|$ is negligible in the game shown in Fig. 11. In the game, $\mathbb{D}_0$ and $\mathbb{D}_1$ are defined in the same way as in Definition 3, but with the following restriction: for $\boldsymbol{id}_0 = (\boldsymbol{id}_0^{(1)}, \boldsymbol{id}_0^{(2)}, \cdots, \boldsymbol{id}_0^{(L)}) \xleftarrow{\mathbb{D}_0} \mathcal{I}^L$ and any $1 \leq i \neq j \leq L$, the probability $\Pr[\boldsymbol{id}_0^{(i)} = \boldsymbol{id}_0^{(j)}]$ is negligible.*

We use $\mathsf{Enc}(\boldsymbol{m}_b, \boldsymbol{id}_b)$ to denote $(\mathsf{Enc}(\boldsymbol{m}_b^{(1)}, \boldsymbol{id}_b^{(1)}), \cdots, \mathsf{Enc}(\boldsymbol{m}_b^{(L)}, \boldsymbol{id}_b)^{(L)})$ for the simplicity of notation. Similar to the definition of forward-secure function privacy for PEKS (i.e. Definition 2), the attacker is given access to the Extract and Enc oracles in Step 4 of the above game. In an Extract oracle query, the attacker has an index $1 \leq i \leq L$ as input and receives $\mathsf{Extract}(Msk, \boldsymbol{id}_b^{(i)})$. In an Enc oracle the attacker has an index $1 \leq j \leq L$ as input and receives $\mathsf{Enc}(m, \boldsymbol{id}_b^{(j)})$ for $m \xleftarrow{\$} \mathcal{M}$.

5   Analysis of Two Existing IBE Schemes

In this section, we analyse an IBE scheme by Boneh et al. [10] and an IBE scheme by Arriaga et al. [4] in our security model.

Setup(λ)	Extract(Msk, id)
$\Gamma = (\mathbb{G}, \mathbb{G}_T, \hat{e}, g, p) = \mathcal{G}_\mathcal{P}(\lambda)$	$id = (id_1, id_2, \cdots, id_n) \in \{0,1\}^n$
$\boldsymbol{A}_0, \boldsymbol{B}, \boldsymbol{A}_1, \cdots, \boldsymbol{A}_n \xleftarrow{\$} \mathbb{Z}_p^{2 \times m}$	$\boldsymbol{S} \xleftarrow{\$} \mathbb{Z}_p^{m \times 2}$
$\boldsymbol{u} \xleftarrow{\$} \mathbb{Z}_p^2, \mathcal{M} = \mathbb{G}_T, \mathcal{I} = \{0,1\}^n$	$\boldsymbol{F}_{id, \boldsymbol{S}} = [\boldsymbol{A}_0 \mid \boldsymbol{B}\boldsymbol{S} + (\sum_{1 \leq j \leq n} id_j \boldsymbol{A}_j)\boldsymbol{S}]$
$Msk = (\boldsymbol{A}_0, \boldsymbol{B}, \boldsymbol{A}_1, \cdots, \boldsymbol{A}_n, \boldsymbol{u})$	$\boldsymbol{v} \xleftarrow{\$} \{\boldsymbol{x} \mid \boldsymbol{F}_{id, \boldsymbol{S}} \cdot \boldsymbol{x} = \boldsymbol{u} \pmod{p}\}$
$params = (\Gamma, g^{\boldsymbol{A}_0}, \boldsymbol{B}, g^{\boldsymbol{A}_1}, \cdots, g^{\boldsymbol{A}_n}, g^{\boldsymbol{u}},$	$\boldsymbol{z} = g^{\boldsymbol{v}} \in \mathbb{G}^{m+2}, sk_{id} = (\boldsymbol{S}, \boldsymbol{z})$
$\mathcal{M}, \mathcal{I})$	
Enc(m, id)	Dec(C, sk_{id})
$id = (id_1, id_2, \cdots, id_n) \in \{0,1\}^n, m \in \mathbb{G}_T$	$\boldsymbol{d}^T = [\boldsymbol{c}_0^T \mid (\boldsymbol{c}_1^T)^{\boldsymbol{S}}] = g^{\boldsymbol{r}^T \boldsymbol{F}_{id, \boldsymbol{S}}}$
$\boldsymbol{D}(id) = \sum_{1 \leq j \leq n} id_j \boldsymbol{A}_j, \boldsymbol{r} \xleftarrow{\$} \mathbb{Z}_p^2$	$\hat{e}(\boldsymbol{d}, \boldsymbol{z}) = \hat{e}(g, g)^{\boldsymbol{r}^T (\boldsymbol{F}_{id, \boldsymbol{S}} \cdot \boldsymbol{v})} = \hat{e}(g, g)^{\boldsymbol{r}^T \boldsymbol{u}}$
$\boldsymbol{c}_0^T = g^{\boldsymbol{r}^T \boldsymbol{A}_0}, \boldsymbol{c}_1^T = g^{\boldsymbol{r}^T [\boldsymbol{B} + \boldsymbol{D}(id)]}$	$m = c_2 \cdot \hat{e}(\boldsymbol{d}, \boldsymbol{z})^{-1}$
$c_2 = m \cdot \hat{e}(g, g)^{\boldsymbol{r}^T \boldsymbol{u}}, C = (\boldsymbol{c}_0, \boldsymbol{c}_1, c_2)$	

Fig. 12. Boneh-Raghunathan-Segev $\mathcal{IBE}_{\mathsf{DLIN2}}$ Scheme

5.1   Boneh-Raghunathan-Segev $\mathcal{IBE}_{\mathsf{DLIN2}}$ Scheme

According to their definitions, the $\mathcal{IBE}_{\mathsf{DLIN2}}$ scheme achieves enhanced function privacy based on the DLIN assumption (see definition in [10]) in the standard model. Next, we show that this scheme does not achieve msk-forward-secure function privacy, namely an attacker wins the attack game in Fig. 11 with overwhelming probability. Note that this does not conflict with the claims from [10] because our security model is stronger. The following attack makes use of the fact that, with Msk, the attacker can transform a ciphertext under an identity id into a ciphertext under another identity id', for some carefully chosen id and id'. In an attack, in step 2 and 4 of the game, the attacker performs as follows.

- In step 2, the attacker sets $L = 2$, which means $\mathbb{D}_0$ and $\mathbb{D}_1$ are the joint distribution of two identity variables. The attacker defines $\mathbb{D}_0$ as follows:

$id_0^{(1)} = (id_1, id_2, \cdots, id_n)$ is defined as $(id_1, id_2, \cdots, id_{n-1}) \xleftarrow{\$} \{0,1\}^{n-1}$ and $id_n = 0$; $id_0^{(2)}$ equals $id_0^{(1)}$ except its $id_n = 1$.

- In step 4, the attacker firstly obtains $Msk = (A_0, B, A_1, \cdots, A_n, u)$. Then, the attacker computes $X \in \mathbb{Z}_p^{m \times m}$ such that $A_n = A_0 X$. Recall that the challenge is (sk_b, C_b). The first ciphertext in C_b, namely $C_b^{(1)} = (c_0, c_1, c_2)$, is in the following form: $c_0{}^T = g^{r^T A_0}, c_1{}^T = g^{r^T[B+D(id_b^{(1)})]}, c_2 = m \cdot \hat{e}(g,g)^{r^T u}$. The attacker has a new ciphertext $C' = (c_0, c_1', c_2)$, where

$$c_1'{}^T = c_1{}^T \otimes (c_0{}^T)^X = g^{r^T[B+D(id_b^{(1)})]} \otimes g^{r^T A_0 X} = g^{r^T[B+D(id_b^{(1)})]} \otimes g^{r^T A_n}$$

Let the secret keys in the challenge sk_b be denoted as $(sk_{id_b^{(1)}}, sk_{id_b^{(2)}})$. The attacker outputs 0 if $\mathsf{Dec}(C', sk_{id_b^{(2)}}) = \mathsf{Dec}(C_b^{(1)}, sk_{id_b^{(1)}})$, and outputs 1 otherwise.

Recall that, $\otimes$ is an operator for pairwise group operations between two the new vectors or matrices. It is clear that if $b = 0$ then we have $c_1'{}^T = g^{r^T[B+D(id_b^{(2)})]}$ and the equality $\mathsf{Dec}(C_b^{(1)}, sk_{id_b^{(1)}}) = \mathsf{Dec}(C', sk_{id_b^{(2)}})$ holds. But, this equality holds with a negligible probability if $b = 1$. As a result, our attack works.

5.2 Arriaga-Tang-Ryan IBE Scheme

The following scheme (in Fig. 13) was proposed by Arriaga et al. [4], based on an anonymous IBE scheme by Boyen and Waters [13]. This scheme has been proven secure with respect to the strong key unlinkability property (under the definition in [4]) in the random oracle model. Compared with our msk-forward-secure key unlinkability property, their definition is weaker in three aspects: (1) the attacker is not allowed to adaptively choose the identity distribution $\mathbb{D}_0$ and it can only specify the identity patterns (i.e. which identities are equal); (2) according to the patterns, the challenger samples the identities uniformly at random from the identity space; (3) there is no forward security.

Similar to the discussions in Section 3.2, an immediate relaxation on Definition 3 and 4 is to make the attacker *RO-non-adaptive*, which means that the attacker can choose the distribution $\mathbb{D}_0$ based on everything except for the random oracle (i.e. the hash function). Following Theorem 6.1 from [10], it is trivial to show that the scheme achieves msk-forward-secure function privacy property in the random oracle model. However, it is non-trivial for the msk-forward-secure key unlinkability property. We have the following theorem. Note that this result is stronger than Lemma 3 from [4] based on a weaker assumption.

Theorem 2. *The scheme achieves the* msk-*forward-secure key unlinkability property against RO-non-adaptive attackers based on the Weak Composite-DDH assumption in the random oracle model.*

Setup(λ)	Extract(Msk, id)
$\Gamma = (p, q, \mathbb{G}, \mathbb{G}_T, \hat{e}, g, g_p, g_q) = \mathcal{G}_c(\lambda)$	$r \xleftarrow{\$} \mathbb{Z}_n$
$\Gamma^* = (n = pq, \mathbb{G}, \mathbb{G}_T, \hat{e}, g, g_p, g_q)$	$x_0, x_1, x_2 \xleftarrow{\$} \mathbb{G}_q$
$x, t_1, t_2 \xleftarrow{\$} \mathbb{Z}_n$	$d_0 = x_0 \cdot g_p^{rt_1 t_2}$
$\Omega = \hat{e}(g_p, g_p)^{xt_1 t_2}$, $v_1 = g_p^{t_1}$, $v_2 = g_p^{t_2}$	$d_1 = x_1 \cdot g_p^{-xt_2} \cdot H(id)^{-rt_2}$
$\mathcal{M} = \mathbb{G}_T$, $\mathcal{I} = \{0,1\}^*$, $H : \{0,1\}^* \to \mathbb{G}_p$	$d_2 = x_2 \cdot g_p^{-xt_1} \cdot H(id)^{-rt_1}$
$Msk = (x, t_1, t_2)$, $params = (\Gamma^*, \Omega, v_1, v_2, \mathcal{M}, \mathcal{I}, H)$	$sk_{id} = (d_0, d_1, d_2)$
Enc(m, id)	Dec(C, sk_{id})
$s, s_1 \xleftarrow{\$} \mathbb{Z}_n$	$e_0 = \hat{e}(c_0, d_0)$, $e_1 = \hat{e}(c_1, d_1)$
$\hat{c} = \Omega^s m$, $c_0 = H(id)^s$, $c_1 = v_1^{s - s_1}$, and $c_2 = v_2^{s_1}$	$e_2 = \hat{e}(c_2, d_2)$,
$C = (\hat{c}, c_0, c_1, c_2)$	$m = \hat{c} \cdot e_0 \cdot e_1 \cdot e_2$

Fig. 13. Arriaga-Tang-Ryan IBE Scheme

6 msk-Forward-Secure IBE Construction

The "extract-combine-augment" concept from [9] is an elegant idea, but it has two drawbacks. One is that it introduces the unrealistic conditional min-entropy restriction on identity distribution when defining enhanced function privacy. The other is that it requires specific modifications to both encryption and decryption algorithms of the underlying IBE scheme. Such modifications may not be an easy task. Moreover, it may introduce *good* algebraic structures into the ciphertexts. This partially makes it possible for us to show that the $\mathcal{IBE}_{\text{DLIN2}}$ scheme does not achieve msk-forward-secure function privacy in Section 5.1.

In the following, we first introduce the concept of correlated-input indistinguishable hash function, which serves as a building block to pre-process identities for any IBE scheme. Similar to the "extract" step in the "extract-combine-augment" approach, such a hash function aims at eliminating the correlations among different inputs so that msk-forward-secure function privacy can be straightforwardly achieved. The advantage is that there is no need to modify the underlying IBE algorithms. We then take the Boyen-Waters scheme [13] as an example to show how to make it msk-forward-secure.

6.1 Correlated-Input Indistinguishable Hash Function

Goyal et al. [21] introduced the concept of correlated-input secure hash functions and gave a few security definitions and instantiations. Unfortunately, their security property definitions are selective and assume certain specific correlations among the inputs (i.e. the inputs are related by polynomials over the input space). Such restrictions conflict with our needs, because we want the inputs to be arbitrarily correlated and full security. Moreover, we want a property which is subtly different from correlated-input pseudorandomness. Very informally, the pseudorandomness property guarantees that the outputs of a hash function look random with respect to correlated inputs, while our desired property is supposed to guarantee that the outputs of a hash function look the same with respect to correlated inputs and random inputs. It seems that our property is weaker than a pseudorandomness property with full security and arbitrary input correlations. We leave the details for future work. Formally, we define the new property as follows.

Definition 5. *A hash function* $H : \mathcal{X} \to \mathcal{Y}$ *is correlated-input indistinguishable if the attacker's advantage* $| \Pr[b' = b] - \frac{1}{2} |$ *is negligible in the attack game, shown in Fig. 14. In the game,* $\mathbb{D}_0$ *is the joint distributions of L (dependent) λ-source random variables over $\mathcal{X}$, while $\mathbb{D}_1$ defines L independent random variables with uniform distribution over $\mathcal{X}$. It is required that, for $(\boldsymbol{x}_0^{(1)}, \boldsymbol{x}_0^{(2)}, \cdots, \boldsymbol{x}_0^{(L)}) \overset{\mathbb{D}_0}{\leftarrow} \mathcal{X}^L$ and any $1 \le i \ne j \le L$, the probability $\Pr[\boldsymbol{x}_0^{(i)} = \boldsymbol{x}_0^{(j)}]$ is negligible. L can be a polynomial of the security parameter.*

---

1. $(\mathbb{D}_0, \mathbb{D}_1, L, state) \overset{\$}{\leftarrow} \mathcal{A}(H)$
2. $b \overset{\$}{\leftarrow} \{0,1\}$, $\boldsymbol{x}_b \overset{\mathbb{D}_b}{\leftarrow} \mathcal{X}^L$, $\boldsymbol{y}_b = (H(\boldsymbol{x}_b^{(1)}), \cdots, H(\boldsymbol{x}_b^{(L)}))$
3. $b' \overset{\$}{\leftarrow} \mathcal{A}(state, \boldsymbol{y}_b)$

Fig. 14. Correlated-Input Indistinguishability

Due to the different security objectives, it is easy to verify that the construction from [21] is not correlated-input indistinguishable. Bellare, Hoang, and Keelveedhi [6] introduced the concept of Universal Computational Extractors(UCEs) and showed how to use this concept to construct selective correlated-input secure hash functions according to the definitions from [21]. However, they noted that UCEs do not guarantee adaptive/full security. It seems difficult to construct correlated-input indistinguishable hash functions based on UCEs. Unseeded deterministic extractors also seem to be a related primitive, but the existing security models do not take into account correlated inputs.

On the positive side, we can instantiate correlated-input indistinguishable hash function based on deterministic encryption (DE) schemes, a primitive proposed in [5]. More specifically, the instantiation should be based on adaptively secure DE schemes, e.g. that from [29]. In a nutshell, an adaptively secure DE scheme guarantees that an attacker cannot distinguish the ciphertexts of arbitrarily correlated plaintexts and random plaintexts. The instantiation has two steps: (1) given an input from domain $\mathcal{X}$, encrypt it with the DE scheme to obtain a ciphertext; (2) hash the ciphertext with a collision-resistant hash function to get an output for the domain $\mathcal{Y}$.

6.2   Example msk-Forward-Secure IBE Construction

With a correlated-input indistinguishable hash function H, we describe an extended variant for the Boyen-Waters scheme [13] in Fig. 15. The extension is from two aspects: (1) pre-processing identities with H; (2) employ composite-order bilinear groups.

Setup(λ)	Extract(Msk, id)
$\Gamma = (p, q, \mathbb{G}, \mathbb{G}_T, \hat{e}, g_p, g_q) = \mathcal{G}_\mathcal{C}(\lambda)$	$r_1, r_2 \xleftarrow{\$} \mathbb{Z}_n,$
$\Gamma^* = (n = pq, \mathbb{G}, \mathbb{G}_T, \hat{e}, g_p, g_q)$	$x_0, x_1, x_2, x_3, x_4 \xleftarrow{\$} \mathbb{G}_q$
$x, t_1, t_2, t_3, t_4 \xleftarrow{\$} \mathbb{Z}_n$	$d_0 = x_0 \cdot g_p^{r_1 t_1 t_2 + r_2 t_3 t_4}$
$\Omega = \hat{e}(g_p, g_p)^{x t_1 t_2}, g_0, g_1 \xleftarrow{\$} \mathbb{G}_p$	$d_1 = x_1 \cdot g_p^{-x t_2} \cdot (g_0 g_1^{\mathsf{H}(id)})^{-r_1 t_2}$
$v_1 = g_p^{t_1}, v_2 = g_p^{t_2}, v_3 = g_p^{t_3}, v_4 = g_p^{t_4}$	$d_2 = x_2 \cdot g_p^{-x t_1} \cdot (g_0 g_1^{\mathsf{H}(id)})^{-r_1 t_1}$
$\mathcal{M} = \mathbb{G}_T, \mathcal{I} = \mathbb{Z}_n, \mathsf{H} : \mathcal{I} \to \mathcal{I}$	$d_3 = x_3 \cdot (g_0 g_1^{\mathsf{H}(id)})^{-r_2 t_4}$
$Msk = (x, t_1, t_2, t_3, t_4)$	$d_4 = x_4 \cdot (g_0 g_1^{\mathsf{H}(id)})^{-r_2 t_3}$
$params = (\Gamma^*, g_0, g_1, \Omega, v_1, v_2, v_3, v_4, \mathcal{M}, \mathcal{I}, \mathsf{H})$	$sk_{id} = (d_0, d_1, d_2, d_3, d_4)$
Enc(m, id)	Dec(C, sk_{id})
$s, s_1, s_2 \xleftarrow{\$} \mathbb{Z}_n$	$e_0 = \hat{e}(c_0, d_0), e_1 = \hat{e}(c_1, d_1)$
$\hat{c} = \Omega^s m, c_0 = (g_0 g_1^{\mathsf{H}(id)})^s, c_1 = v_1^{s - s_1}$	$e_2 = \hat{e}(c_2, d_2), e_3 = \hat{e}(c_3, d_3)$
$c_2 = v_2^{s_1}, c_3 = v_3^{s - s_2}, c_4 = v_4^{s_2}$	$e_4 = \hat{e}(c_4, d_4)$
$C = (\hat{c}, c_0, c_1, c_2, c_3, c_4)$	$m = \hat{c} \cdot e_0 \cdot e_1 \cdot e_2 \cdot e_3 \cdot e_4$

Fig. 15. Extended Boyen-Waters Scheme

If H is correlated-input indistinguishable and collision-resistant, it is straightforward to verify that the extended scheme is IND-CPA, anonymous, and achieves msk-forward-secure function privacy. Next, we prove the scheme also achieves msk-forward-secure key unlinkability.

Theorem 3. *The extended Boyen-Waters scheme achieves* msk-*forward-secure key unlinkability based on the correlated Composite-DDH-II assumption, given that* H *is correlated-input indistinguishable and collision-resistant.*

7 Related Work

In the seminal definition [8], PEKS only supports equality testing of keywords. To support more types of search queries, a number of extensions have been proposed. Among them, [12,23,24] support search queries with conjunctive keywords, [12, 31] support subset and range queries, and [25] supports disjunctions, polynomial equations, and inner products. In contrast to the large number of follow-up works to extend the PEKS functionality, very little has been done to investigate its full security capabilities and the only few we know are [4,9,10,28,30], where [30] only aims at a designated tester.

Forward secrecy is a well-known property for key agreement protocols [19,22], and it ensures that a session key will remain secure even if one of the long-term secret keys is compromised in the future. This concept has also been applied to other primitives, such as signature schemes [3,7] and hierarchical identity based encryption (HIBE) schemes [16,27,33]. It is worth noting that the adapted forward secrecy notions in [3,7,16,27,33] focus on the key evolution problem. In the case of HIBE schemes [16,27,33], the focus is on the secret keys for certain identities instead of the master secret key. The forward security properties, introduced in Section 4, stem from [19,22], and differs from that [16,27,33] in two aspects: the attacker has access to the master secret key and no key evolution is considered. For identity-based cryptography, how to avoid the key escrow problem has been an interesting question, see e.g. [2,20]. Among all, a particularly interesting security notion is the anonymous ciphertext indistinguishability (ACI) property from [17]. The ACI property guarantees that an attacker cannot determine the public key (or, identity) behind a ciphertext even with the knowledge of the master secret key. It is related to the enhanced function privacy property from [9], but they are not comparable.

8   Concluding Remarks

In this paper, we have defined some forward security properties for PEKS and IBE respectively. We have also analyzed several existing PEKS and IBE schemes, and extended the Boyen-Waters anonymous IBE scheme by using a new building block (i.e. correlated-input indistinguishable hash function). Our analysis shows that it is relatively easy to achieve our properties against RO-non-adaptive attackers while it is quite hard to construct secure schemes against adaptive attackers (in particular in the standard model). Our work has motivated many interesting open problems. As to the concept of correlated-input indistinguishable hash function, we only know one method to instantiate it. It is a very interesting task to construct correlated-input indistinguishable hash functions in other ways, e.g. taking into account recent advances in constructing correlated-input secure hash functions [14]. Moreover, it is also useful to investigate the relationships between our definition and those in [21]. Both PEKS and IBE are special types of functional encryption [11]. Hence, the concept of forward security is also valuable for other functional encryption schemes, including other PEKS variants and searchable encryption schemes in the symmetric-key setting.

Acknowledgments. The author is partially supported by a CORE grant from the National Research Fund, Luxembourg. The author appreciates the valuable comments from the ACISP reviewers and will address them in more details in the report [32].

References

1. Abdalla, M., Bellare, M., Catalano, D., Kiltz, E., Kohno, T., Lange, T., Malone-Lee, J., Neven, G., Paillier, P., Shi, H.: Searchable encryption revisited: Consistency properties, relation to anonymous ibe, and extensions. J. Cryptol. **21**(3), 350–391 (2008)
2. Al-Riyami, S.S., Paterson, K.G.: Certificateless public key cryptography. In: Laih, C.-S. (ed.) ASIACRYPT 2003. LNCS, vol. 2894, pp. 452–473. Springer, Heidelberg (2003)
3. Anderson, R.: Two remarks on public key cryptology. Technical Report UCAM-CL-TR-549. Cambridge University (1997)
4. Arriaga, A., Tang, Q., Ryan, P.: Trapdoor privacy in asymmetric searchable encryption schemes. In: Pointcheval, D., Vergnaud, D. (eds.) AFRICACRYPT. LNCS, vol. 8469, pp. 31–50. Springer, Heidelberg (2014)

5. Bellare, M., Boldyreva, A., O'Neill, A.: Deterministic and efficiently searchable encryption. In: Menezes, A. (ed.) CRYPTO 2007. LNCS, vol. 4622, pp. 535–552. Springer, Heidelberg (2007)
6. Bellare, M., Hoang, V.T., Keelveedhi, S.: Instantiating random oracles via UCEs. In: Canetti, R., Garay, J.A. (eds.) CRYPTO 2013, Part II. LNCS, vol. 8043, pp. 398–415. Springer, Heidelberg (2013)
7. Bellare, M., Miner, S.K.: A forward-secure digital signature scheme. In: Wiener, M. (ed.) CRYPTO 1999. LNCS, vol. 1666, pp. 431–448. Springer, Heidelberg (1999)
8. Boneh, D., Di Crescenzo, G., Ostrovsky, R., Persiano, G.: Public key encryption with keyword search. In: Cachin, C., Camenisch, J.L. (eds.) EUROCRYPT 2004. LNCS, vol. 3027, pp. 506–522. Springer, Heidelberg (2004)
9. Boneh, D., Raghunathan, A., Segev, G.: Function-private identity-based encryption: hiding the function in functional encryption. In: Canetti, R., Garay, J.A. (eds.) CRYPTO 2013, Part II. LNCS, vol. 8043, pp. 461–478. Springer, Heidelberg (2013)
10. Boneh, D., Raghunathan, A., Segev, G.: Function-private identity-based encryption: Hiding the function in functional encryption (2013). http://eprint.iacr.org/2013/283.pdf
11. Boneh, D., Sahai, A., Waters, B.: Functional encryption: definitions and challenges. In: Ishai, Y. (ed.) TCC 2011. LNCS, vol. 6597, pp. 253–273. Springer, Heidelberg (2011)
12. Boneh, D., Waters, B.: Conjunctive, subset, and range queries on encrypted data. In: Vadhan, S.P. (ed.) TCC 2007. LNCS, vol. 4392, pp. 535–554. Springer, Heidelberg (2007)
13. Boyen, X., Waters, B.: Anonymous hierarchical identity-based encryption (without random oracles). In: Dwork, C. (ed.) CRYPTO 2006. LNCS, vol. 4117, pp. 290–307. Springer, Heidelberg (2006)
14. Brzuska, C., Mittelbach, A.: Using indistinguishability obfuscation via UCEs. In: Sarkar, P., Iwata, T. (eds.) ASIACRYPT 2014, Part II. LNCS, vol. 8874, pp. 122–141. Springer, Heidelberg (2014)
15. Canetti, R.: Towards realizing random oracles: hash functions that hide all partial information. In: Kaliski Jr., B.S. (ed.) CRYPTO 1997. LNCS, vol. 1294, pp. 455–469. Springer, Heidelberg (1997)
16. Canetti, R., Halevi, S., Katz, J.: A forward-secure public-key encryption scheme. In: Biham, E. (ed.) Advances in Cryptology - EUROCRYPT 2003. LNCS, vol. 2656, pp. 255–271. Springer, Heidelberg (2003)
17. Chow, S.S.M.: Removing escrow from identity-based encryption. In: Jarecki, S., Tsudik, G. (eds.) PKC 2009. LNCS, vol. 5443, pp. 256–276. Springer, Heidelberg (2009)
18. Damgård, I., Hazay, C., Zottarel, A.: Short paper on the generic hardness of DDH-II, May, 2014. http://cs.au.dk/angela/Hardness.pdf
19. Diffie, W., Oorschot, P.C., Wiener, M.J.: Authentication and authenticated key exchanges. Designs, Codes and Cryptography **2**(2), 107–125 (1992)
20. Goyal, V.: Reducing trust in the PKG in identity based cryptosystems. In: Menezes, A. (ed.) CRYPTO 2007. LNCS, vol. 4622, pp. 430–447. Springer, Heidelberg (2007)
21. Goyal, V., O'Neill, A., Rao, V.: Correlated-input secure hash functions. In: Ishai, Y. (ed.) TCC 2011. LNCS, vol. 6597, pp. 182–200. Springer, Heidelberg (2011)
22. Günther, C.G.: An Identity-based key-exchange protocol. In: Quisquater, J.-J., Vandewalle, J. (eds.) EUROCRYPT 1989. LNCS, vol. 434, pp. 29–37. Springer, Heidelberg (1990)

23. Hwang, Y.-H., Lee, P.J.: Public key encryption with conjunctive keyword search and its extension to a multi-user system. In: Takagi, T., Okamoto, T., Okamoto, E., Okamoto, T. (eds.) Pairing 2007. LNCS, vol. 4575, pp. 2–22. Springer, Heidelberg (2007)

24. Iovino, V., Persiano, G.: Hidden-vector encryption with groups of prime order. In: Galbraith, S.D., Paterson, K.G. (eds.) Pairing 2008. LNCS, vol. 5209, pp. 75–88. Springer, Heidelberg (2008)

25. Katz, J., Sahai, A., Waters, B.: Predicate encryption supporting disjunctions, polynomial equations, and inner products. In: Smart, N.P. (ed.) EUROCRYPT 2008. LNCS, vol. 4965, pp. 146–162. Springer, Heidelberg (2008)

26. Lewko, A., Waters, B.: New techniques for dual system encryption and fully secure HIBE with short ciphertexts. In: Micciancio, D. (ed.) TCC 2010. LNCS, vol. 5978, pp. 455–479. Springer, Heidelberg (2010)

27. González Nieto, J.M., Manulis, M., Sun, D.: Forward-secure hierarchical predicate encryption. In: Abdalla, M., Lange, T. (eds.) Pairing 2012. LNCS, vol. 7708, pp. 83–101. Springer, Heidelberg (2013)

28. Nishioka, M.: Perfect keyword privacy in PEKS systems. In: Takagi, T., Wang, G., Qin, Z., Jiang, S., Yu, Y. (eds.) ProvSec 2012. LNCS, vol. 7496, pp. 175–192. Springer, Heidelberg (2012)

29. Raghunathan, A., Segev, G., Vadhan, S.: Deterministic public-key encryption for adaptively chosen plaintext distributions. In: Johansson, T., Nguyen, P.Q. (eds.) EUROCRYPT 2013. LNCS, vol. 7881, pp. 93–110. Springer, Heidelberg (2013)

30. Rhee, H.S., Park, J.H., Susilo, W., Lee, D.H.: Trapdoor security in a searchable public-key encryption scheme with a designated tester. J. Syst. Softw. **83**(5), 763–771 (2010)

31. Shi, E., Bethencourt, J., Chan, T-H.H., Song, D., Perrig, A.: Multi-dimensional range query over encrypted data. In: Proceedings of the 2007 IEEE Symposium on Security and Privacy, pp. 350–364. IEEE Computer Society (2007)

32. Tang, Q.: Towards forward security properties for peks and ibe. Cryptology ePrint Archive: Report 2014/560 (2014)

33. Yao, D., Fazio, N., Dodis, Y., Lysyanskaya, A.: Id-based encryption for complex hierarchies with applications to forward security and broadcast encryption. In: Atluri, V., Pfitzmann, B., McDaniel, P.D. (eds.) Proceedings of the 11th ACM Conference on Computer and Communications Security, CCS 2004, pp. 354–363. ACM (2004)

IBE Under k-LIN with Shorter Ciphertexts and Private Keys

Kaoru Kurosawa[1] and Le Trieu Phong[2](✉)

[1] Ibaraki University, Ibaraki, Japan
kurosawa@mx.ibaraki.ac.jp
[2] NICT, Tokyo, Japan
phong@nict.go.jp

Abstract. Many identity-based encryption schemes under the k-LIN assumption contain $2k + 1$ group elements in the ciphertext overhead and private keys. In this paper,

- We push the limit further by constructing an IBE scheme under the k-LIN assumption with $2k$ group elements in the ciphertext overhead and private keys.
- Our technique additionally expands to the scheme of Boneh, Raghunathan, and Segev (CRYPTO 2013) to yield more efficient function-private IBE under the DLIN assumption.

The shortened size inherently leads to less exponentiations and pairings in encryption and decryption, and hence yielding schemes with better computational efficiency under k-LIN.

Keywords: Identity-based encryption · k-LIN assumption · Function privacy

1 Introduction

1.1 Background

The k-LIN assumption is a gold mine for cryptographers. It is well known that when $k = 2$, the assumption (aka, decision linear) generically holds even in bilinear groups, enabling the usage of bi-linear maps in cryptographic constructions. In general, the k-LIN assumption generically holds even when k-linear maps exist.

We are interested in the use of k-LIN in identity-based encryption. In the literature, the constructions using dual systems [12] in [7,10] need at least $2k + 2$ group elements in the ciphertext overhead and private keys when in prime-order groups. The construction in [9], not involving dual systems, also requires $2k + 2$ group elements. Recently, the work of [3] improves that limit to $2k + 1$.

Function-private IBE (FP-IBE) [5] considers an additional tier of security demanding the private key of each identity leaks no information on that identity (to the extent possible). Under the 2-LIN assumption and in the standard model, the work [5] builds a FP-IBE with 6 (namely $2k + 2$ with $k = 2$) group elements in the ciphertext overhead and private keys.

© Springer International Publishing Switzerland 2015
E. Foo and D. Stebila (Eds.): ACISP 2015, LNCS 9144, pp. 145–159, 2015.
DOI: 10.1007/978-3-319-19962-7_9

1.2   Our Contributions

In this paper, we show that the current barrier $2k + 1$ set by [3] can be reduced further. Specifically, we propose both IBE and FP-IBE schemes which have $2k$ group elements in the ciphertext overhead and private keys, and $2k$ pairings in decryption, under the k-LIN assumption in the standard model. Concrete comparisons with previous works are postponed in Table 1 and Table 3.

Technical Outline. We start from the 2-LIN-based IBE scheme of [9], which has the number $2k + 2$ (with $k = 2$). The proof in [9] ensures the scheme has semantic security, and additionally shows it is leakage-resilient. When considering semantic security *only*, we realize that both the scheme and the proof can be changed so that the employing matrices can be of size $k \times k$ instead of $k \times (k+1)$ as in [9]. Specifying a little deeper, we develop a neat way of using the matrix of size $k \times (k + 1)$ from k-LIN instances in which only a $k \times k$ sub-matrix affects the size of ciphertexts and private keys, which is totally different from the proof in [9]. Therefore we obtain schemes under k-LIN with $2k$ group elements in the ciphertext overhead and private keys, and $2k$ pairings in decryption.

   Our technique of proving semantic security extends to the FP-IBE schemes of [5], as it does not interfere with information-theoretic techniques [5] for proving function privacy.

1.3   More Related Works

Bellare et al. [1, AppendixA] presented an IBE scheme under the 2-LIN assumption and the decisional Bilinear Diffie-Hellman assumption (DBDH) with 4 group elements in the ciphertext overhead and private keys. It is unclear and nontrivial to extend this scheme to the k-LIN assumption since DBDH and k-LIN are generically incompatible as soon as $k > 2$ [2].

2   Notations and Assumptions

Denote $a \xleftarrow{\$} A$ as the process of taking element a randomly from a set A. Vectors and matrices will be in boldface. Let $\mathbb{Z}_q^{m \times n}$ be the matrices of size $m \times n$ over $\mathbb{Z}_q$.

Pairing Groups. Let q be a prime. We call $\mathbb{PG} = (\mathbb{G}, \mathbb{G}_T, g, \hat{e} : \mathbb{G} \times \mathbb{G} \to \mathbb{G}_T)$ a pairing group if $\mathbb{G}$ and $\mathbb{G}_T$ are cyclic groups of order q. The element g is a generator of $\mathbb{G}$, and the mapping $\hat{e}$ satisfies the following properties: $\hat{e}(g, g) \neq 1$, and $\hat{e}(g^a, g^b) = \hat{e}(g, g)^{ab}$.

The k-LIN Assumption. For $u_1, \ldots, u_k \xleftarrow{\$} \mathbb{Z}_q$, with following matrix and vectors

$$\mathbf{L}_k = \begin{bmatrix} u_1 & 0 & \cdots & 0 & 1 \\ 0 & u_2 & \cdots & 0 & 1 \\ \vdots & \vdots & & \vdots & \vdots \\ 0 & 0 & \cdots & u_k & 1 \end{bmatrix} \in \mathbb{Z}_q^{k \times (k+1)}, \mathbf{z} \xleftarrow{\$} \mathbb{Z}_q^{1 \times k}, \mathbf{r} \xleftarrow{\$} \mathbb{Z}_q^{1 \times (k+1)} \tag{1}$$

the k-LIN assumption asserts that tuples

$$\left(g^{\mathbf{L}_k}, g^{\mathbf{z} \cdot \mathbf{L}_k}\right) \text{ and } \left(g^{\mathbf{L}_k}, g^{\mathbf{r}}\right)$$

are computationally indistinguishable. More precisely, for any poly-time distinguisher $\mathcal{D}$, the advantage

$$\mathbf{Adv}_{\mathbb{PG}}^{k-\mathrm{LIN}}(\mathcal{D}) =$$
$$\left| \Pr \left[b' = b : \begin{array}{c} \mathbf{L}_k \text{ as in } (1), \mathbf{z} \xleftarrow{\$} \mathbb{Z}_q^{1 \times k} \\ \mathbf{t}_0 = \mathbf{z} \cdot \mathbf{L}_k \in \mathbb{Z}_q^{1 \times (k+1)}, \mathbf{t}_1 \xleftarrow{\$} \mathbb{Z}_q^{1 \times (k+1)} \\ b \xleftarrow{\$} \{0,1\}, b' \leftarrow \mathcal{D}(\mathbb{PG}, g^{\mathbf{L}_k}, g^{\mathbf{t}_b}) \end{array} \right] - \frac{1}{2} \right|$$

is negligible under the k-LIN assumption. When $k = 2$, the 2-LIN assumption becomes the decision linear assumption originated in [4].

A Remark. Escala et al. [8] generalized the k-LIN assumption to matrix Diffie-Hellman assumptions, and examined their relations. In particular, they showed that one can take $u_1 = \cdots = u_k$ in $\mathbf{L}_k$ without affecting the generic hardness of the assumption (newly called symmetric k-cascade assumption, or k-SCasc, in [8]). In this paper context, under the k-SCasc assumption, the size of public parameter in our schemes will be additionally reduced by $k - 1$ elements (compared to the k-LIN-based counterparts described in the following sections).

3   IBE and Security Definitions

IBE. The scheme consists of algorithms (Setup, Extract, Enc, Dec). Setup generates the public parameters and master key (pp, msk). The public parameter pp is the input to all other algorithms. Extract, on input msk and an identity id, returns the private key sk_{id}. Enc, on input id and a message m, returns a ciphertext c, which will be decrypted by an identity holding sk_{id}, yielding m.

Definition 1 (IND-sID-CPA security). *An IBE scheme is IND-sID-CPA secure if any poly-time adversary succeeds in the following game with probability negligibly close to $1/2$.*

1. **Identity selection***: the adversary decides and sends the target identities id^* to the challenger. Then the challenger runs* Setup *to generate (msk, pp), and sends pp to the adversary.*
2. **Query set 1***: the adversary makes extract queries $id \neq id^*$. The challenger returns $sk_{id} \leftarrow$ Extract(msk, id) to the adversary.*
3. **Challenge***: the adversary gives equal-length m_0, m_1 to the challenger, who computes and sends back $c^* \leftarrow$ Enc(id^*, m_b) for $b \xleftarrow{\$} \{0,1\}$.*
4. **Query set 2***: the adversary issues additional extract queries id with $id \neq id^*$ to which the challenger answers in the same manner as above.*
5. **Finish:** *Finally, the adversary outputs a bit $b' \in \{0,1\}$. It succeeds if $b' = b$.*

Table 1. Comparison of some fully secure IBE schemes

Scheme	Size of ciphertext (C, E)	Size $|sk_{id}|$	Main computation cost in Enc	in Dec	Assum.
[10]	$6|\mathbb{G}| + |\mathbb{G}_T|$	$6|\mathbb{G}|$	6 exp$_{\mathbb{G}}$ $+ 1$ exp$_{\mathbb{G}_T}$	6 pr	2-LIN
[9]	$6|\mathbb{G}| + |\mathbb{G}_T|$	$6|\mathbb{G}|$	6 mexp$_{\mathbb{G}}$ $+ 1$ exp$_{\mathbb{G}_T}$	6 pr	2-LIN
[3]	$(2k+1)|\mathbb{G}| + |\mathbb{G}_T|$	$(2k+1)|\mathbb{G}|$	$(2k+1)$ mexp$_{\mathbb{G}}$ $+ 1$ exp$_{\mathbb{G}_T}$	$2k+1$ pr	k-LIN
Sect.4.2	$2k|\mathbb{G}| + |\mathbb{G}_T|$	$2k|\mathbb{G}|$	$2k$ mexp$_{\mathbb{G}}$ $+ 1$ exp$_{\mathbb{G}_T}$	$2k$ pr	k-LIN

The identity space $\mathcal{ID} = \{0,1\}^n$ where $n \geq 1$. Moreover, (m)exp = (multi)exponentiation, pr = pairing. $|\mathbb{G}|$ and $|\mathbb{G}_T|$ denote the number of bits to represent one element in those groups.

Definition 2 (IND-ID-CPA security). *An IBE scheme is IND-ID-CPA secure if any poly-time adversary succeeds in the following game with probability negligibly close to $1/2$.*

1. *Initially, the challenger runs* Setup *to generate (msk, pp), and sends pp to the adversary.*
2. **Query set 1***: the adversary makes extract queries id. The challenger generates and returns $sk_{id} \leftarrow$ Extract(msk, id) to the adversary.*
3. **Identity selection***: the adversary decides and sends the target identity id^* to the challenger. It is required that id^* does not appear in extract queries above.*
4. **Challenge***: the adversary gives m_0, m_1 of equal length to the challenger, who computes and sends back $c^* \leftarrow$ Enc(id^*, m_b) for $b \xleftarrow{\$} \{0,1\}$.*
5. **Query set 2***: the adversary can ask more of extract queries $id \neq id^*$.*
6. **Finish***: Finally the adversary outputs a bit $b' \in \{0,1\}$. It succeeds if $b' = b$.*

4   IBE Schemes Under k-LIN

We begin with a basic IBE scheme to illustrate the main ideas in Sect.4.1. Then we show how to extend the basic one to a fully secure scheme in Sect.4.2, which is used to compare with some previous schemes in Table 1. All schemes have their own key encapsulation mechanism (identity-based KEM) versions in which $|\mathbb{G}_T|$ is not counted in the encapsulation size.

4.1   Basic Scheme: Selectively Secure IBE

Consider the matrix $\mathbf{L}_k$ at (1) and split it as follows

$$\mathbf{L}_k = \begin{bmatrix} u_1 & 0 & \cdots & 0 & 1 \\ 0 & u_2 & \cdots & 0 & 1 \\ \vdots & \vdots & & \vdots & \vdots \\ 0 & 0 & \cdots & u_k & 1 \end{bmatrix} = \left[\underbrace{\mathbf{A}_0}_{k \times k} \middle| \underbrace{\mathbf{D}}_{k \times 1} \right] \in \mathbb{Z}_q^{k \times (k+1)}. \tag{2}$$

The IBE scheme is described below.

– Setup: The public parameters are $pp = (g^{\mathbf{A}_0}, g^{\mathbf{A}_1}, g^{\mathbf{D}})$, where $\mathbf{A}_0 \in \mathbb{Z}_q^{k \times k}$ and $\mathbf{D} \in \mathbb{Z}_q^{k \times 1}$ are as in (2) and $\mathbf{A}_1 \xleftarrow{\$} \mathbb{Z}_q^{k \times k}$.
The master secret key is $msk = (\mathbf{A}_0, \mathbf{A}_1)$. For an identity $id \in \{0, 1\}^*$, let

$$\mathbf{F}(id) = [\mathbf{A}_0 | \mathbf{A}_1 + H(id) \cdot \mathbf{I}_k] \in \mathbb{Z}_q^{k \times 2k}$$

where $H : \{0, 1\}^* \to \mathbb{Z}_q$ is a collision-resistant hash function and $\mathbf{I}_k$ is the $k \times k$ identity matrix.

– Extract: On input id, return $sk_{id} = g^{\mathbf{v}}$ where $\mathbf{v} \in \mathbb{Z}_q^{2k \times 1}$ is a random vector such that

$$\mathbf{F}(id) \cdot \mathbf{v} = \mathbf{D} \pmod{q}.$$

– Enc: On input id and $M \in \mathbb{G}_T$, take $\mathbf{z} \xleftarrow{\$} \mathbb{Z}_q^{1 \times k}$ and compute

$$C = g^{\mathbf{z} \cdot \mathbf{F}(id)}, \ E = \hat{e}(g, g)^{\mathbf{z} \cdot \mathbf{D}} \cdot M.$$

Return (C, E) as the ciphertext.

– Dec: On input $sk_{id} = g^{\mathbf{v}}$ and $C = g^{\mathbf{c}}$, compute $K = \hat{e}(g, g)^{\mathbf{c} \cdot \mathbf{v}}$ and $M = EK^{-1}$, using the bi-linearity of $\hat{e}$, and return M.

Theorem 1. *Under the k-LIN assumption, the IBE scheme is IND-sID-CPA-secure.*

Proof. Let $\mathbf{Game}_0$ be the real attack game against the IBE scheme (recalled in Sect.3). We will make small subsequent changes on the challenge ciphertext depicted in Table 2.

Table 2. Changes of games in the proof of Theorem 1

Game	Challenge ciphertext	Notes
$\mathbf{Game}_0$:	$C^* = g^{\mathbf{z}^* \mathbf{F}(id^*)}, E^* = \hat{e}(g, g)^{\mathbf{z}^* \mathbf{D}} \cdot M_b$	$\mathbf{z}^* \xleftarrow{\$} \mathbb{Z}_q^{1 \times k}$ by the challenger
$\mathbf{Game}_1$:	$C^* = g^{\mathbf{z}^* \mathbf{F}(id^*)}, E^* = \hat{e}(g, g)^{\mathbf{z}^* \mathbf{F}(id^*) \mathbf{v}^*} \cdot M_b$	$\mathbf{F}(id^*) \mathbf{v}^* = \mathbf{D} \in \mathbb{Z}_q^{k \times 1}$
$\mathbf{Game}_2$:	$C^* = g^{\mathbf{z}^* \mathbf{F}(id^*)}, E^* = R \cdot M_b$	$R \xleftarrow{\$} \mathbb{G}_T$ by the challenger

Note that

– The change from $\mathbf{Game}_0$ to $\mathbf{Game}_1$ is syntactical since $\mathbf{F}(id^*)\mathbf{v}^* = \mathbf{D} \in \mathbb{Z}_q^{k \times 1}$.

– The change from $\mathbf{Game}_1$ to $\mathbf{Game}_2$ is under the k-LIN assumption, proved below. Moreover, the challenge bit b is completely hidden in $\mathbf{Game}_2$, so that the theorem follows.

We now show that $\mathbf{Game}_1$ and $\mathbf{Game}_2$ are indistinguishable under the k-LIN assumption, whose formulation using matrices is in Section 2. Given an adversary $\mathcal{A}$ against the IBE scheme, we build $\mathcal{B}$ with input $g^{\mathbf{L}_k}$ ($\mathbf{L}_k$ as in (1)) and $g^{\mathbf{t}}$ telling whether $\mathbf{t}$ is random in $\mathbb{Z}_q^{1 \times (k+1)}$ or $\mathbf{t} = \mathbf{z}^* \cdot \mathbf{L}_k$ for random $\mathbf{z}^* \in \mathbb{Z}_q^{1 \times k}$.

After $\mathcal{A}$ announces the target identity id^*, $\mathcal{B}$ sets up the public parameter $pp = (g^{\mathbf{A}_0}, g^{\mathbf{A}_1}, g^{\mathbf{D}})$ as follows. Firstly, set

$$[\mathbf{A}_0 \mid \mathbf{D}] = \mathbf{L}_k.$$

Then $\mathcal{B}$ chooses $\mathbf{R}^* \xleftarrow{\$} \mathbb{Z}_q^{k \times k}$, and mentally sets

$$\mathbf{A}_1 = \mathbf{A}_0 \mathbf{R}^* - H(id^*)\mathbf{I}_k \tag{3}$$

so that $g^{\mathbf{A}_1}$ can be computed from $g^{\mathbf{A}_0}$. Note that by the above,

$$\mathbf{F}(id) = [\mathbf{A}_0 | \mathbf{A}_0 \mathbf{R}^* + (H(id) - H(id^*)\mathbf{I}_k] \text{ and } \mathbf{F}(id^*) = [\mathbf{A}_0 | \mathbf{A}_0 \mathbf{R}^*] \tag{4}$$

$\mathcal{B}$ then simulates $\mathcal{A}$ as follows.

- On extract query $id \neq id^*$, $\mathcal{B}$ chooses $\mathbf{w} \xleftarrow{\$} \mathbb{Z}_q^{k \times 1}$ and mentally considers following

$$\mathbf{x} = (H(id) - H(id^*))^{-1} \cdot (\mathbf{D} - \mathbf{A}_0 \mathbf{w}) \in \mathbb{Z}_q^{k \times 1}$$

so that $g^{\mathbf{x}}$ is computable from $g^{\mathbf{A}_0}, g^{\mathbf{D}}$. Let

$$\mathbf{v} = \begin{bmatrix} \mathbf{w} - \mathbf{R}^* \mathbf{x} \\ \mathbf{x} \end{bmatrix} \in \mathbb{Z}_q^{2k \times 1} \tag{5}$$

and set $sk_{id} = g^{\mathbf{v}}$, which is the private key for identity id since

$$\begin{aligned}
\mathbf{F}(id) \cdot \mathbf{v} &= [\mathbf{A}_0 | \mathbf{A}_0 \mathbf{R}^* + (H(id) - H(id^*))\mathbf{I}_k] \cdot \begin{bmatrix} \mathbf{w} - \mathbf{R}^* \mathbf{x} \\ \mathbf{x} \end{bmatrix} \\
&= \mathbf{A}_0(\mathbf{w} - \mathbf{R}^* \mathbf{x}) + (\mathbf{A}_0 \mathbf{R}^* + (H(id) - H(id^*))\mathbf{I}_k)\mathbf{x} \\
&= \mathbf{A}_0 \mathbf{w} + (H(id) - H(id^*)) \cdot \mathbf{x} \\
&= \mathbf{D} \in \mathbb{Z}_q^{k \times 1}
\end{aligned}$$

and $\mathbf{v}$ via the freedom of $\mathbf{w}$ comes from a subspace of dimension k, as expected.

- On challenge query (M_0, M_1), take $b \xleftarrow{\$} \{0,1\}$, and return

$$(C^*, E^*) = \left(g^{[(y_1, \ldots, y_k)|(y_1, \ldots, y_k)\mathbf{R}^*]}, \hat{e}(g, g)^{y_{k+1}} M_b \right) \tag{6}$$

where $(y_1, \ldots, y_{k+1}) = \mathbf{t} \in \mathbb{Z}_q^{1 \times (k+1)}$ is from the input of $\mathcal{B}$.

Finally, $\mathcal{A}$ outputs b'. If $b' = b$, $\mathcal{B}$ bets that $\mathbf{t} = \mathbf{z}^* \mathbf{L}_k$. Otherwise, it guesses $\mathbf{t}$ is random. We will show that (C^*, E^*) is the ciphertext in $\mathbf{Game}_1$ if $\mathbf{t} = \mathbf{z}^* \mathbf{L}_k$; while it is in $\mathbf{Game}_2$ if $\mathbf{t}$ is random. First suppose that $\mathbf{t} = \mathbf{z}^* \mathbf{L}_k$, namely $(y_1, \ldots, y_{k+1}) = \mathbf{z}^*[\mathbf{A}_0|\mathbf{D}]$ so that $(y_1, \ldots, y_k) = \mathbf{z}^* \mathbf{A}_0$ and $y_{k+1} = \mathbf{z}^* \mathbf{D}$. Therefore

$$[(y_1, \ldots, y_k)|(y_1, \ldots, y_k)\mathbf{R}^*] = [\mathbf{z}^* \mathbf{A}_0 | \mathbf{z}^* \mathbf{A}_0 \mathbf{R}^*] = \mathbf{z}^*[\mathbf{A}_0 | \mathbf{A}_0 \mathbf{R}^*] = \mathbf{z}^* \mathbf{F}(id^*)$$
$$y_{k+1} = \mathbf{z}^* \mathbf{F}(id^*)\mathbf{v}^*$$

showing that (C^*, E^*) is exactly the ciphertext in $\mathbf{Game}_1$.

Now suppose that $\mathbf{t} = (y_1, \ldots, y_{k+1})$ is random in $\mathbb{Z}_q^{1 \times (k+1)}$ which particularly means that y_{k+1} is random independently of other elements. Set $R = \hat{e}(g, g)^{y_{k+1}}$, then (C^*, E^*) is the ciphertext in $\mathbf{Game}_2$ as claimed.   □

4.2   Fully Secure Scheme Under DLIN

For an identity id expressed as a bit sequence $id = (id_1, \ldots, id_n)$, consider the KEM in the previous section, yet employing the matrix

$$\mathbf{F}(id) = \left[\mathbf{A}_0 \middle| \mathbf{A}_0' + \sum_{i=1}^{n} id_i \mathbf{A}_i \right] \in \mathbb{Z}_q^{k \times 2k} \tag{7}$$

where $\mathbf{A}_0$ is as in (2), and $\mathbf{A}_1, \ldots, \mathbf{A}_n, \mathbf{A}_0' \in \mathbb{Z}_q^{k \times k}$ are random matrices employed as the master secret key. In the public parameters, the matrices are given in the exponents. Namely, for additional $\mathbf{D}$ as in (2),

$$pp = g^{\mathbf{A}_0}, g^{\mathbf{A}_1}, \ldots, g^{\mathbf{A}_n}, g^{\mathbf{A}_0'}, g^{\mathbf{D}}$$
$$msk = \mathbf{A}_0, \mathbf{A}_1, \ldots, \mathbf{A}_n, \mathbf{A}_0', \mathbf{D}.$$

Theorem 2. *Employing the above* $\mathbf{F}(id)$, *the IBE scheme in Section 4.1 is IND-ID-CPA-secure under the DLIN assumption.*

Proof. We consider identical games as in the proof of Theorem 1, in which function $\mathbf{F}(\cdot)$ is replaced by (7). The only difference is in showing that $\mathbf{Game}_1$ and $\mathbf{Game}_2$ are computationally indistinguishable under the k-LIN assumption from the view of the adversary. Concretely, we construct simulator $\mathcal{B}$ against DLIN as follows. $\mathcal{B}$ first sets $J = 4Q$, where Q is the total number of extract queries of the adversary. $\mathcal{B}$ chooses $k \xleftarrow{\$} \{0, \ldots, n\}$ and $h_i \xleftarrow{\$} \mathbb{Z}_J$ for $i = 0, 1, \ldots, n$. $\mathcal{B}$ then constructs the matrices $\mathbf{A}_0'$ and each $\mathbf{A}_i$ (excluding $\mathbf{A}_0$) as

$$\mathbf{A}_0' = \mathbf{A}_0 \mathbf{R}_0 + (q - kJ + h_0) \mathbf{I}_k, \mathbf{A}_i = \mathbf{A}_0 \mathbf{R}_i + h_i \mathbf{I}_k \ (i \geq 1) \tag{8}$$

where $\mathbf{R}_i \leftarrow \mathbb{Z}_q^{k \times k}$, so that

$$\mathbf{F}(id) = \left[\mathbf{A}_0 \middle| \mathbf{A}_0 \left(\mathbf{R}_0 + \sum_{i=1}^{n} id_i \mathbf{R}_i \right) + \left(q - kJ + h_0 + \sum_{i=1}^{n} id_i h_i \right) \mathbf{I}_k \right]$$

Let $\alpha(id) = q - kJ + h_0 + \sum_{i=1}^{n} id_i h_i$, so that $\mathcal{B}$ can succeed if $\alpha(id^*) = 0 \bmod q$, and for all extract query $id \neq id^*$, $\alpha(id) \neq 0 \bmod q$. This probability λ is lower bounded by $\lambda \geq \frac{1}{(n+1)J} \left(1 - 2\frac{Q}{J} \right)$ similarly to [11, Sect.5.2,eq.(1k)], which is recapped in Appendix A for completeness. With probability λ, and id_i^* as the bits of id^*,

$$\mathbf{F}(id^*) = \left[\mathbf{A}_0 \middle| \mathbf{A}_0 \left(\mathbf{R}_0 + \sum_{i=1}^{n} id_i^* \mathbf{R}_i \right) \right],$$

so that the proof proceeds identically with that of Theorem 1 by letting

$$\mathbf{R}^* = \mathbf{R}_0 + \sum_{i=1}^{n} id_i^* \mathbf{R}_i.$$

Moreover, algorithms $\mathcal{B}$ works as follows.

- The simulation of extract queries id: here we expect $\alpha(id) \neq 0$, and the corresponding $\mathbf{v}$ is set to

$$\mathbf{v} = \begin{bmatrix} \mathbf{w} - (\mathbf{R}_0 + \sum_{i=1}^{n} id_i \mathbf{R}_i)\mathbf{x} \\ \mathbf{x} \end{bmatrix}$$

in which $\mathbf{w} \in \mathbb{Z}_q^{k \times 1}$ is random and $\mathbf{x} = \alpha(id)^{-1} \cdot (\mathbf{D} - \mathbf{A}_0 \mathbf{w}) \in \mathbb{Z}_q^{k \times 1}$. Thus $sk_{id} = g^{\mathbf{v}}$ can be computed and returned to the IBE's adversary $\mathcal{A}$.

- On challenge query id^* and (M_0, M_1), let $\mathbf{y} = (y_1, y_2)$ and $b \xleftarrow{\$} \{0, 1\}$, and return

$$(C^*, E^*) = \left(g^{[(y_1, \ldots, y_k) | (y_1, \ldots, y_k)\mathbf{R}^*]}, \hat{e}(g, g)^{y_{k+1}} M_b \right)$$

where $(y_1, \ldots, y_{k+1}) = \mathbf{t} \in \mathbb{Z}_q^{1 \times (k+1)}$ is from the k-LIN instance.   □

5   Function-Private IBE Schemes

Function-private IBE provides an additional layer of security for IBE, requiring that the private key sk_{id} unconditionally leaks no information on id. Boneh, Raghunathan and Segev [5] proposed the concept and, among other constructions, provided (selective and full) 2-LIN-based IBE schemes having function privacy. Below we revisit their schemes and show that they can be made more efficient using our technique of exploiting the k-LIN assumption when $k = 2$. Concrete comparisons are provided in Table 3.

Table 3. Comparison of 2-LIN-based, *function-private* IBE schemes

Scheme	Ciphertext	Private key sk_{id}	Public parameter	Main computation cost in Enc	Dec	Security
[5, Sect.5.1]	$3(\ell+1)|\mathbb{G}| + |\mathbb{G}_T|$	$6|\mathbb{G}| + \ell|\mathbb{Z}_q|$	$6\ell|\mathbb{G}| + 15|\mathbb{G}|$	$3(\ell+1)$ mexp$_\mathbb{G}$ + 1 exp$_{\mathbb{G}_T}$	1 mexp$_\mathbb{G}$ + 6 pr	selective
Ours	$2(\ell+1)|\mathbb{G}| + |\mathbb{G}_T|$	$4|\mathbb{G}| + \ell|\mathbb{Z}_q|$	$4\ell|\mathbb{G}| + 3|\mathbb{G}|$	$2(\ell+1)$ mexp$_\mathbb{G}$ + 1 exp$_{\mathbb{G}_T}$	1 mexp$_\mathbb{G}$ + 4 pr	selective
[5, Sect.5.3]	$6|\mathbb{G}| + |\mathbb{G}_T|$	$5|\mathbb{G}| + 6|\mathbb{Z}_q|$	$6n|\mathbb{G}| + 15|\mathbb{G}|$	6 mexp$_\mathbb{G}$ + 1 exp$_{\mathbb{G}_T}$	2 mexp$_\mathbb{G}$ + 5 pr	full
Ours	$4|\mathbb{G}| + |\mathbb{G}_T|$	$4|\mathbb{G}| + 4|\mathbb{Z}_q|$	$4n|\mathbb{G}| + 7|\mathbb{G}|$	4 mexp$_\mathbb{G}$ + 1 exp$_{\mathbb{G}_T}$	2 mexp$_\mathbb{G}$ + 4 pr	full

In the selective schemes, the identity space $\mathcal{ID} = \mathbb{Z}_q^\ell$ where $\ell \geq 2$ (to prove function privacy), while in the full schemes $\mathcal{ID} = \{0, 1\}^n$ where $n \geq 1$. Moreover, (m)exp = (multi)exponentiation, pr = pairing.

5.1   Our Function-Private, Selectively Secure IBE

– Setup: Fix $\ell \geq 2$. The public parameters are

$$pp = (g^{\mathbf{A}_0}, g^{\mathbf{D}}, g^{\mathbf{A}_1}, \ldots, g^{\mathbf{A}_\ell})$$

where the matrices are as follows

$$\mathbf{A}_0 = \begin{bmatrix} u & 0 \\ 0 & v \end{bmatrix} \in \mathbb{Z}_q^{2 \times 2}, \mathbf{D} = \begin{bmatrix} 1 \\ 1 \end{bmatrix} \in \mathbb{Z}_q^{2 \times 1}, \text{ and } \mathbf{A}_1, \ldots, \mathbf{A}_\ell \xleftarrow{\$} \mathbb{Z}_q^{2 \times 2}$$

where $u, v \xleftarrow{\$} \mathbb{Z}_q$.

The master secret key is $msk = (\mathbf{A}_0, \mathbf{A}_1, \ldots, \mathbf{A}_\ell)$. For an identity $id = (id_1, \ldots, id_\ell) \in \mathbb{Z}_q^\ell$, let

$$\mathbf{F}(id, s_1, \ldots, s_\ell) = \left[\mathbf{A}_0 \middle| \sum_{i=1}^{\ell} s_i \mathbf{A}_i + \sum_{i=1}^{\ell} s_i id_i \cdot \mathbf{I}_2 \right] \in \mathbb{Z}_q^{2 \times 4}$$

- Extract: on input $id \in \mathbb{Z}_q^\ell$, take $s_1, \ldots, s_\ell \xleftarrow{\$} \mathbb{Z}_q$, and return $sk_{id} = (s_1, \ldots, s_\ell, g^{\mathbf{v}})$ where $\mathbf{v} \in \mathbb{Z}_q^{4 \times 1}$ is a random vector such that

$$\mathbf{F}(id, s_1, \ldots, s_\ell) \cdot \mathbf{v} = \mathbf{D} \pmod{q}.$$

- Enc: on input id and $M \in \mathbb{G}_T$, take $\mathbf{z} \xleftarrow{\$} \mathbb{Z}_q^{1 \times 2}$ and compute

$$C = g^{\mathbf{z} \cdot [\mathbf{A}_0 | \mathbf{A}_1 + id_1 \mathbf{I}_2 | \cdots | \mathbf{A}_\ell + id_\ell \mathbf{I}_2]}, \quad E = \hat{e}(g, g)^{\mathbf{z} \cdot \mathbf{D}} \cdot M.$$

Return (C, E) as the ciphertext.
- Dec: On input $sk_{id} = (s_1, \ldots, s_\ell, g^{\mathbf{v}})$ and $C = g^{[\mathbf{c}_0 | \mathbf{c}_1 | \cdots | \mathbf{c}_\ell]}$, compute $g^{\mathbf{c}} = g^{[\mathbf{c}_0 | s_1 \mathbf{c}_1 + \cdots + s_\ell \mathbf{c}_\ell]}$ and $K = \hat{e}(g, g)^{\mathbf{c} \cdot \mathbf{v}}$ using the bi-linearity of $\hat{e}$, and return $M = EK^{-1}$.

Correctness. Note that if $\mathbf{c}_0 = \mathbf{z}\mathbf{A}_0$ and $\mathbf{c}_i = \mathbf{z}[\mathbf{A}_i + id_i \mathbf{I}_2]$ then $\mathbf{c} = \mathbf{z}[\mathbf{A}_0 | \sum_{i=1}^{\ell} s_i \mathbf{A}_i + \sum_{i=1}^{\ell} s_i id_i \cdot \mathbf{I}_2] = \mathbf{z}\mathbf{F}(id, s_1, \ldots, s_\ell)$, and the completeness follows.

Intuition on Function Privacy. Recall that we need to show that sk_{id} leaks no information on id. The bottom line here is that id needs to be unpredictable, as discussed in [5]. Indeed, if an adversary can predict that $id \in S$ for a small set S of identities, then it can fully recover id as follows: for a fix message m, it computes $CT = \mathsf{Enc}(id', m)$ for all $id' \in S$ and then uses sk_{id} for decryption; if the decrypted message is m, it decides that $id' = id$.

Now as id is assumed unpredictable, it has sufficient entropy. The function $\mathbf{F}(id, s_1, \ldots, s_\ell)$ contains $\mathsf{Ext}_{s_1 \ldots, s_\ell}(id_1, \ldots, id_\ell) = \sum_{i=1}^{\ell} s_i id_i$ which is a randomness extractor, so the output is statistically close to uniform when $id = (id_1, \ldots, id_\ell)$ has enough entropy by the left-over-hash lemma. As $(s_1, \ldots, s_\ell)$ is independent of id, and $\mathbf{F}(id, s_1, \ldots, s_\ell)$ contains almost no information on the identity, so is the extracted secret sk_{id}. The formal proof will be identical to [5, Fullversion,Lemma5.5].

Intuition on IND-sID-CPA Security. Mimicking (3), for challenge identity $id^* = (id_1, \ldots, id_\ell) \in \mathbb{Z}_q^\ell$, set

$$\mathbf{A}_i = \mathbf{A}_0 \mathbf{R}_i^* - id_i^* \mathbf{I}_2 \tag{9}$$

where $\mathbf{R}_i^* \xleftarrow{\$} \mathbb{Z}_q^{2 \times 2}, 1 \leq i \leq \ell$, so that

$$\mathbf{F}(id, s_1, \ldots, s_\ell) = \left[\mathbf{A}_0 \middle| \sum_{i=1}^{\ell} s_i (\mathbf{A}_0 \mathbf{R}_i^* - id_i^* \mathbf{I}_2) + \sum_{i=1}^{\ell} s_i id_i \cdot \mathbf{I}_2 \right]$$

$$= \left[\mathbf{A}_0 \middle| \mathbf{A}_0 \sum_{i=1}^{\ell} s_i \mathbf{R}_i^* + \sum_{i=1}^{\ell} s_i (id_i - id_i^*) \cdot \mathbf{I}_2 \right]$$

which is similar to (4) when putting $\mathbf{R} = \sum_{i=1}^{\ell} s_i \mathbf{R}_i^*$, which enables the simulation of extract queries $id \neq id^*$ as in (5). Moreover,

$$C^* = g^{\mathbf{z}^* \cdot [\mathbf{A}_0 | \mathbf{A}_1 + id_1^* \mathbf{I}_2 | \cdots | \mathbf{A}_\ell + id_\ell^* \mathbf{I}_2]} = g^{\mathbf{z}^* \cdot [\mathbf{A}_0 | \mathbf{A}_0 \mathbf{R}_1^* | \cdots | \mathbf{A}_0 \mathbf{R}_\ell^*]}$$

so that the challenge ciphertext can be simulated as in (6).

Theorem 3. *The above scheme is IND-sID-CPA-secure under the 2-LIN assumption.*

Proof. Game chain is in Table 4 in which the first change is notational. We now

Table 4. Changes of games in the proof of Theorem 3

Game	Challenge ciphertext	Notes
Game$_0$: $C^* = g^{\mathbf{z}^* \cdot [\mathbf{A}_0 | \mathbf{A}_1 + id_1^* \mathbf{I}_2 | \cdots | \mathbf{A}_n + id_\ell^* \mathbf{I}_2]}$ $E^* = \hat{e}(g,g)^{\mathbf{z}^* \mathbf{D}} \cdot M_b$	$\mathbf{z}^* \xleftarrow{\$} \mathbb{Z}_q^{1 \times 2}$ by the challenger
Game$_1$: $C^* = g^{[\mathbf{c}_0^* | \mathbf{c}_1^* | \cdots | \mathbf{c}_\ell^*]}$ $E^* = \hat{e}(g,g)^{[\mathbf{c}_0^* | s_1^* \mathbf{c}_1^* + \cdots + s_\ell^* \mathbf{c}_\ell^*]\mathbf{v}^*} \cdot M_b$	$\mathbf{c}_0^* = \mathbf{z}^* \mathbf{A}_0$ $\mathbf{c}_i^* = \mathbf{z}^*(\mathbf{A}_i + id_i^* \mathbf{I}_2)$ for $1 \le i \le \ell$ $[\mathbf{c}_0^* | s_1^* \mathbf{c}_1^* + \cdots + s_\ell^* \mathbf{c}_\ell^*]\mathbf{v}^* = \mathbf{z}^* \mathbf{D}$
Game$_2$: $C^* = g^{[\mathbf{c}_0^* | \mathbf{c}_1^* | \cdots | \mathbf{c}_\ell^*]}, E^* = R \cdot M_b$	$R \xleftarrow{\$} \mathbb{G}_T$ by the challenger

show that **Game$_1$** and **Game$_2$** are indistinguishable under the DLIN assumption. Given an adversary $\mathcal{A}$ against the IBE scheme, we build $\mathcal{B}$ with input $g^{\mathbf{L}_2}$ ($\mathbf{L}_2$ as in (1) taking $k = 2$) and $g^{\mathbf{t}}$ telling whether $\mathbf{t}$ is random in $\mathbb{Z}_q^{1 \times 3}$ or $\mathbf{t} = \mathbf{z}^* \cdot \mathbf{L}_2$ for random $\mathbf{z}^* \in \mathbb{Z}_q^{1 \times 2}$. After $\mathcal{A}$ announces the target identities id_0^* and id_1^*, $\mathcal{B}$ sets up the public parameter $pp = (g^{\mathbf{A}_0}, g^{\mathbf{D}}, g^{\mathbf{A}_1}, \ldots, g^{\mathbf{A}_\ell})$ using $\mathbf{A}_0 = \mathbf{L}_2$ and $\mathbf{A}_i$ as in (9). The simulation of $\mathcal{B}$ is as follows.

- On extract query $id \neq id^*$, $\mathcal{B}$ takes $s_1, \ldots, s_\ell \xleftarrow{\$} \mathbb{Z}_q$ and random $\mathbf{w} \in \mathbb{Z}_q^{2 \times 1}$ and mentally considers the following

$$\mathbf{x} = \delta^{-1} \cdot (\mathbf{D} - \mathbf{A}_0 \mathbf{w}) \in \mathbb{Z}_q^{2 \times 1}, \mathbf{v} = \begin{bmatrix} \mathbf{w} - \mathbf{R}\mathbf{x} \\ \mathbf{x} \end{bmatrix} \in \mathbb{Z}_q^{4 \times 1}$$

with $\delta = \sum_{i=1}^{\ell} s_i(id_i - id_i^*)$ where id_i^* is the i-th component of $id^* \in \mathbb{Z}_q^\ell$ and $\mathbf{R} = \sum_{i=1}^{\ell} s_i \mathbf{R}_i^*$. Then $sk_{id} = (s_1, \ldots, s_\ell, g^{\mathbf{v}})$ is returned to $\mathcal{A}$. Note δ^{-1} exists since $\delta \neq 0 \pmod{q}$ with overwhelming $1 - 1/q$ probability.
- The challenge ciphertext is

$$(C^*, E^*) = \left(g^{[(y_1, y_2) | (y_1, y_2) \mathbf{R}_1^* | \cdots | (y_1, y_2) \mathbf{R}_\ell^*]}, \hat{e}(g,g)^{y_3} \cdot M_b \right)$$

where $\mathcal{B}$'s input $\mathbf{t} = (y_1, y_2, y_3) \in \mathbb{Z}_q^{1 \times 3}$.

If $\mathbf{t} = \mathbf{z}^* \cdot \mathbf{L}_2$, namely $(\mathbf{y}, y_3) = \mathbf{z}^*[\mathbf{A}_0|\mathbf{D}]$, or equivalently $\mathbf{y} = \mathbf{z}^*\mathbf{A}_0$ and $y_3 = \mathbf{z}^*\mathbf{D}$, we have

$$[\mathbf{y}|\mathbf{y}\mathbf{R}_1^*|\cdots|\mathbf{y}\mathbf{R}_\ell^*] = \mathbf{z}^* \cdot [\mathbf{A}_0|\mathbf{A}_0\mathbf{R}_1^*|\cdots|\mathbf{A}_0\mathbf{R}_\ell^*]$$
$$= \mathbf{z}^* \cdot [\mathbf{A}_0|\mathbf{A}_1 + id_1^*\mathbf{I}_2|\cdots|\mathbf{A}_\ell + id_\ell^*\mathbf{I}_2]$$

as expected, so that the challenge ciphertext is as in **Game₁**.

If $\mathbf{t}$ is random, by $R = \hat{e}(g,g)^{y_3}$, the challenge ciphertext is as in **Game₂**. In this final game, the challenge bit b is perfectly hidden, ending the proof. □

5.2 Our Function-Private, Fully Secure IBE

– Setup: Let the identity space be $\{0,1\}^n$. The public parameters are

$$pp = (g^{\mathbf{A}_0}, g^{\mathbf{A}_0'}, g^{\mathbf{D}}, g^{\mathbf{A}_1}, \ldots, g^{\mathbf{A}_n})$$

where the matrices are as follows

$$\mathbf{A}_0 = \begin{bmatrix} u & 0 \\ 0 & v \end{bmatrix} \in \mathbb{Z}_q^{2\times 2}, \mathbf{D} = \begin{bmatrix} 1 \\ 1 \end{bmatrix} \in \mathbb{Z}_q^{2\times 1}, \text{ and } \mathbf{A}_0', \mathbf{A}_1, \ldots, \mathbf{A}_\ell \xleftarrow{\$} \mathbb{Z}_q^{2\times 2}$$

where $u, v \xleftarrow{\$} \mathbb{Z}_q$.

The master secret key is $msk = (\mathbf{A}_0, \mathbf{A}_0', \mathbf{A}_1, \ldots, \mathbf{A}_\ell)$. For an identity $id \in \{0,1\}^n$, let

$$\mathbf{F}(id, \mathbf{S}) = \left[\mathbf{A}_0 \middle| \mathbf{A}_0'\mathbf{S} + \left(\sum_{i=1}^n id_i \cdot \mathbf{A}_i\right)\mathbf{S}\right] \in \mathbb{Z}_q^{2\times 4}$$

– Extract: on input $id \in \{0,1\}^n$, take $\mathbf{S} \xleftarrow{\$} \mathbb{Z}_q^{2\times 2}$, and return $sk_{id} = (\mathbf{S}, g^{\mathbf{v}})$ where $\mathbf{v} \in \mathbb{Z}_q^{4\times 1}$ is a random vector such that

$$\mathbf{F}(id, \mathbf{S}) \cdot \mathbf{v} = \mathbf{D} \pmod q.$$

– Enc: on input $id \in \{0,1\}^n$ and $M \in \mathbb{G}_T$, take $\mathbf{z} \xleftarrow{\$} \mathbb{Z}_q^{1\times 2}$ and compute

$$C = g^{\mathbf{z}\cdot[\mathbf{A}_0|\mathbf{A}_0'+id_1\mathbf{A}_1+\cdots+id_n\mathbf{A}_n]}, \quad E = \hat{e}(g,g)^{\mathbf{z}\cdot\mathbf{D}} \cdot M.$$

Return (C, E) as the ciphertext.

– Dec: On input $sk_{id} = (\mathbf{S}, g^{\mathbf{v}})$ and $C = g^{[\mathbf{c}_0|\mathbf{c}_1]}$, compute $g^{\mathbf{c}} = g^{[\mathbf{c}_0|\mathbf{c}_1\mathbf{S}]}$ and $K = \hat{e}(g,g)^{\mathbf{c}\cdot\mathbf{v}}$ using the bi-linearity of $\hat{e}$, and return $M = EK^{-1}$.

Correctness. Directly via $[\mathbf{c}_0|\mathbf{c}_1\mathbf{S}] = [\mathbf{z}\mathbf{A}_0|\mathbf{z}(\mathbf{A}_0' + id_1\mathbf{A}_1 + \cdots + id_n\mathbf{A}_n)\mathbf{S}] = \mathbf{z} \cdot \mathbf{F}(id, \mathbf{S})$.

Intuition on Function Privacy. This is similar to the counterpart above, yet is more involved by showing that $\mathsf{Ext}_{\mathbf{S}}(id) = (\sum_{i=1}^n id_i \mathbf{A}_i)\mathbf{S}$ functions as a randomness extractor with overwhelmingly high probability over the choice of

---

156   K. Kurosawa and L.T. Phong

$\mathbf{A}_1, \ldots, \mathbf{A}_n$, which is proved in [5, Claim5.21]. (The change in sizes of $\mathbf{A}_1, \ldots, \mathbf{A}_n$ and $\mathbf{S}$ does not affect the proof by inspection.)

Intuition on IND-ID-CPA Security. Setting up $\mathbf{A}_0', \mathbf{A}_1, \ldots, \mathbf{A}_n$ as in (8), we have

$$\mathbf{F}(id, \mathbf{S}) =$$
$$\left[\mathbf{A}_0 \middle| \mathbf{A}_0 \left(\mathbf{R}_0 + \sum_{i=1}^n id_i \mathbf{R}_i \right) \mathbf{S} + \left(q - kJ + h_0 + \sum_{i=1}^n id_i h_i \right) \mathbf{S} \right] \quad (10)$$

and

$$\mathbf{F}(id^*, \mathbf{S}^*) = \left[\mathbf{A}_0 \middle| \mathbf{A}_0 \mathbf{R}^* \mathbf{S}^* \right] \text{ for } \mathbf{R}^* = \left(\mathbf{R}_0 + \sum_{i=1}^n id_i^* \mathbf{R}_i \right) \quad (11)$$

in which (10) enables the simulation of extract queries, while (11) is used in the challenge query, so that the proof goes along the lines of that of Theorem 2. Below is the details.

Theorem 4. *The above scheme is IND-ID-CPA-secure under the DLIN assumption.*

Proof. The game chain is as in Table 5.

Table 5. Changes of games in the proof of Theorem 4

Game	Challenge ciphertext	Notes
Game$_0$: $C^* = g^{\mathbf{z}^* \cdot [\mathbf{A}_0 \vert \mathbf{A}_0' + id_1^* \mathbf{A}_1 + \cdots + id_n^* \mathbf{A}_n]}$		$\mathbf{z}^* \xleftarrow{\$} \mathbb{Z}_q^{1\times2}$ by the challenger
$E^* = \hat{e}(g,g)^{\mathbf{z}^* \mathbf{D}} \cdot M_b$		
Game$_1$: $C^* = g^{[\mathbf{c}_0^* \vert \mathbf{c}_1^*]}$		$\mathbf{c}_0^* = \mathbf{z}^* \mathbf{A}_0$
$E^* = \hat{e}(g,g)^{[\mathbf{c}_0^* \vert \mathbf{c}_1^* \mathbf{S}^*]\mathbf{v}^*} \cdot M_b$		$\mathbf{c}_1^* = \mathbf{z}^* (\mathbf{A}_0' + id_1^* \mathbf{A}_1 + \cdots + id_n^* \mathbf{A}_n)$
		$[\mathbf{c}_0^* \vert \mathbf{c}_1^* \mathbf{S}^*]\mathbf{v}^* = \mathbf{z}^* \mathbf{F}(id^*, \mathbf{S}^*)\mathbf{v}^* = \mathbf{z}^* \mathbf{D}$
Game$_2$: $C^* = g^{[\mathbf{c}_0^* \vert \mathbf{c}_1^*]}$, $E^* = R \cdot M_b$		$R \xleftarrow{\$} \mathbb{G}_T$ by the challenger

As the first change is notational, we will show that **Game$_1$** and **Game$_2$** are computationally indistinguishable under the DLIN assumption from the view of the adversary. Concretely, we construct simulator $\mathcal{B}$ against DLIN as follows. $\mathcal{B}$ has inputs $g^{\mathbf{L}_2}$ ($\mathbf{L}_2$ as in (1) taking $k = 2$) and $g^{\mathbf{t}}$ and it will tell whether $\mathbf{t}$ is random in $\mathbb{Z}_q^{1\times3}$ or $\mathbf{t} = \mathbf{z}^* \cdot \mathbf{L}_2$ for random $\mathbf{z}^* \in \mathbb{Z}_q^{1\times2}$. Let $\mathbf{A}_0 = \mathbf{L}_2 \in \mathbb{Z}_q^{2\times2}$ and mentally set $\mathbf{A}_0', \mathbf{A}_1, \ldots, \mathbf{A}_n$ as in (8) so that the public parameters can be computable by $\mathcal{B}$ and we have (10) and (11). Moreover, algorithms $\mathcal{B}$ works as follows.

- The simulation of extract queries id: here we expect $\alpha(id) = q - kJ + h_0 + \sum_{i=1}^n id_i h_i \neq 0 \pmod{q}$. Take $\mathbf{S} \xleftarrow{\$} \mathbb{Z}_q^{2\times2}$ and the corresponding $\mathbf{v}$ is set to

$$\mathbf{v} = \begin{bmatrix} \mathbf{w} - (\mathbf{R}_0 + \sum_{i=1}^n id_i \mathbf{R}_i)\mathbf{S}\mathbf{x} \\ \mathbf{x} \end{bmatrix} \in \mathbb{Z}_q^{4\times1}$$

in which $\mathbf{w} \in \mathbb{Z}_q^{2 \times 1}$ is random and $\mathbf{x} = \alpha(id)^{-1} \mathbf{S}^{-1} \cdot (\mathbf{D} - \mathbf{A}_0 \mathbf{w}) \in \mathbb{Z}_q^{2 \times 1}$, which is computable as $\alpha(id) \neq 0 \pmod{q}$ and random $\mathbf{S} \in \mathbb{Z}_q^{2 \times 2}$ is invertible with overwhelming probability. Thus $sk_{id} = (\mathbf{S}, g^{\mathbf{v}})$ can be computed and returned to the IBE's adversary $\mathcal{A}$.

- On challenge query id^* and (M_0, M_1), take $b \xleftarrow{\$} \{0, 1\}$, and return

$$(C^*, E^*) = \left(g^{[(y_1, y_2)|(y_1, y_2)\mathbf{R}^*]}, \hat{e}(g, g)^{y_3} M_b \right)$$

where $\mathbf{t} = (y_1, y_2, y_3) \in \mathbb{Z}_q^{1 \times 3}$ is from the DLIN instance and $\mathbf{R}^*$ is in (11).

We claim that, if $\mathbf{t} = \mathbf{z}^* \mathbf{L}_2$, the challenge ciphertext is as in $\mathbf{Game}_1$; if $\mathbf{t}$ is random, it is as in $\mathbf{Game}_2$. Indeed,

- If $\mathbf{t} = \mathbf{z}^* \mathbf{L}_2$, namely $(y_1, y_2, y_3) = \mathbf{z}^*[\mathbf{A}_0|\mathbf{D}]$, we have $(y_1, y_2) = \mathbf{z}^* \mathbf{A}_0$ and $y_3 = \mathbf{z}^* \mathbf{D}$ so that

$$(C^*, E^*) = \left(g^{[\mathbf{z}^* \mathbf{A}_0 | \mathbf{z}^* \mathbf{A}_0 \mathbf{R}^*]}, \hat{e}(g, g)^{\mathbf{z}^* \mathbf{D}} M_b \right)$$
$$= \left(g^{[\mathbf{c}_0^* | \mathbf{c}_1^*]}, \hat{e}(g, g)^{[\mathbf{c}_0^* | \mathbf{c}_1^* \mathbf{S}^*]\mathbf{v}^*} \cdot M_b \right)$$

where $\mathbf{c}_0^* = \mathbf{z}^* \mathbf{A}_0$, $\mathbf{c}_1^* = \mathbf{z}^* \mathbf{A}_0 \mathbf{R}^*$.

- If $\mathbf{t}$ is random, we have (y_1, y_2) and y_3 are independently random. Put $R = \hat{e}(g, g)^{y_3}$ we obtain the challenge ciphertext in $\mathbf{Game}_2$.

The challenge ciphertext in the final game contains no information on challenge bit b, ending the proof.   □

6   Conclusion and Open Question

We have showed that IBE schemes and function-private ones can have $2k$ group elements in the ciphertext overhead and private keys, and $2k$ pairings in decryption under the k-LIN assumption. In short, under k-LIN, the number is $2k$ which becomes the state-of-the-art.

It is known that public key encryption (PKE) having semantic security under k-LIN has k group elements in the ciphertext overhead. Is the gap between k and $2k$ inherent from the difference of PKE and IBE, or can it be shortened further? This open question is left for future works.

References

1. Bellare, M., Kiltz, E., Peikert, C., Waters, B.: Identity-based (lossy) trapdoor functions and applications. Cryptology ePrint Archive, Report 2011/479 (2011). http://eprint.iacr.org/. Full version of an extended abstract in Eurocrypt 2012
2. Benson, K., Shacham, H., Waters, B.: The k-bdh assumption family: Bilinear map cryptography from progressively weaker assumptions. Cryptology ePrint Archive, Report 2012/687 (2012). http://eprint.iacr.org/. Full version of an extended abstract in CT-RSA 2013

3. Blazy, O., Kiltz, E., Pan, J.: (Hierarchical) identity-based encryption from affine message authentication. In: Garay, J.A., Gennaro, R. (eds.) CRYPTO 2014, Part I. LNCS, vol. 8616, pp. 408–425. Springer, Heidelberg (2014). Full version at http://eprint.iacr.org/2014/581.pdf

4. Boneh, D., Boyen, X., Shacham, H.: Short group signatures. In: Franklin, M. (ed.) CRYPTO 2004. LNCS, vol. 3152, pp. 41–55. Springer, Heidelberg (2004)

5. Boneh, D., Raghunathan, A., Segev, G.: Function-private identity-based encryption: hiding the function in functional encryption. In: Canetti, R., Garay, J.A. (eds.) CRYPTO 2013, Part II. LNCS, vol. 8043, pp. 461–478. Springer, Heidelberg (2013). Full version at http://eprint.iacr.org/2013/283

6. Canetti, R., Garay, J.A. (eds.) Advances in Cryptology - CRYPTO 2013 - Proceedings of the 33rd Annual Cryptology Conference, Santa Barbara, CA, USA, August 18–22, 2013, Part II, vol. 8043. Lecture Notes in Computer Science. Springer (2013)

7. Chen, J., Wee, H.: Fully, (almost) tightly secure IBE and dual system groups. In: Canetti, R., Garay, J.A. (eds.) CRYPTO 2013, Part II. LNCS, vol. 8043, pp. 435–460. Springer, Heidelberg (2013)

8. Escala, A., Herold, G., Kiltz, E., Ràfols, C., Villar, J.: An algebraic framework for Diffie-Hellman assumptions. In: Canetti, R., Garay, J.A. (eds.) CRYPTO 2013, Part II. LNCS, vol. 8043, pp. 129–147. Springer, Heidelberg (2013)

9. Kurosawa, K., Trieu Phong, L.: Leakage resilient IBE and IPE under the DLIN assumption. In: Jacobson, M., Locasto, M., Mohassel, P., Safavi-Naini, R. (eds.) ACNS 2013. LNCS, vol. 7954, pp. 487–501. Springer, Heidelberg (2013)

10. Lewko, A.: Tools for simulating features of composite order bilinear groups in the prime order setting. In: Pointcheval, D., Johansson, T. (eds.) EUROCRYPT 2012. LNCS, vol. 7237, pp. 318–335. Springer, Heidelberg (2012)

11. Waters, B.: Efficient identity-based encryption without random oracles. In: Cramer, R. (ed.) EUROCRYPT 2005. LNCS, vol. 3494, pp. 114–127. Springer, Heidelberg (2005)

12. Waters, B.: Dual system encryption: realizing fully secure IBE and HIBE under simple assumptions. In: Halevi, S. (ed.) CRYPTO 2009. LNCS, vol. 5677, pp. 619–636. Springer, Heidelberg (2009)

A   The Probability λ in Artificial Abort

First define a binary function $\beta(id) = \begin{cases} 0 \text{ if } h_0 + \sum_{i=1}^{n} id_i h_i = 0 \bmod J \\ 1 \text{ otherwise} \end{cases}$, and note that since q is exponential compared to nJ, we have

$$\alpha(id) = 0 \bmod q \Leftrightarrow h_0 + \sum_{i=1}^{n} id_i h_i = kJ \bmod q \Leftrightarrow h_0 + \sum_{i=1}^{n} id_i h_i = kJ$$

$$\Rightarrow h_0 + \sum_{i=1}^{n} id_i h_i = 0 \bmod J \Leftrightarrow \beta(id) = 0$$

Since h_i are random in $\mathbb{Z}_J$, $\Pr[\beta(id) = 0] = 1/J$. Abusing the notation a little, from now on let $id_1, \ldots, id_Q$ be the extract queries, and note that the events

$\beta(id_j) = 0$ and $\beta(id^*) = 0$ are pairwise independent for all $id_j \neq id^*$, we have

$$\lambda = \Pr\left[\left(\wedge_{j=1}^{Q}\alpha(id_j) \neq 0 \bmod q\right) \wedge \alpha(id^*) = 0 \bmod q\right]$$

$$= \Pr\left[\left(\wedge_{j=1}^{Q}\beta(id_j) = 1\right) \wedge \sum_{i=1}^{m} id^*[i]h_i = kJ\right]$$

$$= \frac{1}{m+1}\Pr\left[\left(\wedge_{j=1}^{Q}\beta(id_j) = 1\right) \wedge \beta(id^*) = 0\right]$$

$$= \frac{1}{m+1}\Pr\left[\left(\wedge_{j=1}^{Q}\beta(id_j) = 1\right)\right]\Pr\left[\beta(id^*) = 0 \middle| \left(\wedge_{j=1}^{Q}\beta(id_j) = 1\right)\right]$$

$$= \frac{1}{m+1}\left(1 - \Pr\left[\vee_{j=1}^{Q}\beta(id_j) = 0\right]\right)\Pr\left[\beta(id^*) = 0 \middle| \left(\wedge_{j=1}^{Q}\beta(id_j) = 1\right)\right]$$

$$\geq \frac{1}{m+1}\left(1 - \sum_{j=1}^{Q}\Pr\left[\beta(id_j) = 0\right]\right)\Pr\left[\beta(id^*) = 0 \middle| \left(\wedge_{j=1}^{Q}\beta(id_j) = 1\right)\right]$$

$$= \frac{1}{m+1}\left(1 - \frac{Q}{J}\right)\Pr\left[\beta(id^*) = 0 \middle| \left(\wedge_{j=1}^{Q}\beta(id_j) = 1\right)\right]$$

$$= \frac{1}{m+1}\left(1 - \frac{Q}{J}\right)\frac{\Pr\left[\beta(id^*) = 0\right]}{\Pr\left[\wedge_{j=1}^{Q}\beta(id_j) = 1\right]}\Pr\left[\wedge_{j=1}^{Q}\beta(id_j) = 1 \middle| \beta(id^*) = 0\right]$$

$$\geq \frac{1}{(m+1)}\left(1 - \frac{Q}{J}\right)\frac{1}{J}\Pr\left[\wedge_{j=1}^{Q}\beta(id_j) = 1 \middle| \beta(id^*) = 0\right]$$

$$\geq \frac{1}{(m+1)J}\left(1 - \frac{Q}{J}\right)^2 \geq \frac{1}{(m+1)J}\left(1 - 2\frac{Q}{J}\right),$$

as stated.

Improved Identity-Based Online/Offline Encryption

Jianchang Lai$^{(\boxtimes)}$, Yi Mu, Fuchun Guo, and Willy Susilo

Centre for Computer and Information Security Research,
School of Computing and Information Technology, University of Wollongong,
Wollongong, NSW 2522, Australia
{jl967,ymu,fuchun,wsusilo}@uow.edu.au

Abstract. The notion of online/offline encryption was put forth by Guo, Mu and Chen (FC 2008), where they proposed an identity-based scheme called *identity-based online/offline encryption* (IBOOE). An online/ offline encryption separates an encryption into two stages: offline and online. The offline phase carries much more computational load than the online phase, where the offline phase does not require the information of the message to be encrypted and the identity of the receiver. Subsequently, many applications of IBOOE have been proposed in the literature. As an example, Hobenberger and Waters (PKC 2014) have recently applied it to attribute-based encryption. In this paper, we move one step further and explore a much more efficient variant. We propose an efficient semi-generic transformation to obtain an online/offline encryption from a tradition identity-based encryption (IBE). Our transformation provides a new method to separate the computation of receiver's identity into offline and online phases. The IBOOE schemes using our transformation saves one group element in both offline and online phases compared to other IBOOE schemes in identity computing. The transformed scheme still maintains the same level of security as in the original IBE scheme.

Keywords: Identity-based encryption · Online/offline encryption

1 Introduction

Identity based encryption (IBE) was first introduced by Shamir in 1984 [14]. In an IBE system, each user's public key can be an arbitrary string binding the user's identity, such as an email address or a telephone number. IBE removes the necessity of complex certificate management that exists in traditional public key cryptography. The need to incorporate certificates has been eliminated, and hence, it removes complicated and costly certificate verification processes. If a new user wants to join the network in a network system based on IBE, there is no need for other users in the network to verify its certificate in order to communicate securely.

One of the main concerns in cryptography is the efficiency of computation. However, most IBE schemes [2,7,17] in cryptography involve computations

© Springer International Publishing Switzerland 2015
E. Foo and D. Stebila (Eds.): ACISP 2015, LNCS 9144, pp. 160–173, 2015.
DOI: 10.1007/978-3-319-19962-7_10

including pairings over points on elliptic cure and exponentiations (point multi-plications) in groups. These operations are regarded as the most costly computations in cryptography, which might be too costly to be applied in lightweight devices. One elegant way to solve the problem was proposed to reduce the computational overhead of digital signature schemes by Even, Goldreich and Micali [6], where a signing process is split into two phases. The first phase is called the offline phase and is performed prior to obtaining the message to be signed. The second phase is called the online phase and is executed when the message becomes available. All the heavy computations in signing phase are pre-computed in the offline phase. In the online phase, it only performs the light computations such as modular multiplication.

The notion of online/offline encryption was first introduced by Guo, Mu and Chen [8] in 2008, where they proposed an identity-based construction. The motivation of online/offline encryption is to improve the efficiency of encryption. In the offline phase, most of the heavy computations are conducted without the need to know the recipient's identity and the message to be encrypted. When the recipient's identity and the message become available, the online phase can be accomplished with great efficiency. This seminal work has attracted a lot of attention.

Guo, Mu and Chen [8] constructed the first two identity-based IBOOE schemes based on the IBE schemes of Boneh and Boyen [2] and Gentry [7]. Both IBOOE schemes were proven to be secure against chosen ciphertext attack (CCA) without random oracle. Subsequently, a more efficient IBOOE scheme than Guo et al.'s scheme [8] was proposed by Liu and Zhou [10]. They proved that their proposed scheme was CCA-secure in the random oracle model. However, Selvi, Vivek and Rangan [12,13] found that the scheme proposed by Liu and Zhou [10] actually was not CCA secure and gave a concrete example of an attack on confidentiality. The adversary could easily forge a ciphertext and distinguish the challenge message in the security proof. The authors also proposed a possible fix for the weakness in [10]. This notion has been extended to various areas such as attribute based encryption [9] and signcryption [18].

In an IBE system, the message space is quite limited such as in a cyclic group. To optimize the encryption system for any arbitrary message, one can make use of hybrid encryption. A useful tool called key encapsulation mechanism (KEM) was proposed by Cramer and Shoup [5] to build a hybrid encryption scheme. A KEM is similar to a public key encryption scheme, except that it encrypts a session key K instead of a message. The message is encrypted using the session key with a symmetry encryption system. Identity-based online/offline key encapsulation mechanism (IBOOKEM) is sufficient for practical applications. Therefore, with IBOOKEM, the main work is how to split the encryption into offline phase and online phase, where the identity of receiver only appears in the online phase.

The IBOOKEM was first proposed by Chow, Liu and Zhou [3]. It naturally requires that the KEM is able to divide into online phase and offline phase. Based on their IBOOKEM, they presented a CCA secure IBOOE scheme in the random oracle model and gave the general transformation from a one-way

IBOOKEM scheme into a CCA IBOOE scheme. However, Selvi, Vivek and Rangan [13] showed that there was one weakness in the proof of CCA security in [3], and hence, the scheme is insecure. Selvi, Vivek and Rangan [12,13] proposed a new provably CCA secure and efficient IBOOE scheme in the random oracle model. Subsequently, they revisited their IBOOE and constructed signcryption schemes [13]. A practical IBOOE scheme for wireless sensor network in the selective ID model was proposed by Chu et al. [4]. Recently, Hohenberger and Waters [9] proposed the first online/offline attribute based encryption (OOABE) scheme. Both schemes in their paper were selective chosen plaintext attack (CPA) secure.

A more efficient way to complete encryption and signature at the same time is signcryption. An, Dodis and Rabin [1] proposed online/offline signcryption. But they only gave the general security proof notions and did not give their constructions. Sun et al. [15] provided the definition of the identity-based online/offline signcryption and the corresponding security model. Based on the work by Sun et al., several online/offline signcryption schemes have been proposed in the literature [13,16,18,19].

1.1 Our Contribution

In this paper, we introduce a new semi-generic transformation to split the computation of identity into online and offline. Our transformation is *more efficient* than the previous transformation through the comparison in encryption computation and the ciphertext size. All the previous IBOOE schemes [3,10,12,13] applied the technique introduced by Guo, Mu and Chen [8]. To deal with identity, they require at least two group elements in $\mathbb{G}$ and one element in $\mathbb{Z}_p^*$ while we only need one group element in $\mathbb{G}$ and one element in $\mathbb{Z}_p^*$. We reduce one exponentiation operation in offline computation and save one group element in $\mathbb{G}$ both in offline storage and ciphertext length. We provide the security proof of our semi-generic transformation. We claim that the IBOOE schemes using our semi-generic transformation hold the same security level as in the original IBE schemes. Then we show a natural extension of IBE of Sakai and Kasahara [11], Boneh and Boyen [2], Gentry [7] and Waters [17] applying our transformation.

Organization of the Paper. In Section 2, we review some preliminaries including the definition of bilinear, identity-based online/offline encryption and the security model of IBOOE. Our semi-generic transformation, its security proof and a comparison are provided in Section 3. Four examples of IBOOE schemes converted by our transformation from the classical IBE schemes and our conclusion are presented in Section 4 and Section 5, respectively.

2 Preliminaries

In this section, we define bilinear pairing and identity-based online/offline encryption and then review the definition of security model for an IBOOE system. For simplicity, in this paper, we define an IBOOE as an IBOOKEM.

2.1 Bilinear Pairing

Let $\mathbb{G}$ be a cyclic group of prime order p and $\mathbb{G}_T$ be a multiplicative cyclic group of the same prime order p. Let g be a generator of $\mathbb{G}$. A bilinear pairing is a map $e : \mathbb{G} \times \mathbb{G} \to \mathbb{G}_T$ with the following properties:

1. Bilinear: For all $u, v \in \mathbb{G}$ and $a, b \in \mathbb{Z}_p^*$, we have $e\left(u^a, v^b\right) = e(u, v)^{ab}$.
2. Non-degeneracy: $e\left(g, g\right) \neq 1$.
3. Computability: It is efficient to compute $e\left(u, v\right)$ for all $u, v \in \mathbb{G}$.

2.2 Identity-Based Online/Offline Encryption

An identity-based online/offline encryption scheme consists of the following five algorithms:

Setup(λ): Taking a security parameter λ as input and returns the system parameters mpk and the master key msk. The system parameters mpk includes the descriptions of a finite key space $\mathcal{K}$, a finite message space $\mathcal{M}$ and a finite ciphertext space $\mathcal{CT}$. The system parameters are publicly known, while the master key is kept secretly and known to generator (PKG) only.

KeyGen(mpk, msk, ID): Taking mpk, msk and an arbitrary $ID \in \{0,1\}^*$ as input, returns a private key d_{ID} for ID. Here ID is an arbitrary string which will be used as a public key.

Off-Encrypt(mpk): Taking the system parameter mpk as input, outputs a pair $\left(C_{\mathrm{off}}, K\right)$ where C_{off} is called offline ciphertext and K as the message encryption key.

On-Encrypt(mpk, $C_{\mathbf{off}}$, ID): Taking the system parameters mpk, offline ciphertext C_{off} and an identity $ID \in \{0,1\}^*$ as input, returns a ciphertext CT for K.

Decrypt(mpk, CT, d_{ID}): Taking the system parameters mpk, ciphertext CT and the private key d_{ID} as input, outputs the session key K or a reject symbol $\perp$.

For correctness we require that if for every (mpk, msk) returned by **Setup**(λ), every d_{ID} returned by **KeyGen**(mpk, msk, ID), every $\left(C_{\mathrm{off}}, K\right)$ returned by **Off-Encrypt**(mpk) and every CT returned by **On-Encrypt**(mpk, $C_{\mathbf{off}}$, ID), then **Decrypt**(mpk, CT, d_{ID}) $= K$.

2.3 Security for IBOOE

The semantic security between a challenger and an adversary is defined as follows.

Setup: The challenger takes as input a secure parameter λ and runs the **Setup** algorithm. It gives the adversary $\mathcal{A}$ the system public parameters mpk.

Phase 1: $\mathcal{A}$ issues polynomially private key queries $q_1, \ldots, q_m$. The challenger responds by running key generation algorithm **KeyGen** to generate the private key d_{ID_i} corresponding to ID_i. It sends d_{ID_i} to $\mathcal{A}$. These queries may be asked adaptively, that is, each query q_i may depend on the replies to $q_1, \ldots, q_{i-1}$.

Challenge: Once $\mathcal{A}$ decides that Phase 1 is over, it outputs an identity ID^* on which it wishes to be challenged. $\mathcal{A}$ did not request a private key for ID^* in Phase 1. The challenger chooses a random bit $b \in \{0, 1\}$ and computes a challenge ciphertext CT^* and a session key K_0^* corresponding to ID^*. If $b = 0$, the challenger sends (CT^*, K_0^*) to $\mathcal{A}$. Otherwise, the challenger sends (CT^*, K_1^*) to $\mathcal{A}$, where K_1^* is a random section key from key space.

Phase 2: $\mathcal{A}$ issues more private key queries $q_{m+1}, \ldots, q_n$ on one restriction that $ID_i \neq ID^*$. The challenger responds the same as in Phase 1.

Guess: Finally, $\mathcal{A}$ outputs a guess $b' \in \{0, 1\}$ of b and wins the game if $b' = b$

We define adversary $\mathcal{A}$'s advantage in attacking the above game is

$$Adv_A(\lambda) = \left| \Pr[b = b'] - \frac{1}{2} \right|.$$

Definition 1. *An IBOOE system is semantically secure if for any polynomial time adversary $\mathcal{A}$, the function $Adv_A(\lambda)$ is negligible.*

3   Semi-Generic Transformation

In IBE system, the identity in ciphertext is embedded in some group elements. We refer to those group elements containing identity as ID header. Therefore, the ciphertext of IBE can be written as $CT = (\mathsf{Hdr}, C)$ where Hdr is called ID header and C is the other components of ciphertext excluding ID header.

The IBE schemes in the literature [2,7,11,17] have the same ID headers in the ciphertext, if we do not consider the group which the ID headers belong to. Their ID headers are defined as

$$\left(g_1 g^{ID} \right)^s,$$

where g_1, g are group elements of mpk and $s \in \mathbb{Z}_p^*$ is the random number chosen by the encryptor.

Without loss of generality, the encryption algorithm in IBE system can be written as follow:

$$\mathsf{Hdr} = \left(g_1 g^{ID} \right)^s, \qquad (C, K) \leftarrow \mathcal{E}(\mathsf{mpk}, s),$$

$$CT = (\mathsf{Hdr}, C) = \left(\left(g_1 g^{ID} \right)^s, C \right),$$

where K is the message encryption key and $\mathcal{E}$ is the encryption algorithm without the computation of ID header.

Based on the above scheme, we have the main task of IBOOE is to achieve the online/offline computation on the ID header. Obviously, there is a trivial method to achieve online/offline from IBE. We can compute $C_1 = g_1^s$, $C_2 = g^s$ in the offline phase and perform $C_3 = C_1 \cdot C_2^{ID}$ after one has obtained the identity in the online phase. However, one exponentiation operation is required in the online phase to achieve the online/offline encryption, which is still inefficient.

In the following parts of this session, we first revisit the online/offline computation on the ID header with structure $\mathsf{Hdr} = (g_1 g^{ID})^s$. Then we give our improved semi-generic transformation that only needs two elements to deal with the ID header to achieve online/offline.

3.1 Previous Method of Transformation

We review how the authors dealt with the online/offline computation of the ID header in previous IBOOE schemes [3,8,12,13].

Off-Encrypt: Randomly choose $\alpha, \beta, s \in \mathbb{Z}_p^*$ and compute

$$C_1 = (g_1 g^\alpha)^s, \quad C_2 = g^{s\beta},$$

$$(C, K) \leftarrow \mathcal{E}\,(\mathsf{mpk}, s)\,.$$

Then output the offline ciphertext $C_{\mathrm{off}} = (C_1, C_2, \alpha, \beta^{-1}, C)$ and the message encryption key K.

On-Encrypt: Upon receiving $ID \in \mathbb{Z}_p^*$, compute

$$C_3 = \beta^{-1}\,(ID - \alpha) \bmod p.$$

The ID header is $\mathsf{Hdr}_{\mathrm{on}} = (C_1, C_2, C_3)$. Then output the ciphertext

$$CT = (\mathsf{Hdr}_{\mathrm{on}}, C) = (C_1, C_2, C_3, C)\,.$$

In the decryption algorithm, the receiver first recoves the general ID header in the traditional IBE scheme from the ID header as below:

$$C_1 \cdot C_2^{C_3} = (g_1 g^\alpha)^s \cdot \left(g^{s\beta}\right)^{\beta^{-1}(ID-\alpha)} = \left(g_1 g^{ID}\right)^s.$$

It is the same as the ID header in IBE. Then, the receiver follows the general decryption procedures using its private key as in the traditional encryption scheme to obtain the key K. It needs three elements to handle the ID header.

3.2 Our Method of Transformation

We describe our method to achieve the online/offline encryption, where only two elements are required to deal with the ID header. It saves one group element compared to the previous method.

Off-Encrypt: Randomly choose $s, w \in \mathbb{Z}_p^*$ and compute

$$C_1 = (g_1 g^w)^s,$$

$$(C, K) \leftarrow \mathcal{E}(\mathsf{mpk}, s).$$

Then output the offline ciphertext $C_{\text{off}} = (C_1, w, s, C)$ and the message encryption key K.

On-Encrypt: Upon receiving $ID \in \mathbb{Z}_p^*$, compute

$$C_2 = s(ID - w) \bmod p.$$

The ID header is $\mathsf{Hdr}_{\text{on}} = (C_1, C_2)$. Then output the ciphertext

$$CT = (\mathsf{Hdr}_{\text{on}}, C) = (C_1, C_2, C).$$

Correctness: Given the ID header $\mathsf{Hdr}_{\text{on}} = (C_1, C_2)$, compute

$$C_1 g^{C_2} = (g_1 g^w)^s \cdot g^{s(ID-w)} = \left(g_1 g^{ID}\right)^s.$$

After recovering the original ID header, the recipient follows the general decryption procedures using its private key as in traditional identity-based encryption schemes to obtain the key K.

3.3   Security

Theorem 1. *The identity-based online/offline encryption scheme converted with our transformation is secure if the original identity-based encryption scheme is secure.*

Proof. Let $\mathcal{A}$ be an adversary that has advantage $\varepsilon(\lambda)$ against the IBOOE scheme converted using our transformation. Then, there is a simulator $\mathcal{B}$ that has advantage $\varepsilon(\lambda)$ against the original IBE.

We show how to construct a simulator $\mathcal{B}$ that uses $\mathcal{A}$ to gain advantage $\varepsilon(\lambda)$ against IBE in Fig.1. Here, we refer the IBE as the oracle. The IBE and the simulator $\mathcal{B}$ start the game with the IBE first running the **Setup** algorithm of IBE to generate the system public key mpk. As usual, $\mathbb{G}$ is a cyclic groups of prime order p, and g is the generator of $\mathbb{G}$. Random secret $a \in \mathbb{Z}_p^*$ is the master key and $g_1 = g^a$. The IBE gives mpk to simulator $\mathcal{B}$. Simulator $\mathcal{B}$ is supposed to output an identity ID^* and expects to receive back the IBE challenge ciphertext CT^* and the challenger session key K^* under mpk. Simulator $\mathcal{B}$ outputs its guess $b \in \{0, 1\}$ on K^*.

Simulator $\mathcal{B}$ works by interacting with adversary $\mathcal{A}$ as follows ($\mathcal{B}$ simulates the challenger for $\mathcal{A}$):

Setup: Simulator $\mathcal{B}$ gives mpk to $\mathcal{A}$ as the IBOOE system parameter.

Phase 1: The adversary $\mathcal{A}$ issues polynomially private key queries $q_1, \ldots, q_m$. For the query on ID_i from $\mathcal{A}$, $\mathcal{B}$ queries its private key to IBE, then forwards the results from IBE to $\mathcal{A}$. These queries may be asked adaptively.

IBE		$\mathcal{B}$		$\mathcal{A}$
1. $(\mathsf{mpk}, \mathsf{msk}) \leftarrow Setup(\lambda)$	$\xrightarrow{\quad \mathsf{mpk} \quad}$		$\xrightarrow{\quad \mathsf{mpk} \quad}$	
	$\xleftarrow{\quad ID_i \quad}$		$\xleftarrow{\quad ID_i \quad}$	
2. Generate d_{ID_i} by running $KeyGen(\mathsf{mpk}, \mathsf{msk}, ID_i)$	$\xrightarrow{\quad d_{ID_i} \quad}$		$\xrightarrow{\quad d_{ID_i} \quad}$	
	$\xleftarrow{\quad ID^* \quad}$		$\xleftarrow{\quad ID^* \quad}$	
3. Output (CT^*, K^*) where $CT^* = (\mathsf{Hdr}^*, C^*)$	$\xrightarrow{\quad (CT^*, K^*) \quad}$	Choose $k \in \mathbb{Z}_p^*$ $C_1^* = \mathsf{Hdr}^* \cdot g^{-k}$ $C_2^* = k$ $\mathsf{Hdr}_{\mathsf{ch}}^* = (C_1^*, C_2^*)$ $CT_{\mathsf{ch}}^* = \left(\mathsf{Hdr}_{\mathsf{ch}}^*, C^*\right)$	$\xrightarrow{\quad (CT_{\mathrm{Ch}}^*, K^*) \quad}$	
	$\xleftarrow{\quad b \quad}$		$\xleftarrow{\quad b \quad}$	

Fig. 1. Security Proof

Challenge: Once adversary $\mathcal{A}$ decides that Phase 1 is over, it outputs an ID^* on which it wishes to be challenged. Simulator $\mathcal{B}$ responds as follows:

1. $\mathcal{B}$ gives IBE the challenge identity ID^*. IBE responds with challenge cipher-text CT^* and the corresponding message encryption key K^* where

$$CT^* = (\mathsf{Hdr}^*, C^*) = \left(\left(g_1 g^{ID^*}\right)^s, C^*\right).$$

2. Next, $\mathcal{B}$ randomly chooses $k \in \mathbb{Z}_p^*$ and computes the challenge ID header:

$$\mathsf{Hdr}_{\mathsf{ch}}^* = (C_1^*, C_2^*) = \left(\mathsf{Hdr}^* \cdot g^{-k}, k\right) = \left(\left(g_1 g^{ID^*}\right)^s g^{-k}, k\right).$$

Then, set the online/offline challenge ciphertext as $CT_{\mathsf{ch}}^* = \left(\mathsf{Hdr}_{\mathsf{ch}}^*, C^*\right)$. $\mathcal{B}$ responds to $\mathcal{A}$ with the online/offline challenge ciphertext $\left(CT_{\mathsf{ch}}^*, K^*\right)$.

Note that CT_{ch}^* is a valid IBOOE ciphertext under the identity ID^*. To see this, let $w = ID^* - \frac{k}{s}$, we have

$$C_1^* = \left(g_1 g^{ID^*}\right)^s g^{-k} = (g_1 g^w)^s, \quad C_2^* = k = s(ID^* - w).$$

Therefore,

$$\mathsf{Hdr}_{\mathsf{ch}}^* = (C_1^*, C_2^*) = \left((g_1 g^w)^s, s(ID^* - w)\right)$$

is a valid online/offline challenge ID header for the challenge identity ID^*.

Phase 2: $\mathcal{A}$ issues more private key queries $q_{m+1}, \ldots, q_n$ on one restriction that $ID_i \neq ID^*$. $\mathcal{B}$ responds as in Phase 1.

Guess: Finally, $\mathcal{A}$ outputs a guess $b \in \{0, 1\}$ on K^*. Simulator $\mathcal{B}$ outputs b as its guess.

It is obvious that if the adversary $\mathcal{A}$ has advantage $\varepsilon(\lambda)$ to break the IBOOE scheme converted by our transformation, simulator $\mathcal{B}$ has advantage $\varepsilon(\lambda)$ to break the original IBE scheme.

3.4 Comparison

In an IBOOKEM system, there is no message to be encrypted. Therefore, it is important that how to efficiently compute ID header from KEM system to achieve IBOOKEM, which greatly affects the efficiency of IBOOKEM system. Here, we provide a comparison of computation cost of computing ID header and the ID header size among the traditional IBE, previous transformation and our transformation. We denote by E the exponentiation in group $\mathbb{G}$ and m_c the modular multiplication in $\mathbb{Z}_p^*$.

Table 1. Comparison of Computing ID header for IBOOE

	Traditional IBE	[8],[3],[12],[13]	[10]	Ours
Offline computation	/	3E	5E	2E
Online computation	2E	$1m_c$	$2m_c$	$1m_c$
Offline storage	/	$2\mathbb{G} + 2\mathbb{Z}_p$	$3\mathbb{G} + 4\mathbb{Z}_p$	$1\mathbb{G} + 2\mathbb{Z}_p$
Ciphertext size	1$\mathbb{G}$	$2\mathbb{G} + 1\mathbb{Z}_p$	$3\mathbb{G} + 2\mathbb{Z}_p$	$1\mathbb{G} + 1\mathbb{Z}_p$

From Table 1, it is clear that the online/offline encryption has a larger size of ID header than traditional IBE. However, the online/offline method can greatly reduce the online computation which is the motivation to use the online/offline encryption. Our semi-generic transformation of computing the ID deader is more efficient than the previous transformation to achieve identity-based online/offline encryption. The previous transformation requires two group elements in $\mathbb{G}$ and one element in $\mathbb{Z}_p^*$ to deal with identity while we only need one group element in $\mathbb{G}$ and one element in $\mathbb{Z}_p^*$. We reduce one exponentiation operation in the offline computation and save one group element in $\mathbb{G}$ both in offline storage and ciphertext length. We claim that the identity-based encryption schemes with this kind of ID header can be efficiently converted to online/offline encryption schemes by our method.

4   Identity Based Online/Offline Encryption Schemes

In this section, we give four examples applying our transformation to achieve the online/offline encryption from the classical identity-based encryption schemes

[2,7,11,17]. Four IBOOE schemes are given in the form of key encapsulation. Their security are easy to prove according to the original schemes. We omit their security proofs here. We also claim that the first example is a CPA-secure identity-based online/offline key encapsulation mechanism scheme with the shortest ciphertext.

4.1 IBOOE from Sakai-Kasahara IBE [11]

Setup: The system parameters are generated as follow. The PKG randomly chooses $\alpha \in \mathbb{Z}_p^*$ and sets $g_1 = g^\alpha$. Let $H_1 : \{0,1\}^* \to \mathbb{Z}_p^*$ be the cryptographic hash function. The public parameters mpk and msk are given by

$$\text{mpk} = (\mathbb{G}, \mathbb{G}_T, q, g, g_1, H_1), \quad \text{msk} = \alpha.$$

KeyGen: To generate the private key for $ID \in \{0,1\}^*$, PKG computes

$$d_{ID} = g^{\frac{1}{H_1(ID)+\alpha}}.$$

Off-Encrypt: Randomly choose $x, y \in \mathbb{Z}_p^*$ and compute

$$K = e(g,g)^x, \quad C_1 = (g_1 g^y)^x.$$

Output the offline ciphertext $C_{\text{off}} = (C_1, x, y)$ and the session key K. Note that $e(g,g)$ can be pre-computed by the PKG in **Setup** phase as part of the public parameters mpk. Thus, there is no pairing to be computed in the offline phase.

On-Encrypt: To generate a ciphertext for ID, compute

$$C_2 = x(H_1(ID) - y) \bmod p.$$

Output the ciphertext $CT = (C_1, C_2)$ corresponding to the session key K.

Decrypt: Upon receiving the ciphertext $CT = (C_1, C_2)$, to recover the session key, the recipient decrypts the ciphertext using the private key d_{ID} and computes

$$K = e\left(C_1 \cdot g^{C_2}, d_{ID}\right).$$

According to our transformation, it is easy to check its correctness

$$e\left(C_1 \cdot g^{C_2}, d_{ID}\right) = e\left(\left(g_1 g^{H_1(ID)}\right)^x, g^{\frac{1}{H_1(ID)+\alpha}}\right) = e(g,g)^x = K.$$

4.2 IBOOE from Boneh-Boyen IBE [2]

Setup: PKG randomly chooses a secret $a \in \mathbb{Z}_p$, generators $g, g_2, h_1 \in \mathbb{G}$ and sets $g_1 = g^a$. The system public parameters mpk and master key msk are

$$\text{mpk} = (g, g_1, g_2, h_1), \quad \text{msk} = g_2^a.$$

KeyGen: To generate the private key for $ID \in \mathbb{Z}_p$, PKG picks a random $r \in \mathbb{Z}_p$ and computes

$$d_{ID} = (d_1, d_2) = \left(g_2^a \left(h_1 g_1^{ID}\right)^r, g^r\right).$$

Off-Encrypt: Randomly chooses $w, s \in \mathbb{Z}_p$, compute

$$K = e(g_1, g_2)^s, \quad C_1 = (h_1 g_1^w)^s, \quad C_2 = g^s.$$

Output the offline ciphertext $C_{\text{off}} = (C_1, C_2, w, s)$ and session key K.

On-Encrypt: To generate a ciphertext for an identity $ID \in \mathbb{Z}_p$, compute

$$C_3 = s(ID - w) \bmod p.$$

Then output the ciphertext $CT = (C_1, C_2, C_3)$ corresponding to the session key K.

Decrypt: To decrypt the ciphertext $CT = (C_1, C_2, C_3)$ for $ID \in \mathbb{Z}_p$ and recover the session key, the receiver uses its private key d_{ID} and computes

$$C_0 = C_1 \cdot g_1^{C_3} = \left(h_1 g_1^{ID}\right)^s, \quad K = \frac{e(d_1, C_2)}{e(C_0, d_2)}.$$

For a valid ciphertext, we have

$$\frac{e(d_1, C_2)}{e(C_0, d_2)} = \frac{e\left(g_2^a \left(h_1 g_1^{ID}\right)^r, g^s\right)}{e\left(\left(h_1 g_1^{ID}\right)^s, g^r\right)} = e(g_1, g_2)^s = K.$$

4.3   IBOOE from Gentry IBE [7]

Setup: PKG randomly chooses $a \in \mathbb{Z}_p$ and generators $g, h \in \mathbb{G}$ and sets $g_1 = g^a$. The system parameters mpk and the master key msk are

$$\text{mpk} = (g, g_1, h), \quad \text{msk} = a.$$

KeyGen: To generate the private key for $ID \in \mathbb{Z}_p$, PKG picks a random $r \in \mathbb{Z}_p$ and outputs

$$d_{ID} = (d_1, d_2) = \left(r, \left(hg^{-r}\right)^{\frac{1}{a-ID}}\right).$$

Off-Encrypt: Randomly choose $w, s \in \mathbb{Z}_p$ and compute

$$K = e(g, h)^{-s}, \quad C_1 = \left(g_1 g^{-w}\right)^s, \quad C_2 = e(g, g)^s.$$

Then output the offline ciphertext $C_{\text{off}} = (C_1, C_2, w, s)$ and session key K.

On-Encrypt: To generate a ciphertext for an identity $ID \in \mathbb{Z}_p$, the sender computes

$$C_3 = s(w - ID) \bmod p.$$

Then output the ciphertext $CT = (C_1, C_2, C_3)$ corresponding to the session key K.

Decrypt: To decrypt the ciphertext $CT = (C_1, C_2, C_3)$ with ID and recover the session key, the recipient computes

$$C_0 = C_1 \cdot g^{C_3} = \left(g_1 g^{-w}\right)^s \cdot g^{s(w-ID)} = \left(g_1 g^{-ID}\right)^s,$$

$$K = \frac{1}{e\left(C_0, d_2\right) \cdot C_2^{d_1}}.$$

4.4 IBOOE from Waters' Dual System IBE [17]

Setup: Let $\mathbb{G}$ be a group of prime order p. The PKG chooses generators $g, v, v_1,$ $v_2, w, u, h \in \mathbb{G}$ and $a_1, a_2, b, \alpha \in \mathbb{Z}_p$. Let $\tau_1 = vv_1^{a_1}$, $\tau_2 = vv_2^{a_2}$. The system public parameters mpk and the master key msk are

$$\mathsf{mpk} = \left\{ g^b, g^{a_1}, g^{a_2}, g^{b \cdot a_1}, g^{b \cdot a_2}, \tau_1, \tau_2, \tau_1^b, \tau_2^b, w, u, h, e(g,g)^{\alpha \cdot a_1 \cdot b} \right\},$$

$$\mathsf{msk} = \left\{ g, g^\alpha, g^{\alpha \cdot a_1}, v, v_1, v_2 \right\}.$$

KeyGen: To generate the private key for identity $ID \in \mathbb{Z}_p$, the PKG randomly chooses $r_1, r_2, z_1, z_2, tag_k \in \mathbb{Z}_p$. Let $r = r_1 + r$ and computes

$$D_1 = g^{\alpha \cdot a_1} v^r, \quad D_2 = g^{-\alpha} v_1^r g^{z_1}, \quad D_3 = \left(g^b\right)^{-z_1}, \quad D_4 = v_2^r g^{z_2}, \quad D_5 = \left(g^b\right)^{-z_2},$$

$$D_6 = g^{r_2 \cdot b}, \quad D_7 = g^{r_1}, \quad R = \left(u^{ID} w^{tag_k} h\right)^{r_1}.$$

The private key is

$$d_{ID} = (D_1, \dots, D_7, R, tag_k).$$

Off-Encrypt: Choose random $s_1, s_2, t, x, tag_c \in \mathbb{Z}_p$ and let $s = s_1 + s_2$ and compute:

$$K = \left(e(g,g)^{\alpha \cdot a_1 \cdot b}\right)^{s_2}, \quad C_1 = \left(g^b\right)^{s_1 + s_2}, \quad C_2 = \left(g^{b \cdot a_1}\right)^{s_1}, \quad C_3 = \left(g^{a_1}\right)^{s_1},$$

$$C_4 = \left(g^{b \cdot a_2}\right)^{s_2}, C_5 = \left(g^{a_2}\right)^{s_2}, \quad C_6 = \tau_1^{s_1} \tau_2^{s_2},$$

$$C_7 = \left(\tau_1^b\right)^{s_1} \left(\tau_2^b\right)^{s_2} w^{-t}, \quad E_1 = \left(u^x w^{tag_c} h\right)^t, \quad E_2 = g^t.$$

Then output the offline ciphertext

$$C_{\text{off}} = (C_1, \dots, C_7, E_1, E_2, tag_c)$$

and the session key K.

On-Encrypt: To generate a ciphertext for an identity $ID \in \mathbb{Z}_p$, compute

$$C_8 = t\left(ID - x\right) \bmod p.$$

Then output the ciphertext $CT = (C_1, \ldots, C_8, E_1, E_2, tag_c)$ corresponding to the session key K.

Decrypt: To decrypt the ciphertext $CT = (C_1, \ldots, C_8, E_1, E_2, tag_c)$ with ID, the receiver first checks tag_c, if $tag_c = tag_k$, outputs invalid. Otherwise, the receiver computes

$$E_3 = E_1 \cdot u^{C_8} = \left(u^x w^{tag_c} h\right)^t \cdot u^{t(ID-x)} = \left(u^{ID} w^{tag_c} h\right)^t,$$

$$A_1 = e\left(C_1, D_1\right) \cdot e\left(C_1, D_1\right) \cdot e\left(C_1, D_1\right) \cdot e\left(C_1, D_1\right) \cdot e\left(C_1, D_1\right)$$
$$= e(g,g)^{\alpha \cdot a_1 \cdot b \cdot s_2} e(v,g)^{b(s_1+s_2)r} e(v_1,g)^{a_1 b s_1 r} e(v_2,g)^{a_2 b s_2 r}$$

Since $r = r_1 + r_2$, we have

$$A_2 = e\left(C_6, D_6\right) \cdot e\left(C_7, D_7\right) = e(v,g)^{b(s_1+s_2)r} e(v_1,g)^{a_1 b s_1 r} e(v_2,g)^{a_2 b s_2 r} e(g,w)^{-r_1 t},$$

$$A_3 = \frac{A_1}{A_2} = e(g,g)^{\alpha \cdot a_1 \cdot b \cdot s_2} e(g,w)^{r_1 t},$$

$$A_4 = \left(\frac{e\left(E_3, D_7\right)}{e\left(E_2, R\right)}\right)^{\frac{1}{tag_c - tag_k}} = e(g,w)^{r_1 t}.$$

Finally, the receiver can recover the session key by computing

$$K = \frac{A_3}{A_4}.$$

5   Conclusion

We proposed a semi-generic transformation to transform IBE into IBOOE. Our transformation is applicable to those IBE schemes whose ID header is $\left(g_1 g^{ID}\right)^s$. In comparison with traditional IBOOE schemes, our transformation saves one group element in both offline storage and ciphertext length and reduces one exponentiation operation in offline computation. We proved that our transformation is secure if the IBE scheme is secure. We presented four examples of IBE of Sakai and Kasahara [11], Boneh and Boyen [2], Gentry [7] and Waters [17] by applying our transformation.

References

1. An, J.H., Dodis, Y., Rabin, T.: On the security of joint signature and encryption. In: Knudsen, L.R. (ed.) EUROCRYPT 2002. LNCS, vol. 2332, pp. 83–107. Springer, Heidelberg (2002)
2. Boneh, D., Boyen, X.: Efficient selective-id secure identity-based encryption without random oracles. In: Cachin, C., Camenisch, J.L. (eds.) EUROCRYPT 2004. LNCS, vol. 3027, pp. 223–238. Springer, Heidelberg (2004)

3. Chow, S.S.M., Liu, J.K., Zhou, J.: Identity-based online/offline key encapsulation and encryption. In: Proceedings of the 6th ACM Symposium on Information, Computer and Communications Security, ASIACCS 2011, pp. 52–60 (2011)
4. Chu, C., Liu, J.K., Zhou, J., Bao, F., Deng, R.H.: Practical id-based encryption for wireless sensor network. In: Proceedings of the 5th ACM Symposium on Information, Computer and Communications Security, ASIACCS, pp. 337–340 (2010)
5. Cramer, R., Shoup, V.: Design and analysis of practical public-key encryption schemes secure against adaptive chosen ciphertext attack. SIAM J. Comput. **33**(1), 167–226 (2003)
6. Even, S., Goldreich, O., Micali, S.: On-line/off-line digital signatures. J. Cryptology **9**(1), 35–67 (1996)
7. Gentry, C.: Practical identity-based encryption without random oracles. In: Vaudenay, S. (ed.) EUROCRYPT 2006. LNCS, vol. 4004, pp. 445–464. Springer, Heidelberg (2006)
8. Guo, F., Mu, Y., Chen, Z.: Identity-based online/offline encryption. In: Tsudik, G. (ed.) FC 2008. LNCS, vol. 5143, pp. 247–261. Springer, Heidelberg (2008)
9. Hohenberger, S., Waters, B.: Online/offline attribute-based encryption. In: Krawczyk, H. (ed.) PKC 2014. LNCS, vol. 8383, pp. 293–310. Springer, Heidelberg (2014)
10. Liu, J.K., Zhou, J.: An efficient identity-based online/offline encryption scheme. In: Abdalla, M., Pointcheval, D., Fouque, P.-A., Vergnaud, D. (eds.) ACNS 2009. LNCS, vol. 5536, pp. 156–167. Springer, Heidelberg (2009)
11. Sakai, R., Kasahara, M.: ID based cryptosystems with pairing on elliptic curve. IACR Cryptology ePrint Archive 2003, 54 (2003)
12. Selvi, S.S.D., Vivek, S.S., Rangan, C.P.: Identity based online/offline encryption scheme. IACR Cryptology ePrint Archive 2010, 178 (2010)
13. Selvi, S.S.D., Vivek, S.S., Rangan, C.P.: Identity based online/offline encryption and signcryption schemes revisited. In: Joye, M., Mukhopadhyay, D., Tunstall, M. (eds.) InfoSecHiComNet 2011. LNCS, vol. 7011, pp. 111–127. Springer, Heidelberg (2011)
14. Shamir, A.: Identity-based cryptosystems and signature schemes. In: Blakely, G.R., Chaum, D. (eds.) CRYPTO 1984. LNCS, vol. 196, pp. 47–53. Springer, Heidelberg (1985)
15. Sun, D., Huang, X., Mu, Y., Susilo, W.: Identity-based on-line/off-line signcryption. In: IFIP International Conference on Network and Parallel Computing, NPC, pp. 34–41 (2008)
16. Sun, D., Mu, Y., Susilo, W.: A generic construction of identity-based online/offline signcryption. In: IEEE International Symposium on Parallel and Distributed Processing with Applications, ISPA, pp. 707–712 (2008)
17. Waters, B.: Dual system encryption: realizing fully secure IBE and HIBE under simple assumptions. In: Halevi, S. (ed.) CRYPTO 2009. LNCS, vol. 5677, pp. 619–636. Springer, Heidelberg (2009)
18. Yan, F., Chen, X., Zhang, Y.: Efficient online/offline signcryption without key exposure. IJGUC **4**(1), 85–93 (2013)
19. Zhao, J., Zhao, X., Shi, Y.: Certificateless signcryption with online/offline technique. Journal of Computer Applications **34**, 2659–2663 (2014)

Constructions of CCA-Secure Revocable Identity-Based Encryption

Yuu Ishida[✉], Yohei Watanabe, and Junji Shikata

Graduate School of Environment and Information Sciences,
Yokohama National University, Yokohama, Japan
{ishida-yuu-xg,watanabe-yohei-xs}@ynu.jp,
shikata@ynu.ac.jp

Abstract. Key revocation functionality is important for identity-based encryption (IBE) to manage users dynamically. Revocable IBE (RIBE) realizes such revocation functionality with scalability. In PKC 2013, Seo and Emura first considered decryption key exposure resistance (DKER) as a new realistic threat, and proposed the first RIBE scheme with DKER. Their RIBE scheme is adaptively secure against chosen plaintext attacks (CPA), and there is no concrete RIBE scheme adaptively secure against chosen ciphertext attacks (CCA) even without DKER so far. In this paper, we first propose two constructions of adaptively CCA-secure RIBE schemes with DKER. The first scheme is based on an existing transformation, which is called a BCHK transformation, that a CPA-secure hierarchical IBE scheme can be transformed into a CCA-secure scheme. The second scheme is constructed via the KEM/DEM framework. Specifically, we newly propose a revocable identity-based key encapsulation mechanism (RIB-KEM), and we show a generic construction of a CCA-secure RIBE scheme from the RIB-KEM and a data encapsulation mechanism (DEM). The second scheme is more efficient than the first one in terms of the ciphertext size.

1 Introduction

Identity-based encryption (IBE for short) is a type of public key encryption (PKE for short) to be able to use any string, such as an e-mail address, as a public key. The ability to use identities as public keys eliminates the need for a public key infrastructure (PKI for short). Since Boneh and Franklin have proposed the first secure and practical IBE scheme [6], IBE has been investigated and has become one of the important cryptographic primitives. Revocation functionality in the IBE setting (i.e. without PKIs) is one of the most important issue. For example, in a situation where secret keys of some receivers have to be revoked as soon as possible, when their secret keys are compromised. In the PKE setting, a PKI informs the senders that receivers' keys are revoked or expired via certificate revocation lists and digital certificates. However, in the IBE setting, we have to achieve such revocation functionality without PKIs. Boneh and Franklin [6] first consider a naive solution to such a revocation problem as follows. A key generation center (KGC for short), which is a trusted authority whose role is

© Springer International Publishing Switzerland 2015
E. Foo and D. Stebila (Eds.): ACISP 2015, LNCS 9144, pp. 174–191, 2015.
DOI: 10.1007/978-3-319-19962-7_11

Table 1. Efficiency comparison for two proposed RIBE schemes and the Seo–Emura RIBE. $\mathbb{G}$ is a cyclic group and $|\mathbb{G}|$ denotes the size of a group element in $\mathbb{G}$. $|vk|$ and $|\sigma|$ denote sizes of a verification key and a signature of the underlying one-time signature. An identity space in all schemes is $\{0,1\}^n$. In computational cost analysis, $[\cdot,\cdot,\cdot,\cdot]$ means the number of [pairing, multi-exponentiation, regular exponentiation, fixed-based exponentiation]. Computational costs of the underlying target collision resistant hash function and DEM do not be taken into account here. For comparison we mention that relative tunings for the various operations are as follows: [pairing$\approx$ 5, multi-exp$\approx$ 1.5, regular-exp$\approx$ 1, fixed-based-exp$\ll$ 0.2], and computational costs of the underlying Waters hashing and Boneh–Boyen hashing are approximately one, respectively (description of these hash functions will be given in Section 2). All schemes are secure under the DBDH assumption.

Scheme	Security	Ciphertext Overhead	Public Key Size	Encryption Cost	Decryption Cost
KEM-based RIBE (Section 5)	CCA	$4|\mathbb{G}|$	$(n+8)|\mathbb{G}|$	$[0,1,4,1]$	$[4,1,2,3]$
BCHK-based RIBE (Section 4)	CCA	$4|\mathbb{G}|+|vk|+|\sigma|$	$(n+8)|\mathbb{G}|$	$[0,0,6,1]$ +Sign	$[4,0,1,1]$ +Vrfy
Seo–Emura RIBE [20]	CPA	$3|\mathbb{G}|$	$(n+6)|\mathbb{G}|$	$[0,0,4,1]$	$[3,0,0,0]$

to generate users' secret keys and to distribute them via secure channels, generates a secret key $sk_{ID\|T}$ as a secret key of each non-revoked user ID at each time period T, and distributes them to only corresponding non-revoked users via secure channels at *every* time period. However, this solution does not scale well since the overhead of the KGC is proportional to the number of the non-revoked users, namely, the KGC has to generate $(N-R)$ secret keys, where N is the number of users and R is the number of revoked users. To achieve both the revocation functionality and scalability in IBE, researchers have studied revocable IBE (RIBE for short) schemes [2,7,16,17,19,20] so far.

Related Work. Boldyreva et al. [2] first formalized the security model of RIBE and proposed the first *scalable* RIBE scheme with selective security against chosen plaintext attack, which we call selective CPA-security in this paper. In their scheme, a KGC generates a long-term secret key sk_{ID} and sends it to a user via a secure channel as in IBE, and the KGC broadcasts key update ku_T at each time period T. Note that no secure channel is required for broadcasting ku_T. By using a complete subtree (CS for short) method [18], they succeeded in reducing the overhead of the KGC, specifically, the KGC generates only $O(R\log(N/R))$ number of key update at each time period when $R \geq N/2$. Such a technique for reducing revocation costs is used in all the previous RIBE schemes [7,17,19,20] except for [16]. Lee et al. [16] adopted a subset difference (SD) method [18] and a layered SD method [10] instead of the CS method, and consequently, they achieve $O(R)$ number of key update at each time period. However, their RIBE scheme achieves only selective CPA-security or requires more strong assumption to achieve adaptive CPA-security compared to other adaptively secure RIBE schemes [17, 20]. Libert and Vergnaud [17] proposed the first adaptively CPA-secure RIBE scheme. Seo and Emura [20] captured security for a new realistic threat, which is called decryption key exposure resistance (DKER for short), and proposed an adaptively CPA-secure RIBE scheme with DKER. DKER means that exposure of a decryption key $dk_{ID,T}$ for a user ID at time period T give no information on other decryption keys for the ID at other time periods. Even though the CPA-security with DKER[1] is a stronger security notion than the traditional CPA-security of RIBE [2, 17], their RIBE scheme, which we call a Seo–Emura RIBE, is most efficient in all existing (CPA-secure) RIBE schemes under the same computational assumption, i.e., decisional bilinear Diffie–Hellman (DBDH for short) assumption. In all previous RIBE schemes before the Seo–Emura RIBE, a long-term secret key and key update at the current time are used in a decryption algorithm. To capture DKER, Seo and Emura introduced a decryption key generation algorithm, and hence, a decryption algorithm requires the decryption key at the current time, which is derived from a long-term secret key and key update. Note that such non-interactive updating functionality can be also seen in key-insulated encryption (KIE for short) [8], in particular, identity-based (hierarchical) KIE [11]. However, the main purposes of those schemes are different since the purpose of KIE is to minimize the impact of key leakage, whereas that of RIBE is to revoke users efficiently and securely.

Our Contribution. In this paper, we propose two constructions of CCA-secure RIBE schemes through different approaches, which we call a *BCHK transformation-based approach* and a *KEM-based approach*. The former approach is based on a BCHK transformation [3], which can transform CPA-secure $(\ell + 1)$-level hierarchical IBE (HIBE for short) to a CCA-secure ℓ-level scheme. Although no formal description is given, the former approach was already mentioned in [20] as a way to lifting the Seo–Emura RIBE to a CCA-secure scheme. Therefore, we can say the former seems to be a naive solution. However, it is actually not so straightforward due to its DKER property. Hence, we clarify what the important point to securely construct the CCA-secure scheme via this approach is, and show a concrete construction by applying this approach to the Seo-Emura RIBE [20]. Next, we propose a more efficient construction in terms of the ciphertext size than the first (naive) construction through the latter approach. We first formalize a revocable IB-KEM (RIB-KEM for short), and propose a construction of RIB-KEM. Then, we construct a CCA-secure RIBE scheme from our RIB-KEM and a CCA-secure data encapsulation mechanism (DEM for short). For the above reason, the latter is called the KEM-based approach.

More specifically, the latter approach is as follows. The Seo–Emura RIBE is based on a CPA-secure IBE scheme proposed by Waters in [21], which we call a Waters IBE. Thus, the security of the Seo–Emura RIBE is proved under the that of Waters IBE, and hence the Seo–Emura RIBE is secure under the DBDH assumption. Their proof technique is simple and elegant, and hence,

---

[1] Throughout this paper, we consider CPA-security (and CCA-security) with DKER, and we omit "with DKER" in the following.

we take a similar approach. Namely, our aim is to provide a security reduction from our RIBE scheme to some concrete CCA-secure IBE scheme under the DBDH assumption. Therefore, we adopt an identity-based key encapsulation mechanism (IB-KEM for short) proposed by Kiltz and Galindo in [13,14] (which we call a Kiltz–Galindo IB-KEM) as the underlying scheme since an IBE scheme from their IB-KEM is most efficient in all of the existing CCA-secure IBE schemes under the DBDH assumption. Hence, we first give a model and security definition of RIB-KEM, and we would like to propose a construction of an RIB-KEM so that its security can be proved under that of the Kiltz–Galindo IB-KEM. However, the Kiltz–Galindo IB-KEM is insufficient to provide a security reduction from our proposed RIB-KEM, though the Waters IBE can give a security reduction from the Seo–Emura RIBE. Therefore, we modify the Kiltz–Galindo IB-KEM appropriately, and consider a variant of the Kiltz–Galindo IB-KEM. Then, we propose a construction of an RIB-KEM based on the variant scheme, and thus, we show a security reduction from the RIB-KEM to the variant scheme. Finally, we construct a CCA-secure RIBE scheme through the KEM/DEM framework even in the RIBE setting. Namely, we propose a generic construction of a CCA-secure RIBE scheme from our RIB-KEM and a CCA-secure DEM.

Comparison. For the first time, we propose CCA-secure RIBE schemes. An efficiency comparison between our two RIBE schemes and the Seo–Emura RIBE is given in Table 1. Note that the Seo–Emura RIBE is CPA-secure. We can say that public key sizes, encryption costs, and decryption costs between two our schemes are roughly the same. It is noteworthy that ciphertext size in the KEM-based construction is shorter than that in the BCHK transformation-based construction, and we require only one more group element for the ciphertext in the KEM-based construction compared with that in the Seo–Emura RIBE.

2 Preliminaries

Notation. In this paper, "probabilistic polynomial-time" is abbreviated as "PPT". If we write $(y_1, y_2, \ldots, y_m) \leftarrow \mathcal{A}(x_1, x_2, \ldots, x_n)$ for an algorithm $\mathcal{A}$ having n inputs and m outputs, it means to input $x_1, x_2, \ldots, x_n$ into $\mathcal{A}$ and to get the resulting output $y_1, y_2, \ldots, y_m$. We write $(y_1, y_2, \ldots, y_m) \leftarrow \mathcal{A}^{\mathcal{O}}(x_1, x_2, \ldots, x_n)$ to indicate that an algorithm $\mathcal{A}$ that is allowed to access an oracle $\mathcal{O}$ takes $x_1, x_2, \ldots, x_n$ as input and outputs $(y_1, y_2, \ldots, y_m)$. If $\mathcal{X}$ is a set, we write $x \xleftarrow{\$} \mathcal{X}$ to mean the operation of picking an element x of $\mathcal{X}$ uniformly at random. If x is a string, then $|x|$ denotes its bit-length. We use λ as a security parameter. $\mathcal{M}$, $\mathcal{I}$, $\mathcal{T}$, and $\mathcal{K}$ denote sets of plaintexts, IDs, time periods, and session keys, respectively, which are determined by a security parameter λ.

Bilinear Group. A bilinear group generator $\mathcal{G}$ is an algorithm that takes a security parameter λ as input and outputs a bilinear group $(p, \mathbb{G}, \mathbb{G}_T, e)$, where p is a prime such that $2^{2\lambda} < p$, $\mathbb{G}$ and $\mathbb{G}_T$ are multiplicative cyclic groups of order p, and $\hat{e}$ is an efficiently computable and non-degenerate bilinear map

$\hat{e} : \mathbb{G} \times \mathbb{G} \to \mathbb{G}_T$ with the following bilinear property: For any $u, u', v, v' \in \mathbb{G}$, $\hat{e}(uu', v) = \hat{e}(u, v)\hat{e}(u', v)$ and $\hat{e}(u, vv') = \hat{e}(u, v)\hat{e}(u, v')$, and for any $u, v \in \mathbb{G}$ and any $a \in \mathbb{Z}_p$, $\hat{e}(u^a, v) = \hat{e}(u, v^a) = \hat{e}(u, v)^a$ (for more details, see [6]).

Decisional Bilinear Diffie–Hellman (DBDH) Assumption. Security of all schemes described in this paper are proved under the DBDH problem. In the security proof of our RIBE construction, we provide a reduction from our IND-RID-CCA RIBE scheme to the DBDH problem. We give the definition of the DBDH assumption below. Let $\mathcal{A}$ be a PPT adversary and we consider $\mathcal{A}$'s advantage against the DBDH problem as follows.

$$Adv_{\mathcal{G},\mathcal{A}}^{DBDH}(\lambda, N) := \left| \Pr \left[\beta' = \beta \left| \begin{array}{l} (p, \mathbb{G}, \mathbb{G}_T, \hat{e}) \leftarrow \mathcal{G}, \ a, b, c \xleftarrow{\$} \mathbb{Z}_p, \\ \beta \xleftarrow{\$} \{0,1\}, \text{if } \beta = 1 \text{ then } W := \hat{e}(g,g)^{abc}, \\ \text{else } W \xleftarrow{\$} \mathbb{G}_T, \beta' \leftarrow \mathcal{A}(\lambda, g, g^a, g^b, g^c, W) \end{array} \right. \right] - \frac{1}{2} \right|.$$

Definition 1 (DBDH assumption). *The DBDH assumption relative to a generator $\mathcal{G}$ holds if for all PPT adversaries $\mathcal{A}$, $Adv_{\mathcal{G},\mathcal{A}}^{DBDH}$ is negligible in λ.*

Target Collision Resistant Hash Function (TCRHF). For simplicity, we consider a non-keyed hash function $\mathsf{TCR} : \mathcal{D} \to \mathcal{R}$ that takes $x \in \mathcal{D}$ as input and outputs $y \in \mathcal{R}$, where $|\mathcal{D}| \geq |\mathcal{R}|$.

Definition 2 (TCRHF). *A hash function TCR is said to be target collision resistant if for all PPT adversaries $\mathcal{A}$, the following advantage is negligible in λ:* $Adv_{\mathsf{TCR},\mathcal{A}}^{TCR}(\lambda) := \Pr[(x, x^*) \in \mathcal{D}^2 \wedge x \neq x^* \wedge \mathsf{TCR}(x) = \mathsf{TCR}(x^*) \mid x \xleftarrow{\$} \mathcal{D}, x^* \leftarrow \mathcal{A}(\lambda, x)]$.

Waters Hashing and Boneh–Boyen Hashing. We describe two hash functions used in IBE schemes proposed in [21] and [4], respectively. In this paper, we call the former a *Waters hashing*, and the latter a *Boneh–Boyen hashing*. For $ID = (b_1, \ldots, b_n) \in \{0,1\}^n$ and $u_0, u_1, \ldots, u_n \xleftarrow{\$} \mathbb{G}$, the Waters hashing $\mathsf{F_W} : \{0,1\}^n \to \mathbb{G}$ is defined by $\mathsf{F_W}(ID) = u_0 \prod_{i=1}^n u_i^{b_i}$; and for $T \in \mathbb{Z}_p$ and $v, v' \xleftarrow{\$} \mathbb{G}$, the Boneh-Boyen hashing $\mathsf{F_{BB}} : \mathbb{Z}_p \to \mathbb{G}$ is defined by $\mathsf{F_{BB}}(T) = v'v^T$.

KUNode Algorithm. To reduce costs of a revocation process, we use a binary tree structure and apply the following KUNode algorithm as in the previous RIBE schemes [2,17,20]. KUNode(BT, RL, T) takes as input a binary tree BT, a revocation list RL, and a time period $T \in \mathcal{T}$, and outputs a set of nodes. When η is a non-leaf node, then we write η_L and η_R as the left and right child of η, respectively. When η is a leaf node, $\mathsf{Path}(\eta)$ denotes the set of nodes on the path from η to the *root*. Each user is assigned to a leaf node. If a user who is assigned to η is revoked on a time period $T \in \mathcal{T}$, then $(\eta, T) \in RL$. KUNode(BT, RL, T) is executed as follows. It sets $\mathcal{X} := \emptyset$ and $\mathcal{Y} := \emptyset$. For any $(\eta_i, T_i) \in RL$, if $T_i \leq T$ then it adds $\mathsf{Path}(\eta_i)$ to $\mathcal{X}$ (i.e., $\mathcal{X} := \mathcal{X} \cup \mathsf{Path}(\eta_i)$). Then, for any $\eta \in \mathcal{X}$, if $\eta_L \notin \mathcal{X}$, then it adds η_L to $\mathcal{Y}$. If $\eta_R \notin \mathcal{X}$, then it adds η_R to $\mathcal{Y}$. Finally, it outputs $\mathcal{Y}$ if $\mathcal{Y} \neq \emptyset$. If $\mathcal{Y} = \emptyset$, then it adds *root* to $\mathcal{Y}$ and outputs $\mathcal{Y}$. For the

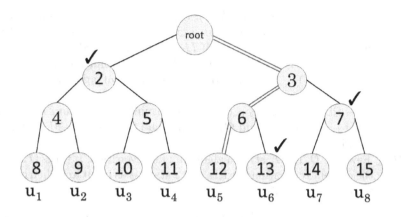

Fig. 1. Example of KUNode algorithm (when u_5 is revoked)

understanding of readers, we give an example in Fig 1 to understand KUNode algorithm easily. In the example, we suppose that a user u_5(assigned to η_{12}) is revoked. Then $\mathcal{X} = \mathsf{Path}(\eta_{12}) = \{\eta_{12}, \eta_6, \eta_3, root = \eta_1\}$, and $\mathcal{Y} = \{\eta_2, \eta_7, \eta_{13}\}$. Intuitively, all users, except u_5, have a node $\eta \in Y$ that is contained in the set of nodes on the path from their assigned node to $root$: e.g., η_2 for u_1, u_2, u_3 and u_4, η_7 for u_7 and u_8, and η_{13} for u_6, whereas $\mathcal{Y} \cap \mathsf{Path}(\eta_{12}) = \emptyset$. When a user joins the system, KGC assigns it to the leaf node η of a complete binary tree, and issues a set of keys, wherein each key is associated with each node on $\mathsf{Path}(\eta)$. At time period T, KGC publishes key updates for a set $\mathsf{KUNode}(BT, RL, T)$. Then, only non-revoked users have at least one key corresponding to a node in $\mathsf{KUNode}(BT, RL, T)$ and are able to generate decryption keys on time T.

3   Revocable Identity-Based Encryption (RIBE)

A revocable identity-based encryption (RIBE) scheme Π_{RIBE} consists of seven-tuple algorithms (Setup, PKG, KeyUp, DKG, REnc, RDec, Revoke) defined as follows:

- $(mpk, msk, RL, st) \leftarrow \mathsf{Setup}(\lambda, N)$: A probabilistic algorithm for setup. It takes a security parameter λ and the number of users N as input and outputs a master public key mpk, a master secret key msk, an initial revocation list $RL = \emptyset$ and a state st.
- $(sk_{ID}, st) \leftarrow \mathsf{PKG}(mpk, msk, ID, st)$: An algorithm for private key generation. It takes mpk, msk, an identity $ID \in \mathcal{I}$, and st as input and outputs a secret key sk_{ID} associated with ID and an updated state st.
- $ku_T \leftarrow \mathsf{KeyUp}(mpk, msk, T, RL, st)$: An algorithm for key update generation. It takes mpk, msk, a time period $T \in \mathcal{T}$, a current revocation list RL, and st as input and then outputs a key update ku_T.

- $dk_{ID,T}$ or $\perp \leftarrow \mathsf{DKG}(mpk, sk_{ID}, ku_T)$: A probabilistic algorithm for decryption key generation. It takes mpk, sk_{ID} and ku_T as input and then outputs a decryption key $dk_{ID,T}$ at T or $\perp$ if ID has been revoked.
- $CT \leftarrow \mathsf{REnc}(mpk, ID, T, M)$: A probabilistic algorithm for encryption. It takes mpk, $(ID, T) \in \mathcal{I} \times \mathcal{T}$, and $M \in \mathcal{M}$ as input and then outputs a ciphertext CT.
- M or $\perp \leftarrow \mathsf{RDec}(mpk, dk_{ID,T}, CT)$: A deterministic algorithm for decryption. It takes mpk, $dk_{ID,T}$ and CT as input and then outputs M or $\perp$ if CT is an invalid ciphertext.
- $RL \leftarrow \mathsf{Revoke}(ID, T, RL, st)$: An algorithm for revocation. It takes $(ID, T) \in \mathcal{I} \times \mathcal{T}$, the current revocation list RL, and a state st as input and then outputs an updated revocation list RL.

In the above model, we assume that Π_{RIBE} meets the following correctness property: For all security parameter λ, all $(mpk, msk, RL, st) \leftarrow \mathsf{Setup}(\lambda, N)$, all $M \in \mathcal{M}$, if $ID \in \mathcal{I}$ is not revoked on $T \in \mathcal{T}$, it holds that $M = \mathsf{RDec}(mpk, dk_{ID,T}, \mathsf{REnc}(mpk, ID, T, M))$, where $(sk_{ID}, st) \leftarrow \mathsf{PKG}(mpk, msk, ID, st)$, $ku_T \leftarrow \mathsf{KeyUp}(mpk, msk, T, RL, st)$ and $dk_{ID,T} \leftarrow \mathsf{DKG}(mpk, sk_{ID}, ku_T)$.

We describe the notion of indistinguishability against chosen ciphertext attack for RIBE (IND-RID-CCA) with DKER, which was first captured in [20]. Note that the decryption key exposure can be considered for realistic threats, therefore we consider RIBE schemes having DKER in addition to CCA-security. Let $\mathcal{A}$ be a PPT adversary, and $\mathcal{A}$'s advantage against IND-RID-CCA security is defined by

$$Adv_{\Pi_{RIBE}, \mathcal{A}}^{IND\text{-}RID\text{-}CCA}(\lambda, N) :=$$

$$\left| \Pr \left[\beta' = \beta \begin{vmatrix} (mpk, msk, RL, st) \leftarrow \mathsf{Setup}(\lambda, N), \\ (M_0^*, M_1^*, ID^*, T^*, st) \leftarrow \mathcal{A}^{\mathcal{O}(\cdot)}(\mathsf{find}, mpk, RL, st), \\ \beta \xleftarrow{\$} \{0, 1\}, CT^* \leftarrow \mathsf{REnc}(mpk, ID^*, T^*, M_\beta^*), \\ \beta' \leftarrow \mathcal{A}^{\mathcal{O}(\cdot)}(\mathsf{guess}, CT^*, st) \end{vmatrix} \right] - \frac{1}{2} \right|.$$

Here, $\mathcal{O}$ is a set of oracles $\{PKG(\cdot),\ KeyUp(\cdot),\ Revoke(\cdot, \cdot),\ DKG(\cdot, \cdot),\ RDec(\cdot, \cdot, \cdot)\}$ defined as follows.

PKG($\cdot$): For a query $ID \in \mathcal{I}$, it stores and returns sk_{ID} by running $\mathsf{PKG}(mpk, msk, ID, st)$ (if sk_{ID} was already generated and stored by DKG or $RDec$, then PKG returns the stored sk_{ID}).

KeyUp($\cdot$): For a query $T \in \mathcal{T}$, it stores and returns $\mathsf{KeyUp}(mpk, msk, T, RL, st)$.

Revoke($\cdot, \cdot$): For a query $((ID, T) \in \mathcal{I} \times \mathcal{T})$, it updates and returns a revocation list RL by running $\mathsf{Revoke}(ID, T, RL, st)$.

DKG($\cdot, \cdot$): For a query $((ID, T) \in \mathcal{I} \times \mathcal{T})$, it returns $\mathsf{DKG}(mpk, sk_{ID}, ku_T)$ and stores it unless it is $\perp$ (if $dk_{ID,T}$ was already generated and stored by $RDec$, then DKG returns the stored $dk_{ID,T}$).

RDec($\cdot, \cdot, \cdot$): For a query (ID, T, CT), it returns $\mathsf{RDec}(mpk, dk_{ID,T}, CT)$. Note that in DKG and $RDec$, sk_{ID} and/or $dk_{ID,T}$ may not have been generated yet. If not, they are generated and stored by running PKG and/or DKG, respectively.

$\mathcal{A}$ is allowed to access the above oracles with the following restrictions.

1. KeyUp($\cdot$) and Revoke($\cdot, \cdot$) can be queried at a time period which is later than or equal to that of all previous queries.
2. Revoke($\cdot, \cdot$) cannot be queried at a time period T if KeyUp($\cdot$) was queried at T.
3. If PKG(ID^*) was queried, then Revoke(ID^*, T) must be queried at $T \leq T^*$.
4. DKG($\cdot, \cdot$) and RDec($\cdot, \cdot, \cdot$) cannot be queried before KeyUp($\cdot$) was queried at time T.
5. DKG(ID^*, T^*) cannot be queried.
6. RDec(ID^*, T^*, CT^*) cannot be queried.

Definition 3 (CCA-security of RIBE). *An RIBE scheme Π_{RIBE} is said to be IND-RID-CCA secure if for all PPT adversaries $\mathcal{A}$, $Adv_{\Pi_{RIBE}, \mathcal{A}}^{IND\text{-}RID\text{-}CCA}(\lambda, N)$ is negligible in λ.*

4   Naive Approach to Constructing CCA-Secure RIBE

First, we show a naive approach based on the BCHK transformation [3], which can transform Hierarchical IBE (HIBE for short) from a CPA-secure $(\ell+1)$-level scheme and a one-time signature (OTS for short) to a CCA-secure ℓ-level scheme, and in this paper it is called *the BCHK transformation-based approach*. In [20], Seo and Emura also mentioned that a CCA-secure RIBE scheme may be easily obtained through the BCHK transformation-based approach above, however, we show that it is actually not so straightforward as expected. Therefore, in this section we clarify an important point to apply the BCHK transformation-based approach and show a concrete construction based on this approach.

The BCHK Transformation. We recall the BCHK transformation [3]. In particular, we here consider the BCHK transformation from a CPA-secure 2-level HIBE scheme and an OTS. In the 2-level HIBE, a user id_1 having a secret key sk_{id_1} can generate a secret key $sk_{(id_1, id_2)}$ for his descendant (id_1, id_2) (note that the descendant *cannot* generate his descendant's secret key). In the BCHK transformation, a fresh key-pair (sk, vk) of an OTS is generated in each encryption. We regard vk as not only a verification key of the OTS but also a part of an identity (by being encoded as an n-bit string). Then, a ciphertext C is generated by the encryption algorithm of the CPA-secure HIBE and the identity (ID, vk). Hence, the resulting ciphertext is (C, vk, σ), where σ is a signature of C. For decryption, a user having a secret key sk_{ID} generates $sk_{(ID, vk)}$ and decrypts C after validity checking of C by the verification algorithm of the OTS.

Details of the BCHK Transformation-Based Approach (Also Mentioned in [20]). The Seo–Emura RIBE is based on the Waters IBE [21], and consequently, the CPA security of the Seo–Emura RIBE is proved by a polynomial-time reduction to that of the Waters IBE. In [20, Section6], Seo and Emura referred to the BCHK transformation-based approach as follows:

"Due to the property of the underlying Waters IBE scheme, we can extend our RIBE scheme to a HIBE scheme with efficient revocation only for the first level users. There is a well-known transformation from a two-level HIBE scheme to a CCA-secure IBE scheme [3]. Therefore, we can obtain CCA-secure RIBE scheme by applying this transformation."

Since any CPA-secure 2-level HIBE with *selective security* regarding the second level of the hierarchy and *adaptive security* regarding the first level is sufficient to obtain a CCA-secure IBE scheme (showed in [3,21]), we brush up the above approach by efficiently constructing the underlying 2-level HIBE scheme from the Boneh–Boyen IBE [4] and the Waters IBE [21]. For convenience, such a CPA-secure 2-level HIBE scheme using the Boneh–Boyen IBE at the second level and the Waters IBE at the first level is called a *Hybrid HIBE* scheme in this paper.

Important Point to Apply the BCHK Transformation-Based Approach. The reason why the BCHK transformation-based approach cannot be easily applied is due to its DKER property, namely, the existence of the DKG algorithm.

We give intuition of an important point to construct a *secure* RIBE scheme through this approach. Suppose that a ciphertext C is encrypted by using a 2-dimensional ID-vector (ID, vk) at a time period T, and the resulting ciphertext CT is (C, vk, σ). Therefore, $dk_{(ID,vk),T}$ is needed to decrypt C. As a natural way of trying to take this approach, one may come up with the following approach: First, a secret key at the second level of hierarchy (i.e. $sk_{(ID,vk)}$) is generated, then a decryption key at T is generated from it (i.e. $dk_{(ID,vk),T}$). This means that the DKG algorithm takes sk_{ID} and ku_T as input and outputs $dk_{ID,T} := (sk_{ID}, ku_T)$ directly. However, it is obvious that the resulting RIBE scheme is insecure since an adversary can obtain both sk_{ID} and ku_T by querying $dk_{ID^*,T}$ and dk_{ID,T^*} to the *DKG* oracle, respectively, in the IND-RID-CCA game. For the above reason, we take the following approach: As in the Seo–Emura RIBE, a decryption key at the first level at T (i.e. $dk_{ID,T}$) is generated in the DKG algorithm, and then $dk_{(ID,vk),T}$ is calculated from $dk_{ID,T}$ and vk in the RDec algorithm. As seen above, we have to pay attention to such a *generating flow of decryption keys*. Taking into account above, we construct a CCA-secure RIBE scheme based on the BCHK transformation-based approach as follows.

Let $\mathcal{T} := \mathbb{Z}_p$, $\mathcal{I} := \{0,1\}^n$, and $\mathcal{M} := \mathbb{G}_T$. Let $\Pi_{OTS} = (\mathsf{Setup}, \mathsf{Sign}, \mathsf{Ver})$ be a one-time signature.[2] Let $\mathsf{F_W} : \{0,1\}^n \to \mathbb{G}$ be the Waters hashing which consists of $u_0, u_1, \ldots, u_n \in \mathbb{G}$, and $\mathsf{F}_{\mathsf{BB}}^{(i)} : \mathbb{Z}_p \to \mathbb{G}$ ($i = 1, 2$) be two Boneh-Boyen hashing which consist of $v_1, v_1' \in \mathbb{G}$ and $v_2, v_2' \in \mathbb{G}$, respectively. To avoid confusion, we denote them by $\mathsf{F}_{\mathsf{BB}}^{(i)}(x) := v_i' v_i^x$. We assume vk is appropriately encoded as an element of $\mathbb{Z}_p$ when it is used in $\mathsf{F}_{\mathsf{BB}}^{(1)}$.

---

[2] We omit description of an OTS (and a DEM, which will appear in Section 5.4) since we believe readers are familiar with it.

- Setup(λ, N): First, it gets $(p, \mathbb{G}, \mathbb{G}_T, \hat{e}) \leftarrow \mathcal{G}(\lambda)$. Let g be a generator of $\mathbb{G}$. It chooses $g_2, u_0, u_1, \ldots, u_n, v_1', v_1, v_2', v_2 \xleftarrow{\$} \mathbb{G}$ and $\alpha \xleftarrow{\$} \mathbb{Z}_p$, and sets $g_1 := g^\alpha$. It outputs $mpk := (g, g_1, g_2, u_0, u_1, \ldots, u_n, v_1', v_1, v_2', v_2)$, $msk := \alpha$, $RL := \emptyset$ and $st := BT$ where BT is a binary tree with N leaves.
- PKG(mpk, msk, ID, st): It randomly chooses an unassigned leaf η from BT, and stores ID in the node η. For each node $\theta \in \mathsf{Path}(\eta)$, it recalls g_θ if it was defined. Otherwise, it chooses $g_\theta \xleftarrow{\$} \mathbb{G}$ and stores g_θ in the node θ. Then, it chooses $r_\theta \xleftarrow{\$} \mathbb{Z}_p$ and computes

$$(D_\theta^{(0)}, D_\theta^{(1)}) = (g_\theta^\alpha \mathsf{F_W}(ID)^{r_\theta}, g^{r_\theta}).$$

Finally, it outputs $sk_{ID} := \left\{ (\theta, D_\theta^{(0)}, D_\theta^{(1)}) \right\}_{\theta \in \mathsf{Path}(\eta)}$ and $st := BT$.
- KeyUp(mpk, msk, T, RL, st): Parse st as $st := BT$. For each node $\theta \in \mathsf{KUNode}(BT, RL, T)$, it computes as follows. It retrieves g_θ and computes $\tilde{g}_\theta := w_1/g_\theta$. Note that g_θ is always pre-defined in PKG. It chooses $s_\theta \xleftarrow{\$} \mathbb{Z}_p$ and computes

$$(\tilde{D}_\theta^{(0)}, \tilde{D}_\theta^{(1)}) := (\tilde{g}_\theta^\alpha \mathsf{F_W}(ID)^{s_\theta}, g^{s_\theta}).$$

Finally, it outputs $ku_T := \left\{ (\theta, \tilde{D}_\theta^{(0)}, \tilde{D}_\theta^{(1)}) \right\}_{\theta \in \mathsf{KUNode}(BT, RL, T)}$.
- DKG(mpk, sk_{ID}, ku_T): Parse sk_{ID} as $sk_{ID} = \{(\theta, D_\theta^{(0)}, D_\theta^{(1)})\}_{\theta \in \Theta_{sk}}$ and ku_T as $ku_T = \{(\theta, \tilde{D}_\theta^{(0)}, \tilde{D}_\theta^{(1)})\}_{\theta \in \Theta_{ku}}$. If $\Theta_{sk} \cap \Theta_{ku} = \emptyset$, then it outputs $\bot$. Otherwise, it chooses $\theta \in \Theta_{sk} \cap \Theta_{ku}$ and $r, s \xleftarrow{\$} \mathbb{Z}_p$, and outputs

$$dk_{ID,T} = (D_\theta^{(0)} \tilde{D}_\theta^{(0)} \mathsf{F_W}(ID)^r \mathsf{F_{BB}^{(2)}}(T)^s, D_\theta^{(1)} g^r, \tilde{D}_\theta^{(1)} g^s)$$
$$= (w_1^\alpha \mathsf{F_W}(ID)^{r+r_\theta} \mathsf{F_{BB}^{(2)}}(T)^{s+s_\theta}, g^{r+r_\theta}, g^{s+s_\theta}).$$

- REnc(mpk, ID, T, M) : It first runs $(vk, sk) \leftarrow \mathsf{Setup}(\lambda)$. It chooses $t \xleftarrow{\$} \mathbb{Z}_p$ and computes

$$C_0 := M \cdot \hat{e}(g_1, g_2)^t, C_1 := g^{-t}, C_2 := \mathsf{F_W}(ID)^t, C_3 := \mathsf{F_{BB}^{(1)}}(vk)^t, C_4 := \mathsf{F_{BB}^{(2)}}(T)^t.$$

It also runs $\sigma \leftarrow \mathsf{Sign}(sk, (C_0, C_1, \ldots, C_4))$ and outputs $CT := (vk, C_0, C_1, \ldots, C_4, \sigma)$.
- RDec($mpk, dk_{ID,T}, CT$): Parse $dk_{ID,T}$ as $dk_{ID,T} = (DK_1, DK_2, DK_3)$ and CT as $CT = (vk, C_0, C_1, \ldots, C_4, \sigma)$. If $\mathsf{Ver}(vk, C_0, \ldots, C_4, \sigma) \to 0$, then it outputs $\bot$. Otherwise, it chooses $\tilde{r} \xleftarrow{\$} \mathbb{Z}_p$ and computes

$$dk_{(ID,vk),T} = (D_1, D_2, D_3, D_4)$$
$$= (DK_1 \cdot \mathsf{F_{BB}^{(1)}}(vk)^{\tilde{r}}, DK_2, g^{\tilde{r}}, DK_3)$$
$$= (g_2^\alpha \mathsf{F_W}(ID)^{r+r_\theta} \mathsf{F_{BB}^{(1)}}(vk)^{\tilde{r}} \cdot \mathsf{F_{BB}^{(2)}}(T)^{s+s_\theta}, g^{r+r_\theta}, g^{\tilde{r}}, g^{s+s_\theta}).$$

Finally, it outputs $M = C_0 \prod_{i=1}^4 \hat{e}(C_i, D_i)$.

- Revoke(mpk, ID, T, RL, st) : Let η be a leaf node associated with ID. It updates the revocation list by $RL \leftarrow RL \cup \{(\eta, T)\}$ and outputs the updated revocation list RL.

We obtain the following theorem. Due to space limitation, the proof will appear in the full version of this paper.

Theorem 1. *If the underlying 2-level Hybrid HIBE scheme is IND-ID-CPA secure and Π_{OTS} is OT-sEUF-CMA secure, then our RIBE scheme constructed above is IND-RID-CCA secure.*

In general, the BCHK transformation is one of *generic* transformations, whereas the above construction is a direct one (i.e. a construction from scratch). Therefore, there seem to be some redundant points. In particular, due to the underlying OTS, the ciphertext contains vk and σ, and hence the overhead seems to be a redundant length. Thus, in the next section, we propose a more efficient CCA-secure RIBE scheme by taking another approach.

5   KEM-Based Approach: CCA-Secure Revocable ID-Based KEM

We introduce a revocable identity-based key encapsulation mechanism (RIB-KEM for short), and show a construction of a CCA-secure RIB-KEM. As mentioned earlier, in [20], Seo–Emura RIBE scheme is proved to be IND-RID-CPA secure under the DBDH assumption through the reduction to the Waters IBE [21]. The proof technique is simple and elegant, and further, their construction based on the Waters IBE and the Boneh–Boyen IBE [4,5] is also simple and most efficient among all existing CPA-secure RIBE schemes (under the DBDH assumption). Therefore, we would like to use a similar approach so that security of our RIBE scheme is proved under that of a certain concrete CCA-secure IBE scheme, and for doing so, we consider a CCA-secure IBE scheme from the Kiltz–Galindo IB-KEM [13,14]. The Kiltz–Galindo IB-KEM is based on the Waters IBE and is the most efficient construction among existing CCA-secure IB-KEMs (and IBE schemes) under the DBDH assumption.[3] However, we cannot apply Seo and Emura's proof technique to the *original* Kiltz–Galindo IB-KEM, whereas it can be applied to the Waters IBE. Therefore, we first consider a variant of the Kiltz–Galindo IB-KEM in such a way that it suits our aim (i.e., to be able to give a reduction from the security of our RIB-KEM), and show the resulting IB-KEM is also IND-ID-CCA secure under the DBDH assumption (i.e. the same as the original one). Then, we construct a CCA-secure RIB-KEM based on the variant IB-KEM. Finally, we construct a CCA-secure RIBE scheme from our CCA-secure RIB-KEM and a CCA-secure DEM via the KEM/DEM framework in the RIBE setting. Therefore, as a by-product we will show that the KEM/DEM framework works well in the RIBE setting.

---

[3] Of course we may construct more efficient IBE schemes than the Kiltz–Galindo scheme if we allow to use more strong assumptions or add other assumptions (e.g. [9,15,22]). However, we consider the DBDH assumption only in this paper, since it is the standard assumption used for utilizing pairing techniques in cryptography.

5.1 Syntax of Revocable IB-KEM

An RIB-KEM, which is based on RIBE [20] and IB-KEMs [1,13,14], is defined as follows. An RIB-KEM $\Pi_{RIB\text{-}KEM}$ consists of seven-tuple algorithms (Setup, PKG, KeyUp, DKG, REncaps, RDecps, Revoke). All algorithms except for REncaps and RDecaps are the same as those of RIBE. Therefore, we here describe only these two algorithms.

- $(C, K) \leftarrow$ REncaps(mpk, ID, T): A probabilistic algorithm for encapsulation. It takes mpk, $ID \in \mathcal{I}$, $T \in \mathcal{T}$ and as input and then outputs a session key $K \in \mathcal{K}$ and a ciphertext C.
- $K \leftarrow$ RDecaps($mpk, ID, T, dk_{ID,T}, C$): A deterministic algorithm for decapsulation. It takes mpk, $dk_{ID,T}$ and C as input and then outputs K.

We assume that $\Pi_{RIB\text{-}KEM}$ meets the following correctness property: For all security parameter λ, all $(mpk, msk, RL, st) \leftarrow$ Setup(λ, N), and all $(C, K) \leftarrow$ REncaps (mpk, ID, T), if $ID \in \mathcal{I}$ is not revoked at time $T \in \mathcal{T}$, it holds that $K \leftarrow$ RDecaps($mpk, dk_{ID,T}, C$), where $(sk_{ID}, st) \leftarrow$ PKG(mpk, msk, ID, st), $ku_T \leftarrow$ KeyUp(mpk, msk, T, RL, st) and $dk_{ID,T} \leftarrow$ DKG(mpk, sk_{ID}, ku_T).

We describe a KEM-version of the IND-RID-CCA security. Let $\mathcal{A}$ be a PPT adversary and $\mathcal{A}$'s advantage for IND-RID-CCA security is defined by

$$Adv_{\Pi_{RIB\text{-}KEM},\mathcal{A}}^{IND\text{-}RID\text{-}CCA}(\lambda, N) :=$$

$$\left| \Pr\left[\beta' = \beta \left| \begin{matrix} (mpk, msk, RL, st) \leftarrow \text{Setup}(\lambda, N), \\ (ID^*, T^*, st) \leftarrow \mathcal{A}^{\mathcal{O}(\cdot)}(\text{find}, mpk, RL, st), \\ K_0^* \xleftarrow{\$} \mathcal{K}, \\ (C^*, K_1^*) \leftarrow \text{REncaps}(mpk, ID^*, T^*), \\ \beta \xleftarrow{\$} \{0,1\}, \beta' \leftarrow \mathcal{A}^{\mathcal{O}(\cdot)}(\text{guess}, K_\beta^*, C^*, st) \end{matrix} \right. \right] - \frac{1}{2} \right|.$$

Here, $\mathcal{O}$ is a set of oracles $\{PKG(\cdot), KeyUp(\cdot, \cdot), Revoke(\cdot), DKG(\cdot), RDe\text{-}caps(\cdot, \cdot, \cdot)\}$, which are the same as those in the case of RIBE except for $RDe\text{-}caps(\cdot, \cdot, \cdot)$. For a query (ID, T, C), $RDecaps(\cdot, \cdot, \cdot)$ returns K by running $sk_{ID} \leftarrow$ PKG(mpk, msk, ID, st), $dk_{ID,T} \leftarrow$ DKG(mpk, sk_{ID}, ku_T) (or taking stored sk_{ID} and $dk_{ID,T}$ if they have been already generated), and $K \leftarrow$ RDecaps($mpk, ID, T, dk_{ID,T}, C$). Restrictions on queries for oracles are also the same as those of RIBE by replacing the $RDec$ oracle with the $RDecaps$ oracle.

Definition 4 (CCA-security of RIB-KEM). *An RIB-KEM $\Pi_{RIB\text{-}KEM}$ is said to be IND-RID-CCA secure if for all PPT adversaries $\mathcal{A}$, $\mathcal{A}$'s advantage $Adv_{\Pi_{RIB\text{-}KEM},\mathcal{A}}^{IND\text{-}RID\text{-}CCA}(\lambda, N)$ is negligible in λ.*

5.2 A Variant of the Kiltz–Galindo IB-KEM

We modify the Kiltz–Galindo IB-KEM [13,14]. Let $\mathsf{TCR} : \mathbb{G} \to \mathbb{Z}_p$ be a target collision resistant hash function and $\mathsf{F_W} : \{0,1\}^n \to \mathbb{G}$ be the Waters hashing which consists of $u_0, u_1, \ldots, u_n$. We construct an IB-KEM $\Pi_{\mathsf{vKG}} = \{\mathsf{KG}_{\mathsf{vKG}},$

$\mathsf{Extract}_{\mathsf{vKG}}$, $\mathsf{Encaps}_{\mathsf{vKG}}$, $\mathsf{Decaps}_{\mathsf{vKG}}\}$ with $\mathcal{I} := \{0,1\}^n$, and $\mathcal{K} := \mathbb{G}_T$ as follows. In this construction, we say that a tuple $(g, u, v, w) \in \mathbb{G}^4$ is a DH tuple if it satisfies $\hat{e}(g, w) = \hat{e}(v, u)$.

- $\mathsf{KG}_{\mathsf{vKG}}(\lambda)$: First, it gets $(p, \mathbb{G}, \mathbb{G}_T, \hat{e}) \leftarrow \mathcal{G}(\lambda)$. Let g be a generator of $\mathbb{G}$. It chooses $\alpha \xleftarrow{\$} \mathbb{Z}_p$, $w_1, w_2, u_0, u_1, \ldots, u_n \xleftarrow{\$} \mathbb{G}$, and sets $g_1 := g^\alpha$ and $z := \hat{e}(g, w_1)^\alpha$. It outputs $mpk := (g, g_1, w_1, w_2, u_0, u_1, \ldots, u_n, z)$ and $msk := \alpha$.
- $\mathsf{Extract}_{\mathsf{vKG}}(mpk, msk, ID)$: It chooses $s \xleftarrow{\$} \mathbb{Z}_p$ and computes $SK_{ID} := (w_1^\alpha \mathsf{F_W}(ID)^s, g^s)$.
- $\mathsf{Encaps}_{\mathsf{vKG}}(mpk, ID)$: It chooses $r \xleftarrow{\$} \mathbb{Z}_p$ and computes $c_1 := g^r$, $c_2 := \mathsf{F_W}(ID)^r$, $c_3 := (w_1^t w_2)^r$, where $t \leftarrow \mathsf{TCR}(c_1)$. It also computes a random session key $K := z^r \in \mathbb{G}_T$. Finally, it outputs a session key K and a ciphertext $C := (c_1, c_2, c_3)$.
- $\mathsf{Decaps}_{\mathsf{vKG}}(mpk, ID, SK_{ID}, C)$: Parse C and SK_{ID} as $C = (c_1, c_2, c_3)$ and $SK_{ID} = (d_1, d_2)$ respectively. It first runs $t \leftarrow \mathsf{TCR}(c_1)$ and checks whether $(g, c_1, w_1^t w_2, c_3)$ and $(g, c_1, \mathsf{F_W}(ID), c_2)$ are DH tuples. If both of them are DH tuples, then it outputs $K = \hat{e}(c_1, d_1)/\hat{e}(c_2, d_2)$. Otherwise, it outputs $K \xleftarrow{\$} \mathbb{G}_T$.

The above scheme satisfies the following correctness property: For all $\lambda \in \mathbb{N}$, all $ID \in \mathcal{I}$, all $(mpk, msk) \leftarrow \mathsf{KG}_{\mathsf{vKG}}(\lambda)$, all $SK_{ID} \leftarrow \mathsf{Extract}_{\mathsf{vKG}}(mpk, msk, ID)$, and all $(C, K) \leftarrow \mathsf{Encaps}_{\mathsf{vKG}}(mpk, ID)$, it holds that $K \leftarrow \mathsf{Decaps}_{\mathsf{vKG}}(mpk, ID, SK_{ID}, C)$.

Roughly speaking, the important point for this modification is that we add a one element of $\mathbb{G}$ (i.e., $g_1 := g^\alpha$) to a public parameter of the original scheme and then replace a secret key $\alpha \in \mathbb{Z}_p$ with $\alpha \in \mathbb{G}$. The reason why the above modification is needed is that in the security proof of our RIB-KEM, an adversary of IB-KEM needs to embed information on a secret key into a key update ku_T without knowing the secret key $msk = \alpha$ and he/she has to answer a query from an adversary of RIB-KEM. To achieve this, we need to add information on α as exponent in the public parameter (i.e. g_1), and we can prove the following theorem.

Theorem 2. *The above IB-KEM Π_{vKG} is IND-ID-CCA secure under the DBDH assumption.*

Proof (Sketch). We can give the proof in a similar way to that of the original scheme [14] with a slight modification. Due to space limitation, we here give intuition about the proof. We can construct an adversary $\mathcal{B}$ against the DBDH problem by using an adversary $\mathcal{A}$ against the IND-RID-CCA security. After receiving g, g^a, g^b, g^c, and W, where $W = \hat{e}(g, g)^{abc}$ or $W \xleftarrow{\$} \mathbb{G}_T$, $\mathcal{A}$ sets $w_1 := g^a$, $w_2, u_0, u_1, \ldots, u_n \xleftarrow{\$} \mathbb{G}$, $z := \hat{e}(g^a, g^b)$, and $g_1 := g^b$. When receiving a challenge query ID^*, $\mathcal{B}$ chooses $\beta \xleftarrow{\$} \{0, 1\}$ and sets a challenge ciphertext $c_1^* := g^c$, $c_2^* := \mathsf{F_W}(ID^*)^c$, $c_3^* := (w_1^{t^*} w_2)^c$ and a session key $K_\beta := W$ (if $\beta = 0$ then W is a random element of $\mathbb{G}_T$, otherwise $W = z^c$), where $t^* \leftarrow \mathsf{TCR}(c_1^*)$. Since c_2^* and c_3^* have to be computed without knowing the exact value of c, we need to change values of c_2^* and c_3^* by a sequence of games. We can also prove that differences between games are negligible.   □

5.3 Proposed CCA-Secure RIB-KEM

A basic idea of our construction is similar to that in the Seo–Emura RIBE scheme [20]. Namely, we consider a simple 2-level hierarchical IB-KEM (without delegating property), and we assign the first level of hierarchy for identities and the second level for time periods. Interestingly, a 2-level hierarchical IB-KEM with our adaptively CCA-secure variant scheme Π_{vKG} (as seen in the previous subsection) at the first level and the selectively CPA-secure Boneh-Boyen IBE at the second level is sufficient for constructing a CCA-secure RIB-KEM. We propose a construction of an RIB-KEM $\Pi_{RIB\text{-}KEM}$ ={Setup, PKG, KeyUp, DKG, REncaps, RDecaps, Revoke} with $\mathcal{T} := \mathbb{Z}_p$, $\mathcal{I} := \{0,1\}^n$, and $\mathcal{K} := \mathbb{G}_T$ as follows. Let TCR : $\mathbb{G} \to \mathbb{Z}_p$ be a target collision resistant hash function, $\mathsf{F_W} : \{0,1\}^n \to \mathbb{G}$ be the Waters hashing which consists of $u_0, u_1, \ldots, u_n$, and $\mathsf{F_{BB}} : \mathbb{Z}_p \to \mathbb{G}$ be the Boneh-Boyen hashing which consists of v, v'.

- Setup(λ, N): First, it gets $(p, \mathbb{G}, \mathbb{G}_T, \hat{e}) \leftarrow \mathcal{G}(\lambda)$. Let g be a generator of $\mathbb{G}$. It chooses $\alpha \xleftarrow{\$} \mathbb{Z}_p$, $w_1, w_2, u_0, u_1, \ldots, u_n, v', v \xleftarrow{\$} \mathbb{G}$, $g_1 := g^\alpha$ and $z := \hat{e}(g, w_1)^\alpha$. It outputs $mpk := (g, g_1, w_1, w_2, u_0, u_1, \ldots, u_n, v', v, z)$, $msk := \alpha$, $RL := \emptyset$, $st := BT$ where BT is a binary tree with N leaves.
- PKG(mpk, msk, ID, st): It randomly chooses an unassigned leaf η from BT, and stores ID in the node η. For each node $\theta \in \mathsf{Path}(\eta)$, it recalls g_θ if it was defined. Otherwise, it chooses $g_\theta \xleftarrow{\$} \mathbb{G}$ and stores g_θ in the node θ. Then, it chooses $\hat{r}_\theta \xleftarrow{\$} \mathbb{Z}_p$ and it computes

$$(D_\theta^{(0)}, D_\theta^{(1)}) = (g_\theta^\alpha \mathsf{F_W}(ID)^{\hat{r}_\theta}, g^{\hat{r}_\theta}).$$

Finally, it outputs $sk_{ID} := \left\{ (\theta, D_\theta^{(0)}, D_\theta^{(1)}) \right\}_{\theta \in \mathsf{Path}(\eta)}$ and $st := BT$.
- KeyUp(mpk, msk, T, RL, st): For each node $\theta \in \mathsf{KUNode}(BT, RL, T)$, it computes as follows. It retrieves g_θ and computes $\tilde{g}_\theta := w_1/g_\theta$. Note that g_θ is always pre-defined in PKG. It chooses $\hat{s}_\theta \xleftarrow{\$} \mathbb{Z}_p$ and computes

$$(\tilde{D}_\theta^{(0)}, \tilde{D}_\theta^{(1)}) = (\tilde{g}_\theta^\alpha \mathsf{F_W}(ID)^{\hat{s}_\theta}, g^{\hat{s}_\theta}).$$

Finally, it outputs $ku_T = \left\{ (\theta, \tilde{D}_\theta^{(0)}, \tilde{D}_\theta^{(1)}) \right\}_{\theta \in \mathsf{KUNode}(BT, RL, T)}$.
- DKG(mpk, sk_{ID}, ku_T): Parse sk_{ID} and ku_T as $sk_{ID} = \{(\theta, D_\theta^{(0)}, D_\theta^{(1)})\}_{\theta \in \Theta_{sk}}$ and $ku_T = \{(\theta, \tilde{D}_\theta^{(0)}, \tilde{D}_\theta^{(1)})\}_{\theta \in \Theta_{ku}}$, respectively. If $\Theta_{sk} \cap \Theta_{ku} = \emptyset$, then it outputs $\perp$. Otherwise, it chooses $\theta \in \Theta_{sk} \cap \Theta_{ku}$, $\hat{r}, \hat{s} \xleftarrow{\$} \mathbb{Z}_p$ and outputs

$$dk_{ID,T} = (D_\theta^{(0)} \cdot \tilde{D}_\theta^{(0)} \cdot \mathsf{F_W}(ID)^{\hat{r}} \cdot \mathsf{F_{BB}}(T)^{\hat{s}}, D_\theta^{(1)} \cdot g^{\hat{r}}, \tilde{D}_\theta^{(1)} \cdot g^{\hat{s}})$$
$$= (w_1^\alpha \mathsf{F_W}(ID)^{\hat{r}+\hat{r}_\theta} \mathsf{F_{BB}}(T)^{\hat{s}+\hat{s}_\theta}, g^{\hat{r}+\hat{r}_\theta}, g^{\hat{s}+\hat{s}_\theta}).$$

- REncaps(mpk, ID, T): It chooses $r \xleftarrow{\$} \mathbb{Z}_p$ and computes

$$c_1 := g^r, \quad c_2 := \mathsf{F_W}(ID)^r, \quad c_3 := \mathsf{F_{BB}}(T)^r, \quad c_4 := (w_1^t w_2)^r, \quad K := z^r \in \mathbb{G}_T,$$

where $t \leftarrow \mathsf{TCR}(c_1)$. It outputs K and $C := (c_1, c_2, c_3, c_4)$.
- RDecaps($mpk, ID, dk_{ID,T}, C$): Parse $dk_{ID,T}$ and C as $dk_{ID,T} = (d_1, d_2, d_3)$ and $C = (c_1, c_2, c_3, c_4)$, respectively. It computes $t \leftarrow \mathsf{TCR}(c_1)$ and chooses $r_1, r_2, r_3 \xleftarrow{\$} \mathbb{Z}_p$. Then, it computes

$$K = \frac{\hat{e}(c_1, d_1 \cdot (w_1^t w_2)^{r_1} \cdot \mathsf{F_W}(ID)^{r_2} \cdot \mathsf{F_{BB}}(T)^{r_3})}{\hat{e}(c_3, d_3 \cdot g^{r_3})\hat{e}(c_2, d_2 \cdot g^{r_2})\hat{e}(g^{r_1}, c_4)}.$$

- Revoke(mpk, ID, T, RL, st): Let η be a leaf node associated with ID. It updates the revocation list by $RL \leftarrow RL \cup \{(\eta, T)\}$ and outputs the updated revocation list RL.

First, we show the correctness of our $\Pi_{RIB\text{-}KEM}$. Before that, we show that the above RDecaps algorithm always outputs a random group element of $\mathbb{G}_T$ if C is not a valid ciphertext. In fact, we have

$$
\begin{aligned}
K &= \frac{\hat{e}(c_1, d_1 \cdot (w_1^t w_2)^{r_1} \cdot \mathsf{F_W}(ID)^{r_2} \cdot \mathsf{F_{BB}}(T)^{r_3})}{\hat{e}(c_3, d_3 \cdot g^{r_3})\hat{e}(c_2, d_2 \cdot g^{r_2})\hat{e}(g^{r_1}, c_4)} \\
&= \frac{\hat{e}(c_1, d_1)\hat{e}(c_1, (w_1^t w_2)^{r_1})\hat{e}(c_1, \mathsf{F_W}(ID)^{r_2})\hat{e}(c_1, \mathsf{F_{BB}}(T)^{r_3})}{\hat{e}(c_3, d_3)\hat{e}(c_2, d_2)\hat{e}(g^{r_1}, c_4)\hat{e}(c_2, g^{r_2})\hat{e}(c_3, g^{r_3})} \\
&= \frac{\hat{e}(c_1, d_1)}{\hat{e}(c_3, d_3)\hat{e}(c_2, d_2)} \cdot \frac{\hat{e}(c_1, (w_1^t w_2)^{r_1})}{\hat{e}(g^{r_1}, c_4)} \cdot \frac{\hat{e}(c_1, \mathsf{F_W}(ID)^{r_2})}{\hat{e}(c_2, g^{r_2})} \cdot \frac{\hat{e}(c_1, \mathsf{F_{BB}}(T)^{r_3})}{\hat{e}(c_3, g^{r_3})} \\
&= \frac{\hat{e}(c_1, d_1)}{\hat{e}(c_3, d_3)\hat{e}(c_2, d_2)} \cdot \Delta_1(C)^{r_1} \cdot \Delta_2(C)^{r_2} \cdot \Delta_3(C)^{r_3},
\end{aligned}
$$

where $\Delta_1(C) := \frac{\hat{e}(c_1, (w_1^t w_2))}{\hat{e}(g, c_4)}$, $\Delta_2(C) := \frac{\hat{e}(c_1, \mathsf{F_W}(ID))}{\hat{e}(c_2, g)}$, and $\Delta_3(C) := \frac{\hat{e}(c_1, \mathsf{F_{BB}}(T))}{\hat{e}(c_3, g)}$. Then, $\Delta_1(C) = \Delta_2(C) = \Delta_3(C) = 1$ if and only if C is valid ciphertext, and therefore, K is a random group element of $\mathbb{G}_T$ if C is not valid. Such an *implicit rejection* technique can be also seen in [12,14]. We then show that $\Pi_{RIB\text{-}KEM}$ satisfies the correctness. Suppose that $dk_{ID,T} = (d_1, d_2, d_3)$ is a correctly-generated decryption key of a non-revoked user ID at T, and that $C = (c_1, c_2, c_3, c_4)$ is a valid ciphertext for the user ID. Then, we have

$$
\begin{aligned}
\frac{\hat{e}(c_1, d_1)}{\hat{e}(c_3, d_3)\hat{e}(c_2, d_2)} &= \frac{\hat{e}(g^r, w_1^\alpha \mathsf{F_W}(ID)^{\hat{r}+\hat{r}_\theta} \mathsf{F_{BB}}(T)^{\hat{s}+\hat{s}_\theta})}{\hat{e}(\mathsf{F_{BB}}(T)^r, g^{\hat{s}+\hat{s}_\theta})\hat{e}(\mathsf{F_W}(ID)^r, g^{\hat{r}+\hat{r}_\theta})} \\
&= \frac{\hat{e}(g^r, w_1^\alpha)\hat{e}(g^r, \mathsf{F_W}(ID)^{\hat{r}+\hat{r}_\theta})\hat{e}(g^r, \mathsf{F_{BB}}(T)^{\hat{s}+\hat{s}_\theta})}{\hat{e}(\mathsf{F_{BB}}(T)^r, g^{\hat{s}+\hat{s}_\theta})\hat{e}(\mathsf{F_W}(ID)^r, g^{\hat{r}+\hat{r}_\theta})} \\
&= z^r.
\end{aligned}
$$

Next, we show security of our $\Pi_{RIB\text{-}KEM}$ as follows. The formal proof will appear in the full version of this paper.

Theorem 3. *If the IB-KEM Π_{vKG} described in Section 5.2 is IND-ID-CCA secure, then our proposed $\Pi_{RIB\text{-}KEM}$ is IND-RID-CCA secure.*

Proof (Sketch). We can prove it through a similar approach of the security proof in [20]. We construct adversary $\mathcal{B}$ who breaks IND-ID-CCA security for Π_{vKG} using an adversary $\mathcal{A}$ who breaks IND-RID-CCA security for $\Pi_{RIB\text{-}KEM}$. $\mathcal{CH}$ denotes the challenger of IND-ID-CCA game of Π_{vKG}. First, $\mathcal{B}$ receives $g, g_1, w_1, w_2, u_0, u_1, \ldots, u_n, z$ as a public parameter of Π_{vKG} from $\mathcal{CH}$. Then, $\mathcal{B}$ chooses $\nu, \nu' \xleftarrow{\$} \mathbb{Z}_p$ and computes $v = g_1 g^{\nu}$ and $v' = g_1^{-T^*} g^{\nu'}$, and $\mathcal{B}$ sends $mpk := (g, g_1, w_1, w_2, u_0, u_1, \ldots, u_n, v', v, z)$ to $\mathcal{A}$. Next, we need to consider two types of adversaries for simulating *PKG*, *KeyUp* and *DKG* oracles.

- Type-1 adversary: $\mathcal{A}$ can issue a query for sk_{ID^*} to the *PKG* oracle, however, then ID^* will be revoked before T^*. (For $T \neq T^*$, $\mathcal{A}$ may query $dk_{ID^*, T}$.)
- Type-2 adversary: $\mathcal{A}$ does not query sk_{ID^*}, however $\mathcal{A}$ may issue $dk_{ID^*, T}$ for $T \neq T^*$.

We omit how $\mathcal{B}$ simulates them since we can take a similar approach to that in [20]. Therefore, we here describe how $\mathcal{B}$ simulates the *RDecaps* oracle. When $\mathcal{B}$ receives $(ID, T, CT = (c_1, c_2, c_3, c_4))$ from $\mathcal{A}$, it checks whether a form of c_3 is vaild or not. Namely, $\mathcal{B}$ checks whether $(g, c_1, \mathsf{F}_{\mathsf{BB}}(T), c_3)$ is a DH tuple or not. If not so, then $\mathcal{B}$ returns a random element of $\mathbb{G}_T$ to $\mathcal{A}$. Otherwise, $\mathcal{B}$ sends (c_1, c_2, c_4) to the *Decaps* oracle of the IND-ID-CCA game for Π_{vKG}. Then, the ciphertext (c_1, c_2, c_4) is the same form as that in Π_{vKG} if the ciphertext is valid. Therefore, $\mathcal{B}$ can perfectly simulate the *RDecaps* oracle by transferring a session key K received from the *Decaps* oracle. □

5.4   Proposed CCA-Secure RIBE Based on the KEM/DEM Framework

We show that the KEM/DEM framework works well even in the RIBE setting though it is known that the framework works well in the PKE setting and the IBE setting. Specifically, a CCA-secure RIBE scheme $\Pi_{RIBE} = (\mathsf{Setup}, \mathsf{PKG}, \mathsf{KeyUp}, \mathsf{DKG}, \mathsf{REnc}, \mathsf{RDec}, \mathsf{Revoke})$ can be constructed from a CCA-secure RIB-KEM $\Pi_{RIB\text{-}KEM} = (\mathsf{Setup}, \mathsf{PKG}, \mathsf{KeyUp}, \mathsf{DKG}, \mathsf{REncaps}, \mathsf{RDecaps}, \mathsf{Revoke})$ and a CCA-secure DEM $\Pi_{DEM} = (\mathsf{E}, \mathsf{D})$. The construction is simple. All algorithms except for REnc and RDec can be constructed by algorithms with the same name.

- $\mathsf{Enc}(mpk, ID, T, M)$: It executes $(K, C) \leftarrow \mathsf{REncaps}(mpk, ID, T)$ and $C' \leftarrow \mathsf{E}(M, K)$. It outputs $CT := (C, C')$.
- $\mathsf{Dec}(mpk, dk_{ID,T}, CT)$: It executes $K \leftarrow \mathsf{RDecaps}(mpk, dk_{ID,T}, C)$, and then outputs M or $\perp \leftarrow \mathsf{D}(C', K)$.

Security of the resulting RIBE scheme can be shown as follows. The proof will appear in the full version of this paper.

Theorem 4. *If an RIB-KEM $\Pi_{RIB\text{-}KEM}$ is IND-RID-CCA secure and a DEM Π_{DEM} is IND-CCA secure, then the resulting RIBE scheme Π_{RIBE} is IND-RID-CCA secure.*

6   Concluding Remarks

We first proposed two adaptively CCA-secure RIBE constructions with DKER. The first one is constructed through a naive approach based on the BCHK transformation. The second one is constructed through a KEM-based approach. Specifically, we newly proposed an RIB-KEM, and we showed a generic construction of a CCA-secure RIBE scheme from the RIB-KEM and a DEM. As seen in Section 1, it is noteworthy that ciphertext size in the KEM-based construction is shorter than that in the BCHK transformation-based construction.

Acknowledgments. We would like to thank anonymous referees for their helpful comments. We would also like to thank Keita Emura for his valuable comments for the preliminary version of this paper. The second author is supported by JSPS Research Fellowships for Young Scientists.

References

1. Bentahar, K., Farshim, P., Malone-Lee, J., Smart, N.: Generic constructions of identity-based and certificateless kems. Journal of Cryptology **21**(2), 178–199 (2008)
2. Boldyreva, A., Goyal, V., Kumar, V.: Identity-based encryption with efficient revocation. In: Proceedings of the 15th ACM conference on Computer and communications security, pp. 417–426. ACM, New York (2008)
3. Boneh, D., Canetti, R., Halevi, S., Katz, J.: Chosen ciphertext security from identity based encryption. SIAM Journal on Computing **36**(5), 1301–1328 (2007)
4. Boneh, D., Boyen, X.: Efficient selective-ID secure identity-based encryption without random oracles. In: Cachin, C., Camenisch, J.L. (eds.) EUROCRYPT 2004. LNCS, vol. 3027, pp. 223–238. Springer, Heidelberg (2004)
5. Boneh, D., Boyen, X.: Efficient selective identity-based encryption without random oracles. Journal of Cryptology **24**(4), 659–693 (2011)
6. Boneh, D., Franklin, M.: Identity-based encryption from the Weil pairing. In: Kilian, J. (ed.) CRYPTO 2001. LNCS, vol. 2139, pp. 213–229. Springer, Heidelberg (2001)
7. Chen, J., Lim, H.W., Ling, S., Wang, H., Nguyen, K.: Revocable identity-based encryption from lattices. In: Susilo, W., Mu, Y., Seberry, J. (eds.) ACISP 2012. LNCS, vol. 7372, pp. 390–403. Springer, Heidelberg (2012)
8. Dodis, Y., Katz, J., Xu, S., Yung, M.: Key-insulated public key cryptosystems. In: Knudsen, L.R. (ed.) EUROCRYPT 2002. LNCS, vol. 2332, pp. 65–82. Springer, Heidelberg (2002)
9. Gentry, C.: Practical identity-based encryption without random oracles. In: Vaudenay, S. (ed.) EUROCRYPT 2006. LNCS, vol. 4004, pp. 445–464. Springer, Heidelberg (2006)
10. Halevy, D., Shamir, A.: The LSD broadcast encryption scheme. In: Yung, M. (ed.) CRYPTO 2002. LNCS, vol. 2442, pp. 47–60. Springer, Heidelberg (2002)
11. Hanaoka, Y., Hanaoka, G., Shikata, J., Imai, H.: Identity-based hierarchical strongly key-insulated encryption and its application. In: Roy, B. (ed.) ASIACRYPT 2005. LNCS, vol. 3788, pp. 495–514. Springer, Heidelberg (2005)

12. Kiltz, E.: Chosen-ciphertext security from tag-based encryption. In: Halevi, S., Rabin, T. (eds.) TCC 2006. LNCS, vol. 3876, pp. 581–600. Springer, Heidelberg (2006)

13. Kiltz, E., Galindo, D.: Direct chosen-ciphertext secure identity-based key encapsulation without random oracles. In: Batten, L.M., Safavi-Naini, R. (eds.) ACISP 2006. LNCS, vol. 4058, pp. 336–347. Springer, Heidelberg (2006)

14. Kiltz, E., Galindo, D.: Direct chosen-ciphertext secure identity-based key encapsulation without random oracles. Theoretical Computer Science **410**(47–49), 5093–5111 (2009)

15. Kiltz, E., Vahlis, Y.: CCA2 secure IBE: Standard model efficiency through authenticated symmetric encryption. In: Malkin, T. (ed.) CT-RSA 2008. LNCS, vol. 4964, pp. 221–238. Springer, Heidelberg (2008)

16. Lee, K., Lee, D.H., Park, J.H.: Efficient revocable identity-based encryption via subset difference methods. Cryptology ePrint Archive, Report 2014/132 (2014). http://eprint.iacr.org/

17. Libert, B., Vergnaud, D.: Adaptive-ID secure revocable identity-based encryption. In: Fischlin, M. (ed.) CT-RSA 2009. LNCS, vol. 5473, pp. 1–15. Springer, Heidelberg (2009)

18. Naor, D., Naor, M., Lotspiech, J.: Revocation and tracing schemes for stateless receivers. In: Kilian, J. (ed.) CRYPTO 2001. LNCS, vol. 2139, pp. 41–62. Springer, Heidelberg (2001)

19. Seo, J.H., Emura, K.: Revocable identity-based encryption with rejoin functionality. IEICE Transactions **97–A**(8), 1806–1809 (2014)

20. Seo, J.H., Emura, K.: Revocable identity-based encryption revisited: security model and construction. In: Kurosawa, K., Hanaoka, G. (eds.) PKC 2013. LNCS, vol. 7778, pp. 216–234. Springer, Heidelberg (2013). http://eprint.iacr.org/2013/016.pdf

21. Waters, B.: Efficient identity-based encryption without random oracles. In: Cramer, R. (ed.) EUROCRYPT 2005. LNCS, vol. 3494, pp. 114–127. Springer, Heidelberg (2005)

22. Waters, B.: Dual system encryption: realizing fully secure IBE and HIBE under simple assumptions. In: Halevi, S. (ed.) CRYPTO 2009. LNCS, vol. 5677, pp. 619–636. Springer, Heidelberg (2009)

Digital Signatures

Linkable Message Tagging: Solving the Key Distribution Problem of Signature Schemes

Felix Günther[1](✉) and Bertram Poettering[2]

[1] Cryptoplexity Group, Technische Universität Darmstadt, Darmstadt, Germany
guenther@cs.tu-darmstadt.de
[2] Foundations of Cryptography, Ruhr-Universität Bochum, Bochum, Germany
http://www.foc.rub.de

Abstract. Digital signatures guarantee practical security only if the corresponding verification keys are distributed authentically; however, arguably, satisfying solutions for the latter haven't been found yet. This paper introduces a novel approach for cryptographic message authentication where this problem does not arise: A *linkable message tagging* scheme (LMT) identifies pairs of messages and accompanying authentication tags as related if and only if these tags were created using the same secret key. Importantly, our primitive fully avoids public keys, and hence elegantly sidesteps the key distribution problem of signature schemes.

As an application of LMT we envision an email authentication system with minimal user interaction. Email clients could routinely equip all outgoing messages with corresponding tags and verify for incoming messages whether they indeed originate from the same entity as previously or subsequently received messages with identical sender address.

As technical contributions we formalize the notions of LMT and its (more efficient) variant CMT (*classifiable message tagging*), including corresponding notions of unforgeability. For both variants we propose a range of provably secure constructions, basing on different hardness assumptions, with and without requiring random oracles.

Keywords: Message authentication · Key distribution problem · Message tagging · Digital signatures

1 Introduction

Digital Signature Schemes. Digital signatures are an omnipresent cryptographic primitive in today's security landscape. Most prominently they find application as building blocks in message authentication, entity authentication, and in establishing trust relations in hierarchical public key infrastructures (PKIs). The first formal treatment of the security of signature schemes was given in 1984 when Goldwasser, Micali, and Rivest coined the notion of *existential unforgeability*, requiring that it be infeasible for any adaptive forging adversary to come up with a valid signature on a fresh message, even in the presence of a signing oracle. Despite the apparent strength of this notion, research effort in the past 30 years resulted in a wide range of efficient and provably secure constructions available today.

© Springer International Publishing Switzerland 2015
E. Foo and D. Stebila (Eds.): ACISP 2015, LNCS 9144, pp. 195–212, 2015.
DOI: 10.1007/978-3-319-19962-7_12

Public Key Infrastructures. A remaining challenge for the practical security of signature schemes is the authentic distribution of verification keys: Trustworthy authentication of messages or entities via signatures seems out of reach if assurances on the genuineness of available verification keys cannot be provided. Indeed, if the adversary manages to replace real verification keys by keys of its own, all security is lost.

A variety of proposals to resolve this challenge exist. As a prime example, hierarchical PKIs like those building on the X.509 standard [10] provide certificate-based attestation that a given public key belongs to a certain real-world user. Social PKIs, like the 'web of trust' underlying OpenPGP [5], constitute an alternative approach towards the authentic distribution of keys. Here, putting trust into centralized CAs is not required; instead, users establish trust relationships by deciding on the genuineness of keys with the help and judgment of 'socially close' other users.

Practical Obstacles in Email Authentication. On first sight the two discussed approaches towards the authentic distribution of cryptographic keys appear sound and reliable. Moreover, when considering authentic email communication, software implementations based on the S/MIME (i.e., X.509) and OpenPGP standards are freely available as plugins for all modern mail clients. However, in practice, large-scale deployment of email authentication for individuals, i.e., outside of organizations, fails to appear. Indeed, only a negligible fraction of Internet users secures their email correspondence using cryptography. Partly responsible for this might be the following technical and social obstacles:

- In respect to hierarchical PKIs: a practically unmanageable number of root CAs, unclear trust relations to the CAs (see the compromises of DigiNotar in 2011 [7], TURKTRUST in 2013 [17], and National Informatics Centre of India in 2014 [8]), unclear authentication procedures during certificate requests, and unclear revocation procedures.
- In respect to social PKIs: barriers introduced by time-consuming and error-prone authentication procedures (e.g., in 'key-signing parties'), complicated user guidance in encryption software [19], and the privacy problem introduced by publicly revealing social relationships on the key servers.

To summarize, all currently established approaches towards strong email authentication come with specific usability barriers that seem insurmountable by the broader public in practice.

A Novel Approach: History-Based Message Authentication. Assume a setting in which two users, Alice and Bob, routinely communicate via email and at some point have accumulated a communication history of, say, one year. Assume further that an adversary wants to intervene in this communication by injecting her own messages and making Bob accept them as originating from Alice. Such an attack could clearly be recognized and thwarted if Alice would sign all her outgoing messages and Bob would validate all incoming ones using an authentic copy of Alice's public key; however, motivated by the discussion above, in the following we abstain from assuming that Alice and Bob actively exchange any verification keys or follow any comparable explicit setup routine.

Our new concept of *history-based message authentication* builds on the idea that the strong authentication of regularly occurring message transmissions can be boot-strapped from a single authentic delivery (even if it is not known which out of many transmissions the authentic one is). These preconditions are met in the context of email communication where, arguably, a large fraction of messages reaches its destination in unmodified form. As we will elaborate, our new paradigm of authentication does not involve any kind of interaction between computer and user (except, possibly, if identified forgeries shall be reported), and in particular does not require an explicit exchange of verification keys. As our method completely side-steps the obstacles of key distribution discussed above, we envision that our new authentication model could contribute to make email authentication practically accessible to the masses.

Theoretical Contributions. We explore the concept of history-based message authentication by introducing the notion of *linkable message tagging (LMT)*. Briefly, such schemes allow users holding a *tagging key* to equip given messages with corresponding *tags*; a dedicated *linking predicate* can then be used to decide whether any two message-tag pairs originate from the same (anonymous) sender, i.e., were created using the same key. Importantly, and in contrast to signature schemes, users of LMT schemes do not have explicit identities, e.g., in the form of public keys. However, if required, LMT schemes can be 'upgraded' to the functionality and security properties of signature schemes by authentically exchanging a specific reference token (that takes precisely the role of a verification key). Observe that this can be done at any time and seems particularly helpful to resolve cases where LMT schemes identify forged messages.

An interesting subclass of LMT is given by *classifiable message tagging (CMT)*. Corresponding schemes are optimized for situations where messages shall be automatically *classified* according to their origin. More concretely, in CMT schemes, a dedicated algorithm computes for messages-tag pairs a corresponding *class identifier*; the LMT linking predicate then reports matching origins if and only if the respective class identifiers match. As we argue below, this extended functionality is attractive in applications like email authentication.

To model security of LMT and CMT, we formalize notions of *unforgeability*: Intuitively, schemes are unforgeable if no adversary can create, for any message of its choosing, a tag that is identified by the scheme as originating from the same source as a genuinely crafted message-tag pair.

Practical Contributions. On the constructive side we unveil tight connections between the new primitives on the one hand and signature schemes on the other (this might be surprising at first sight, as the new primitives *per se* do not involve public keys). These connections not only allow for generic constructions of LMT and CMT schemes from signature schemes and vice versa, but also explain notable similarities between our constructions and some well-known signature schemes.

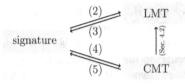

Type Scheme	Setting	Assumption	Model
LMT BLS-LMT (1)	Pairing	CDH	ROM
CMT Waters-CMT (FV)	Pairing	CDH	CRS
CMT Schnorr-CMT (6)	Cyclic group	DLP	ROM
LMT Sig-LMT (2)	as signature	euf-cma	STD
CMT Sig-CMT (4)	as signature	euf-cma	STD

Fig. 1. The figure on the left shows the conceptual relationship between signature schemes, LMT schemes, and CMT schemes. The table on the right gives an overview over the proposed direct (top) and generic (bottom) LMT and CMT constructions, indicating whether proofs are in the standard (STD), random oracle (ROM), or common reference string (CRS) model. The numbers in parentheses indicate the respective constructions (Waters-CMT is only defined in the full version [9]).

We additionally put forward a couple of direct constructions of LMT and CMT schemes, with and without random oracles, based on different hardness assumptions. An overview over our direct constructions and the (less efficient) generic signature-based constructions is given in Figure 1.

Envisioned Application: Automated Email Authentication. We consider the concept of linkable message tagging valuable for implementing easy-to-use and fully-automated cryptographic authentication of email communication; notably, LMT and CMT do not rely on trusted third parties or on verification keys exchanged a priori. More concretely, we envision that email client software would automatically setup tagging keys upon its first execution, equip all outgoing emails with corresponding LMT tags, and visually group together incoming emails according to their origin (e.g., by color or position) without requiring any user interaction. By consequence, adversarially crafted or manipulated emails would be displayed differently than the authentic ones.

Pitfalls with naïve Constructions Using Signature Schemes. We discuss why the following ad-hoc approach towards linkable message tagging is insecure in general: Using a regular signature scheme, users sign all outgoing emails and append the signatures to the messages; after some time, users additionally disclose to each other their respective verification keys. Authenticity of these keys is then verified by checking the validity of all signatures received so far; if all signatures are valid, the corresponding key is considered authentic. What might at first seem to be a sound approach is in fact not: (strongly) unforgeable signature schemes can be vulnerable to so-called *duplicate-signature key selection* (DSKS) attacks in which the adversary aims at finding verification keys that are valid for given message-signature pairs [3,11,13]. Clearly, a DSKS-vulnerable signature scheme will not yield a secure LMT scheme when employed in the construction just described.

Related Work. Cryptographic solutions for message authentication in settings without pre-shared keys are generally based on signature schemes [6], most often in conjunction with hierarchical or non-hierarchical PKIs (like in X.509 [10] or OpenPGP [5]). As argued above, such approaches suffer from a variety of usability problems, particularly when used outside of organizations [19].

An alternative to public-key-based message authentication is given by *identity-based signatures* [16] that side-step the key distribution problem by replacing participants' verification keys by just their identities. Problematic here, however, is the required trustworthiness of the central authority (CA) that issues the private keys: the *key escrow problem*, namely that the CA can compute secret keys for any identity and thus impersonate it, is inherent to id-based cryptography.

Certificateless signatures [1] can be seen as hybrid between PKI-based and identity-based signatures, avoiding both the use of certificates and the key escrow problem. Here, the CA issues only partial private keys; these need to be complemented by the corresponding user to obtain the actual private/public key pair. The public key can then be distributed non-authentically.

We note that the concept of *message recognition* [12,18] partially aims in the direction of linkable message tagging. It was coined for settings where devices with low computational power and communication bandwidth should, after exchanging a small amount of authentic data, be able to afterwards recognize each other's messages. Comparable goals were also approached in ad-hoc networks based on location-limited side channels [2]. Note that both these notions require an a priori or side-channel-based exchange of authenticated data.

2 Preliminaries

Notation. Let A, B be sets. For $Q \subseteq A \times B$ and $a \in A$ we write $(a, \cdot) \in Q$ if $\exists b \in B : (a, b) \in Q$; we write $(a, \cdot) \notin Q$ if $\forall b \in B : (a, b) \notin Q$.

Fact 1 (Equivalence Kernel). *Let A, B be sets and let $f \colon A \to B$ be a function. The equivalence relation $\sim_f$ on A defined by $a_1 \sim_f a_2 \Leftrightarrow f(a_1) = f(a_2)$ is said to be the* equivalence kernel *of f. For all equivalence relations $\sim$ on A we observe that $\sim$ is the equivalence kernel of projection $A \to A/{\sim}; \; a \mapsto [a]$, where $[a]$ denotes the equivalence class of a.*

Definition 1 (Reflexive Closure). *Let A be a set and let $R \subseteq A \times A$ be a relation on A. We define $\mathrm{Fix}(A) = \{(a, a) : a \in A\}$ and say that $R \cup \mathrm{Fix}(A)$ is the* reflexive closure *of R.*

We refer to the full version of this paper [9] for the notions of digital signature schemes $\Sigma = (\mathsf{KGen}, \mathsf{Sign}, \mathsf{Ver})$. Among others, we introduce symbols for the message space $\mathcal{M} = \{0, 1\}^*$, the signature space $\mathcal{S}ig$, and the verification key space $\mathcal{VK}$, and recall the security notions of (strong) existential unforgeability under chosen-message attacks (euf-cma/suf-cma security).

3 Linkable Message Tagging Schemes

Our central contribution is the introduction of linkable message tagging (LMT) schemes. This novel cryptographic primitive allows users, after having generated a (secret) tagging key, to take arbitrary messages and compute corresponding LMT tags; other users can test for any two such message-tag pairs whether they have the same origin, i.e., were generated using the same key. Notably, this verification is done without any further (public or secret) inputs. Briefly speaking, security requires that tags be unforgeable, i.e., no adversary can find a message-tag pair that appears to have the same origin as a genuine one.

3.1 Syntax and Security

We formalize LMT schemes by specifying their syntax, correctness, and security properties.

Definition 2 (LMT Scheme). *A linkable message tagging (LMT) scheme* $\mathsf{L} =$ $(\mathsf{KGen}, \mathsf{Tag}, \mathsf{Link})$ *consists of a message space* $\mathcal{M} = \{0,1\}^*$, *a tag space* $\mathcal{T}$, *and the following efficient algorithms:*

$\mathsf{KGen}(1^\lambda)$: *On input the security parameter, this probabilistic algorithm outputs a tagging key* tk.

$\mathsf{Tag}(tk, m)$: *On input a tagging key* tk *and message* $m \in \mathcal{M}$, *this algorithm outputs a tag* $\tau \in \mathcal{T}$.

$\mathsf{Link}(m_1, \tau_1, m_2, \tau_2)$: *On input message-tag pairs* $(m_1, \tau_1), (m_2, \tau_2) \in \mathcal{M} \times \mathcal{T}$, *this deterministic algorithm outputs either 0 or 1. As a shortcut, we write* $(m_1, \tau_1) \sim (m_2, \tau_2)$ *if* $\mathsf{Link}(m_1, \tau_1, m_2, \tau_2) = 1$, *otherwise* $(m_1, \tau_1) \not\sim (m_2, \tau_2)$.

An LMT scheme shall offer a meaningful way to partition messages-tag pairs according to their origin. We hence require that the Link algorithm defines an equivalence relation on $\mathcal{M} \times \mathcal{T}$, and that all message-tag pairs created using a fixed tagging key belong to the same equivalence class.

Definition 3 (Correctness of LMT Schemes). *An LMT scheme* L *is correct if (a) for all* $\lambda \in \mathbb{N}$, *all* $tk \leftarrow_R \mathsf{KGen}(1^\lambda)$, *all* $m_1, m_2 \in \mathcal{M}$, *and all* $\tau_1 \leftarrow_R \mathsf{Tag}(tk, m_1)$ *and* $\tau_2 \leftarrow_R \mathsf{Tag}(tk, m_2)$, *we have* $(m_1, \tau_1) \sim (m_2, \tau_2)$, *i.e.,* $\mathsf{Link}(m_1, \tau_1, m_2, \tau_2) = 1$, *and (b) the Link algorithm defines an equivalence relation on* $\mathcal{M} \times \mathcal{T}$, *i.e., if for all* $(m_1, \tau_1), (m_2, \tau_2), (m_3, \tau_3) \in \mathcal{M} \times \mathcal{T}$ *we have*

- $(m_1, \tau_1) \sim (m_1, \tau_1)$ *(Reflexivity)*
- $(m_1, \tau_1) \sim (m_2, \tau_2) \Leftrightarrow (m_2, \tau_2) \sim (m_1, \tau_1)$ *(Symmetry)*
- $(m_1, \tau_1) \sim (m_2, \tau_2) \wedge (m_2, \tau_2) \sim (m_3, \tau_3) \Rightarrow (m_1, \tau_1) \sim (m_3, \tau_3)$ *(Transitivity)*

The essential security property of LMT schemes is unforgeability: Given a collection Q of genuine message-tag pairs, it shall be impossible to come up with a tag τ^* on a fresh message m^* such that $(m^*, \tau^*) \sim (m, \tau)$ for any pair $(m, \tau) \in Q$. Akin to the security notions for signature schemes, we distinguish between two variants of unforgeability: lmt-euf, and the (strictly) stronger lmt-suf.

Definition 4 (Unforgeability of LMT Schemes). *An LMT scheme* L *is (strongly) unforgeable (*lmt-euf, *respectively* lmt-suf*) if for all efficient adversaries* $\mathcal{A}$ *the success probability* $\mathrm{Succ}_{\mathsf{L},\mathcal{A}}^{\mathsf{lmt-euf}}$ *(resp.,* $\mathrm{Succ}_{\mathsf{L},\mathcal{A}}^{\mathsf{lmt-suf}}$*) is a negligible function where*

$$\mathrm{Succ}_{\mathsf{L},\mathcal{A}}^{\mathsf{lmt-euf}}(\lambda) = \Pr\left[\mathrm{Expt}_{\mathsf{L},\mathcal{A}}^{\mathsf{lmt-euf}}(1^\lambda) = 1\right], \mathrm{Succ}_{\mathsf{L},\mathcal{A}}^{\mathsf{lmt-suf}}(\lambda) = \Pr\left[\mathrm{Expt}_{\mathsf{L},\mathcal{A}}^{\mathsf{lmt-suf}}(1^\lambda) = 1\right]$$

Expt$_{L,A}^{\text{lmt-euf}}(1^\lambda)$:
  (a) $tk \leftarrow_R \text{KGen}(1^\lambda)$
  (b) $(m^*, \tau^*) \leftarrow_R \mathcal{A}^{\mathcal{O}_{\text{Tag}}}(1^\lambda)$
  (c) Return 1 iff all hold:
    – $(m^*, \cdot) \notin Q$
    – $\exists (m, \tau) \in Q : (m^*, \tau^*) \sim (m, \tau)$

Expt$_{L,A}^{\text{lmt-suf}}(1^\lambda)$:
  (a) $tk \leftarrow_R \text{KGen}(1^\lambda)$
  (b) $(m^*, \tau^*) \leftarrow_R \mathcal{A}^{\mathcal{O}_{\text{Tag}}}(1^\lambda)$
  (c) Return 1 iff all hold:
    – $(m^*, \tau^*) \notin Q$
    – $\exists (m, \tau) \in Q : (m^*, \tau^*) \sim (m, \tau)$

Processing of $\mathcal{O}_{\text{Tag}}(m)$:
  (a) $\tau \leftarrow_R \text{Tag}(tk, m)$
  (b) $Q \leftarrow Q \cup \{(m, \tau)\}$
  (c) Return τ

Fig. 2. Experiments for (strong) unforgeability of LMT schemes. We assume that queries to $\mathcal{O}_{\text{Tag}}$ oracle are answered as specified on the right, and that set Q is initialized as $Q \leftarrow \emptyset$.

are defined in respect to the experiments from Figure 2, and the probabilities are taken over the random coins of the respective experiment and the adversary.

3.2 A Direct LMT Construction

We show the existence of LMT schemes by giving a simple yet efficient example. Our construction is loosely related to the BLS signature scheme by Boneh, Lynn, and Shacham [4] (cf. Figure 3) which enjoys strong unforgeability under the CDH assumption in a pairing-friendly group, in the random oracle model.

Construction 1 (LMT Scheme BLS-LMT). *The LMT scheme BLS-LMT is defined in respect to a (symmetric) bilinear group $\mathbb{G}$ and a hash function $H: \mathcal{M} \to \mathbb{G} \setminus \{1\}$. More precisely, for a set $(\mathbb{G}, \mathbb{G}_T, q, g, e)$ it is assumed that $\mathbb{G} = \langle g \rangle$ is a cyclic group of prime order q and that $e: \mathbb{G} \times \mathbb{G} \to \mathbb{G}_T$ is a bilinear map. The tag space of BLS-LMT is $\mathcal{T} = \mathbb{G}$, and its algorithms are specified in Figure 3.*

Proof of Correctness. Consider function $f: \mathcal{M} \times \mathcal{T} \to \mathbb{Z}_q; (m, \tau) \mapsto \log_{H(m)}(\tau)$. For arbitrary $(m_1, \tau_1), (m_2, \tau_2) \in \mathcal{M} \times \mathcal{T}$ let $\alpha = f(m_1, \tau_1)$ and $\beta = f(m_2, \tau_2)$, i.e., $\tau_1 = H(m_1)^\alpha$ and $\tau_2 = H(m_2)^\beta$. By bilinearity and symmetry of e we obtain

$$(m_1, \tau_1) \sim (m_2, \tau_2) \Leftrightarrow e(H(m_1), H(m_2))^\beta = e(H(m_2), H(m_1))^\alpha \Leftrightarrow \alpha = \beta. (1)$$

Together with Fact 1 this characterization of the Link algorithm allows an immediate verification of the requirements from Definition 3. □

We next analyze the security properties of BLS-LMT.

Theorem 1 (Security of BLS-LMT). *The LMT scheme BLS-LMT is strongly unforgeable (lmt-suf) if the CDH assumption holds in $\mathbb{G}$ and H is modeled as a random oracle. By consequence, the scheme is also unforgeable (lmt-euf).*

Proof. We reduce the strong unforgeability of the BLS-LMT scheme to the strong unforgeability of the BLS signature scheme (defined over the same bilinear group). Together with Fact 2 below, this establishes the statement.

KGen(1^λ):	Sign(sk, m):	Ver(vk, m, σ):
$x \leftarrow_R \mathbb{Z}_q$	Output $\sigma = H(m)^x$	If $e(\sigma, g) = e(H(m), X)$
$X \leftarrow g^x$		output 1,
Output $(sk, vk) = (x, X)$		else output 0

KGen(1^λ):	Tag(tk, m):	Link(m_1, τ_1, m_2, τ_2):
$x \leftarrow_R \mathbb{Z}_q$	Output $\tau = H(m)^x$	If $e(H(m_1), \tau_2) = e(H(m_2), \tau_1)$
Output $tk = x$		output 1,
		else output 0

Fig. 3. Signature scheme BLS (top) and LMT scheme BLS-LMT (bottom). For further details see Construction 1.

From an efficient adversary $\mathcal{A}$ against lmt-suf of BLS-LMT we construct an efficient adversary $\mathcal{B}$ against suf-cma of BLS. Concretely, $\mathcal{B}(vk)$ runs $\mathcal{A}(1^\lambda)$ as a subroutine. Each oracle query $\mathcal{O}_{\mathsf{Tag}}(m)$ posed by $\mathcal{A}$ is forwarded by $\mathcal{B}$ as $\mathcal{O}_{\mathsf{Sign}}(m)$ to its own oracle, and the result is relayed to $\mathcal{A}$ (observe that this is a perfect simulation). Finally, when $\mathcal{A}$ outputs a candidate tag forgery (m^*, τ^*), $\mathcal{B}$ outputs the same pair and stops.

Assume $\mathcal{A}$ is successful, i.e., (m^*, τ^*) is a valid tag forgery. By definition we then have $e(H(m^*), H(m)^x) = e(H(m), \tau^*)$ for $x = \log_g vk$ and some m. This equation can only hold if $\tau^* = H(m^*)^x$, i.e., τ^* is a valid BLS signature on m^*. Further on, as τ^* is not the result of an $\mathcal{O}_{\mathsf{Tag}}(m^*)$ query, this signature was also not output on input m^* by $\mathcal{B}$'s $\mathcal{O}_{\mathsf{Sign}}$ oracle, i.e., adversary $\mathcal{B}$ is successful in forging a signature. We hence have $\mathrm{Succ}^{\mathsf{suf\text{-}cma}}_{\mathsf{BLS},\mathcal{B}}(\lambda) = \mathrm{Succ}^{\mathsf{lmt\text{-}suf}}_{\mathsf{BLS\text{-}LMT},\mathcal{A}}(\lambda)$. As the left-hand side is negligible by assumption, this completes the proof. □

Fact 2 (Unforgeability of BLS Signature Scheme [4]). *The BLS signature scheme is existentially unforgeable (euf-cma) if the CDH assumption holds in $\mathbb{G}$ and H is modeled as a random oracle. Moreover, the scheme has unique signatures and is hence strongly unforgeable (suf-cma).*

3.3 On the Generic Relation Between Signature and LMT Schemes

We now explore the relationship between signature schemes and LMT schemes. Perhaps surprisingly, from an engineer's point of view, the notions are quite close: LMT schemes and signature schemes can be constructed from each other, and the corresponding transformations are natural and efficient. On the other side of the coin this tight connection implies that there is little hope to obtain practical LMT constructions from just symmetric primitives like blockciphers, hash functions, or PRFs, although LMT schemes *per se* do not require public keys.

We begin with transforming signature schemes into LMT schemes. The idea behind our construction is to use signing keys as tagging keys and signatures with attached verification keys as tags, i.e., $\mathcal{T} = \mathcal{S}ig \times \mathcal{VK}$; precisely, a tag for a message m is a pair $\tau = (\sigma, vk)$ such that σ is a signature on m in respect to verification key vk. Intuitively, in order to test whether two message-tag pairs are in LMT relation, one checks that the verification keys match and both signatures are valid. This minimum requirement on the Link algorithm is formally expressed by binary relation R_M, defined on $\mathcal{M} \times \mathcal{T} = \mathcal{M} \times \mathcal{Sig} \times \mathcal{VK}$ as follows:

$$(m_1, \sigma_1, vk_1)\, R_M\, (m_2, \sigma_2, vk_2) \Leftrightarrow vk_1 = vk_2 \wedge \mathsf{Ver}(vk_1, m_1, \sigma_1) = 1 = \mathsf{Ver}(vk_2, m_2, \sigma_2).$$

Observe that this relation is symmetric and transitive. However, it is not reflexive, and hence does not induce a· correct LMT scheme, as message-tag pairs with invalid signatures are not in relation to themselves. Fixing this problem by adding further elements to R_M requires special care: intuitively, LMT security is diluted by putting valid and invalid tags into relation. Generic candidate elements that can be safely added to R_M seem to be those from binary relation R_0, defined on $\mathcal{M} \times \mathcal{Sig} \times \mathcal{VK}$ such that

$$(m_1, \sigma_1, vk_1)\, R_0\, (m_2, \sigma_2, vk_2) \quad \Leftrightarrow \quad \mathsf{Ver}(vk_1, m_1, \sigma_1) = 0 = \mathsf{Ver}(vk_2, m_2, \sigma_2).$$

Concluding, we say that an equivalence relation R on $\mathcal{M} \times \mathcal{Sig} \times \mathcal{VK}$ is *admissible* if $R_M \subseteq R \subseteq R_M \cup R_0$. Many such relations exist in general, but two natural choices for R are

- $R_M^{1:1} = R_M \cup \mathrm{Fix}(\mathcal{M} \times \mathcal{Sig} \times \mathcal{VK})$, i.e., the reflexive closure of R_M (see Definition 1). This is the finest possible admissible relation, where no invalid message-tag pair is related to any other (valid or invalid) message-tag pair.
- $R_M^{*:1} = R_M \cup R_0$, i.e., the coarsest possible admissible relation. Here, all invalid message-tag pairs are in relation to each other, i.e., belong to the same equivalence class.

Lemma 1. $R_M^{1:1}$ and $R_M^{*:1}$ are admissible equivalence relations.

Proof. Let $\mathcal{X} = \mathcal{M} \times \mathcal{Sig} \times \mathcal{VK}$. Observe that for each $a = (m, \sigma, vk) \in \mathcal{X}$ we have either $\mathsf{Ver}(vk, m, \sigma) = 1$ and $(a, a) \in R_M$, or $\mathsf{Ver}(vk, m, \sigma) = 0$ and $(a, a) \in R_0$. In other words, $\mathrm{Fix}(\mathcal{X}) \subseteq R_M \cup R_0$.

We first consider $R_M^{1:1}$. Reflexivity and symmetry are clear. To show transitivity, let $a, b, c \in \mathcal{X}$ with $(a, b), (b, c) \in R_M^{1:1}$. Nothing is to show if $(a, b) \in \mathrm{Fix}(\mathcal{X})$ or $(b, c) \in \mathrm{Fix}(\mathcal{X})$. Thus assume $(a, b), (b, c) \in R_M$. Transitivity of R_M implies $(a, c) \in R_M \subseteq R_M^{1:1}$. Admissibility follows from $\mathrm{Fix}(\mathcal{X}) \subseteq R_M \cup R_0$.

We next consider $R_M^{*:1}$. Reflexivity follows from $\mathrm{Fix}(\mathcal{X}) \subseteq R_M \cup R_0 = R_M^{*:1}$. Symmetry is clear. To show transitivity, let $a, b, c \in \mathcal{X}$ with $(a, b), (b, c) \in R_M^{*:1}$. Then either $(a, b), (b, c) \in R_M$ or $(a, b), (b, c) \in R_0$. In both cases $(a, c) \in R_M^{*:1}$ follows. Admissibility is clear. □

We are now ready to specify our signature-based LMT scheme. More precisely, we define a family of schemes, parameterized by an admissible equivalence relation R. We stress that the security achieved by our LMT construction is independent of the specific relation in use (as long as it is admissible) as the latter influences only how *invalid* message-tag pairs are grouped together. Defining our construction in respect to arbitrary admissible relations leaves flexibility to the user of the scheme—it is the application that determines whether $R_M^{1:1}$, $R_M^{*:1}$, or any other admissible relation is the favorable one.

Construction 2 (LMT Scheme Sig-LMT from a Generic Signature Scheme). *Let Σ be a signature scheme with message space $\mathcal{M} = \{0,1\}^*$, signature space Sig, and verification key space $\mathcal{VK}$. Let R be an admissible equivalence relation on $\mathcal{M} \times Sig \times \mathcal{VK}$. Define the LMT scheme Sig-LMT in respect to R with tag space $\mathcal{T} = Sig \times \mathcal{VK}$ as follows:*

KGen(1^λ): *Set* $(sk, vk) \leftarrow_R \Sigma.\mathsf{KGen}(1^\lambda)$ *and output tagging key* $tk = (sk, vk)$.
Tag(tk, m): *Compute* $\sigma \leftarrow_R \mathsf{Sign}(sk, m)$ *and output tag* $\tau = (\sigma, vk)$.
Link(m_1, τ_1, m_2, τ_2): *Parse* τ_1 *as* (σ_1, vk_1) *and* τ_2 *as* (σ_2, vk_2). *Output 1 if* (m_1, σ_1, vk_1) R (m_2, σ_2, vk_2). *Otherwise, output 0.*

Correctness of Sig-LMT follows directly from the definition of admissibility. The scheme's unforgeability properties are analyzed in Theorem 2; as mentioned above, they are independent of the particular choice of relation R.

Theorem 2 (Security of Sig-LMT). *For any admissible equivalence relation R, the LMT scheme Sig-LMT defined in respect to R is (strongly) unforgeable if the underlying signature scheme Σ is (strongly) unforgeable.*

Proof. We reduce the unforgeability of the Sig-LMT scheme to the unforgeability of the Σ signature scheme. The proof can easily be adapted to cover the strong variants of the corresponding security notions.

From an efficient adversary $\mathcal{A}$ against lmt-euf of Sig-LMT we construct an efficient adversary $\mathcal{B}$ against euf-cma of Σ. Concretely, $\mathcal{B}(vk)$ runs $\mathcal{A}(1^\lambda)$ as a subroutine. Each oracle query $\mathcal{O}_{\mathsf{Tag}}(m)$ posed by $\mathcal{A}$ is forwarded by $\mathcal{B}$ as $\sigma \leftarrow \mathcal{O}_{\mathsf{Sign}}(m)$ to its own oracle, and $\tau = (\sigma, vk)$ is answered to $\mathcal{A}$ (observe that this is a perfect simulation). Let Q denote the collection of all occurring such pairs (m, σ). Finally, when $\mathcal{A}$ outputs a candidate tag forgery (m^*, τ^*), $\mathcal{B}$ parses τ^* as (σ^*, vk^*), outputs σ^*, and stops.

Assume $\mathcal{A}$ is successful, i.e., (m^*, τ^*) is a valid tag forgery. By definition we then have (m^*, σ^*, vk^*) R (m, σ, vk) for some $(m, \sigma) \in Q$. As $\mathsf{Ver}(vk, m, \sigma) = 1$ by construction, we particularly have (m^*, σ^*, vk^*) R_M (m, σ, vk), i.e., $\mathsf{Ver}(vk, m^*, \sigma^*) = 1$. Further on, as m^* was never queried to the $\mathcal{O}_{\mathsf{Tag}}$ oracle, it was also not queried to $\mathcal{B}$'s $\mathcal{O}_{\mathsf{Sign}}$ oracle, i.e., adversary $\mathcal{B}$ is successful in forging a signature. We hence have $\mathsf{Succ}_{\Sigma, \mathcal{B}}^{\mathsf{euf\text{-}cma}}(\lambda) = \mathsf{Succ}_{\mathsf{Sig\text{-}LMT}, \mathcal{A}}^{\mathsf{lmt\text{-}euf}}(\lambda)$. As the left-hand side is negligible by assumption, this completes the proof. $\square$

We next transform LMT schemes into signature schemes. The intuition behind our construction is to use tags as signatures and to include a reference message-tag pair in the verification key against which candidate signatures (i.e., tags) can be aligned. However, doing so naïvely would not result in an unforgeable signature scheme: an adversary could just output the reference pair as a forgery. We deploy a technical solution to this problem in Construction 3: the fixed prefix "1" is prepended to all signed messages, preventing collision with the "0" message used for the reference tag.

Construction 3 (Signature Scheme LMT-Sig from a Generic LMT Scheme). *Let L be an LMT scheme with tag space $\mathcal{T}$. Define the signature scheme LMT-Sig with $Sig = \mathcal{VK} = \mathcal{T}$ as follows:*

KGen(1^λ): *Set $tk \leftarrow_R$ L.KGen(1^λ), compute $\tau_0 \leftarrow$ Tag(tk, "0"), and output key pair $(sk, vk) = (tk, \tau_0)$.*

Sign(sk, m): *Compute $\tau \leftarrow$ Tag(tk, "1" $\| m$) and output signature $\sigma = \tau$.*

Ver(vk, m, σ): *Output* Link("1" $\| m, \sigma$, "0", τ_0).

Correctness of LMT-Sig follows from correctness of L. The unforgeability of Construction 3 is assessed as follows.

Theorem 3 (Security of LMT-Sig). *The signature scheme LMT-Sig is (strongly) unforgeable if the underlying LMT scheme L is (strongly) unforgeable.*

Proof. We reduce the unforgeability of the LMT-Sig signature scheme to the unforgeability of LMT scheme L. The proof can easily be adapted to cover the strong variants of the corresponding security notions.

From an efficient adversary $\mathcal{A}$ against euf-cma of LMT-Sig we construct an efficient adversary $\mathcal{B}$ against lmt-euf of L. Concretely, $\mathcal{B}(1^\lambda)$ starts by posing a $\tau_0 \leftarrow \mathcal{O}_{\text{Tag}}$("0") query to its tagging oracle. Then $\mathcal{B}$ runs $\mathcal{A}$, on input $vk = \tau_0$, as a subroutine. Each oracle query $\mathcal{O}_{\text{Sign}}(m)$ posed by $\mathcal{A}$ is forwarded by $\mathcal{B}$ as $\mathcal{O}_{\text{Tag}}$("1" $\| m$) to its own oracle, and the result is relayed to $\mathcal{A}$ (observe that this is a perfect simulation). Finally, when $\mathcal{A}$ outputs a candidate signature forgery (m^*, σ^*), $\mathcal{B}$ outputs ("1" $\| m^*, \sigma^*$) and stops.

Assume $\mathcal{A}$ is successful, i.e., (m^*, σ^*) is a valid signature forgery. By definition we then have Link("1" $\| m^*, \sigma^*$, "0", τ_0) = 1. Further on, as m^* was never queried to the $\mathcal{O}_{\text{Sign}}$ oracle, "1" $\| m^*$ was also not queried to the $\mathcal{O}_{\text{Tag}}$ oracle, i.e., adversary $\mathcal{B}$ is successful in forging a tag. We hence have $\text{Succ}_{\text{L},\mathcal{B}}^{\text{lmt-euf}}(\lambda) = \text{Succ}_{\text{LMT-Sig},\mathcal{A}}^{\text{euf-cma}}(\lambda)$. As the left-hand side is negligible by assumption, this completes the proof. □

4 Classifiable Message Tagging Schemes

The main functionality of LMT schemes is the partitioning of message-tag pairs into sets according to their origin. Correspondingly, Definition 3 requires the Link algorithm to induce an equivalence relation $\sim$ on the message-tag space $\mathcal{M} \times \mathcal{T}$ such that, essentially, each equivalence class corresponds to one origin. Note that, so far, the used notion of origin is only virtual: it does not explicitly appear in syntax, correctness, or security definition of LMT schemes. In other words, although the Link algorithm always implies existence of projection

$$\pi \colon \mathcal{M} \times \mathcal{T} \to (\mathcal{M} \times \mathcal{T})/\!\sim; \ (m, \tau) \mapsto [m, \tau]$$

that maps message-tag pairs to their 'origin' (cf. Fact 1), there is no formal requirement in Section 3 that demands that this mapping be effectively computable.

We argue that for many natural applications of the LMT primitive the direct computability of π would be quite desirable. Assume, for instance, a mail client that is instructed to automatically classify received emails according to their origin. In such a setting, for each incoming email m with corresponding tag τ, the Link algorithm of a plain LMT scheme would have to be invoked several times, namely at least once for each priorly identified class of origin. If, however, we assume existence of an efficient projection π as defined above, the mail client could sort any email directly, i.e., without any further pair-wise computation, into a folder of name $\rho \circ \pi(m, \tau)$, where injective function $\rho \colon (\mathcal{M} \times \mathcal{T})/_\sim \rightarrow \{0,1\}^*$ assigns a (unique) label to each origin.

In this section we introduce an LMT variant called classifiable message tagging (CMT); such schemes are equipped with a dedicated algorithm for the efficient computation of $\rho \circ \pi$, for an adequate labeling scheme ρ. We will define the adapted syntax and security notions, study formal relations between the CMT and LMT primitives, and finally identify generic CMT constructions. We leave the direct construction of (more efficient) instances to Section 5.

4.1   Syntax and Security

The syntactical difference between LMT and CMT schemes is that the Link algorithm is replaced by the new Classify algorithm that shall compute $\rho \circ \pi$. In contrast to the introduction given above, we assume that the labels output by Classify are elements of an abstract set $\mathcal{C}$ of *class identifiers*; the only restriction on $\mathcal{C}$ is that its elements can be tested for equality.

Definition 5 (CMT Scheme). *A* classifiable message tagging (CMT) *scheme* $\mathsf{C} = (\mathsf{KGen}, \mathsf{Tag}, \mathsf{Classify})$ *consists of a message space* $\mathcal{M} = \{0,1\}^*$, *a tag space* $\mathcal{T}$, *a class identifier space* $\mathcal{C}$, *and the following efficient algorithms:*

$\mathsf{KGen}(1^\lambda)$: *On input the security parameter, this probabilistic algorithm outputs a tagging key tk.*

$\mathsf{Tag}(tk, m)$: *On input a tagging key tk and message $m \in \mathcal{M}$, this algorithm outputs a tag $\tau \in \mathcal{T}$.*

$\mathsf{Classify}(m, \tau)$: *On input a message-tag pair $(m, \tau) \in \mathcal{M} \times \mathcal{T}$, this deterministic algorithm outputs a class identifier $cid \in \mathcal{C}$.*

Correctness of CMT schemes requires that for any two pairs of message and corresponding tag (created with the same tagging key) the Classify algorithm outputs the same class identifier:

Definition 6 (Correctness of CMT Schemes). *A CMT scheme* C *is correct if for all* $\lambda \in \mathbb{N}$, *all* $tk \leftarrow_R \mathsf{KGen}(1^\lambda)$, *all* $m_1, m_2 \in \mathcal{M}$, *and all* $\tau_1 \leftarrow_R \mathsf{Tag}(tk, m_1)$ *and* $\tau_2 \leftarrow_R \mathsf{Tag}(tk, m_2)$, *we have* $\mathsf{Classify}(m_1, \tau_1) = \mathsf{Classify}(m_2, \tau_2)$.

Definition 7 (Key-Specific Class Identifier cid_{tk}). *Consider a (correct) CMT scheme* C *and a fixed key* $tk \leftarrow_R \mathsf{KGen}(1^\lambda)$. *For any message* $m \in \mathcal{M}$, *compute* $\tau \leftarrow_R \mathsf{Tag}(tk, m)$ *and* $cid \leftarrow \mathsf{Classify}(m, \tau)$. *Then the correctness of* C *ensures that cid is independent of both m and the randomness used in the* Tag *algorithm. In other words, for each tagging key tk there exists a (uniquely) corresponding* key-specific class identifier cid_{tk} *defined in this way.*

$\text{Expt}_{C,\mathcal{A}}^{\text{cmt-euf}}(1^\lambda)$:
  (a) $tk \leftarrow_R \text{KGen}(1^\lambda)$
  (b) $(m^*, \tau^*) \leftarrow_R \mathcal{A}^{\mathcal{O}_{\text{Tag}}}(1^\lambda)$
  (c) Return 1 iff all hold:
    $- (m^*, \cdot) \notin Q$
    $- \text{Classify}(m^*, \tau^*) = cid_{tk}$

$\text{Expt}_{C,\mathcal{A}}^{\text{cmt-suf}}(1^\lambda)$:
  (a) $tk \leftarrow_R \text{KGen}(1^\lambda)$
  (b) $(m^*, \tau^*) \leftarrow_R \mathcal{A}^{\mathcal{O}_{\text{Tag}}}(1^\lambda)$
  (c) Return 1 iff all hold:
    $- (m^*, \tau^*) \notin Q$
    $- \text{Classify}(m^*, \tau^*) = cid_{tk}$

Processing of $\mathcal{O}_{\text{Tag}}(m)$:
  (a) $\tau \leftarrow_R \text{Tag}(tk, m)$
  (b) $Q \leftarrow Q \cup \{(m, \tau)\}$
  (c) Return τ

Fig. 4. Experiments for (strong) unforgeability of CMT schemes. We assume that queries to $\mathcal{O}_{\text{Tag}}$ oracle are answered as specified on the right, and that set Q is initialized as $Q \leftarrow \emptyset$.

Similarly to LMT schemes, we define unforgeability as the essential security property of CMT schemes: Given a collection of genuine message-tag pairs for a fixed class identifier cid_{tk}, it shall be impossible to come up with a tag τ^* on a fresh message m^* such that $\text{Classify}(m^*, \tau^*) = cid_{tk}$. We again distinguish two variants of unforgeability, namely cmt-euf, and the (strictly) stronger cmt-suf.

Definition 8 (Unforgeability of CMT Schemes). *A CMT scheme C is (strongly) unforgeable (cmt-euf, respectively cmt-suf) if for all efficient adversaries $\mathcal{A}$ the success probability $\text{Succ}_{C,\mathcal{A}}^{\text{cmt-euf}}$ (resp., $\text{Succ}_{C,\mathcal{A}}^{\text{cmt-suf}}$) is a negligible function where*

$$\text{Succ}_{C,\mathcal{A}}^{\text{cmt-euf}}(\lambda) = \Pr\left[\text{Expt}_{C,\mathcal{A}}^{\text{cmt-euf}}(1^\lambda) = 1\right], \text{Succ}_{C,\mathcal{A}}^{\text{cmt-suf}}(\lambda) = \Pr\left[\text{Expt}_{C,\mathcal{A}}^{\text{cmt-suf}}(1^\lambda) = 1\right]$$

are defined in respect to the experiments from Figure 4, and the probabilities are taken over the random coins of the respective experiment and the adversary.

4.2 CMT Schemes are Special LMT Schemes

We motivated the introduction of CMT schemes with the interest in a specially optimized LMT variant. However, it is not immediately apparent that schemes defined in accordance with Definitions 5–8 are indeed of the LMT type. We next give formal evidence for this relation, both syntax-wise and security-wise. Interestingly, as we elaborate in the full version, the reverse relation does not hold in general, i.e., there exist LMT schemes that do not have a CMT analogue.

Let $C = (\text{KGen}, \text{Tag}, \text{Classify})$ be an arbitrary CMT scheme with message space $\mathcal{M}$ and tag space $\mathcal{T}$. Define the following auxiliary algorithm:

$\text{Link}(m_1, \tau_1, m_2, \tau_2)$: On input message-tag pairs $(m_1, \tau_1), (m_2, \tau_2) \in \mathcal{M} \times \mathcal{T}$ output 0 or 1 such that the following condition is met:

$$\text{Link}(m_1, \tau_1, m_2, \tau_2) = 1 \quad \Leftrightarrow \quad \text{Classify}(m_1, \tau_1) = \text{Classify}(m_2, \tau_2). \quad (2)$$

Given this, define the LMT scheme corresponding to C as $L = (\text{KGen}, \text{Tag}, \text{Link})$. Regarding its correctness, note that condition (a) of Definition 3 is fulfilled due to the correctness of C, and that condition (b) follows from (2) in conjunction with Fact 1. In addition, a comparison of Figures 2 and 4 readily establishes the following relation between security notions.

Lemma 2 (Unforgeability of C is Equivalent to Unforgeability of L). *A CMT scheme is* cmt-euf *(resp.* cmt-suf*) if and only if the corresponding LMT scheme is* lmt-euf *(resp.* lmt-suf*).*   □

4.3 On the Generic Relation Between Signature and CMT Schemes

In Section 3.3 we showed how to construct LMT schemes from signature schemes and vice versa. We analyze next if similar results also hold in the CMT setting.

We will first focus on how to generically obtain CMT schemes from signature schemes. Recall that we based our corresponding transformation in the LMT setting on an arbitrary admissible equivalence relation R that determines how invalid tags are grouped together (cf. Construction 2). This offers a degree of freedom that we implicitly exploit when constructing our signature-based CMT scheme Sig-CMT presented below: the key observation is that Construction 2 with $R = R_M^{*1}$ yields exactly the same LMT scheme as is obtained by understanding Sig-CMT as an LMT scheme in the terms of Section 4.2. Indeed, in both cases message-tag pairs are in relation exactly when either both tags are valid and the verification keys match (the latter serve as key-specific class identifiers in Sig-CMT), or when the tags are both invalid.

Construction 4 (CMT Scheme Sig-CMT from a Generic Signature Scheme). *Let Σ be a signature scheme with signature space Sig and verification key space $\mathcal{VK}$. Define the CMT scheme* Sig-CMT *with tag space $\mathcal{T} = Sig \times \mathcal{VK}$ and class identifier space $\mathcal{C} = \mathcal{VK} \,\dot\cup\, \{\bot\}$ (where $\dot\cup$ denotes the disjoint union) as follows:*

KGen(1^λ): *Set $(sk, vk) \leftarrow_R \Sigma.\mathsf{KGen}(1^\lambda)$ and output tagging key $tk = (sk, vk)$.*
Tag(tk, m): *Compute $\sigma \leftarrow_R \mathsf{Sign}(sk, m)$ and output tag $\tau = (\sigma, vk)$.*
Classify(m, τ): *Parse τ as (σ, vk). Output $cid = vk$ if $\mathsf{Ver}(vk, m, \sigma) = 1$. Otherwise, output $cid = \bot$.*

Correctness of the scheme is obvious. Concerning its security claim, by Lemma 2 it suffices to prove the (strong) unforgeability of the LMT scheme corresponding to Sig-CMT. Following the observations above, as the latter scheme results from Construction 2 with $R = R_M^{*1}$, Theorem 2 and Lemma 1 establish the following security result.

Theorem 4 (Security of Sig-CMT). *The CMT scheme* Sig-CMT *is (strongly) unforgeable if the underlying signature scheme Σ is (strongly) unforgeable.*   □

The next step is to generically construct a signature scheme from a CMT scheme. That this works in principle is not surprising by our earlier results: CMT schemes are just special LMT schemes, and the latter already imply signature schemes. We observe, however, that the following generic construction is slightly more efficient.

Construction 5 (Signature Scheme CMT-Sig from a Generic CMT Scheme). *Let C be a CMT scheme with tag space $\mathcal{T}$ and class identifier space $\mathcal{C}$. Define the signature scheme* CMT-Sig *as follows:*

$\mathsf{KGen}(1^\lambda)$: *Set* $tk \leftarrow_R \mathsf{C.KGen}(1^\lambda)$ *and compute corresponding key-specific class identifier* cid_{tk}. *Output key pair* $(sk, vk) = (tk, cid_{tk})$.

$\mathsf{Sign}(sk, m)$: *Compute* $\tau \leftarrow_R \mathsf{Tag}(tk, m)$ *and output signature* $\sigma = \tau$.

$\mathsf{Ver}(vk, m, \sigma)$: *Output* 1 *if* $\mathsf{Classify}(m, \tau) = cid_{tk}$. *Otherwise, output* 0.

Correctness of CMT-Sig follows from the correctness of C. Observe that, regarding its security statement, we had to strengthen the precondition in comparison to Theorem 3 for a technical reason.

Theorem 5 (Security of CMT-Sig). *If $\mathcal{M}$ has super-polynomial cardinality, the signature scheme CMT-Sig is (strongly) unforgeable if the underlying CMT scheme C is (strongly) unforgeable.*

Proof. We reduce the unforgeability of the CMT-Sig signature scheme to the unforgeability of CMT scheme C. The proof can easily be adapted to cover the strong variants of the corresponding security notions.

From an efficient adversary $\mathcal{A}$ against euf-cma of CMT-Sig we construct an efficient adversary $\mathcal{B}$ against cmt-euf of C. Concretely, after fixing a finite subset $\mathcal{M}_0 \subseteq \mathcal{M}$ of super-polynomial size, $\mathcal{B}(1^\lambda)$ starts by picking a random message $m_0 \leftarrow_R \mathcal{M}_0$, posing a $\tau_0 \leftarrow \mathcal{O}_{\mathsf{Tag}}(m_0)$ query to its tagging oracle, and computing key-specific class identifier $cid \leftarrow \mathsf{Classify}(m_0, \tau_0)$. Then $\mathcal{B}$ runs $\mathcal{A}$, on input $vk = cid$, as a subroutine. Each oracle query $\mathcal{O}_{\mathsf{Sign}}(m)$ posed by $\mathcal{A}$ is forwarded by $\mathcal{B}$ as $\mathcal{O}_{\mathsf{Tag}}(m)$ to its own oracle, and the result is relayed to $\mathcal{A}$ (observe that this is a perfect simulation). Finally, when $\mathcal{A}$ outputs a candidate signature forgery (m^*, σ^*), $\mathcal{B}$ outputs the same pair and stops.

Assume $\mathcal{A}$ is successful, i.e., (m^*, σ^*) is a valid signature forgery. By definition we then have $\mathsf{Classify}(m^*, \sigma^*) = cid$. Further on, as m^* was never queried to the $\mathcal{O}_{\mathsf{Sign}}$ oracle, either we have $m^* = m_0$ (with negligible probability $\epsilon \leq 1/|\mathcal{M}_0|$), or m^* was not queried to $\mathcal{B}$'s $\mathcal{O}_{\mathsf{Tag}}$ oracle, i.e., adversary $\mathcal{B}$ is successful in forging a tag. We hence have $\mathsf{Succ}_{\mathsf{C},\mathcal{B}}^{\mathsf{cmt\text{-}euf}}(\lambda) = \mathsf{Succ}_{\mathsf{CMT\text{-}Sig},\mathcal{A}}^{\mathsf{euf\text{-}cma}}(\lambda) - \epsilon$. As both the left-hand side and ϵ are negligible by assumption, this completes the proof. □

5 Practical Classifiable Message Tagging Constructions

We focus next on practical, efficiency-optimized CMT constructions. Our motivation comes from the observation that the generic methods from Construction 4 demand a signature scheme's verification key to be included in every tag; as we reveal, this is not required in direct, i.e., non-generic constructions. Indeed, we propose a CMT scheme with more compact tags, defined over a prime-order cyclic group with security under the DLP assumption in the random oracle model. Interestingly, the construction is implicitly based on a signature scheme where the verification key can be *uniquely reconstructed* from any (valid) signature.

In the full version of this paper [9] we further present an efficient CMT scheme that does not require random oracles, discuss our (fruitless) efforts of finding factoring-based CMT or LMT constructions, and explore whether signatures from standardized email authentication schemes (OpenPGP and S/MIME) can be reinterpreted in the CMT or LMT sense.

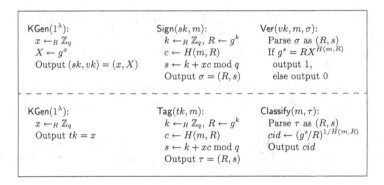

Fig. 5. Signature scheme Schnorr (top) and CMT scheme Schnorr-CMT (bottom). For further details see Construction 6.

5.1 A Highly Practical CMT Scheme Based on the DLP

Our direct CMT construction is based on the Schnorr signature scheme (cf. Schnorr [15] and Figure 5) and exploits the fact that in the latter the verification key can be reconstructed from any valid signature, requiring only one (multi-)exponentiation. Interestingly this does not hold for the related signature schemes DSA and ECDSA, as we explore in the full version of this paper [9]. We specify the new scheme as follows:

Construction 6 (CMT   Scheme   Schnorr-CMT). *The   CMT   scheme* Schnorr-CMT *is defined in respect to a cyclic group* $\mathbb{G} = \langle g \rangle$ *of prime order* q *and a hash function* $H \colon \mathcal{M} \times \mathbb{G} \to \mathbb{Z}_q$. *The tag space of* Schnorr-CMT *is* $\mathcal{T} = \mathbb{G} \times \mathbb{Z}_q$, *the class identifier space is* $\mathcal{C} = \mathbb{G}$, *and its algorithms are specified in Figure 5.*

For the correctness of Schnorr-CMT observe that for all $m_1, m_2 \in \mathcal{M}$ and $r_1, r_2 \in \mathbb{Z}_q$ we have

$$(g^{s_1}/R_1)^{1/H(m_1, R_1)} = (g^{k_1 + xc_1}/g^{k_1})^{1/c_1} = g^x = (g^{k_2 + xc_2}/g^{k_2})^{1/c_2} = (g^{s_2}/R_2)^{1/H(m_2, R_2)}.$$

In other words, for tagging key tk we have the key-specific class identifier $cid_{tk} = g^{tk}$ (which corresponds exactly with the verification key in the Schnorr scheme). We establish the security of Schnorr-CMT as follows.

Theorem 6 (Security of Schnorr-CMT**).** *The CMT scheme* Schnorr-CMT *is strongly unforgeable (*cmt-suf*) if the DLP is hard in* $\mathbb{G}$ *and* H *is modeled as a random oracle. By consequence, the scheme is also unforgeable (*cmt-euf*).*

Proof. We reduce the strong unforgeability of Schnorr-CMT to the strong existential unforgeability of the Schnorr signature scheme. Together with Fact 3 below, this establishes the statement.

From an efficient adversary $\mathcal{A}$ against cmt-suf of Schnorr-CMT we construct an efficient adversary $\mathcal{B}$ against suf-cma of Schnorr. Concretely, $\mathcal{B}(vk)$ runs $\mathcal{A}(1^\lambda)$ as a subroutine. Each oracle query $\mathcal{O}_{\mathsf{Tag}}(m)$ posed by $\mathcal{A}$ is forwarded by $\mathcal{B}$ as

$\mathcal{O}_{\text{Sign}}(m)$ to its own oracle, and the result is relayed to $\mathcal{A}$ (observe that this is a perfect simulation). Finally, when $\mathcal{A}$ outputs a candidate tag forgery (m^*, τ^*), $\mathcal{B}$ outputs the same pair and stops.

Assume $\mathcal{A}$ is successful, i.e., (m^*, τ^*) with $\tau^* = (R^*, s^*)$ is a valid tag forgery. By definition we then have $(g^{s^*}/R^*)^{1/H(m^*, R^*)} = cid_{tk} = g^{tk}$, i.e., $g^{s^*} = R^*(g^{tk})^{H(m^*, R^*)}$, hence in particular τ^* is a valid Schnorr signature on m^*. Further on, as m^* was never queried to the $\mathcal{O}_{\text{Tag}}$ oracle with answer τ^*, it was also not queried to $\mathcal{B}$'s $\mathcal{O}_{\text{Sign}}$ oracle with that answer, i.e., adversary $\mathcal{B}$ is successful in forging a signature. We hence have $\text{Succ}^{\text{suf-cma}}_{\text{Schnorr}, \mathcal{B}}(\lambda) = \text{Succ}^{\text{cmt-suf}}_{\text{Schnorr-CMT}, \mathcal{A}}(\lambda)$. As the left-hand side is negligible by assumption, this completes the proof.   □

Fact 3 (Unforgeability of Schnorr Signature Scheme [14]). *The Schnorr signature scheme is strongly existentially unforgeable (*suf-cma*) if DLP is hard in $\mathbb{G}$ and H is modeled as a random oracle.*[1]

6 Conclusion and Open Problems

This paper approaches the key distribution problem of classical signature schemes from an entirely new direction: Our notions of linkable and classifiable message tagging (LMT and CMT) allow to unambiguously decide whether pairs of messages and authentication tags originate from the same source (i.e., tagging key). This is achieved without requiring a special setup (e.g., a pre-shared authentic verification key or a PKI). We construct secure instantiations of the new primitives, both with and without random oracles (for the latter see the full version [9]), based on different hardness assumptions.

Acknowledgments. The authors thank all anonymous reviewers for their valuable comments. Both authors were supported by the German Federal Ministry of Education and Research (BMBF) within EC SPRIDE, and Bertram Poettering additionally by EPSRC Leadership Fellowship EP/H005455/1 and a Sofja Kovalevskaja Award of the Alexander von Humboldt Foundation. This work has been co-funded by the German Research Foundation (DFG) as part of project S4 within the CRC 1119 CROSSING.

References

1. Al-Riyami, S.S., Paterson, K.G.: Certificateless public key cryptography. In: Laih, C.-S. (ed.) ASIACRYPT 2003. LNCS, vol. 2894, pp. 452–473. Springer, Heidelberg (2003)
2. Balfanz, D., Smetters, D.K., Stewart, P., Wong, H.C.: Talking to strangers: authentication in ad-hoc wireless networks. In: NDSS 2002. The Internet Society, February 2002

---

[1] Although the statement proven by Pointcheval and Stern [14] considers only euf-cma security, their results can readily be extended to also cover the suf-cma notion.

3. Blake-Wilson, S., Menezes, A.: Unknown key-share attacks on the station-to-station (STS) protocol. In: Imai, H., Zheng, Y. (eds.) PKC 1999. LNCS, vol. 1560, pp. 154–170. Springer, Heidelberg (1999)

4. Boneh, D., Lynn, B., Shacham, H.: Short signatures from the weil pairing. In: Boyd, C. (ed.) ASIACRYPT 2001. LNCS, vol. 2248, pp. 514–532. Springer, Heidelberg (2001)

5. Callas, J., Donnerhacke, L., Finney, H., Shaw, D., Thayer, R.: OpenPGP Message Format. RFC 4880 (Proposed Standard), November 2007. http://www.ietf.org/rfc/rfc4880.txt. Updated by RFC 5581

6. Diffie, W., Hellman, M.E.: New directions in cryptography. IEEE Transactions on Information Theory 22(6), 644–654 (1976)

7. Fox-IT: Black Tulip – Report of the investigation into the DigiNotar Certificate Authority breach, August 2012. http://www.rijksoverheid.nl/bestanden/documenten-en-publicaties/rapporten/2012/08/13/black-tulip-update/black-tulip-update.pdf

8. Google Online Security Blog: Maintaining digital certificate security, July 2014. http://googleonlinesecurity.blogspot.de/2014/07/maintaining-digital-certificate-security.html

9. Günther, F., Poettering, B.: Linkable Message Tagging: Solving the key distribution problem of signature schemes. Cryptology ePrint Archive, Report 2014/014 (2014). http://eprint.iacr.org/2014/014

10. Kaliski, B.: PKCS #7: Cryptographic Message Syntax Version 1.5. RFC 2315 (Informational), March 1998. http://www.ietf.org/rfc/rfc2315.txt

11. Koblitz, N., Menezes, A.: Another look at security definitions. Advances in Mathematics of Communications 7(1), 1–38 (2013)

12. Mashatan, A., Vaudenay, S.: A message recognition protocol based on standard assumptions. In: Zhou, J., Yung, M. (eds.) ACNS 2010. LNCS, vol. 6123, pp. 384–401. Springer, Heidelberg (2010)

13. Menezes, A., Smart, N.P.: Security of signature schemes in a multi-user setting. Designs, Codes and Cryptography 33(3), 261–274 (2004)

14. Pointcheval, D., Stern, J.: Security arguments for digital signatures and blind signatures. Journal of Cryptology 13(3), 361–396 (2000)

15. Schnorr, C.P.: Efficient signature generation by smart cards. Journal of Cryptology 4(3), 161–174 (1991)

16. Shamir, A.: Identity-based cryptosystems and signature schemes. In: Blakely, G.R., Chaum, D. (eds.) CRYPTO 1984. LNCS, vol. 196, pp. 47–53. Springer, Heidelberg (1985)

17. TURKTRUST Information Security Services Inc.: Public Announcements, January 2013. http://www.turktrust.com.tr/en/about-us/news-detail/kamuoyu-aciklamalari

18. Weimerskirch, A., Westhoff, D.: Zero common-knowledge authentication for pervasive networks. In: Matsui, M., Zuccherato, R.J. (eds.) SAC 2003. LNCS, vol. 3006, pp. 73–87. Springer, Heidelberg (2004)

19. Whitten, A., Tygar, J.D.: Why Johnny can't encrypt: a usability evaluation of PGP 5.0. In: Proceedings of the 8th Conference on USENIX Security Symposium, SSYM 1999, vol. 8, p. 14. USENIX Association, Berkeley (1999). http://dl.acm.org/citation.cfm?id=1251421.1251435

Generic Transformation to Strongly Existentially Unforgeable Signature Schemes with Continuous Leakage Resiliency

Yuyu Wang$^{(\boxtimes)}$ and Keisuke Tanaka

Tokyo Institute of Technology, Tokyo, Japan
wang.y.ar@m.titech.ac.jp,
keisuke@is.titech.ac.jp

Abstract. In ProvSec 2014, Wang and Tanaka proposed a transformation which converts weakly existentially unforgeable (wEUF) signature schemes into strongly existentially unforgeable (sEUF) ones in the bounded leakage model. To obtain the construction, they combined the leakage resilient (LR) chameleon hash functions with the Generalised Boneh-Shen-Waters (GBSW) transformation proposed by Steinfeld, Pieprzyk, and Wang. However, their transformation cannot be used in a more realistic model called continual leakage model since the secret key of the LR chameleon hash functions cannot be updated.

In this paper, we propose a transformation which can convert wEUF signature schemes into sEUF ones in the continual leakage model. To achieve our goal, we give a new definition of continuous leakage resilient (CLR) chameleon hash function and construct it based on the CLR signature scheme proposed by Malkin, Teranishi, Vahlis, and Yung. Although the CLR chameleon hash functions satisfy the property of strong collision-resistance, because of the existence of the updating algorithm, an adversary may find the kind of collisions such that messages are the same but randomizers are different. From this fact, we cannot combine our chameleon hash functions with the GBSW transformation directly, or the sEUF security of the transformed signature schemes cannot be achieved. To solve this problem, we improve the original GBSW transformation by making use of the Groth-Sahai proof system and then combine it with our CLR chameleon hash functions.

Keywords: Generic transformation · Strong existential unforgeability · Continual leakage model · Continuous leakage resilient chameleon hash function

Department of Mathematical and Computing Sciences, Graduate School of Information Science and Engineering, Tokyo Institute of Technology, and CREST, JST, W8-55, 2-12-1 Ookayama, Meguro-ku, Tokyo 152-8552, Japan. Supported by the Ministry of Education, Science, Sports and Culture, Grant-in-Aid for Scientific Research (A) No.24240001 and (C) No.23500010, a grant of I-System Co. Ltd., and NTT Secure Platform Laboratories.

© Springer International Publishing Switzerland 2015
E. Foo and D. Stebila (Eds.): ACISP 2015, LNCS 9144, pp. 213–229, 2015.
DOI: 10.1007/978-3-319-19962-7_13

1   Introduction

1.1   Background

For a signature scheme, if it is hard to forge signatures on messages not signed before, then we say this signature scheme satisfies the security of weak existential unforgeability (wEUF). Furthermore, if it is also hard to forge signatures on messages signed before, then the strong existential unforgeability (sEUF) security is said to be satisfied, which is known as the strongest security for the forgery of signatures and required by some applications. There have already been several transformations proposed to convert wEUF signature schemes into sEUF ones (c.f. [4,6,17,23,24]). Specially, In [23], Steinfeld, Pieprzyk, and Wang presented a generic transformation called Generalised Boneh-Shen-Waters (GBSW) transformation which exploits the chameleon hash functions.

In [26], Wang and Tanaka presented a generic transformation that can convert fully leakage resilient (FLR) signature schemes which are wEUF into ones which are sEUF. For FLR signature schemes, information of signing keys and randomness may be leaked. However, this transformation only works well in the bounded leakage model, in which the adversary is allowed to learn some bounded leakage on the secret information. We hope there may be a transformation that can convert wEUF-FLR signature schemes into sEUF-FLR ones in a more realistic model called continual leakage model.

The continual leakage model was suggested by Dodis, Haralambiev, López-Alt, and Wichs [11] and Brakerski, Kalai, Katz, and Vaikuntanathan [8], which is an extension of the bounded leakage model introduced by Akavia, Goldwasser, and Vaikuntanathan [2]. In the continual leakage model, the signing key is periodically updated, and there is only bound on the leakage between two successive key updates, but no bound on the total leakage during the lifetime of the system. There has been a lot of research for cryptographic primitives in the continual leakage model (c.f., [8,10,11,14,19,20]). As far as we know, the only previously presented sEUF-FLR signature scheme in this model is proposed by Wang et al. [27]. However, they did not provide a generic transformation to sEUF-FLR signature schemes. Furthermore, The reason why the transformation proposed in [26] cannot be used in the continual leakage model is that the secret key of the leakage resilient (LR) chameleon hash functions used in that transformation cannot be updated.

1.2   Our Results

First, we give the definition of continuous leakage resilient (CLR) chameleon hash function as an extension of the definition of LR chameleon hash function [26]. For the LR chameleon hash functions, collisions can be found efficiently by making use of the secret key, and it is hard to find any collisions if the total leakage obtained during the lifetime of the system is bounded. In the case of CLR chameleon hash functions, it is hard to find collisions even when the secret key is continuously leaked, without bound of total leakage. To construct the CLR chameleon hash functions, we exploit the signature scheme in [20], in which the tuple of key generation algorithm, updating algorithm, and relation of the public/secret key pair satisfies the CLR one-way relation (OWR) defined by Dodis et al. [11]. Our construction inherits the properties of this instantiation of CLR-OWR scheme, and can tolerate any leakage of $\ell = (1 - o(1))L$ bits between every two successive key updating, where L is the length of the secret key.

Then, we make use of the CLR chameleon hash functions and the GBSW transformation to obtain a generic transformation from wEUF-FLR signature schemes into sEUF-FLR ones. Although the CLR chameleon hash functions satisfy the property of strong collision-resistance, an adversary may find message/randomizer pairs for the CLR chameleon hash functions such that the hash values and messages are the same but randomizers are different, because of the existence of updating algorithms. From this fact, we cannot combine the CLR chameleon hash functions with the GBSW transformation directly or the sEUF security cannot be satisfied, while Wang et al. combined the LR chameleon hash functions with the GBSW transformation directly to obtain their transformation in the bounded leakage model [26]. To solve this problem, we improve the original GBSW transformation by making use of the Groth-Sahai proof system.

If the wEUF-FLR signature scheme can tolerate leakage of ℓ_w bits in each round, then the converted signature scheme is resilient to any leakage of $min\{\ell, \ell_w\}$ bits in each round. Assume that $\ell_w = (1 - o(1))L$ (such as the signature scheme in [20]), then we can obtain a signature scheme that tolerates leakage of $(\frac{1}{2} - o(1))L'$ bits, where $L' = 2L$ is the length of the signing key. The same as [26], we argue that we can obtain an ℓ_s-sEUF-FLR signature scheme with signing key of length L'' where $\ell_s = (1 - o(1))L''$ by applying our technique to the wEUF-FLR signature scheme in [14].

As far as we know, this is the first generic transformation that can convert wEUF(-FLR) signature schemes into sEUF(-FLR) ones in the continual leakage model.

2 Preliminaries

2.1 CLR One-Way Relation

A OWR scheme usually consists of two algorithms KeyGen and $\mathcal{R}$, where KeyGen generates a public/secret key pair (y, x) satisfying $\mathcal{R}(y, x) = 1$. It is said to be secure if for any probabilistic polynomial time (PPT) adversary $\mathcal{A}$, given y, it is difficult to find x^* such that $\mathcal{R}(y, x^*) = 1$. In the case of CLR-OWR scheme, there is one more algorithm Update which is used to update the secret key periodically while the public key does not change. Furthermore, a CLR-OWR scheme keeps secure even if an adversary can learn leakage of the secret keys continuously. We now give the formal definition of CLR-OWR schemes, following [11].

Definition 1 (CLR-OWR schemes [11]). *A CLR-OWR scheme consists of three algorithms* (KeyGen, Update, $\mathcal{R}$). KeyGen *takes as input* 1^k *and outputs a* *public/secret key pair* (y, x). Update *takes as input a secret key* x *and outputs a refreshed secret key* x'. $\mathcal{R}$ *takes as input a public/secret key pair* (y, x) *and outputs* 1 *if* (y, x) *is "correct", and outputs* 0 *otherwise. The* ℓ-*CLR-OWR scheme must satisfy two properties, which are* correctness *property and* security *property.*

The correctness property is satisfied if for any polynomial $q = q(k)$, *we compute* $(y, x^{[0]}) \leftarrow \mathsf{KeyGen}(1^k)$, $x^{[1]} \leftarrow \mathsf{Update}(y, x^{[0]})$, ..., $x^{[q]} \leftarrow \mathsf{Update}(y, x^{[q-1]})$, *then we have* $\mathcal{R}(y, x^{[0]}) = ... = \mathcal{R}(y, x^{[q]}) = 1$.

The security property is satisfied if for any PPT adversary $\mathcal{A}$, *we have* $\Pr[\mathcal{A} \ wins] \leq \mathrm{negl}(k)$ *in the following game:*

1. *The challenger computes* $(y, x^{[0]}) \leftarrow \mathsf{KG}(1^k)$ *and sets* $L = 0$.
2. *On input* $(1^k, y)$, $\mathcal{A}$ *runs for arbitrarily many leakage rounds* $i = 0, ..., q$. *In each round* i:
   (a) $\mathcal{A}$ *makes adaptive queries to the challenger. Every time on receiving the description of a polynomial-time computable function* f_j, *if* $L + |f_j(x^{[i]})| \leq \ell$, *the challenger sends* $f_j(x^{[i]})$ *back to* $\mathcal{A}$ *and updates* $L = L + |f_j(x^{[i]})|$. *Otherwise it aborts.*
   (b) *The challenger samples* $x^{[i+1]} \leftarrow \mathsf{Update}(y, x^{[i]})$ *and sets* $L = 0$ *at the end of the round.*
3. $\mathcal{A}$ *wins if it outputs* x^* *such that* $\mathcal{R}(y, x^*) = 1$.

2.2 FLR Signature Scheme in the Continual Leakage Model

We now recall the definition of FLR signature scheme in the continual leakage model from [7,14].

A signature scheme in the continual leakage model consists of four PPT algorithms (KG, Update, Sign, Verify). KG takes as input 1^k and outputs a signing/verification key pair (pk, sk). Update takes as input a verification/signing key pair (pk, sk) and outputs a refreshed signing key sk'. Sign takes as input a signing key sk and a message m and returns a signature σ. Verify takes as input a verification key pk, a message m, and a signature σ and outputs 1 if the signature is valid, outputs 0 otherwise. In addition to the correctness, we require the following property.

Definition 2 (wEUF-FLR signature schemes [7]). *A signature scheme* (KG, Update, Sign, Verify) *is said to be* wEUF *and* ℓ-*FLR in the continual leakage model if for any PPT adversary* $\mathcal{A}$, *we have* $\Pr[\mathcal{A} \ wins] \leq \mathrm{negl}(k)$ *in the following game:*

1. *Compute* $(pk, sk) \leftarrow \mathsf{KG}(1^k, \ell)$, *set state* $= sk$ *and* $L = 0$.
2. *Run the adversary* $\mathcal{A}$ *on input* $(1^k, pk)$. *The adversary may make adaptive queries to the signing oracle, the leakage oracle and the updating oracle, defined as follows:*
   − *Signing oracle: On receiving a query* m_i, *the signing oracle samples* $r_i \leftarrow \{0, 1\}^*$, *and computes* $\sigma_i \leftarrow \mathsf{Sign}_{sk}(m_i; r_i)$. *It updates state* $= state \| r_i$ *and outputs* σ_i.

- Leakage oracle: On receiving a polynomial-time computable function f_j : $\{0,1\}^* \to \{0,1\}^{\ell_j}$, if $L + |f_j(state)| \leq \ell$, then outputs $f_j(state)$ and sets $L = L + |f_j(state)|$. Otherwise it aborts.
- Updating oracle: On receiving an updating query, the updating oracle computes $sk' \leftarrow \mathsf{Update}(pk, sk)$. It resets $sk = sk'$, $state = sk$, and $L = 0$.

3. $\mathcal{A}$ outputs (m^*, σ^*) and wins if : (a) $\mathsf{Verify}_{pk}(m^*, \sigma^*) = 1$, (b) m^* was not queried to the signing oracle.

The definition of *sEUF-FLR signature schemes* is the same as the above one, except the winning condition (b) being set as follows.

- the pair (m^*, σ^*) is new, that is, either m^* was not queried to the signing oracle or it was, σ^* is not the one(s) generated as a signature of m^* by the signing oracle.

Without loss of generality, we can assume that the adversary makes a leakage query every time after making a signing query.

The definition described above does not consider the leakage on key generation and key updating since generating key and updating key may be conducted "off-line", according to [7].

2.3   Assumptions in Bilinear Group

In this paper, we let $\mathcal{G}$ be an algorithm takes as input 1^k and outputs $gk = (p, \mathbb{G}_1, \mathbb{G}_2, \mathbb{G}_T, e)$ such that p is prime, $(\mathbb{G}_1, \mathbb{G}_2, \mathbb{G}_T)$ are descriptions of groups of order p, and $e : \mathbb{G}_1 \times \mathbb{G}_2 \to \mathbb{G}_T$ is a non-degenerate efficiently computable bilinear map. It is required that there is no efficient computable mapping between $\mathbb{G}_1$ and $\mathbb{G}_2$.

The same as [20], we use additive notation for pairings, such as $e((a + b)A, B) = a \cdot e(A, B) + b \cdot e(A, B)$. We denote $e(\mathbf{A}^T, \mathbf{B}) = \sum_{i=1}^{n} e(A_i, B_i)$, where $\mathbf{A} = (A_1, ..., A_n)^T \in \mathbb{G}_1$, $\mathbf{B} = (B_1, ..., B_n)^T \in \mathbb{G}_2$.

We now recall the *Decisional Diffie-Hellman (DDH) assumption*, the *Symmetric External Diffie-Hellman (SXDH) assumption*, and the *Double Paring Assumption*.

Definition 3 (DDH assumption). *Let $\mathbb{G}$ be a group of primer order p. For any PPT adversary $\mathcal{A}$, we have*

$$\Pr[G_1, G_2 \leftarrow \mathbb{G}; r \leftarrow \mathbb{Z}_p : \mathcal{A}(\mathbb{G}, G_1, G_2, rG_1, rG_2) = 1]$$
$$\approx \Pr[G_1, G_2 \leftarrow \mathbb{G}; r_1, r_2 \leftarrow \mathbb{Z}_p : \mathcal{A}(\mathbb{G}, G_1, G_2, r_1G_1, r_2G_2) = 1].$$

SXDH assumption [3, 5, 12, 13, 21, 25]. Let $gk = (p, \mathbb{G}_1, \mathbb{G}_2, \mathbb{G}_T, e)$ be the tuple generated by $\mathcal{G}$ as we introduced earlier, the SXDH assumption states that the DDH problem is hard in both groups $\mathbb{G}_1$ and $\mathbb{G}_2$.

Definition 4 (Double Paring Assumption [1, 12, 15]). *For any PPT adversary $\mathcal{A}$, we have*

$$\Pr[G_1, G_2 \leftarrow \mathbb{G}_1; (Z_1, Z_2) \leftarrow \mathcal{A}(gk, G_1, G_2) :$$
$$Z_1, Z_2 \in \mathbb{G}_2 \wedge (Z_1, Z_2) \neq (0, 0) \wedge e(G_1, Z_1) + e(G_2, Z_2) = 0] \leq negl(k).$$

The double pairing assumption is implied by the SXDH assumption (ref., [1, 12, 15]).

Now we give a lemma on which our construction will be based.

Lemma 1 (Simular to [12]). *For any PPT adversary $\mathcal{A}$, we have*

$$\Pr[(p, \mathbb{G}_1, \mathbb{G}_2, \mathbb{G}_T, e) \leftarrow \mathcal{G}(1^k); \boldsymbol{B} \leftarrow \mathbb{G}_1^n; \boldsymbol{M} \leftarrow \mathbb{G}_2^n; \boldsymbol{M}^* \leftarrow \mathcal{A}(gk, \boldsymbol{B}, \boldsymbol{M}) :$$
$$e(\boldsymbol{B}^T, \boldsymbol{M}^*) = e(\boldsymbol{B}^T, \boldsymbol{M}) \wedge \boldsymbol{M}^* \neq \boldsymbol{M}] \leq negl(k).$$

The proof of this lemma is based on the SXDH assumption and almost the same as the proof of the second preimage relation in [12]. We give the proof as follows.

Proof. Assume that there exists an adversary $\mathcal{A}$ that given $\boldsymbol{B} = (B_1, ..., B_n)^T$ and $\boldsymbol{M} = (M_1, ..., M_n)^T \in \mathbb{G}_2^n$, finds $\boldsymbol{M}^* \in \mathbb{G}_2^n$ such that $\boldsymbol{M} \neq \boldsymbol{M}^*$ and $e(\boldsymbol{B}^T, \boldsymbol{M}) = e(\boldsymbol{B}^T, \boldsymbol{M}^*)$ with non-negligible probability ϵ. By making use of $\mathcal{A}$, we construct an adversary $\mathcal{B}$ that breaks the double-pairing assumption.

$\mathcal{B}$ takes as input G_1, G_2, chooses $\alpha_1, \beta_1, ..., \alpha_n, \beta_n \leftarrow \mathbb{Z}_p$, and sets $\boldsymbol{B} = (\alpha_1 G_1 + \beta_1 G_2, ..., \alpha_n G_1 + \beta_n G_2)^T$. Then $\mathcal{B}$ chooses $\boldsymbol{M} \leftarrow \mathbb{G}_2^n$ and gives $\boldsymbol{B}, \boldsymbol{M}$ to $\mathcal{A}$. With probability ϵ, $\mathcal{A}$ returns $\boldsymbol{M}^*$ such that $\boldsymbol{M}^* \neq \boldsymbol{M}$ and $e(\boldsymbol{B}^T, \boldsymbol{M}^*) = e(\boldsymbol{B}^T, \boldsymbol{M})$. Then $\mathcal{B}$ outputs $(Z_1, Z_2) = (\sum_{i=1}^n \alpha_i(M_i - M_i^*), \sum_{i=1}^n \beta_i(M_i - M_i^*))$. We have

$$e(G_1, Z_1) + e(G_2, Z_2) = e(G_1, \sum_{i=1}^n \alpha_i(M_i - M_i^*)) + e(G_2, \sum_{i=1}^n \beta_i(M_i - M_i^*))$$
$$= e(\boldsymbol{B}^T, \boldsymbol{M} - \boldsymbol{M}^*) = 0.$$

Furthermore, there exists $j \in [1, ..., n]$ for which $M_j - M_j^* \neq 0$. Since α_j is information theoretically hidden, we have $Z_1 \neq 0$ with probability $(1 - 1/q)$. Thus, $\mathcal{B}$ breaks the double pairing assumption with non-negligible probability.

2.4 Groth-Sahai Proofs

In [20], Malkin et al. made use of the Groth-Sahai Proof system [16] to construct their signature scheme. Inspired by them, we will construct our transformation based on this system.

In this paper, the statements are of the form $e(\boldsymbol{A}^T, \boldsymbol{M}) = T$ for $(\boldsymbol{A}, \boldsymbol{M}, T) \in \mathbb{G}_1^n \times \mathbb{G}_2^n \times \mathbb{G}_T$, where $\boldsymbol{M}$ is the witness.

The proof system consists of four algorithms (HideCRS, BindCRS, Prf, Vrf). HideCRS takes as input gk (ref., Section 2.3) and outputs the common reference string (CRS) $crs = (\boldsymbol{G}, \boldsymbol{H}) \leftarrow \mathbb{G}_2^2$. BindCRS takes as input gk, chooses $\boldsymbol{G} \leftarrow \mathbb{G}_2^2$, $\alpha \leftarrow \mathbb{Z}_p$, and outputs the CRS and trapdoor information $(crs = (\boldsymbol{G}, \boldsymbol{H} = \alpha\boldsymbol{G}), \alpha)$. Prf takes as input $(gk, crs, (\boldsymbol{A}, T), \boldsymbol{M})$, chooses $R \leftarrow \mathbb{Z}_p^{n \times 2}$, and outputs $\sigma = (\boldsymbol{C}, \boldsymbol{D}, \boldsymbol{\Pi}) = (R \cdot \boldsymbol{G}, \boldsymbol{M} + R \cdot \boldsymbol{H}, R^T \boldsymbol{A})$. Vrf takes as input $(gk, crs, (\boldsymbol{A}, T), \sigma)$ and outputs 1 if $(e(\boldsymbol{A}^T, \boldsymbol{C}), e(\boldsymbol{A}^T, \boldsymbol{D})) = (e(\boldsymbol{\Pi}^T, \boldsymbol{G}), T + e(\boldsymbol{\Pi}^T, \boldsymbol{H}))$, outputs 0 otherwise. Groth and Sahai showed that the two types of CRS are indistinguishable under the SXDH assumption.

The scheme described above satisfies two properties, which are *perfect witness indistinguishability property* and *perfect extractability* property. Their definitions are as follow.

The perfect witness indistinguishability property is satisfied if for all PPT adversaries $\mathcal{A}$,

$$\Pr[gk \leftarrow \mathcal{G}(1^k), crs \leftarrow \mathsf{HideCRS}(gk), (\boldsymbol{A}, T, \boldsymbol{M}_0, \boldsymbol{M}_1, st) \leftarrow \mathcal{A}(gk, CRS),$$
$$\sigma \leftarrow \mathsf{Prf}(gk, CRS, (\boldsymbol{A}, T), \boldsymbol{M}_0) : 1 \leftarrow \mathcal{A}(\sigma, st)]$$
$$= \Pr[gk \leftarrow \mathcal{G}(1^k), crs \leftarrow \mathsf{HideCRS}(gk), (\boldsymbol{A}, T, \boldsymbol{M}_0, \boldsymbol{M}_1, st) \leftarrow \mathcal{A}(gk, CRS),$$
$$\sigma \leftarrow \mathsf{Prf}(gk, CRS, (\boldsymbol{A}, T), \boldsymbol{M}_1) : 1 \leftarrow \mathcal{A}(\sigma, st)],$$

where it is required that $e(\boldsymbol{A}^T, \boldsymbol{M}_0) = e(\boldsymbol{A}^T, \boldsymbol{M}_1) = T$.

The perfect extractability property is satisfied if for all possible output gk of $\mathcal{G}(1^k)$, all possible output (crs, α) of $\mathsf{BindCRS}(gk)$, all $(\boldsymbol{A}, T) \in \mathbb{G}_1^n \times \mathbb{G}_T$ and all $\sigma = (\boldsymbol{C}, \boldsymbol{D}, \boldsymbol{\Pi}) \in \mathbb{G}_2^{n \times 1} \times \mathbb{G}_2^{n \times 1} \times \mathbb{G}_1^2$ satisfying $\mathsf{Vrf}(gk, crs, (\boldsymbol{A}, T), \sigma) = 1$, we set $\boldsymbol{M}^* = \boldsymbol{D} - \alpha\boldsymbol{C}$, then $e(\boldsymbol{A}^T, \boldsymbol{M}^*) = T$ always holds.

3 CLR Chameleon Hash Functions

In this section, we define the CLR chameleon hash function. This definition is an extension of the notion of chameleon hash function [18,22] and LR chameleon hash function [26]. Then we give our construction of CLR chameleon hash functions based on a CLR-OWR scheme from [20].

3.1 Definition

An ℓ-CLR chameleon hash function scheme consists of four PPT algorithms $(\mathsf{KG}_F, \mathsf{TC}_F, F, \mathsf{UD}_F)$.

KG_F is a *key generation* algorithm that takes as input $(1^k, \ell)$, and outputs a public/private key pair (pk_F, sk_F). F is a *hash function evaluation* algorithm that takes as input pk_F, a message m, and a randomizer r, and outputs a hash value $h = F_{pk_F}(m; r)$. TC_F is a *trapdoor collision finder* algorithm that takes as input sk_F, an arbitrary message pair (m, m'), and a randomizer r, and outputs $r' = \mathsf{TC}_F(sk_F, (m, r), m')$ such that $F_{pk_F}(m; r) = F_{pk_F}(m'; r')$. UD_F is a *key update* algorithm takes as input (pk_F, sk_F) and samples a refreshed secret key sk_F' for pk_F.

An ℓ-CLR chameleon hash function scheme must satisfy four properties, which are *reversibility, correctness, random trapdoor collision*, and ℓ-CLR strong *collision-resistance*.

The reversibility property is satisfied if $r' = \mathsf{TC}_F(sk_F, (m, r), m')$ is equivalent to $r = \mathsf{TC}_F(sk_F, (m', r'), m)$.

The correctness property is satisfied if for any polynomial $i = i(k)$, any message pair (m, m'), and a randomizer r, if we compute $(pk_F, sk_F^{[0]}) \leftarrow \mathsf{KG}_F(1^k)$, $sk_F^{[1]} \leftarrow \mathsf{UD}_F(pk_F, sk_F^{[0]})$, ..., $sk_F^{[i]} \leftarrow \mathsf{UD}_F(pk_F, sk_F^{[i-1]})$, and $r' = \mathsf{TC}_F(sk_F^{[i]}, (m, r), m')$, we have $F_{pk_F}(m; r) = F_{pk_F}(m'; r')$. If the r' has a uniform probability distribution on the randomness space, then the random trapdoor collision property is also satisfied.

The ℓ-CLR strong collision-resistance property is satisfied if for any PPT adversary $\mathcal{A}$, we have $\Pr[\mathcal{A} \text{ wins}] \leq \mathsf{negl}(k)$ in the following game:

1. the challenger computes $(pk_F, sk_F^{[0]}) \leftarrow \mathsf{KG}_F(1^k)$ and sets $L = 0$.
2. On input $(1^k, pk_F, F)$, $\mathcal{A}$ runs for arbitrarily many leakage rounds $i = 0, ..., q$. In each round i:
   (a) $\mathcal{A}$ makes adaptive queries to the challenger. Every time on receiving the description of a polynomial-time computable function f_j, if $L + |f_j(sk_F^{[i]})| \leq \ell$, then the challenger sends $f_j(sk_F^{[i]})$ back to $\mathcal{A}$ and updates $L = L + |f_j(sk_F^{[i]})|$. Otherwise it aborts.
   (b) the challenger refreshes the secret key by sampling $sk_F^{[i+1]} \leftarrow \mathsf{Update}(pk_F, sk_F^{[i]})$ and resets $L = 0$ at the end of the round.
3. $\mathcal{A}$ wins if it outputs (m, r) and (m', r') such that $m \neq m'$ and $F_{pk_F}(m, r) = F_{pk_F}(m', r')$.

The definition of standard chameleon hash function is the same as the definition of CLR one except that there exists no key updating algorithm and the adversary is not allowed to make leakage queries to learn any information about the secret keys. Furthermore, although the original definition of chameleon hash function scheme just require that $m \neq m'$, it is required that the adversary cannot find a collision that $(m, r) \neq (m', r')$ for the standard chameleon hash function here. As far as we know, all of the previously presented chameleon functions satisfy this stronger version of strong collision-resistance naturally.

3.2   Construction of CLR One-Way Relation Scheme

Theorem 1. *The scheme described in Figure 1 is an ℓ-CLR-OWR scheme for $\ell = n \log p - (2 + \Theta(1/\sqrt{k})) \log p$ if the SXDH assumption holds.*

If we add $(\boldsymbol{G}, \boldsymbol{H})$ where $\boldsymbol{G} \leftarrow \mathbb{G}_2^2$ and $\boldsymbol{H} = (\boldsymbol{H}_0, ... \boldsymbol{H}_t) \leftarrow (\mathbb{G}_2^2)^{t+1}$ to the public key, then the public/secret key pair of our CLR-OWR scheme is the same as the verification/signing key pair of the continuous leakage resilient signature scheme in [20].

For the signature scheme in [20], a PPT adversary can make three kinds of queries, which are updating queries, leakage queries, and signing queries, and the probability to output a valid forgery against the wEUF experiment is negligible if the SXDH assumption holds (we refer the reader to [20] for details of the

---

- Key generation algorithm $\mathsf{KG}(1^k)$:
    1. Run $gk = (p, \mathbb{G}_1, \mathbb{G}_2, \mathbb{G}_T, e) \leftarrow \mathcal{G}(1^k)$.
    2. Choose $A \leftarrow \mathbb{G}_1$, $Q \leftarrow \mathbb{G}_2$, $\boldsymbol{a}, \boldsymbol{q} \leftarrow \mathbb{Z}_p^n$ satisfying $\langle \boldsymbol{a}^T, \boldsymbol{q} \rangle = 0$. $\boldsymbol{A} = \boldsymbol{a}A, \boldsymbol{Q} = \boldsymbol{q}Q$.
    3. Choose $\boldsymbol{W}^{[0]} \leftarrow \mathbb{G}_2^n$.
    4. Compute $T = e(\boldsymbol{A}^T, \boldsymbol{W}^{[0]})$.
    5. Return $y = (gk, \boldsymbol{A}, T, \boldsymbol{Q})$ and $x^{[0]} = \boldsymbol{W}^{[0]}$.
- Updating algorithm $\mathsf{Update}(y, x^{[i]})$:
    1. Parse $pk = (gk, \boldsymbol{A}, T, \boldsymbol{Q})$ and $x^{[i]} = \boldsymbol{W}^{[i]}$.
    2. Choose $s \leftarrow \mathbb{Z}_p$.
    3. Return $x^{[i+1]} = \boldsymbol{W}^{[i+1]} = \boldsymbol{W}^{[i]} + s\boldsymbol{Q}$.
- Verification algorithm $\mathcal{R}(y, x^{[i]})$:
    1. Parse $y = (gk, \boldsymbol{A}, T, \boldsymbol{Q})$ and $x^{[i]} = \boldsymbol{W}^{[i]}$.
    2. Output 1 if $T = e(\boldsymbol{A}^T, \boldsymbol{W}^{[i]})$, and output 0 otherwise.

Fig. 1. CLR-OWR scheme

proof). Now we assume that the adversary only makes updating queries and leakage queries for the signing key. It is clear that the advantage of the adversary becomes even smaller than before.

Furthermore, according to [20], the signatures output by the signing algorithms are Groth-Sahai proofs which prove statements of the form $e(\boldsymbol{A}^T, \boldsymbol{W}) = T$ where $\boldsymbol{W}$ is the witness (and signing key), and the CRSs depend on the messages. It is not hard to see that if an adversary can obtain $\boldsymbol{W}^*$ such that $e(\boldsymbol{A}^T, \boldsymbol{W}^*) = T$, then it is able to forge signatures against the wEUF game by using $\boldsymbol{W}^*$ as the signing key. As a result, the adversary cannot output a valid signing key (or secret key) after making updating queries and leakage queries.

Since the signature scheme in [20] can tolerate $n \log p - (2 + \Theta(1/\sqrt{k})) \log p$ bits of leakage on the signing key in each leakage round, the probability that any PPT adversary $\mathcal{A}$, who can learn $n \log p - (2 + \Theta(1/\sqrt{k})) \log p$ bits of leakage on the secret key in each leakage round, outputs a valid secret key is negligible. Furthermore, if we set $n = k$, we have $n \log p - (2 + \Theta(1/\sqrt{k})) \log p = (1 - o(1))L$ where L is the length of secret key.

3.3 Construction of CLR Chameleon Hash Function

We present our construction of CLR chameleon hash functions in Figure 2.

Theorem 2. *The scheme described in Figure 2 is an ℓ-CLR chameleon hash function for $\ell = n \log p - (2 + \Theta(1/\sqrt{k})) \log p$ if the SXDH assumption holds.*

To prove that our scheme is a CLR chameleon hash function scheme, we have to show that this scheme satisfies the properties of *correctness, reversibility, random trapdoor collision,* and *CLR strong collision-resistance.* It is not hard

- Key generation algorithm $\mathsf{KG}_F(1^k)$:
  1. Run $gk = (p, \mathbb{G}_1, \mathbb{G}_2, \mathbb{G}_T, e) \leftarrow \mathcal{G}(1^k)$.
  2. Choose $A \leftarrow \mathbb{G}_1, Q \leftarrow \mathbb{G}_2, \boldsymbol{a}, \boldsymbol{q} \leftarrow \mathbb{Z}_p^n$ satisfying $\langle \boldsymbol{a}, \boldsymbol{q} \rangle = 0$. $\boldsymbol{A} = \boldsymbol{a}A, \boldsymbol{Q} = \boldsymbol{q}Q$.
  3. Choose $\boldsymbol{W}^{[0]} \leftarrow \mathbb{G}_2^n$.
  4. Compute $T = e(\boldsymbol{A}^T, \boldsymbol{W}^{[0]})$.
  5. Return $pk_F = (gk, \boldsymbol{A}, T, \boldsymbol{Q})$ and $sk_F^{[0]} = \boldsymbol{W}^{[0]}$.
- Hash function evaluation algorithm $F_{pk_F}(m, \boldsymbol{R})$ where $\boldsymbol{R} \leftarrow \mathbb{G}_2^n$:
  1. Return $h = J(m)(T + e(\boldsymbol{A}^T, \boldsymbol{R}))$, where J denotes a strongly collision resistant hash function from $\{0,1\}^*$ to $\mathbb{Z}_p/\{0\}$.
- Trapdoor collision finder algorithm $\mathsf{TC}_F(sk_F^{[i]}, (m, \boldsymbol{R}), m')$:
  1. Parse $sk_F^{[i]} = \boldsymbol{W}^{[i]}$.
  2. Return $\boldsymbol{R}' = \frac{J(m)}{J(m')}(\boldsymbol{W}^{[i]} + \boldsymbol{R}) - \boldsymbol{W}^{[i]}$.
- Updating algorithm $\mathsf{UD}_F(pk_F, sk_F^{[i]})$:
  1. Parse $pk = (gk, \boldsymbol{A}, T, \boldsymbol{Q})$ and $sk_F^{[i]} = \boldsymbol{W}^{[i]}$.
  2. Choose $s \leftarrow \mathbb{Z}_p$.
  3. Return $sk_F^{[i+1]} = \boldsymbol{W}^{[i+1]} = \boldsymbol{W}^{[i]} + s\boldsymbol{Q}$.

Fig. 2. CLR Chameleon Hash Function Scheme

to prove that our scheme satisfies the properties of correctness, reversibility, random trapdoor collision, and we will argue that if there exists an adversary that breaks the CLR strong collision-resistance for this scheme, then we can construct another adversary that breaks the security property of the CLR-OWR scheme in Figure 1.

Proof. First we argue that the correctness property is satisfied for our scheme.

For any polynomial integer $i \geq 0$, if we compute $((gk, \boldsymbol{A}, T, \boldsymbol{Q}), \boldsymbol{W}^{[0]}) \leftarrow \mathsf{KG}_F(1^k), \boldsymbol{W}^{[1]} = \boldsymbol{W}^{[0]} + s_0\boldsymbol{Q}, ..., \boldsymbol{W}^{[i]} = \boldsymbol{W}^{[i-1]} + s_{i-1}\boldsymbol{Q}$, where $s_0, ..., s_{i-1}$ are randomly chosen from $\mathbb{Z}_p$, we have $e(\boldsymbol{A}^T, \boldsymbol{W}^{[i]}) = e(\boldsymbol{A}^T, \boldsymbol{W}^{[0]} + (s_0 + ... + s_{i-1})\boldsymbol{Q}) = T + (s_0 + ... + s_{i-1})e(\boldsymbol{A}^T, \boldsymbol{Q}) = T$. According to the trapdoor collision finder algorithm described above, if $\boldsymbol{R}' = \mathsf{TC}_F(sk_F^{[i]}, (m, \boldsymbol{R}), m')$, we have $J(m')(\boldsymbol{W}^{[i]} + \boldsymbol{R}') = J(m)(\boldsymbol{W}^{[i]} + \boldsymbol{R})$, which means that we have $J(m')(e(\boldsymbol{A}^T, \boldsymbol{W}^{[i]}) + e(\boldsymbol{A}^T, \boldsymbol{R}')) = J(m)(e(\boldsymbol{A}^T, \boldsymbol{W}^{[i]}) + e(\boldsymbol{A}^T, \boldsymbol{R}))$, equivalently, $F_{pk_F}(m', \boldsymbol{R}') = F_{pk_F}(m, \boldsymbol{R})$.

Since $\boldsymbol{R}' = \frac{J(m)}{J(m')}(\boldsymbol{W}^{[i]} + \boldsymbol{R}) - \boldsymbol{W}^{[i]}$ is equivalent to $\boldsymbol{R} = \frac{J(m')}{J(m)}(\boldsymbol{W}^{[i]} + \boldsymbol{R}') - \boldsymbol{W}^{[i]}$, if $\boldsymbol{R}' = \mathsf{TC}_F(sk_F, (m, \boldsymbol{R}), m')$ holds, $\boldsymbol{R} = \mathsf{TC}_F(sk_F, (m', \boldsymbol{R}'), m)$ holds as well, which makes our scheme satisfy the reversibility property. Furthermore, it is apparent that $\boldsymbol{R}'$ has a uniform probability distribution on $\mathbb{G}_2^n$ if $\boldsymbol{R}$ is chosen randomly from $\mathbb{G}_2^n$, which makes our scheme also satisfy the random trapdoor collision property.

Since we have shown that our scheme satisfies the properties of correctness, reversibility, and random trapdoor collision, what we are left to do is to prove that our scheme also satisfies the property of CLR strong collision-resistance.

Let VR_F be a deterministic algorithm which takes as input $(gk, \boldsymbol{A}, T, \boldsymbol{Q}, \boldsymbol{W})$, and outputs 1 if $T = e(\boldsymbol{A}^T, \boldsymbol{W})$, outputs 0 otherwise. It is clear that $(\mathsf{KG}_F, \mathsf{UD}_F, \mathsf{VR}_F)$ is the same as the ℓ-CLR-OWR that we have stated in Figure 1. We argue that if there exists a PPT adversary $\mathcal{B}$ that breaks the ℓ-CLR strong collision-resistance property, then there exists a PPT adversary $\mathcal{A}$ that wins the ℓ-security experiment of CLR-OWR (c.f., Section 2.1).

The challenger generates $((gk, \boldsymbol{A}, T, \boldsymbol{Q}), \boldsymbol{W}^{[0]})$ and gives $(gk, \boldsymbol{A}, T, \boldsymbol{Q})$ to $\mathcal{A}$. Then $\mathcal{A}$ gives $(gk, \boldsymbol{A}, T, \boldsymbol{Q})$ to $\mathcal{B}$ as the public key.

Every time $\mathcal{B}$ runs for a new leakage round, $\mathcal{A}$ asks the challenger to update the secret key. After getting a leakage query $f_i(\cdot)$ from $\mathcal{B}$, $\mathcal{A}$ sends the query to the challenger and gives the answer back to $\mathcal{B}$. Since the number of leaked bits obtained by $\mathcal{B}$ in each round should be less than ℓ, all of the queries from $\mathcal{B}$ can be answered. After getting the output of $\mathcal{B}$ denoted by $(m, \boldsymbol{R})$ and $(m', \boldsymbol{R}')$, $\mathcal{A}$ computes $\boldsymbol{W}^* = \frac{J(m')\boldsymbol{R}' - J(m)\boldsymbol{R}}{J(m) - J(m')}$ (Since $m' \neq m$ and $J(\cdot)$ is a strongly collision resistant hash function, we know the probability that $(J(m) - J(m')) \bmod p = 0$ is negligible). Then $\mathcal{A}$ outputs $\boldsymbol{W}^*$.

If $\mathcal{B}$ has found the collision successfully, we have $J(m)(T + e(\boldsymbol{A}^T, \boldsymbol{R})) = J(m')(T + e(\boldsymbol{A}^T, \boldsymbol{R}'))$. Furthermore, since $J(m)(\boldsymbol{W}^* + \boldsymbol{R}) = J(m')(\boldsymbol{W}^* + \boldsymbol{R}')$, which means $J(m)(e(\boldsymbol{A}^T, \boldsymbol{W}^*) + e(\boldsymbol{A}^T, \boldsymbol{R})) = J(m')(e(\boldsymbol{A}^T, \boldsymbol{W}^*) + e(\boldsymbol{A}^T, \boldsymbol{R}'))$, we have $T = e(\boldsymbol{A}^T, \boldsymbol{W}^*) = \frac{J(m')e(\boldsymbol{A}^T, \boldsymbol{R}') - J(m)e(\boldsymbol{A}^T, \boldsymbol{R})}{J(m) - J(m')}$.

As a result if $\mathcal{B}$ can find a collision successfully with probability ϵ in polynomial time t, then $\mathcal{A}$ can break the security of CLR one-way relation with the same probability in the same running time, completing the proof.

Notice that it is very easy to find a collision $((m, \boldsymbol{R}_1), (m, \boldsymbol{R}_2))$ for this CLR chameleon hash function such that $F_{pk_F}(m, \boldsymbol{R}_1) = F_{pk_F}(m, \boldsymbol{R}_2)$ and $\boldsymbol{R}_1 \neq \boldsymbol{R}_2$, since for any m, $s \in \mathbb{Z}_p$, and $\boldsymbol{R}_1 \in \mathbb{G}_2^n$, we have $F_{pk_F}(m, \boldsymbol{R}_1) = J(m)(T + e(\boldsymbol{A}^T, \boldsymbol{R}_1)) = J(m)(T + e(\boldsymbol{A}^T, \boldsymbol{R}_2)) = F_{pk_F}(m, \boldsymbol{R}_2)$ where $\boldsymbol{R}_2 = \boldsymbol{R}_1 + s\boldsymbol{Q}$. As a result, this CLR chameleon hash function scheme does not satisfy the stronger version of strong collision-resistance that we talked about in Section 3.1.

4   Generic Transformation

We now give the construction of the generic transformation that can convert any wEUF-FLR signature schemes into sEUF-FLR ones in the continual leakage model. Our construction is inspired by the transformation in [26]. In [26], Wang et al. improved the GBSW transformation in [23] by substituting the standard chameleon hash functions with the LR ones. However, substituting the standard chameleon hash functions in the GBSW transformation with the CLR ones is not enough to obtain the transformation we want. The reason is that it is very hard to achieve the chameleon hash functions satisfying the stronger version of strong collision-resistance as [23, 26] in the continual leakage model. To solve this problem, we make use of the Groth-Sahai proof system.

Let $\Sigma = (\mathsf{KG}, \mathsf{Sign}, \mathsf{Verify}, \mathsf{Update})$ be an arbitrary ℓ_w-wEUF-FLR signature scheme with randomness space Ω_Σ in the continual leakage model, $\mathcal{F} = (\mathsf{KG}_F, F, \mathsf{TC}_F, \mathsf{UD}_F)$ the ℓ-CLR chameleon hash function scheme with randomness space $\mathcal{R}_F$, where $\ell = n \log p - (2 + \Theta(1/\sqrt{k})) \log p$, and $\mathcal{H} = (\mathsf{KG}_H, H, \mathsf{TC}_H)$ a standard chameleon hash function with randomness space $\mathcal{R}_H$. We make use of the Groth-Sahai proof system and the GBSW scheme [23] to construct an ℓ_s-sEUF-FLR signature scheme Σ' as shown in Figure 3.

For Σ', the signature is a tuple of (σ, r, s, π, T). $\pi = (\boldsymbol{\Pi}, \boldsymbol{C}, \boldsymbol{D})$ is a Groth-Sahai proof for the statement $T = e(\boldsymbol{B}^T, \boldsymbol{M})$ where $\boldsymbol{B}$ is a part of the public key and $\boldsymbol{M}$ is a randomizer generated in the signing process. σ is the signature depending on m, σ, $\boldsymbol{\Pi}$, and T.

Inspired by [20], we use the Water's hash function to generate the CRS of the Groth-Sahai proof system. Water's hash function is defined as $h_{gk}(\mathbf{H}, x) = \boldsymbol{H}_0 + \sum_{i=1}^t x_i \boldsymbol{H}_i$, where $gk = (p, \mathbb{G}_1, \mathbb{G}_2, \mathbb{G}_T, e)$, $\mathbf{H} = (\boldsymbol{H}_0, ..., \boldsymbol{H}_t) \in (\mathbb{G}_2^2)^{t+1}$, $x \in \{0,1\}^t$, and x_i is the ith bit of x. We generate the CRS as $(\boldsymbol{G}, \boldsymbol{H}_r = h_{gk}(\mathbf{H}, J'(r)))$. Notice that to make the signature depend on $\boldsymbol{\Pi}$, we have to compute $\boldsymbol{\Pi}$ before generating r and the CRS.

By making use of the Groth-Sahai proof system, we can make sure that if there exists an adversary that can forge a message/signature pair which is the same as a pair generated by the signing oracle except that r or π is different, then we can extract $\boldsymbol{M}^*$ such that $e(\boldsymbol{B}^T, \boldsymbol{M}^*) = T = e(\boldsymbol{B}^T, \boldsymbol{M}) \wedge \boldsymbol{M}^* \neq \boldsymbol{M}$ from the forged π (in the hybrid game) with non-negligible probability, breaking Lemma 1.

Theorem 3. *The signature scheme described in Figure 3 is an ℓ_s-sEUF-FLR signature scheme for $\ell_s = \min\{\ell, \ell_w\}$.*

To prove that Σ' is secure in the continual leakage model, we show that if there is an adversary that can break the sEUF-FLR property, then there exist five adversaries against the wEUF-FLR property of Σ, the strong collision-resistance of $\mathcal{H}$ and $\mathcal{F}$, and Lemma 1, respectively. Some parts of our proof are similar to [23]. The proof sketch is given as follows.

Proof sketch. For $i = 1, ..., q$, let m_i be the ith signing query, $\sigma_i' = (\sigma_i, r_i, s_i, \pi_i = (\boldsymbol{\Pi}_i, \boldsymbol{C}_i, \boldsymbol{D}_i), T_i)$ be the answer to the ith signing query, $\boldsymbol{H}_{ri} = h_{gk}(\mathbf{H}, J'(r_i))$, $h_i = F_{pk_F}(m_i||\sigma_i||\boldsymbol{\Pi}_i||T_i; r_i)$, and $\bar{m}_i = H_{pk_H}(h_i; s_i)$. We denote f_j as the jth leakage query of $\mathcal{A}$. At some point, $\mathcal{A}$ outputs (m^*, σ'^*) where $\sigma'^* = (\sigma^*, r^*, s^*, \pi^* = (\boldsymbol{\Pi}^*, \boldsymbol{C}^*, \boldsymbol{D}^*), T^*)$ as the forgery. In the same way, $\boldsymbol{H}_r^* = h_{gk}(\mathbf{H}, J'(r^*))$, $h^* = F_{pk_F}(m^*||\sigma^*||\boldsymbol{\Pi}^*||T^*; r^*)$ and $\bar{m}^* = H_{pk_H}(h^*; s^*)$.

If $\mathcal{A}$ wins the sEUF-FLR experiment with non-negligible probability ϵ, then $\mathcal{A}$ outputs a forgery, which is one of the following five types with probability $\epsilon/5$ in the sEUF-FLR experiment:

- $\mathsf{KG}'(1^k)$:
    1. Run $gk = (p, \mathbb{G}_1, \mathbb{G}_2, \mathbb{G}_T, e) \leftarrow \mathcal{G}(1^k)$.
    2. Run $(pk, sk) \leftarrow \mathsf{KG}(1^k)$.
    3. Run $(pk_F, sk_F) \leftarrow \mathsf{KG}_F(1^k)$.
    4. Run $(pk_H, sk_H) \leftarrow \mathsf{KG}_H(1^k)$.
    5. Randomly choose $\boldsymbol{G} \leftarrow \mathbb{G}_2^2$, $\mathbf{H} = (\boldsymbol{H}_0, \boldsymbol{H}_1, ..., \boldsymbol{H}_t) \leftarrow (\mathbb{G}_2^2)^{t+1}$, $\boldsymbol{B} \leftarrow \mathbb{G}_1^n$.
    6. Output public key $pk_s = (gk, pk, pk_F, pk_H, \boldsymbol{G}, \mathbf{H}, \boldsymbol{B}, m', \sigma')$ and secret key $sk_s = (sk, sk_F)$, where m' and σ' are arbitrary fixed strings.
- $\mathsf{Sign}'_{sk_s}(m)$:
    1. Parse $sk_s = (sk, sk_F)$.
    2. Randomly choose $\omega \leftarrow \Omega_\Sigma$, $s \leftarrow \mathcal{R}_H$, $r' \leftarrow \mathcal{R}_F$, $R \leftarrow \mathbb{Z}_p^{n \times 2}$, and $\boldsymbol{M} \leftarrow \mathbb{G}_2^n$.
    3. Compute $h = F_{pk_F}(m' || \sigma'; r')$.
    4. Compute $\bar{m} = H_{pk_H}(h; s)$.
    5. Compute $\sigma = \mathsf{Sign}_{sk}(\bar{m}; \omega)$.
    6. Compute $\boldsymbol{\Pi} = R^T \boldsymbol{B}$, $T = e(\boldsymbol{B}^T, \boldsymbol{M})$.
    7. Compute $r = \mathsf{TC}_F(sk_F, (m' || \sigma', r'), m || \sigma || \boldsymbol{\Pi} || T)$.
    8. Compute $\boldsymbol{H}_r = h_{gk}(\mathbf{H}, J'(r))$, where J' denotes a strongly collision resistant hash function from $\{0, 1\}^*$ to $\{0, 1\}^t$.
    9. Compute $(\boldsymbol{C}, \boldsymbol{D}) = (RG, \boldsymbol{M} + R\boldsymbol{H}_r)$, $\pi = (\boldsymbol{\Pi}, \boldsymbol{C}, \boldsymbol{D})$.
    10. Output $\sigma' = (\sigma, r, s, \pi, T)$.
- $\mathsf{Verify}'(pk_s, m, \sigma')$:
    1. Parse $pk_s = (gk, pk, pk_F, pk_H, \boldsymbol{G}, \mathbf{H}, \boldsymbol{B}, m', \sigma')$, $\sigma' = (\sigma, r, s, \pi, T)$, and $\pi = (\boldsymbol{\Pi}, \boldsymbol{C}, \boldsymbol{D})$.
    2. Compute $h = F_{pk_F}(m || \sigma || \boldsymbol{\Pi} || T; r)$.
    3. Compute $\bar{m} = H_{pk_H}(h; s)$.
    4. Compute $\boldsymbol{H}_r = h_{gk}(\mathbf{H}, J'(r))$.
    5. Output 1 if $\mathsf{Verify}(pk, \bar{m}, \sigma) = 1$ and $(e(\boldsymbol{B}^T, \boldsymbol{C}), e(\boldsymbol{B}^T, \boldsymbol{D})) = (e(\boldsymbol{\Pi}^T, \boldsymbol{G}), T + e(\boldsymbol{\Pi}^T, \boldsymbol{H}_r))$, and output 0 otherwise.
- $\mathsf{Update}'(pk_s, sk_s)$:
    1. Parse $pk_s = (gk, pk, pk_F, pk_H, \boldsymbol{G}, \mathbf{H}, \boldsymbol{B}, m', \sigma')$ and $sk_s = (sk, sk_F)$.
    2. Compute $sk' \leftarrow \mathsf{Update}(pk, sk)$ and $sk'_F \leftarrow \mathsf{UD}_F(pk_F, sk_F)$.
    3. Output $sk'_s = (sk', sk'_F)$.

Fig. 3. GBSW Transformation in the Continuous Leakage Model

- **type I** forgery: $\bar{m}^* \notin \{\bar{m}_1, ..., \bar{m}_q\}$.
- **type II** forgery: there exists $i^* \in \{1, ..., q\}$ such that $\bar{m}^* = \bar{m}_{i^*}$, but $(h^*, s^*) \neq (h_{i^*}, s_{i^*})$.
- **type III** forgery: there exists $i^* \in \{1, ..., q\}$ such that $\bar{m}^* = \bar{m}_{i^*}$ and $(h^*, s^*) = (h_{i^*}, s_{i^*})$, but $(m^*, \sigma^*, \boldsymbol{\Pi}^*, T^*) \neq (m_{i^*}, \sigma_{i^*}, \boldsymbol{\Pi}_{i^*}, T_{i^*})$.
- **type IV** forgery: there exists $i^* \in \{1, ..., q\}$ such that $\bar{m}^* = \bar{m}_{i^*}$, $(h^*, s^*) = (h_{i^*}, s_{i^*})$, and $(m^*, \sigma^*, \boldsymbol{\Pi}^*, T^*) = (m_{i^*}, \sigma_{i^*}, \boldsymbol{\Pi}_{i^*}, T_{i^*})$, but $r^* \neq r_{i^*}$.
- **type V** forgery: there exists $i^* \in \{1, ..., q\}$ such that $\bar{m}^* = \bar{m}_{i^*}$, $(h^*, s^*) = (h_{i^*}, s_{i^*})$, $(m^*, \sigma^*, \boldsymbol{\Pi}^*, T^*) = (m_{i^*}, \sigma_{i^*}, \boldsymbol{\Pi}_{i^*}, T_{i^*})$, and $r^* = r_{i^*}$, but $\pi^* \neq \pi_{i^*}$.

What we have to do is to show how to construct PPT adversary $\mathcal{A}_I$ against the ℓ_w-wEUF-FLR of Σ, adversary $\mathcal{A}_{II}$ against the strong collision-resistance of $\mathcal{H}$, adversary $\mathcal{A}_{III}$ against the ℓ-CLR strong collision-resistance of $\mathcal{F}$, and adversaries $\mathcal{A}_{IV}$ and $\mathcal{A}_V$ against Lemma 1, by making use of $\mathcal{A}$. Each of the adversaries $\mathcal{A}_I$, $\mathcal{A}_{II}$, $\mathcal{A}_{III}$, $\mathcal{A}_{IV}$, and $\mathcal{A}_V$ succeeds if $\mathcal{A}$ outputs a **type I**, **type II**, **type III**, **type IV**, and **type V** forgery, respectively.

Now we give the overview of $\mathcal{A}_I$, $\mathcal{A}_{II}$, $\mathcal{A}_{III}$, $\mathcal{A}_{IV}$, and $\mathcal{A}_V$.

There are five games for $\mathcal{A}_I$, $\mathcal{A}_{II}$, $\mathcal{A}_{III}$, $\mathcal{A}_{IV}$, and $\mathcal{A}_V$, respectively. In each game, the adversary (which is one of $\mathcal{A}_I$, $\mathcal{A}_{II}$, $\mathcal{A}_{III}$, $\mathcal{A}_{IV}$, and $\mathcal{A}_V$) gets some public information from the challenger and simulates the signing oracle of $\mathcal{A}$. If $\mathcal{A}$ makes leakage queries to the adversary, the adversary answers by making use of the leakage oracle and the secret information generated by itself.

The final outputs of the adversaries are as follows.

Game of $\mathcal{A}_I$. $\mathcal{A}_I$ outputs $(\bar{m}^*, \sigma'^*)$ as the forgery for Σ and succeeds when $\mathcal{A}$ outputs the **type I** forgery.

Game of $\mathcal{A}_{II}$. $\mathcal{A}_{II}$ outputs (h^*, s^*) and (h_{i^*}, s_{i^*}) as a collision for $\mathcal{H}$ and succeeds when $\mathcal{A}$ outputs the **type II** forgery.

Game of $\mathcal{A}_{III}$. $\mathcal{A}_{III}$ outputs $((m^*, \sigma^*, \Pi^*, T^*), r^*)$ and $((m_{i^*}, \sigma_{i^*}, \Pi_{i^*}, T_{i^*}), r_{i^*})$ as a collision for $\mathcal{F}$ and succeeds when $\mathcal{A}$ outputs the **type III** forgery.

Game of $\mathcal{A}_{IV}$. When $\mathcal{A}$ outputs the **type IV** forgery, we have that the probability that $r^* = r_i$ for some i is negligible. Depending on this fact, we build a hybrid game for the game of $\mathcal{A}_{IV}$, in which, $h_{gk}(\mathbf{H}, J'(r^*))$ is a binding CRS and $h_{gk}(\mathbf{H}, J'(r_i))$ for $i = 1, ..., q$ are hiding CRSs. As a result, M_i is hidden for $i = 1, ..., q$ and M^* can be extracted with non-negligible probability where $M^* \neq M_{i^*} \wedge T^* = T_{i^*}$. Then $\mathcal{A}_{IV}$ outputs M^*, breaking Lemma 1.

Game of $\mathcal{A}_V$. When $\mathcal{A}$ outputs the **type V** forgery, we can extract M^* in almost the same way, and we have $M^* \neq M_{i^*}$ since $\Pi^* = \Pi_{i^*}$, $r^* = r_{i^*}$, and $\pi^* \neq \pi_{i^*}$. Then $\mathcal{A}_V$ outputs $M^* \neq M_{i^*}$ where $M^* \neq M_{i^*} \wedge T^* = T_{i^*}$, breaking Lemma 1.

We show how these five adversaries run in the full version of this paper.

Remark. We do not discuss the leakage on key generation and key updating. If the wEUF-FLR signature scheme can tolerate leakage on key generation and key updating, then the resulting scheme can also tolerate this kind of leakage to some extent. The CLR-OWR scheme (c.f., Figure 1) from [20] can tolerate leakage of length $c \log k$ bits[1] during the key generation and key updating where $c \geq 0$ is some constant, and the public key can be sampled without knowledge of the secret key for some instantiations of chameleon hash functions, such as the well-known Discrete-log based instantiation by Chaum, van Heijst, and Pfitzmann [9].

---

[1] This is also counted in the leakage on secret key.

Furthermore, the same as [26], we can obtain a $(1 - o(1))L$-sEUF-FLR signature scheme by setting $sk_F = sk$ if we apply our technique to the $(1 - o(1))L$-wEUF-FLR signature scheme proposed in [14] where L is the length of secret key. We refer the reader to [26] for details of the discussion[2].

5   Conclusions

In this paper, we have first defined the continuous leakage resilient chameleon hash function and given the construction of it based on the signature scheme proposed in [20]. Then we have combined this new kind of chameleon hash function with the Groth-Sahai proof system [16] and the GBSW [23] transformation to obtain a transformation which converts wEUF-FLR schemes into sEUF-FLR ones in the continual leakage model.

However, the transformed signature scheme is only resilient to any leakage of $min\{\ell, \ell_w\}$ in each round, where ℓ is the leakage parameter of the CLR chameleon hash function and ℓ_w is the leakage parameter of the original wEUF-FLR signature scheme, for most cases. We leave a transformation from ℓ_w-wEUF-FLR signature scheme into ℓ_w-sEUF-FLR ones in the continual leakage model without loosing the efficiency as a future work.

References

1. Abe, M., Fuchsbauer, G., Groth, J., Haralambiev, K., Ohkubo, M.: Structure-preserving signatures and commitments to group elements. In: Rabin, T. (ed.) CRYPTO 2010. LNCS, vol. 6223, pp. 209–236. Springer, Heidelberg (2010)
2. Akavia, A., Goldwasser, S., Vaikuntanathan, V.: Simultaneous hardcore bits and cryptography against memory attacks. In: Reingold, O. (ed.) TCC 2009. LNCS, vol. 5444, pp. 474–495. Springer, Heidelberg (2009)
3. Ballard, L., Green, M., de Medeiros, B., Monrose, F.: Correlation-resistant storage via keyword-searchable encryption. Cryptology ePrint Archive, Report 2005/417 (2005). http://eprint.iacr.org/
4. Bellare, M., Shoup, S.: Two-tier signatures, strongly unforgeable signatures, and fiat-shamir without random oracles. In: Okamoto, T., Wang, X. (eds.) PKC 2007. LNCS, vol. 4450, pp. 201–216. Springer, Heidelberg (2007)
5. Boneh, D., Boyen, X., Shacham, H.: Short group signatures. In: Franklin, M. (ed.) CRYPTO 2004. LNCS, vol. 3152, pp. 41–55. Springer, Heidelberg (2004)
6. Boneh, D., Shen, E., Waters, B.: Strongly unforgeable signatures based on computational Diffie-Hellman. In: Yung, M., Dodis, Y., Kiayias, A., Malkin, T. (eds.) PKC 2006. LNCS, vol. 3958, pp. 229–240. Springer, Heidelberg (2006)
7. Boyle, E., Segev, G., Wichs, D.: Fully leakage-resilient signatures. In: Paterson, K.G. (ed.) EUROCRYPT 2011. LNCS, vol. 6632, pp. 89–108. Springer, Heidelberg (2011)

---

[2] The discussion in [26] is totally suitable for our situation although we consider two more adversaries in this paper.

8. Brakerski, Z., Kalai, Y.T., Katz, J., Vaikuntanathan, V.: Overcoming the hole in the bucket: public-key cryptography resilient to continual memory leakage. In: 2010 51st Annual IEEE Symposium on Foundations of Computer Science (FOCS), pp. 501–510, October 2010
9. Chaum, D., van Heijst, E., Pfitzmann, B.: Cryptographically strong undeniable signatures, unconditionally secure for the signer. In: Feigenbaum, J. (ed.) CRYPTO 1991. LNCS, vol. 576, pp. 470–484. Springer, Heidelberg (1992)
10. Dodis, Y., Lewko, A., Waters, B., Wichs, D.: Storing secrets on continually leaky devices. In: 2011 IEEE 52nd Annual Symposium on Foundations of Computer Science (FOCS), pp. 688–697, October 2011
11. Dodis, Y., Haralambiev, K., López-Alt, A., Wichs, D.: Cryptography against continuous memory attacks. In: Proceedings of the 2010 IEEE 51st Annual Symposium on Foundations of Computer Science, FOCS 2010, pp. 511–520. IEEE Computer Society, Washington (2010)
12. Dodis, Y., Haralambiev, K., López-Alt, A., Wichs, D.: Efficient public-key cryptography in the presence of key leakage. In: Abe, M. (ed.) ASIACRYPT 2010. LNCS, vol. 6477, pp. 613–631. Springer, Heidelberg (2010)
13. Galbraith, S.D., Rotger, V.: Easy decision-diffie-hellman groups. LMS Journal of Computation and Mathematics 7(2004) (2004)
14. Garg, S., Jain, A., Sahai, A.: Leakage-resilient zero knowledge. In: Rogaway, P. (ed.) CRYPTO 2011. LNCS, vol. 6841, pp. 297–315. Springer, Heidelberg (2011)
15. Groth, J.: Homomorphic trapdoor commitments to group elements. IACR Cryptology ePrint Archive 2009, 7 (2009)
16. Groth, J., Sahai, A.: Efficient non-interactive proof systems for bilinear groups. In: Smart, N.P. (ed.) EUROCRYPT 2008. LNCS, vol. 4965, pp. 415–432. Springer, Heidelberg (2008)
17. Huang, Q., Wong, D.S., Zhao, Y.: Generic transformation to strongly unforgeable signatures. In: Katz, J., Yung, M. (eds.) ACNS 2007. LNCS, vol. 4521, pp. 1–17. Springer, Heidelberg (2007)
18. Krawczyk, H., Rabin, T.: Chameleon signatures. In: NDSS. The InternetSociety (2000)
19. Lewko, A., Lewko, M., Waters, B.: How to leak on key updates. In: Proceedings of the Forty-third Annual ACM Symposium on Theory of Computing, STOC 2011, pp. 725–734. ACM, New York (2011)
20. Malkin, T., Teranishi, I., Vahlis, Y., Yung, M.: Signatures resilient to continual leakage on memory and computation. In: Ishai, Y. (ed.) TCC 2011. LNCS, vol. 6597, pp. 89–106. Springer, Heidelberg (2011)
21. Scott, M.: Authenticated id-based key exchange and remote log-in with simple token and pin number. Cryptology ePrint Archive, Report 2002/164 (2002). http://eprint.iacr.org/
22. Shamir, A., Tauman, Y.: Improved online/offline signature schemes. In: Kilian, J. (ed.) CRYPTO 2001. LNCS, vol. 2139, pp. 355–367. Springer, Heidelberg (2001)
23. Steinfeld, R., Pieprzyk, J., Wang, H.: How to strengthen any weakly unforgeable signature into a strongly unforgeable signature. In: Abe, M. (ed.) CT-RSA 2007. LNCS, vol. 4377, pp. 357–371. Springer, Heidelberg (2006)
24. Teranishi, I., Oyama, T., Ogata, W.: General conversion for obtaining strongly existentially unforgeable signatures. In: Barua, R., Lange, T. (eds.) INDOCRYPT 2006. LNCS, vol. 4329, pp. 191–205. Springer, Heidelberg (2006)

25. Verheul, E.R.: Evidence that XTR is more secure than supersingular elliptic curve cryptosystems. In: Pfitzmann, B. (ed.) EUROCRYPT 2001. LNCS, vol. 2045, pp. 195–210. Springer, Heidelberg (2001)
26. Wang, Y., Tanaka, K.: Generic transformation to strongly existentially unforgeable signature schemes with leakage resiliency. In: Chow, S.S.M., Liu, J.K., Hui, L.C.K., Yiu, S.M. (eds.) ProvSec 2014. LNCS, vol. 8782, pp. 117–129. Springer, Heidelberg (2014)
27. Wang, Y., Tanaka, K.: Strongly simulation-extractable leakage-resilient NIZK. In: Susilo, W., Mu, Y. (eds.) ACISP 2014. LNCS, vol. 8544, pp. 66–81. Springer, Heidelberg (2014)

Constant Size Ring Signature
Without Random Oracle

Priyanka Bose[✉], Dipanjan Das, and Chandrasekharan Pandu Rangan

Indian Institute of Technology, Madras, Adyar, Chennai 600036, Tamilnadu, India
{priyab,dipanjan,rangan}@cse.iitm.ac.in

Abstract. Ring signature enables an user to anonymously sign a message on behalf of a group of users termed as 'ring' formed in an 'ad-hoc' manner. A naive scheme produces a signature linear in the size of the ring, but this is extremely inefficient when ring size is large. Dodis *et al.* proposed a constant size scheme in EUROCRYPT'13, but its security is provided in random oracle model. Best known result without random oracle is a sub-linear size construction by Chandran *et al.* in ICALP'07 and a follow-up work by Essam Ghadafi in IMACC'13. Therefore, construction of a constant size ring signature scheme without random oracle meeting stringent security requirement still remained as an interesting open problem.

Our first contribution is a generic technique to convert a *compatible* signature scheme to a constant-sized ring signature scheme. The technique employs a constant size set membership check that may be of independent interest. Our construction is instantiated with asymmetric pairing over groups of composite order and meets strongest security requirements, *viz.* anonymity under full key exposure and unforgeability against insider-corruption without using random oracle under simple hardness assumptions. We also demonstrate a concrete instantiation of the scheme with Full Boneh-Boyen signature scheme.

Keywords: Ring signature · Constant size · Groth-sahai protocol · Set membership · Zero-knowledge

1 Introduction

The idea of ring signature was introduced by Rivest, Shamir and Tauman [26]. Ring signature leaks no information more than the endorsement of the message by *some* ring member. Unlike a group in a group signatures [12], a ring is not administered by a manager. In practice, ring members may be completely unaware of each others' inclusion in the ring. To form a ring, the real signer arbitrarily chooses a set of *potential signers* including himself, thus concealing his identity. Since rings are formed on-the-fly, notions such as addition or deletion of users, revocation of signing rights or divulging the anonymity of the actual signer etc. are irrelevant.

© Springer International Publishing Switzerland 2015
E. Foo and D. Stebila (Eds.): ACISP 2015, LNCS 9144, pp. 230–247, 2015.
DOI: 10.1007/978-3-319-19962-7_14

Apart from regular properties, e.g. correctness and unforgeability that any signature scheme must have, ring signature [2] mandates anonymity. Correctness allows a ring member to sign on a message on behalf of the ring. Unforgeability is defined by the impossibility of a new signature to be generated by an adversary on behalf of the ring. Finally, anonymity demands a signature not being traceable to its signer. In other words, signatures produced on a message by any two members of the ring have identical distributions.

The prime application of ring signature is in anonymous leaking of sensitive secrets as suggested in the original paper [26]. Another application is designated verifier signatures [19], where the verifier designated by confirmer/prover can obtain validity or invalidity of the proof. For more applications, refer to [14][24]. Such protocol, often with additional blindness requirement, finds its relevance in e-voting or e-cash.

Table 1 gives a quick survey on PKI based ring signatures.

1.1 Motivation

Most of the ring signature constructions [26][1][5][18][2][13][28][8][27][9] are of linear size with respect to the size of the ring. First four constructions are in random oracle model (ROM), remaining ones but the last are without random

Table 1. Survey of Ring Signatures in PKI Setting

Author	Reference	Size	Model	Remarks
Rivest *et al.*	[26]	$O(N)$	ROM	Trapdoor permutation
Abe *et al.*	[1]	$O(N)$	ROM	RSA and DL based signatues
Boneh *et al.*	[5]	$O(N)$	ROM	Co-GDH based signature
Herranz *et al.*	[18]	$O(N)$	ROM	Based on Schnorr ring signature
Bender *et al.*	[2]	$O(N)$	w/o ROM	ZAP based, inefficient
Chow *et al.*	[13]	$O(N)$	w/o ROM	(q, n)-DsjSDH assumption
Shacham *et al.*	[28]	$O(N)$	w/o ROM	User keys belong to same group
Boyen	[8]	$O(N)$	w/o ROM	First unconditional anonymity
Schage *et al.*	[27]	$O(N)$	w/o ROM	Weak notion of unforgeability
Brakerski *et al.*	[9]	$O(N)$	Standard	Weak notion of unforgeability
Chandran *et al.*	[10]	$O(\sqrt{N})$	w/o ROM	FBB scheme in composite order
Yuen *et al.*	[30]	$O(\sqrt{N})$	Standard	Stronger definition of anonymity
Ghadafi	[16]	$O(\sqrt{N})$	w/o ROM	Uses GS NIZK protocol
Dodis *et al.*	[14]	$O(1)$	ROM	Fiat-Shamir transformation
Our construction	-	$O(1)$	w/o ROM	Composite order group

oracle (RO) and the last one is in standard model. Often there are some limitations, e.g. [2] makes use of generic ZAP, which is a 2-round, public-coin, witness-indistinguishable proof system for any language in $\mathcal{NP}$, hence inefficient and far from being practical. Chow *et al.* introduced a new strong assumption in [13]. First sub-linear size ring signature scheme with $O(\sqrt{N})$ signature size was proposed by Chandran, Groth and Sahai [10] followed by Ghadafi [16]. Both the schemes are provably secure without random oracle. To the best of our knowledge, only constant size ring signature scheme in PKI setting known so far is by Dodis *et al.* [14]. But, their approach uses Fiat-Shamir transformation and provably secure in random oracle model. So the challenge of achieving constant-size ring signature without random oracle motivated our research.

1.2 Our Contribution

Our major contribution is to present a generic technique to build a ring signature scheme on top of any *compatible* signature scheme, (such as Full-Boneh-Boyen [3]) having size independent of the cardinality of the ring. The scheme is instantiable in the most efficient Type-3 bilinear setting without any compromise in efficiency. We have attained the strongest possible security [2], e.g. anonymity under full key exposure and unforgeability against insider-corruption without using random oracle. Also we present a concrete instantiation of the technique to compare it with the existing schemes.

Lastly, our ring signature uses an $O(1)$ size membership checking protocol to test the containment of an integer in a public set. It makes use of Groth-Sahai [17] commitment to realize witness indistinguishability and zero-knowledgeness. The protocol as well as its proof may be of independent interest.

1.3 Paper Organization

The paper is organized as follows: section 2 provides the necessary background pertaining to the ideas used in the paper. In section 3, we introduce a non-interactive, constant size membership proof to prove the knowledge of an element of a public set. Our main contribution, the construction of a constant-sized ring signature for PKI based cryptosystems is outlined in section 4. We have instantiated our construction in section 5. Conclusion and future directions are offered in section 6.

2 Preliminaries

2.1 Notations

By PPT, we mean a probabilistic polynomial time algorithm with respect to a security parameter κ. All adversaries defined here will be PPT except stated otherwise. Given a probability distribution $\mathcal{D}$ and an element y, $y \leftarrow \mathcal{D}$ denotes selecting an element y according to $\mathcal{D}$. Let $\mathcal{A}$ be a probabilistic algorithm, then

$\mathcal{A}(x_1...x_n)$ describes the output distribution of $\mathcal{A}$ based on inputs $x_1, x_1, ..., x_n$. $\mathbb{Z}_n$ denotes set of all integers modulo n, where n is composite, product of two safe primes. The set of all polynomials in x with coefficients in $\mathbb{Z}_n$ is represented by $\mathbb{Z}_n[x]$. Let $\mathbb{G}$ be a group and $m \in \mathbb{Z}$. $\mathbb{Z}_n^m = \{x_i | x_i \in \mathbb{Z}_n, i \in [0, m-1]\}$ and $\mathbb{G}^m = \{X_i | X_i \in \mathbb{G}, i \in [0, m-1]\}$. A function $\nu : \mathbb{N} \to \mathbb{R}^+$ is said to be negligible if $\forall c > 0, \exists k'$ such that $\nu(k) < k^{-c}$ for all $k > k'$.

2.2 Bilinear Groups

A bilinear pairing is defined to be $\mathcal{G} = (n, \mathbb{G}_1, \mathbb{G}_2, \mathbb{G}_T, e, g_1, g_2)$ where we choose $\mathbb{G}_1 = \langle g_1 \rangle$, $\mathbb{G}_2 = \langle g_2 \rangle$ and $\mathbb{G}_T$ as multiplicative groups of order n. A bilinear pairing e is a map $e : \mathbb{G}_1 \times \mathbb{G}_2 \to \mathbb{G}_T$ having the following properties.

- **Bilinearity**: For $g_1 \in \mathbb{G}_1$, $g_2 \in \mathbb{G}_2$ and $a, b \in \mathbb{Z}_n$ the following holds true: $e(g_1^a, g_2^b) = e(g_1, g_2)^{ab}$.

- **Non-degeneracy**: For any $\mathcal{X} \in \mathbb{G}_1$ and $\mathcal{Y} \in \mathbb{G}_2$, if $e(\mathcal{X}, \mathcal{Y}) = 1_T$, the identity element of $\mathbb{G}_T$, then either $\mathcal{X}$ is the identity of $\mathbb{G}_1$ or $\mathcal{Y}$ is the identity of $\mathbb{G}_2$, but not both.

- **Efficiently Computable**: The map e should be efficiently computable.

  Three main types of pairings exist in the literature [15][29].

  - **Type-1**. The groups $\mathbb{G}_1$ and $\mathbb{G}_2$ are the same.
  - **Type-2**. $\mathbb{G}_1 \neq \mathbb{G}_2$, but an efficiently computable isomorphism $\zeta : \mathbb{G}_2 \to \mathbb{G}_1$ exists.
  - **Type-3**. $\mathbb{G}_1 \neq \mathbb{G}_2$ and no efficiently computable isomorphism are known to exist between $\mathbb{G}_1$ and $\mathbb{G}_2$.

We will use asymmetric pairing over groups of composite order which can be shown to be generated efficiently using the method in [21]. Meiklejohn *et al.* have shown that this setting has an advantage of the resulting curve having an embedding degree $k = 1$ and thus optimally efficient.

2.3 Hardness Assumptions

All the hardness assumptions are stated below:

- **Decisional Diffie-Hellman Assumption (DDH)**.[25] Given a cyclic group $\mathbb{G} = \langle g \rangle$, a tuple $\langle g, g^a, g^b, g^{ab}, g^c \rangle$ where $a, b, c \in_R \mathbb{Z}_n$ and for all PPT adversaries $\mathcal{A}_{DDH}$, the probability

$$|Pr[\mathcal{A}_{DDH}(g, g^a, g^b, g^{ab}) = 1] - Pr[\mathcal{A}_{DDH}(g, g^a, g^b, g^c) = 1]| < \nu(\kappa)$$

- **Symmetric External Diffie-Hellman Assumption (SXDH)**.[25] DDH holds in both groups $\mathbb{G}_1$ and $\mathbb{G}_2$.

- **Decisional Linear Assumption (DLIN)**.[4] For Type-1 bilinear groups where $\mathbb{G}_1 = \mathbb{G}_2 = \mathbb{G} = \langle g \rangle$, given $\langle g^a, g^b, g^{ra}, g^{sb}, g^t \rangle$ and $a, b, s, r, t \in \mathbb{Z}_p$ being unknown, it is hard to tell whether $t = r + s$ or t is random.

- **Subgroup Hiding Assumption (SGH)**.[6] Given a generation algorithm $\mathcal{G}$, which takes security parameter κ as input and gives output a tuple $\langle \mathbb{G}, \mathbb{G}_T, e, sk \rangle$, where $sk = (p, q)$ such that $e : \mathbb{G} \times \mathbb{G} \to \mathbb{G}_T$ and $\mathbb{G}$ and $\mathbb{G}_T$ are both groups of order $n = pq$, it is computationally in feasible to distinguish between an element of $\mathbb{G}$ and an element of $\mathbb{G}_p$. Formally, for all PPT adversaries $\mathcal{A}_{SGH}$, the probability

$$|Pr[(sk, \mathbb{G}, \mathbb{G}_T, e) \leftarrow \mathcal{G}(1^\kappa); n = pq; sk = (p, q); x \leftarrow \mathbb{G} :$$
$$\mathcal{A}_{SGH}(n, \mathbb{G}, \mathbb{G}_T, e, x) = 0] - Pr[(sk, \mathbb{G}, \mathbb{G}_T, e) \leftarrow \mathcal{G}(1^\kappa);$$
$$n = pq; sk = (p, q); x \leftarrow \mathbb{G} : \mathcal{A}_{SGH}(n, \mathbb{G}, \mathbb{G}_T, e, x^q) = 0]| < \nu(\kappa)$$

  where $\mathcal{A}_{SGH}$ outputs 1 if it believes $x \in \mathbb{G}_p$ and 0 otherwise. **SGH** being hard in asymmetric pairing over composite order groups means, it is hard in both $\mathbb{G}_1$ and $\mathbb{G}_2$.

- **q-Strong Diffie-Hellman Assumption (q-SDH)**.[3] Let $\alpha \in_R \mathbb{Z}_p$. Given a $(q + 1)$-tuple $\langle g, g^\alpha, g^{\alpha^2}, ..., g^{\alpha^q} \rangle \in \mathbb{G}^{q+1}$ as input, for every adversary $\mathcal{A}_{q\text{-}SDH}$, the probability

$$Pr[\mathcal{A}_{q\text{-}SDH}(g, g^\alpha, g^{\alpha^2}, ..., g^{\alpha^q}) = \langle c, g^{\frac{1}{\alpha+c}} \rangle] < \nu(\kappa)$$

  for any value of $c \in \mathbb{Z}_p \backslash \{-\alpha\}$. Though naturally q-type assumptions are defined on prime order groups, it has been shown in [11] that all q-type assumptions can also be proven to be secure in composite order groups provided subgroup hiding assumption (SGH) holds.

- **Square Root Modulo Composite (SQROOT)**[22]. Given a composite integer n and $a \in Q_n$ (the set of quadratic residues modulo n), it is computationally hard to find a square root of $a \mod n$; that is an integer x such that $x^2 \equiv a \pmod{n}$, where $n = pq$, product of two safe primes.

In all the definitions above, $\nu(\kappa)$ is negligible in the security parameter κ.

2.4 Groth-Sahai Proofs

Groth-Sahai[17] introduced a highly efficient and flexible proof system in common reference string (CRS) model that yields Non-Interactive Witness-Indistinguishable (NIWI) and Zero-Knowledge (NIZK) proofs. It can be used for proving satisfiability of certain types of equations under various cryptographic assumptions. This proof system can be instantiated both in prime and composite order bilinear groups. The set of equations provable in this framework are as follows:

$\mathcal{X}_1, ..., \mathcal{X}_m \in \mathbb{G}_1; \mathcal{Y}_1, ..., \mathcal{Y}_n \in \mathbb{G}_1; x_1, ..., x_{m'} \in \mathbb{Z}_n$ and $y_1, ..., y_{n'} \in \mathbb{Z}_n$ are variables.

Pairing Product Equation (PPE):

$$\prod_{i=1}^{n} e(\mathcal{A}_i, \underline{\mathcal{Y}}_i) \cdot \prod_{i=1}^{m} e(\underline{\mathcal{X}}_i, \mathcal{B}_i) \cdot \prod_{i=1}^{m} \prod_{j=1}^{n} e(\underline{\mathcal{X}}_i, \underline{\mathcal{Y}}_j)^{\gamma_{ij}} = t_T$$

For constants $\mathcal{A}_i \in \mathbb{G}_1, \mathcal{B}_i \in \mathbb{G}_2, t_T \in \mathbb{G}_T, \gamma_{ij} \in \mathbb{Z}_n$

Multi-scalar Multiplication Equation (MSME) in $\mathbb{G}_1$:

$$\sum_{i=1}^{n'} \underline{y}_i \mathcal{A}_i + \sum_{i=1}^{m} b_i \underline{\mathcal{X}}_i + \sum_{i=1}^{m} \sum_{j=1}^{n'} \gamma_{ij} \underline{y}_j \underline{\mathcal{X}}_i = T_1$$

For constants $\mathcal{A}_i, T_1 \in \mathbb{G}_1$ and $b_i, \gamma_{ij} \in \mathbb{Z}_n$

Multi-scalar Multiplication Equation (MSME) in $\mathbb{G}_2$:

$$\sum_{i=1}^{n} a_i \underline{\mathcal{Y}}_i + \sum_{i=1}^{m'} \underline{x}_i \mathcal{B}_i + \sum_{i=1}^{m'} \sum_{j=1}^{n} \gamma_{ij} \underline{x}_i \underline{\mathcal{Y}}_j = T_2$$

For constants $\mathcal{B}_i, T_2 \in \mathbb{G}_2$ and $a_i, \gamma_{ij} \in \mathbb{Z}_n$

Quadratic Equation (QE) in $\mathbb{Z}_n$:

$$\sum_{i=1}^{n'} a_i \underline{y}_i + \sum_{i=1}^{m'} \underline{x}_i b_i + \sum_{i=1}^{m'} \sum_{j=1}^{n'} \gamma_{ij} \underline{x}_i \underline{y}_j = t$$

For constants $a_i, b_i, \gamma_{ij}, t \in \mathbb{Z}_n$

With multiplicative notation, multi-scalar multiplication equations will be multi-scalar multi-exponential equations. For the sake of clarity, we have under-lined the elements of the witness in the description of the equations.

Groth-Sahai proof system consists of the following four PPT algorithms as defined in [16]

- **GSSetup**(1^κ): It takes security parameter κ as input and produces description of bilinear group $\mathcal{G}$ and secret key sk as output.

- **GSCRSGen**($\mathcal{G}, sk$): Given group description $\mathcal{G}$ as input, it outputs common reference string (CRS) crs and an extraction key xk.

- **GSCommit**(w, τ_w): Given a witness $w \in \mathbb{G}$ and randomness τ_w, it produces a commitment to w with randomness τ_w. We denote the commitment to a witness w as Υ_w in this paper.

- **GSProve**$(\mathcal{G}, crs, x, w)$: It uses `GSCommit(.,.)` internally and outputs proof $\phi = \langle \Upsilon, \Gamma \rangle$, where $\Upsilon = \langle c, d \rangle$ and $\Gamma = \langle \pi, \theta \rangle$ as defined in [17, p. 12]. In symmetric setting $\Upsilon = \langle c \rangle$ and $\Gamma = \langle \pi \rangle$. In asymmetric setting for linear equation $\Upsilon = \langle c \rangle$. Here, Υ is called commitment to witnesses.

- **GSVerify**$(\mathcal{G}, crs, x, \phi)$: It takes the tuple $\langle \mathcal{G}, crs, x, \phi \rangle$ as input and outputs 1 if proof ϕ is accepted or 0 if rejected.

In addition to the algorithms above, we also define the following ones:

- **GSExtract**$(\mathcal{G}, crs, xk, \phi)$: It takes the tuple $\langle \mathcal{G}, crs, xk, \phi \rangle$ as input and outputs the witness w used in the proof ϕ.

- **GSCRSSimGen**$(\mathcal{G})$: It takes group description $\mathcal{G}$ and outputs simulated CRS crs_{sim} and a trapdoor key td.

- **GSSimProve**$(\mathcal{G}, crs_{sim}, td, x)$: It takes $\mathcal{G}$, simulated CRS crs_{sim} and a trapdoor key td and generates simulated proofs ϕ_{sim}.

The system works by first committing to the elements of the witness and then producing the proof of satisfiability of all equations. If one witness component is involved in more than one equation, then same commitment is used during verification, thereby making the proofs correlated.

2.5 Ring Signatures - Definitions

Definition 1 (Ring Signature): A ring signature scheme is a quadruple of PPT algorithms `RSig := (RSetup, RKeyGen, RSign, RVerify)` which generates public parameters, keys for users, signs message and verifies the validity of signature on a message produced by user.

- **RSetup**(1^κ): It takes security parameter κ as input and produces public parameters $rParam$ as output.

- **RKeyGen**$(rParam)$: Given $rParam$ as input, it produces a secret key SK and a public key PK.

- **RSign**$(m, SK_s, \mathcal{R})$: Given a private signing key SK_s as input, it outputs a signature Σ on message m with respect to a ring $\mathcal{R} := (PK_1, PK_2, ..., PK_n)$. We require that $PK_s \in \mathcal{R}$ for $s \in [1, n]$ where $n \in \mathbb{N}$ and $\langle PK_s, SK_s \rangle$ is a valid key pair.

- **RVerify**$(m, \Sigma, \mathcal{R})$: It verifies a signature Σ on message m with respect to a set of public keys in $\mathcal{R}$ and outputs 1 if succeeds, otherwise 0.

The quadruple `RSig := (RSetup, RKeyGen, RSign, RVerify)` is a secure ring signature scheme if it satisfies the following properties from the literatures [2][10].

Definition 2 (Correctness): [2] A ring signature scheme RSig := (RSetup, RKeyGen, RSign, RVerify) is correct if for any polynomial $p(.)$, a set of secret-public key pairs $\{(PK_i, SK_i)\}_{i=1}^{p(\kappa)}$ generated by RKeyGen(.), any message m and any index $j \in [1, p(\kappa)]$, the signature Σ produced by RSign$(m, SK_j, \mathcal{R})$ will be accepted by RVerify$(m, \Sigma, \mathcal{R})$. Here $\mathcal{R} = (PK_1, PK_2...PK_{p(\kappa)})$

Definition 3 (Anonymity Against Full Key Exposure): [2] A ring signature scheme RSig := (RSetup, RKeyGen, RSign, RVerify) is anonymous (with respect to full key exposure) if for any adversary $\mathcal{A}$ and for any polynomial $p(.)$, the probability that $\mathcal{A}$ succeeds in the following game is negligibly close to $1/2$:

1. Key pairs $(PK_i, SK_i)_{i=1}^{p(\kappa)}$ are generated by the challenger using $rParam \leftarrow$ RSetup(1^κ) and RKeyGen$(rParam, \omega_i)$ for randomly chosen ω_i. $\mathcal{A}$ is given $S := (PK_i)_{i=1}^{p(\kappa)}$.
2. Throughout the game, $\mathcal{A}$ has access to a signing oracle Osign$(s,m,\mathcal{R})$ that outputs RSign$(m, SK_s, \mathcal{R})$. Here, we require $PK_s \in \mathcal{R}$ and $s \in [1, p(\kappa)]$.
3. $\mathcal{A}$ is also given access to the corrupt oracle Corrupt(i) that outputs ω_i, the random coins associated with user i.
4. $\mathcal{A}$ outputs a message m, two distinct indices i_0 and i_1 and a ring $\mathcal{R}$ with the only condition that $PK_{i_0}, PK_{i_1} \in \mathcal{R}$. It interacts with the challenger to obtain a signature $\Sigma \leftarrow$ RSign$(m, SK_{i_b}, \mathcal{R})$ where $b \leftarrow \{0,1\}$.
5. $\mathcal{A}$ outputs a bit b' and succeeds if $b = b'$.

Definition 4 (Unforgeability with Respect to Insider Corruption): [2] A ring signature scheme RSig := (RSetup, RKeyGen, RSign, RVerify) is unforgeable (with respect to insider corruption) if for any adversary $\mathcal{A}$ and for any polynomial $p(.)$, the probability that $\mathcal{A}$ succeeds in the following game is negligible:

1. Key pairs $(PK_i, SK_i)_{i=1}^{p(\kappa)}$ are generated by the challenger using RKeyGen$(rParam)$. $\mathcal{A}$ is given $S := (PK_i)_{i=1}^{p(\kappa)}$
2. Throughout the game, $\mathcal{A}$ has access to a signing oracle Osign$(s,m,\mathcal{R})$ that outputs RSign$(m, SK_s, \mathcal{R})$. Here, we require $PK_s \in \mathcal{R}$.
3. $\mathcal{A}$ is also given access to the corrupt oracle Corrupt(i) that outputs SK_i.
4. $\mathcal{A}$ outputs $\langle \mathcal{R}^\star, m^\star, \Sigma^\star \rangle$ and succeeds if RVerify$(m^\star, \Sigma^\star, \mathcal{R}^\star) = 1$, $\mathcal{A}$ never queried $\langle \star, m^\star, \mathcal{R}^\star \rangle$ and $\mathcal{R}^\star \subseteq S - C$, where C is the set of corrupted users.

2.6 Polynomial Commitments

Polynomial commitment is committing to a polynomial with a short string used by some verifier to confirm the claimed evaluations of the committed polynomial. An efficient polynomial commitment scheme can be found in the literature in [20]. The main idea of this paper was to commit to the polynomial $F(x)$ over a bilinear group with two different types of commitment schemes based on discrete log and Pedersen commitments. It ensures the size of the commitment to be constant, a single group element.

We can apply the above polynomial commitment scheme to construct Zero Knowledge Set (ZKS) [23]. ZKS allows a committer to create a short commitment to the set of values contained in a set S and later prove statements like $s_j \in S$ or $s_j \notin S$ without revealing S or the upper bound of $|S|$. In a slightly different notion of ZKS, called *nearly* ZKS, upper bound of $|S|$ is revealed. Kate *et al.* [20] have shown an application of his polynomial commitment scheme in *nearly* ZKS. Our primary idea of constructing a constant size membership proof of an element in a public set is derived from [20].

3   Constant Size Set Membership Proof

We provide a non-interactive, constant-sized set membership proof technique based on the application of polynomial commitment scheme in ZKS [20] and Groth-Sahai NIZK proof system [17]. The technique allows a prover to prove the containment of an element α_δ in a set $S = \{\alpha_1, \alpha_2, ..., \alpha_\delta, ...\alpha_N\} \in \mathbb{Z}_n^N$.

The sub-linear size membership proof in [16] arranges the set elements in the form of a square matrix. Each element of a vertical and horizontal bit vector is committed using Groth-Sahai (GS) scheme resulting in an expensive sub-linear blowup both in number of proofs and commitment components. GS proofs for $O(\sqrt{|S|})$ number of MSME and QE equations as well as corresponding GS commitments contribute to the final size of the proof.

Our formulation constructs a polynomial $F(x)$ having only $\alpha_i \in S, \forall i \in [1, |S|]$ as roots. The prover aims to demonstrate the existence of *some* secret value $\alpha_\delta \in S$ to the verifier in a non-interactive manner without revealing its value. While correctness of the proof system follows from the construction itself, soundness relies on the hardness of q-SDH assumption. Verification equations are in the form of Pairing Product Equation (PPE) and Multi-scalar Multiplication Equation (MSME) as defined by GS framework. Variables which could potentially leak out the secret value α_δ are committed using GS commitment scheme to provide required zero-knowledgeness. Our proof works both in prime and composite order groups. However, to be able to fit it *as-is* in our ring signature scheme, we use asymmetric pairing of composite order in the presentation.

Our membership proof consists of following four algorithms:

- **MemSetup**$(1^\kappa, q)$: This algorithm is run by a trusted authority (possibly a distributed one to enhance security) to generate required q-SDH tuple and initialize GS protocol.
  - Initialize GS protocol $\langle \mathcal{G}, sk \rangle \leftarrow \texttt{GSSetup}(1^\kappa)$ in asymmetric setting of composite order $n = p.q$ where $sk = \langle p, q \rangle$, $\mathcal{G} = \langle n, \mathbb{G}_1, \mathbb{G}_2, \mathbb{G}_T, e, g_1, g_2 \rangle$ and q-SDH assumption holds in $\mathbb{G}_1$. p and q are large prime numbers.
  - Generate common reference string $\langle crs, xk \rangle \leftarrow \texttt{GSCRSGen}(\mathcal{G}, sk)$
  - Choose a secret key $\beta \in_R \mathbb{Z}_n^*$

- Generate a $(q+1)$ tuple $qSDH = \langle g_1, g_1^{\beta}, g_1^{\beta^2}, ..., g_1^{\beta^q} \rangle \in \mathbb{G}_1^{q+1}$ to accommodate a set of cardinality $\leq q$. Note that the secret key is not needed any more and can be discarded.
- Publish public parameters $mParam = \langle \mathcal{G}, crs, qSDH, g_2^{\beta} \rangle$

- **MemWitness**$(mParam, \alpha_\delta, S)$: This algorithm is run by the prover to generate witness W testifying the presence of $\alpha_\delta \in S$.
  - Compute the polynomial $F(x) = \prod_{i=1}^{|S|}(x - \alpha_i) = \sum_{j=0}^{|S|} F_j x^j, \alpha_i \in S$
  - Compute the polynomial $\psi(x) = \frac{F(x)}{(x - \alpha_\delta)} = \sum_{i=0}^{|S|-1} \psi_i x^i$
  - Compute $w = g_1^{\psi(\beta)} = \prod_{i=0}^{|S|-1}(g_1^{\beta^i})^{\psi_i}$. Note that the components of the form $g_1^{\beta^i}$ are available to the prover as part of $qSDH$ tuple.
  - Compute $D = g_2^{\alpha_\delta}$
  - Output the tuple $W = \langle \alpha_\delta, w, D \rangle$ as witness.

- **MemProve**$(mParam, S, W)$: This algorithm is run by the prover to generate commitments for variables and GS proofs for verification equations.
  - Compute $C = g_1^{F(\beta)} = \prod_{i=0}^{|S|}(g_1^{\beta^i})^{F_i}$. Note that the components of the form $g_1^{\beta^i}$ are available to the prover as part of $qSDH$ tuple.
  - Compute $t = e(C, g_2)$
  - Compute the membership proof $\phi_{mem} = \langle \{\Upsilon_w, \Upsilon_{\alpha_\delta}, \Upsilon_D\}, \Gamma_{mem} \rangle$

  $$\phi_{mem} \leftarrow \texttt{GSProve}\{\mathcal{G}, crs, \{e(\underline{w}, g_2^{\beta}/\underline{D}) = t \wedge \underline{D} = g_2^{\underline{\alpha_\delta}}\}, (\alpha_\delta, w, D)\}$$

  - Send the proof ϕ_{mem} to the verifier.

- **MemVerify**$(mParam, S, \phi_{mem})$: This algorithm is run by the verifier to verify the presence of the element α_δ chosen by the prover in the set S.
  - Compute $F(x), C$ and t in the same way as the prover did from publicly available information.
  - Compute $c \leftarrow \texttt{GSVerify}\{\mathcal{G}, crs, \{e(\underline{w}, g_2^{\beta}/\underline{D}) = t \wedge \underline{D} = g_2^{\underline{\alpha_\delta}}\}, \phi_{mem}\}$
  - Announce 'Success' if $c = 1$, 'Failure' otherwise

Theorem 1. *The set membership proof technique is correct, perfectly sound and zero-knowledge.*

Proof: Due to space constraint, detailed proof of the theorem above will be presented in the full version of the paper [7].

Cost of the Membership Proof: We present the cost of membership proof and associated commitments of our construction in terms of group elements of $\mathbb{G}_1$ and $\mathbb{G}_2$ in Table 2. Due to space constraint, detailed calculation of the sizes of the proof elements will be presented in the full version of the paper [7].

Table 2. Cost of our membership proofs

Components | Instantiations	DLIN$_{\mathbb{G}}$	DDH$_{\mathbb{G}_1}$ + DLIN$_{\mathbb{G}_2}$		SXDH$_{\mathbb{G}_1,\mathbb{G}_2}$	
	$\mathbb{G}$	$\mathbb{G}_1$	$\mathbb{G}_2$	$\mathbb{G}_1$	$\mathbb{G}_2$
GS Commitments	9	4	3	4	2
GS Proofs	18	8	6	8	6
Membership Proofs	27	21		20	

4 Generic Construction of Ring Signature

We now present a construction of constant size ring signature scheme based on our membership proof outlined in section 3. Signature scheme is a four algorithm protocol Sig := (SSetup, SKeyGen, SSign, SVerify). Let $\mathcal{G}$ be a bilinear group, $\mathcal{M}$ be the message space, $\langle SK_i = \{sk_{i1}, sk_{i2}, ..., sk_{iM}\}, PK_i = \{pk_{i1}, pk_{i2}, ..., pk_{iN}\}\rangle$ be the secret and public keys (N and M are independent of each other) of the signer i with respect to the signature scheme Sig. Let $\Delta = \langle \Delta_1, \Delta_2, ..., \Delta_n \rangle$ be the signature on message $m \in \mathcal{M}$ and $\mathcal{R}$ be the ring. The signature scheme must be a *compatible* one satisfying the following characteristics:

- Our construction requires $\mathcal{G} = \langle n, \mathbb{G}_1, \mathbb{G}_2, \mathbb{G}_T, e, g_1, g_2 \rangle$ to be a bilinear group of composite order in asymmetric setting [21] to be able to instantiate GS commitment scheme under SXDH assumption. Apparently for composite order groups, SGH instantiation of GS scheme in symmetric setting could have been the most obvious choice. But, the reason such a construction wouldn't work in our case is GS commitments are not fully extractable in this setting as we require in the unforgeability game. Moreover, proofs are L_{co} sound rather than being perfectly sound in this case.
- q-SDH assumption must be hard in $\mathbb{G}_1$ for our constant size set membership proof to be plugged-in.
- Secret key $SK_i \in \mathbb{Z}_n^M$ and public key $PK_i \in \mathbb{G}_k^N$, $k \in [1, 2]$
- Verification equations of the scheme must be MSME or PPE committable in GS framework.
- We commit signature components in GS framework. Signature component Δ_i that depends on SK_i must be a group element of $\mathbb{G}_1$ or $\mathbb{G}_2$ committable in GS framework. Unless committed, an adversary may trivially break the signature anonymity by test verifying Δ_i with $\forall PK_j \in \mathcal{R}$. Extractability is important to demonstrate the impossibility of forgery by the challenger in the unforgeability game.

Our ring signature construction is as follows:

- **RSetup**($1^\kappa, q$): This algorithm is run by a trusted authority (possibly a distributed one to enhance security). GS proof system is instantiated and a suitable hash function is chosen to associate message to ring information.

- $mParam \leftarrow$ MemSetup$(1^\kappa, q)$. Parse $mParam$ as public parameters $\langle \mathcal{G}, crs, qSDH, g_2^\beta \rangle$ of the constant size membership proof technique as outlined in section 3. Parse $\mathcal{G}$ as a description of a bilinear group $\langle n, \mathbb{G}_1, \mathbb{G}_2, \mathbb{G}_T, e, g_1, g_2 \rangle$ of composite order $n = p.q$ where q-SDH assumption holds in $\mathbb{G}_1$. p and q are large prime numbers.

- Choose a collision-resistant hash function $\mathcal{H} : \{0,1\}^* \rightarrow \mathcal{M}$ used to map the concatenation of some pre-agreed representation of message m and $\mathcal{R}$ to $\mathcal{M}$

- $sParam \leftarrow$ SSetup(1^κ)

- Publish public parameters $rParam = \langle sParam, mParam, \mathcal{H} \rangle$

- **RKeyGen**$(rParam)$: Key generation protocol is assumed to have run by each of the prospective ring members to generate their own secret-public key pairs.

  - Generate key-pair $(SK_i, PK_i) \leftarrow$ SKeyGen$(sParam, \mathcal{G})$ for all prospective ring member $i \in \mathcal{R}$

  - Extend the public key of the signature scheme by computing public integers $q_{ij} = sk_{ij}^2 \pmod{n} \in \mathbb{Z}_n, \forall sk_{ij} \in SK_i$ for all prospective ring member $i \in \mathcal{R}$. Going ahead, these components will help us in showing the correlation between the public key PK_i and ring $\mathcal{R}$. Augment the public key PK_i by including $q_i = \{q_{ij}\}$, $j \in [1, M]$. $PK_i' = \langle PK_i, q_{i1}, q_{i2}, ..., q_{iM} \rangle$ acts as the extended public key for signer i of our signature algorithm.

  - Publish extended public keys $\{PK_i'\}$ to the world.

- **RSign**$(m, SK_s, rParam)$: This algorithm is run by the *real* signer s having key-pair (SK_s, PK_s). A ring is an M-tuple $\mathcal{R} = \langle \mathcal{R}_1, \mathcal{R}_2, ..., \mathcal{R}_M \rangle$. $\mathcal{R}$ is formed by s choosing a set of k *potential* signers, which includes himself. There are as many ring components as q-components present in extended public key. We denote j-th ring component as $\mathcal{R}_j = \{q_{1j}, q_{2j}, ...q_{sj}, ..., q_{kj}\}$. Message m and ring information $\mathcal{R}$ are made available for public verification.

  - Associate the message to the ring by computing $m' \leftarrow \mathcal{H}(m||\mathcal{R})$, $m \in \{0,1\}^*$

  - Signer s runs $\Delta \leftarrow$ SSign$(m', SK_s, sParam)$

  - Generate GS proofs for the signature:

  $$\phi_{sig} \leftarrow \text{GSProve}(\mathcal{G}, crs, \{\text{SVerify}(\underline{PK_s}, m', \underline{\Delta}) = 1\}, (PK_s, \Delta'))$$

  - Compute witnesses:

  $$W_j = \text{MemWitness}(mParam, \underline{q_{sj}}, \mathcal{R}_j), \forall j \in [1, M]$$

  Define $W = \{W_j\}, \forall j \in [1, M]$

- Generate the membership proof:

$$\phi_{mem_j} \leftarrow \texttt{MemProve}(mParam, \mathcal{R}_j, W_j), \forall j \in [1, M]$$

  Define $\phi_{mem} = \{\phi_{mem_j}\}, \forall j \in [1, M]$.

- Generate proofs of correlation between q_{sj} and sk_{sj}:

$$\phi_{q_j} \leftarrow \texttt{GSProve}(\mathcal{G}, crs, \{\underline{q_{sj}} = \underline{sk_{sj}}^2\}, (q_{sj}, sk_{sj})), \forall j \in [1, M]$$

  Define $\phi_q = \{\phi_{q_j}\}, \forall j \in [1, M]$

- Generate proofs of correlation between $SK'_{si} \subseteq SK_s$ and PK_s where $pk_{si} = f_{pk_i}(SK'_{si}), \bigcup_i SK'_{si} = SK_s$:

$$\phi_{pk_i} \leftarrow \texttt{GSProve}(\mathcal{G}, crs, \{\underline{pk_{si}} = f_{pk_i}(\underline{SK'_{si}})\}, (pk_{si}, SK'_{si})), \forall pk_{si} \in PK_s$$

  Define $\phi_{pk} = \{\phi_{pk_i}\}, \forall pk_{si} \in PK_s$. Note that computing $f_{pk_i}^{-1}$ is always hard.

- Publish message m, ring signature $\Sigma \leftarrow \langle \phi_{sig}, \phi_{mem}, \phi_q, \phi_{pk}, \Delta \backslash \Delta' \rangle$ and ring information $\mathcal{R}$

- **RVerify**$(m, \mathcal{R}, \Sigma, rParam)$: The verifier runs this algorithm to verify the validity of the ring signature on the message with respect to the ring information published.
  - Let $VE = \{VE_i\}$ be the set of verification equations of the signature scheme Sig. Verify the consistency of the signature,

$$c_{sig} \leftarrow \texttt{GSVerify}(\mathcal{G}, crs, \{VE\}, \phi_{sig})$$

  - Verify the membership of each q-component of signer's extended public key in the ring,

$$c_{mem_i} \leftarrow \texttt{MemVerify}(mParam, \mathcal{R}, \phi_{mem_i}), \forall \phi_{mem_i} \in \phi_{mem}$$

  - Verify proofs of correlation between q_{sj} and sk_{sj}:

$$c_{q_j} \leftarrow \texttt{GSVerify}(\mathcal{G}, crs, \{\underline{q_{sj}} = \underline{sk_{sj}}^2\}, \phi_{q_j}), \forall j \in M$$

  - Verify proofs of correlation between $SK'_{si} \subseteq SK_s$ and PK_s where $pk_{si} = f_{pk}(SK'_{si}), \bigcup_i SK'_{si} = SK_s$:

$$c_{pk_i} \leftarrow \texttt{GSVerify}(\mathcal{G}, crs, \{\underline{pk_{si}} = f_{pk}(\underline{SK'_s})\}, \phi_{pk_i}), \forall pk_{si} \in PK_s$$

  - Announce 'Success' if $(c_{sig} \wedge (\bigwedge_i c_{mem_i}) \wedge (\bigwedge_i c_{q_i}) \wedge (\bigwedge_i c_{pk_i})) = 1$, 'Failure' otherwise

The idea of the proof system above is to show correlation among commitments shared across equations. If a witness is involved in more than one equation, prover must use the same set of randomness to commit to that particular witness throughout. On the other hand, verifier re-uses the same commitment during verification which makes the proofs correlated. Intuitively, public key

$$PK_s \xrightarrow{\phi_{pk}} SK_s \xrightarrow{\phi_q} q_s \xrightarrow{\phi_{mem}} \text{ring } \mathcal{R}$$

Theorem 2. *The generic construction of ring signature scheme outlined above is a secure one satisfying correctness, anonymity and unforgeability.*

Proof: Due to space constraint, detailed proof of the theorem above will be presented in the full version of the paper [7].

5   Instantiation Based on Full Boneh-Boyen Signature (FBB) Scheme

To quantify the reduction in size our construction offers, we will now pick up FBB scheme for a concrete instantiation. [3] proves the security of the signature scheme for prime order groups. Their proof translates directly to composite order model as shown by [10]. Our construction is in asymmetric setting over composite order group [21] where both q-SDH [11] and SXDH assumptions hold.

- **RSetup**$(1^\kappa, q)$: This algorithm is run by a trusted authority (possibly a distributed one to enhance security).
  - $mParam \leftarrow$ MemSetup$(1^\kappa, q)$. Parse $mParam$ as public parameters $\langle \mathcal{G}, crs, qSDH, g_2^\beta \rangle$ of the constant size membership proof technique as outlined in section 3. Parse $\mathcal{G}$ as a description of a bilinear group $\langle n, \mathbb{G}_1, \mathbb{G}_2, \mathbb{G}_T, e, g_1, g_2 \rangle$ of composite order $n = p.q$ where q-SDH assumption holds in $\mathbb{G}_1$. p and q are large prime numbers.
  - Choose a collision-resistant hash function $\mathcal{H} : \{0,1\}^* \rightarrow \mathbb{Z}_n$
  - Publish public parameters $rParam \leftarrow \langle mParam, \mathcal{H} \rangle$

- **RKeyGen**$(rParam)$: Key generation protocol is assumed to have run by each of the prospective ring member $i \in \mathcal{R}$ to generate their own secret-public key pairs.
  - Uniformly choose secret key $SK_i = \langle a_i, b_i \rangle \in \mathbb{Z}_n^2$
  - Generate FBB public key $PK_i = \langle A_i, B_i \rangle = \langle g_2^{a_i}, g_2^{b_i} \rangle$. Compute $q_{ia} = a_i^2 \pmod{n}$ and $q_{ib} = b_i^2 \pmod{n}$. Extended public key $PK_i' = \langle PK_i, q_{ia}, q_{ib} \rangle$
  - Publish extended public keys $\{PK_i'\}$ to the outer world.

- **RSign**$(m, SK_s, rParam)$: This algorithm is run by the *real* signer s having key-pair $(SK_s = \langle a_s, b_s \rangle, PK_s = \langle A_s, B_s \rangle)$. Choose k potential signers to construct a ring $\mathcal{R} = \{\mathcal{R}_a, \mathcal{R}_b\}$. Message m and ring information $\mathcal{R}$ are made available for public verification. Rename $a = a_s, b = b_s, A = A_s, B = B_s$
  - Compute $m' \leftarrow \mathcal{H}(m\|\mathcal{R})$, $m \in \{0,1\}^*$
  - Uniformly choose $r \leftarrow \mathbb{Z}_n \setminus \{\frac{-a+m'}{b}\}$
  - Generate the signature $\Delta \leftarrow g_1^{\frac{1}{a+r.b+m'}}$

- Generate GS proofs for the signature:

$$\phi_{sig} \leftarrow \texttt{GSProve}(\mathcal{G}, crs, \{\underline{B}^r = \underline{B}' \wedge$$
$$e(\underline{\Delta}, \underline{A})e(\underline{\Delta}, \underline{B}')e(\underline{\Delta}, g_2^{m'}) = e(g_1, g_2)\}, (\Delta, A, B, B'))$$

- Compute witnesses $W = \langle W_a, W_b \rangle$:

$$W_a \leftarrow \texttt{MemWitness}(mParam, q_{sa}, \mathcal{R}_a)$$
$$W_b \leftarrow \texttt{MemWitness}(mParam, q_{sb}, \mathcal{R}_b)$$

- Generate the membership proof $\phi_{mem} = \langle \phi_{mem_a}, \phi_{mem_b} \rangle$:

$$\phi_{mem_a} \leftarrow \texttt{MemProve}(mParam, \mathcal{R}_a, W_a)$$
$$\phi_{mem_b} \leftarrow \texttt{MemProve}(mParam, \mathcal{R}_b, W_b)$$

- Generate proofs of correlation $\phi_q = \langle \phi_{q_a}, \phi_{q_b} \rangle$ between $q_s = \langle q_{sa}, q_{sb} \rangle$ and $SK_s = \langle a, b \rangle$:

$$\phi_{q_a} \leftarrow \texttt{GSProve}(\mathcal{G}, crs, \{\underline{q_{sa}} = \underline{a}^2\}, (q_{sa}, a))$$
$$\phi_{q_b} \leftarrow \texttt{GSProve}(\mathcal{G}, crs, \{\underline{q_{sb}} = \underline{b}^2\}, (q_{sb}, b))$$

- Generate proofs of correlation $\phi_{pk} = \langle \phi_{pk_A}, \phi_{pk_B} \rangle$ between SK_s and PK_s:

$$\phi_{pk_A} \leftarrow \texttt{GSProve}(\mathcal{G}, crs, \{\underline{A} = g_2^{\underline{a}}\}, (A, a))$$
$$\phi_{pk_B} \leftarrow \texttt{GSProve}(\mathcal{G}, crs, \{\underline{B} = g_2^{\underline{b}}\}, (B, b))$$

- Publish message m, ring signature $\Sigma \leftarrow \langle \phi_{sig}, \phi_{mem}, \phi_q, \phi_{pk}, \Delta \backslash \Delta', r \rangle$ and ring information $\mathcal{R}$

- **RVerify**$(m, \Sigma, \mathcal{R})$: The verifier runs this algorithm to verify the validity of the ring signature on the message with respect to the ring information published.

  - Verify the consistency of the signature

$$c_{sig} \leftarrow \texttt{GSVerify}(\mathcal{G}, crs, \{\underline{B}^r = \underline{B}' \wedge$$
$$e(\underline{\Delta}, \underline{A})e(\underline{\Delta}, \underline{B}')e(\underline{\Delta}, g_2^{m'}) = e(g_1, g_2)\}, \phi_{sig})$$

  - Verify the membership of each q-component of signer's extended public key in the ring,

$$c_{mem_a} \leftarrow \texttt{MemVerify}(mParam, \mathcal{R}_a, \phi_{mem_a})$$
$$c_{mem_b} \leftarrow \texttt{MemVerify}(mParam, \mathcal{R}_b, \phi_{mem_b})$$

  - Verify proofs of correlation between q_s and SK_s:

$$c_{q_a} \leftarrow \texttt{GSVerify}(\mathcal{G}, crs, \{\underline{q_{sa}} = \underline{a}^2\}, \phi_{q_a})$$
$$c_{q_b} \leftarrow \texttt{GSVerify}(\mathcal{G}, crs, \{\underline{q_{sb}} = \underline{b}^2\}, \phi_{q_b})$$

- Verify proofs of correlation between SK_s and PK_s:

$$c_{pk_A} \leftarrow \texttt{GSVerify}(\mathcal{G}, crs, \{\underline{A} = g_2^{\underline{a}}\}, \phi_{pk_A})$$
$$c_{pk_B} \leftarrow \texttt{GSVerify}(\mathcal{G}, crs, \{\underline{B} = g_2^{\underline{b}}\}, \phi_{pk_B})$$

- Announce 'Success' if $(c_{sig} \wedge (c_{mem_a} \wedge c_{mem_b}) \wedge (c_{q_a} \wedge c_{q_b}) \wedge (c_{pk_A} \wedge c_{pk_B})) = 1$, 'Failure' otherwise

Theorem 3. *The construction of ring signature scheme outlined above is a secure if SXDH assumption holds, q-SDH assumption holds in $\mathbb{G}_1$ and the hash function $\mathcal{H}$ is collision-resistant.*

Proof: The proof for the theorem above follows directly from Theorem 2 and the security proof for FBB scheme [3].

Cost of the Signature Instantiation: We present the cost of our signature instantiation in terms of group elements of $\mathbb{G}_1$, $\mathbb{G}_2$ and $\mathbb{Z}_p$ in Table 3. Our ring signature construction will consist of 50 elements from $\mathbb{G}_1$, 42 elements from $\mathbb{G}_2$ and 3 elements from $\mathbb{Z}_p$.

Table 3. Cost split up under SXDH assumption[17, p. 23,28]

Item Type	Item	$\text{Cost}_{\mathbb{G}_1} + \text{Cost}_{\mathbb{G}_2}$		$\text{Cost}_{\mathbb{Z}_p}$
Commitment	Υ_Δ	$\mathbb{G}_1^2$	-	-
Commitment	Υ_A	-	$\mathbb{G}_2^2$	-
Commitment	Υ_B	-	$\mathbb{G}_2^2$	-
Commitment	$\Upsilon_{B'}$	-	$\mathbb{G}_2^2$	-
Commitment	Υ_a	$\mathbb{G}_1^2$	$\mathbb{G}_2^2$	-
Commitment	Υ_b	$\mathbb{G}_1^2$	$\mathbb{G}_2^2$	-
PPE Proof	$\Gamma_{sig_{PPE}}$	$\mathbb{G}_1^4$	$\mathbb{G}_2^4$	-
Linear MSME($\mathbb{G}_2$)	$\Gamma_{sig_{MSME}}$	-	-	$\mathbb{Z}_p^2$
Constant	r	-	-	$\mathbb{Z}_p^1$
Membership Proof	ϕ_{mem_a}	$\mathbb{G}_1^{12}$	$\mathbb{G}_2^8$	-
Membership Proof	ϕ_{mem_b}	$\mathbb{G}_1^{12}$	$\mathbb{G}_2^8$	-
Correlation Proof	Γ_{q_a}	$\mathbb{G}_1^2$	$\mathbb{G}_2^2$	-
Correlation Proof	Γ_{q_b}	$\mathbb{G}_1^2$	$\mathbb{G}_2^2$	-
QE Equality Proof*	-	$\mathbb{G}_1^2$	$\mathbb{G}_2^2$	-
QE Equality Proof*	-	$\mathbb{G}_1^2$	$\mathbb{G}_2^2$	-
Correlation Proof	Γ_{pk_A}	$\mathbb{G}_1^4$	$\mathbb{G}_2^2$	-
Correlation Proof	Γ_{pk_B}	$\mathbb{G}_1^4$	$\mathbb{G}_2^2$	-
Total Cost	-	$\mathbb{G}_1^{50} + \mathbb{G}_2^{42} + \mathbb{Z}_p^3$		

*We considered correlation QEs to be of the form $x_1 y_1 - x_2 = 0$ having $\langle \{a, a\}, q_{sa} \rangle$ and $\langle \{b, b\}, q_{sb} \rangle$ as witnesses. To deal with only one group of variables in $\mathbb{Z}_n$, we implicitly added equations of the form $x_1 = y_1$

6 Conclusion and Open Problems

We construct a ring signature without random oracle where the signature size is independent of the size of the ring. Each user has a Full-Boneh-Boyen signature key pair. To make a ring signature, the user computes a FBB signature, but outputs a Groth-Sahai zero-knowledge proof that he created a valid signature from one of the keys in a designated ring without revealing which. The key step is to construct a GS proof whose size remains constant, using an accumulation technique discussed in section 3.

It would be interesting to explore the possibility of applying the generic construction to signature schemes other than FBB to achieve the same objective. Achieving a scheme yielding signature of size shorter than our construction is also a problem which deserves to be studied further.

Acknowledgments. The authors of this paper are grateful to Dr. Jens Groth and anonymous reviewers of ACISP 2015 for their valuable suggestions.

References

1. Abe, M., Ohkubo, M., Suzuki, K.: 1-out-of-n signatures from a variety of keys. In: Zheng, Y. (ed.) ASIACRYPT 2002. LNCS, vol. 2501, pp. 415–432. Springer, Heidelberg (2002)
2. Bender, A., Katz, J., Morselli, R.: Ring signatures: stronger definitions, and constructions without random oracles. In: Halevi, S., Rabin, T. (eds.) TCC 2006. LNCS, vol. 3876, pp. 60–79. Springer, Heidelberg (2006)
3. Boneh, D., Boyen, X.: Short signatures without random oracles and the sdh assumption in bilinear groups. Journal of Cryptology **21**(2), 149–177 (2008)
4. Boneh, D., Boyen, X., Shacham, H.: Short group signatures. In: Franklin, M. (ed.) CRYPTO 2004. LNCS, vol. 3152, pp. 41–55. Springer, Heidelberg (2004)
5. Boneh, D., Gentry, C., Lynn, B., Shacham, H.: Aggregate and verifiably encrypted signatures from bilinear maps. In: Biham, E. (ed.) EUROCRYPT 2003. LNCS, vol. 2656, pp. 416–432. Springer, Heidelberg (2003)
6. Boneh, D., Goh, E.-J., Nissim, K.: Evaluating 2-dnf formulas on ciphertexts. In: Kilian, J. (ed.) TCC 2005. LNCS, vol. 3378, pp. 325–341. Springer, Heidelberg (2005)
7. Bose, P., Das, D., Rangan, C.P.: Constant size ring signature without random oracle. Cryptology ePrint Archive, Report 2015/164 (2015). http://eprint.iacr.org/2015/164
8. Boyen, X.: Mesh signatures. In: Naor, M. (ed.) EUROCRYPT 2007. LNCS, vol. 4515, pp. 210–227. Springer, Heidelberg (2007)
9. Brakerski, Z., Kalai, Y.T.: A framework for efficient signatures, ring signatures and identity based encryption in the standard model. In: IACR Eprint archive (2010). http://eprint.iacr.org/2010/086
10. Chandran, N., Groth, J., Sahai, A.: Ring signatures of sub-linear size without random oracles. In: Arge, L., Cachin, C., Jurdziński, T., Tarlecki, A. (eds.) ICALP 2007. LNCS, vol. 4596, pp. 423–434. Springer, Heidelberg (2007)
11. Chase, M., Meiklejohn, S.: Déjà Q: using dual systems to revisit q-type assumptions. In: Nguyen, P.Q., Oswald, E. (eds.) EUROCRYPT 2014. LNCS, vol. 8441, pp. 622–639. Springer, Heidelberg (2014)

12. Chaum, D., van Heyst, E.: Group signatures. In: Davies, D.W. (ed.) EUROCRYPT 1991. LNCS, vol. 547, pp. 257–265. Springer, Heidelberg (1991)
13. Chow, S.S.M., Liu, J.K., Wei, V.K., Yuen, T.H.: Ring signatures without random oracles. In: ASIACCS 2006, pp. 297–302. ACM Press (2005)
14. Dodis, Y., Kiayias, A., Nicolosi, A., Shoup, V.: Anonymous identification in *ad hoc* groups. In: Cachin, C., Camenisch, J.L. (eds.) EUROCRYPT 2004. LNCS, vol. 3027, pp. 609–626. Springer, Heidelberg (2004)
15. Galbraith, S.D., Paterson, K.G., Smart, N.P.: Pairings for cryptographers. Discrete Appl. Math. **156**(16), 3113–3121 (2008)
16. Ghadafi, E.M.: Sub-linear blind ring signatures without random oracles. In: Stam, M. (ed.) IMACC 2013. LNCS, vol. 8308, pp. 304–323. Springer, Heidelberg (2013)
17. Groth, J., Sahai, A.: Efficient non-interactive proof systems for bilinear groups. In: Smart, N.P. (ed.) EUROCRYPT 2008. LNCS, vol. 4965, pp. 415–432. Springer, Heidelberg (2008)
18. Herranz, J., Sáez, G.: Forking lemmas for ring signature schemes. In: Johansson, T., Maitra, S. (eds.) INDOCRYPT 2003. LNCS, vol. 2904, pp. 266–279. Springer, Heidelberg (2003)
19. Jakobsson, M., Sako, K., Impagliazzo, R.: Designated verifier proofs and their applications. In: Maurer, U.M. (ed.) EUROCRYPT 1996. LNCS, vol. 1070, pp. 143–154. Springer, Heidelberg (1996)
20. Kate, A., Zaverucha, G.M., Goldberg, I.: Constant-size commitments to polynomials and their applications. In: Abe, M. (ed.) ASIACRYPT 2010. LNCS, vol. 6477, pp. 177–194. Springer, Heidelberg (2010)
21. Meiklejohn, S., Shacham, H.: New trapdoor projection maps for composite-order bilinear groups. Cryptology ePrint Archive, Report 2013/657 (2013). http://eprint.iacr.org/
22. Menezes, A.J., Vanstone, S.A., Oorschot, P.C.V.: Handbook of Applied Cryptography, 1st edn. CRC Press Inc, Boca Raton, FL, USA (1996)
23. Micali, S., Rabin, M., Kilian, J.: Zero-knowledge sets. In: Proceedings of the 44th Annual IEEE Symposium on Foundations of Computer Science, pp. 80–91 (2003)
24. Naor, M.: Deniable ring authentication. In: Yung, M. (ed.) CRYPTO 2002. LNCS, vol. 2442, pp. 481–498. Springer, Heidelberg (2002)
25. Naor, M., Reingold, O.: On the construction of pseudorandom permutations: Luby-rackoff revisited. Journal of Cryptology **12**(1), 29–66 (1999)
26. Rivest, R.L., Shamir, A., Tauman, Y.: How to leak a secret: theory and applications of ring signatures. In: Goldreich, O., Rosenberg, A.L., Selman, A.L. (eds.) Theoretical Computer Science. LNCS, vol. 3895, pp. 164–186. Springer, Heidelberg (2006)
27. Schäge, S., Schwenk, J.: A CDH-based ring signature scheme with short signatures and public keys. In: Sion, R. (ed.) FC 2010. LNCS, vol. 6052, pp. 129–142. Springer, Heidelberg (2010)
28. Shacham, H., Waters, B.: Efficient ring signatures without random oracles. In: Okamoto, T., Wang, X. (eds.) PKC 2007. LNCS, vol. 4450, pp. 166–180. Springer, Heidelberg (2007)
29. Smart, N.P., Vercauteren, F.: On computable isomorphisms in efficient asymmetric pairing-based systems. Discrete Appl. Math. **155**(4), 538–547 (2007)
30. Yuen, T.H., Liu, J.K., Au, M.H., Susilo, W., Zhou, J.: Efficient linkable and/or threshold ring signature without random oracles. The Computer Journal (2012)

Security Protocols

Constant-Round Leakage-Resilient Zero-Knowledge Argument for NP from the Knowledge-of-Exponent Assumption

Tingting Zhang[1,2,3]($\boxtimes$), Hongda Li[1,2,3], and Guifang Huang[1,2,3]

[1] State Key Laboratory of Information Security, Institute of Information Engineering of Chinese Academy of Sciences, Beijing, China
{zhangtingting,lihongda,huangguifang}@iie.ac.cn
[2] Data Assurance and Communication Security Research Center of Chinese Academy of Sciences, Beijing, China
[3] University of Chinese Academy of Sciences, Beijing, China

Abstract. In this paper, we study the design of constant-round or even 3-round zero-knowledge protocols for all NP languages resistant against side channel attack. Garg, Jain, and Sahai firstly formalize a meaningful definition of $(1 + \epsilon)$-leakage-resilient zero-knowledge(LRZK), and give a construction of $(1 + \epsilon)$-LRZK, for every constant $\epsilon > 0$. Then, with Barak's non-black-box (NBB) simulation technique, Pandey presents the first construction of constant-round LRZK satisfying the ideal requirement $\epsilon = 0$. In this paper, we focus on the construction of constant-round (especially 3-round) LRZK protocols for all NP languages satisfying the ideal requirement $\epsilon = 0$, by means of other techniques. Specially, based on extended Knowledge-of-Exponent Assumption over bilinear groups, we obtain a constant-round LRZK argument for Hamiltonian Cycle (HC) problem, and a 3-round LRZK arguments for circuit satisfiability, which is the first 3-round LRZK protocol for NP.

Keywords: Leakage-resilient zero-knowledge · Knowledge of exponent assumption · Bilinear map

1 Introduction

Zero-knowledge proof, introduced by Goldwasser et al. [14], has been a fundamental cryptographic primitive used in modern cryptography. A zero-knowledge proof for a language L is an interactive proof where a prover $\mathcal{P}$ proves a statement x to a verifier $\mathcal{V}$ such that the interaction doesn't reveal any additional information besides the validity of the statement. It is formalized by requiring that for every malicious verifier $\mathcal{V}^*$, there exists a probabilistic polynomial time

This research is supported by the National Natural Science Foundation of China (Grant No. 61003276) and the Strategic Priority Program of Chinese Academy of Sciences (Grant No. Y2W0012203).

© Springer International Publishing Switzerland 2015
E. Foo and D. Stebila (Eds.): ACISP 2015, LNCS 9144, pp. 251–269, 2015.
DOI: 10.1007/978-3-319-19962-7_15

(PPT) simulator $\mathcal{S}$ such that on input only the common input x, $\mathcal{S}$ can simulate a "real looking" interaction for $\mathcal{V}^*$. $\mathcal{V}^*$ cannot distinguish the simulated interaction with $\mathcal{S}$ and the real interaction with an honest prover $\mathcal{P}$.

Traditionally, it is assumed that the prover's internal state, including the witness and the random coins, is perfectly hidden from $\mathcal{V}^*$. However, in the presence of side channel attack [19,21,25] where an adversary $\mathcal{V}^*$ can learn useful information about the internal state of a cryptographic device, the traditional notion of security becomes meaningless. To handle this problem, many recent works considered stronger adversarial models in which the adversary can learn some leakage on the internal state of the honest party. Now, interest has been growing in studying leakage-resilient cryptographic primitives [1,3,6,10,12,13].

Garg et al. [13] initiated a study of leakage-resilient zero-knowledge (LRZK), where $\mathcal{V}^*$ is allowed to learn arbitrary amount of leakage on the internal state of the honest prover by making leakage queries $F_1, F_2, \ldots$ during the protocol execution. Intuitively, the definition of LRZK should guarantee that no such $\mathcal{V}^*$ can learn anything beyond the validity of the statement and the leakage. To formalize this intuition, [13] considers a leakage oracle, $\mathcal{L}_w^n(\cdot)$, which is parameterized by the witness w and the security parameter n; the simulator $\mathcal{S}$ is then given access to such a leakage oracle, which means that during the simulation, $\mathcal{S}$ can answer leakage queries of $\mathcal{V}^*$ by querying $\mathcal{L}_w^n$ on leakage functions of its choice. Of course, the length of bits that the simulator can read from $\mathcal{L}_w^n$ must be bounded by some parameters. Formally speaking, the LRZK definition requires that for any malicious verifier $\mathcal{V}^*$ with total ℓ-bits leakage, there exists a simulator $\mathcal{S}$ which can obtain at most $(1 + \epsilon)\ell$-bits leakage from $\mathcal{L}_w^n$, and finally outputs a view of $\mathcal{V}^*$ that is computationally indistinguishable from that in the real execution. Besides, to prevent the simulator from simply choosing to leak on the witness instead of using the leakage oracle to only answer the leakage queries of the verifier, [13] also requires that the simulator is leakage-oblivious which means that the oracle's responses are sent directly to the verifier and the simulator does not get to see them. [13] presents a protocol of $\frac{n}{\epsilon}$ rounds, which satisfies the $(1 + \epsilon)$-LRZK for Hamiltonian Cycle (HC) problem for any $\epsilon > 0$. After that, using Barak's non-black-box (NBB) simulation technique, Pandey [22] first presents a constant-round LRZK argument for NP, and Li Hongda et al. [20] give a constant-round LRZK argument of knowledge for NP, both of which satisfy the ideal requirement $\epsilon = 0$. Up to now, most of constant-round LRZK protocols are obtained by using Barak's NBB simulation technique. However, using Barak's NBB simulation technique, it is difficult to achieve a 3-round LRZK protocol for NP. In this paper, we mainly focus on how to construct 3-round LRZK protocols for NP satisfying the ideal requirement $\epsilon = 0$.

1.1   Our Contributions

In this paper, we mainly study how to construct 3-round LRZK protocols. Finally, under the Knowledge-of-Exponent Assumption over bilinear groups (KEA)[2], we present a constant-round LRZK argument for HC problem, and under the extended Knowledge-of-Exponent Assumption over bilinear groups

(XKEA)[2], we construct a 3-round LRZK argument for circuit satisfiability, which is the first 3-round LRZK protocol for NP. And both of our protocols satisfy the ideal requirement $\epsilon = 0$.

Let HC be all directed graphs that contain a Hamiltonian cycle. We first recall Bellare and Palacio's three-round zero-knowledge protocol for HC (BPtzk) from the Knowledge-of-Exponent Assumption [7].

Let q be a prime such that $p = 2q + 1$ is also a prime and the length of the binary representation of p is n bits. It also assumes that if p is an n-bit prime then any $x \in \mathbb{Z}_p$ can be represented by a unique n-bit string. Let G_q denote the subgroup of quadratic residues of $\mathbb{Z}_p^*$, and g is its generator. The Knowledge-of-Exponent Assumption (KEA1) says that for any adversary $\mathcal{A}$ that takes as input q, g, g^a and returns (C, Y) with $Y = C^a$, there exists an extractor $\bar{A}$ which given the same inputs as $\mathcal{A}$ returns c such that $C = g^c$.

Let nBHP denote a protocol which is constructed by running n parallel repetitions of the 3-round Blum Hamiltonicity protocol for HC, and (M_1, Y, M_2) denote the three messages exchanged in nBHP. Informally speaking, if the simulator $\mathcal{S}$ can decide the challenge string Y before it generates the first message M_1, then it can simulate correctly by generating M_1 depending on Y. Therefore, BPtzk is constructed by modifying the way of generating Y in nBHP: in the first round, the prover $\mathcal{P}$ generates M_1 and p, q, g, g^a; then the verifier $\mathcal{V}$ sends (B, X) such that $X = B^a$; finally, $\mathcal{P}$ generates C, Y such that $Y = C^b$, and computes M_2 using Y as the challenge string. From KEA1, there exists an extractor for $\mathcal{V}$ which can output b such that $B = g^b$, which means that the simulator $\mathcal{S}$ can control over the final challenge Y by computing $C = Y^{\frac{1}{b}}$. Thus, $\mathcal{S}$ can simulate correctly. That is, $\mathcal{S}$ can generate M_1 depending on a random selected challenge Y, and then makes the final challenge string be equal to Y.

To make BPtzk be leakage-resilient zero-knowledge, there are two problems to be considered. The first problem is that KEA1 will not hold when the adversary can launch leakage attacks. Since if the adversary can query the leakage of a, he can compute a with just one bit leakage, which means that the adversary can generate B without knowing b. The second problem is that to respond leakage queries during simulation, the simulator $\mathcal{S}$ needs to "explain its actions" so far by maintaining that the relation between its messages and state is the same as the relation between an honest prover's messages and state, which means that to emulate an honest prover's behavior, after sending M_1, $\mathcal{S}$ must be able to explain its randomness used in generating commitments in M_1, in a way that is consistent with the prover's input and the commitments it generated so far in the protocol. To this end, $\mathcal{S}$ is required to be able to reveal the commitment to 1 (or 0) as the commitment to 0 (or 1). This contradicts the binding property of the commitment scheme.

To deal with the first problem, we require that A is not generated by first choosing $a \in \mathbb{Z}_q$ and then computing $A = g^a$, but is directly selected from G_q. Then, to decide the correctness of the pair (B, X), we use the property of bilinear groups. Thus, we need the KEA assumption [2]. To solve the second problem, we follow the idea of [13] by making the commitment scheme used in generating M_1

be a trapdoor commitment scheme. We use a new bit commitment scheme $\langle C, R \rangle$ (presented in Fig.1), which is modified from Pedersen's commitment scheme. Let $\mathsf{BG} = (\mathbb{G}, \mathbb{H}, q, g, e)$ be a bilinear group (described in Section 2.2). The commitment key is $\mathsf{CRS} = (\mathsf{BG}, h = g^t)$ and the trapdoor is t. In the protocol, the commitment key can be jointly generated by the prover $\mathcal{P}$ and the verifier $\mathcal{V}$ where $\mathcal{P}$ generates (BG, Z) with $Z \leftarrow \mathbb{G}$, and then $\mathcal{V}$ generates a pair $(h, \hat{h})$ such that $e(g, \hat{h}) = e(h, Z)$. Then, if the KEA holds, there exists an extractor for $\mathcal{V}$ that can extract t so that $h = g^t$. Combining the above analysis, we can construct a constant-round LRZK protocol for HC. However, it is not 3-round. And we find it is difficult to construct a 3-round LRZK protocol by modifying nBHP. Since to make the simulator $\mathcal{S}$ get the trapdoor, we need extra rounds.

To construct a 3-round LRZK protocol for NP, we must seek for other solutions. We consider the idea of constructing non-interactive zero-knowledge (NIZK) for circuit satisfiability problem in [2,15]. Recall that in the protocol, the prover $\mathcal{P}$ first commits to the value in each circuit wire, and then for every gate g with input wires a, b and output wire c, $\mathcal{P}$ generates a proof to prove that c is equal to $\mathsf{g}(a, b)$. Following this idea, we construct our 3-round LRZK protocol by generating the common reference string of the NIZK protocol in the first two round, and then generating the commitments and proofs in the third round. For soundness, we need the commitment scheme to be extractable. This can be satisfied by using the XKEA assumption which says that for any adversary $\mathcal{A}$ that takes as input $(\mathsf{BG}, h, g^x, h^x)$ and returns $(A, \hat{A})$, there exists an extractor $\mathcal{X}_\mathcal{A}$ which given the same inputs as $\mathcal{A}$ and returns (a, α) such that $A = g^a h^\alpha$. Thus, $\mathsf{CRS} = (\mathsf{BG}, h = g^t, \hat{g}, \hat{h})$ satisfying $e(g, \hat{h}) = e(\hat{g}, h)$, and the trapdoor is t. The scheme is presented in Fig.2. Roughly speaking, our 3-round LRZK protocol is constructed as following: in the first two round, the prover and the verifier jointly generate the commitment key; in the third round, the prover generates corresponding commitments and proofs. Since XKEA holds, the zero-knowledge simulator can obtain the trapdoor t before generating the third message, which means that the leakage query can be handled as in [13].

1.2   Related Works

Since being conceptualizing by Goldwasser et al. [14], zero-knowledge proof systems have been studied in various adversarial settings such as concurrency attacks [11], malleability attacks [9], reset attacks [5], and so on. KEA1 was firstly introduced and used by Damgård in [8]. And later, Hada and Tanaka [18] extended the KEA1 to KEA2, and used it to show the existence of 3-round, negligible-error zero-knowledge for NP. But after that, Bellare and Palacio [7] showed that KEA2 is false, and presented a new version called KEA3 for saving Hada and Tanaka's results. In past few years, there have been a number of interesting researches applying these knowledge of exponent assumptions to zero-knowledge [2,16,17,24].

The study of leakage-resilient cryptography is initiated by Dziembowski and Pietrzak [12]. In recent years, a few works focus on the leakage-resilient interactive protocols have been worked out, such as leakage-resilient identification schemes [1,10], leakage-resilient multiparty computation [6], leakage-resilient interactive proofs [3,4,13,20,22] and so on.

2   Preliminaries

We first give some standard notations used in this paper. The set of natural numbers is represented by $\mathbb{N}$. In the following section, we will use $n \in \mathbb{N}$ to denote the security parameter, and we always implicitly require the size of the input of all the algorithms in this paper to be bounded by some polynomial in n. For non-uniform probabilistic poly-time (PPT) algorithms, we mean algorithms which together with 1^n also get some poly-size auxiliary input aux_n. For brevity, we usually leave the dependency on n (and on aux_n) implicit. By $y \leftarrow \mathcal{A}(x)$, we mean that algorithm $\mathcal{A}$ is executed on input x (and 1^n, in the non-uniform case, aux_n) and the output is y. Similarly, for any finite set S, we write $y \leftarrow S$ to denote that y is sampled uniformly from S.

Besides, we assume familiarity with standard concepts such as interactive Turing machines, interactive proof system, computational indistinguishability, commitment schemes, NP-languages, witness relations and so on.

2.1   Leakage-Resilient Zero-Knowledge

Let $\langle \mathcal{P}, \mathcal{V} \rangle$ be an interactive proof system. In this paper, we will only refer to argument systems which means that the soundness condition holds only against polynomial time machines $\mathcal{P}^*$.

Now, we start to present some description about leakage attacks. It is assumed that the random coins used by a party in any particular round are determined only at the beginning of that round. Let state denote the internal state of the prover $\mathcal{P}$, which is initialized to be the private input w of $\mathcal{P}$. At the beginning of each round i, $\mathcal{P}$ selects a random coins r_i to be used for round i, and then updates the current state state = state $\|$ r_i. A leakage query on prover's state in round i is denoted as a leakage function F_i, to which the prover responds with $F_i(\text{state})$. The leakage attack of $\mathcal{V}^*$ is modeled as any number of arbitrary leakage queries on prover's state throughout the interaction.

To formulate zero-knowledge under a leakage attack, we model the zero-knowledge simulator $\mathcal{S}$ as a PPT machine that has access to a leakage oracle $\mathcal{L}_w^n$ parameterized by the witness w and the security parameter n. A query to the oracle consists of an efficiently computable function F, to which the oracle responds with $F(w)$. Finally, LRZK requires that the the output of $\mathcal{S}$ (denoted by $\mathcal{S}^{\mathcal{L}_w^n(\cdot)}(x, z)$ where z is the auxiliary input) is computationally indistinguishable from the verifier's view in the real interaction (denoted by $\text{view}_{\mathcal{V}^*}(x, z)$).

Definition 1 (Leakage-Resilient Zero-Knowledge[22]). *We say that an interactive proof system $\langle \mathcal{P}, \mathcal{V} \rangle$ for a language $L \in$ NP with a witness relation R, is* leakage-resilient zero-knowledge *if for every PPT machine $\mathcal{V}^*$ that makes any arbitrary polynomial number of leakage queries on $\mathcal{P}$'s state, there exists a PPT algorithm $\mathcal{S}$ such that the following two conditions hold:*

1. *For every $x \in L$, every w such that $R(x, w) = 1$, and every $z \in \{0,1\}^*$, $\mathrm{view}_{\mathcal{V}^*}(x, z)$ and $\mathcal{S}^{\mathcal{L}^n_w(\cdot)}(x, z)$ are computationally indistinguishable.*
2. *For every $x \in L$, every w such that $R(x, w) = 1$, and every $z \in \{0,1\}^*$, and every sufficiently long $r \in \{0,1\}^*$, it holds that $\ell_{\mathcal{S}}(v, r) \le \ell_{\mathcal{V}^*}(v)$, where $\ell_{\mathcal{S}}(v, r)$ is the number of bits that $\mathcal{S}$ receives from $\mathcal{L}^n_w$ when generating the view v with randomness r, and $\ell_{\mathcal{V}^*}(v)$ denote the total length of leakage answers that $\mathcal{V}^*$ receives in the output v.*

2.2 Bilinear Groups and Hardness Assumptions

Definition 2 (Bilinear Groups). *Let $\mathcal{BGG}$ be a bilinear group generator that outputs a tuple $\mathsf{BG} = (\mathbb{G}, \mathbb{H}, q, g, e)$, where $\mathbb{G}$ and $\mathbb{H}$ are cyclic groups of prime order q, g is a generator of $\mathbb{G}$ and $e : \mathbb{G} \times \mathbb{G} \to \mathbb{H}$ is a non-degenerate bilinear map, i.e., $\forall X, Y \in \mathbb{G}, \forall a, b \in \mathbb{Z}_q : e(X^a, Y^b) = e(X, Y)^{ab}$, and $e(g, g)$ generates $\mathbb{H}$. In this paper, we assume that given $\mathsf{BG} = (\mathbb{G}, \mathbb{H}, q, g, e)$, one can efficiently verify that BG is a valid bilinear map. Let L^n_{BG} denote the set of $\{(\mathbb{G}, \mathbb{H}, q, g, e)\}$, where $(\mathbb{G}, \mathbb{H}, q, g, e)$ is a bilinear group and q is an n-bit prime. Besides, we also assume that if q is an n-bit prime then any $x \in \mathbb{Z}_q$ can be represented by a unique n-bit string, and for simply, we just use x to denote this unique string.*

In some cases, we assume the Diffie-Hellman Inversion Assumption, DHIA, which states that given a random $h = g^w \in \mathbb{G}$, it is infeasible to compute $g^{1/w}$.

Assumption 1 (DHIA[2]). *For every non-uniform PPT algorithm $\mathcal{A}$,*

$$\Pr[\mathsf{BG} \leftarrow \mathcal{BGG}, h \leftarrow \mathbb{G}, g^{1/w} \leftarrow \mathcal{A}(\mathsf{BG}, h) : h = g^w] \le negl.$$

Next, we will describe a new assumption, called VDHIA, which is very similar to DHIA. VDHIA says that given a Diffie-Hellman tuple (g^a, g^b, g^{ab}), it is difficult to compute $g^{1/b}$ even when a is chosen maliciously by the adversary. Clearly, any adversary that can break DHIA can also be used to break VDHIA. This indicates that VDHIA is an extension of DHIA.

Assumption 2 (VDHIA). *For every non-uniform PPT algorithm $\mathcal{A}$, consider the following probabilistic experiment:*

- *$\mathcal{A}$ on input $('Step1', 1^n)$ outputs (BG, A), where $A \in \mathbb{G}$;*
- *Given (BG, A) as input, the experiment selects $b \in \mathbb{Z}_q^*$, and outputs $(B = g^b, X = A^b)$ to $\mathcal{A}$.*

The VDHIA says that, if (g, A, B, X) is a Diffie-Hellman tuple, then for sufficiently large n,

$$\Pr[B^* \leftarrow \mathcal{A}('Step2', g, A, B, X) : B^* = g^{1/b}] \le negl.$$

Besides, we need the KEA assumption, which states that given $h = g^w \in \mathbb{G}$ with unknown discrete-log w, it is infeasible to create $A, \hat{A}$ so $\hat{A} = A^w$ without knowing a so $A = g^a$, and the XKEA assumption, which says that given (g, h, g^x, h^x), it is infeasible to create $A, \hat{A}$ so $\hat{A} = A^x$ without knowing a, α so $A = g^a h^\alpha$ [2].

Assumption 3 (KEA). *For every non-uniform PPT algorithm $\mathcal{A}$, there exists a non-uniform PPT algorithm $\mathcal{X}_\mathcal{A}$, the extractor, such that*

$$\Pr\left[\begin{array}{l} \mathsf{BG} \leftarrow \mathcal{BGG}, x \leftarrow \mathbb{Z}_q \\ (A, \hat{A}; a) \leftarrow (\mathcal{A} \parallel \mathcal{X}_\mathcal{A})(\mathsf{BG}, g^x) \end{array} : \hat{A} = A^x \wedge A \neq g^a \right] \leq negl.$$

Where $(A, \hat{A}; a) \leftarrow (\mathcal{A} \parallel \mathcal{X}_\mathcal{A})(\mathsf{BG}, g^x)$ means that $\mathcal{A}$ and $\mathcal{X}_\mathcal{A}$ are executed on the same input (BG, g^x) and the same random tape, and $\mathcal{A}$ outputs $(A, \hat{A})$ whereas $\mathcal{X}_\mathcal{A}$ outputs a.

Assumption 4 (XKEA). *For every non-uniform PPT algorithm $\mathcal{A}$, there exists a non-uniform PPT algorithm $\mathcal{X}_\mathcal{A}$, the extractor, such that*

$$\Pr\left[\begin{array}{l} \mathsf{BG} \leftarrow \mathcal{BGG}, h \leftarrow \mathbb{G}, x \leftarrow \mathbb{Z}_q \\ (A, \hat{A}; a, \alpha) \leftarrow (\mathcal{A} \parallel \mathcal{X}_\mathcal{A})(\mathsf{BG}, h, g^x, h^x) \end{array} : \hat{A} = A^x \wedge A \neq g^a h^\alpha \right] < negl.$$

3   Extractable and Trapdoor Bit Commitment Scheme Based on DHIA and XKEA

In the Pedersen's commitment scheme [23], given a group $\mathbb{G}$ of prime order q, its generator g and an element $h = g^w$, to commit to $m \in \mathbb{Z}_q$, the committer chooses $r \leftarrow \mathbb{Z}_q$, and sends $C = g^m h^r$; to open, the committer sends (m, r). This commitment scheme is perfectly hiding and computationally binding. And if the committer holds w (the discrete log of h), it can open $C = g^m h^r$ as being a commitment to any $m' \in \mathbb{Z}_q$ by computing $r' = (m + r \cdot w - m') \cdot w^{-1}$.

In our protocol, we require that the committed value m is exactly in $\{0, 1\}$. However, if just given a commitment $C = g^m h^r$, the receiver cannot verify whether $m \in \{0, 1\}$. Thus, we add a proof for $m \in \{0, 1\}$ to the commitment. We present the trapdoor bit commitment scheme $\langle \mathcal{C}, \mathcal{R} \rangle$ in Fig.1.

Key generation: Pick $\mathsf{BG} \leftarrow \mathcal{BGG}$, $w \leftarrow \mathbb{Z}_q$ and let $h = g^w$. The commitment key is $\mathsf{CRS} = (\mathsf{BG}, h)$, and the trapdoor key is $\tau = w$.

Commitment: To commit to $m \in \{0, 1\}$, the committer $\mathcal{C}$ randomly chooses $r \leftarrow \mathbb{Z}_q$, and computes the commitment (C, P) as follows:

$$C = g^m h^r, \quad P = g^{r(2m-1)} h^{r^2}.$$

After receiving the commitment (C, P), the receiver $\mathcal{R}$ verifies whether $e(C, Cg^{-1}) = e(h, P)$. If not, the receiver aborts. Else, the receiver believes that the message committed in (C, P) is 0 or 1.

Opening: The committer $\mathcal{C}$ sends (m, r), and then the receiver $\mathcal{R}$ accepts if $C = g^m h^r$ and $P = g^{r(2m-1)} h^{r^2}$.

Fig. 1. Commitment Scheme $\langle \mathcal{C}, \mathcal{R} \rangle$

Theorem 1. *If the* DHIA *holds,* $\langle \mathcal{C}, \mathcal{R} \rangle$ *is a perfectly hiding and computationally trapdoor bit commitment scheme.*

Proof. The required security properties can be seen as follows.

Correctness: It is easy to verify that an honest receiver always accepts the commitment of an honest committer. Besides, we also need to prove that for any accepted commitment (C, P), the message hidden in it is equal to 0 or 1. Suppose there exists a non-uniform PPT adversary that can create a pair $(C = g^m h^r, P)$ such that $e(C, Cg^{-1}) = e(h, P)$ but $m \notin \{0, 1\}$. Then, we have

$$e(h, P) = e(C, Cg^{-1}) = e(g, g^{m(m-1)+(2m-1)wr+(wr)^2}).$$

This implies $g^{m(m-1)w^{-1}} = Pg^{-((2m-1)r+wr^2)}$. Thus, when $m \notin \{0, 1\}$, we can get $g^{\frac{1}{w}} = (Pg^{(1-2m)r}h^{-r^2}))^{\frac{1}{m(m-1)}}$. Therefore, given the opening of C, we can compute $g^{\frac{1}{w}}$, which contradicts the DHIA.

Perfectly Hiding: For any valid commitment (C, P), we assume that $C = g^\alpha$ and $P = g^\beta$. Consider the following equations where m, r are variables,

$$\begin{cases} \alpha = m + wr \\ \beta = r(2m - 1) + wr^2 \\ \beta = \alpha(\alpha - 1)w^{-1} \end{cases}$$

Clearly, computing the message hidden in (C, P) is equivalent to compute the solution of the above equations. It is easy to see that these equations only have two solutions: $(m = 0, r = \alpha w^{-1})$ and $(m = 1, r' = (\alpha - 1)w^{-1})$. Thus, the probability that the committed value in (C, P) is 0 is identical to the probability that the committed value in (C, P) is 1.

Computationally Binding: Suppose a non-uniform PPT adversary creates two different openings (m, r) and (m', r') for a commitment (C, P), i.e., $g^m h^r = g^{m'} h^{r'}$. Then one can easily compute $w = (m - m')(r - r')^{-1}$ such that $h = g^w$.

Computationally Trapdoor: To generate a trapdoor commitment, the simulator just randomly chooses $r \leftarrow \mathbb{Z}_q$, and computes $(C = h^r, P = g^{-r}h^{r^2})$. To open to 0, the simulator just sends $(0, r)$. To open to 1, the simulator just computes $r' = (r \cdot w - 1) \cdot w^{-1}$, and sends $(1, r')$. Since r is randomly selected, it is easy to see that the trapdoor commitment (C, P) is also random, which is just the same as the commitment generated by an honest committer.   □

In our 3-round LRZK protocol, we need a commitment scheme which is extractable and equivocal. From the XKEA, we know that given BG, $h \leftarrow \mathbb{G}$, $\hat{g} = g^x$, and $\hat{h} = h^x$ where $x \leftarrow \mathbb{Z}_q$, if an adversary can produce a pair $(A, \hat{A})$ such that $\hat{A} = A^x$, then there exists a non-uniform poly-time algorithm $\mathcal{X}_A$, the extractor, that can extract a pair (a, α) such that $A = g^a h^\alpha$. Following this idea, we add a commitment $\hat{C} = \hat{g}^m \hat{h}^r$ to the commitment pair (C, P). The details are in Fig.2.

Key generation: Pick BG $\leftarrow \mathcal{BGG}$, $w \leftarrow \mathbb{Z}_q$, $\hat{g} \leftarrow \mathbb{G}$, and let $h = g^w$, $\hat{h} = \hat{g}^w$. The commitment key is CRS $= (\text{BG}, h, \hat{g}, \hat{h})$, and the trapdoor key is $\tau = w$.
Commitment: To commit to $m \in \{0, 1\}$, the committer $\mathcal{C}$ randomly chooses $r \leftarrow \mathbb{Z}_q$, and computes the commitments $(C, \widehat{C}, P)$ as follows:

$$C = g^m h^r, \quad \widehat{C} = \hat{g}^m \hat{h}^r, \quad P = g^{r(2m-1)} h^{r^2}.$$

After receiving the commitments $(C, \widehat{C}, P)$, the receiver $\mathcal{R}$ verifies whether $e(C, Cg^{-1}) = e(h, P)$ and $e(g, \widehat{C}) = e(\hat{g}, C)$. If not, the receiver abort. Else, the receiver accepts that the message committed in $(C, \widehat{C}, P)$ is 0 or 1.
Opening: The committer $\mathcal{C}$ sends (m, r), and then the receiver $\mathcal{R}$ verifies whether $C = g^m h^r$, $\widehat{C} = \hat{g}^m \hat{h}^r$ and $P = g^{r(2m-1)} h^{r^2}$.

Fig. 2. Commitment scheme $\langle \widetilde{\mathcal{C}}, \widetilde{\mathcal{R}} \rangle$

Theorem 2. *If the* XKEA *and* DHIA *hold,* $\langle \widetilde{\mathcal{C}}, \widetilde{\mathcal{R}} \rangle$ *is a perfectly hiding, extractable and computationally trapdoor bit commitment scheme.*

The proof is easy to get from the above analysis, and we omit it here. In the following section, by $(C, P) = \text{Com}(m; r)$, we mean that (C, P) is a commitment to m with randomness r under the commitment scheme $\langle \mathcal{C}, \mathcal{R} \rangle$, and by $(C, \widehat{C}, P) = \widetilde{\text{Com}}(m; r)$, we mean that $(C, \widehat{C}, P)$ is a commitment to m with randomness r under the commitment scheme $\langle \widetilde{\mathcal{C}}, \widetilde{\mathcal{R}} \rangle$.

4   Constant-Round LRZK Arguments for HC

4.1   Our Protocol

In this section, we will present our constant-round protocol $\langle \mathcal{P}, \mathcal{V} \rangle$. The protocol consists of two stages. In Stage 1, $\mathcal{P}$ and $\mathcal{V}$ jointly generate the commitment key CRS $= (\text{BG}, h)$ for the commitment scheme $\langle \mathcal{C}, \mathcal{R} \rangle$ (in section 3). The Stage 2 is a variant of Blum's Hamiltionicity protocol, where instead of using Naor's commitment scheme, $\mathcal{P}$ uses the commitment scheme $\langle \mathcal{C}, \mathcal{R} \rangle$ to generate its commitment messages. Besides, in this stage, $\mathcal{P}$ and $\mathcal{V}$ also engage in coin-flipping to jointly generate the challenge for Blum's Hamiltionicity protocol. The details are presented in Fig.3.

Theorem 3. *If* KEA *and* VDHIA *hold, Protocol* $\langle \mathcal{P}, \mathcal{V} \rangle$ *is a constant-round leakage-resilient zero-knowledge argument for* HC *problem.*

The completeness is obvious, and we present the proof of soundness and leakage-resilient zero-knowledge property respectively in Section 4.2 and Section 4.3.

Common Input: $G = (V, E) \in HC$, $|V| = n$.
Private Input to $\mathcal{P}$: A Hamiltonian cycle H in G.
Protocol:

- **Stage 1 : Jointly Generating the Parameters of** $\langle \mathcal{C}, \mathcal{R} \rangle$
    - $\mathcal{P} \to \mathcal{V}$: Generate $\mathsf{BG} \leftarrow \mathcal{BGG}$, and $Z \leftarrow \mathbb{G}$. Send (BG, Z) to $\mathcal{V}$.
    - $\mathcal{V} \to \mathcal{P}$: If BG is not a valid bilinear group or $A \notin \mathbb{G}$ then abort. Else, choose $t \leftarrow \mathbb{Z}_q$, and compute $(h = g^t, \hat{h} = Z^t)$. Send $(h, \hat{h})$ to $\mathcal{P}$.
- **Stage 2: A Variant of Blum's Hamiltonicity Protocol**
    - $\mathcal{P} \to \mathcal{V}$: If $e(g, \hat{h}) \neq e(h, Z)$ then abort. Else, let $\mathsf{CRS} = (\mathsf{BG}, h)$, and $\mathcal{P}$ does as follows:
        (1) Select $\bar{\mathsf{BG}} = (\bar{\mathbb{G}}, \bar{\mathbb{H}}, \bar{q}, \bar{g}, \bar{e},) \leftarrow L_{BG}^n$, and $A \leftarrow \bar{\mathbb{G}}$;
        (2) For every $i \in [n]$,
            - Choose a random permutation π_i and set $G_i = \pi_i(G)$.
            - For every $j \in [n^2]$, $\mathcal{P}$ commits to each bit b_j in G_i using the commitment scheme $\langle \mathcal{C}, \mathcal{R} \rangle$ with $\mathsf{CRS} = (\mathsf{BG}, h)$.
        Let M_1 be the set of all the commitments.
        $\mathcal{P}$ sends $(M_1, \bar{\mathsf{BG}}, A)$ to $\mathcal{V}$.
    - $\mathcal{V} \to \mathcal{P}$: If $\bar{\mathsf{BG}} \notin L_{BG}^n$, or $A \notin \bar{\mathbb{G}}$, or any commitment in M_1 is invalid, then abort. Else, choose $b \leftarrow \mathbb{Z}_{\bar{q}}$, and compute $B = \bar{g}^b, X = A^b$. Send (B, X) to $\mathcal{P}$.
    - $\mathcal{P} \to \mathcal{V}$: If $\bar{e}(\bar{g}, X) \neq \bar{e}(A, B)$ then abort. Else, select $c \in \{0, 1\}^n$, and send it to $\mathcal{V}$.
    - $\mathcal{V} \to \mathcal{P}$: Send b to $\mathcal{P}$.
    - $\mathcal{P} \to \mathcal{V}$: If $B \neq \bar{g}^b$ then abort. Else, Let $ch = c \oplus b = ch_1, ..., ch_n$. For each $i \in [n]$, if $ch_i = 0$, P decommits to every edge in G_i and reveals π_i; else, it decommits to the edges in the Hamiltonian Cycle in G_i. Let M_2 be the set of all the opening messages. $\mathcal{P}$ sends M_2 to $\mathcal{V}$.
    - $\mathcal{V}$: Output 1 (i.e., accept) if using $ch = c \oplus b$ as the challenge message, each opening message in M_2 is valid. Otherwise output 0.

Fig. 3. Constant-round Protocol for LRZK $\langle \mathcal{P}, \mathcal{V} \rangle$

4.2 Proving Computationally Soundness

If protocol $\langle \mathcal{P}, \mathcal{V} \rangle$ is not computationally sound, then there exists a PPT cheating prover $\mathcal{P}^*$ and an infinite set $\mathcal{I} = \{(x, w) : x \notin L\}$ such that for every $(x, w) \in \mathcal{I}$, there exists a polynomial $p_0(\cdot)$ satisfying that $\Pr[\langle \mathcal{P}^*, \mathcal{V} \rangle(x) = 1] > 1/p_0(|x|)$, where $\langle \mathcal{P}^*, \mathcal{V} \rangle(x)$ represents the output of $\mathcal{V}$ at the end of the protocol.

In the following section, we let pi denote the prover's i-th message, and similarly, vi denote the verifier's i-th message. To prove the soundness of protocol $\langle \mathcal{P}, \mathcal{V} \rangle$, we just need to prove the following three facts:

- Firstly, we prove that $\mathcal{P}^*$ cannot equivocate its commitments, and each opening message in M_2 must be 0 or 1.
- Secondly, we can prove that if the commitment scheme $\langle \mathcal{C}, \mathcal{R} \rangle$ is computationally binding, then for every common input $G \notin L$ and every possible prefix (p1, v1, p2), there exist at most one challenge string ch such that the prover $\mathcal{P}^*$ can answer properly in its opening message M_2.

– Finally, under the above two conditions, we can prove that if $\mathcal{P}^*$ can succeed with a noticeable probability, then we can use it to construct an adversary for VDHIA which can also succeed with a noticeable probability.

Firstly, it is easy to verify that under the VDHIA, the first fact holds (referring to Section 3 for more details).

Secondly, if there exist a false statement $G \notin L$ and a prefix $(\mathsf{p1}, \mathsf{v1}, \mathsf{p2})$ such that there exist at least two challenges that $\mathcal{P}^*$ can answer properly in its opening message, then it is easy to compute a Hamiltonian Cycle for G, which contradicts $G \notin L$.

Now, we start to prove the third fact. We first construct an adversary $\mathcal{A}$ for VDHIA. $\mathcal{A}$ uses $\mathcal{P}^*$ as a subroutine, and does as following:

Step 1: Internally interact with $\mathcal{P}^*$ as an honest verifier on some $(G, w) \in \mathcal{I}$ till $\mathcal{P}^*$ successfully completes the protocol. Let $\mathsf{trans} = (\mathsf{p1}, \mathsf{v1}, \mathsf{p2})$, $\mathsf{p2} = (M_1, \bar{\mathsf{BG}}, A)$, $\mathsf{v2} = (B_1 = g^{b_1}, X_1)$ and the challenge be ch^*. Go to Step 2.

Step 2: $\mathcal{A}$ forwards $(\bar{\mathsf{BG}}, A)$ to the external challenger of VDHIA, and then receives a challenge pair (B, X). Go to Step 3.

Step 3: $\mathcal{A}$ does as following:
   (1) $\mathcal{A}$ selects $b' \leftarrow \mathbb{Z}_{\bar{q}}$ and sets $B' = B\bar{g}^{b'}, X' = XA^{b'}$. If $B' = B_1$, $\mathcal{A}$ computes $b = b_1 - b'$, outputs $g^{\frac{1}{b}}$ and stops. Otherwise, continue.
   (2) $\mathcal{A}$ runs $\mathcal{P}^*$ on (trans, B', X') to get its response c'. Let $b^* = ch^* \oplus c'$. If $\bar{g}^{b^*} \neq B'$, $\mathcal{A}$ goes back to (1) of Step 3. Otherwise, $\mathcal{A}$ computes $b = b^* - b'$, outputs $g^{\frac{1}{b}}$ and stops.

Now, we have completed the description of $\mathcal{A}$. Intuitively, in Step 1, we first find an accepted transcript and the unique challenge ch^* for the prefix trans. Then, from the above analysis, we know that if $\mathcal{P}^*$ wants to successfully prove a false statement, it must output a c' such that $c' \oplus (b + b') = ch^*$. As a result, it is easy to compute b.

Besides, we need to analyze the expected running time of $\mathcal{A}$. Recall that we have assumed that $Pr[\langle \mathcal{P}^*, \mathcal{V} \rangle (x) = 1] > 1/p_0(|x|)$. Thus, the probability that $\mathcal{A}$ passes the checks in Step 1 is at least $1/p_0(n)$. In Step 2, the running time of $\mathcal{A}$ is obviously polynomial. From the above analysis, we know that if $\mathcal{P}^*$ can successfully prove a false statement, it must output a c' such that $c' \oplus (b + b') = ch^*$. Then, the probability that $\mathcal{A}$ passes the checks in (2) of Step 3 is at least $1/p_0(n)$. Therefore, the expected running time of $\mathcal{A}$ is $O(t_2(n) + p_0(n)(t_1(n) + t_3(n)))$, where $t_i(n)$ is a polynomial bounding the running time of Step i.

Now, we can conclude that if there exists a cheating prover $\mathcal{P}^*$ can succeed with a noticeable probability, then there exists a PPT adversary attacking the VDHIA that can also succeed with a noticeable probability. This completes the proof of the computationally soundness.

4.3   Proving Leakage-Resilient Zero-Knowledge

The Simulator $\mathcal{S}$. Let $\mathcal{V}^*$ be a PPT cheating verifier, and $\mathcal{X}_{\mathcal{V}^*}$ be the KEA extractor for $\mathcal{V}^*$. The simulator receives as input the security parameter 1^n, an

n vertex Hamiltonian graph G, and uses $\mathcal{X}_{\mathcal{V}^*}$ as a subroutine. By $\mathcal{A} \to \mathcal{B}$, we mean that $\mathcal{A}$ sends a message to $\mathcal{B}$, and similarly, $\mathcal{A} \leftarrow \mathcal{B}$ means that $\mathcal{A}$ receives a message from $\mathcal{B}$. tape is initialized with the null string.

- **Stage 1 : Jointly Generating the Parameter of $\langle \mathcal{C}, \mathcal{R} \rangle$**
  - $\mathcal{S} \to \mathcal{V}^*$: Generate $\mathsf{BG} \leftarrow \mathcal{BGG}$, and $Z \leftarrow \mathbb{G}$. Send (BG, Z) to $\mathcal{V}$.

    Leakage query : Update tape = tape $\|$ (BG, Z). After receiving a leakage function F from $\mathcal{V}^*$, $\mathcal{S}$ answers it by querying $\mathcal{L}_H^n$ with $F'(H) = F(H, \mathsf{tape})$.
  - $\mathcal{S} \leftarrow \mathcal{V}^*$: $\mathcal{S}$ runs $(\mathcal{V}^* \| \mathcal{X}_{\mathcal{V}^*})(\mathsf{BG}, Z)$ to get $(h, \hat{h}; t)$. If $e(g, \hat{h}) = e(h, Z)$ but $h \neq g^t$ then output abort.
- **Stage 2: Blum Hamiltonicity Protocol**
  - $\mathcal{S} \to \mathcal{V}^*$: If $e(g, \hat{h}) \neq e(h, Z)$ then abort. Else, let $\mathsf{CRS} = (\mathsf{BG}, h), \tau = t$. $\mathcal{S}$ does as following:
    (1) Select $\bar{\mathsf{BG}} = (\bar{\mathbb{G}}, \bar{\mathbb{H}}, \bar{q}, \bar{g}, \bar{e},) \leftarrow L_{\bar{BG}}^n$, and $A \leftarrow \bar{\mathbb{G}}$;
    (2) Choose $ch \leftarrow \{0,1\}^n$. For $i \in [n]$, if $ch_i = 0$, it commits to a random $G_i = \pi_i(G)$; otherwise, it commits to a random n-cycle graph G_i. Let M_1 be the set of all the commitments.
    $\mathcal{S}$ sends $(M_1, \bar{\mathsf{BG}}, A)$ to $\mathcal{V}^*$.

    Leakage query : Note that since $\mathcal{S}$ holds the trapdoor key τ, it can equivocate the commitments, i.e., it can compute both the random coins that result in a commitment to bit 0 and the random coins that result in a commitment to bit 1, and let ρ be a string that consists of the random coins for both cases. Besides, $\mathcal{S}$ also knows the final challenge string ch. That is to say, $\mathcal{S}$ can learn the double trapdoor (ch, τ) before it sends the commitments. Thus, we can handle the leakage queries just the same as in [13]: first define a special deterministic function $R(G, \rho, H)$, which uses ρ and H to construct randomness r' such that the honest prover uses H and r' will result in the exact same transcript as output by $\mathcal{S}$ (i.e., the message M_1). Set tape = tape $\|$ $(\bar{\mathsf{BG}}, A) \| r'$. After receiving a leakage query F, $\mathcal{S}$ answers it by sending $F'(H) = F(H, \mathsf{tape})$ to $\mathcal{L}_H^n$.
  - $\mathcal{S} \leftarrow \mathcal{V}^*$: Run $(\mathcal{V}^* \| \mathcal{X}_{\mathcal{V}^*})(\bar{\mathsf{BG}}, A)$ to get $(B, X; b)$. If $\bar{e}(\bar{g}, X) = \bar{e}(A, B)$ but $B \neq \bar{g}^b$ then output abort.
  - $\mathcal{S} \to \mathcal{V}$: If $\bar{e}(\bar{g}, X) \neq \bar{e}(A, B)$ then abort. Else, let $c = ch \oplus b$, and send it to $\mathcal{V}^*$.

    Leakage query : Set tape = tape $\|$ c. After receiving a leakage function F from $\mathcal{V}^*$, $\mathcal{S}$ answers it by querying $\mathcal{L}_H^n$ with $F'(H) = F(H, \mathsf{tape})$.
  - $\mathcal{S} \leftarrow \mathcal{V}^*$: Receive b^* from $\mathcal{V}^*$.
  - $\mathcal{S} \to \mathcal{V}$: If $B \neq \bar{g}^{b^*}$ then abort. Else, $\mathcal{S}$ does as following: Open the commitments in M_1 corresponding to the challenge ch. Let M_2 be the set of all the opening messages. $\mathcal{S}$ sends M_2 to $\mathcal{V}^*$.

    Leakage query : Note that no new random coins are generated, i.e., tape is unchanged. Upon receiving a leakage function F, $\mathcal{S}$ answers it by querying $\mathcal{L}_H^n$ with $F'(H) = F(H, \mathsf{tape})$.

Now, we have completed the description of $\mathcal{S}$. $\mathcal{S}$ outputs whatever is the final view of $\mathcal{V}^*$.

Lemma 1. *Protocol* $\langle \mathcal{P}, \mathcal{V} \rangle$ *is a leakage-resilient zero-knowledge protocol.*

Proof. Now, we need to prove that the view of $\mathcal{V}^*$ generated when interacting with the simulator $\mathcal{S}$ is computationally indistinguishable from that generated when interacting with the real prover. Consider the following hybrids:

H_0: In this hybrid, the simulator $\mathcal{S}$ holds the witness H and interacts with $\mathcal{V}^*$ just like the honest prover. Leakage queries are answered directly based on H and the random coins it used. This corresponds to the real interaction.

H_1: This hybrid is same as H_0 except that in Stage 1, $\mathcal{S}$ runs $(\mathcal{V}^* \parallel \mathcal{X}_{\mathcal{V}^*})(\mathsf{BG}, Z)$ to get $(h, \hat{h}; t)$. If $e(g, \hat{h}) = e(h, Z)$ but $h \neq g^t$, then output abort. Leakage queries are answered in the same way as in H_0.

H_2: This hybrid is just like in H_1 except that in the fourth-round, $\mathcal{S}$ runs $(\mathcal{V}^* \parallel \mathcal{X}_{\mathcal{V}^*})(\overline{\mathsf{BG}}, A)$ to get $(B, X; b)$. If $\bar{e}(\bar{g}, X) = \bar{e}(A, B)$ but $B \neq \bar{g}^b$ then output abort. Leakage queries are answered in the same way as in H_1.

H_3: This hybrid is just like in H_2 except that instead of using the witness H, $\mathcal{S}$ generates the commitment messages M_1 according to a randomly selected challenge string $ch \in \{0, 1\}^n$, i.e., generates M_1 by the way of simulation. Leakage queries are handled as follows. With the witness H, $\mathcal{S}$ uses the function $R(G, \rho, H)$ (described above) to select corresponding random strings, and let r' be the final output of R. The simulator answers a leakage query F by computing $F(H, \mathsf{tape} \parallel (\overline{\mathsf{BG}}, A) \parallel r')$.

H_4: This hybrid is same as H_3 except that the simulator $\mathcal{S}$ doesn't hold a witness any more, and thus it handles leakage queries slightly differently. After receiving F, it creates a function $F'(H) = F(H, \mathsf{tape})$, and then sends $F'(\cdot)$ to the leakage oracle $\mathcal{L}_H^n$. Note that this hybrid corresponds to our final simulation.

Now, we just need to prove the indistinguishability of H_0 and H_4, which is satisfied if H_i is computationally indistinguishable from H_{i+1} for $i = 0, ..., 3$.

Indistinguishability of hybrids H_0 and H_1 directly follows the KEA assumption. Similarly, under the KEA assumption, hybrids H_1 and H_2 are also computationally indistinguishable.

Now, let we see hybrids H_2 and H_3. From the computationally hiding property of $\langle \mathcal{C}, \mathcal{R} \rangle$, we know that the messages M_1 generated in H_2 is indistinguishable from that in H_3. Besides, R outputs uniform randomness consistent with the witness used in hybrid H_3, that is to say, the leakage queries are also answered (and distributed) correctly. Thus, H_2 and H_3 are also indistinguishable.

Finally, obviously, the output of hybrids H_3 and H_4 are identically distributed. This completes the proof. □

5   3-Round LRZK Arguments for Circuit Satisfiability

In this section, we will present our 3-Round LRZK protocol for circuit satisfiability. Since any circuit can be linearly reduced to a circuit built from NAND-gates, without loss of generality, we will focus on this simpler case. Before giving the full protocol, we first see the following observation about evaluating NAND-gates from [15], which is easily proved by constructing a truth table.

Claim 1. *Let $a, b, c \in \{0, 1\}$, then $a + b + 2c - 2 \in \{0, 1\}$ if and only if $c = a$ NAND b.*

5.1 Protocol

We now present our 3-round LRZK protocol $\langle \overline{\mathcal{P}}, \overline{\mathcal{V}} \rangle$, which consists of three stages. In Stage 1, the prover $\mathcal{P}$ and the verifier $\mathcal{V}$ jointly generate the commitment key $\mathsf{CRS} = (\mathsf{BG}, h, \hat{g}, \hat{h})$ for the commitment scheme $\langle \widetilde{\mathcal{C}}, \widetilde{\mathcal{R}} \rangle$ (in Fig.2). In Stage 2, the prover $\mathcal{P}$ first generates commitments to the value of every wire, and then generate a proof for each NAND-gate using Claim 1. In Stage 3, $\mathcal{V}$ verify the validity of $\mathcal{P}$'s messages. Details are presented in Fig.4.

Theorem 4. *Assuming XKEA and VDHIA hold, protocol $\langle \overline{\mathcal{P}}, \overline{\mathcal{V}} \rangle$ is a 3-round leakage-resilient zero-knowledge argument for circuit satisfiability.*

Proof. We first give the proof of completeness and soundness, and present the proof of leakage-resilient zero-knowledge property in Section 5.2

Completeness. Firstly, every honest prover $\mathcal{P}$ holding a valid witness w for C, can compute correct commitments for all wires and correct proofs for all NAND-gates. Secondly, the correctness of $\langle \widetilde{\mathcal{C}}, \widetilde{\mathcal{R}} \rangle$ guarantees that every committed value is other 0 or 1. Finally, for every NAND-gate, if the associated commitments and proof are valid, from Claim 1, the operation of NAND is also correct.

Soundness. Assume there exists a PPT adversary $\mathcal{P}^*$ that succeeds in proving an unsatisfiable circuit C with probability at least p_0, we can use it to construct an adversary $\mathcal{A}$ for VDHIA as follows:

1. Internally interact with $\mathcal{P}^*$ by acting as an honest verifier. After receiving the first message (BG, A) from $\mathcal{P}^*$, if BG is not a valid bilinear group or $A \notin \mathbb{G}$, abort. Otherwise, $\mathcal{A}$ forwards it to an external challenger $\mathcal{C}$ of VDHIA.
2. After externally receiving a valid challenge pair (h, B) from $\mathcal{C}$, choose $y, x \leftarrow \mathbb{Z}_q$, and set $h' = h^y, B' = B^y, \hat{g} = g^x, \hat{h} = h'^x$. Send $(h', B', \hat{g}, \hat{h})$ to $\mathcal{P}^*$.
3. After receiving $\mathcal{P}^*$'s proof messages π, if π is invalid then abort. Else, $\mathcal{A}$ runs the extractor $\mathcal{X}_{\mathcal{P}^*}$ to extract all the opening information in π. If $\mathcal{X}_{\mathcal{P}^*}$ fails, $\mathcal{A}$ outputs Fail1. Else, check all the NAND-gates, and
   - If there exists invalid opening messages such that $C = g^m h'^r$, $e(C, Cg^{-1}) = e(h', P)$ but $m \notin \{0, 1\}$, $\mathcal{A}$ outputs $h^* = g^{\frac{1}{t}} = (Pg^{(1-2m)r} h^{-r^2})^{\frac{y}{m(m-1)}}$.
   - If there exists an inconsistent NAND-gate with associated commitments $(C_0, \widehat{C}_0, P_0), (C_1, \widehat{C}_1, P_1), (C_2, \widehat{C}_2, P_2)$ and the proof P such that $M = C_0 C_1 C_2{}^2 g^{-2} = g^m h'^r$, $e(M, Mg^{-1}) = e(h', P)$ but $m = c_0 + c_1 + 2c_2 - 2 \notin \{0, 1\}$, $\mathcal{A}$ outputs $h^* = g^{\frac{1}{t}} = (Pg^{(1-2m)r} h^{-r^2})^{\frac{y}{m(m-1)}}$.
   - Otherwise, $\mathcal{A}$ outputs Fail2.

Common Input: A circuit C built from NAND-gates.
Private Input to P: An n-bit string $w = w_1, ..., w_n$ such that $C(w) = 1$.

- **Stage 1 : Jointly Generating Parameter of Commitment Scheme** $\langle \widetilde{\mathcal{C}}, \widetilde{\mathcal{R}} \rangle$
  - $\mathcal{P} \rightarrow \mathcal{V}$: Generate $\mathsf{BG} \leftarrow \mathcal{BGG}$, and choose $A \leftarrow \mathbb{G}$. Send (BG, A) to $\mathcal{V}$.
  - $\mathcal{V} \rightarrow \mathcal{P}$: If BG is not a valid bilinear group or $A \notin \mathbb{G}$ then abort. Else, randomly choose $t \leftarrow \mathbb{Z}_q$, $\hat{g} \leftarrow \mathbb{G}$, and compute $h = g^t, B = A^t, \hat{h} = \hat{g}^t$. Send $(h, B, \hat{g}, \hat{h})$ to $\mathcal{P}$.
- **Stage 2 : Generating the Proof**
  - $\mathcal{P} \rightarrow \mathcal{V}$: If $e(g, B) \neq e(h, A)$, or $e(g, \hat{h}) \neq e(\hat{g}, h)$ then abort. Else, let $\mathsf{CRS} = (\mathsf{BG}, h, \hat{g}, \hat{h})$ be the commitment key of $\langle \widetilde{\mathcal{C}}, \widetilde{\mathcal{R}} \rangle$. $\mathcal{P}$ does as following:
    (1) Compute commitments for each bit w_i as $\widetilde{\mathsf{Com}}(w_i; r_i) = (W_i, \widehat{W}_i, P_i)$, where $W_i = g^{w_i} h^{r_i}$, $\widehat{W}_i = \hat{g}^{w_i} \hat{h}^{r_i}$, $P_i = g^{r_i(2w_i-1)} h^{r_i^2}$.
    (2) For the output of the circuit, let the commitment be $C_{op} = g, \widehat{C}_{op} = \hat{g}$.
    (3) For every NAND-gate in C with two input values c_0 and c_1 which are committed by $(C_0, \widehat{C}_0, P_0) = \widetilde{\mathsf{Com}}(c_0; \alpha)$ and $(C_1, \widehat{C}_1, P_1) = \widetilde{\mathsf{Com}}(c_1; \beta)$, the prover $\mathcal{P}$ computes commitments $(C_2, \widehat{C}_2, P_2) = \widetilde{\mathsf{Com}}(c_2; \gamma)$ for the corresponding output value $c_2 = c_0 \mathsf{NAND} c_1$. Besides let $C_0 C_1 C_2^2 g^{-2} = g^m h^r$ where $m = c_0 + c_1 + 2c_2 - 2$ and $r = \alpha + \beta + 2\gamma$, then $\mathcal{P}$ computes a proof $P = g^{r(2m-1)} h^{r^2}$ for this gate.
    (4) Let π consist of commitments for all wires and proofs for all gates. $\mathcal{P}$ sends π to $\mathcal{V}$.
- **Stage 3 : Verification.**
  - V : Output 1 if all of the following holds, otherwise output 0.
    (1) Every wire's commitment is correct.
    (2) For every NAND-gate, with associated commitments $(C_0, \widehat{C}_0, P_0)$, $(C_1, \widehat{C}_1, P_1)$, $(C_2, \widehat{C}_2, P_2)$ and the proof P, let $M = C_0 C_1 C_2^2 g^{-2}$, and then M satisfies $e(M, Mg^{-1}) = e(h, P)$.

Fig. 4. Protocol $\langle \overline{\mathcal{P}}, \overline{\mathcal{V}} \rangle$

Obviously, $\mathcal{A}$ runs in poly-time. Then, we analyze the success probability of $\mathcal{A}$.

First, note that $\mathcal{A}$ may abort in Steps 1 and 3 if $\mathcal{P}^*$'s messages are invalid. Since the distribution of the messages sent by $\mathcal{A}$ are identical to the messages generated by an honest verifier, $\Pr[\mathcal{A} \text{ not abort}] \geq p_0$.

Then, we analyze the probability that $\mathcal{A}$ outputs Fail1 and Fail2. Clearly, under the XKEA assumption, $\Pr[\mathcal{A} \text{ outputs Fail1}] \leq negl$. Besides, the event that $\mathcal{A}$ outputs Fail2 means that there do not exist invalid opening messages and inconsistent NAND-gate, which implies that $\mathcal{C}$ must be a satisfiable circuit.

As a result, the success probability of $\mathcal{A}$ is at least $p_0 - negl(n)$, which contradicts the VDHIA. This proves the soundness. □

5.2 Leakage-Resilient Zero-Knowledge

The Simulator $\mathcal{S}$. Let $\mathcal{V}^*$ be a PPT cheating verifier, and $\mathcal{X}_{\mathcal{V}^*}$ be the KEA extractor for $\mathcal{V}^*$. The simulator receives as input 1^n, a circuit C with n input wires, and uses $\mathcal{X}_{\mathcal{V}^*}$ as a subroutine. tape is initialized with the null string.

- **Stage 1: Jointly generating parameter of commitment scheme** $\langle \widetilde{\mathcal{C}}, \mathcal{R} \rangle$:
  - $\mathcal{S} \to \mathcal{V}^*$: Generate BG $\leftarrow \mathcal{BGG}$, and pick $A \leftarrow \mathbb{G}$, and send (BG, A) to $\mathcal{V}$.
    Leakage query : Set tape = tape $\|$ (BG, A). After receiving a leakage function F from $\mathcal{V}^*$, answer it by querying $\mathcal{L}_w^n$ with $F'(w) = F(w, \text{tape})$.
  - $\mathcal{S} \leftarrow \mathcal{V}^*$: Run $\mathcal{V}^*$ and $\mathcal{X}_{\mathcal{V}^*}$ on input (BG, A) to get $(h, B; t)$ and $(\hat{g}, \hat{h})$. If $e(g, B) = e(h, A)$ but $g^t \neq h$ then output abort.
- **Stage 2 : Generating the Proof:**
  - $\mathcal{S} \to \mathcal{V}^*$: If $e(g, B) \neq e(h, A)$ or $e(g, \hat{h}) \neq e(\hat{g}, h)$ then $\mathcal{S}$ aborts. Else, let CRS = (BG, $h, \hat{g}, \hat{h}$), $\tau = t$. $\mathcal{S}$ does as following:
    (1) For the output wire of the circuit, let the commitment be $C_{op} = g, \widehat{C}_{op} = \hat{g}$. For every other wire, $\mathcal{S}$ just commits to 0.
    (2) For every NAND-gate in C with two input commitments $(C_0 = g^{c_0} h^\alpha, \widehat{C}_0, P_0)$ and $(C_1 = g^{c_1} h^\beta, \widehat{C}_1, P_1)$, and an output commitment $(C_2 = g^{c_2} h^\gamma, \widehat{C}_2, P_2)$, $\mathcal{S}$ computes $r = \alpha + \beta + 2\gamma + (c_0 + c_1 + 2c_2 - 2)t^{-1}$, and then computes a simulated proof $P = g^{-r} h^{r^2}$ for this gate.
    (3) Let π consist of commitments for all wires and proofs for all gates. Send π to $\mathcal{V}^*$.

    Leakage query : Note that since $\mathcal{S}$ holds the trapdoor key τ, it can equivocate the commitments, i.e., it can compute both the random coins that result in a commitment to bit 0 and the random coins that result in a commitment to bit 1. Let ρ be a string that consists of the random coins for both cases. Define a function $R(\mathsf{C}, \rho, w)$ as follows:
    (a) For the commitments corresponding to the input wires of C, R selects from ρ the random coins corresponding to witness w.
    (b) For the commitments corresponding to the middle wires of C (i.e., the wires between the input gates and the output gate), R first computes the values of the middle wires using the witness w, and then selects the random coins corresponding to these values from ρ.

    Let r' denote the concatenation of all the random coins selected from ρ in the above manner. Finally, R outputs r'. Now, the simulator $\mathcal{S}$ answers by querying $\mathcal{L}_w^n$ with $F'(w) = F(w, \text{tape} \| R(\mathsf{C}, \rho, w))$.

Now, we have completed the description of $\mathcal{S}$. $\mathcal{S}$ outputs whatever is the final view of $\mathcal{V}^*$.

Lemma 2. *Protocol* $\langle \overline{\mathcal{P}}, \overline{\mathcal{V}} \rangle$ *is a leakage-resilient zero-knowledge protocol.*

Proof. To prove this lemma, we need to prove that the view of $\mathcal{V}^*$ generated when interacting with the simulator $\mathcal{S}$ is indistinguishable from the view generated when interacting with the real prover. Let us consider the following hybrids.

H_0: In this hybrid, the simulator $\mathcal{S}$ holds the witness w and interacts with $\mathcal{V}^*$ just as the honest prover. Leakage queries are answered directly based on w and the random coins it used. Clearly, this corresponds to the real interaction.

H_1: This hybrid is same as H_0 except that in the second round, $\mathcal{S}$ runs $\mathcal{V}^*$ and $\mathcal{X}_{\mathcal{V}^*}$ to get $(h, B; t)$ and $(\hat{g}, \hat{h})$. If $e(g, B) = e(h, A)$ but $g^t \neq h$ then output abort. Leakage queries are answered in the same way as in H_0.

H_2: This hybrid is just like in H_1 except that instead of using the witness w, $\mathcal{S}$ commits to 0 for all the input wires and middle wires, and generates a simulated proof using the trapdoor $\tau = t$. Leakage queries are handled as follows. With the witness w, $\mathcal{S}$ uses the function $R(\mathsf{C}, \rho, w)$ (described above) to select corresponding random strings, and let r' be the final output of R. The simulator answers a leakage query F by computing $F(w, \mathsf{tape} \parallel r')$.

H_3: This hybrid is same as H_2 except that the simulator $\mathcal{S}$ doesn't hold a witness any more. Thus it handles leakage queries slightly differently. After receiving F, it creates a function $F'(w) = F(w, \mathsf{tape})$, and then sends $F'(\cdot)$ to the leakage oracle $\mathcal{L}^n_w$. Note that this hybrid corresponds to our final simulation.

Now, we just need to prove that the indistinguishability of H_0 and H_3.

Firstly, indistinguishability of hybrids H_0 and H_1 directly follows the KEA assumption.

Secondly, H_2 is different from H_1 only in the way of generating the commitments and proofs, and answering the leakage queries.

(1) In H_2, the commitments are generated by committing to 0. From the computationally hiding of the commitment scheme, the commitments generated in hybrids H_1 and H_2 are computationally indistinguishable.

(2) Note that the proof for $C = g^m h^r$ just can proving $m \in \{0, 1\}$. If $m = 0, C = h^r, P = g^{-r} h^{r^2}$. If $m = 1, C = gh^{r_1} = g^{(1+tr_1)} = h^r$ where $r_1 = r - t^{-1}$, $P' = g^{r_1} h^{r_1^2} = g^{(r-t^{-1}+t(r-t^{-1})^2)} = g^{-r} h^{r^2} = P$. Thus, the distribution of proofs generated in H_2 is equal to that of proofs generated in H_1.

(3) Finally, since R outputs uniform randomness consistent with the witness used in hybrid H_1, it holds that the leakage queries are also answered and distributed correctly.

Thus, the outputs of H_1 and H_2 are computationally indistinguishable.

Finally, note that the simulator in hybrid H_3 having access to the leakage oracle can also answer the leakage queries correctly, i.e., the outputs of H_2 and H_3 are identical.

This completes the proof. $\square$

References

1. Alwen, J., Dodis, Y., Wichs, D.: Leakage-resilient public-key cryptography in the bounded-retrieval model. In: Halevi, S. (ed.) CRYPTO 2009. LNCS, vol. 5677, pp. 36–54. Springer, Heidelberg (2009)
2. Abe, M., Fehr, S.: Perfect NIZK with adaptive soundness. In: Vadhan, S.P. (ed.) TCC 2007. LNCS, vol. 4392, pp. 118–136. Springer, Heidelberg (2007)
3. Ananth, P., Goyal, V., Pandey, O.: Interactive proofs under continual memory leakage. In: Garay, J.A., Gennaro, R. (eds.) CRYPTO 2014, Part II. LNCS, vol. 8617, pp. 164–182. Springer, Heidelberg (2014)

4. Bitansky, N., Canetti, R., Halevi, S.: Leakage-tolerant interactive protocols. In: Cramer, R. (ed.) TCC 2012. LNCS, vol. 7194, pp. 266–284. Springer, Heidelberg (2012)

5. Barak, B., Goldreich, O., Goldwasser, S., Lindell, Y.: Resettably-sound zero-knowledge and its applications. In: FOCS 2002, pp. 116–125 (2001)

6. Boyle, E., Goldwasser, S., Jain, A., Kalai, Y.T.: Multiparty computation secure against continual memory leakage. In: STOC, pp. 1235–1254. ACM (2012)

7. Bellare, M., Palacio, A.: The knowledge-of-exponent assumptions and 3-round zero-knowledge protocols. In: Franklin, M. (ed.) CRYPTO 2004. LNCS, vol. 3152, pp. 273–289. Springer, Heidelberg (2004)

8. Damgård, I.: Towards practical public key systems secure against chosen ciphertext attacks. In: Feigenbaum, J. (ed.) CRYPTO 1991. LNCS, vol. 576, pp. 445–456. Springer, Heidelberg (1992)

9. Dolev, D., Dwork, C., Naor, M.: Non-malleable cryptography (extended abstract). In: STOC, pp. 542–552 (1991)

10. Dodis, Y., Haralambiev, K., Lpez-Alt, A., Wichs, D.: Cryptography against continuous memory attacks. In: FOCS, pp. 511–520 (2010)

11. Dwork, C., Naor, M., Sahai, A.: Concurrent zero-knowledge. J. ACM 51(6), 851–898 (2004)

12. Dziembowski, S., Pietrzak, K.: Leakage-resilient cryptography. In: FOCS, pp. 293–302 (2008)

13. Garg, S., Jain, A., Sahai, A.: Leakage-resilient zero knowledge. In: Rogaway, P. (ed.) CRYPTO 2011. LNCS, vol. 6841, pp. 297–315. Springer, Heidelberg (2011)

14. Goldwasser, S., Micali, S., Rackoff, C.: The knowledge complexity of interactive proof systems. In: STOC, pp. 291–304 (1985)

15. Groth, J., Ostrovsky, R., Sahai, A.: Perfect non-interactive zero knowledge for NP. In: Vaudenay, S. (ed.) EUROCRYPT 2006. LNCS, vol. 4004, pp. 339–358. Springer, Heidelberg (2006)

16. Groth, J.: Short pairing-based non-interactive zero-knowledge arguments. In: Abe, M. (ed.) ASIACRYPT 2010. LNCS, vol. 6477, pp. 321–340. Springer, Heidelberg (2010)

17. Gupta, D., Sahai, A.: On Constant-Round Concurrent Zero-Knowledge from a Knowledge Assumption. In Cryptology ePrint Archive, Report 2012/572

18. Hada, S., Tanaka, T.: On the existence of 3-round zero-knowledge protocols. In: Krawczyk, H. (ed.) CRYPTO 1998. LNCS, vol. 1462, pp. 408–423. Springer, Heidelberg (1998)

19. Kocher, P.C.: Timing attacks on implementations of diffie-hellman, RSA, DSS, and other systems. In: Koblitz, N. (ed.) CRYPTO 1996. LNCS, vol. 1109, pp. 104–113. Springer, Heidelberg (1996)

20. Li, H., Niu, Q., Liang, B.: Leakage-resilient zero-knowledge proofs of knowledge for NP. In: Lopez, J., Huang, X., Sandhu, R. (eds.) NSS 2013. LNCS, vol. 7873, pp. 365–380. Springer, Heidelberg (2013)

21. Osvik, D.A., Shamir, A., Tromer, E.: Cache attacks and countermeasures: the case of AES. In: Pointcheval, D. (ed.) CT-RSA 2006. LNCS, vol. 3860, pp. 1–20. Springer, Heidelberg (2006)

22. Pandey, O.: Achieving constant round leakage-resilient zero-knowledge. In: Lindell, Y. (ed.) TCC 2014. LNCS, vol. 8349, pp. 146–166. Springer, Heidelberg (2014)

23. Pedersen, T.P.: Non-interactive and information-theoretic secure verifiable secret sharing. In: Feigenbaum, J. (ed.) CRYPTO 1991. LNCS, vol. 576, pp. 129–140. Springer, Heidelberg (1992)
24. Prabhakaran, M., Xue, R.: Statistically hiding sets. In: Fischlin, M. (ed.) CT-RSA 2009. LNCS, vol. 5473, pp. 100–116. Springer, Heidelberg (2009)
25. Quisquater, J.-J., Samyde, D.: Electromagnetic analysis (EMA): measures and counter-measures for smart cards. In: Attali, S., Jensen, T. (eds.) E-smart 2001. LNCS, vol. 2140, pp. 200–210. Springer, Heidelberg (2001)

Modelling Ciphersuite and Version Negotiation in the TLS Protocol

Benjamin Dowling$^{(\boxtimes)}$ and Douglas Stebila

Queensland University of Technology, Brisbane, Australia
{b1.dowling,stebila}@qut.edu.au

Abstract. Real-world cryptographic protocols such as the widely used Transport Layer Security (TLS) protocol support many different combinations of cryptographic algorithms (called ciphersuites) and simultaneously support different versions. Recent advances in provable security have shown that most modern TLS ciphersuites are secure authenticated and confidential channel establishment (ACCE) protocols, but these analyses generally focus on single ciphersuites in isolation. In this paper we extend the ACCE model to cover protocols with many different sub-protocols, capturing both multiple ciphersuites and multiple versions, and define a security notion for secure negotiation of the optimal sub-protocol. We give a generic theorem that shows how secure negotiation follows, with some additional conditions, from the authentication property of secure ACCE protocols. Using this framework, we analyse the security of ciphersuite and three variants of version negotiation in TLS, including a recently proposed mechanism for detecting fallback attacks.

Keywords: Transport layer security (tls) · Ciphersuite negotiation · Version negotiation · Downgrade attacks · Cryptographic protocols

1 Introduction

The security of much communication on the Internet depends on the Transport Layer Security (TLS) protocol [1–3], previously known as the Secure Sockets Layer (SSL) protocol [4]. TLS allows two parties to authenticate each other using public keys and subsequently establish a secure channel which provides confidentiality and integrity of messages. The general structure of all versions of SSL and TLS is that a *handshake protocol* is run, in which a set of cryptographic preferences are first negotiated, then an authenticated key exchange protocol is used to perform mututal or server-to-client authentication and establish a shared session key; and then the *record layer* is active, in which the shared session key is used with authenticated encryption for secure communication. TLS supports many combinations of cryptographic parameters, called *ciphersuites*: as of this writing, more than 300 ciphersuites have been standardized, with various combinations of digital signature algorithms, key exchange methods, hash functions, ciphers and modes, and authentication codes.

© Springer International Publishing Switzerland 2015
E. Foo and D. Stebila (Eds.): ACISP 2015, LNCS 9144, pp. 270–288, 2015.
DOI: 10.1007/978-3-319-19962-7_16

Given the paramount importance of TLS, formal understanding of its security is an important goal of cryptography. Wagner and Schneier [5] were among the first to study SSL, and in particular compared SSLv3 [4] to SSLv2 [6]. A key difference was that SSLv3 provided authentication of the full handshake, whereas SSLv2 omitted the ciphersuite negotiation messages, leaving SSLv2 vulnerable to ciphersuite rollback attacks: an active attack could force clients and servers to negotiate weaker ciphersuites than the best they mutually support.

Provable Security of TLS. A significant body of work is devoted to studying the provable security of TLS: the majority of it focuses on individual ciphersuites. Early work on the provable security of TLS analyzed truncated forms of the TLS handshake [7,8] and a simplified record layer [9]. More recently, unmodified versions of the TLS constructions have been studied by introducing suitable security definitions. Paterson et al. [10] showed that certain modes of authenticated encryption in the TLS record layer satisfy a property known as *secure length-hiding authenticated encryption.* In 2012, Jager et al. [11] showed that, under suitable assumptions on the underlying cryptographic primitives, the signed-Diffie–Hellman TLS ciphersuite is a secure *authenticated and confidential channel establishment (ACCE) protocol,* yielding the first full proof of security of an unmodified TLS ciphersuite. Subsequent efforts [12–14] have shown that most other TLS ciphersuites (using static or ephemeral Diffie–Hellman, RSA key transport, or pre-shared keys) are also secure. Other recent approaches to analyzing TLS include an alternative composability notion [15] and formal verification of an implementation [16].

Previous security results on TLS all focus on analyzing a single ciphersuite in isolation. Among other things, TLS allows for versions and ciphersuites to be negotiated within the protocol, sessions to be resumed, renegotiation within a session. Moreover, in practice servers often use the same long-term key in many different ciphersuites, and browsers re-attempt failed handshakes with lower versions. This variety of complex functionality leaves a gap between single-ciphersuite results and real-world security. Some work has tried to bridge that gap: Giesen et al. [17] extended the ACCE model to analyze the renegotiation security of TLS in light of the attack of Ray and Dispensa [18]; Mavrogiannopoulos et al. [19] demonstrated a cross-ciphersuite attack first suggested by Wagner and Schneier [5] when the same long-term signing key is used in two different key exchange methods; Bergsma et al. [20] developed an ACCE-based model for multi-ciphersuite security and showed that the Secure Shell (SSH) protocol is multi-ciphersuite security, though the Mavrogiannopolous et al. attack rules out a general proof that TLS is multi-ciphersuite secure; and Bhargavan et al. [21] showed that some combinations of ciphersuites do support key agility (a concept related to multi-ciphersuite security).

Ciphersuite and Version Negotiation. This work aims to give a formal treatment of the negotiation of ciphersuites and versions in real-world protocols like TLS. For *ciphersuite negotiation* in TLS, the client sends in its first handshake message a list of its supported ciphersuites in order of preference, and the server responds with one of those that it also supports. With regards to *version negotiation*, most browsers and servers support multiple versions of SSL and TLS, with the majority supporting and accepting SSLv3 and TLSv1.0 (with more modern software also supporting TLSv1.1 and TLSv1.2). The differences between versions can significantly affect security: TLSv1.1 and TLSv1.2 are less vulnerable to certain weaknesses in record layer encryption in some ciphersuites; SSLv3 does not support extensions in the `ClientHello` and `ServerHello` negotiation messages; and some extensions such as the Renegotiation Information Extension [22] are essential to prevent certain types of attacks; and some ciphersuites with newer, more efficient and secure algorithms are only supported in TLSv1.2.

The TLS protocol standards support a limited version negotiation mechanism at present: the client sends the highest version it supports, and the server responds with the highest version it supports that is less than or equal to the client's version, and that is the version the parties continue to use. However, some server implementations do not correctly respond to `ClientHello` messages containing higher versions, and instead of returning their highest supported version in the `ServerHello` message will instead fail and return an error. Thus, in practice a more complex version negotiation mechanism is often employed by web browsers, sometimes called the "downgrade dance". The client's browser will try to negotiate the highest version it supports (say, TLSv1.2); if the handshake fails, then the browser will retry with each lower enabled version (TLSv1.1, TLSv1.0, SSLv3) until it succeeds. This improved compatibility with incorrect server implementation comes at the cost of decreased efficiency and more importantly decreased security: the client and server have no way of detecting whether the negotiated version is actually the highest version they both support or a lower version due to an attacker maliciously injecting failure messages. In light of this potential downgrade attack, a very recent Internet-Draft by Möller and Langley has proposed a new backwards-compatible mechanism for detecting such attacks [23], but as of this writing has yet to be standardized or deployed. The SCSV extension is proposed to work as follows: If the client is falling back to an earlier version due to a handshake failure, the client includes the SCSV value indicating that it has fallen back; if the server observes the fallback SCSV but supports a higher version than the client requests, the server returns an error indicating that inappropriate fallback has been detected.

Contributions. We investigate the security of version and ciphersuite negotiation in TLS. We do so by introducing an extension to the ACCE security model that generically captures negotiation of "sub-protocols". In particular, using ideas from the multi-ciphersuite ACCE security experiment of Bergsma et al. [20], we extend the ACCE security experiment to include "sub-protocols": a single protocol (such as TLS) consists of a *negotiation protocol* NP and several *sub-protocols* $\overrightarrow{\text{SP}}$ (such as different ciphersuites or different versions), and in each session the parties use the negotiation protocol to identify which sub-protocol they will use for that session. We define **secure negotiation** for a negotiable protocol, and use this to derive a negotiation-authentication theorem which allows us to relate the security of sub-protocol negotiation to ACCE authentication under certain conditions. Intuitively, if each sub-protocol individually is a secure ACCE protocol with an independent long-term key, and if the transcript of all of the messages in the negotiation protocol is authenticated by the sub-protocol, then the authentication detects any attempt by an attacker to carry out a downgrade attack. It is important to note that the aforementioned cross-ciphersuite attack breaks ACCE authentication security under long-term key reuse setting; thus, in order to obtain results on multi-ciphersuite TLS, our framework assume long-term keys are independent for each sub-protocol. Existing analyses of TLS show ([11–14]) that authentication security of TLS holds under independent long-term key assumptions.

Having established the secure negotiation framework and tools we proceed to study **version and ciphersuite negotiation in TLS** in several forms:

1. *Ciphersuite negotiation within a single version:* For a fixed version of TLS, by application of the negotiation-authentication theorem we show that TLS provides secure ciphersuite negotiation.
2. *Version negotiation, no fallback:* For clients and servers that support multiple versions of TLS but do not attempt to fallback to earlier versions upon handshake failure, we show that TLS also provides secure version negotiation via the negotiation-authentication theorem.
3. *Version negotiation, with fallback:* For clients and servers that support multiple versions of TLS and where the client *will* fallback to earlier versions if the handshake fails, we see that secure negotiation is not provided demonstrating that our secure negotiation definition does detect this undesired behaviour.
4. *Version negotiation, with fallback using signalling ciphersuite value (SCSV):* A recent Internet-Draft [23] proposes the use of a special flag in the ClientHello message. We show that this SCSV does provide TLS with a secure version negotiation mechanism even when fallbacks are used.

2   The TLS Protocol

In this section, we give the details for ciphersuite negotiation and three variants of version negotiation in the TLS protocol. The following is a description of the two messages most relevant to TLS ciphersuite and version negotiation: the ClientHello and ServerHello messages; descriptions of the subsequent messages can be found in the TLS protocol specification [3].

- ClientHello: Sent by the client to begin the TLS handshake. Consists of: the highest version that the client supports v; a random nonce r_c; the optional identifier of previous session that the client wishes to resume; a list of client ciphersuite preferences $\vec{c}$; and an optional list of extensions extensions describing additional options or functionality.
- ServerHello: Sent by the server in response to ClientHello. Consists of: the negotiated choice of version v; a random nonce r_s; a session identifier; the negotiated choice of ciphersuite c^*; and an optional list of extensions.

2.1   Ciphersuite Negotiation in TLS

As indicated above, in TLS the client sends in $\mathtt{ClientHello}.\vec{c}$ a list of supported ciphersuites, ordered from most preferred to least preferred. The server also has a list of supported ciphersuites ordered by preference, and selects its most preferred ciphersuite that the client also supports. This ciphersuite negotiation protocol $\mathrm{NP_{cs}}$ is described algorithmically in Figure 1. In our formalism, the adversary activates each party with the vector $\vec{c}$ of their ordered ciphersuite preferences for that session.

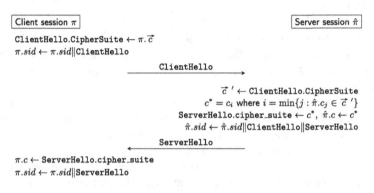

Fig. 1. $\mathrm{NP_{cs}}$: Ciphersuite negotiation protocol in TLS

2.2   Version Negotiation in TLS

As indicated in the standards, in TLS the client sends in $\mathtt{ClientHello}.v$ the highest version of TLS supports, and the server responds in its $\mathtt{ServerHello}$ message with the chosen version. In practice, buggy TLS server implementations sometimes reject unrecognised versions rather than negotiating a lower version, so some TLS clients will carry out fallback, where they try again with a lower supported version. We identify three variants of TLS version negotiation as follows. Recall again that in our formalism, the adversary activates each party with a vector $\vec{v}$ of their supported versions for that session.

- *No-fallback version negotiation*, denoted $\mathrm{NP_v}$: Version negotiation as defined by the TLS standards (Figure 1).
- *Fallback version negotiation (the "downgrade dance")*, denoted $\mathrm{NP_{v\text{-}fb}}$: Version negotiation as defined by the TLS standards, but allowing version fallback (Figure 3).
- *Fallback version negotiation with SCSV*, denoted $\mathrm{NP_{v\text{-}fb\text{-}scsv}}$: The client proceeds as in fallback version negotiation, but when falling back to a lower version, the client also includes in its ciphersuite list a *fallback signalling ciphersuite value* (SCSV) to indicate that it has fallen back; this ciphersuite cannot be negotiated, and instead simply serves as a flag. If the server sees that it would negotiate a version lower than its highest version and the

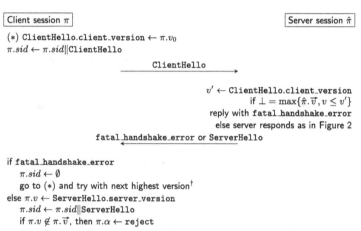

Fig. 2. NP_v: No-fallback version negotiation protocol in standard TLS

Client session π		Server session $\hat{\pi}$
$(*)$ ClientHello.client_version $\leftarrow \pi.v_0$		
$\pi.sid \leftarrow \pi.sid\|$ClientHello		
	ClientHello $\longrightarrow$	
		$v' \leftarrow$ ClientHello.client_version
		if $\perp = \max\{\hat{\pi}.\vec{v}, v \leq v'\}$
		reply with fatal_handshake_error
		else server responds as in Figure 2
	$\longleftarrow$ fatal_handshake_error or ServerHello	
if fatal_handshake_error		
$\quad \pi.sid \leftarrow \emptyset$		
$\quad$ go to $(*)$ and try with next highest version†		
else $\pi.v \leftarrow$ ServerHello.server_version		
$\quad \pi.sid \leftarrow \pi.sid\|$ServerHello		
$\quad$ if $\pi.v \notin \pi.\vec{v}$, then $\pi.\alpha \leftarrow$ reject		

† Note that the "go to $(*)$" step in the client execution means that execution remains in the same session for the client; however, the server, receiving a new ClientHello, will start a new session.

Fig. 3. $NP_{v\text{-fb}}$: Fallback version negotiation in TLS (the "downgrade dance")

client has included the fallback SCSV, the server aborts and responds with inappropriate_fallback (Figure 4).

Note that the transcript ($\pi.sid$ in our formalism) "resets" in fallback version negotiation: matching conversations are based solely on the last handshake, rather than all handshakes that may have fallen back.

3 Security Definitions

We begin by introducing the standard *authenticated and confidential channel establishment (ACCE)* protocol framework as introduced by Jager et al. [11].

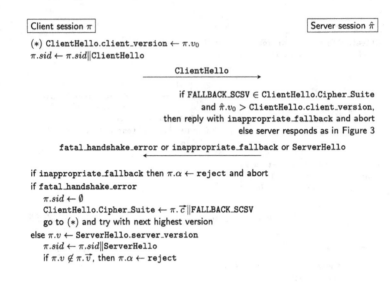

Fig. 4. $NP_{v\text{-fb-scsv}}$: Fallback negotiation in TLS with signalling ciphersuite value

We then extend the definition to cover protocols which negotiate a sub-protocol, and define the secure negotiation property.

3.1 Authenticated and Confidential Channel Establishment (ACCE) Protocols

An ACCE protocol is a multi-party protocol. Each instance of the protocol is executed between two parties: during the *pre-accept phase*, the parties establish a shared secret key and mutually authenticate each other; this is followed by a *post-accept phase*, which allows parties to transmitted authenticated and encrypted payload data. We now proceed to describe the ACCE security model in detail, beginning with the per-session variables and adversary interaction. Note that, for simplicity, we restrict to the mutual authentication setting as in the original ACCE definition of Jager et al. [11], but our results apply equally to server-only authenticated ACCE [12,13]. Each ciphersuite in TLS is considered a separate ACCE protocol with independent long-term keys, which limits the application of the framework to implementations of TLS with no long-term key reuse.

Parties and Sessions. The execution environment consists of n_P parties, denoted $P_1, P_2, \ldots P_{n_P}$. Each party P_i has a long-term public/private key pair (pk_i, sk_i), generated according to the protocol specification. Each party can execute multiple runs of the protocol either sequentially or in parallel; each run is referred to as a *session*, and π_i^s denotes the sth session at party i. For each session, the party maintains a collection of the following *per-session variables*, and we overload the notation π_i^s to refer to both the session itself and the corresponding collection of per-session variables.

- $\rho \in \{\texttt{init}, \texttt{resp}\}$: The role of the party in the session.
- $\mathsf{pid} \in [n_P]$: The index of the intended peer of this session.
- $\alpha \in \{\texttt{in-progress}, \texttt{accept}, \texttt{reject}\}$: The execution status of the session.
- k: A session key, or $\bot$; k may for example consist of sub-keys for bi-directional authentication and encryption.
- T: Transcript of all messages sent and received by the party in this session.
- sid: A *session identifier*, consisting of an ordered subset of messages in T as defined by the protocol specification.[1]
- Any additional state specific to the protocol (such as ephemeral Diffie–Hellman exponents).
- Any additional state specific to the security experiment.

We use the notation $\pi_i^s.\rho$ etc. to denote each variable of a particular session.

While a session has set $\alpha \leftarrow \texttt{in-progress}$, we say that the session is in the *pre-accept phase*; after the session has set $\alpha \leftarrow \texttt{accept}$, we say that the session is in the *post-accept phase*.

Definition 1 (ACCE Protocol). *An ACCE protocol* P *consists of a probabilistic long-term public-private key pair generation algorithm, as well as probabilistic algorithms defining how the party generates and responds to protocol messages. The protocol specification also includes a* stateful length-hiding authenticated encryption (sLHAE) *scheme* StE *[10, 11] for sending and receiving payload data on the record layer.*

Adversary Interaction. In the security experiment, the adversary controls all interactions between parties: the adversary activates sessions with initialization information; it delivers messages to parties, and can reorder, alter, delete, replace, and create messages. The adversary can also compromise certain long-term and per-session values. The adversary interacts parties using the following queries.

The first query models normal, unencrypted operation of the protocol, generally corresponding to the pre-accept phase.

- $\mathsf{Send}(i, s, m) \xrightarrow{\$} m'$: The adversary sends message m to session π_i^s. Party P_i processes m according to the protocol specification and its per-session variables π_i^s, updates its per-session state, and optionally outputs an outgoing message m'.

  There is a distinguished initialization message which allows the adversary to activate the session with certain information, such as the intended role ρ the party in the session, the intended communication partner pid, and any additional protocol-specific information; when we extend to the negotiable setting in the next subsection, this will include ciphersuite and/or version preferences.

  This query may return error symbol $\bot$ if the session has entered state $\alpha = \texttt{accept}$ and no more protocol messages are to be transmitted over the unencrypted channel.

---

[1] Our separation of the transcript and session identifier follows [20] and is a slight change compared to the original ACCE model [11] to allow for consideration of protocols where some messages are not authenticated.

The next two queries model adversarial compromise of long-term and per-session secrets.

- Corrupt$(i) \xrightarrow{\$} sk_i$: Returns long-term secret key sk_i of party P_i.
- Reveal$(i, s) \xrightarrow{\$} \pi_i^s.k$: Returns session key $\pi_i^s.k$.

The final two queries, Encrypt and Decrypt, model communication over the encrypted channel. The adversary can direct parties to encrypt plaintexts and obtains the corresponding ciphertext. The adversary can deliver ciphertexts to parties, which are then decrypted. To accommodate defining the security property of indistinguishability of ciphertexts, the Encrypt query takes two messages, and one of the tasks of the adversary is to distinguish which was encrypted. The exact specification of Encrypt and Decrypt is specified in Figure 4 of [24] (the full version of [11]), and is omitted in this paper as these queries are not required for defining negotiable security.

ACCE Security Definitions. We now present the two sub-properties that define security of ACCE protocols. Like authenticated key exchange (AKE) security definitions, the ACCE framework requires that the protocol provides secure mutual authentication. The difference lies in the encryption-challenge: instead of key indistinguishability (found in AKE experiments) the ACCE framework requires that all payload data transmitted between parties (during the post-accept stage) is over an authenticated and confidential channel. The original motivation for this distinction is that real-world protocols often have key confirmation messages (for example, TLS's `Finished` message), which can act as a key-distinguisher in a AKE security framework. ACCE solves this by focusing on message confidentiality and integrity instead of key indistinguishability.

We start by defining matching conversations and the mutual authentication property of an ACCE protocol. Matching conversations is a property useful for describing the correctness and authentication of a protocol, first introduced by Bellare and Rogaway [25]. [2]

Definition 2 (Matching Sessions). *A session π_j^t matches session π_i^s if:*

- *if P_i sent the last message in $\pi_i^s.sid$, then $\pi_j^t.sid$ is a prefix of $\pi_i^s.sid$; or*
- *if P_i received the last message in $\pi_i^s.sid$, then $\pi_i^s.sid = \pi_j^t.sid$,*

where X is a prefix of Y if X contains at least one message and the messages in X are identical to and in the same order as the first $|X|$ messages in Y.

Definition 3 (Mutual Authentication). *A session π_i^s accepts maliciously if*

- $\pi_i^s.\alpha = \mathsf{accept}$;
- $\pi_i^s.\mathsf{pid} = j$ *and no* Corrupt(j) *query was issued before $\pi_i^s.\alpha$ was updated to* accept; *and*
- *there is not a unique session π_j^t that matches π_i^s.*

---

[2] Our formulation is a slight variant of Jager et al. [11]: we match on *session identifiers* (a well-defined subset of messages sent and received) rather than the full transcript.

We define $\mathrm{Adv}_{\mathsf{P}}^{\mathrm{acce\text{-}auth}}(\mathcal{A})$ *as the probability that, when probabilistic adversary algorithm* $\mathcal{A}$ *terminates in the ACCE experiment for protocol* P, *there exists a session that has accepted maliciously.*

Channel security for ACCE protocols is defined as the ability of the adversary to break confidentiality or integrity of the channel. As the channel security definition does not play a role in the remainder of this paper, we omit the definition and refer the reader to Definition 5.2 of [11] for details. Using the notation of Bergsma et al. [20], the expression $\mathrm{Adv}_{\mathsf{P}}^{\mathrm{acce\text{-}aenc}}(\mathcal{A})$ denotes the probability that the adversary $\mathcal{A}$ breaks channel security of protocol P.

Definition 4 (ACCE-Secure). *A protocol* P *is said to be* ϵ-*ACCE-secure against an adversary* $\mathcal{A}$ *if we have that* $\mathrm{Adv}_{\mathsf{P}}^{\mathrm{acce\text{-}auth}}(\mathcal{A}) \leq \epsilon$ *and* $\mathrm{Adv}_{\mathsf{P}}^{\mathrm{acce\text{-}aenc}}(\mathcal{A}) \leq \epsilon$.

3.2 Negotiable ACCE Protocols

In this section we define formally a negotiable ACCE protocol and the corresponding security notions. We do so by explaining the differences with Section 3.1. The basis of our definition is the multi-ciphersuite ACCE definition of Bergsma et al. [20], but like the ACCE definitions above we do not consider use of the same long-term key in multiple sub-protocols. We then define the secure negotiation property.

Differences in Execution Environment. A *negotiable ACCE protocol* is composed of a *negotiation protocol* NP and a collection of *sub-protocols* $\overrightarrow{\mathsf{SP}}$; we use the notation $\mathsf{NP}\|\overrightarrow{\mathsf{SP}}$ to denote the combined protocol. For example:

- In TLS with multiple ciphersuites, the negotiation protocol $\mathsf{NP}_{\mathsf{cs}}$ consists of the sending and receiving of the ClientHello and ServerHello messages as shown in Figure 1, and each sub-protocol SP_i corresponds to the remaining messages in ciphersuite i.
- For TLS with multiple versions, each sub-protocol SP_i corresponds to a different version of TLS; the description of the negotiation protocol depends on whether and how fallback is handled, and is described in Section 2.

Parties and Sessions. In a negotiable ACCE protocol, each party P_i has a vector of long-term public/private key pairs $(\overrightarrow{pk_i}, \overrightarrow{sk_i})$, one for each sub-protocol.

Each session in a negotiable ACCE protocol maintains two additional per-session variables:

- $\overrightarrow{n}$: An ordered list of negotiation preferences.
- n: The index of the negotiated sub-protocol.

In the execution of $\mathsf{NP}\|\overrightarrow{\mathsf{SP}}$, the protocol begins by running the negotiation protocol NP, which has as input the ordered list $\overrightarrow{n}$ of negotiation preferences; the negotiation protocol updates per-session variables, and in particular updates the index n of the negotiated sub-protocol. Once the negotiation protocol completes, subprotocol SP_n is run, operating on the same per-session variables.

Adversary Interaction. The adversary can interact with parties exactly as in Section 3.1. The only difference is that in the distinguished initialization message in the Send query, the adversary also includes an ordered list $\vec{n}$ of the sub-protocol preferences that the party should use in that session. For example, in ciphersuite negotiation, the adversary may direct the party to prefer RSA over Diffie–Hellman in one session and Diffie–Hellman over RSA in another session. For version negotiation in TLS, order of the list is descending and contiguous (i.e., if TLSv1.2 and TLSv1.0 are listed as supported, TLSv1.1 must be listed).

Secure Negotiation. Intuitively, a negotiable protocol has secure negotiation if the adversary cannot cause the parties to successfully negotiate a worse sub-protocol than the best one they both support. We formalize this via an optimality function, which will be different for each protocol (for example, the optimality function for TLS ciphersuite negotiation is different from that of TLS version negotiation).

Definition 5 (Optimal Negotiation). *Let* $\omega(\vec{x}, \vec{y}) \to z$ *be a function taking as input two ordered lists and outputting an element of one of the lists or* $\bot$. *We say that two sessions* π_i^s *and* π_j^t *do not have optimal negotiation with respect to* ω *unless* $\pi_i^s.n = \pi_j^t.n = \omega(\pi_i^s.\vec{n}, \pi_j^t.\vec{n})$.

For TLS ciphersuite negotiation, the optimality function yields the first ciphersuite in the server's ordered list of preferences also supported by the client:

$$\omega_{\text{cs}}(\vec{x}, \vec{y}) = y_i, \text{ where } i = \min\{j : y_j \in \vec{x}\} \ . \tag{1}$$

For TLS version negotiation, the optimality function yields the highest version that is supported by both the client and the server:

$$\omega_{\text{vers}}(\vec{x}, \vec{y}) = \max\{\vec{x} \cap \vec{y}\} \ . \tag{2}$$

For TLS version negotiation, we impose the order TLSv1.2 > TLSv1.1 > TLSv1.0 > SSLv3.0 > SSLv2.0.

We can now define what it means for a protocol to have secure negotiation, either of a particular sub-protocol or over all sub-protocols.

Definition 6 (Secure Negotiation of a Sub-Protocol). *We say that a session* π_i^s *has negotiated a sub-protocol* n^* *insecurely with respect to* ω *if*

- $\pi_i^s.\alpha = \text{accept}$;
- $\pi_i^s.n = n^*$;
- π_i^s *has not accepted maliciously (in the sense of Definition 3); and*
- π_i^s *and* π_j^t *do not have optimal negotiation with respect to* ω, *where* π_j^t *is the unique session that matches* π_i^s.

We define $\text{Adv}_{\text{NP}\|\vec{\text{SP}},n^*}^{\text{neg},\omega}(\mathcal{A})$ as the probability that, when $\mathcal{A}$ terminates in the negotiable-ACCE experiment for $\text{NP}\|\vec{\text{SP}}$, there exists a session that has negotiated sub-protocol n^* insecurely with respect to ω.

Remark 1 (Secure Negotiation vs. Authentication). Secure negotiation, as defined is a stronger property than authentication: the third condition of Definition 6 effectively incorporates the authentication security definition. Recall that authentication is based on matching session identifiers; if a protocol uses the full transcript as the session identifier, then negotiation generally reduces to authentication, which is shown in the theorem in the next section. However, if a protocol uses some subset of the transcript as the session identifier, or for example "resets" the session identifier partway through the handshake as in TLS version fallback, then negotiation becomes non-trivially different from authentication and requires further consideration, as we shall see in Section 6.

4   Negotiation-Authentication Theorem

We now present our negotiation-authentication theorem, which allows us under certain conditions to relate the probability of an adversary forcing a user to insecurely negotiate to $\mathtt{NP}\|\mathtt{SP}_n$ to the probability of an adversary breaking authentication in $\mathtt{NP}\|\mathtt{SP}_n$. At first glance, this seems obvious: if all of the messages in a protocol are securely authenticated, then it should be impossible for an adversary to trick the parties into negotiating something sub-optimal. There is a reason why the application of the theorem is not trivial: In practise, not all protocols authenticate all messages in the handshake. As we will see Section 6, version fallback in TLS results in some parts of the negotiation not being authenticated. Historically, ciphersuite downgrade in SSLv2 was possible as the negotiation phase wasn't entirely authenticated.

To be able to apply this theorem, the protocol P has to satisfy certain conditions as shown in the theorem statement below. Precondition 1 captures the notion that protocols where all handshake message are authenticated, or at least all handshake messages related to negotiation are authenticated, should allow us to reduce negotiation security to authentication security. Precondition 2 is a simply that, in the absence of an active adversary, parties negotiate correctly.

Theorem 1. *Let* $\mathtt{NP}\|\overrightarrow{\mathtt{SP}}$ *be a negotiable ACCE protocol and let ω be an optimality function. Suppose that:*

1. *all message sent and received by a party in the negotiation phase are included in the session identifier; and*
2. *in the absence of an active adversary, negotiation is always optimal with respect to ω,*

then for all algorithms $\mathcal{A}$ and for all sub-protocols $\mathtt{SP}_n$, $\mathrm{Adv}_{\mathtt{NP}\|\overrightarrow{\mathtt{SP}},n}^{\mathrm{neg},\omega}(\mathcal{A}) = \mathrm{Adv}_{\mathtt{NP}\|\mathtt{SP}_n}^{\mathrm{acce\text{-}auth}}(\mathcal{A})$.

The proof of Theorem 1 appears in the full version [26]. The brief description of the argument is as follows: By condition 1, both parties can verify that in presence of a passive adversary that negotiation was optimal with respect to ω. Since both parties can verify (via the session identifier) that the negotiation sub-protocol $\mathtt{SP}_n$ is the optimal sub-protocol, and $\mathtt{NP}\|\mathtt{SP}_n$ itself is an ACCE protocol with negligible adversary advantage over a passive adversary, then negotiating to NP||SP$_n$ is both optimal and authenticated with negligible adversary advantage. Once we have related the security of negotiation to the security of authentication as in the equation in the theorem, we can make use of existing results on ACCE authentication security, for example the bounds on $\mathrm{Adv}_{\mathsf{P}}^{\mathsf{acce\text{-}auth}}(\mathcal{B})$ given for ACCE authentication security of P = TLS signed-Diffie–Hellman ciphersuites [11], P = TLS RSA key transport and P = TLS static Diffie–Hellman ciphersuites [12,13].

5   Analysis of TLS Ciphersuite Negotiation

Using our negotiation-authentication theorem from Section 4, we can show that TLS is ciphersuite-negotiation secure. We do this by showing that ciphersuite negotiation in TLS satisfies the two preconditions outlined in our negotiation-authentication theorem, and hence secure negotiation of ciphersuites is, not surprisingly, guaranteed by security of authentication. All outputs of ciphersuite negotiation are included in the session identifier (as seen in Figure 1), thus precondition 1 is satisfied, provided the ciphersuite has secure authentication. In addition, TLS ciphersuite negotiation is optimal in the presence of a passive adversary, so precondition 2 is also satisfied. Details appear in the full version [26].

Corollary 1. *For the TLS protocol with ciphersuite negotiation* NP$_{cs}$ *as described in Figure 1 and TLS ciphersuites* $\overrightarrow{\mathsf{SP}}$, *an adversary* $\mathcal{A}$ *who can force a user to negotiate insecurely to ciphersuite* SP$_n$ *with respect to the TLS ciphersuite optimality function* ω_{cs} *from equation (1) can also break authentication of that ciphersuite:* $\mathrm{Adv}_{\mathsf{NP}_{cs}||\overrightarrow{\mathsf{SP}},n}^{\mathsf{neg},\omega_{cs}}(\mathcal{A}) = \mathrm{Adv}_{\mathsf{SP}_n}^{\mathsf{acce\text{-}auth}}(\mathcal{A}).$

6   Analysis of TLS Version Negotiation

In this section, we consider the three variants of TLS version negotiation identified in Section 2.2. The no-fallback version negotiation mechanism specified by the TLS standard, can easily be seen to be secure using our negotiation-authentication mechanism. When version fallback is permitted, version negotiation is no longer secure, as we demonstrate with a counterexample, and thus our model successfully captures this weakness of fallback. Finally, when the signalling ciphersuite value (SCSV) version fallback detection mechanism is used, we can show that TLS becomes version-negotiable secure.

6.1   TLS No-Fallback Version Negotiation is Secure

It is straightforward to apply our negotiation-authentication theorem to show that TLS with no-fallback version negotiation (NP$_v$ described in Figure 2), provides secure version negotiation. Here the session identifier consists of the entire transcript, which includes the client and server's version information, so precondition 1 of Theorem 1 is satisfied. It is clear that TLS provides optimal version negotiation in the presence of a passive adversary, so precondition 2 is satisfied. Thus the negotiation-authentication theorem yields Corollary 2. Details appear in the full version [26].

Corollary 2. *For the TLS protocol with no-fallback version negotiation* $\mathsf{NP_v}$ *as described in Figure 2 and TLS versions* $\overrightarrow{\mathsf{SP}}$, *an adversary* $\mathcal{A}$ *who can force a user to negotiate insecurely to version* SP_n *with respect to the TLS version optimality*
• *function* ω_{vers} *from equation (2) can also break authentication of that version:*
$$\mathrm{Adv}^{\mathsf{neg},\omega_{\mathsf{vers}}}_{\mathsf{NP_v}\|\overrightarrow{\mathsf{SP}},n}(\mathcal{A}) = \mathrm{Adv}^{\mathsf{acce\text{-}auth}}_{\mathsf{SP}_n}(\mathcal{A}).$$

6.2   TLS Fallback Version Negotiation is Not Secure

When examining version negotiation in TLS with fallback ($\mathsf{NP_{v\text{-}fb}}$ from Figure 3), notice that many different ClientHello messages may be sent by the client before the handshake is accepted by the server. An active adversary may force this behaviour: instead of delivering the first few ClientHello attempts at handshake messages to the server, the adversary responds with fatal_handshake_error, until the client sends a ClientHello which has a sufficiently low version that the adversary is satisfied. In practise, this may mean a client and a server both supporting TLSv1.2 may be downgraded to TLSv1.0 by an adversary returning a handshake error until the client attempts a TLSv1.0 ClientHello with a successful response. In this scenario, the session clearly has sub-optimal version-negotiation—the client and server both support TLSv1.2, but the adversary has caused a version 1.0 negotiation—and this provides a example that TLS with fallback is not version-negotiable secure.

In terms of our negotiation-authentication theorem, it fails to apply here because not every output of the negotiation phase is authenticated by the sub-protocol: only the successful ClientHello message is included in the transcript and is considered for matching sessions. Much like the ciphersuite-downgrade vulnerability in SSLv2, this allows an active adversary to modify and delete any of the previous exchanges between the server and client.

6.3   TLS Fallback Version Negotiation with SCSV is Secure

Similar to TLS fallback version negotiation, TLS fallback version negotiation with SCSV ($\mathsf{NP_{v\text{-}fb\text{-}scsv}}$ as described in Figure 4) does not acknowledge or authenticate any messages previous to the fatal_handshake_message in the session identifier, and as such does not satisfy precondition 1 of Theorem 1. Thus, we cannot use the negotiation-authentication theorem to show that that fallback version negotiation with SCSV securely negotiates version. Instead, we provide a direct argument to show that fallback version negotiation with SCSV is secure provided that no-fallback TLS version negotiation is secure.

Theorem 2. *For the TLS protocol with fallback version negotiation with SCSV* $\mathrm{NP}_{\text{v-fb-scsv}}$ *as described in Figure 4 and TLS versions* $\overrightarrow{\mathrm{SP}}$, *an adversary who can force a user to negotiate insecurely to version* SP_n *with respect to the TLS version optimality function* ω_{vers} *from equation 2 can also break authentication of that version:* $\mathrm{Adv}^{\text{neg},\omega_{\text{vers}}}_{\mathrm{NP}_{\text{v-fb-scsv}}\|\overrightarrow{\mathrm{SP}},n}(\mathcal{A}) \leq \mathrm{Adv}^{\text{acce-auth}}_{\mathrm{SP}_n}(\mathcal{A})$.

Proof. The security argument proceeds by showing that an adversary who is successful in breaking fallback version negotiation with SCSV is also successful in breaking authentication of the underlying ACCE protocol. We give a high-level description of the simulator behaviour below.

The simulator $\mathcal{B}$ in our argument recreates the SCSV mechanisms described in Figure 4 and ref. [23] using a version negotiation TLS challenger $\mathcal{C}$ for TLS with no-fallback version negotiation; more precisely, $\mathcal{B}$ simulates the neg experiment for $\mathrm{NP}_{\text{v-fb-scsv}}\|\overrightarrow{\mathrm{SP}}$ using a challenger for $\mathrm{NP}_{\text{v}}\|\overrightarrow{\mathrm{SP}}$.

$\mathcal{B}$ initially forwards all adversarial queries to the challenger $\mathcal{C}$ for each session. After receiving the ClientHello message for a session π from the adversary $\mathcal{A}$, the simulator is able to determine whether the version in the ClientHello would cause a handshake error. If the error would occur, $\mathcal{B}$ replies to $\mathcal{A}$ directly with fatal_handshake_error. If the error would not occur, $\mathcal{B}$ faithfully forwards all queries for that session between $\mathcal{A}$ and $\mathcal{C}$.

Upon receiving a fatal_handshake_error from $\mathcal{A}$ intended for a session π, the simulator uses a Send query to activate a new session π' that is activated identically to π except FALLBACK_SCSV is also included in the list of supported ciphersuites and the list of supported versions for π' is modified to no longer include the highest supported version v of the session π. $\mathcal{B}$ also adds π to a fallback list FL to determine which sessions have performed version-fallback.

Note that from $\mathcal{A}$'s point-of-view, π' and π are the same continuous session, and $\mathcal{B}$ now directs all queries sent to π to π' instead.

As well, $\mathcal{B}$, upon receiving a ClientHello from $\mathcal{A}$ that contains FALLBACK_SCSV in the list of supported ciphersuites, determines if the server's highest supported version is higher than the client's indicated version in the ClientHello. If so, $\mathcal{B}$ replies with an inappropriate_fallback error message. Note that the alert is fatal, so the simulator $\mathcal{B}$ will disregard all further Send queries directed to the server's session. If not, $\mathcal{B}$ forwards the ClientHello to $\mathcal{C}$ and continues to forward all messages for these sessions between $\mathcal{A}$ and $\mathcal{C}$.

This describes the simulator's behaviour during the experiment. Suppose at some point $\mathcal{A}$ breaks the negotiable security of a session π^*. There are two cases:

1. If π^* does not appear on $\mathcal{B}$'s fallback list FL, then all messages were forwarded faithfully between $\mathcal{A}$ and $\mathcal{C}$. An insecure version fallback to version SP_n in $\mathcal{B}$'s simulation of $\mathrm{NP}_{\text{v-fb-scsv}}\|\overrightarrow{\mathrm{SP}}$ thus directly translates to insecure version negotiation to version SP_n in $\mathcal{C}$'s execution of $\mathrm{NP}_{\text{v}}\|\overrightarrow{\mathrm{SP}}$. Hence, $\mathrm{Adv}^{\text{neg},\omega_{\text{vers}}}_{\mathrm{NP}_{\text{v-fb-scsv}}\|\overrightarrow{\mathrm{SP}},n}(\mathcal{A}) \leq \mathrm{Adv}^{\text{neg},\omega_{\text{vers}}}_{\mathrm{NP}_{\text{v}}\|\overrightarrow{\mathrm{SP}},n}(\mathcal{A})$. By Corollary 2, $\mathrm{Adv}^{\text{neg},\omega_{\text{vers}}}_{\mathrm{NP}_{\text{v-fb-scsv}}\|\overrightarrow{\mathrm{SP}},n}(\mathcal{A}) \leq \mathrm{Adv}^{\text{acce-auth}}_{\mathrm{SP}_n}(\mathcal{A})$.

2. If π^* does appear on $\mathcal{B}$'s fallback list FL, then the simulator will have rejected any non-optimal handshakes containing the SCSV. It follows then that the session must have accepted maliciously (either by the $\mathcal{A}$ impersonating the server party or by modifying the handshake of the fallback session $\pi^{*\prime}$). Thus an insecure fallback to version SP_n in $\mathcal{B}$'s simulation of $\mathrm{NP}_{\text{v-fb-scsv}} \| \overrightarrow{\mathrm{SP}}$ directly translates to an authentication break in SP_n. Hence, $\mathrm{Adv}_{\mathrm{NP}_{\text{v-fb-scsv}} \| \overrightarrow{\mathrm{SP}}, n}^{\mathrm{neg}, \omega_{\mathrm{vers}}}(\mathcal{A}) \leq \mathrm{Adv}_{\mathrm{SP}_n}^{\mathrm{acce\text{-}auth}}(\mathcal{A})$. □

Need for Contiguous Support of TLS Versions for Fallback with SCSV.
As shown above, SCSV does give additional protection against version downgrade attacks in TLS implementations that support version fallback. However, we observe that there is a drawback to the SCSV proposal as it stands: Non-contiguous support of versions in TLS implementations (a viable scenario in practise) can hamper interoperability between systems supporting checking for insecure fallback using SCSV.

In some implementations of TLS,[3] users can select a non-contiguous subset of TLS version support. For example, a user could—for some reason—enable TLSv1.2 and TLSv1.0, but not TLSv1.1.

In relation to the SCSV, this can result in a connection attempt that could fail to accept without adversarial interaction. Consider the following scenario: suppose a client user selects TLSv1.2 and TLSv1.0 to support, and attempts to connect to a server that only supports TLSv1.1 and TLSv1.0, and will return a `fatal_handshake_error` for TLSv1.2. The client sends a `ClientHello` with TLSv1.2. After the server fails to parse the TLSv1.2 handshake correctly, it reply with a `fatal_handshake_error` message. The client falls back, sending a new `ClientHello` message with its next highest supported version, TLSv1.0, and includes `FALLBACK_SCSV` in the ciphersuite list to indicate it is falling back. The server notes the SCSV and rejects the handshake with `inappropriate_fallback` as recommended in the SCSV proposal because the server's highest supported version (TLSv1.1) is higher than the client's indicated version (TLSv1.0), despite the fact that the optimal negotiated version would be TLSv1.0.

An alternative mechanism for secure version fallback would be to include a signalling ciphersuite value for each version it supports, allow the parties to detect insecure fallback while allowing non-contiguous version support.

7   Discussion

We have introduced provable security notions for negotiation in Internet protocols, and extended the definition of ACCE protocols to utilise previous

---

[3] The current version of Microsoft Internet Explorer (11) and previous versions allow users to configure which subset of SSL/TLS versions are enabled (Internet options → Advanced → Security); Mozilla Firefox up to version 22 did as well. On the server side, Apache mod_ssl, Microsoft IIS, and nginx all allow the server administrate to select which subset of SSL/TLS versions to enable.

comprehensive ACCE proofs of TLS ciphersuites. We develop a negotiation-authentication theorem and show that ciphersuite negotiation in TLS is secure, under certain conditions about long-term key reuse. We follow by showing that the version negotiation in standards-defined TLS and the TLS implementation with the SCSV is also secure, but demonstrate that TLS implementations that utilise browser-based version fallback mechanisms are not version-negotiable secure. This analysis holds for TLS configurations that exclude sharing long-term keys across multiple versions. In practice, our analysis requires that TLS configurations (in order to have ciphersuite negotiation security) must use independent long-term keys and thus distinct digital certificates for each ciphersuite; this is currently a necessary cost in order to prevent cross-ciphersuite-like attacks from breaking authentication in TLS. To the best of our knowledge, no web server software currently permits configuring different certificate for different TLS ciphersuites with the same signing/key transport algorithm, nor different certificates for different TLS versions.

Future Work. It seems possible that one could extend our analysis to include TLS configurations where long-term keys are shared across multiple *versions* but a single *fixed ciphersuite* (i.e. that TLS 1.2 and TLS 1.0 can reuse long-term keys in the same ciphersuite configuration). However in order to do so requires extensive modification of the negotiation framework to more closely resemble the multi-ciphersuite setting [20]. This remains a significant practical limitation on long-term key reuse across ciphersuites.

Proposed revisions to TLS in the current draft of TLS 1.3 [27] seem to make the protocol resistant to cross-ciphersuite and cross-version attacks. The main change is that, in TLS 1.3, the value signed using the long-term secret key now includes (the hash of) all handshake messages, including the negotiated version and ciphersuite. As a result, the multi-ciphersuite composition framework of Bergsma et al. [20] should be applicable to both multi-version and multi-ciphersuite configurations of TLS: a signing oracle for a single sub-protocol could be constructed to avoid signing objects that would be valid in another sub-protocol, defeating the first step of the cross-ciphersuite attack. This could then imply negotiation-authentication security of TLS 1.3 with shared long-term keys. A thorough analysis is required to show this categorically, however.

Our techniques can also be applied to other protocols that negotiate cryptographic parameters or versions, the Secure Shell (SSH) protocol being a prime candidate. While SSH does have two versions, they are largely incompatible, and current best-practices including disabling v1 support, so there is little value in studying SSH version negotiation. However, SSH also supports multiple cryptographic algorithms, and our framework can easily be applied to SSH algorithm negotiation. Since the parties authenticate their entire transcript, including both the client's and server's algorithm preferences, our negotiation-authentication theorem readily implies that SSH has secure ciphersuite negotiation if it has secure authentication, which it does by the recent results of Bergsma et al. [20].

Acknowledgments. This research has been supported by Australian Research Council (ARC) Discovery Project grant DP130104304.

References

1. Dierks, T., Allen, C.: The TLS protocol version 1.0. RFC 2246 (1999)
2. Dierks, T., Rescorla, E.: The Transport Layer Security (TLS) protocol version 1.1. RFC 4346 (2006)
3. Dierks, T., Rescorla, E.: The Transport Layer Security (TLS) protocol version 1.2. RFC 5246 (2008)
4. Freier, A.O., Karlton, P., Kocher, P.C.: The Secure Sockets Layer (SSL) protocol version 3.0. RFC 6101 (2011). Republication of original SSL 3.0 specification by Netscape of November 18, 1996
5. Wagner, D., Schneier, B.: Analysis of the SSL 3.0 protocol. In: Proc. 2nd USENIX Workshop on Electronic Commerce (1996)
6. Hickman, K.E.B.: The SSL protocol (version 0.2) (1995). http://www-archive. mozilla.org/projects/security/pki/nss/ssl/draft02.html
7. Jonsson, J., Kaliski Jr., B.S.: On the security of RSA encryption in TLS. In: Yung, M. (ed.) CRYPTO 2002. LNCS, vol. 2442, pp. 127–142. Springer, Heidelberg (2002)
8. Morrissey, P., Smart, N.P., Warinschi, B.: A modular security analysis of the TLS handshake protocol. In: Pieprzyk, J. (ed.) ASIACRYPT 2008. LNCS, vol. 5350, pp. 55–73. Springer, Heidelberg (2008)
9. Krawczyk, H.: The order of encryption and authentication for protecting communications (or: How Secure Is SSL?). In: Kilian, J. (ed.) CRYPTO 2001. LNCS, vol. 2139, p. 310. Springer, Heidelberg (2001)
10. Paterson, K.G., Ristenpart, T., Shrimpton, T.: Tag size does matter: attacks and proofs for the TLS record protocol. In: Lee, D.H., Wang, X. (eds.) ASIACRYPT 2011. LNCS, vol. 7073, pp. 372–389. Springer, Heidelberg (2011)
11. Jager, T., Kohlar, F., Schäge, S., Schwenk, J.: On the security of TLS-DHE in the standard model. In: Safavi-Naini, R., Canetti, R. (eds.) CRYPTO 2012. LNCS, vol. 7417, pp. 273–293. Springer, Heidelberg (2012)
12. Krawczyk, H., Paterson, K.G., Wee, H.: On the security of the TLS protocol: a systematic analysis. In: Canetti, R., Garay, J.A. (eds.) CRYPTO 2013, Part I. LNCS, vol. 8042, pp. 429–448. Springer, Heidelberg (2013)
13. Kohlar, F., Schäge, S., Schwenk, J.: On the security of TLS-DH and TLS-RSA in the standard model. Cryptology ePrint Archive, Report 2013/367 (2013). http:// eprint.iacr.org/2013/367
14. Li, Y., Schäge, S., Yang, Z., Kohlar, F., Schwenk, J.: On the security of the pre-shared key ciphersuites of TLS. In: Krawczyk, H. (ed.) PKC 2014. LNCS, vol. 8383, pp. 669–684. Springer, Heidelberg (2014)
15. Brzuska, C., Fischlin, M., Smart, N.P., Warinschi, B., Williams, S.C.: Less is more: Relaxed yet composable security notions for key exchange. International Journal of Information Security **12**, 267–297 (2013)
16. Bhargavan, K., Fournet, C., Kohlweiss, M., Pironti, A., Strub, P.Y.: Implementing TLS with verified cryptographic security. In: 2013 IEEE Symposium on Security and Privacy, pp. 445–459. IEEE Computer Society Press (2013)
17. Giesen, F., Kohlar, F., Stebila, D.: On the security of TLS renegotiation. In: Sadeghi, A.R., Gligor, V.D., Yung, M. (eds.) ACM CCS 2013, pp. 387–398. ACM Press (2013)

18. Ray, M., Dispensa, S.: Renegotiating TLS (2009) http://extendedsubset.com/Renegotiating_TLS.pdf
19. Mavrogiannopoulos, N., Vercauteren, F., Velichkov, V., Preneel, B.: A cross-protocol attack on the TLS protocol. In: Yu, T., Danezis, G., Gligor, V.D. (eds.) ACM CCS 2012, pp. 62–72. ACM Press (2012)
20. Bergsma, F., Dowling, B., Kohlar, F., Schwenk, J., Stebila, D.: Multi-ciphersuite security of the secure shell (SSH) protocol. In: Ahn, G.J., Yung, M., Li, N. (eds.) ACM CCS 2014, pp. 369–381. ACM Press (2014)
21. Bhargavan, K., Fournet, C., Kohlweiss, M., Pironti, A., Strub, P.-Y., Zanella-Béguelin, S.: Proving the TLS handshake secure (As It Is). In: Garay, J.A., Gennaro, R. (eds.) CRYPTO 2014, Part II. LNCS, vol. 8617, pp. 235–255. Springer, Heidelberg (2014)
22. Rescorla, E., Ray, M., Dispensa, S., Oskov, N.: Transport Layer Security (TLS) renegotiation indication extension. RFC 5746 (2010)
23. Möller, B., Langley, A.G.: TLS fallback Signaling Cipher Suite Value (SCSV) for preventing protocol downgrade attacks (2015). https://tools.ietf.org/html/draft-ietf-tls-downgrade-scsv-05. Internet-Draft -05
24. Jager, T., Kohlar, F., Schäge, S., Schwenk, J.: On the security of TLS-DHE in the standard model. Cryptology ePrint Archive, Report 2011/219 (2011). http://eprint.iacr.org/2011/219
25. Bellare, M., Rogaway, P.: Entity authentication and key distribution. In: Stinson, D.R. (ed.) CRYPTO 1993. LNCS, vol. 773, pp. 232–249. Springer, Heidelberg (1994)
26. Dowling, B., Stebila, D.: Modelling ciphersuite and version negotiation in the TLS protocol (full version). Cryptology ePrint Archive (2015)
27. Rescorla, E.: The Transport Layer Security (TLS) protocol version 1.3 (2015). https://tools.ietf.org/html/draft-ietf-tls-tls13-05. Internet-Draft -05

VisRAID: Visualizing Remote Access for Intrusion Detection

Leliel Trethowen[1], Craig Anslow[2], Stuart Marshall[1], and Ian Welch[1]([✉])

[1] School of Engineering and Computer Science,
Victoria University of Wellington, Wellington, New Zealand
`leliel.trethowen@gmail.com`,
`{stuart,ian}@ecs.vuw.ac.nz`
[2] Department of Computer Science,
University of Calgary, Calgary, Canada
`craig.anslow@ucalgary.ca`

Abstract. Detecting malicious attempts to access computers is difficult with current security applications. Many current applications do not give the user the right information to find and analyze possible attempts. We present *VisRAID* – a novel visual analytics web application for detecting intrusions via remote access attempts, and a user study to evaluate the effectiveness and usability of the application with security professionals. The implications of the study will help inform the design of future security visualization applications.

1 Introduction

As computer networks have become ubiquitous, threats to the integrity of the networks and data have multiplied and diversified. The proliferation of threats has lead to the development of intrusion detection systems [14]. Intrusions are defined as access to systems resources for purposes contrary to the intended use of the system, or access to the system by an unauthorized person.

There are two main methods of operation for intrusion detection systems. Rule based systems flag any attempt that matches defined rules as malicious. These systems are extremely effective at detecting and blocking known attack patterns, particularly for outsider access as rules are written for the known attack patterns. Insider attacks are more difficult to control with rules based systems, as blanket access blocks are often not suitable as it is not clear if a user is legitimate. Anomaly based systems use machine learning techniques to automatically classify incoming events as normal or anomalous. Normal events are ignored, while anomalous events are flagged for operator attention.

Anomaly based systems are able to recognize new intrusion methods but not able to provide much if any context about events, while Rule based systems identify which rule was matched. Anomaly based systems are harder to disguise existing intrusions from, as their classification systems are flexible enough to recognize small changes in patterns, whereas Rule based systems cannot do this as easily.

E. Foo and D. Stebila (Eds.): ACISP 2015, LNCS 9144, pp. 289–306, 2015.
DOI: 10.1007/978-3-319-19962-7_17

Intrusion detection system can suffer from false positives and false negatives. False negatives are undesirable as each represents an intrusion that went undetected and potentially un-countered. Note that not all undetected intrusions will achieve their goals, however security administrators are not able to effectively ensure the vulnerabilities used are addressed as they may remain unaware of the intrusion indefinitely unless traces are left elsewhere in the system.

Large numbers of false positives are problematic for secure systems as they quickly undermine the trust of users [11]. Many intrusion detection systems offer very limited forms of alerting with email mostly used, and SMS for critical alerts. The limited range of sensory urgency available via alerting mechanisms is problematic, as it causes a mismatch between the apparent and importance of a message [11].

Despite new intrusion techniques and rapidly growing networks, ensuring that actual intrusions are being detected is important. Existing intrusion detection systems have a number of problems: they do not scale well to large networks, cause information overload, and often fail to reveal important information about logged events.

In this paper we present *VisRAID* – a novel visual analytics web application that addresses these problems by allowing security administrators to effectively monitor remote access attempts to their systems to detect intrusions. VisRAID currently monitors SSH remote access attempts as the ports used for SSH traffic are often the focus of intrusion attempts. We present the design, user interface, and implementation of VisRAID, a preliminary user study with security professionals, and discuss implications for the design of security visualization applications.

2   Related Work

Related work on visualization of intrusion detection has primarily focused on two major areas: techniques used to visualize and explore the results of data mining, and visualization driven techniques. We treat intrusion detection systems (IDS) as data mining systems. Most of the research to date has focused on network intrusion detection logs, and relatively little work has considered access or system log visualization which is the primary focus of our research.

2.1   Data Mining with Visualization

LogView is a visualization application designed to support the understanding of information extracted through data-mining techniques applied to systems logs [9]. The visualization component uses treemaps to show clusters of events in a space efficient manner, with leaf nodes representing events, and branches showing clusters the events belong to. All leaf nodes are coloured in green, with shade darkening in four steps representing different statuses: OK, WARN, FAIL, and OUTLIER. The application allows filtering based on time, and search terms. Time filtering shows only events occurring on the specified day in the map. Nodes matching search terms are highlighted red. Detailed information about a given event is available via a mouseover. The simple filtering and interaction methods, coupled with very similar shades for clusters leaves the system very vulnerable to producing information overload in users. The overload potential grows rapidly as the logs grow, as there is very little information hiding present in this application.

Itoh et al. created a hierarchical system for visualizing intrusion system detection logs [7]. Intrusion detection system messages are lacking in the context needed to support an evaluation of the priority and accuracy of the report. The application shows the entire network under surveillance using a rectangle packing algorithm to group machines by subnets. The number of incidents sent and received from a given machine are displayed as a coloured bar rising out of the plane. The amount of data produced quickly leads to navigability and readability problems as the number of incidents reported grows. Simple filtering applications are available to limit by severity, time, IP, and signature ID. The application is highly reliant on an IDS with both a low false positive, and false negative rate, as almost all information about the actual events is hidden, and there is no easy method to drill down to detailed information.

Xu et al. present a system log data mining application [13]. The log syntax is automatically recovered through source code analysis, allowing the system to be applied to any source available. Once log syntax is extracted, logs are parsed and machine learning algorithms used to perform feature extraction. Once the features are extracted the principle component analysis anomaly detection algorithm are applied to this data, to find interesting patterns in log messages. This approach identified many issues in the tested software, but was forced to be extended from a pure data-mining approach as users found the black box nature of data-mining algorithms caused difficulty in understanding why the results were as they are. To assist with this, a very simple decision tree visualization was added. This visualization was created with the intention of showing the logic used by the data-mining systems to give context for decisions. As the processing required for feature extraction and anomaly detection is highly parallel this approach readily scales to millions of entries, and shows very strong performance in detecting anomalous patterns in logs. From a security standpoint, however, decision trees alone do not give sufficient context to easily determine if an anomaly represents an intrusion as the the trees depends on data not always included in the raw logs.

2.2 Visualization Driven Techniques

Picvis is an application created to generate parallel co-ordinate plots of log data [12]. Picviz has features to automate data extraction from several common log formats for use with their plot description language. This language allows a great deal of control over what variables are shown on a plot. Parallel co-ordinate plots can show strong clustering extremely well. However there are issues of scalability, as clusters and patterns can easily be hidden in background noise unless axes are well chosen. Filtering features are available to help address this limitation, but still require significant knowledge of the data structure and content. This application would be excellent for confirmatory analyses however.

Spiralview is an application that displays time-series data which uses a spiral visualization technique and has been used to visualize static logs and dynamic data streams [1]. The aim of Spiralview is to reveal repeating patterns in time series data from intrusion detection system reports and access logs. An evaluation of the spiral technique asked participants to identify regions of high and low activity in cellphone calling records [3]. Participants were also asked to estimate the time period of patterns in the cellphone data. Participants were presented with both a spiral view and linear timeline views of the data. The study claims that the spiral view approach will offer higher performance than a linear timeline due to the reinforcement of repeating patterns. The results showed that users were significantly faster, more accurate, and more satisfied with a linear timeline presentation for identifying regions of high and low activity. Users were significantly more accurate at identifying time periods for repeating patterns with the Spiralview.

The integrated visualization system is an IDS log based visualization application, focusing on attacks originating inside the monitored network [10]. The application provides a unified logical, geographic and temporal display of data, using three orthogonal planes. Multiple layouts of the three planes are available, with animated transitions. The timeline plane in the visualization shows events for the entire subnet. Individual IP's can be chosen by shifting the timeline plane along the IP plane. Filtering features are made available to control what kinds of events are shown. The application relies on colour to distinguish ports on the timeline frame, which is easily subject to visual overload, as the human eye is not able to reliably distinguish fine differences in colours. Vertical position of the line indicates the number of events. With poorly described filtering systems and reliance on colour coding to distinguish ports, this system is extremely vulnerable to producing information overload. This leads to missing important events. The lack of data hiding creates visual clutter which can easily mask important intrusions composed of a small number of events. The application appears interesting as an attempt to correlate attack information with machine location through GeoIP systems. Where the number of events is "low enough" lines are drawn from IP plane to physical location on the lower plane. The exact number of lines drawn is not clear.

3   VisRAID

VisRAID is a novel web application for network security professionals to visually explore monitoring of network traffic for intrusion detection. VisRAID adopts a visualization driven technique design. There are several goals we have used to help guide the design of VisRAID:

G1: Deploy visualizations over the web.
G2: Strong filtering and highlighting options.

G3: Show surrounding context for anomalous accesses.
G4: Support sharing of work and saving work in progress.
G5: GeoIP support to add context to login attempts.
G6: Allow the user control over which machine is monitored at any given time.
G7: Show network context for currently monitored machine.
G8: Support extensible log parsing.

3.1   User Interface and Timeline Visualization

Figure 1 shows the web-based user interface of VisRAID. The main features are a timeline overview, vertical scaling, colour-coding of event types, and mouseover tooltips. Within each timeline, blocks are vertically scaled proportional to the block with the largest number of events to help with information hiding so important data is not masked. In Figure 1 the first block consists of 5 events total, the second block is absent indicating no events occurred in that time, and the third block shows 25 events of three different classes.

As networks can become extremely busy by producing lots of activity the information can overwhelm an analyst's ability to comprehend and detect meaningful patterns. To address this problem we adopted data hiding techniques, used a time series based approach for displaying the data, and used time binning to aggregate entities. In our approach all entries in a short time period are displayed as a single entity, with icons indicating some simple features of the hidden data. Such features include superuser accesses, number of abnormal failed access attempts, number of abnormal access attempts, abnormal login locations for a user, abnormal login times for a user. Each time a bin can be zoomed in on, allowing the analyst to see greater detail within the bin. For busy systems and longer time periods there may be multiple levels of binning to aggregate sufficiently. This approach reduces the visual complexity, but allows access to detailed information on demand.

Flags for abnormal login time and location are the most complicated flags, as they require creating a profile of each user's access times over repeated access attempts. This complexity can produce false positives while a user is learning the application and may be tripped up by a legitimate change in their behaviour.

Timelines are required to have independent vertical scales as the number of events in a given time period may be highly variable. This is demonstrated in Figure 1 where the top timeline shows 25 events in the largest bin, and the third timeline shows in excess of 20K events. Without independent scaling for each timeline all features of the upper two lines would be overwhelmed by the third. This led to the inclusion of the black scale indicators found between the controls and timelines. They are logarithmically scaled such that the timeline with the highest maximum events per bin is represented by a full bar. These provide a quick visual indication of how much variability there is between scales.

Each block is subdivided into four colours to represent different classes of events. Each event must be in exactly one event class, this allows the colour sections to be linearly scaled to block height (i.e. if half the events are failed connections, half of the block will be red). The colour coding was added to give an

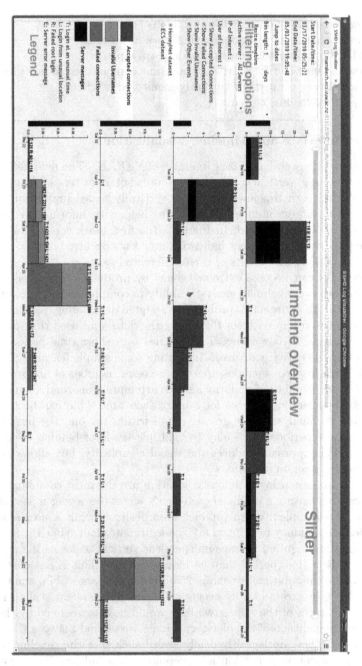

Fig. 1. VisRAID - showing an overview of the Honeynet dataset, slider to navigate, filtering options to make changes, and legend for different types of events

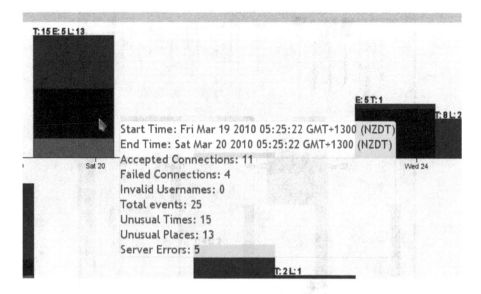

Fig. 2. VisRAID - Tooltip showing statistics for a block

instant overview of the breakdown of event types within each bin. Hovering the mouse over a block produces a tooltip showing a detailed statistical breakdown of the events within that block (see Figure 2). Double-clicking on any block zooms in on that block, with all four timelines reloading to show only data from the selected block. Zooming can be performed until either there is only one event in the chosen block, or each block covers 1 second. Where there is only one event to display, mousing over the block will show the raw log line in a popup.

Above the timelines a slider can be used to navigate the dataset. The position of the slider gives an approximate indication of how far through the timeline the view is currently at. The extreme left is when the first log event occurred. The extreme right is the latest log event. The slider can be dragged and moved in steps. Each step covers exactly as long as is currently shown in the timelines (see Figure 3).

3.2 Implementation

While there are many kinds of events, and metadata about connections that can be logged, extended information is highly dependent on SSH demon configuration. The listed message types can be relied on to be present in all useful logging levels. A log event will typically be represented by a single log line at the standard level of logging for OpenSSH. A typical user interaction may generate between two and three log events: connection, disconnection, and transferring files across the secure connection. Malicious access attempts may generate between two and

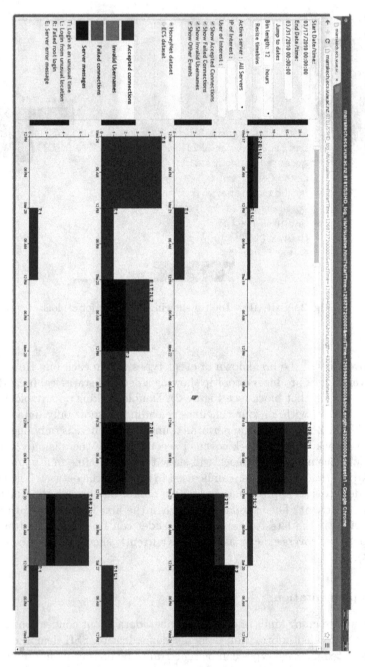

Fig. 3. VisRAID - Showing 2 weeks of the Honeynet dataset

```
Mar 16 08:25:22 app-1 sshd[4884]: Server listening on :: port 22.
Mar 16 08:25:22 app-1 sshd[4884]: error: Bind to port 22 on 0.0.0.0 failed: Address already in use.
Apr 19 05:55:20 app-1 sshd[12996]: Accepted password for root from 219.150.161.20 port 55545 ssh2
Apr 19 05:55:20 app-1 sshd[12997]: Invalid user pauline from 219.150.161.20
Apr 19 05:55:21 app-1 sshd[12990]: Failed password for root from 219.150.161.20 port 54890 ssh2
Apr 20 00:00:51 app-1 sshd[24442]: subsystem request for sftp
Jun 8 01:03:34 machine0 sshd[1796]: Received disconnect from 38.165.101.19: 11: Bye Bye
```

Fig. 4. Examples of SSHD logs, showing each type of message

three log events: connection, disconnection, and if the username provided is not recognised. Rates of log generation can vary widely between networks.

We used the following event types from the SSHD logs: connection attempts, disconnection messages, subsystem requests, invalid usernames, and system messages. All events contain a timestamp, server name, service name, and process ID. The remainder of a message is free text. Each entry contains metadata, for example a connection attempt contains information about authentication method, username, source address, and status. Whereas a disconnection message contains a code, and source IP. Figure 4 shows an example of some of the messages contained in the SSHD log files.

A log parsing tool was implemented in two layers: log reader and writer/analyser. The reader layer is responsible for reading any number of log files into a sorted list of events. The list of events is then passed to the analyzer/writer layer, which is responsible for checking connection attempts to see if the location and time are frequently used by the user and writing the analyzed metadata to the datastore. The results of the parser are stored in a MySQL database.

To address the design goal of deploying visualizations over the web we implemented a web-based application. The user interface was implemented with JQuery and visualizations with D3 [2]. Apache Tomcat was used for the server along with SQL generation from the jOOQ library [4]. The server contained two layers implemented as servlets. The data access servlet was responsible for fetching data from the underlying datastore. The servlet takes values from the client communication layer and returns lists of matching log entries. The servlet can be easily modified to communicate with different kinds of datastores. The client communication servlet was responsible for aggregating data returned by the data access layer, and building HTTP(S) responses from the aggregated data.

4   Evaluation

To evaluate the effectiveness of VisRAID we performed a preliminary user study with security professionals. We obtained human ethics approval from our University to conduct this user study.

4.1   Participants

Six people were recruited for the user study. Four of the participants were security professionals who had security components as part of their day jobs, and are regularly involved in log analysis tasks. The other two were computer science students who had passed a graduate security course.

4.2 Datasets

Two datasets were used in this study which represent real systems exposed to the public internet.

Honeynet Forensic Data: from Challenge 10 which is publicly available and anonymized [6]. The data covers a single server, with 35K log entries covering 16 March to 2 May (approx. 729 events/day).

ECS Data: from our computer science department which are network logs, anonymized, cover three servers for two disjoint weeks, and contain 74K log entries. (approx. 5300 events/day).

The Honeynet dataset has been extensively analyzed, over the course of two forensic challenges. Multiple successful brute force and scattergun attacks have been identified in this dataset. There were few usernames which showed a pattern of usage in the log data gathered. The Honeynet dataset was from the GMT-5 timezone.

The ECS dataset is more complex than the Honeynet dataset. The ECS dataset covers three separate servers, with more active users. The ECS dataset shows approximated 5300 events/day, more than seven times as many as the Honeynet dataset. The ECS dataset contains disconnection messages absent from the Honeynet dataset. These messages can account for at most a doubling of event rates, as there may be at most one disconnection per connection attempt, and a connection attempt may produce more than one event. As disconnection messages are not currently useful, they add a significant amount of noise. This dataset was extensively analyzed before the user study to search for existing attacks. Several attempted brute force and scattergun attacks were found, though all were unsuccessful.

The difference in attack success rates between datasets reflects differences in the purposes of the networks. The ECS network is provided for use by staff and students in our department at our university. This network can reasonably be expected to have significant amounts of sensitive information stored. Therefore the school expends significant effort in protecting these systems. In contrast, the Honeynet system is deliberately exposed to lure in attackers, and as such has significantly less effort expended on securing it.

The ECS dataset was altered, to introduce a successful scattergun attack on one server. This was introduced, as there were no naturally occurring successful attacks discovered after thorough analysis with both VisRAID, and direct exploration through the database. The introduced scattergun attack in the ECS dataset had a relatively small attack signature, with only 204 log entries involved, of 4.7K entries for that day. Some successful attacks on Honeynet had similar numbers of access attempts, though often a much higher proportion of invalid or failed attempts for a given day.

The ECS dataset is recorded from a live network in normal operation. The log produced contains IP addresses and usernames of everyone to use the system during the recording period. As this information could easily be used to identify people, it requires being anonymized to be ethically used without each user's consent. SSHD logs contain usernames and raw IP addresses. Both usernames and IP addresses can be useful to malicious people. IP addresses allow for approximate location of a user's home through GeoIP databases, as well as direct attacks on the security of their computers. Usernames do not carry as significant a risk to the owner, though these could be useful to mount an attack on the ECS system directly.

Both datasets were anonymized, but the procedures were different. The Honeynet dataset is publicly available in an anonymized form, hence we did not have to do anything further to the data [6]. The ECS dataset was recorded from Internet facing servers in the ECS network. The ECS dataset was anonymized by system admin staff within our department. The data required anonymizing both usernames and IP addresses. IP addresses were anonymized with CryptoPAN a prefix preserving IP address anonymize tool extended with support for IPv6 addresses [5]. CryptoPAN uses strong encryption to generate codes which are combined with the IP address to produce a new valid IP address. This cannot be reversed without knowledge of the key, or an efficient means of cracking AES encryption. Usernames were anonymized through a script, where each username was replaced with the string "user" and a unique number.

4.3   Procedure

The user study was conducted in a controlled lab, with only the participant and session instructor present. Audio recordings were made as a record of events during the study as an addition to handwritten observational notes. Participants were provided with a desktop computer running at 1920x1080 resolution and the Chrome web browser.

Participants were given up to ten minutes to familiarize themselves with VisRAID. After familiarization, participants were asked to answer four questions about each dataset for a total of eight tasks. Questions were presented to users in a random order to avoid any learning bias. Participants were given up to eight minutes for each task. The participants were not given the opportunity to read questions before the study began which limited their opportunity to learn the answers to later questions while answering a question.

The four questions are listed below. Tasks 1 through 4 were based on questions 1 and 2, with tasks 1 and 4 using the ECS dataset, and tasks 2 and 3 using the Honeynet dataset. Tasks 5 through 8 were based on questions 3 and 4, with tasks 5 and 7 using the ECS dataset, and tasks 6 and 8 using the Honeynet dataset. Table 1 lists the combinations of tasks, questions, and datasets.

Q1 Find an instance of a successful brute force attack on root.
Q2 Find an instance of a successful scattergun attack. (an instance where the attacker attempts many common username/password pairs at random).

Q3 Find an instance of a legitimate user logging in from an abnormal location.
Q4 Find an instance of a legitimate user logging in at an abnormal time.

Q1 and Q2 are based on the most commonly found attack signatures in SSH logs with many botnets and automated systems carrying out brute force or scattergun attacks against any IP address responding to connection requests. As these attacks are very common and can lead to serious compromises determining success or failure of such attacks is a core function of any log analysis tool. Q3 and Q4 are based on finding anomalous behaviour by legitimate accounts. Anomalous behaviour by legitimate accounts can be an indication that their account has been compromised, or that the account owner has become malicious.

For each task a brief questionnaire was completed indicating participants' subjective opinions about different aspects of VisRAID [8]. Participants were asked to complete the following three questions using a 7 point likert scale, where 7 is Strongly Disagree, and 1 Strongly Agree.

1. I am satisfied with the *ease* of completing this task.
2. I am satisfied with the amount of *time* it took to complete this task.
3. I am satisfied with the *support* information (e.g. online help, documentation) when completing this task.

Timing and accuracy for each task was recorded. For each task a date, time, source IP, and where applicable username involved were recorded. This information combined with the dataset provides sufficient details to allow checking of answers for accuracy from the raw logs, database directly, or using VisRAID.

4.4   Results

Each Task was given a pass/fail grade based on accuracy. Time taken to complete each task was also measured. Results are shown in Table 1. A dash indicates the task was not completed in time, hence an incorrect answer. Ticks represents correct answers and crosses incorrect answers.

Table 1. Time and accuracy results for each task by participant (Professionals and Students). Dashes represent tasks not completed within 8 mins. Ticks represents correct answers and Crosses incorrect answers.

T#	Q	Dataset	P1- P		P2 - P		P3 - S		P4 - S		P5 - P		P6 - P		Correct
1	Q1	ECS	3:05	✓	5:46	✗	-	✗	-	✗	-	✗	-	✗	1
2	Q1	Honeynet	-	✗	-	✗	2:26	✓	2:09	✓	3:55	✓	3:08	✓	4
3	Q2	Honeynet	5:10	✓	-	✗	4:18	✓	4:51	✓	8:00	✓	2:20	✗	4
4	Q2	ECS	-	✗	-	✗	4:18	✓	3:18	✗	-	✗	-	✗	1
5	Q3	ECS	1:09	✓	1:22	✓	1:07	✓	0:39	✓	1:04	✓	1:10	✓	6
6	Q3	Honeynet	0:31	✓	1:07	✓	1:02	✓	1:13	✗	1:00	✓	2:15	✓	5
7	Q4	ECS	0:45	✓	1:59	✓	0:42	✗	0:44	✓	2:06	✓	-	✗	4
8	Q4	Honeynet	0:32	✓	1:10	✗	1:32	✗	1:07	✓	1:15	✓	0:55	✓	4
		Total	26.32	6/8	34.44	3/8	22.45	5/8	20.81	5/8	32.8	6/8	33.08	4/8	29/48

When participants were working on Tasks 1 and 4 (ECS), they had difficulties in navigating the timeline which was a significant aspect for carrying out these tasks. Task 1 involved finding a brute force attack which compromised root. There was no such attack present in the dataset. Demonstrating the absence of an item in a dataset can be significantly harder than finding the presence of it similar to finding bugs in software. Only one participant was successful in completing Task 1 and we believe the combination of navigation difficulties in the visualization with increased task difficulty was the cause of the very high failure rate for this task. Task 4 involved participants looking for a successful scattergun attack in the ECS dataset. Only one participant was successful in completing Task 4. Poor navigation support caused problems as the relatively small attack signature was easily swamped in other data.

Tasks 2 and 3 (Honeynet) were to find a brute force and scattergun attack respectively. There were multiple successful brute force attacks, and scattergun attacks with much larger attack signatures (higher number of attempts). These questions were quickly and reliably answered by most participants. Poor accuracy, and significantly slower times with the ECS data coupled with observations of participants attempting these tasks suggest that navigation difficulties and limited filtering options were a greater issue in the more complicated dataset, with smaller attack signatures, and greater noise. Participants performed much better for tasks 5–8.

The introduced scattergun attack in the ECS dataset had a relatively small attack signature, with only 204 log entries involved, of 4.7K entries for that day. Some successful attacks on the Honeynet dataset had similar numbers of access attempts, though often a much higher proportion of invalid or failed attempts for a given day. There were many more legitimate access attempts to the ECS network, and much higher event density. Logging of disconnect messages introduced further noise to the system.

Participant 2 (Professional) had a great deal of difficulty in identifying brute force and scattergun attacks on both datasets. Feedback and observation of the participant in action suggest severe difficulties with navigation, combined with the lack of ability to hide all attempts from a specified set of IP addresses caused significant difficulties for this participant. Participant 2 commented that in the normal course of investigating such incidents using tools such as grep, they would build up a blacklist of IP's to hide from results as they were fully investigated and discarded. VisRAID does not currently support this analysis feature. Participant 2 has significantly more experience in analyzing SSHD logs using traditional tools where stronger filtering tools are available, such as regular expressions.

Figure 5 shows the perceived effectiveness for the questions in the survey participants completed at the end of each task. Each question in the survey was answered with a score on a 7 point likert scale, where 1 is Strongly Agree and 7 is Strongly Disagree. There were variations between participants as could be expected in an early prototype, which can be caused by many factors. The results of the survey match well with the accuracy and time results, as each participant gave a higher score (Disagree) for tasks they found difficult. For ease and amount of time to complete a task the perceived effectiveness had a similar range with median of 2 and an outlier at 7. Amount of time did not have any outliers. For support the perceived effectiveness had a smaller range with a median of 3. The results shows that participants felt VisRAID was easy to use, allowed them to find the answers within a reasonable amount of time, but better support was required for helping participants to use VisRAID.

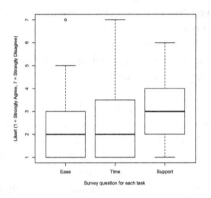

Fig. 5. Perceived Effectiveness of Ease of use, completion Time, and Support available

5   Discussion

Based on our evaluation we discuss how VisRAID meets the design goals, weaknesses, suggested improvements, and limitations of the user study.

5.1   Design Goals

Several goals were presented to help guide the design of VisRAID. Some design goals were met while others were not.

G1: Deploy visualizations over the web. VisRAID was developed as a web-based application and can display visualizations using JQuery and D3 inside a web browser.

G2: Strong filtering and highlighting options. Participants were able to successfully answer questions about both datasets with VisRAID. Highlighting is not currently implemented. Extensions could be added to make the filtering stronger and implementing highlighting.

G3: Show surrounding context for anomalous accesses. The timeline display shows the surrounding time, with each level of zoom reducing the surrounding time that is visible. This provides context to users, but requires improvement due to navigation difficulties when transitioning.

G4: Support sharing of work and saving work in progress. These goals were not tested, but VisRAID is designed to support sharing of work through URL passing and saving work in progress through browser bookmarking.

G5: GeoIP support to add context to login attempts This is currently used for abnormal location detection, but is not currently made available to the user directly.

G6: User control over machine monitoring. Users have direct control over which machine's log data is shown at any time through the server menu, which is populated with a list of all servers known to the database.

G7: Show network context for currently monitored machine. Due to time this design goal was not met.

G8: Extensible log parsing. Only SSHD logs are supported, but integration of other syslog formats is possible.

5.2 Weaknesses

Navigation. Difficulties were experienced by most participants, where abrupt transitions between zoom levels lead to loss of context, and difficulty building up a mental map of the timeline. Most users demonstrated improved navigation as they became more familiar with VisRAID. These issues could be addressed in two major ways: showing a radar view to assist users in maintaining context, and animating transitions to build up a mental map of the log.

Filtering. Analysis of the difficulties experienced by participant 2, and suggestions from other participants several new filtering options would significantly enhance the ability to deal with potential information overload. Implementing IP blacklisting would be extremely useful for some users, as it would support an interaction model where one IP is fully investigated, then hidden, and the process repeated until all suspicious IP's have been investigated. One participant suggested allowing filtering by an authentication method. This is strongly supported by the difficulties users had in Task 1, as on multiple occasions, a successful root login would occur mixed in with many failed attempts. This successful login would be from a different IP address, using an authentication method not amenable to brute force, such as host-based authentication. Allowing filtering by authentication method, would assist users in avoiding this pitfall, by hiding a class of logins which cannot be involved in attacks.

Information Hiding. Information hiding is an issue for VisRAID as the timezone display caused all participants to query the discrepancy in times for the Honeynet dataset. This caused some confusion at first, however, results suggest that once informed of the issue users could compensate.

5.3 Suggested Improvements

Animated Zooming. Users complained that they get lost when zooming. A common feature used to smooth out such transitions and ease navigation is animating the zoom level. Animated zooming offers the potential for improvements by helping to address the navigation issues experienced by participants. As each timeline is currently updated independently and zooming replaces the contents of all timelines. The most common zooming action would be for the selected block to grow to fill all four timelines, replacing their data with a detailed breakdown.

Filtering by subnet. Adding options to filter IP addresses by subnet would potentially be useful, as it would allow more controllable filtering on IP than is currently present. Currently filters are restricted to matching against dotted quad forms of address. There would be some difficulty in implementing the filtering approach, as IP addresses are currently stored in human readable formats, not suitable for matching against less common subnets. Matching against subnets in 1 byte increments (/8, /16, /24) would be easy, as these match with the dotted quad format used.

IP Address Hiding. The inverse of the IP of interest filter is IP address hiding which shows all addresses except those selected. This would allow support of another interaction model, as used by participant 2. Implementing IP hiding, or blacklisting is relatively simple from a server side perspective, as the datastore is able to efficiently handle complex selection criteria. The difficulty is maintaining the stateful URL for this filter. Blacklists can grow potentially quite large, and URLs have an implementation defined maximum size. Larger URLs can be too long to email, hence a new approach may be needed.

Filter events by authentication type. This will help reduce false detection rates for brute force and similar attacks, as some authentication methods are not vulnerable to these attacks. Adding filtering for authentication type would offer the ability to hide all events that cannot be involved in specific types of attacks. This would be straightforward to implement but requires changes in several places. The data access layer of the server would have to be modified with an optional where clause in the query, and the URL would have to be modified with another optional filtering clause.

Suppress abnormal time and place warnings for invalid and failed attempts. This will cut down the number of abnormalities reported, and help to reduce false positives and information overload. The ability to spot abnormal logins would be improved. Implementation would require a change to the server, to ignore time and location flags when producing the aggregated data.

Separate disconnection messages into their own type. This would allow hiding of disconnection messages in the same way failed and successful connections can be hidden, reducing noise in the dataset. Implementation would require changes in the aggregation code to count disconnections separately, and draw a 5th category of event.

Scaling to larger datasets. VisRAID was only tested on two datasets, where ECS was the largest and contained up to 75K log entries. Testing on much larger datasets will determine how well VisRAID scales and performs.

Larger Evaluation. Once VisRAID has been improved a further evaluation should be conducted with a larger scope, statistically significant sample size, and larger and more varied datasets to address the weaknesses. A further improvement to the evaluation procedure would be the inclusion of a training dataset to allow participants to become familiar with the application.

5.4 Limitations

There were some limitations with the user study and the datasets. The user study was conducted in a controlled lab environment, for a set period of time, and an application that the participants were not familiar with. Only six participants were involved, two of whom were computer science students. Students are less ideal for this kind of study, as their experience and domain knowledge are more limited than those that have been working in the industry for some time. Obtaining security professionals for user studies is difficult as we found there were a limited number in the city where the study was conducted. We could obtain more participants by evaluating in different locations. Small, exploratory evaluations have advantages in cost and time required. With small numbers of participants, the evaluation can be conducted in a short time and non-viable approaches can be discarded before significant development effort is invested.

Both datasets are in the 10's of thousands of entries, We have not tested VisRAID with much larger networks such as over 100K log entries. The addition of a successful scattergun attack to the ECS dataset represents a potential weakness of this study, however, great care was taken to ensure that the inserted log entries matched the patterns found in other scattergun attacks on both datasets. Participants were using datasets that they were not familiar with. Testing on much larger datasets in the future will determine how VisRAID scales.

6   Conclusion

Detecting malicious attempts to access computers is difficult with current security applications. Many current applications do not give the user the right information to find and analyze possible attempts. In this paper we presented *VisRAID* – a novel visual analytics web application for detecting intrusions via remote access attempts, and conducted a preliminary user study to evaluate the effectiveness and usability of the application with security professionals.

The user study involved six participants four of whom were security professionals. Participants were able to effectively answer the questions in the user tasks using different sized data sets. Some questions proved to be more difficult than others. The results showed that participants felt VisRAID was easy to use, allowed them to find the answers within a reasonable amount of time, but better support was required for helping users learn the application. VisRAID could be improved by allowing easier navigation of the visualizations, providing better support for filtering by IP, and the ability to hide information more effectively.

References

1. Bertini, E., Hertzog, P., Lalanne, D.: SpiralView: towards security policies assessment through visual correlation of network resources with evolution of alarms. In: Proc. of Conference on Visual Analytics Science and Technology (VAST), pp. 139–146. IEEE (2007)
2. Bostock, M., Ogievetsky, V., Heer, J.: D^3 Data-Driven Documents. IEEE Transactions on Visualization and Computer Graphics **17**(12), 2301–2309 (2011)
3. Chin, G., Singhal, M., Nakamura, G., Gurumoorthi, V., Freeman-Cadoret, N.: Visual analysis of dynamic data streams. Information Visualization **8**(3), 212–229 (2009)
4. Data Geekery. jOOQ: Get back in control of your SQL, October 30, 2013. http://jooq.org
5. Fan, J., Xu, J., Ammar, M., Moon, S.: Prefix-preserving ip address anonymization: Measurement-based security evaluation and a new cryptography-based scheme. Computer Networks **46**(2), 253–272 (2004)
6. Honeynet Project. Forensic Challenge 10 - Attack Visualization, June 05, 2013. http://www.honeynet.org/challenges/attack_visualization_challenge
7. Itoh, T., Takakura, H., Sawada, A., Koyamada, K.: Hierarchical visualization of network intrusion detection data. IEEE Computer Graphics Applications **26**(2), 40–47 (2006)
8. Lewis, J.R.: IBM computer usability satisfaction questionnaires: psychometric evaluation and instructions for use. International Journal of Human-Computer Interaction **7**(1), 57–78 (1995)
9. Makanju, A., Brooks, S., Zincir-Heywood, A., Milios, E.: LogView: visualizing event log clusters. In: Proc. of Conference on Privacy, Security and Trust (PST), pp. 99–108. IEEE (2008)
10. Mukosaka, S., Koike, H.: Integrated visualization system for monitoring security in large-scale local area network. In: Proc. of the Asia-Pacific Symposium on Information Visualisation (APVIS), pp. 41–44. IEEE (2007)
11. Stanton, N.: Human factors in alarm design. CRC Press (1994)
12. Tricaud, S.: PicViz: finding a needle in a haystack. In: Proc. of the USENIX Conference on Analysis of System Logs. USENIX Association (2008)
13. Xu, W., Huang, L., Fox, A., Patterson, D., Jordan, M.I.: Detecting large-scale system problems by mining console logs. In: Proc. of the Symposium on Operating Systems Principles (SIGOPS), pp. 117–132. ACM (2009)
14. Zhang, Y., Xiao, Y., Chen, M., Zhang, J., Deng, H.: A survey of security visualization for computer network logs. Security and Communication Networks **5**(4), 404–421 (2012)

BP-XACML an Authorisation Policy Language for Business Processes

Khalid Alissa[1,2]($\boxtimes$), Jason Reid[1], Ed Dawson[1], and Farzad Salim[1]

[1] Institute of Future Environment, Queensland University of Technology,
Brisbane, QLD, Australia
{Khalid.alissa,jf.reid,e.dawson,f.salim}@qut.edu.au
[2] King Abdulaziz City for Science and Technology (KACST), Riyadh, Saudi Arabia

Abstract. XACML has become the defacto standard for enterprise-wide, policy-based access control. It is a structured, extensible language that can express and enforce complex access control policies. There have been several efforts to extend XACML to support specific authorisation models, such as the OASIS RBAC profile to support Role Based Access Control. A number of proposals for authorisation models that support business processes and workflow systems have also appeared in the literature. However, there is no published work describing an extension to allow XACML to be used as a policy language with these models. This paper analyses the specific requirements of a policy language to express and enforce business process authorisation policies. It then introduces BP-XACML, a new profile that extends the RBAC profile for XACML so it can support business process authorisation policies. In particular, BP-XACML supports the notion of tasks, and constraints at the level of a task instance, which are important requirements in enforcing business process authorisation policies.

Keywords: XACML · BPM · Workflow · Authorisation management · Authorisation policy language

1 Introduction

The domain of 'Business Process Management (BPM)' is an important and maturing domain. A survey by Gartner [6] showed that BPM is the number one concern of many senior executives. This increasing interest in BPM has prompted research in a variety of directions, including the domain of access control. Several access control models designed specifically for the business process environment have been presented in the literature including [3], [11], and [16]. Most of these proposals focus on the authorisation model itself, and do not specify an authorisation policy language, which is an important aspect of authorisation management. One of the most accepted and widely discussed authorisation policy languages is the eXtensible Access Control Markup Language (XACML) [8].

XACML is an XML defined standard language for access control policies. XACML uses rules, which are defined in policies, in conjunction with a standard

© Springer International Publishing Switzerland 2015
E. Foo and D. Stebila (Eds.): ACISP 2015, LNCS 9144, pp. 307–325, 2015.
DOI: 10.1007/978-3-319-19962-7_18

component called a Policy Decision Point (PDP). The PDP evaluates access requests against the policies to decide whether to allow or deny the request [9].

The XACML RBAC Profile [2] was proposed to extend the initial version of XACML. It supports the notion of roles to be able to support role-based access control policies [2]. The RBAC profile supports both core and hierarchical RBAC, but it explicitly states that it does not support separation of duty (SoD) constraints [2], although an earlier draft of the profile [1] did mention SoD, but it was removed in the final release. To the best of the author's knowledge, currently there is no published work that aims to extend the XACML language to support authorisation policies for business processes.

This paper proposes BP-XACML, an extension to XACML to express authorisation policies for business processes. The proposed extension builds on the RBAC profile to support the notion of tasks and task instances, to support instance level restrictions, and separation of duty (SoD) constraints. The paper identifies the features that the language should support, defines the needed extension, and describes the new XACML profile, BP-XACML. The paper introduces a new function called 'performers list' along with new authorities to support the history-based instance-level restrictions. It also proposes a new policy set to support tasks, and a new attribute to recognise the task instances. It introduces new conditions and functions to support SoD. Figure 1 shows the complete framework of BP-XACML showing all 'policy-sets' and authorities. Elements shaded in white are from the XACML standard. Those with dotted background are added in the RBAC-XACML profile, while the ones with dark background are introduced in this paper (BP-XACML).

The rest of the paper is organized as follows. Section 2 provides an example scenario to illustrate the need for a new policy language. Section 3 discusses the characteristics of the language. The structure of the policy language is explained

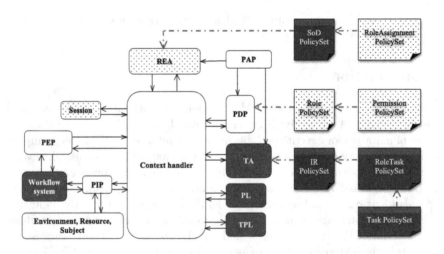

Fig. 1. BP-XACML Authorities and policy sets

in section 4. Section 5 discusses the policy model. The language semantics are explained in section 6. Section 7 provides a review of related works. Finally, section 8 concludes the paper.

2   Example Scenario

In order to illustrate the various policy language requirements for an access control system for business processes, this section will consider the access control policies for a hypothetical business process that runs across a number of systems. The example scenario is of a process of fixing a pump malfunction in an air-conditioning system in a high-security facility such as an airport.

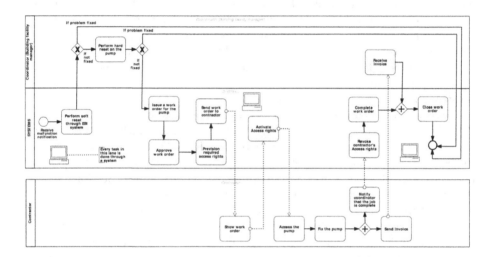

Fig. 2. Business process model for fixing pump malfunction

As can be seen in Figure 2, no one can perform a 'soft reset' on the pump unless a malfunction notification was received, and it has to be done by someone with the role 'coordinator'. If both 'soft reset' and 'hard reset' fail to solve the problem, a work order is issued. Only users with the role 'coordinator' can issue the work order. The approval of that work order should be done by a different user with the role 'Manager'. A user with the role 'contractor' needs to show the work order to gain access to the pump room. Once the issue has been resolved the user who fixed the problem will notify the user who issued the work order. This notification will result in revoking the access rights granted to the coordinator. The user who created the work order is the only one allowed to close it, and will only be able to do so after receiving the notification and the invoice.

The policy language must support the definition of policies that reflect these access control restrictions and conditions. Some of these access control policies cannot be expressed directly in XACML.

3   Business Process Authorisation Policy Requirements

With its focus on tasks and their controlled, sequenced execution, an authorisation model for business processes introduces a range of capabilities not found in the standard RBAC model [15]. Similarly, an authorisation policy language for business processes requires more than what RBAC-XACML currently provides. This section will identify the important concepts and constraints that such a policy language should be able to express by describing the significant functionalities that business process authorisation models support.

Role-Based access control (RBAC) [5] is a widely used authorisation concept. It assigns access privileges to 'roles' instead of directly assigning them to users, which reduces management overhead [13]. Users indirectly acquire permissions through their membership of roles. RBAC is an important concept to be supported in business process authorisation [7]. Support for RBAC among the published business process authorisation models including [16] and [11] is widespread. For a policy language to be able to support the RBAC concept it should support the notion of user, role, and permission. Moreover, the policy language should have the ability to represent Separation of Duties (SoD) constraints to assist in preventing fraud [5].

Tasks are a fundamental concept in business process management. They are the building blocks of business processes, so business process authorisation models such as [11] and [16] typically focus on extending RBAC with the notion of tasks. Reflecting this, authorisation policy language for business processes should support the notion of 'tasks' as a group of permissions. The example in Section 2 shows that requests are to perform a 'task', rather than to acquire a permission. So, it is important to be able to deal with tasks as well as permissions.

An important functionality that is supported by the more expressive business process authorisation models such as [16] is history-based restrictions between tasks on the instance-level, which we will refer to as 'Instance-level Restrictions (IR)'. These are restrictions that apply only within a unique execution instance of a process [16]. For example, consider the policy from section 2, which states that the person who closes a 'work order' must be the same user who issued it. So, a user will only be allowed to close the work order if he previously performed the issue function within the same process instance. This is an example of Binding of Duty (BoD) at the instance level. Separation of duty (SoD) on an instance-level requires that two tasks within an execution instance of a process, be performed by different users.

A first step to support instance-level restrictions is to be able to distinguish between instances. Some authorisation models such as [16] and [17] support the notion of 'task instance', which allows different execution instances to be distinguished. So, a policy language should be able to represent a 'task instance'. The language should also have the ability to represent the 'instance-level restrictions' themselves by specifying a separation or binding of duty relation between two tasks. Moreover, in order to enforce this condition (an instance-level restriction) the language should have the ability to retrieve history based information on an instance level [17], such as, who issued a specific 'work order'.

The key concepts that an authorisation policy language for business processes should be able to represent are: Users, Roles, Operations, Tasks, Task instance, Instance-level restrictions, and SoD. The RBAC profile of XACML supports representation of the first three characteristics. The proposed policy language extends RBAC-XACML to provide support for representation of tasks, task instances, SoD, and instance-level restrictions.

4   BP-XACML: Policy Structure

BP-XACML is based on XACML which implements rule-based access control [12]. An authorisation policy may contain multiple authorisation rules (AR), which are the basic building blocks for stating authorisation restrictions. Each AR consists of four elements: Subject, Object, Action, and Condition, the evaluation of which results in a Allow or Deny decision. $AR = \{S, O, A, C\} \rightarrow \{Allow, Deny\}$.

Action (A) is implementation specific. Condition (C) is a boolean expression that is evaluated based on the value of variables determined at run time as either true or false. Conditions can be used to represent complex constraints. The rule has its specified effect (allow or deny) if the condition evaluates as true. Rules are grouped together in 'policies', which may contain a target that limits the applicability of rules to requests which match the target's subject, object and action [9]. Policies also specify a rule-combining algorithm, which resolves potential conflicts when more than one rule is applicable [9]. Policies can be grouped together in a 'policySet' that also contains a target, and a policy-combining algorithm. It may also contain other policy sets included by reference[9].

4.1   Request and Decision

An XACML request message is sent to the PDP when a user tries to access a controlled resource. The PDP identifies matching policies and evaluates the request against them to arrive at an authorisation decision. The Request (RQ) is in the form of $\{S, O, A\}$. In BP-XACML there are three types of resource whose related policies are defined in three different policy sets (see Section 4.2). In the context of the request, the interpretation of S, O and A is different for each type. Because of this, each type of request is processed by a different authority. Firstly, in the case of a user requesting to perform a workflow task, the subject (S), will be the identifier for the specific user making the request. The object (O), is the task that the user wants to perform. Since a task explicitly defines its associated permissions (object, action pair), they are not separately identified in the request. The Action (A), is simply the request to 'perform'. In the second case a user requests access to a resource object that is not a workflow 'task', for example, to access the 'pump room'. In this case, O will be the 'pump room', and A will be 'access'. The third type of request is to activate a role, for example, 'Adam' wants to activate the role 'coordinator'. In such requests, S is 'Adam', O is the role 'coordinator', and A is 'activate'. The decision (DS) will be either {Allow}, {Deny}, or {Not applicable} if no matching policies are found.

4.2   Policy Sets

In XACML 'Policy sets' are used to group related policies, which contain, groups of related access control rules. The RBAC profile of XACML predefines some policy sets and makes use of them to determine the access control decision. For example, a `RoleAssignment<PolicySet>` will include all policies and rules related to role assignment. In this extended profile we will make use of these policy sets and introduce new policy sets.

BP-XACML includes seven types of access control policy sets. The PDP will use two policy sets, the `Role<PolicySet>`, and the `Permission<PolicySet>` to make decisions on the requests directed to the PDP. The `task<PolicySet>`, and `RoleTask<PolicySet>` are used to state the tasks that a role is allowed to perform. `IR<PolicySet>` is used to state instance-level restrictions. The `SoD <PolicySet>`, and `RoleAssignment<PolicySet>`, are used for stating and activating roles of each user. The `Role<PolicySet>`, `Permission<PolicySet>`, and `RoleAssignment<PolicySet>` are adopted from the XACML RBAC profile [9]. The rest of the `PolicySets` are newly introduced in this paper, and will be discussed in this section. The mechanism and application of these policy sets will be discussed in more detail in section 6. Figure 3 shows the relation between IRPS, RTPS, and TPS, and gives a summary of the structure of each policy set.

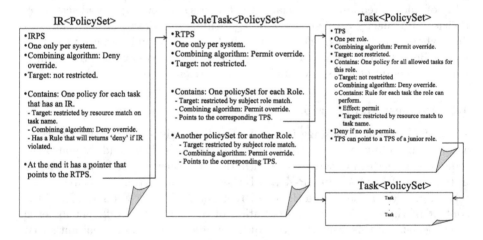

Fig. 3. New Policy Sets

`Task<PolicySet>` (TPS) is a `<PolicySet>` that contains the actual tasks authorised for a given role. The `<Target>` element of a TPS, should not limit the applicability of the `<PolicySet>` as the `IR<PolicySet>` and the `RoleTask<Policy Set>` restrict access (see Figure 3). To achieve role hierarchy, a TPS associated with a senior role may also contain references to TPSs associated with junior roles, thereby allowing the senior role to inherit all access to tasks associated with the junior roles. In a TPS, (S) refers to user's role, and (O) refers to task.

RoleTask<PolicySet> (RTPS) is a <PolicySet> that contains the Roles, and for each role it points to the corresponding Task<PolicySet> (i.e. the TPS is included in the RTPS by reference). The <Target> element of a RTPS, should not restrict the applicability of the <PolicySet>, but the <PolicySet>s for each role (that are included within the RTPS) has a target restricting applicability for the specified role only. The RTPS is used to achieve role hierarchy. In the RTPS Subject (S) refers to the user's role, and Object (O) refers to the task.

IR<PolicySet> (IRPS) is a <PolicySet> that describes instance-level restrictions. The RTPS and TPS can only be reached through the IRPS where they are included by reference. The Task Authority will first access this policy set to check if there is no violation of an IR constraint, then it will be pointed via the RoleTask<PolicySet> to the related Task<PolicySet>. Section 6.3 explains this in more detail. In the IRPS, the subject (S) is not restricted because IR constraints deal with task instances regardless of the subject. The object (O) is the task, and the action (A) is 'perform'. For example, no user is allowed to perform both 'issue work order' and 'approve work order'. In this case the IRPS will have both tasks in one policy making sure that the user does not perform both for the same instance.

SoD<PolicySet> (SoDPS) is a <PolicySet> that describes separation of duties constraints. It restricts access to the RoleAssignment<PolicySet>. The Role Enablement Authority will first access this policy set to check if there is no violation of SoD constraint, then it will be pointed to the RoleAssignment <PolicySet>. In a SoDPS, the subject (S) is not restricted because SoD constraints deal with roles regardless of the subject. The object (O) is a role. Each policy in the SoD<PolicySet> includes a pair of conflicting roles.

4.3   Conditions

A condition is specified as a Boolean expression that is evaluated at runtime. There are two main types of policy conditions of interest in specifying access restrictions in this policy model. The first one is dynamic Separation of Duties (SoD) conditions on role level. The other one is instance-level restrictions (IR).

A dynamic SoD condition is an expression that can be evaluated for user-role relation by testing the current active roles for this user. It is used to prevent a user from activating two conflicting roles by the same user at the same time. They are defined as policies in the SoD<PolicySet>. $SoD : (Role1, Role2)$. The Role enablement authority (REA) will be able to know the SoD restriction before enabling a role. It will use the 'session' component to check the current status of role enablement for a user requesting role activation. Session maintains the list of active roles for each user.

An 'instance-level restriction' (IR) condition is an expression that can be evaluated to check the relation between two objects within the same instance. They are defined as policies within the IR<PolicySet>. $IR : (\{Task1, Task2\}, type)$. IR is a type of SoD (or BoD) restriction on a task level that only applies within the same instance. It makes sure that the restriction is met within the same instance. For example, the task of 'closing work order' should have a restriction that it can be only done by the same user who performed 'issue work order' for this same instance.

5   BP-XACML: Policy Model

BP-XACML is designed to be backward-compatible with the RBAC-XACML policy structure. This has an important benefit: It means that role-based authorisation policies can be defined and managed independently of the workflow authorisation system. These policies will still be applied when a user requires access to a controlled resource to execute an instance of a business process. This design approach introduces some complexity, most notably in the inclusion of the Task Authority as a separate PDP to authorise task activation. But it is necessary because the role-based authorisation policies that control access to an organisation's valuable resources, (e.g. customer records, financial records etc.) are typically created and maintained independently of the business processes. They will often exist before a workflow is created that uses the controlled resources. These policies still need to be applied in the context of the workflow but we argue that this should not be done by a parallel and duplicated workflow authorisation system, since this would be inefficient and difficult to maintain. Accordingly, we have designed the BP-XACML policy structure to work with an existing RBAC-XACML policy set. This results in an integrated system which can handle both workflow and non-workflow requests from a single (and therefore consistent) set of policies.

After explaining the structure of the BP-XACML policy language, this section will describe the BP-XACML policy model. It shows how access decisions are made using the defined 'policy sets', describes the needed authorities and repositories, and explains the policy model framework.

5.1   Authorities and Repositories

In this policy model we are introducing a new authority and two repositories that are needed to fulfill the requirements. They are the Task authority (TA), Performers list (PL), and Task-permissions list (TPL). We also include the 'Role Enablement Authority (REA)', and 'session' concept from the XACML RBAC profile, and we elaborate on how to use them, as the RBAC profile does not provide these details.

It might appear unnecessarily complex to add these authorities, where some of them are essentially a specialised PDP. One might argue that one PDP should be enough. However, the RBAC-XACML profile [2], which is proposed by OASIS, adopts this approach in introducing the REA. The RBAC profile shows that role enablement should be out of the scope of the PDP, that is why REA was introduced to be responsible for role assignment and enablement [2]. The justification for having a specialised PDP for role enablement can be understood by looking at the basic request concept of XACML, where each request contains a subject and an object. The PDP is designed to deal with one interpretation of each aspect of the request (subject, object, action). For example, in RBAC-XACML if the PDP receives a request it will look at the subject as the user's role, and the object as the resource that the user wants to perform an action on. Adam, who is a manager, wants to read file2. The PDP will use the permission policy to determine if managers are allowed to read file2. A request to activate a role has the subject as the user ID, and the object as the role that needs to be activated. That is why it was necessary to have a specialised PDP called REA. This REA is designed to look at the subject as the user's ID, and the object is the role that the user wants to activate. Therefore it will be able to deal with activation requests.

BP-XACML deals with three different type of requests, where each type of request has a different interpretation of subject and object. The change in subject and object interpretation, makes it necessary to have a different authority to deal with each different type of request. The request to perform a task has the user's role as the subject and the task ID as the object. Therefore, the authorisation of task performance is out of the scope of the PDP. TA is introduced in this model to be the specialised PDP responsible for making a task performance decisions. It permits backward compatibility with the role and permission policy sets defined in RBAC-XACML. TA deals with requests on the basis that the subject is the user's role and the object as the task ID. Therefore, it is able to deal with requests to perform a task.

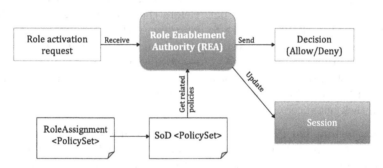

Fig. 4. Role Enablement Authority

Role Enablement Authority (REA) uses the SoD<PolicySet>, and Role Assignment<PolicySet> to either allow or deny activation of a specific role for a specific user.

Session provides a quarryable service, which maintains and continuously refreshes the state of user role enablement relations.

Figure 4 shows how REA uses the RoleAssignment<PolicySet> to know if the user is allowed to enable a role or not. Before reaching the RoleAssignment <PolicySet>, REA checks the SoD<PolicySet> to check if a SoD policy is available for this role. If such a policy exists, REA needs to know the status of the user's activated roles. This information can be retrieved from the user's session.

The information allows REA to evaluate if the condition is met or not. Based on that REA will send the final decision on the role enablement request.

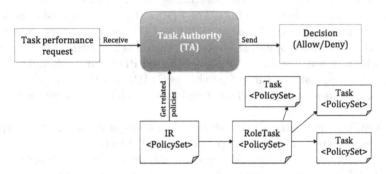

Fig. 5. Task Authority

Task Authority (TA) uses the IR<PolicySet>, and Task<Policy Set> to either allow or deny a user's request to perform a specific task.

Performers list is introduced to provide a quarryable service to report the user that performed a completed task instance. It maintains the state of user 'task instance' performance relations, and continuously refreshes the state.

As can be seen in Figure 5, TA uses Task<PolicySet> to check if the role is allowed to perform the task or not. Before checking the Task<PolicySet>, TA first checks the IR<PolicySet> to determine if there are any instance-level restrictions on such task. If a restriction is found TA needs to retrieve extra information to assess the restriction. This information can be found through the 'Performers list (PL)'. It is important to be able to check IR restrictions. In order for an IR condition to be evaluated, it is necessary to know the performer of a given task instance.

Task-permissions list (TPL) is a new proposal. It maintains the state of task-permission relations. TPL is used by the context handler (CH) to determine the permissions associated with each task. TPL provides a list of permissions for each task, where a permission is an action on a resource.

5.2   Access Control

BP-XACML model controls three types of access control requests: activating a role (controlled by the REA), performing a task (controlled by the TA), and performing action on a resource (controlled by the PDP). The context handler is responsible for forwarding the request to the corresponding authority depending on its type.

A single SoD<PolicySet> is defined in the system, which contains all SoD restrictions. The policy set itself is not limited (i.e. the target is empty and therefore does not restrict the applicability of the included policies), but each policy is limited to a specific role. It contains a single <PolicySetIdReference>

element, which refers to the `RoleAssignment<PolicySet>` (RAPS). There is a single RAPS in a system, which contains the information on whether to allow or deny the role activation for a specific user.

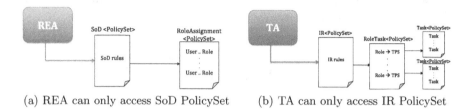

(a) REA can only access SoD PolicySet   (b) TA can only access IR PolicySet

Fig. 6. New PDPs access

As shown in Figure 6-a, the RAPS must be stored in a policy repository in such a way that it can never be reached directly by the REA; RAPS must be reachable only through the SoDPS. This is because, in order to support separation of duties, it is important that the SoD policies are satisfied before reaching the RAPS. For REA to achieve a decision on role activation request it accesses the SoDPS and only check the RAPS if the SoD rules were satisfied.

A single `IR<PolicySet>` is defined in the system, which contains all IR restrictions. The policy set itself is not limited, as the policy set target is empty, but each policy is limited to a specific task. The policy set contains a single `<PolicySetIdReference>` element, which refers to the `RoleTask<PolicySet>`. For the system there is a single `RoleTask<Policy Set>`, which contains a `<PolicySet>` for each role, which points to the corresponding `Task<PolicySet>`. A user will be authorised to perform a task if there is a permit rule for the task in the TPS for a role that the user has active.

As shown in Figure 6-b, TPS instances, and the RTPS must be stored in a policy repository in such a way that they can never be reached directly by the TA. RTPS must be reachable only through the IRPS. This is because, in order to support 'role hierarchy', the TPS depends on the RTPS to ensure that only subjects holding the corresponding role attribute (or senior role) will gain access to perform tasks in the given TPS. For TA to achieve a decision on a request to 'perform a task', it first must access the IRPS, and check if there are any related IR policies. IRPS will then point to RTPS. Using the user's role, RTPS points to the corresponding TPS, which contains rules stating whether this role is allowed to perform a task or not. These `<PolicySet>` relationships and constrains are summarised in Figure 3.

5.3 Policy Framework

Figure 7 shows the complete BP-XACML framework without the 'policy sets'. It includes all the authorities, components, and repositories. As explained earlier, the policy model should be unified and deal with all authorisation requests, regardless of whether or not they arise in the context of a workflow. For this reason, the BP-XACML policy model is designed to deal with several types of requests. It could be either a request to activate a role for a user, a request to perform a task, or a standard RBAC request to perform an action on a resource. In this section we will discuss each type of request by it self, and show how it is handled within the framework.

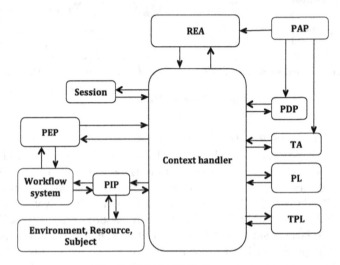

Fig. 7. BP-XACML framework

The role activation requests are directed to the 'role enablement authority (REA)' by the context handler. The REA will use theSoD<PolicySet> to check for any SoD restrictions on this role. Then it will point to the RAPS to decide if this user is allowed to activate this role or not. If there was an SoD constraint on the role, REA will require extra information. For example, if there is a SoD condition on activating this role, REA needs to make sure that activating this role will not breach the SoD condition. Information about the activated roles of this user will be obtained from the 'session' through the CH. Figure 8 shows the steps related to this type of request.

The standard RBAC request is a request to perform an action on a resource, where the resource is not a role or a task (e.g. read a file). This type of request is directed to the PDP, and will be handled exactly how access requests are handled in the RBAC-XACML profile [9] using the Role<PolicySet> and permission<PolicySet>. For more information please refer to [9]. In BP-XACML, a request to perform a task, will produce a set of one or more requests of this type (standard request).

If the request was to perform a specific task, the context handler will forward the requests to the TA. The TA will use the IRPS to check if there are any IR restrictions on this task. Violation of an IR results in a deny decision. Then it will use the user's role to identify the proper TPS through the RTPS. TPS identifies

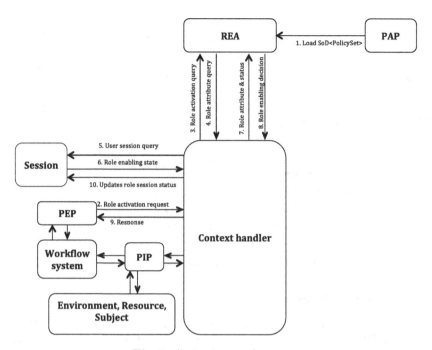

Fig. 8. Activating a role request

the tasks that this user is allowed to perform based on the role activated at the request time. If an IR is restricting the assigning of a task, the TA will obtain extra information from the 'performers list (PL)' through the CH to evaluate the IR condition. If the TA allows the user to perform the task, CH will use the Task Permissions List (TPL) to retrieve all permissions associated with the task. Each permission is a pair of an action and a resource. CH will create a request for each permission, with requests containing the user's role, action, and resource. These requests will be sent to the PDP and dealt with as standard requests to perform an action on a resource. PDP will send back each decision individually. CH will combine the decisions, where deny over rides. So, if one request was denied, the whole request to perform the task will be denied. If all requests were allowed, the CH will then send back to the PEP that this user is allowed to perform the task. Figure 9 shows the steps for this type of request.

6   BP-XACML: Policy Semantics

In this section, we will refine the previously described policy structure with specific data and language representations. Users, roles, operations and permission are all part of the RBAC profile of XACML. In this paper we adopt these entities and the way they are expressed from the RBAC-XACML [2]. Refer to [2] for information on the representation of users, roles, operation, and permissions.

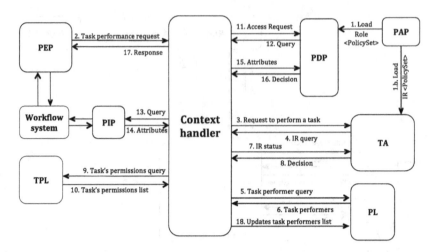

Fig. 9. A request to perform a task

6.1   Task and Task Instances

Task and task instances are new features that are not supported in RBAC-XACML. In BP-XACML tasks are expressed as an XACML Resource. Listing 1 shows an example `Task<PolicySet>` showing the task as a resource.

```
<PolicySet ... PolicySetId="TPS:coordinator:role" PolicyCombiningAlgId="&policy-combine;permit-overrides">
 <Target>  <Subjects><AnySubject/></Subjects>   <Resources><AnyResource/></Resources>   <Actions><AnyAction
          /></Actions>  </Target>
<Policy PolicyId="Allowed tasks"  RuleCombiningAlgId="&policy-combine;permit-overrides">
<Target>
 <Target>  <Subjects><AnySubject/></Subjects>   <Resources><AnyResource/></Resources>   <Actions><AnyAction
          /></Actions>  </Target>
 <Rule Effect="Permit" RuleId="issue:work:order:task">
<Subjects><AnySubject/></Subjects>
<Resources>
 <ResourceMatch MatchId="&function;string-match">
  <AttributeValue DataType="&xml;string">issue work order</AttributeValue>
  <ResourceAttributeDesignator AttributeId="&resource;resource-id" DataType="&xml;string"/>
 </ResourceMatch> </Resources>
<Actions>
 <ActionMatch MatchId="&function;string-match">
 <AttributeValue DataType="&xml;string">perform</AttributeValue>
  <ActionAttributeDesignator AttributeId="&action;action-id" DataType="&xml;string"/>
 </ActionMatch>  </Actions>  </Target> </Rule>
 <Rule Effect="Deny" RuleId="DenyRule"/>
</Policy>  </PolicySet>
```

Listing 1. Task Policy set

In listing 1 task was represented as an object in the policy, because TPSs are linking the user's role to the task, so the task is the object. To be able to represent 'Task instance' a new object attribute is introduced, it is called 'instance'. It is similar to the 'role' attribute from the RBAC-XACML profile. In section 6.3 an example listing showing instance-level restriction will show how to make use of the new attribute 'instance".

As it can be seen the `Task<PolicySet>` will include a policy for each task the role is allowed to perform. The example includes a policy for the task 'issue work order' as a part of the policy set. The policy says if someone wants to perform the action 'perform' on the object 'task: issue work order' they will be allowed. As can be seen in the listing, the policy set target is not limiting the applicability of the policy set. `RoleTask<PolicySet>` will limit the applicability to users with the role 'coordinator' and then point to this policySet. Listing 2 is an example `RoleTask<PolicySet>` for the role 'coordinator'.

```
<PolicySet ... PolicySetId="RTPS" PolicyCombiningAlgId="&policy-combine;permit-overrides">
 <Target> <Subjects><AnySubject/></Subjects> <Resources><AnyResource/></Resources> <Actions><AnyAction/></
    Actions> </Target>
 <Policy PolicyId="Coordinator:Role" RuleCombiningAlgId="&rule-combine;permit-overrides">
 <Target>
  <Subjects>
   <SubjectMatch MatchId="&function:any-of">
    <Apply FunctionId="urn:oasis:names:tc:xacml:3.0:function;string-equal"
     <AttributeValue DataType="&xml;string">coordinator</AttributeValue>
     <SubjectAttributeDesignator AttributeId="urn:someapp:attributes:role" DataType="&xml;string"/>
    </Apply> </SubjectMatch> </Subjects>
  <Resources><AnyResource/></Resources>
  <Actions><AnyAction/></Actions>
 </Target>
 <!-- Use tasks associated with the "coordinator" role -->
 <PolicySetIdReference> TPS:coordinator:role </PolicySetIdReference>
 </policy> </PolicySet>
```

Listing 2. The Role Task Policy Set

6.2   SoD on a Role Level

In BP-XACML SoD is expressed as policies in the `SoD<PolicySet>`. SoD refers to the dynamic role level separation of duties, which is used to make sure that no one user activates two conflicting roles at the same time. Listing 3 shows an example SoD policy set. The policy set includes policies stating conflicting roles. For example, the policy set in listing 3 includes a policy stating that in order to activate the role 'coordinator, the role 'manager' should not be in the activated roles of the same user.

The function 'Session' is a new function that helps to check that the given role is not available in the activated roles of the given user. This function takes one argument of data-type "..#string", which is the user's ID. It returns a list of all roles currently activated for this user. Then the predefined function "any-of" will compare the given string with the list retrieved by the session function. If the role was found the function will return the result 'true', and if it was not found, it will return 'false'. If the condition was true the rule will return 'deny' and the request will be denied. If the condition returns false, the rule will not do anything and continue to the `RoleAssignment<PolicySet>`.

```
<PolicySet ... PolicySetId="SoD" PolicyCombiningAlgId="&policy-combine;deny-overrides">
 <Target> <Subjects><AnySubject/></Subjects> <Resources><AnyResource/></Resources> <Actions><AnyAction
    /></Actions> </Target>
 <Policy PolicyId="Coordinator:Role" RuleCombiningAlgId="&rule-combine;deny-overrides">
 <Target> <Subjects><AnySubject/></Subjects>
  <Resources>
   <ResourceMatch MatchId="&function;string-match">
    <AttributeValue DataType="&xml;string"> Coordinator </AttributeValue>
    <ResourceAttributeDesignator AttributeId="&resource;resource-id" DataType="&xml;string"/>
   </ResourceMatch> </Resources>
  <Actions> activate </Actions>
 </Target>
 <Rule RuleId="role:manager:not:active" Effect="Deny">
  <Target> <Subjects><AnySubject/></Subjects> <Resources><AnyResource/></Resources> <Actions><AnyAction
    /></Actions> </Target>
  <Condition FunctionId="urn:oasis:names:tc:xacml:3.0:function:any-of">
   <AttributeValue DataType=&xml;string"> manager </AttributeValue>
   <Apply FunctionId="http://localhost/BPXACML/function#function;Session">
   <SubjectAttributeDesignator AttributeId="urn:someapp:attributes:role" DataType="&xml;string"/>
   </Apply> </Condition>    </Rule> </Policy>
 <PolicySetIdReference> Role:Assignment </PolicySetIdReference>
</PolicySet>
```

Listing 3. SoD policy set example

Listing 4 shows an example `RoleAssignment<PolicySet>`. The `<PolicySet>` contains a policy for each user, which contains rules for each role the user can activate. The policy set in listing 4 includes an example policy for the user Adam, which includes an example rule for activating the role 'coordinator'.

```
<PolicySet ... PolicySetId="Role:Assignment" PolicyCombiningAlgId="&policy-combine;deny-overrides">
  <Target>  <Subjects><AnySubject/></Subjects>  <Resources><AnyResource/></Resources>  <Actions><AnyAction
          /></Actions>  </Target>
<Policy PolicyId="Roles:For:user:Adam" RuleCombiningAlgId="&rule-combine;deny-overrides">
  <Target>
  <Subjects>
   <SubjectMatch MatchId="&function;string-match">
    <AttributeValue DataType="&xml;string"> Adam </AttributeValue>
    <SubjectAttributeDesignator AttributeId="&subject;subject-id" DataType="&xml;string"/>
   </SubjectMatch> </Subjects>
  <Resources><AnyResource/></Resources>
  <Actions><AnyAction/></Actions>
  </Target>
<Rule RuleId="Permission:to:activate:coordinator:role" Effect="Permit">
  <Target>
  <Subjects><AnySubject/></Subjects>
  <Resources>
   <ResourceMatch MatchId="&function;string-equal">
    <AttributeValue DataType="&xml;string"> Coordinator </AttributeValue>
    <ResourcesAttributeDesignator AttributeId="&resource;resource-id" DataType="&xml;string"/>
   </ResourcetMatch>  </Resources>
  <Actions> Activate </Actions>  </Target>  </Rule>  </Policy> </PolicySet>
```

Listing 4. Role Assignment policy set example

6.3   Instance-Level Restrictions (IR)

Instance-level restrictions (IR) are used to fulfill the need to apply history based restrictions within the same instance. For example, the scenario states that the user who close the 'work order' should be the same user who issued it. So, for the same 'work order' (same instance), the user to perform 'close work order' must be the same user who performed 'issue work order'. IR restrictions are written as policies in the IR policy set.

Listing 5 is an example `IR<PolicySet>` that includes instance-level restriction using the BP-XACML language. The IR policy set has a policy for the task 'close work order'. The policy has a rule stating that the user must be the same user who issued the work order for the same instance.

The function 'PL' is a new function that retrieves the performers list of a specific task for a specific instance. This function takes two arguments of datatype "..#string", which are a task name and an instance number. It returns a list of all users who performed the task for this instance. Then the predefined function "any-of" will compare the given string, which is the username of the user who requests to perform the task, with the list retrieved by the PL function. The function "any-of" will return 'true' if the user was in the performers list, and it will return 'false' if it was not found in the performers list. If it was a SoD-IR then this condition will be satisfied and the user will be denied if he was part of the list. Because it is a binding of duties constraint in this case, we want the rule to deny only if the user was not found in the list (i.e. the function 'any-of' returned false), and permit it if he was in the list (i.e. the function 'any-of' returned true). For this reason the function "not" has been added to reverse the output of the function.

```
<PolicySet ... PolicySetId="IR" PolicyCombiningAlgId="&policy-combine;deny-overrides">
  <Target>   <Subjects><AnySubject/></Subjects>   <Resources><AnyResource/></Resources>   <Actions><AnyAction
    /></Actions>   </Target>
<Policy PolicyId="close:work:order:task RuleCombiningAlgId="&rule-combine;deny-overrides""
<Target>   <Subjects><AnySubject/></Subjects>
       <Resources>
       <ResourceMatch MatchId="&function;string-match">
          <AttributeValue DataType="&xml;string"> close work order</AttributeValue>
          <ResourceAttributeDesignator AttributeId="&resource;resource-id" DataType="&xml;string"/>
       </ResourceMatch>   </Resources>
     <Actions>
     <ActionMatch MatchId="&function;string-match">
     <AttributeValue DataType="&xml;string"> perform </AttributeValue>
     <ActionAttributeDesignator AttributeId="&action;action-id" DataType="&xml;string"/>
     </ActionMatch>  </Actions>  </Target>
   <Rule RuleId="Must:be:who:issued:work:order" Effect="Deny">
<Target> <Subjects><AnySubject/></Subjects>   <Resources><AnyResource/></Resources>   <Actions><AnyAction/></
          Actions> </Target>
       <Condition FunctionId=urn:oasis:names:tc:xacml:1.0:function:not>
          <Apply FunctionId="urn:oasis:names:tc:xacml:3.0:function:any-of">
          <SubjectAttributeDesignator AttributeId="&subject;subject-id" DataType="&xml;string"/>
          <Apply FunctionId="http://localhost/BPXACML/function#function;PL">
          <AttributeValue DataType=&xml;string"> issue work order </AttributeValue>
          <ResourceAttributeDesignator AttributeId="urn:someapp:attributes:instance" DataType="&xml;string"/>
       </Apply>  </Apply> </Condition>  </Policy>
<!-- Point to the RoleTask policy set -->
<PolicySetIdReference> RoleTask:PolicySet </PolicySetIdReference>
</PolicySet>
```

Listing 5. Example IR Policy set

7 Related Literature

To the best of the authors' knowledge, currently there is no published work that aims to extend XACML to support business process authorisation policies. There are several published works that extend XACML to support different models but none of them focus on 'business processes'. For example, Wolter et. al. in [19] developed a XACML customised profile that supports RBAC concept, mandatory access control, and permission-based separation of duty policies. The work does not take into consideration the special requirements that 'business process' authorisation policies need such as 'tasks', and it does not extend XACML to support business process authorisation policies.

The work in [4], [10], [18], and [19] all focus on proposing a model transformation framework that focuses on deriving security policies from the process model, using a form of extended BPMN as a process modeling language and XACML as a policy language. These papers start by proposing a new extension to the process modeling language BPMN, and then propose a model-driven extraction of the policies based on a mapping between the new modeling language and the policy language. All four proposals are limited to the BPMN extension proposed in the corresponding paper ("seBPMN"[19], "ConstrainedBPMN"[18] "SecureBPMN"[4], and "BPMS"[10]) and they do not extend XACML. Sinha et. al. [14] also propose a method of translating security requirements into XACML, by making use of the obligation feature in XACML. It does not provide an extension to XACML. A draft version of the RBAC-XACML profile [1] proposed a policy structure to handle dynamic SoD. We use the same policy structure, but implement the SoD restriction in a different way. We also provide more details on the way it should be used.

8 Conclusion

This paper introduced BP-XACML, a new profile that extends the RBAC-XACML and enables the specification of business process authorisation policies. In addition to supporting the XACML RBAC profile, the extended language also supports the representation of tasks and tasks instance. It proposes a new policy set called Task<PolicySet> for the incorporation of business process tasks. BP-XACML also supports separation of duties and binding of duties constraints at the level of process instances. It supports the representation of the instance-level restrictions in a way that can be linked to the related tasks and can be evaluated. The paper proposes a new policy set IR<PolicySet>. The new repository 'performers list' helps in evaluating the instance-level restrictions. The new repository TPL links tasks to permissions. Finally, it supports the 'separation of duties' on the role level, making use of the 'REA' and 'sessions' to find, and evaluate the SoD restrictions.

As a future work, it is intended to do an experimental implementation to test the efficiency, feasibility and usability of this design.

References

1. Anderson, A.: Xacml profile for role based access control (rbac), committee draft 01. Standard, OASIS, February 2004
2. Anderson, A.: Core and hierarchical role based access control (rbac) profile of xacml version 2.0, oasis standard. Standard, OASIS Open, February 2005
3. Atluri, V., Kuang Huang, W.: An authorization model for workflows. In: Bertino, E., Kurth, H., Martella, G., Montolivo, E. (eds.) European Symposium on Research in Computer Security. LNCS, vol. 1146, pp. 44–64. Springer, Heidelberg (1996)
4. Brucker, A.D., Hang, I., Lückemeyer, G., Ruparel, R.: Securebpmn: Modeling and enforcing access control requirements in business processes. In: Proceedings of the 17th ACM Symposium on Access Control Models and Technologies, SACMAT 2012, pp. 123–126. ACM, New York (2012)
5. Ferraiolo, D., Kuhn, D.: Role-Based Access Control. In: 15th National Computer Security Conference, pp. 554–563, October 1992
6. Gartner. Leading in times of transition: The 2010 CIO agenda. In Gartner EXP CIO report (2010)
7. Leitner, M., Rinderle-Ma, S., Mangler, J.: Aw-rbac: access control in adaptive workflow systems. In: Sixth International Conference on Availability, Reliability and Security, ARES, pp. 27–34. IEEE (2011)
8. Liu, A.X., Chen, F., Hwang, J., Xie, T.: Xengine: A fast and scalable xacml policy evaluation engine. In: Proceedings of the 2008 ACM SIGMETRICS International Conference on Measurement and Modeling of Computer Systems, SIGMETRICS 2008, pp. 265–276. ACM, New York (2008)
9. Moses, T.: Extensible access control markup language (xacml) version 2.0. oasis standard. Technical report, OASIS Open (2005)
10. Mülle, J., Stackelberg, S.V., Böhm, K.: A security language for bpmn process models. In: Karlsruhe Reports in Informatics, Karlsruhe (2011)

11. Oh, S., Park, S.: Task-Role Based Access Control (T-RBAC): An Improved Access Control Model for Enterprise Environment. In: Ibrahim, M., Küng, J., Revell, N. (eds.) DEXA 2000. LNCS, vol. 1873, pp. 264–273. Springer, Heidelberg (2000)
12. Samarati, P., di Vimercati, S.C.: Access Control: Policies, Models, and Mechanisms. In: Focardi, R., Gorrieri, R. (eds.) FOSAD 2000. LNCS, vol. 2171, pp. 137–196. Springer, Heidelberg (2001)
13. Sandhu, R., Coyne, E., Feinstein, H., Youman, C.: Role - based access control models. IEEE Computer **29**, 38–47 (1996)
14. Sinha, S., Sinha, S.K., Purkayastha, B.S.: Synchronization of Authorization Flow with Work Object Flow in a Document Production Workflow Using XACML and BPEL. In: Das, V.V., Vijaykumar, R. (eds.) ICT 2010. CCIS, vol. 101, pp. 365–370. Springer, Heidelberg (2010)
15. Strembeck, M., Mendling, J.: Modeling process-related rbac models with extended uml activity models. Information & Software Technology **53**, 456–483 (2011)
16. Wainer, J., Kumar, A., Barthelmess, P.: WRBAC a work-flow security model incorporating controlled overriding of constraints. International Journal of Cooperative Information Systems (IJCIS) **4**, 455–486 (2003)
17. Wainer, J., Kumar, A., Barthelmess, P.: DW-RBAC: A formal security model of delegation and revocation in workflow systems. Inf. Syst. **32**(3), 365–384 (2007)
18. Wolter, C., Schaad, A., Meinel, C.: Deriving XACML Policies from Business Process Models. In: Weske, M., Hacid, M.-S., Godart, C. (eds.) WISE Workshops 2007. LNCS, vol. 4832, pp. 142–153. Springer, Heidelberg (2007)
19. Wolter, C., Weiss, C., Meinel, C.: An xacml extension for business process-centric access control policies. In: IEEE International Symposium on Policies for Distributed Systems and Networks, POLICY 2009, pp. 166–169, July 2009

Symmetric Cryptanalysis

How TKIP Induces Biases of Internal States of Generic RC4

Ryoma Ito[(✉)] and Atsuko Miyaji

Japan Advanced Institute of Science and Technology,
1-1 Asahidai, Nomi-shi, Ishikawa 923-1292, Japan
ryoma.ito.shs@gmail.com,
miyaji@jaist.ac.jp

Abstract. RC4, designed by Rivest, is widely used including WPA, which is one of the security protocols for IEEE 802.11 wireless standard. The first 3-byte RC4 keys in WPA generated by IV are *known* since IV can be obtained by observing a packet. In 2014, Sen Gupta et al. found linear correlations between the keystream byte and *known* RC4 key bytes. In 2015, Our previous work extended linear correlations to include *unknown* internal states as well as the keystream byte and *known* RC4 key bytes. They found more than 150 linear correlations experimentally, and proved only 6 cases theoretically. In this paper, we will provide theoretical proof of 15 cases out of their unproven linear correlations. These theoretical results demonstrated how TKIP key generation procedure in WPA induces biases on internal states different from generic RC4.

Keywords: RC4 · WPA · TKIP · Linear correlation

1 Introduction

RC4 is the stream cipher designed by Rivest in 1987, and is widely used in various standard protocols such as Secure Socket Layer/Transport Layer Security (SSL/TLS), Wired Equivalent Privacy (WEP) and Wi-fi Protected Access (WPA), etc. Due to its popularity and simplicity, RC4 has been intensively analyzed since its specification was made public on the internet in 1994 [1–11]. RC4 consists of two algorithms: the Key Scheduling Algorithm (KSA) and the Pseudo Random Generation Algorithm (PRGA). Both the KSA and the PRGA update a secret internal state S which is a permutation of all N (typically, $N = 2^8$) possible bytes and two 8-bit indices i and j. The KSA generates the initial state from a secret key K of l bytes to become the input of the PRGA. Once the initial state is generated in the KSA, the PRGA outputs a pseudo-random sequence (keystream) $Z_1, Z_2, \ldots, Z_r$, where r is the number of rounds. The KSA and the

A. Miyaji—Supported by the project "The Security infrastructure Technology for Integrated Utilization of Big Data" of Japan Science and Technology Agency CREST.

E. Foo and D. Stebila (Eds.): ACISP 2015, LNCS 9144, pp. 329–342, 2015.
DOI: 10.1007/978-3-319-19962-7_19

PRGA are shown in Algorithms 1 and 2, respectively, where $\{S_i^K, i, j_i^K\}$ and $\{S_r, i_r, j_r\}$ are $\{S, i, j\}$ in the i-th and r-th round of the KSA and the PRGA, respectively; t_r is a 8-bit index of Z_r. All addition used in both the KSA and the PRGA are arithmetic addition modulo N.

Algorithm 1. KSA	Algorithm 2. PRGA
1: **for** $i = 0$ to $N - 1$ **do**	1: $r \leftarrow 0$, $i_0 \leftarrow 0$, $j_0 \leftarrow 0$
2: $S_0^K[i] \leftarrow i$	2: **loop**
3: **end for**	3: $r \leftarrow r + 1$, $i_r \leftarrow i_{r-1} + 1$
4: $j_0^K \leftarrow 0$	4: $j_r \leftarrow j_{r-1} + S_{r-1}[i_r]$
5: **for** $i = 0$ to $N - 1$ **do**	5: Swap($S_{r-1}[i_r], S_{r-1}[j_r]$)
6: $j_{i+1}^K \leftarrow j_i^K + S_i^K[i] + K[i \bmod l]$	6: $t_r \leftarrow S_r[i_r] + S_r[j_r]$
7: Swap($S_i^K[i], S_i^K[j_{i+1}^K]$)	7: **Output:** $Z_r \leftarrow S_r[t_r]$
8: **end for**	8: **end loop**

WPA is the security protocol for IEEE 802.11 wireless networks standardized as a substitute for WEP in 2003, and uses RC4 for encryption. WPA improves a 16-byte RC4 key generation procedure known as the Temporary Key Integrity Protocol (TKIP) to prevent an attack against WEP by Fluhrer et al. [2]. One of characteristic features in TKIP is that the first 3-byte RC4 keys, $K[0]$, $K[1]$ and $K[2]$, are generated by the last 16-bit Initialization Vector (IV16), which is a sequence counter as follows:

$$K[0] = (\text{IV16} >> 8) \ \& \ 0\text{xFF},$$
$$K[1] = ((\text{IV16} >> 8) \ | \ 0\text{x20}) \ \& \ 0\text{x7F},$$
$$K[2] = \text{IV16} \ \& \ 0\text{xFF}.$$

Note that these RC4 key bytes in WPA are *known* since IV can be obtained by observing a packet.

In 2014, Sen Gupta et al. showed that there exists a characteristic distribution related to $K[0] + K[1]$ in WPA [3]. They also found some linear correlations between the keystream byte and *known* RC4 key bytes in WPA such as $Z_1 = -K[0] - K[1]$, $Z_3 = K[0] + K[1] + K[2] + 3$, etc. They applied these linear correlations to a plaintext recovery attack against WPA in the same way as the attack against SSL/TLS by Isobe et al. [4], and reduced the computational complexity necessary for the attack. In 2015, We extended linear correlations to include *unknown* internal states as well as the keystream byte and *known* RC4 key bytes [5]. Here, *unknown* internal states mean $S_r[i_{r+1}]$, $S_r[j_{r+1}]$, j_{r+1} and t_{r+1} for $r \geq 0$. Then, more than 150 linear correlations have been found experimentally, although only 6 correlations have been proved theoretically such as: $S_0[i_1] = K[0]$, $K[0] - K[1] - 3$ or $K[0] - K[1] - 1$; $S_{255}[i_{256}] = K[0]$ or $S_{255}[i_{256}] = K[1]$; $S_r[i_{r+1}] = K[0] + K[1] + 1$ $(0 \leq r \leq N)$.

We focus on these correlations remain unproven theoretically. [5]. Actually, linear correlations including internal states could contribute to reducing the computational complexity necessary for the state recovery attacks against RC4 proposed in [1,6,9] especially with WPA. Furthermore, theoretical proofs on linear correlations including internal states can make clear how TKIP induces biases as pointed out above. In the previous results, biases related to the first round internal state $S_0[i_1]$ were intensively investigated but other internal states in more than second round are still unknown. If we see how many round these biases have been kept in internal states, then key generation procedure in WPA could be reconstructed securely while keeping congruity with TKIP. In fact, TKIP should have been constructed in such a way that it can keep or further enhance original security level of generic RC4. Our analysis would be also useful to investigate a generic construction of key generation procedure including IV in such a way that it can keep or further enhance security level of an original encryption.

In this paper, we will provide theoretical proofs of 15 cases out of remaining linear correlations. Our contributions of 10 theorems can be summarized as follows:

- Theorems 1, 4 and 5 show that $\Pr(S_0[i_1] = -K[0] - K[1] - 3)$, $\Pr(S_1[i_2] = -K[0] - K[1] + K[2] - 1)$ and $\Pr(S_1[i_2] = K[0] - K[1] + K[2] + x)$ ($x \in \{-3, -1, 1\}$) are double probabilities of random association $\frac{1}{N}$ in WPA.
- Theorem 2 shows that $\Pr(S_0[i_1] = K[0] + K[1] + K[2] + 3)$ is less than half of the probability of random association $\frac{1}{N}$ in both generic RC4 and WPA.
- Theorem 3 shows that $\Pr(S_1[i_2] = K[0] + K[1] + K[2] + 3)$ is pretty high probability in comparison to the probability of random association $\frac{1}{N}$ in both generic RC4 and WPA. This probability is induced by Roos' bias, that is

$$\Pr(S_0[i_2] = K[0] + K[1] + K[2] + 3) \approx \left(1 - \frac{2}{N}\right) \cdot \left(1 - \frac{1}{N}\right)^{N+3} + \frac{1}{N}.$$

- Theorems 6-10 provide theoretical analysis related to the second round index j_2.

This paper is organized as follows: Section 2 summarizes the previous works necessary for both theoretical proofs and experiments such as Roos' biases [10, 11], biases of the initial state of the PRGA in generic RC4 [7], the distribution of $K[0] + K[1]$ and the initial state of PRGA in WPA [3] and the number of samples necessary for distinguishing two distributions [8]. Section 3 shows the theoretical proofs of biases based on linear equations and the experimental results. Section 4 concludes this paper.

2   Preliminary for Our Proofs and Experiments

Let us summarize some previous results which will be used in both theoretical proofs and experiments. Proposition 1 shows Roos' biases [11], correlations between the RC4 key bytes and S_0, proved by Paul and Maitra [10]. Proposition 2 shows biases of S_0, proved by Mantin [7]. Proposition 3 shows a distribution of $K[0] + K[1]$ in WPA, proved by Sen Gupta et al. [3]. By combining Proposition 3 with Proposition 1 (Roos' biases), a characteristic bias on the distribution of $S_0[1]$ is given as Proposition 4 [3]. Finally, Mantin and Shamir showed Proposition 5 related to the number of samples necessary for distinguishing two distributions with a constant probability of success [8].

Proposition 1 ([10, Corollary 2]). *In the initial state of the PRGA for* $0 \leq y \leq N - 1$, *we have*

$$\Pr(S_0[y] = \tfrac{y(y+1)}{2} + \textstyle\sum_{x=0}^{y} K[x]) \approx \left(1 - \tfrac{y}{N}\right) \cdot \left(1 - \tfrac{1}{N}\right)^{\left[\frac{y(y+1)}{2} + N\right]} + \tfrac{1}{N}.$$

Proposition 2 ([7, Theorem 6.2.1]). *In the initial state of the PRGA for* $0 \leq u \leq N - 1$, $0 \leq v \leq N - 1$, *we have*

$$\Pr(S_0[u] = v) = \begin{cases} \frac{1}{N}\left(\left(1 - \frac{1}{N}\right)^v + \left(1 - \left(1 - \frac{1}{N}\right)^v\right)\left(1 - \frac{1}{N}\right)^{N-u-1}\right) & \text{if } v \leq u, \\ \frac{1}{N}\left(\left(1 - \frac{1}{N}\right)^{N-u-1} + \left(1 - \frac{1}{N}\right)^v\right) & \text{if } v > u. \end{cases}$$

Proposition 3 ([3, Theorem 1]). *For* $0 \leq v \leq N - 1$, *the distribution of the sum* v *of* $K[0]$ *and* $K[1]$ *generated by the temporal key hash function in WPA is given as follows:*

$$\Pr(K[0] + K[1] = v) = 0 \qquad \text{if } v \text{ is odd,}$$
$$\Pr(K[0] + K[1] = v) = 0 \qquad \text{if } v \text{ is even and } v \in [0, 31] \cup [128, 159],$$
$$\Pr(K[0] + K[1] = v) = 2/256 \quad \text{if } v \text{ is even and}$$
$$\qquad\qquad\qquad v \in [32, 63] \cup [96, 127] \cup [160, 191] \cup [224, 255],$$
$$\Pr(K[0] + K[1] = v) = 4/256 \quad \text{if } v \text{ is even and } v \in [64, 95] \cup [192, 223].$$

Proposition 4 ([3, Theorem 2]). *In the initial state of the PRGA in WPA for* $0 \leq v \leq N - 1$, *we have*

$$\Pr(S_0[1] = v) = \alpha \cdot \Pr(K[0] + K[1] = v - 1)$$
$$+ (1 - \alpha) \cdot (1 - \Pr(K[0] + K[1] = v - 1)) \cdot \Pr(S_0[1] = v)_{\text{RC4}}$$
$$+ \tfrac{(1-\alpha)}{N-1} \cdot \textstyle\sum_{x \neq v} \Pr(K[0] + K[1] = x - 1) \cdot \Pr(S_0[1] = x)_{\text{RC4}}.$$

where, $\alpha = \frac{1}{N} + \left(1 - \frac{1}{N}\right)^{N+2}$, *and both* $\Pr(S_0[1] = v)_{\text{RC4}}$ *and* $\Pr(S_0[1] = x)_{\text{RC4}}$ *are taken from Proposition 2.*

Proposition 5 ([8, Theorem 2]). *Let* X *and* Y *be two distributions, and suppose that the event* e *occurs in* X *with a probability* p *and* Y *with a probability* $p \cdot (1 + q)$. *Then, for small* p *and* q, $\mathcal{O}(\frac{1}{p \cdot q^2})$ *samples suffice to distinguish* X *from* Y *with a constant probability of success.*

3   Newly Proved Linear Correlations

3.1   Biases Based on Linear Equations

In 2014, Sen Gupta et al. found some linear correlations between the keystream byte and *known* RC4 key bytes in WPA using the following linear equations for $a, b, c \in \{0, \pm 1\}$ and $d \in \{0, \pm 1, \pm 2, \pm 3\}$:

$$Z_r = a \cdot K[0] + b \cdot K[1] + c \cdot K[2] + d \quad \text{for } r \geq 1 \ [3]. \tag{1}$$

In 2015, we further extended linear correlations on *known* RC4 key bytes in both generic RC4 and WPA to those among *unknown* state information, *known* RC4 key bytes and the keystream byte such as

$$X_r = a \cdot Z_{r+1} + b \cdot K[0] + c \cdot K[1] + d \cdot K[2] + e \quad \text{for } r \geq 1, \tag{2}$$

where $X_r \in \{S_r[i_{r+1}], S_r[j_{r+1}], j_{r+1}, t_{r+1}\}$, $a, b, c, d \in \{0, \pm 1\}$, and $e \in \{0, \pm 1, \pm 2, \pm 3\}$ [5]. Then, 6 correlations out of more than 150 linear correlations have been shown theoretically as follows:

$$S_0[i_1] = K[0], K[0] - K[1] - 3 \text{ or } K[0] - K[1] - 1;$$
$$S_{255}[i_{256}] = K[0] \text{ or } K[1];$$
$$S_r[i_{r+1}] = K[0] + K[1] + 1 \text{ for } 0 \leq r \leq N.$$

In this paper, we will provide newly theoretical proofs of 15 linear correlations listed in Table 1. Actually, the first state recovery attack proposed by Knudsen et al. reconstructs the internal state of RC4 by computing optimum solutions of four *unknown* variables in each round such as $S_r[i_{r+1}]$, $S_r[j_{r+1}]$, j_{r+1} and t_{r+1} for $r \geq 0$ [6]. Therefore, these linear correlations could contribute to finding a correct internal state of RC4 in WPA.

We often use Roos' biases shown in Proposition 1 through proofs. Roos' biases are denoted by $\alpha_y = \Pr(S_0[y] = \frac{y(y+1)}{2} + \sum_{x=0}^{y} K[x])$. We assume through proofs that the probability of certain events, confirmed experimentally that there are no significant biases, is that of random association $\frac{1}{N}$ (e.g. events related to the internal state). We also assume that the RC4 key K is generated uniformly at random in both generic RC4 and WPA, except $K[0]$, $K[1]$ and $K[2]$ in WPA generated by IV using a sequence counter.

Table 1. Newly proved linear correlations in both generic RC4 and WPA

X_r	Linear correlations	RC4	WPA	Remarks
$S_0[i_1]$	$-K[0] - K[1] - 3$	0.005336	0.008437	Theorem 1
	$K[0] + K[1] + K[2] + 3$	0.001492	0.001491	Theorem 2
$S_1[i_2]$	$K[0] + K[1] + K[2] + 3$	0.360357	0.361718	Theorem 3
	$-K[0] - K[1] + K[2] - 1$	0.005305	0.008197	Theorem 4
	$K[0] - K[1] + K[2] - 3$	0.005295	0.008163	Theorem 5
	$K[0] - K[1] + K[2] - 1$	0.005290	0.008171	Theorem 5
	$K[0] - K[1] + K[2] + 1$	0.005309	0.008171	Theorem 5
j_2	$K[2]$	0.004428	0.005571	Theorem 6
	$-K[0] - K[1] + K[2] - 2$	0.003921	0.004574	Theorem 7
	$-K[0] - K[1] + K[2]$	0.003919	0.005573	Theorem 7
	$-K[0] - K[1] + K[2] + 2$	0.003912	0.004545	Theorem 7
	$-K[0] + K[1] + K[2]$	0.003921	0.005501	Theorem 8
	$-K[1] + K[2] - 2$	0.003911	0.005479	Theorem 9
	$-K[1] + K[2] + 3$	0.003899	0.005476	Theorem 9
	$K[0] - K[1] + K[2]$	0.003918	0.005618	Theorem 10

3.2   Proof of Biases in $S_0[i_1]$

In this section, we prove Theorems 1 and 2 theoretically. Theorem 1 shows that event $(S_0[i_1] = -K[0] - K[1] - 3)$ yields a positive bias in both generic RC4 and WPA. We note that Theorem 1 means the first round internal state $S_0[i_1]$ can be guessed in a double probability of random association $\frac{1}{N}$ by using *known* $K[0]$ and $K[1]$ in WPA. Theorem 2 shows that event $(S_0[i_1] = K[0] + K[1] + K[2] + 3)$ yields a negative bias in both generic RC4 and WPA.

Theorem 1. *In the initial state of the PRGA, we have*

$$
\Pr(S_0[i_1] = -K[0] - K[1] - 3) \approx \begin{cases} \frac{2}{N}\alpha_1 + \frac{1}{N}\left(1 - \frac{2}{N}\right)(1 - \alpha_1) & \text{for RC4,} \\ \frac{4}{N}\alpha_1 + \frac{1}{N}\left(1 - \frac{4}{N}\right)(1 - \alpha_1) & \text{for WPA.} \end{cases}
$$

Proof. The probability of event $(S_0[i_1] = -K[0] - K[1] - 3)$ can be decomposed in two paths: $K[0] + K[1] = 126, 254$ (Path 1) and $K[0] + K[1] \neq 126, 254$ (Path 2). These paths include all events in order to compute $Pr(S_0[i_1] = -K[0] - K[1] - 3)$. In the following proof, we use $S_0[1]$ instead of $S_0[i_1]$ ($i_1 = 1$) for simplicity.

Path 1. In $K[0] + K[1] = 126, 254$, event $(S_0[1] = -K[0] - K[1] - 3)$ occurs if and only if $S_0[1] = K[0] + K[1] + 1$. Therefore, we get

$$
\Pr(S_0[1] = -K[0] - K[1] - 3 \mid \text{Path 1}) = \alpha_1.
$$

Path 2. In $K[0] + K[1] \neq 126, 254$, event $(S_0[1] = -K[0] - K[1] - 3)$ never occurs if $S_0[1] = K[0] + K[1] + 1$. If $S_0[1] \neq K[0] + K[1] + 1$ holds, then we assume that event $(S_0[1] = -K[0] - K[1] - 3)$ occurs with the probability of random association $\frac{1}{N}$. Therefore, we get

$$
\Pr(S_0[1] = -K[0] - K[1] - 3 \mid \text{Path 2}) = \frac{1}{N} \cdot (1 - \alpha_1).
$$

The probability of $K[0] + K[1] = 126$ and 254 in WPA is $\frac{2}{N}$, twice as high as that of random association, although that in generic RC4 is $\frac{1}{N}$ since K is generated uniformly at random. By substituting each $\Pr(K[0] + K[1] = 126, 254)$ in both generic RC4 and WPA, we get

$$
\begin{aligned}
\Pr(S_0[i_1] &= K[0] - K[1] - 3) \\
&= \Pr(S_0[1] = K[0] - K[1] - 3 \mid \text{Path 1}) \cdot \Pr(\text{Path 1}) \\
&\quad + \Pr(S_0[1] = K[0] - K[1] - 3 \mid \text{Path 2}) \cdot \Pr(\text{Path 2}) \\
&\approx \begin{cases} \frac{2}{N}\alpha_1 + \frac{1}{N}\left(1 - \frac{2}{N}\right)(1 - \alpha_1) & \text{for RC4,} \\ \frac{4}{N}\alpha_1 + \frac{1}{N}\left(1 - \frac{4}{N}\right)(1 - \alpha_1) & \text{for WPA.} \end{cases}
\end{aligned}
$$

$\square$

Theorem 2. *In the initial state of the PRGA, we have*

$$
\Pr(S_0[i_1] = K[0] + K[1] + K[2] + 3) \approx \frac{1}{N}\left(1 - \frac{2}{N}\right)\left(1 - \frac{1}{N}\right)^{N-2} + \frac{1}{N^2}\left(3 - \frac{2}{N}\right).
$$

Proof. Since both $S_1^K[1] = 1$ and $S_2^K[2] = 2$ hold with high probability from Algorithm 1, we get

$$j_1^K = K[0], \tag{3}$$
$$j_2^K = K[0] + K[1] + S_1^K[1] = K[0] + K[1] + 1, \tag{4}$$
$$j_3^K = K[0] + K[1] + K[2] + S_1^K[1] + S_2^K[2] = K[0] + K[1] + K[2] + 3. \tag{5}$$

In this case, $S_3^K[2] = K[0] + K[1] + K[2] + 3$ always holds from step 7 in Algorithm 1, and thus, event $(S_0[i_1] = K[0] + K[1] + K[2] + 3)$ never occurs because $S_r^K[i_1] \neq K[0] + K[1] + K[2] + 3$ always holds for $r \geq 3$. Then, the probability of event $(S_0[i_1] = K[0] + K[1] + K[2] + 3)$ can be decomposed in two paths: $j_1^K = 1, 2$ (Path 1) and $j_1^K \neq 1, 2$ (Path 2). Path 2 is further divided into three subpaths: $j_2^K = 2$ (Path 2-1), $j_2^K \neq 2 \wedge K[2] = 254$ (Path 2-2) and $j_2^K \neq 2 \wedge K[2] \neq 254$ (Path 2-3). These paths include all events in order to compute $Pr(S_0[i_1] = K[0] + K[1] + K[2] + 3)$. In the following proof, we use $S_0[1]$ instead of $S_0[i_1]$ ($i_1 = 1$) for simplicity.

Path 1. If $j_1^K = 1$, then $S_1^K[1] \neq 1$ from step 7 in Algorithm 1. Thus, $S_3^K[2] \neq K[0] + K[1] + K[2] + 3$ always holds since $j_3^K \neq K[0] + K[1] + K[2] + 3$ from Eq. (5). Similarly, if $j_1^K = 2$, then $S_3^K[2] \neq K[0] + K[1] + K[2] + 3$ always holds. Then, we assume that event $(S_0[1] = K[0] + K[1] + K[2] + 3)$ occurs with the probability of random association $\frac{1}{N}$. Therefore, we get

$$\Pr(S_0[1] = K[0] + K[1] + K[2] + 3 \mid \text{Path 1}) \approx \frac{1}{N}.$$

Path 2-1. As with the discussion in Path 1, if $j_2^K = 2$, then $S_3^K[2] \neq K[0] + K[1] + K[2] + 3$ always holds. We then assume that event $(S_0[1] = K[0] + K[1] + K[2] + 3)$ with the probability of random association $\frac{1}{N}$. Therefore, we get

$$\Pr(S_0[1] = K[0] + K[1] + K[2] + 3 \mid \text{Path 2-1}) \approx \frac{1}{N}.$$

Path 2-2. Except the cases in Paths 1 and 2-1, Eqs. (3)-(5) always hold since we get both $S_1^K[1] = 1$ and $S_2^K[2] = 2$. Here, if $K[2] = 254$, then $j_2^K = j_3^K = K[0] + K[1] + K[2] + 3$ holds since $K[2] + 3 = 1$. Thus, we get both $S_3^K[1] = K[0] + K[1] + K[2] + 3$ and $S_3^K[2] = 1$ from step 7 in Algorithm 1. After the third round of KSA, $S_r^K[1] = S_3^K[1]$ for $4 \leq r \leq N$ if $j_r^K \neq 1$ during the subsequent $N - 3$ rounds, whose probability is approximately $\left(1 - \frac{1}{N}\right)^{N-3}$ since we assume that $j_r^K = 1$ holds with the probability of random association $\frac{1}{N}$. Therefore, we get

$$\Pr(S_0[1] = K[0] + K[1] + K[2] + 3 \mid \text{Path 2-2}) \approx \left(1 - \frac{1}{N}\right)^{N-3}.$$

Path 2-3. As with the discussion in Path 2-2, Eqs. (3)-(5) always hold, and $j_2^K \neq j_3^K$ since $K[2] \neq 254$ from the assumption in Path 2-3. Thus, event $(S_0[i_1] = K[0] + K[1] + K[2] + 3)$ never occurs since $S_3^K[2] = K[0] + K[1] + K[2] + 3$ always holds. Therefore, we get

$$\Pr(S_0[1] = K[0] + K[1] + K[2] + 3 \mid \text{Path 2-3}) = 0.$$

In summary, event $(S_0[i_1] = K[0] + K[1] + K[2] + 3)$ occurs only in Paths 1, 2-1 and 2-2. Therefore, we get

$$
\begin{aligned}
&\Pr(S_0[1] = K[0] + K[1] + K[2] + 3) \\
&= \Pr(S_0[1] = K[0] + K[1] + K[2] + 3 \mid \text{Path 1}) \cdot \Pr(\text{Path 1}) \\
&\quad + \Pr(S_0[1] = K[0] + K[1] + K[2] + 3 \mid \text{Path 2-1}) \cdot \Pr(\text{Path 2-1}) \\
&\quad + \Pr(S_0[1] = K[0] + K[1] + K[2] + 3 \mid \text{Path 2-2}) \cdot \Pr(\text{Path 2-2}) \\
&\approx \tfrac{1}{N} \cdot \tfrac{2}{N} + \tfrac{1}{N} \cdot \tfrac{1}{N}\left(1 - \tfrac{2}{N}\right) + \left(1 - \tfrac{1}{N}\right)^{N-3} \cdot \tfrac{1}{N}\left(1 - \tfrac{1}{N}\right)\left(1 - \tfrac{2}{N}\right) \\
&= \tfrac{1}{N}\left(1 - \tfrac{2}{N}\right)\left(1 - \tfrac{1}{N}\right)^{N-2} + \tfrac{1}{N^2}\left(3 - \tfrac{2}{N}\right),
\end{aligned}
$$

where we assume that 4 events, $(j_1^K = 1)$, $(j_1^K = 2)$, $(j_2^K = 2)$ and $(K[2] = 254)$, occur with the probability of random association $\tfrac{1}{N}$, respectively.   □

3.3   Proof of Biases in $S_1[i_2]$

In this section, we prove Theorems 3-5 theoretically. Theorem 3 shows that event $(S_1[i_2] = K[0] + K[1] + K[2] + 3)$ occurs with pretty high probability in both generic RC4 and WPA. This high probability is induced by Roos' bias, that is $\alpha_2 = \Pr(S_0[2] = K[0] + K[1] + K[2] + 3)$. Theorems 4 and 5 show that 4 events related to $S_1[i_2]$ yield a positive bias in both generic RC4 and WPA. We note that Theorems 3-5 mean the second round internal state of $S_1[i_2]$ can be guessed in pretty high probability or double probabilities of random association $\tfrac{1}{N}$ by using *known* $K[0]$, $K[1]$ and $K[2]$ in WPA. Here, we show only the proofs of Theorems 3 and 4. Theorem 5 is proved in the same way as Theorem 4. In order to prove the following theorems, let us denote the results of Theorems 2 and 3 as $\beta = \Pr(S_0[1] = K[0]+K[1]+K[2]+3)$ and $\gamma = \Pr(S_1[2] = K[0]+K[1]+K[2]+3)$, respectively.

Theorem 3. *After the first round of the PRGA, we have*

$$
\Pr(S_1[i_2]=K[0]+K[1]+K[2]+3) \approx \beta \cdot \Pr(S_0[1]=2) + \alpha_2 \cdot \left(1 - \Pr(S_0[1]=2)\right).
$$

Proof. The probability of event $(S_1[i_2] = K[0] + K[1] + K[2] + 3)$ can be decomposed in two paths: $j_1 = 2$ (Path 1) and $j_1 \neq 2$ (Path 2). These paths include all events in order to compute $\Pr(S_1[i_2] = K[0] + K[1] + K[2] + 3)$. Note that $j_1 = S_0[1]$ from step 4 in Alforithm 2. In the following proof, we use $S_1[2]$ instead of $S_1[i_2]$ ($i_2 = 2$) for simplicity.

Path 1. In $j_1 = 2$, event $(S_1[2] = K[0] + K[1] + K[2] + 3)$ occurs if and only if $S_0[1] = K[0] + K[1] + K[2] + 3$ from step 5 in Algorithm 2. We assume that both events $(j_1 = 2)$ and $(S_0[1] = K[0] + K[1] + K[2] + 3)$ are mutually independent. Therefore, we get

$$
\Pr(S_1[2] = K[0] + K[1] + K[2] + 3 \mid \text{Path 1}) = \beta.
$$

Path 2. In $j_1 \neq 2$, event $(S_1[2] = K[0] + K[1] + K[2] + 3)$ occurs if and only if $S_0[2] = K[0] + K[1] + K[2] + 3$ from step 5 in Algorithm 2. We assume that both events $(j_1 \neq 2)$ and $(S_0[2] = K[0] + K[1] + K[2] + 3)$ are mutually independent. Therefore, we get

$$\Pr(S_1[2] = K[0] + K[1] + K[2] + 3 \mid \text{Path 2}) = \alpha_2.$$

In summary, we get

$$
\begin{aligned}
&\Pr(S_1[i_2] = K[0] + K[1] + K[2] + 3) \\
&= \Pr(S_1[2] = K[0] + K[1] + K[2] + 3 \mid \text{Path 1}) \cdot \Pr(\text{Path 1}) \\
&\quad + \Pr(S_1[2] = K[0] + K[1] + K[2] + 3 \mid \text{Path 2}) \cdot \Pr(\text{Path 2}) \\
&\approx \beta \cdot \Pr(S_0[1] = 2) + \alpha_2 \cdot (1 - \Pr(S_0[1] = 2)),
\end{aligned}
$$

where the probability of event $(S_0[1] = 2)$ is taken from Propositions 2 and 4 in generic RC4 and WPA, respectively. □

Theorem 4. *After the first round of the PRGA, we have*

$$
\Pr(S_1[i_2] = -K[0] - K[1] + K[2] - 1) \approx
\begin{cases}
\frac{2}{N}\gamma + \frac{1}{N}\left(1 - \frac{2}{N}\right)(1 - \gamma) & \text{for RC4,} \\
\frac{4}{N}\gamma + \frac{1}{N}\left(1 - \frac{4}{N}\right)(1 - \gamma) & \text{for WPA.}
\end{cases}
$$

Proof. The probability of event $(S_1[i_2] = -K[0] - K[1] + K[2] - 1)$ can be decomposed in two paths: $K[0] + K[1] = 126,254$ (Path 1) and $K[0] + K[1] \neq 126,254$ (Path 2). These paths include all events in order to compute $Pr(S_1[i_2] = -K[0] - K[1] + K[2] - 1)$. In the following proof, we use $S_1[2]$ instead of $S_1[i_2]$ $(i_2 = 2)$ for simplicity.

Path 1. In $K[0] + K[1] = 126,254$, event $(S_1[2] = -K[0] - K[1] + K[2] - 1)$ occurs if and only if $S_1[2] = K[0] + K[1] + K[2] + 3$. Therefore, we get

$$\Pr(S_1[2] = -K[0] - K[1] + K[2] - 1 \mid \text{Path 1}) = \gamma.$$

Path 2. In $K[0] + K[1] \neq 126,254$, event $(S_1[2] = -K[0] - K[1] + K[2] - 1)$ never occurs if $S_1[2] = K[0] + K[1] + K[2] + 3$. If $S_1[2] \neq K[0] + K[1] + K[2] + 3$ holds, then we assume that event $(S_1[2] = -K[0] - K[1] + K[2] - 1)$ occurs with the probability of random association $\frac{1}{N}$. Therefore, we get

$$\Pr(S_1[2] = -K[0] - K[1] + K[2] - 1 \mid \text{Path 2}) = \frac{1}{N} \cdot (1 - \gamma).$$

The probability of $K[0] + K[1] = 126$ and 254 in WPA is $\frac{2}{N}$, twice as high as that of random association, although that in generic RC4 is $\frac{1}{N}$ since K is generated uniformly at random. By substituting each $\Pr(K[0] + K[1] = 126,254)$ in both generic RC4 and WPA, we get

$$
\begin{aligned}
&\Pr(S_1[i_2] = -K[0] - K[1] + K[2] - 1) \\
&= \Pr(S_1[2] = -K[0] - K[1] + K[2] - 1 \mid \text{Path 1}) \cdot \Pr(\text{Path 1}) \\
&\quad + \Pr(S_1[2] = -K[0] - K[1] + K[2] - 1 \mid \text{Path 2}) \cdot \Pr(\text{Path 2}) \\
&\approx
\begin{cases}
\frac{2}{N}\gamma + \frac{1}{N}\left(1 - \frac{2}{N}\right)(1 - \gamma) & \text{for RC4,} \\
\frac{4}{N}\gamma + \frac{1}{N}\left(1 - \frac{4}{N}\right)(1 - \gamma) & \text{for WPA.}
\end{cases}
\end{aligned}
$$

□

Theorem 5. *After the first round of the PRGA for* $x \in \{-3, -1, 1\}$, *we have*

$$\Pr(S_1[i_2] = K[0] - K[1] + K[2] + x) \approx \begin{cases} \frac{2}{N}\gamma + \frac{1}{N}(1 - \frac{2}{N})(1 - \gamma) & \text{for RC4,} \\ \frac{4}{N}\gamma + \frac{1}{N}(1 - \frac{4}{N})(1 - \gamma) & \text{for WPA.} \end{cases}$$

3.4   Proof of Biases in j_2

In this section, we prove Theorems 6-10 theoretically. Theorem 6 shows that event $(j_2 = K[2])$ yields a positive bias in both generic RC4 and WPA. On the other hand, Theorems 7-10 show that 7 events related to j_2 yield positive biases in WPA but those are not biases in generic RC4. Here, we show only the proof of Theorem 6. Theorems 7-10 are proved in the same way as Theorem 6. In order to prove the following theorems, let us denote the result of Theorem 3 as $\gamma = \Pr(S_1[2] = K[0] + K[1] + K[2] + 3)$.

Theorem 6. *After the second round of the PRGA, we have*

$$\Pr(j_2 = K[2]) \approx \begin{cases} \frac{2}{N}\alpha_1\gamma + \frac{1}{N}(1 - \frac{2}{N})(1 - \alpha_1\gamma) & \text{for RC4,} \\ \frac{4}{N}\alpha_1\gamma + \frac{1}{N}(1 - \frac{4}{N})(1 - \alpha_1\gamma) & \text{for WPA.} \end{cases}$$

Proof. The probability of event $(j_2 = K[2])$ can be decomposed in two paths: $K[0]+K[1] = 126, 254$ (Path 1) and $K[0]+K[1] \neq 126, 254$ (Path 2). These paths include all events in order to compute $Pr(j_2 = K[2])$. Note that $j_2 = S_0[1]+S_1[2]$ from step 4 in Algorithm 2.

Path 1. If two events $(S_0[1] = K[0] + K[1] + 1)$ and $(S_1[2] = K[0] + K[1] + K[2] + 3)$ occur simultaneously, we get

$$j_2 = S_0[1] + S_1[2] = (K[0] + K[1] + 1) + (K[0] + K[1] + K[2] + 3)$$
$$= 2K[0] + 2K[1] + K[2] + 4.$$

Then, in $K[0] + K[1] = 126, 254$, event $(j_2 = K[2])$ occurs if and only if $j_2 = 2K[0] + 2K[1] + K[2] + 4$, that is both $S_0[1] = K[0] + K[1] + 1$ and $S_1[2] = K[0] + K[1] + K[2] + 3$ hold simultaneously. We assume that both events $(S_0[1] = K[0] + K[1] + 1)$ and $(S_1[2] = K[0] + K[1] + K[2] + 3)$ are mutually independent. Therefore, we get

$$\Pr(j_2 = K[2] \mid \text{path 1}) = \alpha_1\gamma.$$

Path 2. In $K[0] + K[1] \neq 126, 254$ event $(j_2 = K[2])$ never occurs if and only if $j_2 = 2K[0] + 2K[1] + K[2] + 4$. If either $S_0[1] \neq K[0] + K[1] + 1$ or $S_1[2] \neq K[0] + K[1] + K[2] + 3$ hold, then we assume that event $(j_2 = K[2])$ occurs with the probability of random association $\frac{1}{N}$. Therefore, we get

$$\Pr(j_2 = K[2] \mid \text{Path 2}) = \frac{1}{N} \cdot (1 - \alpha_1\gamma).$$

The probability of $K[0] + K[1] = 126$ and 254 in WPA is $\frac{2}{N}$, twice as high as that of random association, although that in generic RC4 is $\frac{1}{N}$ since K is generated uniformly at random. By substituting each $\Pr(K[0] + K[1] = 126, 254)$ in both generic RC4 and WPA, we get

$$\Pr(j_2 = K[2]) = \Pr(j_2 = K[2] \mid \text{Path 1}) \cdot \Pr(\text{Path 1})$$
$$+ \Pr(j_2 = K[2] \mid \text{Path 2}) \cdot \Pr(\text{Path 2})$$
$$\approx \begin{cases} \frac{2}{N}\alpha_1\gamma + \frac{1}{N}\left(1 - \frac{2}{N}\right)(1 - \alpha_1\gamma) & \text{for RC4,} \\ \frac{4}{N}\alpha_1\gamma + \frac{1}{N}\left(1 - \frac{4}{N}\right)(1 - \alpha_1\gamma) & \text{for WPA.} \end{cases}$$ □

Theorem 7. *After the second round of the PRGA for $x \in \{-2, 0, 2\}$, we have*

$$\Pr(j_2 = -K[0] - K[1] + K[2] + x)$$
$$\approx \begin{cases} \frac{1}{N}\alpha_1\gamma + \frac{1}{N}\left(1 - \frac{1}{N}\right)(1 - \alpha_1\gamma) & \text{for RC4,} \\ \frac{2}{N}\alpha_1\gamma + \frac{1}{N}\left(1 - \frac{2}{N}\right)(1 - \alpha_1\gamma) & \text{if } x = -2, 2 \text{ for WPA,} \\ \frac{4}{N}\alpha_1\gamma + \frac{1}{N}\left(1 - \frac{4}{N}\right)(1 - \alpha_1\gamma) & \text{if } x = 0 \text{ for WPA.} \end{cases}$$

Theorem 8. *After the second round of the PRGA, we have*

$$\Pr(j_2 = -K[0] + K[1] + K[2]) \approx \begin{cases} \frac{1}{N}\alpha_1\gamma + \frac{1}{N}\left(1 - \frac{1}{N}\right)(1 - \alpha_1\gamma) & \text{for RC4,} \\ \frac{4}{N}\alpha_1\gamma + \frac{1}{N}\left(1 - \frac{4}{N}\right)(1 - \alpha_1\gamma) & \text{for WPA.} \end{cases}$$

Theorem 9. *After the second round of the PRGA for $x \in \{-2, 3\}$, we have*

$$\Pr(j_2 = -K[1] + K[2] + x) \approx \begin{cases} \frac{1}{N}\alpha_1\gamma + \frac{1}{N}\left(1 - \frac{1}{N}\right)(1 - \alpha_1\gamma) & \text{for RC4,} \\ \frac{4}{N}\alpha_1\gamma + \frac{1}{N}\left(1 - \frac{4}{N}\right)(1 - \alpha_1\gamma) & \text{for WPA.} \end{cases}$$

Theorem 10. *After the second round of the PRGA, we have*

$$\Pr(j_2 = K[0] - K[1] + K[2]) \approx \begin{cases} \frac{1}{N}\alpha_1\gamma + \frac{1}{N}\left(1 - \frac{1}{N}\right)(1 - \alpha_1\gamma) & \text{for RC4,} \\ \frac{4}{N}\alpha_1\gamma + \frac{1}{N}\left(1 - \frac{4}{N}\right)(1 - \alpha_1\gamma) & \text{for WPA.} \end{cases}$$

3.5 Experimental Results

We have conducted experiments on Theorems 1-10 in the following environment in order to confirm the accuracy of theorems: Intel(R) Core(TM) i3-3220M CPU with 3.30 GHz, 3.8 GiB memory, gcc 4.8.2 compiler and C language. The number of samples necessary for our experiments is at least $\mathcal{O}(N^3)$ according to Proposition 5. This is why each correlation has a relative bias with the probability of at least $\mathcal{O}(\frac{1}{N})$. Then, we have used N^5 randomly generated RC4 keys in both generic RC4 and WPA. The number of these samples satisfies a condition to distinguish each correlation from random distribution with constant probability of success. We also evaluate the percentage of relative error ϵ of experimental values compared with theoretical values in the same way as [5]:

$$\epsilon = \frac{|\text{experimental value} - \text{theoretical value}|}{\text{experimental value}} \times 100(\%).$$

Tables 2 and 3 show experimental and theoretical values and percentage of relative error ϵ in both generic RC4 and WPA.

We see that ϵ is small enough in each case in generic RC4 such as $\epsilon \leq$ 0.730 (%). From this results, we have convinced that theoretical values closely reflects the experimental values in generic RC4.

Table 2. Comparison between experimental and theoretical results for generic RC4

Linear correlation		Experimental value	Theoretical value	ϵ (%)
$S_0[i_1]$	$-K[0] - K[1] - 3$	0.005333309	0.005325263	0.151
	$K[0] + K[1] + K[2] + 3$	0.001490745	0.001479853	0.730
$S_1[i_2]$	$K[0] + K[1] + K[2] + 3$	0.360360690	0.362016405	0.459
	$-K[0] - K[1] + K[2] - 1$	0.005305673	0.005302926	0.052
	$K[0] - K[1] + K[2] - 3$	0.005295155	0.005302926	0.147
	$K[0] - K[1] + K[2] - 1$	0.005289180	0.005302926	0.260
	$K[0] - K[1] + K[2] + 1$	0.005309594	0.005302926	0.126
j_2	$K[2]$	0.004430372	0.004401230	0.658
	$-K[0] - K[1] + K[2] - 2$	0.003920799	0.003893028	0.708
	$-K[0] - K[1] + K[2]$	0.003919381	0.003893028	0.672
	$-K[0] - K[1] + K[2] + 2$	0.003910929	0.003893028	0.458
	$-K[0] + K[1] + K[2]$	0.003920399	0.003893028	0.698
	$-K[1] + K[2] - 2$	0.003910053	0.003893028	0.435
	$-K[1] + K[2] + 3$	0.003897939	0.003893028	0.126
	$K[0] - K[1] + K[2]$	0.003917895	0.003893028	0.635

Table 3. Comparison between experimental and theoretical results for WPA

Linear correlation		Experimental value	Theoretical value	ϵ (%)
$S_0[i_1]$	$-K[0] - K[1] - 3$	0.008408305	0.008182569	2.685
	$K[0] + K[1] + K[2] + 3$	0.001491090	0.001479853	0.754
$S_1[i_2]$	$K[0] + K[1] + K[2] + 3$	0.361751935	0.362723221	0.268
	$-K[0] - K[1] + K[2] - 1$	0.008174625	0.008115732	0.720
	$K[0] - K[1] + K[2] - 3$	0.008140906	0.008115732	0.309
	$K[0] - K[1] + K[2] - 1$	0.008147205	0.008115732	0.386
	$K[0] - K[1] + K[2] + 1$	0.008150390	0.008115732	0.425
j_2	$K[2]$	0.005560613	0.005417633	2.571
	$-K[0] - K[1] + K[2] - 2$	0.004573276	0.004401230	3.762
	$-K[0] - K[1] + K[2]$	0.005562336	0.005417633	2.601
	$-K[0] - K[1] + K[2] + 2$	0.004543826	0.004401230	3.138
	$-K[0] + K[1] + K[2]$	0.005490766	0.005417633	1.332
	$-K[1] + K[2] - 2$	0.005468425	0.005417633	0.929
	$-K[1] + K[2] + 3$	0.005468472	0.005417633	0.930
	$K[0] - K[1] + K[2]$	0.005607004	0.005417633	3.377

We also see that theoretical biases in $S_0[i_1]$ and j_2 in WPA produce slightly large ϵ such as 3.762 (%) but those in $S_1[i_2]$ in WPA is quite small in the same way as generic RC4. Let us investigate why such differences on the percentage of relative error are produced between generic RC4 and WPA. Actually, difference between generic RC4 and WPA exist only in a relation between $K[0]$ and $K[1]$. Therefore, these difference influence theoretical biases in the early round, but seem to attenuate in the second or more round as we see in results to $S_0[i_1]$ and $S_1[i_2]$.

4   Conclusion

In this paper, we have focused on linear correlations including *unknown* internal states as well as the keystream byte and *known* RC4 key bytes in both generic RC4 and WPA, and provided newly theoretical proofs of 15 linear correlations related to $S_0[i_1]$, $S_1[i_2]$ and j_2. For example, event $(S_1[i_2] = K[0]+K[1]+K[2]+3)$ yields a pretty high probability in both generic RC4 and WPA, influenced directly by Roos' bias; and the probability of 5 linear correlations such as $\Pr(S_0[i_1] = -K[0] - K[1] - 3)$, $\Pr(S_1[i_2] = -K[0] - K[1] + K[2] - 1)$ and $\Pr(S_1[i_2] = K[0] - K[1] + K[2] + x)$ for $x \in \{-3, -1, 1\}$ is a double probability of random association $\frac{1}{N}$ in WPA.

Our theoretical analysis are expected to contribute from the following two viewpoints. One is to contribute to reducing the computational complexity necessary for the state recovery attacks against RC4 proposed in [1,6,9] especially with WPA since our linear correlations includes internal states. The other is to contribute to construct a key generation procedure with IV in such a way that it keeps or further enhance the security level of its original symmetric cipher. In our analysis, we have seen how TKIP downgrades security level of generic RC4 theoretically. These discussions could be generalized to reconstruct a key generation procedure with IV.

References

1. Das, A., Maitra, S., Paul, G., Sarkar, S.: Some Combinatorial Results towards State Recovery Attack on RC4. In: Jajodia, S., Mazumdar, C. (eds.) ICISS 2011. LNCS, vol. 7093, pp. 204–214. Springer, Heidelberg (2011)
2. Fluhrer, S.R., Mantin, I., Shamir, A.: Weaknesses in the Key Scheduling Algorithm of RC4. In: Vaudenay, S., Youssef, A.M. (eds.) SAC 2001. LNCS, vol. 2259, pp. 1–24. Springer, Heidelberg (2001)
3. Sen Gupta, S., Maitra, S., Meier, W., Paul, G., Sarkar, S.: Dependence in IV-Related Bytes of RC4 Key Enhances Vulnerabilities in WPA. In: Cid, C., Rechberger, C. (eds.) FSE 2014. LNCS, vol. 8540, pp. 350–369. Springer, Heidelberg (2015)
4. Isobe, T., Ohigashi, T., Watanabe, Y., Morii, M.: Full Plaintext Recovery Attack on Broadcast RC4. In: Moriai, S. (ed.) FSE 2013. LNCS, vol. 8424, pp. 179–202. Springer, Heidelberg (2014)

5. Ito, R., Miyaji, A.: New Linear Correlations related to State Information of RC4 PRGA using IV in WPA. In: Fast Software Encryption, FSE 2015 (to appear, 2015)

6. Knudsen, L.R., Meier, W., Preneel, B., Rijmen, V., Verdoolaege, S.: Analysis Methods for (Alleged) RC4. In: Ohta, K., Pei, D. (eds.) ASIACRYPT 1998. LNCS, vol. 1514, pp. 327–341. Springer, Heidelberg (1998)

7. Mantin, I.: Analysis of the Stream Cipher RC4. Master's thesis, The Weizmann Institute of Science, Israel (2001). http://www.wisdom.weizmann.ac.il/itsik/RC4/rc4.html

8. Mantin, I., Shamir, A.: Practical Attack on Broadcast RC4. In: Matsui, M. (ed.) Fast Software Encryption - FSE 2001. LNCS, vol. 2355, pp. 152–164. Springer, Berlin Heidelberg (2002)

9. Maximov, A., Khovratovich, D.: New State Recovery Attack on RC4. In: Wagner, D. (ed.) CRYPTO 2008. LNCS, vol. 5157, pp. 297–316. Springer, Heidelberg (2008)

10. Paul, G., Maitra, S.: Permutation After RC4 Key Scheduling Reveals the Secret Key. In: Adams, C., Miri, A., Wiener, M. (eds.) SAC 2007. LNCS, vol. 4876, pp. 360–377. Springer, Heidelberg (2007)

11. Roos, A.: A class of weak keys in the RC4 stream cipher. Posts in sci.crypt. http://marcel.wanda.ch/Archive/WeakKeys (1995)

Preventing Fault Attacks Using Fault Randomization with a Case Study on AES

Shamit Ghosh$^{(\boxtimes)}$, Dhiman Saha, Abhrajit Sengupta,
and Dipanwita Roy Chowdhury

Indian Institute of Technology, Kharagpur, India
{raaz714,saha.dhiman,abhrajit.sengupta}@gmail.com,
drc@cse.iitkgp.ernet.in

Abstract. Infective countermeasures have been shown to be the most efficient way to prevent fault attacks which are one of the most effective side-channel attacks on symmetric key ciphers. However, none of the countermeasures have been found to last in terms of security. Battistello *et al.* [1] has broken the last two surviving infective methods against fault attacks on AES and emphasized on the need of a better security framework for fault attack countermeasures. The current work is the first such step towards achieving the design of a secure infective countermeasure as suggested by [1]. We develop a theoretical framework based on fault randomization to formalize the infective approach used in fault attack countermeasures. On the basis of this formalization, a new infective countermeasure is proposed which employs a randomized non-linear mixing coupled with a linear diffusion function. A case study on AES with a practical construction of the countermeasure is presented. The full design is implemented on Xilinx SPARTAN-3 FPGA platform and compared favorably with a related scheme in literature.

Keywords: Infective countermeasure · AES · Differential fault attack · Fault attack countermeasure · Randomized mixing

1 Introduction

Since their inception in 1996 by Boneh *et. al* [2], Fault Attacks (FA) have gained considerable attention of the research community. This popularity is primarily attributed to the power that these attacks put at the hands of an attacker. The feasibility of fault injection techniques further make these attacks very practical. Consequently, preventing such attacks is a very challenging area of research. The primary idea behind the attack is to intentionally inject a fault in an intermediate state of the algorithm and then study the resulting faulty outputs for possible exploits. One of the most popular targets of fault attacks has been the Advanced Encryption Standard (AES) [3]. Differential Fault Analysis (DFA) was introduced by Biham *et. al.* [4] on the Data Encryption Standard (DES) and later mounted on AES by Giraud [5]. Among other improved DFA on AES are

© Springer International Publishing Switzerland 2015
E. Foo and D. Stebila (Eds.): ACISP 2015, LNCS 9144, pp. 343–355, 2015.
DOI: 10.1007/978-3-319-19962-7_20

[6–8]. In the light of highly sophisticated and realistic fault attacks, it becomes imperative to design effective countermeasures against them.

The fault attack countermeasures can be divided into two classes, *detection* and *infection*. In case of detection countermeasure, some redundant computation is always added to the encryption module. But irrespective of the redundancy, it has been shown in [9] that fault injection during verification, aids the attacker to bypass the comparison altogether. Even if the verification stage itself is redundant, it can be avoided using three fault injections as described in [10]. To overcome these limitations of fault detection techniques, infective countermeasure has been introduced in [11] for RSA and later adapted for other encryption schemes as well. Numerous attempts of protecting AES against fault attacks using fault infection have been proposed. But those attempts have failed for various reasons, the primary being the deterministic nature of the infection techniques. This issue has been addressed by recent works [12,13] that have tried to incorporate randomness into their schemes. In [13], the authors show that the deterministic diffusion used in infective countermeasures are not secure and thus emphasize on the need of randomness. Indeed the countermeasure of AES proposed in [12] infects the faulty computation with random values using dummy rounds. However, both the randomized infective countermeasures have been attacked by [1]. Further, [14] shows some additional weakness in the infection mechanism of [12] which makes the attack of [1] more feasible. Additionally, [14] presents a modified countermeasure algorithm proposed in [12].

Before introducing our approach we briefly outline the vulnerabilities of randomized schemes mentioned above. In [1], the authors have shown that using the same fault model assumed in [13], the attack complexity can be reduced from 2^{128} to 16×2^8. The scheme proposed in [12] that uses some additional dummy rounds, has also been shown to be vulnerable in [1]. This attack requires 36 faults to recover the full AES-128 key if any row except the top one is infected. The attack is further improved in [14] by including the top row while reducing the number of faults to 8. In addition to this, the authors also presented a modified version of the countermeasure proposed in [12]. However, like previous works, as pointed out by Battistello and Giraud[1], this is yet another patch work and hence the need of a theoretical framework is imperative. Moreover, existing literature lacks a study of practical implementation of any infective countermeasure. The work presented in this paper is the first such attempt to develop a theoretical framework to formalize the infective countermeasure and at the same time to present a practical construction based on this.

In the current work, a formalization of fault attacks on symmetric ciphers is done. Referring to the classical IND-CPA security, we introduce a term called IND_f-CPA security to take into account an adversary that has the power of fault injection. The idea behind IND_f-CPA security is to randomize the induced fault. To achieve this, we propose a model which uses a linear diffusion layer and a nonlinear mixing function. To validate the proposed method, we show a case study choosing AES as the crypto primitive. The design rationale of the model is

Table 1. Comparative Study with Existing DFA Countermeasures

Algorithm	Fault Model	Vulnerability
Parity/Error Detecting Codes	Multibyte	Inject more faults than the error correcting capability
Duplication	Singlebyte, penultimate round of key scheduling	Combined Attack [15]
Deterministic Infection	Single or Multibyte	Fixed fault diffusion[16]
Multiplicative Infection[13]	Single byte, 8th round	Repetition of Same fault[1]
Dummy Round [12]	Singlebyte at last effective round	Localization of fault infection [1,14]
Proposed Model	**Single or Multibyte**	**No Known vulnerabilities**

also furnished. A comparative study with some of the existing countermeasures is depicted in Table 1.

Contribution: The contribution of the paper is listed as follows:

– Formalized fault randomization as an effective countermeasure against fault attacks.
– Proposed a practical solution using a linear diffusion function (realized by a maximum length cellular automata) and a nonlinear mixing (achieved by nonlinear mixing function NMix [17]) following the theoretical model.
– Presented a detailed case study on AES implementing and validating the entire scheme on Xilinx FPGA platform.
– Furnished a comparative study to show that the proposed method is better than the only secure scheme in the existing literature.

The rest of the paper is organized as follows. Section 2 formalizes the fault attack model and the security notions. A theoretical construction based on the formalized model is discussed in Section 3. Then we sketch a case study on AES with a practical construction of the countermeasure in Section 4. The implementation details of the proposed scheme on Xilinx FPGA along with a comparative study with the countermesure [13] is shown in Section 5. Section 6 concludes the work.

2   A Security Model for Fault Randomization

In order to formalize our approach, we refer to the classical IND-CPA game. However, to take into account the additional access to the faulty ciphertext(s), we modify the IND-CPA and refer to the modified game as IND_f-CPA. In IND_f-CPA an adversary has access to an additional oracle which simulates the faulty encryption. So when the adversary queries his oracle with a plaintext, it returns a faulty ciphertext following some predefined fault attack model. Let $\Pi = (K, E, D)$ be an IND-CPA secure symmetric encryption scheme with key-space $\mathcal{K}$, message-space $\mathcal{M}$ and ciphertext-space $\mathcal{C}$ and the security parameter n. The encryption oracle $E_k(\cdot)$ on input $m \in \mathcal{M}$ returns $E_k(m) \in \mathcal{C}$. The fault simulating oracle $E_k^f(\cdot, \cdot)$ takes as input (m, L) and returns a faulty ciphertext $E_k^f(m, L) \in \mathcal{C}$, where L is a collection of parameters associated with the fault and is directly determined by the underlying fault model. We now formally introduce the IND_f-CPA game.

Game 1. $\text{IND}_f\text{-CPA}(A, \Pi)$

1: **procedure** INITIALIZE
2:     $k \xleftarrow{\$} \mathcal{K}$ ▷ Chosen by encryption oracle
3:     $m_0, m_1 \xleftarrow{\$} \mathcal{M}$ ▷ Chosen by adversary
4:     $b \in_\$ \{0, 1\}$ ▷ Chosen by encryption oracle
5:     $c \leftarrow E_k(m_b)$
6:     $win = 0$
7: **end procedure**

8: **procedure** ADVERSARY$(c, E_k(\cdot)E_k^f(\cdot, \cdot))$
9:     **for** $i \leftarrow 1$ to $q(n)$ **do**   ▷ $q(n)$ is a polynomial in n
10:         $c'_{i_0} \leftarrow E_k^f(m_0, L_i)$ ▷ Returned by fault simulating oracle
             $c'_{i_1} \leftarrow E_k^f(m_1, L'_i)$
11:     **end for**
12:     **return** $b' \in \{0, 1\}$ ▷ Using $\{c, \{c'_{i_0}\}, \{c'_{i_1}\}\}$, adversary guesses b
13: **end procedure**

14: **procedure** FINALIZE
15:     **if** $b' = b$ **then**
16:         $win = 1$
17:     **end if**
18:     **return** win
19: **end procedure**

With respect to the IND_f-CPA game defined above, an adversary wins if he is able to correctly guess the value of b. Let $\mathcal{A}$ be some class of computationally bounded adversaries. The following expression gives the maximum of the distinguishing advantages over all adversaries.

$$Adv_\Pi^{\text{IND}_f\text{-CPA}}(A) = \max_{A \in \mathcal{A}} \left| \Pr[A^{E_k(m_0), E_k^f(\cdot, \cdot)} = 0] - \right.$$
$$\left. \Pr[A^{E_k(m_1), E_k^f(\cdot, \cdot)} = 1] \right|$$

Thus for a symmetric key encryption scheme Π to be IND_f-CPA secure $Adv_\Pi^{\text{IND}_f\text{-CPA}}(A)$ must be upper bounded by a negligible function of the security parameter n. This leads us to the following definition for IND_f-CPA security.

Definition 1. *A symmetric encryption scheme $\Pi = (K, E, D)$ is said to be **IND_f-CPA** secure if for any computationally bounded adversary A who has the additional capability of inducing polynomial number of random faults in E and observe corresponding outputs, there exists a negligible function ϵ such that*

$$\max_{A \in \mathcal{A}} \left| Pr[A^{E_k(m_0), E_k^f(\cdot, \cdot)} = 0] - Pr[A^{E_k(m_1), E_k^f(\cdot, \cdot)} = 1] \right|$$
$$\leq \epsilon(n)$$

where, $\mathcal{A}$ represents some class of computationally bounded adversaries.

It is clear from the above definition that IND_f-CPA security $\implies$ IND-CPA security. However, the converse may not be true. In order to achieve IND-CPA $\implies \text{IND}_f$-CPA we give the following theorem.

Theorem 1. *An IND-CPA secure symmetric encryption scheme $\Pi = (K, E, D)$ is also IND_f-CPA secure if there exists a randomized transformation T such that*

$$E_k^f(\cdot, \cdot) \xrightarrow{T} \mathcal{R}(\cdot, \cdot)$$

where the oracle $\mathcal{R}$ returns $\left| E_k^f(\cdot, \cdot) \right|$ random bits.

Proof. Let $A \in \mathcal{A}$ be any computationally bounded adversary. Given the randomized transformation T, the following derivation explains how we reduce $Adv_\Pi^{\text{IND}_f\text{-CPA}}(A)$ to $Adv_\Pi^{\text{ind-cpa}}(A)$ thereby achieving IND_f-CPA security from IND-CPA security.

$$\begin{aligned}
&Adv_\Pi^{\text{IND}_f\text{-CPA}}(A) \\
&= \left| \Pr[A^{E_k(m_0), E_k^f(\cdot, \cdot)} = 0] - \Pr[A^{E_k(m_1), E_k^f(\cdot, \cdot)} = 1] \right| \\
&= \left| \Pr[A^{E_k(m_0), \mathcal{R}(\cdot, \cdot)} = 0] - \Pr[A^{E_k(m_1), \mathcal{R}(\cdot, \cdot)} = 1] \right| \\
&\qquad [\because E_k^f(\cdot, \cdot) \xrightarrow{T} \mathcal{R}(\cdot, \cdot)] \\
&= \left| \Pr[A^{E_k(m_0)} = 0] - \Pr[A^{E_k(m_1)} = 1] \right| \\
&\qquad [\because A^{E_k(\cdot), \mathcal{R}(\cdot, \cdot)} \Leftrightarrow A^{E_k(\cdot)}] \\
&= Adv_\Pi^{\text{ind-cpa}}(A) \\
&\leq \epsilon(n) \qquad [\because \Pi \text{ is IND-CPA secure}]
\end{aligned}$$

The interpretation of Theorem (1) in real-world terms is that if we can obfuscate the faulty output of an encryption algorithm then the advantage gained by the adversary due to the fault induction is completely nullified. In the next section of the paper we introduce a theoretical construction of the randomized transformation T. Later we give a practical construction of T. We finally show that if we apply T on AES, we are able to achieve IND_fCPA security.

3   A Theoretical Construction for $\mathcal{T}$

Our principle objective while designing $\mathcal{T}$ is to disperse the fault induced by an attacker into the entire state of the encryption scheme in a non-deterministic way. So the function $\mathcal{T}$ will be of the following form:

$$\mathcal{T}(f(\delta), r) = \begin{cases} 0, \text{if } f(\delta) = 0 \\ \text{random}, \ f(\delta) \neq 0 \end{cases}$$

where f is a function of the fault value δ and r is a random mask.

In order to achieve non-deterministic fault dispersion, we use both linear and nonlinear layers in the design of $\mathcal{T}$ along with a random mask. The construction is detailed in Fig. 1.

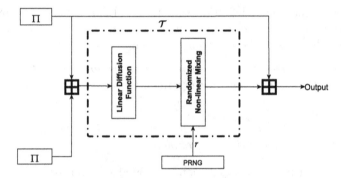

Fig. 1. Construction of $\mathcal{T}$

We use two instances of the encryption algorithm. The fault model assumed in this work states that the attacker can inject single or multibyte random fault at anywhere in the intermediate state of the AES. The only assumption is that faults cannot be induced in both the instances such that they cancel each other out. We next combine the outputs of both the instances using some combiner ⊞ (typically the XOR function) and feed it to a Linear Diffusion Function (LDF) followed by a Randomized Non-linear Mixing (RNLM). Finally, we combine the output of RNLM with original output of one of the instances to form the final output. The LDF and RNLM functions are the building blocks of $\mathcal{T}$. In the next subsection, we discuss about the design rationale behind these building blocks.

3.1   Design Rationale

The functions LDF and RNLM have been introduced to achieve the desired randomization as discussed in Section 2. These functions cater to specific requirements that are to ensured to achieve the goal of $\mathcal{T}$. Existing works that address these requirements have failed due to various reasons, the primary causes being low diffusion or localized diffusion [12,13] and lack of randomness [18,19]. Below we briefly discuss the effect of these vulnerabilities and the analyze the remedies.

Linear Diffusion Layer. Low or localized diffusion results in low dispersion of the fault. This in turn reduces the effect of the random mask used [12,13] and may lead to the retrieval of the original faulty ciphertext. This precludes the need for a state dependent high diffusion function which is ensured by LDF in $\mathcal{T}$. This layer aims at dispersing the fault thereby denying any advantage the attacker could gain from the locality of the faults. It is well-known that linear functions can achieve better diffusion. So we propose that the underlying primitive be linear in nature satisfying the *strict avalanche criterion*.

Randomized Nonlinear Mixing. The deterministic nature of the earlier fault attack countermeasures like [18,19] was a major limitation. The authors of [13] first highlighted the need of randomness while handling fault based attacks. Thus a random parameter is essential. This is also evident from the requirement of Theorem 1, where we need to transform $E_k^f(\cdot, \cdot)$ to a random oracle $\mathcal{R}(\cdot, \cdot)$. RNLM layer of $\mathcal{T}$ achieves this goal by using a unique random mask in every iteration of the encryption. In addition we also propose that random mask be mixed with the diffused fault from LDF using some nonlinear function. Nonlinearity will help protect against reverse engineering and also other differential attacks.

The final combiner ⊞ mixes the output value from the previous stage with the result of one of the encryption modules. This is done to ensure that, in absence of any fault value, the genuine ciphertext forms the final output. In all other cases the attacker receives an obfuscated version of the actual faulty ciphertext. In the next section, we present a case-study on the AES with a practical construction for $\mathcal{T}$ followed by a detailed hardware analysis on FPGA.

4 Fault Randomization: A Case-Study on AES

It is known that AES, when used with a proper mode of operation, is IND-CPA secure. However, as discussed earlier, there are many attacks on AES that exploit faults to recover the secret key. This renders AES insecure under IND_f-CPA. There have been many attempts to protect AES against these attacks. Still those countermeasures are proved to be vulnerable. In this section, we construct a countermeasure based on the design rationale discussed in the previous section and choosing $\Pi = \text{AES}$. The overall structure is depicted in Fig. 2. It is interesting to note that this construction is applicable to any cipher in place of AES.

4.1 The Combiner to Get the Differential Value Δ

A simple bitwise XOR operation is used to get the difference between the outputs of two AES modules.

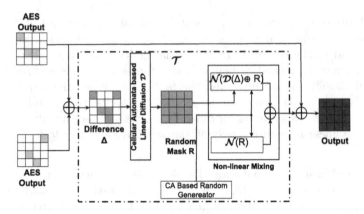

Fig. 2. Countermeasure on AES[†]
[†]AES can be replaced by any iterative block cipher

4.2 Cellular Automata Based Linear Diffusion

In this design, the linear diffusion function $\mathcal{D}$ is implemented using three neighborhood[1] *maximum length*[2] Cellular Automata (CA) where the input is an 128 bit register. The motivation of using 3-neighborhood CA is stated below.

- The evolution of each cell at each iteration is dependent only upon the current state of its left, right and itself as in Fig. 3b which is a very optimized hardware structure.
- Synthesis of maximum length 3-neighborhood CA from a primitive polynomial is well defined in [20].

We have synthesized a maximum length CA from the primitive polynomial shown in Eq. (1) using the technique stated in [20].

$$x^{128} + x^{29} + x^{27} + x^2 + 1 \tag{1}$$

CAs are known to provide good diffusion property when iterated sufficient number of times. So our next task is to ascertain the minimum number of iterations of the CA to achieve optimal diffusion. In order to do this we rely on the *Strict Avalanche Criterion* (SAC). The following lemma gives us an idea about the maximum number of iterations that will definitely violate SAC.

Lemma 1. *If the number of iterations of an n-cell three neighborhood CA is less than $n - 1$, then the output of the CA **violates** the Strict Avalanche Criterion.*

---

[1] The evolution of each cell of a 3-neighborhood CA is based on the value of the cell to its left, the value of the cell itself, and the value of the cell to its right.
[2] An n-cell maximum length CA has a period $2^n - 1$, period of a CA is the number of cycles after which the CA returns to its initial state.

Proof. Let $C^t : \{0,1\}^n \to \{0,1\}^n$ represents t iterations of the n-cell three neighborhood CA. If the initial state of the CA is $X = \{x_0, x_1, \cdots, x_{n-1}\}$ and the output after t iterations is $Y = \{y_0, y_1, \cdots, y_{n-1}\}$, then

$$C^t(x_0, x_1, \cdots, x_{n-1}) = (y_0, y_1, \cdots, y_{n-1}),$$

$$\text{where} \begin{cases} y_i = f_i^t(\mathbb{S}_i^t) : \mathbb{S}_i^t \subseteq X \\ f_i^t : \{0,1\}^{|\mathbb{S}_i^t|} \to \{0,1\} \end{cases}$$

Here $\mathbb{S}_i^t$ is the set of cells driving the function f_i^t. Initially, the function f_i is dependent upon only x_{i-1}, x_i and x_{i+1}. The following set of equations shows the change of $\mathbb{S}_i^t$ with number of iterations t.

$$\begin{aligned} \mathbb{S}_i^1 &= \{x_{i-1}, x_i, x_{i+1}\} \\ \mathbb{S}_i^2 &= \{x_{i-2}, x_{i-1}, x_i, x_{i+1}, x_{i+2}\} \\ &\vdots \\ \mathbb{S}_i^t &= \{x_{i-t}, \cdots, x_i, \cdots, x_{i+t}\}, \quad i \geq t, \ i+t \leq n \end{aligned} \tag{2}$$

Now, if $t < n-1$, then it is clear from Eq. (2), that $x_0 \notin \mathbb{S}_{n-1}^t$ and $x_{n-1} \notin \mathbb{S}_0^t$. This implies that, if the number of iterations is less than $n-1$, then the output bits y_{n-1}, y_0 are independent of the input bits x_0, x_{n-1} respectively which is a straightforward violation of SAC.

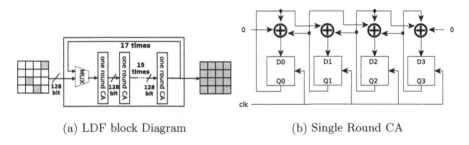

(a) LDF block Diagram   (b) Single Round CA

Fig. 3. Design of LDF

So, to satisfy SAC in our case, the number of iterations for the 128 cell CA cannot be less than $128 - 1 = 127$. Now, to get an experimental lower bound, we perform the SAC test on the output with increasing number of iterations. The experiments reveal that iterating the CA for an additional 128 times is sufficient making a total of $127 + 128 = 255$ iterations. However, if each iteration corresponds to one clock cycle, the throughput of the scheme will reduce substantially. So we avoid the iterative design strategy. We now look into the prospect of using a combinatorial logic that realizes multiple rounds in a single iteration. But, using a logic that realizes 255 rounds in only one iteration will have a high area footprint and at the same time increase the circuit depth, thereby increasing the maximum path delay. We address this problem by using a partially unrolled design to strike a trade off between area and latency. We do so by realizing 15 iterations of the CA with a combinatorial logic and then iterate this logic for 17 clock cycles. This reduces the circuit depth which results in increase of both maximum operating frequency and throughput. The design is shown in Fig. 3.

4.3   Randomized Non-Linear Mixing Using NMix Function

For non-linear mixing purpose, we have used a cryptographically secure and hardware optimized Bent Function called NMix which was introduced in [17]. For the sake of clear understanding the NMix function is briefly revisited here.

Definition 2. *For two n-bit variables* $X = (x_{n-1}, x_{n-2}, \cdots, x_0)$ *and* $R = (r_{n-1}, r_{n-2}, \cdots, r_0)$, *NMix produces an n-bit output variable* $Y = (y_{n-1}, y_{n-2}, \cdots, y_0)$, *where* $Y = \mathcal{N}(X, R)$ *and* $\mathcal{N}$ *is the NMix function. Each output bit of the NMix is related to the input bits by the following relation:*

$$y_i = x_i \oplus r_i \oplus c_{i-1}$$

$$c_i = \bigoplus_{j=0}^{i} x_j r_j \oplus x_{i-1} x_i \oplus r_{i-1} r_i$$

where $0 \le i \le n-1, c_{-1} = 0, x_{-1} = 0, r_{-1} = 0$.

The security properties of NMix is depicted in Table 2 as given in [17].

Table 2. Security Properties of NMix[17]

Parameters	Value
Nonlinearity of output bit y_i	$2^{2i+1} - 2^{i+2}$
Bias for best linear approx. of output bit y_i	2^{-i}
Bias for best linear approx. of $y_i \oplus y_{i+1}$	0.0625
Provide differential resistance	Yes
Algebraic degree of output bit y_i	2

For our purpose we slightly modify the NMix function by taking $c_{-1} = c_{n-1}$. This way the bias of the 0-th bit is omitted. Being a *Bent Function*, the nonlinearity of NMix is $2^{n-1} - 2^{\frac{n}{2}-1}$ which is the maximum possible nonlinearity.

We also compute $\mathcal{N}(0, R)$ and finally we XOR the outputs of the two NMix functions. This step is required to make sure that the correct ciphertext remains unaltered if no fault is injected. The PRNG to generate the random mask is also implemented using a CA in our case. But, this can be replaced by any other PRNGs as, the implementation of PRNG is not our principle concern.

4.4   The Final Combiner

The output from the last step is mixed with the result of one of the AES modules using a bitwise XOR operation.

5   Hardware Implementation

The proposed countermeasure is implemented on Xilinx Spartan-3 XC3S1500-4FG676C FPGA platform choosing AES as the encryption function as depicted in Section 4. The architecture of the design follows the structure in Fig. 2. As discussed earlier, the multiplicative countermeasure in [13] has been cryptanalyzed [1] when $\mathbb{F}_8$ multiplication is used but no cryptanalysis exists of the same scheme when using $\mathbb{F}_{128}$ multiplication. So we have taken the $\mathbb{F}_{128}$ multiplicative version of [13] for comparison. However, as no implementation details was given in [13], we also implemented their scheme in the same FPGA platform. For a fair comparison, the underlying AES primitive used is kept same across all the implementations. The results are given in Table 3.

Table 3. Implementation Summary and Comparison in Altium NB-2

	Unprotected AES	Countermeasure in FDTC '12 with $\mathbb{F}_{128}$ multiplication	Proposed Scheme
Number of LUTs	2214	5881	**5669**
Number of Slices	1292	3543	**3010**
Frequency (MHz)	82	70	**77**
Throughput (Mbit/s)	20.78	14.11	**17.52**
Efficiency (Mbit/s/slice)	0.016	0.004	**0.005**

It is evident from the table that proposed design clearly outperforms the multiplicative countermeasure. The increase in hardware requirement compared to the basic AES is also optimal considering that the scheme uses two AES modules.

6   Conclusion

In this paper we introduce a formal model of fault attacks on symmetric ciphers and their countermeasures based on the infective approach. This model captures the notion of security irrespective of the fault attack strategy. Our design takes the localization of fault, low diffusion and deterministic nature of the countermeasures into account which were not addressed properly in the existing literature. In support of our model, we have also shown a case study on AES and its implementation details on FPGA platform. The hardware results are shown to be better than the multiplicative countermeasure.

References

1. Battistello, A., Giraud, C.: Fault Analysis of Infective AES Computations. In: 2013 Workshop on Fault Diagnosis and Tolerance in Cryptography (FDTC), pp. 101–107, August 2013
2. Boneh, D., Demillo, R.A., Lipton, R.J.: On the Importance of Checking Cryptographic Protocols for Faults. In: Fumy, W., (ed.) Advances in Cryptology EURO-CRYPT 1997. LNCS, vol. 1233, pp. 37–51. Springer, Heidelberg (1997)
3. Daemen, J., Rijmen, V.: The Design of Rijndael. Springer-Verlag New York Inc., Secaucus, NJ, USA (2002) ISBN: 3540425802
4. Biham, E., Shamir, A.: Differential Fault Analysis of Secret Key Cryptosystems. In: Kaliski Jr, B.S. (ed.) CRYPTO 1997. LNCS, vol. 1294, pp. 513–525. Springer, Heidelberg (1997)
5. Giraud, C.: DFA on AES. In: Dobbertin, H., Rijmen, V., Sowa, A. (eds.) AES 2005. LNCS, vol. 3373, pp. 27–41. Springer, Heidelberg (2005)
6. Tunstall, M., Mukhopadhyay, D., Ali, S.: Differential Fault Analysis of the Advanced Encryption Standard Using a Single Fault. In: Ardagna, C.A., Zhou, J. (eds.) WISTP 2011. LNCS, vol. 6633, pp. 224–233. Springer, Heidelberg (2011)
7. Mukhopadhyay, D.: An Improved Fault Based Attack of the Advanced Encryption Standard. In: Preneel, B. (ed.) AFRICACRYPT 2009. LNCS, vol. 5580, pp. 421–434. Springer, Heidelberg (2009)
8. Saha, D., Mukhopadhyay, D., Roy Chowdhury, D.: A Diagonal Fault Attack on the Advanced Encryption Standard. Cryptology ePrint Archive, Report 2009/581 (2009). http://eprint.iacr.org/
9. Kim, C.H., Quisquater, J.-J.: Fault Attacks for CRT Based RSA: New Attacks, New Results, and New Countermeasures. In: Sauveron, D., Markantonakis, K., Bilas, A., Quisquater, J.-J. (eds.) WISTP 2007. LNCS, vol. 4462, pp. 215–228. Springer, Heidelberg (2007)
10. Van Woudenberg, J., Witteman, M., Menarini, F.: Practical Optical Fault Injection on Secure Microcontrollers. In: 2011 Workshop on Fault Diagnosis and Tolerance in Cryptography (FDTC), pp. 91–99, September 2011
11. Yen, S.M., Joye, M.: Checking before output may not be enough against fault-based cryptanalysis. IEEE Transactions on Computers **49**(9), 967–970 (2000)
12. Gierlichs, B., Schmidt, J.-M., Tunstall, M.: Infective Computation and Dummy Rounds: Fault Protection for Block Ciphers without Check-before-Output. In: Hevia, A., Neven, G. (eds.) LatinCrypt 2012. LNCS, vol. 7533, pp. 305–321. Springer, Heidelberg (2012)
13. Lomne, V., Roche, T., Thillard, A.: On the Need of Randomness in Fault Attack Countermeasures - Application to AES. In: Proceedings of the 2012 Workshop on Fault Diagnosis and Tolerance in Cryptography, FDTC 2012, pp. 85–94. IEEE Computer Society Washington, DC (2012)
14. Tupsamudre, H., Bisht, S., Mukhopadhyay, D.: Destroying fault invariant with randomization - A countermeasure for AES against differential fault attacks. In: Proceedings of the Cryptographic Hardware and Embedded Systems, CHES 2014–16th International Workshop, Busan, South Korea, September 23–26, pp. 93–111 (2014)
15. Roche, T., Lomné, V., Khalfallah, K.: Combined Fault and Side-Channel Attack on Protected Implementations of AES. In: Prouff, E. (ed.) CARDIS 2011. LNCS, vol. 7079, pp. 65–83. Springer, Heidelberg (2011)

16. Piret, G., Quisquater, J.-J.: A Differential Fault Attack Technique against SPN Structures, with Application to the AES and KHAZAD. In: Walter, C.D., Koç, Ç.K., Paar, C. (eds.) CHES 2003. LNCS, vol. 2779, pp. 77–88. Springer, Heidelberg (2003)
17. Bhaumik, J., Roy Chowdhury, D.: Nmix: An Ideal Candidate for Key Mixing. In: SECRYPT, pp. 285–288 (2009)
18. Fournier, J., Rigaud, J.B., Bouquet, S., Robisson, B., Tria, A., Dutertre, J.M., Agoyan, M.: Design and characterisation of an AES chip embedding countermeasures. IJIEI **1**(3/4), 328–347 (2011)
19. Joye, M., Manet, P., Rigaud, J.B.: Strengthening hardware AES implementations against fault attacks. Information Security, IET **1**(3), 106–110 (2007)
20. Cattell, K., Muzio, J.C.: Synthesis of one-dimensional linear hybrid cellular automata. IEEE Transactions on Computer-Aided Design of Integrated Circuits and Systems **15**(3), 325–335(1996)

Analysis of Rainbow Tables with Fingerprints

Gildas Avoine[1,2], Adrien Bourgeois[1], and Xavier Carpent[1(✉)]

[1] Université catholique de Louvain, 1348 Louvain-la-Neuve, Belgium
xavier.carpent@uclouvain.be
[2] INSA de Rennes, IRISA UMR 6074, 35043 Rennes, France

Abstract. Cryptanalytic time-memory tradeoffs were introduced by Martin Hellman in 1980 to perform key-recovery attacks on cryptosystems. *Rainbow tables* are a variant and a major advance presented by Philippe Oechslin at Crypto 2003. Checkpoints for rainbow tables have been proposed in Indocrypt 2005 as a method to reduce the cost of false alarms. Endpoints truncation has also been suggested to reduce their memory consumption.

This article shows that checkpoints and endpoints share the same nature and unifies checkpoints and endpoint truncation in a single model. An analysis of the average cryptanalysis time is presented and validated experimentally, and a method to determine fingerprint configuration systematically is proposed.

Rainbow tables with fingerprints exhibit a speedup of about two with respect to their classical counterparts in average cryptanalysis time.

Keywords: Cryptanalysis · Time-memory tradeoff · Rainbow tables

1 Introduction

1.1 Motivations

Fundamental problems in cryptanalysis such as recovering encrypted data without the key, or inverting a hash function can be done by exhaustive search. However, the search needs to be carried out from scratch with each new instance of the problem. Moreover, it suffers from scalability issues in practice, with instances of interesting size requiring too much time or computational power. Alternatively, one could precompute and store a lookup table, but again interesting instances require unrealistic storage capabilities.

The *cryptanalytic time-memory tradeoff* (TMTO) is a technique introduced by Hellman in 1980 [13] that allows an adversary to carry out efficient brute-force attacks in practice. As its name suggests, it is a tradeoff between an on-the-fly exhaustive search and a precomputed lookup table. A TMTO particularly makes sense when a known plaintext attack is performed more than once (because the initial precomputation costs more than a single exhaustive search), with a keyspace that does not allow the adversary to store all the pairs (key, ciphertext). A TMTO is also quite relevant when the attack is time-constrained once the adversary receives the ciphertext.

© Springer International Publishing Switzerland 2015
E. Foo and D. Stebila (Eds.): ACISP 2015, LNCS 9144, pp. 356–374, 2015.
DOI: 10.1007/978-3-319-19962-7_21

Cryptanalytic time-memory tradeoffs are thus the keystone of many practical attacks, for example against A5/1 (GSM) in 2000 [7], LILI-128 in 2002 [22], Windows LM Hash in 2003 [19], Unix passwords in 2005 [17], and Texas Instruments DST in 2005 [8]. In 2010, the attack against A5/1 was resurrected and a world-wide distributed TMTO-based attack was launched during Black Hat 2010 [18]. The weakness exploited in all these cases is twofold: the key entropy is not high enough, and a known (constant) plaintext attack is feasible.

In spite of the wide use of cryptanalytic time-memory tradeoffs, few significant advances have been done since Oechslin introduced the rainbow tables at Crypto 2003 [19], illustrated with the instant cracking of alphanumerical Windows LM Hash passwords. However, any improvement of their efficiency may render attacks more practical, especially when they are time-constrained. It is thus very important to minimize their cost.

1.2   Background

A Hellman-type cryptanalytic time-memory tradeoff consists of a *precomputation phase* that is done once, and an *online phase* that is expected to be much faster than a brute-force attack.

Precomputation Phase. To invert a function $h : A \rightarrow B$, a set of m chains of t elements in A is precomputed. A chain starts with an arbitrary value S_j belonging to A, known as its *starting point*. Each subsequent element is computed by iterating a function $f : A \rightarrow A$, $x \mapsto r(h(x))$, where $r : B \rightarrow A$ is a *reduction function*, which aim is to assign an arbitrary value in A to any value of B. The i-th ($1 \leq i \leq t$) element of the j-th ($1 \leq j \leq m$) chain is denoted $X_{j,i}$, where $X_{j,i+1} = f(X_{j,i})$ and $X_{j,1} = S_j$. The values $X_{j,t}$ are denoted E_j and called the *endpoints*. The trick of the TMTO technique consists in only storing the m pairs (S_j, E_j) in a so-called *table*. A single table cannot fully cover the set A, and several tables are consequently required to reach a success rate close to 1.

Online Phase. Given a value y in B, the goal of the online phase is to retrieve x in A such that $h(x) = y$ (provided such a point exists)[1]. As the table does not contain the intermediate points, the adversary computes instead a chain from y and searches for a match with an endpoint. More precisely, she starts by reducing y and searching through the m endpoints. If there exists j such that $r(y) = E_j$, then she re-computes $X_{j,t-1}$ from S_j and verifies whether $h(X_{j,t-1}) = y$. If this holds, the attack succeeds and $x = X_{j,t-1}$. Otherwise, the match is called a *false alarm*. When a false alarm occurs, or when no matching endpoint is found, the attack proceeds on the next column: the attacker computes $y \leftarrow f(y)$ and repeats the operations. The attack goes on until a correct value is found, or until the end of the table is reached, in which case the attack fails for this table.

---

[1] In the following, it is assumed that x is chosen uniformly at random in A.

A major drawback of Hellman's method is that two colliding chains in a given table lead to a *fusion*. Such artifacts substantially decrease the tradeoff performance. Two significant improvements have been introduced to mitigate this problem: the *distinguished points* in 1982 by Rivest [10] and the *rainbow table* in 2003 by Oechslin [19]. This article focuses on the latter, which is significantly faster in practice [16, 19].

1.3   Related Works

Although not the focus of this paper, the following works are also relevant.

Hellman's technique is designed to invert random functions. Fiat and Naor provide in [11] a construction for inverting any function, at the price of a less efficient tradeoff. De, Trevisan and Tulsiani propose in [9] a similar construction for inverting any function on a fraction of their input. They also suggest using time-memory tradeoffs for distinguishing the output of pseudorandom generators from random.

Time-memory tradeoffs have also been applied to stream cipher independently by Babbage in [3] and Golić in [12]. These tradeoffs typically require more data than attacks on block ciphers. Biryukov and Shamir improve in [6] the efficiency of this attack on stream ciphers by combining the Babbage/Golić and the Hellman techniques. Finally, Biryukov, Mukhopadhyay and Sarkar generalize these different approaches in [5], and propose a way to use Hellman's technique with multiple data.

In [4], Barkan, Biham, and Shamir showed that the performance of existing time-memory tradeoffs can not be improved by more than a logarithmic factor.

1.4   Contributions

This paper revisits the regular rainbow tables and introduces the rainbow tables with *fingerprints*. They form a generalization of rainbow tables and bring a new vision of them.

The keystone of the rainbow tables with fingerprints is that the endpoints are no longer stored in the table. Instead, a *fingerprint* of each chain is stored along with the starting point. We show that the fingerprint is an alternative characterization of a chain that behaves better in the online phase than the endpoint. The fingerprints may be thought of as the concatenation of a truncated endpoint (as described for instance in [16]), and a series of checkpoints (see [1]). However, we develop a framework in which the checkpoints and the (truncated or not) endpoint have the same nature, and analyze them together. We show that this approach makes sense and that it is more general. This sheds new light on the problem, and we trust this might lead to further improvements.

We present a theoretical analysis of the average performance of rainbow tables with fingerprints, and propose a way to efficiently and systematically compute good configurations.

Rainbow tables are reviewed in Sect. 2, along with existing relevant analysis and improvements on them. The fingerprint model is introduced in Sect. 3, and is analyzed in Sect. 4. A technique for finding fingerprint configurations is described in Sect. 5. Finally, Sect. 6 presents theoretical results on different comparison between rainbow tables with fingerprint and their regular version, along with experimental validation.

2 Rainbow Tables

2.1 Description

Oechslin introduced in 2003 [19] an improvement that outperforms the distinguished points. In this variant, a different reduction function is used per column, which leads to the so-called rainbow tables. This new organization of the tables eases the detection of fusions, while keeping constant the chain length, and also divides the number of lookups by a factor t in comparison with Hellman's tables. The online phase is similar to the one of Hellman's method, but the difference is that it is necessary to start the online chains iteratively from the last column at the right of the table to the first column at the left of the table. Indeed, as the column that contains the expected key is unknown, the first reduction function that must be applied is unknown as well, and each possibility must be tested. This means that in the worst case, $t^2/2$ operations are necessary to browse all the table, without taking false alarms into account. A thorough analysis of the rainbow tables has been done by Avoine, Junod, and Oechslin [2]. The rainbow tables are currently used by most of the password crackers, and have been implemented by Mentens, Batina, Preneel, and Verbauwhede [17] using FPGAs to retrieve UNIX passwords.

Precomputation Phase. The precomputation phase is very similar to that of the Hellman method. Instead of iterating a function $f : x \mapsto r(h(x))$ to compute a chain, a different reduction function is used in each column. Chains therefore consists of elements computed iteratively using $f_i : x \mapsto r_i(h(x))$, where r_i is the reduction function associated with column i. A typical reduction function family is $r_i : y \mapsto (y + i) \bmod N$, with $N = |A|$. A series of chains is computed in order to form a table.

In order to build a *clean*[2] table, only one chain per different endpoint is kept. These endpoints, along with their corresponding starting points, are stored in memory. Furthermore, a table of *maximal size* is obtained when all (or almost all) the possible endpoints are saved, which happens when the number of chains computed is sufficiently large (i.e. when any new chain would have a negligible probability of having an endpoint that is not yet saved). The structure of a rainbow table is shown in Fig. 1.

As highlighted by Theorem 2, the probability of success of a single rainbow table is bounded. In the case of rainbow tables of maximal size, this probability is about 86.47%. In order to obtain a higher probability of success, multiple tables

---

[2] Although the word "perfect" is usually attributed to tables without merges in the literature, we find this terminology more intuitive and more adapted.

	$\xrightarrow{r_1 \circ h}$		$\xrightarrow{r_2 \circ h}$				$\xrightarrow{r_{t-2} \circ h}$		$\xrightarrow{r_{t-1} \circ h}$	
$S_1 = X_{1,1}$	$\xrightarrow{r_1 \circ h}$	$X_{1,2}$	$\xrightarrow{r_2 \circ h}$	$\cdots$		$X_{1,t-1}$	$\xrightarrow{r_{t-1} \circ h}$			$X_{1,t} = E_1$
$S_2 = X_{2,1}$	$\xrightarrow{r_1 \circ h}$	$X_{2,2}$	$\xrightarrow{r_2 \circ h}$	$\cdots$		$X_{2,t-1}$	$\xrightarrow{r_{t-1} \circ h}$			$X_{2,t} = E_2$
$\vdots$		$\vdots$		$\ddots$		$\vdots$				$\vdots$
$S_j = X_{j,1}$	$\xrightarrow{r_1 \circ h}$	$X_{j,2}$	$\xrightarrow{r_2 \circ h}$	$\cdots$		$X_{j,t-1}$	$\xrightarrow{r_{t-1} \circ h}$			$X_{j,t} = E_j$
$\vdots$		$\vdots$		$\ddots$		$\vdots$				$\vdots$
$S_m = X_{m,1}$	$\xrightarrow{r_1 \circ h}$	$X_{m,2}$	$\xrightarrow{r_2 \circ h}$	$\cdots$		$X_{m,t-1}$	$\xrightarrow{r_{t-1} \circ h}$			$X_{m,t} = E_m$

Fig. 1. Structure of a rainbow table. The framed columns, respectively the starting points and the endpoints, are the parts stored in memory.

are used, with a different family of reduction functions per table. A typical number is 4 (achieving a total probability of success of about 99.97%).

In the following, clean rainbow tables of maximal size are assumed, because they offer the best efficiency for a given memory.

Online Phase. The online phase in rainbow tables is again very similar to that of the Hellman method. In order to invert a given y, one starts by computing $r_{t-1}(y)$ and searching through the endpoint list whether there exists j such that $E_j = r_{t-1}(y)$. If so, a chain is rebuilt from the corresponding starting point S_j in order to compute $X_{j,t-1}$ and verify whether $h(X_{j,t-1}) = y$. If so, the attack succeeds with $x = X_{j,t-1}$, and if not, this match was a false alarm. In that case, or when no matching endpoint is found, the attack proceeds to the next table. Once all tables are cycled[3], the attack proceeds with the next column, computing $r_{t-1}(h(r_{t-2}(y)))$, and so on until the search succeeds or that all columns are searched through.

2.2 Analysis

For the sake of clarity, the notations provided in [2] and [19] for rainbow tables are also used below, and summarized in Tab. 1. In addition, some theoretical results from [2] are provided.

Theorem 1. *The number of possible points in column i for a chain generated from the starting column is*

$$m_{i+1} = N \left(1 - \left(1 - \frac{1}{N} \right)^{m_i} \right). \tag{1}$$

When using tables of maximum size, this can be approximated by $m_i^{max} = \frac{2N}{i+1}$.

---

[3] The search procedure for rainbow tables works "vertically" (all tables for each column) rather than "horizontally" (all columns for each table) because the search is increasingly more expensive towards the left of the tables. In the Hellman method, this does not matter.

Table 1. Notations used in this paper

Symbol	Meaning
$h : A \to B$	The function to invert
N	$|A|$
m	Number of chains in one table
t	Number of columns per table
ℓ	Number of tables
q_c	Probability of a false alarm occuring when the search is at column c
m_i	Number of possible points in column i in a precomputed rainbow table

Proof. See Theorem 1 in [2].

Theorem 2. *The success probability of a set of ℓ rainbow tables is*

$$P^* = 1 - \left(1 - \frac{m}{N}\right)^{\ell t}. \tag{2}$$

When using tables of maximum size, this can be approximated by $P^* \approx 1 - e^{-2\ell}$.

Proof. See Theorem 2 in [2].

Theorem 3. *The probability of occurrence of a false alarm when the search is at column c is*

$$q_c = 1 - \prod_{i=c}^{t}\left(1 - \frac{m_i^{max}}{N}\right) \approx 1 - \frac{(c-1)c}{t(t+1)} \tag{3}$$

Proof. See Theorem 2 in [2].

2.3 Improvements

Checkpoints. In 2005, Avoine, Junod, and Oechslin [1] introduced a new feature to the rainbow tables, known as the *checkpoints*. The authors observed that more than 50% of the cryptanalysis time is devoted to rule out the false alarms. Their technique consists in storing information (e.g., a parity bit) on some intermediate points of the chains alongside the endpoints. During the online phase, when a match with an endpoint occurs, its checkpoints must be compared with the checkpoints of the chain which construction is ongoing. When there is a match of the endpoints, but no match of the checkpoints, the adversary can conclude that a false alarm occurred without re-computing the colliding chain. Although the checkpoints increase the performance of the tradeoff, their impact is limited given that their storage consumes additional memory.

Endpoint Truncation. In an effort to lower the memory consumption of the rainbow tables, an idea is to truncate the endpoints by a fixed amount of bits. It is not clear where this idea first appeared in the literature, but it most likely originated from the (more straightforward) truncation in the distinguished points method [10]. In the case of rainbow tables, it was hinted in [4]. As noted in [16], endpoint truncation however comes with a cost in the form of an increase in false alarms (due to fortuitous matching endpoints).

3   Fingerprints

Despite having been analyzed separately (see e.g. [16]), checkpoints and end-point truncation have never been addressed together. Moreover, and more importantly, good checkpoint positions and truncation amount were up to now found empirically. In this section, a new model is proposed. It encompasses these two improvements of rainbow tables in a sensible and unified way. A technique for determining configurations is discussed in Sect. 5.

3.1   Rationale

In regular rainbow tables, chains are composed of the starting points, which allows one to rebuild that chain without ambiguity, and the endpoints, which are used to select the chain to rebuild in each step of the online phase. Although it is necessary for the starting points to be points in A for the chain reconstruction to be meaningful, it is not necessary for endpoints to have that property. Indeed, their purpose is solely to compare the online chain with each chain of the table, in order to determine which should be rebuilt (if there is one). An issue with using the endpoint as characterization is that when the online chain merges with a precomputed chain, they cannot be distinguished. This leads to the false alarms, which are the pet hate of the time-memory tradeoffs. The fingerprints reduce this problem by providing a better way to characterize the chains.

3.2   Description

Definition. In the model presented in this paper, the characterization of a chain is the list of checkpoints, and the endpoint is considered as a regular checkpoint. Formally, a fingerprint F_j is defined as the concatenation of the outputs of the functions Φ_i applied to each element $X_{j,i}$ of the chain:

$$F_j = \Phi_1(X_{j,1}) \;||\; \Phi_2(X_{j,2}) \;||\; \cdots \;||\; \Phi_t(X_{j,t})$$

where $j \in [1, m]$, "$||$" denotes the concatenation, and Φ_i ($1 \le i \le t$) is a *checkpoint function*, used in column i. A checkpoint function is such that:

$$\Phi_i : A \to \begin{cases} \{0,1\}^{\sigma_i} & \text{if } \sigma_i > 0 \\ \epsilon & \text{otherwise} \end{cases}$$

with $0 \leq \sigma_i \leq \lceil \log_2 N \rceil$ and ϵ representing no information. The output of the checkpoint function is called a *checkpoint*. A fingerprint is therefore the concatenation of the checkpoints of the points in the chain. Note that a checkpoint function is expected to have a uniform distribution of its output, as it is the case with reduction functions. A typical checkpoint function $\Phi_i(x)$ returns the σ_i least significant bits of x for instance.

Note that, depending on the configuration (i.e. the value of σ_i in all columns), a fingerprint F_j is not necessarily $\lceil \log_2 N \rceil$ bits long. In fact, fingerprints are typically smaller than the endpoints in regular rainbow tables, as shown in Sect. 6. This allows the rainbow table with fingerprints to contain more chains than what a regular rainbow table would, for the same memory.

Precomputation Phase. Precomputation in rainbow tables with fingerprints is very similar to that of regular rainbow tables. The difference is that during the computation of a chain, the checkpoint functions are applied on each point, such that a fingerprint is computed for that chain. Once a chain is complete, the starting point, the fingerprint, as well as the endpoint (i.e. the last point of the chain) are all temporarily stored. Similarly to rainbow tables, chains are then sorted according to their endpoints in order to remove the merging chains. The table thus becomes clean (or perfect). Endpoints are then discarded, as they are no longer required. A final step consists in sorting the chains according to their fingerprints, in order to make the search more efficient[4]. Note that at this point, there might be several chains sharing the same fingerprint even though they had different endpoints. However, this is marginal for reasonable configurations. This final step (sorting fingerprints) requires negligible time with respect to the earlier work, much like sorting the endpoints requires negligible time over the computation of the chains. Rainbow tables with fingerprints therefore require the same amount of precomputation as their regular counterparts.

Online Phase. Again, the algorithm for performing the search in rainbow tables with fingerprints is very close to the one described in 2.1. However, the checkpoint functions are applied to the online chain, which gives a *partial fingerprint* (rather than an endpoint). The fingerprint is partial because the online chain is shorter than chains of the table, and therefore it might be that not all checkpoints are part of it. The partial fingerprint is then compared to stored fingerprints (the comparison is done for the available bits only). A second particularity is that there might be several fingerprints matching the partial fingerprint of the online chain, leading to possibly several false alarms per step (there can only be one in regular rainbow tables).

The fact that endpoints are possibly not completely part of the fingerprint means that it is possible that two non-merging chains share the same fingerprint.

---

[4] The sort is performed in reverse order, that is the fingerprints are considered flipped, because partial fingerprints $\Phi_c(X_{j,c}) || \ldots || \Phi_t(X_{j,t})$ are searched in the online phase. This ensures that multiple candidate matching fingerprints are contiguous in the list, making the search more efficient.

This leads to false alarms, although they are not of the same type as false alarms caused by merges. Consequently, false alarms are divided into two types: Type-I false alarms are those that are merge-induced, and Type-II false alarms are those that are caused by partial fingerprint matching of non-merging chains. Although Type-II false alarms do not appear in regular rainbow tables, the additional cost they incur in tables with fingerprints is more than made up for by the other benefits.

4   Analysis

This section provides an analysis of rainbow tables with fingerprints. Theorem 4 presents preliminary results regarding fortuitous collisions in checkpoint functions, and Theorem 5 presents the average execution cost of a rainbow table with fingerprints, for a given configuration.

Let ϕ_c be the probability that two different points have the same checkpoint in a given column c:

$$\phi_c := \Pr\left[\Phi_c(x) = \Phi_c(y) | x, y \in A : x \neq y\right]. \qquad (4)$$

This probability is useful to describe the event of two non-merging chains having the same partial fingerprint.

Theorem 4. *If $N \equiv 0 \pmod{2^{\sigma_c}}$, given a column c, the probability that two different points chosen uniformly at random in A have the same checkpoint in c is:*

$$\phi_c = \frac{N/2^{\sigma_c} - 1}{N - 1}. \qquad (5)$$

Proof. Given a value x and its corresponding checkpoint $\Phi_c(x)$, there are $N - 1$ different possible values $y \neq x$. Among those, there are on average $N/2^{\sigma_c} - 1$ values y such that $\Phi_c(x) = \Phi_c(y)$. □

This theorem assumes that both the points in a column and the checkpoints are uniformly distributed. This is for instance ensured if the reduction and checkpoint functions are modulos, and if the h function has a uniformly distributed output, which is the case in virtually all practical cases. Note that this assumption is already made in previous analyses, such as [2] and [19].

The following theorem gives the average cost of a search using a rainbow table with fingerprints. Its lengthy proof is given in Appendix A.

Theorem 5. *The average amount of evaluations of h during the online phase using the rainbow tables with fingerprints is:*

$$T = \sum_{k=1}^{\ell t} \frac{m}{N} \left(1 - \frac{m}{N}\right)^{k-1} (W_k + Q_k) + \left(1 - \frac{m}{N}\right)^{\ell t} (W_{\ell t} + Q_{\ell t}), \qquad (6)$$

with

$$c_i = \left\lceil \frac{i-1}{\ell} \right\rceil, \qquad\qquad q_c = 1 - \prod_{i=t-c+1}^{t} \left(1 - \frac{m_i}{N}\right),$$

$$W_k = \sum_{i=1}^{k} c_i, \qquad\qquad Q_k = \sum_{i=1}^{k} (t - c_i)(P_{c_i} + E_{c_i}),$$

$$P_c = \frac{1}{N} \sum_{i=1}^{c} \left(\prod_{j=t-c}^{t-i} \phi_j \right) (z_{i-1,c} - z_{i,c}), \qquad E_c = (m - q_c) \prod_{i=t-c+1}^{t} \phi_i,$$

$$z_{i,c} = m(1 + c - i) + \frac{(c-i)(c-i+2)}{i^2} \left[mi + 2N \log\left(1 - \frac{mi}{2N}\right) \right],$$

$$z_{0,c} = m(1 + c) \left(1 - \frac{mc}{4N}\right).$$

Proof. See Appendix A.

5   Algorithm for Finding Optimal Configurations

This section presents an algorithm for determining the configuration of a rainbow table with fingerprints. Up to now, the configurations for checkpoints and endpoint truncation were found empirically.

5.1   Hill Climbing

Hill Climbing [21] is a local search technique designed to obtain a local optimum of a function f using an iterative procedure. If f has a single local optimum which is thus the global optimum (in our case, minimum), it will be found by in a finite (and small) number of steps with Hill Climbing. The idea is the following. Let $f : X \rightarrow \mathbb{R}$ be the target function of which one wants to find the global minimum. We start with an initial $x_0 \in X$, and each step consists in exploring the neighbors of the current point, evaluating f in these neighbor positions, and comparing these values to that of the current position. The new current point is then set to be the neighbor that minimized f among all the neighbors. The search goes on until a situation where all neighbor have small values through f than the current point, which consists in a local minimum.

The definition of neighbor depends on the application, but when minimizing a discrete function, it is rather straightforward. An additional improvement that we used in order to accelerate the search is starting with a large step, and decreasing it gradually whenever the search stalls, until the step is sufficiently small.

See [21] for a more thorough description of the Hill Climbing algorithm.

5.2 Application to Checkpoint Functions

As shown in Sect. 4, the performance of the rainbow tables with fingerprints strongly depends on their configuration.

One way to find the best configuration for the checkpoint functions is to apply a brute-force technique to compute T for the $(1 + \lceil \log_2 N \rceil)^t$ possibilities (from 0 to $\lceil \log_2 N \rceil$ bits included for each column), and keep the one that minimizes T. This however is not feasible for any practical instance, because the parameter space is too large. Instead, Hill climbing is used, as described in Sect. 5.1, to compute these configurations efficiently. In order to apply it, the two following assumptions are made.

First, all the non-ϵ checkpoint functions, except the one in column t, output exactly one bit. This hypothesis makes sense because one two-bit checkpoint in a column or two one-bit checkpoints in adjacent columns give nearly identical results. Moreover, we observed experimentally that good configurations tend to have their non-ϵ checkpoints scattered, except in the last column where a more important concentration is more efficient. This tendency is most likely explained by Type-II false alarms.

Then, it is assumed that the local minimum is a global minimum (that is, T is unimodal with respect to the positions of the one-bit checkpoints). This has been observed experimentally.

Note that this technique is conservative in the sense that if either assumption is not verified, then the real optimal configuration can only lead to yet better performance. In the following, the "optimal configurations" refer to the best solutions found using this approach. The determination of the configuration is of course only done once, before the precomputation phase, and adds a marginal overhead to its cost.

The overall technique that we used to find the optimal configurations is displayed in Algorithm 1. The variables nbits and ncp represent respectively the number of bits for a fingerprint (that is, $\text{nbits} = \sum_{i=1}^{t} \sigma_i$) and the number of one-bit non-final checkpoints (that is, $\text{ncp} = \text{nbits} - \sigma_t$). The values $\text{nbits}^{\min}$ and $\text{nbits}^{\max}$ represent the range of search of nbits. In theory, this goes from 1 up to $t \times \lceil \log_2 N \rceil$, but it is impractical to explore that range. These bounds need to be defined heuristically. In our experiments, we found out that it is hardly necessary to search beyond, say $[0.75 \lceil \log_2 N \rceil, \ldots, 1.25 \lceil \log_2 N \rceil]$. The same holds for the values $\text{ncp}^{\min}$ and $\text{ncp}^{\max}$, which represent the range of search of ncp. Again, in theory these bounds are respectively 0 and nbits, but in practice, we observed that the optimal configuration is in most cases in a range of about $[0.1\,\text{nbits}, \ldots, 0.4\,\text{nbits}]$.

Finally, we observed that there is an clear constancy in the optimal positions for the one-bit checkpoints, as represented in Fig. 2. One can notice that, for a given ncp^{opt}, the relative positions of the one-bit checkpoints remain the same. When ncp^{opt} changes (as is the case between $N = 2^{44}$ and $N = 2^{46}$ for instance), the relative checkpoint positions change as well, although they retain the same structure. Although we did not find an analytic way to use this, one could spare the somewhat tedious procedure exposed in this section by using known optimal

Algorithm 1. Algorithm for finding optimal configurations of rainbow tables with fingerprints.

Input: N, M, ℓ

  bestcfg $\leftarrow \emptyset$

  for nbits $\in [\text{nbits}^{\min}, \ldots, \text{nbits}^{\max}]$ **do**

    $m \leftarrow M/(\ell \times \text{nbits})$

    $t \leftarrow 2N/m - 1$

    for ncp $\in [\text{ncp}^{\min}, \ldots, \text{ncp}^{\max}]$ **do**

      newcfg $\leftarrow$ Hill Climbing on T with ncp one-bit checkpoints and a final (nbits $-$ ncp)-bits checkpoint

      if $T(\text{newcfg}) < T(\text{bestcfg})$ **then**

        bestcfg $\leftarrow$ newcfg

      end if

    end for

  end for

  return bestcfg

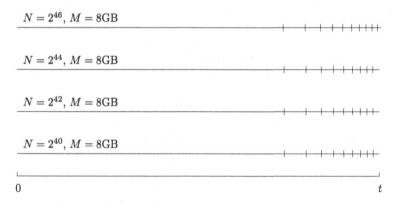

Fig. 2. Repartition of one-bit checkpoints relatively to t

relative checkpoint positions, or using them as initial starting points for the Hill Climbing search.

6 Theoretical and Experimental Results

6.1 Theoretical Results

Table 2 presents the gain $1 - T_{\text{fingerprint}}/T_{\text{regular}}$ between rainbow tables with fingerprints in optimal configurations and regular rainbow tables, for different sizes of key space and memory dedicated to the tradeoff. The value $\ell = 4$ is considered in both cases[5], and m and t are set for regular rainbow tables to the

---

[5] This value for ℓ represents an overwhelming success probability, and is the default in Ophcrack [20], for instance. Other values of ℓ lead to very similar results.

Table 2. Gain of rainbow tables with fingerprints over regular rainbow tables for various N and M

	2^{38}	2^{40}	2^{42}	2^{44}	2^{46}	2^{48}
2GB	32.48%	35.94%	39.01%	41.73%	44.16%	46.35%
4GB	30.76%	34.36%	37.54%	40.36%	42.88%	45.14%
8GB	29.04%	32.76%	36.05%	38.97%	41.58%	43.93%

optimal values as presented in [2]. For the fingerprint version, Algorithm 1 is used to find the optimal configurations.

Table 2 is filled with memory sizes that belong to a reasonable range for an average personal computer. Note that M denotes the memory dedicated for endpoints/fingerprints only (adding the starting points about doubles the memory required). The problem sizes are also driven by practical considerations, to avoid a prohibitive online search time. Analyzing the results leads to two trends. The advantage of the rainbow tables with fingerprints over the regular version tends to increase as the memory decreases. Secondly, the gain increases with the problem size. This behavior can be explained by the fact that when N is large, or when M is small, t and therefore T increases, and there is thus more freedom in the configuration of the checkpoint functions.

Table. 3 lists differences in the parameters and results between rainbow tables with fingerprints in optimal configuration and regular rainbow tables in several settings. Again, the memory M is the one dedicated to endpoint/fingerprint storage (identical in both cases). The row "Positions" corresponds to the set of columns associated with a one-bit checkpoint. In the optimal configurations found, all checkpoints but the one in the last column consist of at most one bit, as described in Sect. 5.2. The use of the following checkpoint functions are assumed:

$$\Phi_i : A \to \{0,1\}^{\sigma_i}$$
$$x \mapsto \begin{cases} \mathrm{lsb}_{\sigma_i}(x) & \text{if } \sigma_i > 0 \\ \epsilon & \text{otherwise,} \end{cases}$$

where $\mathrm{lsb}_n(x)$ is a function that outputs the n least significant bits of x.

One can observe that when additional memory is available, the optimal solutions tend to use some extra memory per chain, and vice versa. Additionally, it is noteworthy that the cost of a false alarm for rainbow tables with fingerprints is around one third of the one for regular rainbow tables.

6.2 Experimental Validation

A time-memory tradeoff with rainbow tables with fingerprints has been implemented in order to illustrate the theory with experimental results. We considered

Table 3. Analytical performance for the best configurations of rainbow tables with fingerprints

(a) $N = 2^{48}$, $M = 2\text{GB}$

	regular rainbow tables	rainbow tables with fingerprints
m	4.47×10^7	4.88×10^7
$|E_j|, |F_j|$	48	40
t	1.26×10^7	1.15×10^7
T	2.32×10^{13}	1.24×10^{13} (-46.35%)
Average FA cost	1.33×10^{13}	0.41×10^{13} (-68.88%)
Positions		8476358, 9172110, 9663530, 10050060, 10371170, 10647046, 10889558, 11106326, 11302572, 11482032

(b) $N = 2^{48}$, $M = 4\text{GB}$

	regular rainbow tables	rainbow tables with fingerprints
m	8.95×10^7	9.65×10^7
$|E_j|, |F_j|$	48	41
t	6.29×10^6	5.83×10^6
T	5.79×10^{12}	3.18×10^{12} (-45.14%)
Average FA cost	3.33×10^{12},	1.06×10^{12} (-68.20%)
Positions		4285001, 4636802, 4885286, 5080733, 5243100, 5382597, 5505222, 5614831, 5714062, 5804807

(c) $N = 2^{48}$, $M = 8\text{GB}$

	regular rainbow tables	rainbow tables with fingerprints
m	1.79×10^8	1.89×10^8
$|E_j|, |F_j|$	48	43
t	3.15×10^6	2.98×10^6
T	1.45×10^{12}	0.81×10^{12} (-43.93%)
Average FA cost	8.31×10^{11}	2.58×10^{11} (-68.99%)
Positions		2155147, 2334199, 2460731, 2560281, 2642997, 2714070, 2776554, 2832410, 2882981, 2929230, 2971872

NTLM Hash alphanumeric (both lowercase and uppercase) passwords of length 1 to 7, which represents a search space of $N = \sum_{i=1}^{7} 62^i \approx 2^{41.70}$. Considering longer passwords would better emphasize the performance of the rainbow tables with fingerprints, but we were time-constrained for the precomputation of the tables.

The parameters are $m = 5.03 \times 10^8$, $t = 13554$, $\ell = 4$. Prefix/suffix decomposition [1] was also used in order to save some extra memory, but this has no influence on the online performance (it decreases M, the memory used in practice, but not m, the number of chains). The four tables take up about 14.8GB in total. Using the methodology described in Sect. 5.2, the following configuration was found:

$$\Phi_i(x) = \begin{cases} \mathrm{lsb}_1(x) & \text{if } i \in \{10077, 10928, 11530, 12004, \\ & \qquad 12398, 12736, 13034, 13301\} \\ \mathrm{lsb}_{34}(x) & \text{if } i = 13554 \\ \epsilon & \text{otherwise.} \end{cases}$$

The results of our experiment are presented in Table 4. It shows that the practice matches with the theoretical estimations.

Table 4. Theoretical and experimental (average of 25000 searches) results for NTLM problem

	Theoretical	Experimental
# operations total ($\times 10^6$)	19.88	19.29
# operations for false alarms ($\times 10^6$)	7.28	7.15
# false alarms	716.57	697.15

The precomputing phase for these tables took roughly a month on about a hundred machines. The online phase takes place on a machine with a i7-3770 CPU and 16GB of RAM. Recovering any alphanumeric NTLM Hash password (whose length is 1 to 7 characters) in this setting takes 3.5 seconds on average.

7   Conclusion

This paper unifies checkpoints and endpoint truncation improvements for rainbow tables in a new model, in which fingerprints of chains are stored rather than endpoints. This new model highlights that endpoints (truncated or not) and checkpoints have the same nature. An analysis of the average search time of rainbow tables with fingerprints is presented, and corroborated with implementation results. A method to search for optimal parameters is proposed. Up to our knowledge, there was up to now no systematic method to find checkpoint positions. Rainbow tables with fingerprint present, in optimal configuration, a speedup of about two, with respect to the regular rainbow tables.

References

1. Avoine, G., Junod, P., Oechslin, P.: Time-Memory Trade-Offs: False Alarm Detection Using Checkpoints. In: Maitra, S., Veni Madhavan, C.E., Venkatesan, R. (eds.) INDOCRYPT 2005. LNCS, vol. 3797, pp. 183–196. Springer, Heidelberg (2005)

2. Avoine, G., Junod, P., Oechslin, P.: Characterization and improvement of time-memory trade-off based on perfect tables. ACM Trans. Inf. Syst. Secur., 11:17:1–17:22, July 2008

3. Babbage, S.: A space/time tradeoff in exhaustive search attacks on stream ciphers. In: European Convention on Security and Detection **408** (1995)

4. Barkan, E., Biham, E., Shamir, A.: Rigorous Bounds on Cryptanalytic Time/Memory Tradeoffs. In: Dwork, C. (ed.) CRYPTO 2006. LNCS, vol. 4117, pp. 1–21. Springer, Heidelberg (2006)

5. Biryukov, A., Mukhopadhyay, S., Sarkar, P.: Improved Time-Memory Trade-Offs with Multiple Data. In: Preneel, B., Tavares, S. (eds.) SAC 2005. LNCS, vol. 3897, pp. 110–127. Springer, Heidelberg (2006)

6. Gentry, C., Jonsson, J., Stern, J., Szydlo, M.: Cryptanalysis of the NTRU Signature Scheme (NSS) from Eurocrypt 2001. In: Boyd, C. (ed.) ASIACRYPT 2001. LNCS, vol. 2248, pp. 1–13. Springer, Heidelberg (2001)

7. Biryukov, A., Shamir, A., Wagner, D.: Real Time Cryptanalysis of A5/1 on a PC. In: Schneier, B. (ed.) FSE 2000. LNCS, vol. 1978, pp. 1–18. Springer, Heidelberg (2001)

8. Bono, S., Green, M., Stubblefield, A., Juels, A., Rubin, A., Szydlo, M.: Security Analysis of a Cryptographically-Enabled RFID Device. In: 14th USENIX Security Symposium - USENIX 2005, , Baltimore, Maryland, USA, pp. 1–16. USENIX, July-August 2005

9. De, A., Trevisan, L., Tulsiani, M.: Time Space Tradeoffs for Attacks against One-Way Functions and PRGs. In: Rabin, T. (ed.) CRYPTO 2010. LNCS, vol. 6223, pp. 649–665. Springer, Heidelberg (2010)

10. Denning, D.: Cryptography and Data Security, page 100. Addison-Wesley, Boston (1982)

11. Fiat, A., Naor, M.: Rigorous time/space tradeoffs for inverting functions. In: ACM Symposium on Theory of Computing, STOC 1991, New Orleans, Louisiana, USA, pp. 534–541. ACM (May 1991)

12. Golić, J.D.: Cryptanalysis of Alleged A5 Stream Cipher. In: Fumy, W. (ed.) EURO-CRYPT 1997. LNCS, vol. 1233, pp. 239–255. Springer, Heidelberg (1997)

13. Hellman, M.: A cryptanalytic time-memory trade off. IEEE Transactions on Information Theory, IT-26(4), 401–406 (1980)

14. Hong, J.: The cost of false alarms in hellman and rainbow tradeoffs. Designs, Codes and Cryptography **57**(3), 293–327 (2010)

15. Kim, J.W., Seo, J., Hong, J., Park, K., Kim, S.-R.: High-Speed Parallel Implementations of the Rainbow Method in a Heterogeneous System. In: Galbraith, S., Nandi, M. (eds.) INDOCRYPT 2012. LNCS, vol. 7668, pp. 303–316. Springer, Heidelberg (2012)

16. Lee, G.W., Hong, J.: A comparison of perfect table cryptanalytic tradeoff algorithms. Cryptology ePrint Archive, Report 2012/540 (2012)

17. Mentens, N., Batina, L., Preneel, B.: Ingrid Verbauwhede. Cracking Unix passwords using FPGA platforms. SHARCS - Special Purpose Hardware for Attacking Cryptographic Systems, February 2005

18. Nohl, K.: Attacking phone privacy. Blackhat - White Paper (2010)

19. Oechslin, P.: Making a Faster Cryptanalytic Time-Memory Trade-Off. In: Boneh, D. (ed.) CRYPTO 2003. LNCS, vol. 2729, pp. 617–630. Springer, Heidelberg (2003)

20. Oechslin, P.: The ophcrack password cracker (2013). http://ophcrack.sourceforge.net/

21. Russell, S.J., Norvig, P.: Artificial intelligence: a modern approach, vol. 2. Pearson
    Education (2003)
22. Saarinen, M.-J.O.: A Time-Memory Tradeoff Attack Against LILI-128. In: Daemen,
    J., Rijmen, V. (eds.) FSE 2002. LNCS, vol. 2365, pp. 231–236. Springer, Heidelberg
    (2002)

A   Proof of Theorem 5

Given the online phase described in Sect. 3, we have:

$$T = \sum_{k=1}^{\ell t} p_k T_k + p_{\text{fail}} T_{\ell t}, \tag{7}$$

with p_{fail} and p_k the probabilities that the attack fails, and that it succeeds after
k steps respectively. Here, T_k denotes the average amount of evaluations of h
when the attack stops after k steps.

Determination of p_k and p_{fail}:
The probability that the current point is found in a column is m/N, and p_k is
the probability that the current point is found in a column, but is not found in
the preceding $k - 1$ searches:

$$p_k = \frac{m}{N} \left(1 - \frac{m}{N}\right)^{k-1}. \tag{8}$$

The probability of failure p_{fail} is simply the probability that the current point is
not found in any of the ℓt previous searches, that is:

$$\left(1 - \frac{m}{N}\right)^{\ell t}. \tag{9}$$

Determination of T_k:
At each step, h is computed for the following reasons: when building the online
chain (this work is noted W), and when filtering false alarms (noted Q), hence
$T_k = W_k + Q_k$.

Determination of W_k:
At step k, we begin the fingerprint comparison at column

$$c_k = \left\lceil \frac{k-1}{\ell} \right\rceil.$$

The number of h computations needed for the online chain is simply c_k. Consequently,

$$W_k = \sum_{i=1}^{k} c_i. \tag{10}$$

Determination of Q_k:
Similarly, for each false alarm, a chain has to be computed from the start to the current column, needing $t - c_k$ computations. Hence, we have:

$$Q_k = \sum_{i=1}^{k}(t - c_i)FA_{c_i}, \tag{11}$$

with FA_c the average number of false alarms after c columns. False alarms in rainbow tables with fingerprints are of two types. Type-I false alarms are the same as the ones in rainbow tables and occur because of merges induced by reduction functions. Type-II false alarms occur because two chains may have the same partial fingerprint. We will respectively denote by P_c and E_c the average number of Type-I and Type-II false alarms after c columns. In the following, all alarms (that is, including the one true alarm) are counted as false alarms, for the sake of simplicity. The resulting loss in accuracy is negligible.

Determination of P_c:
Because the tables are perfect, there can be at most one Type-I false alarm per step. This false alarm, if it exists, is due to a chain merging with the online chain, somewhere between the start of the online chain and the last column. Moreover, for this chain to cause a false alarm, the partial fingerprint must match before the merge as well. That is,

$$P_c = \sum_{i=1}^{c} \Pr(\text{partial fingerprints match} \mid \text{not merged up to } i)$$

$$\times \Pr(\text{Online chain merges in } i)$$

$$= \sum_{i=1}^{c} \left(\prod_{j=t-c}^{t-i} \phi_j \right) \frac{z_{i-1,c} - z_{i,c}}{N}, \tag{12}$$

with

$$z_{i,c} = m(1 + c - i) + \frac{(c-i)(c-i+2)}{i^2}\left[mi + 2N\log\left(1 - \frac{mi}{2N}\right)\right], \tag{13}$$

$$z_{0,c} = m(1 + c)\left(1 - \frac{mc}{4N}\right).$$

Equation (13) represents the number of chains in column $t - c$ that merge with one of the m chains of the precomputed table in column $t - i$. It was computed in Propositions 4 and 5 of [14]. Equation (12) is a generalization of equation (1) in [15] for where checkpoints appear in every column and are of potentially more than one bit. The first factor of each term represents the probability that the online chain (which has not yet merged with any chain of the precomputed table) shares partial fingerprints with the chain of the precomputation table it will eventually merge with. The second factor represents the probability that the online chain will merge at that step.

374   G. Avoine et al.

Determination of E_c:

The probability of having a merge between columns c and t, already identified in [2], is $q_c = 1 - \prod_{i=c}^{t} \left(1 - \frac{m_i}{N}\right)$. Considering that the probability that the online chain merges with a chain of the table is q_c, there are, on average, $m - q_c$ non-merging chains. Among those, each creates a Type-II FA with probability $\prod_{i=c}^{t} \phi_i$, which gives:

$$E_c = (m - q_c) \prod_{i=c}^{t} \phi_i. \tag{14}$$

Using equations (8), (9), (10), (11), (12), (13), and (14) into (7) gives (6), allowing us to conclude. □

Privacy Protocols

A New Public Remote Integrity Checking Scheme with User Privacy

Yiteng Feng[1], Yi Mu[1], Guomin Yang[1]([✉]), and Joseph K. Liu[2]

[1] Centre for Computer and Information Security Research,
School of Computing and Information Technology,
University of Wollongong, Wollongong, Australia
yf579@uowmail.edu.au, {ymu,gyang}@uow.edu.au
[2] Faculty of Information Technology, Monash University, Melbourne, Australia
joseph.liu@monash.edu

Abstract. With a cloud storage, users can store their data files on a remote cloud server with a high quality on-demand cloud service and are able to share their data with other users. Since cloud servers are not usually regarded as fully trusted and the cloud data can be shared amongst users, the integrity checking of the remote files has become an important issue. A number of remote data integrity checking protocols have been proposed in the literature to allow public auditing of cloud data by a third party auditor (TPA). However, user privacy is not taken into account in most of the existing protocols. We believe that preserving the anonymity (i.e., identity privacy) of the data owner is also very important in many applications. In this paper, we propose a new remote integrity checking scheme which allows the cloud server to protect the identity information of the data owner against the TPA. We also define a formal security model to capture the requirement of user anonymity, and prove the anonymity as well as the soundness of the proposed scheme.

Keywords: Data integrity · Identity privacy · Public auditing · Cloud storage

1 Introduction

Cloud computing offers various kinds of computation and storage services to end users via computer networks, and is becoming very popular nowadays. One of the major services is cloud storage which allows users to store their data files remotely and access the files anywhere any time. It has greatly reduced the burden for local storage management and maintenance. Some commerical products such as Google Drive and Dropbox have become very popular for both individuals and enterprises.

However, after the data owners outsource their files to the cloud server and delete the local copies, the server may not store the files correctly due to various

J.K. Liu—Joseph K. Liu is supported by National Natural Science Foundation of China (61472083).

© Springer International Publishing Switzerland 2015
E. Foo and D. Stebila (Eds.): ACISP 2015, LNCS 9144, pp. 377–394, 2015.
DOI: 10.1007/978-3-319-19962-7_22

reasons such as system crash or deliberately deleting some data blocks that are seldom or never used in order to save the cost. Moreover, the server may try to hide the accidents or misbehaviours to the end users. In order to detect or prevent this kind of situations, we need to audit the integrity of remote files either periodically or before downloading. Many protocols have been proposed for auditing the file integrity and retrievability in remote storage, such as Proof of Data Possession (PDP) [1] and Proof of Retrievability (PoR) [6,7]. These protocols utilised spot-checking techniques such as homomorphic authenticators to make the auditing more efficient.

Recently, some additional security and usability properties have been proposed and formalised for Remote Integrity Checking (RIC) protocols [4,11,12], including public auditing (i.e., the data auditing can be performed by a third-party auditor), batch auditing, and privacy-preserving auditing (i.e., the third-party auditor cannot learn any information about the file during the auditing process). These properties are achieved by extending the previous work on homomorphic authenticators and zero-knowledge proof systems.

Since users may frequently modify the files by inserting, updating and deleting the file blocks, data dynamic operations have also been considered in some recent RIC protocols. In [13,14], a Merkle Hash Tree (MHT) is employed to achieve this goal where the structure of a file is represented using a MHT. Later, a more efficient scheme was proposed by Yang and Jia in [15] where an index table is maintained by a *fixed* TPA in order to keep track of the data changes. Although Yang and Jia's scheme is more efficient than the MHT approach proposed in [14], the TPA must be fixed for a specific file, which can be considered as a limitation of the scheme. Some RIC protocols [9] have also considered file sharing among a group of users, where the technique of proxy-resign is used to allow authenticators to be transferred from a leaving member to another staying member in the group.

In this paper, we focus on another important and desirable property of RIC protocols: identity privacy (i.e., anonymity) of the data owner against outsiders and the TPA. Such a problem has been studied in [10] where a ring signature (i.e., authenticator) rather than an ordinary one is generated for each data block by the data owner. Nevertheless, there is an issue in this protocol: in order to allow data dynamic operations, a virtual index is used for each file block. Since the cloud server maintains the virtual index table, it can always redirect the challenge for a corrupted file block to an uncorrupted one in order to pass the verification. Details of this issue will be shown in Appendix A. A similar problem has also been considered in [8] where a group signature is used as the authenticator for each block. However, the group manager is still able to reveal the identity of signer and it is not easy to set up that kind of group.

Identity privacy is essential in many scenarios. For example, a group of users may prefer anonymous file sharing for some reasons such as fear of retribution for disclosure. Besides, censorship is usually required in local, organizational or national level applications such as anonymous bidding. A group of bidders will place their bids which are actually files on the cloud storage and the identity of bidders should be confidential during assessment. At the same time, the assessment community would like to ensure the integrity of files periodically or before they retrieve a file.

In this paper, we propose a new RIC protocol with user anonymity. Differing from the protocol in [10], we consider the user anonymity in file level instead of data block level in order to save the storage and communication overheads. In the current work, we only focus on static files and leave the support of data dynamic operations as the future work.

Our Contribution. We formalise the notion of user anonymity for RIC protocols. In our RIC anonymity model, we consider the TPA as the adversary who aims to discover the identity of the file owner during the RIC proof with the cloud server. Then we construct an identity privacy-preserving RIC protocol based on the ring signature scheme proposed by Boneh et al. in [2], which is a variant of BLS signature [3]. The protocol is very practical because of the homomorphic property of the underlying signature scheme. Moreover, the protocol also supports batch verification such that the TPA can verify several proofs simultaneously using one verification equation. We prove that the proposed protocol can ensure data integrity while preserving identity privacy. In addition, this protocol can be also extended to support the privacy of audited files (which is defined as IND-Privacy in [4]).

Paper Organisation. The rest of the paper is organised as follows. In Section 2, we give the system model and security definition of the protocol. In Section 3, we present our identity privacy preserving remote integrity check protocol. We analyse the security of the proposed scheme in Section 4. We provide some extensions in Section 5. We conclude the paper in Section 6. The details of an attack on an existing scheme and the security proofs of the proposed scheme are given in Appendices.

2   System Model and Security Definition

Fig. 1 is an overview of the system. The basic case is that d users stored d files on the cloud server, and each of them owns one file. None of the users wants the TPA to link their identity with the file. The system can be easily extended to a more general setting where one user stores multiple files on the cloud server.

Users first form a group to preserve anonymity from the TPA. Then they outsource their files to the cloud individually. From the file level point of view, a file has one file tag, one glue value, some auxiliary information. From the block level point of view, one authenticator is attached to each block. During the auditing process, the file tags are public to the TPA but other information is kept secret.

After that, this group of users delegate the auditing task for the outsourced files to any TPA. Either periodically or at specific times, the TPA will challenge the cloud server for the storage of the outsourced files. The cloud server will then generate a short response for the challenge based on the information it has.

Fig. 1. System Model

Now we are going to describe the formal definition of an RIC protocol as well as the soundness and anonymity game.

2.1 Anonymous RIC Protocols

There are three types of parties in an anonymous RIC protocol: a group of users, the cloud server, and the TPA. An anonymous RIC scheme consists of the following algorithms:

- **Setup:** This algorithm takes a security parameter λ and generates the public parameters mpk for the whole system.
- **KeyGen:** This algorithm takes as input mpk and generates the public and private key pair (pk_i, sk_i) for each user.
- **TokenGen:** This algorithm takes as input a file F, and the owner's private key sk, to generate a file tag t, and the authenticator σ for each file block.
- **GlueGen:** This algorithm takes as input the public keys of all group users $\{pk_i\}$ and the owner's private key sk to generate a glue value θ and auxiliary information $\{b\}$ for anonymous public auditing.
- **Challenge:** Given the file tag t, this algorithm generates the challenge $chal$ for cloud server.
- **Response:** Taking as input $(F, t, \{\sigma\}, \theta, \{b\}, chal, mpk)$, this algorithm outputs a proof P to prove the integrity of the file.
- **Verify:** Taking as input $(\{pk_i\}, mpk, t, chal, P)$, this algorithm outputs true or false to indicate whether the file is stored correctly.

2.2 RIC Anonymity

Since we want to ensure that the TPA cannot distinguish the identity of the real file owner from other users in the group during multiple runs of the protocol, we fix the owner at the beginning of the adversarial game, and then allow the adversary to ask multiple proof queries. The Anonymity for an RIC scheme is defined via an *Anonymity* game between a challenger $\mathcal{C}$ (i.e. the cloud server or prover) and an Adversary $\mathcal{A}$ (i.e. the TPA or verifier) as follows.

- **Setup:** The challenger $\mathcal{C}$ runs **Setup** and **KeyGen** to generate the public parameters and the key pairs for a group of users $U_1, U_2, ..., U_d$ and passes all the public keys to the Adversary $\mathcal{A}$. Also, $\mathcal{C}$ randomly chooses a user $b \in [1, d]$ to be the real signer.
- **Phase 1:** $\mathcal{A}$ can ask for tag queries. In each query, $\mathcal{A}$ can choose a file F to be stored and $\mathcal{C}$ generates the file tag, the authenticators, the glue value and the auxiliary information for the file. Only the file tag t is returned to $\mathcal{A}$. $\mathcal{A}$ can ask multiple tag queries for different files.
- **Phase 2:** $\mathcal{A}$ uses the file tag t of file F which appeared in **Phase 1** to generates the *chal* to ask for proof from $\mathcal{C}$. Then, $\mathcal{C}$ generates the proof P and sends P to $\mathcal{A}$. In this phase, $\mathcal{A}$ can also ask multiple proof queries.
- **Decision:** $\mathcal{A}$ output b' as the guess of b.

Define the advantage of adversary $\mathcal{A}$ as $Adv_{\mathcal{A}}(\lambda) = |\Pr[b' = b] - 1/d|$.

Definition 1. *We say an RIC scheme has anonymity if for any polynomial-time algorithm $\mathcal{A}$, $Adv_{\mathcal{A}}(\lambda)$ is a negligible function of the security parameter λ.*

2.3 RIC Soundness

We say a protocol is sound if it is infeasible for the cloud server to modify the content of a file without being detected by the TPA in the auditing. We define the soundness games between a challenger $\mathcal{C}$ and an adversary $\mathcal{A}$ as follows:

- **Setup:** $\mathcal{C}$ runs **Setup** and **KeyGen** to generate the key pairs for a group of users. $\mathcal{C}$ then chooses the first user as the real signer and passes all the public keys to the Adversary.
- **Phase 1:** $\mathcal{A}$ makes multiple queries to $\mathcal{C}$ for **TokenGen** and **GlueGen** on any file F. $\mathcal{C}$ generates the file tag t, authenticators σ, and the glue value θ and auxiliary information $\{b\}$ using the secret key of the first user, and then returns $(t, \{\sigma\}, \theta, \{b\})$ to $\mathcal{A}$.
- **Phase 2:** $\mathcal{A}$ outputs a file F' and a file tag t' such that $t' = t$ but $F' \neq F$ for some (F, t) appeared in Phase 1 (i.e., at least one block of F is corrupted). $\mathcal{C}$ then plays the role as the verifier and executes the RIC protocol with $\mathcal{A}$ by sending a challenge *chal* which contains at least one corrupted block.
- **Decision:** $\mathcal{C}$ makes a decision which is either True or False after verifying the proof P' generated by the adversary $\mathcal{A}$.

Definition 2. *We say a RIC protocol is ε-sound if $\Pr[\mathcal{C}\ outputs\ True] \leq \varepsilon$.*

3   The Proposed Scheme

3.1   Notation

Let G_1, G_2 and G_T be three multiplicative cyclic groups of prime order p. Let g_1 and g_2 be the generators of G_1 and G_2 respectively. The bilinear map $e : G_1 \times G_2 \to G_T$ should have the following properties:

- Bilinear: We say that the map is bilinear if $e(u^a, h^b) = e(u, h)^{ab}$ for all $u \in G_1, h \in G_2, a, b \in Z_p$.
- Non-degenerate: The map does not send all pairs in $G_1 \times G_2$ to the identity in G_T. As they are prime order groups, $e(g_1, g_2)$ is a generator of G_T.
- Computable: There is an efficient algorithm to compute $e(u, h)$ for any $u \in G_1, h \in G_2$.
- Isomorphism: In addition, there should be a computable isomorphism ψ from G_2 to G_1, with $\psi(g_2) = g_1$ and $e(\psi(u), h) = e(\psi(h), u)$ for any $u, h \in G_2$.

3.2   Our Anonymous RIC Scheme

We present the details of our anonymous RIC scheme.

Setup: Let $(e, p, G_1, G_2, G_T, g_1, g_2, \psi)$ be the bilinear map and associated group parameters defined as above. Choose a cryptographic hash functions $H : \{0,1\}^* \to G_1$. Choose another generator $h \in G_1$. Choose two random numbers $\alpha, \tau \in Z_p$ to generate the commitment keys: $\boldsymbol{u} = (u_1, u_2)$ where $u_1 = (g_1, g_1^\alpha), u_2 = (g_1^\tau, g_1^{\tau\alpha})$. The public parameters are $mpk = (e, p, G_1, G_2, G_T, g_1, g_2, \psi, H, h, u_1, u_2)$.

KeyGen: Each user U_i randomly chooses $x_i \in Z_p$ and computes $y_i = g_2^{x_i}$. Besides, each user generates a key pair (spk_i, ssk_i) for a secure ring signature scheme. The user U_i's public key is (y_i, spk_i), and the private key is (x_i, ssk_i).

TokenGen: The outsourced file F is first divided into n blocks, and the file owner s chooses a random file name $name$ from some sufficiently large domain (e.g., Z_p). Let t_0 be "$name||n$"; the file tag t is t_0 together with a ring signature on t_0 under the private key ssk_s and the public keys $\{spk_i\}_{i \neq s}$: $t \leftarrow t_0 || Sig_{ssk_s}(t_0)$. For each block m_j, the signer computes: $\sigma_j = (H(name||j) \cdot h^{m_j})^{1/x_s}$.

GlueGen: For each user $U_i \neq U_s$, the signer chooses $a_i \in Z_p$, and computes the auxiliary information: $b_i = g_1^{a_i}$. Then the signer computes a glue value

$$\theta = 1 \bigg/ \psi\left(\prod_{i \neq s}^{n} y_i^{a_i}\right)^{1/x_s}.$$

Finally, the user sends $\{F, t, \{\sigma_j\}_{j \in [1,n]}, \{b_i\}_{i \in [1,d]}, \theta\}$ to the cloud server. We shows the computation and communication between client and server in Fig. 2.

Challenge: The TPA first retrieves the file tag t and verifies the ring signature $Sig_{ssk_s}(t_0)$ based on the user public keys of all the users in the ring. The TPA quits by emitting False if the verification fails. Otherwise, the TPA recovers

Client	Communication	Cloud Server
1. Divide F into n block. Choose $name \in Z_p$. Let $t_0 = name\|\|n$, $t \leftarrow t_0\|\|Sig_{ssk_s}(t_0)$.		
2. For each block m_j, compute: $\sigma_j = (H(name\|\|j) \cdot h^{m_j})^{1/x_s}$		
3. For user $u_i \neq u_s$, choose $a_i \in Z_p$, compute: $b_i = g_1^{a_i}$		
4. Compute a glue value: $\theta = 1 \Big/ \psi \left(\prod_{i \neq s}^{n} y_i^{a_i} \right)^{1/x_s}$		
5. Outsource the file to Cloud.	$\{F, t, \{\sigma\}, \{b\}, \theta\}$ $\longrightarrow$	
6. Delegate the auditing to TPA.		

Fig. 2. Storing a file

$name, n$. Then the TPA picks c elements in set $[1, n]$, where n is the total number of file blocks, to indicate the blocks that will be checked. J denotes the subset of $[1, n]$ that contains all the chosen indices. For $j \in J$, the TPA randomly chooses $c_j \in Z_p$. Finally the TPA sends $\{(j, c_j)\}_{j \in J}$ to the cloud server as a challenge.

Response: Upon receiving the challenge $\{(j, c_j)\}_{j \in J}$, the cloud server computes $\mu = \sum_{j \in J} c_j m_j$, and $\Sigma_s = \prod_{j \in J} \sigma_j^{c_j} \cdot \theta$, $\Sigma_i = b_i$ for all $i \neq s$. Given $(\mu, \{\Sigma\})$, the TPA can use the following equation to check the integrity of the file $e \left(\prod_{j \in J} H(name\|\|j)^{c_j} \cdot h^{\mu}, g_2 \right) = \prod_{i=1}^{d} e(\Sigma_i, y_i)$.

However, if we run the above protocol for multiple times, the values of μ and Σ_s will change depending on the challenge, while other Σ_i will remain static, which will reveal the identity of the file owner. To address this issue, we make use of the Groth-Sahai Proof System [5] to hide all the $\{\Sigma\}$ while convincing the TPA they are correct. So in the modified **Response** algorithm, using the system public key u as the commitment key, the cloud server computes commitments as: $c = (c_1, c_2, ..., c_d)$, where

$$c_1 = (c_{11}, c_{12}) = (g_1^{r_{11}+r_{12}\tau}, g_1^{\alpha(r_{11}+r_{12}\tau)}\Sigma_1) = (u_{11}^{r_{11}} u_{12}^{r_{12}}, u_{21}^{r_{11}} u_{22}^{r_{12}}\Sigma_1)$$

$$c_2 = (c_{21}, c_{22}) = (g_1^{r_{21}+r_{22}\tau}, g_1^{\alpha(r_{21}+r_{22}\tau)}\Sigma_2) = (u_{11}^{r_{21}} u_{12}^{r_{22}}, u_{21}^{r_{21}} u_{22}^{r_{22}}\Sigma_2)$$

$$\dots$$

$$c_d = (c_{d1}, c_{d2}) = (g_1^{r_{d1}+r_{d2}\tau}, g_1^{\alpha(r_{d1}+r_{d2}\tau)}\Sigma_d) = (u_{11}^{r_{d1}} u_{12}^{r_{d2}}, u_{21}^{r_{d1}} u_{22}^{r_{d2}}\Sigma_d)$$

where $r_{ij}(i \in [1, d], j \in \{1, 2\})$ is randomly selected from Z_p.

The proof becomes: $\boldsymbol{\pi} = (\pi_1, \pi_2)$ where $\pi_1 = (1, y_1^{r_{11}} y_2^{r_{21}} ... y_d^{r_{d1}})$ and $\pi_2 = (1, y_1^{r_{12}} y_2^{r_{22}} ... y_d^{r_{d2}})$. Finally, $(\mu, \boldsymbol{c}, \boldsymbol{\pi})$ are sent to TPA instead of $(\mu, \{\Sigma\})$.

Verify: First, we define the $\star$ operator as $\boldsymbol{x} \star \boldsymbol{y} = F(x_1, y_1)F(x_2, y_2)...F(x_n, y_n)$, where

$$F(x_i, y_i) = \begin{pmatrix} e(x_{i1}, y_{i1}) & e(x_{i1}, y_{i2}) \\ e(x_{i2}, y_{i1}) & e(x_{i2}, y_{i2}) \end{pmatrix}$$

for $(x_{i1}, x_{i2}) \in G_1^2, (y_{i1}, y_{i2}) \in G_2^2, i \in [1, n]$.

To do the verification, TPA first performs the transformation on the original verification equation as follows.

- Transform Left Hand Side: $\boldsymbol{l} = (l_1, l_2)$ where $l_{11} = (1, 1)$ and $l_{12} = (1, L)$, where $L = e\left(\prod_{j \in J} H(name||j)^{c_j} \cdot h^\mu, g_2\right)$.
- Transform Public Keys: $\boldsymbol{k} = (k_1, k_2, ..., k_d)$ where $k_1 = (1, y_1)$ and $k_2 = (1, y_2) ... k_d = (1, y_d)$

The verifier then performs the verification via the following equation: $\boldsymbol{l}(\boldsymbol{u} \star \boldsymbol{\pi}) = \boldsymbol{c} \star \boldsymbol{k}$. Please note that here we use the Hadamard product of the matrix. We show the computations and message flows between TPA and cloud server in Fig. 3. The correctness of both the non-anonymous and anonymous verification equations are proved in Appendix B.

4 Security Analysis

4.1 Anonymity of the Protocol

External Diffie-Hellman (XDH) Assumption: Groth-Sahai proof system in [5] is under the assumption SXDH, where the DDH problem is hard in both G_1 and G_2. But we need to have isomorphism to generate the glue value, so we will just assume DDH is hard in G_1. Let $gk = (\lambda, p, G_1, G_2, G_T, e, g_1, g_2)$, define a bilinear map $e : G_1 \times G_2 \to G_T$ and isomorphism from G_2 to G_1, with $\psi(g_2) = g_1$. The XDH assumption holds if we have

$$| \Pr[A(gk, \psi, g_1^x, g_1^y, g_1^{xy}) = 1] - \Pr[A(gk, \psi, g_1^x, g_1^y, g_1^z) = 1] | \leq \epsilon$$

where $x, y, z \leftarrow Z_p^*$.

Theorem 1. *Our new anonymous RIC protocol has identity privacy if XDH assumption holds.*

4.2 Soundness of the Protocol

Co-CDH Problem: Given $(G_1, G_2, g_1, g_2, h = g_1^a, u = g_2^b)$, Compute g_1^{ab}. Similar to [2], we can solve the Co-CDH problem by solving two instances of the following problem: given $(G_1, G_2, g_1, g_2, u = g_2^a, h = g_1^{ab})$, compute g_1^b. We will use this version of the Co-CDH problem to prove the soundness of our protocol.

Theorem 2. *The proposed RIC scheme is negl(λ)-sound, where negl(λ) is a negligible function of the security parameter λ, if the Co-CDH problem is hard.*

The proofs of the theorems are presented in Appendix C and D.

TPA	**Communication**	**Cloud Server**
1. Retrieve the file tag t. Verify the signature, and recover $name, n$.		
2. Pick c elements in $[1, n]$ to form a subset J. For each $j \in J$, choose $c_j \in Z_p$.		
3. Send Challenge to Cloud.	$\{(j, c_j)\}_{j \in J}$ $\xrightarrow{\hspace{2cm}}$	

1. Compute: $\mu = \sum_{j \in J} c_j m_j$

2. Compute:
$\Sigma_s = \prod_{j \in J} \sigma_j^{c_j} \cdot \theta$
and $\Sigma_i = b_i$ for all $i \neq s$.

3. Commit $\{\Sigma\}$ to c:
$c_i = (c_{i1}, c_{i2})$
$\quad = (u_{11}^{r_{i1}} u_{12}^{r_{i2}}, u_{21}^{r_{i1}} u_{22}^{r_{i2}} \Sigma_i)$
where $r_{ij}(i \in [1, d], j \in \{1, 2\})$
is randomly selected from Z_p.

4. Compute the Proof:
$\boldsymbol{\pi} = (\pi_1, \pi_2)$.
$\pi_1 = (1, y_1^{r_{11}} y_2^{r_{21}} ... y_d^{r_{d1}})$
$\pi_2 = (1, y_1^{r_{12}} y_2^{r_{22}} ... y_d^{r_{d2}})$

5. Send Response to TPA.

$\xleftarrow{\{\mu, \boldsymbol{c}, \boldsymbol{\pi}\}}$

4. Transform left hand side:
$\boldsymbol{l} = (l_1, l_2)$.
$l_{11} = (1, 1), l_{12} = (1, L)$,
while $L = e \left(\prod_{j \in J} H(name||j)^{c_j} \cdot h^\mu, g_2 \right)$.

5. Transform Public Keys:
$\boldsymbol{k} = (k_1, k_2, ..., k_d)$,
where $k_i = (1, y_i)$.

6. Verify the proof with commitment key $\boldsymbol{u}$:
$\boldsymbol{l}(\boldsymbol{u} \star \boldsymbol{\pi}) = \boldsymbol{c} \star \boldsymbol{k}$.

Fig. 3. Auditing

5   Extension

5.1   Batch Auditing

Our scheme can be easily extended to support batch auditing, which can audit multiple files for the group at the same time and save the pairing computations. For example, for non-anonymous auditing, given two challenges for different files $\{(j, c_j)\}_{j \in J}$ and $\{(j', c'_j)\}_{j' \in J'}$, the cloud server can calculate $(\mu, \{\Sigma\}$ and $(\mu', \{\Sigma'\})$, and verification equation becomes

$$e\left(\left(\prod_{j \in J} H(name||j)^{c_j}\right) \cdot \left(\prod_{j' \in J'} H(name'||j')^{c'_j}\right) \cdot h^{\mu+\mu'}, g_2\right) = \prod_{i=1}^{d} e\left(\Sigma_i \cdot \Sigma'_i, y_i\right).$$

For anonymous auditing, the equation for the verification is still

$$l(u \star \pi) = c \star k \ .$$

As a result, the response from the cloud server still contains three parts $(\mu + \mu', c, \pi)$ where the commitment c will hide $\Sigma_i \cdot \Sigma'_i$ instead of Σ_i.

It is also worth noting that during TPA verification, L inside l will be changed to

$$\left(\prod_{j \in J} H(name||j)^{c_j}\right) \cdot \left(\prod_{j' \in J'} H(name'||j')^{c'_j}\right) \cdot h^{\mu+\mu'} \ .$$

5.2   IND-Privacy

We have addressed the identity privacy of users, and we can also extend the scheme to provide the privacy of the audited files, which is defined as IND-Privacy in [4]. With IND-Privacy, the TPA is not able to distinguish which file is being audited. The Groth-Sahai proof system [5] is also used in [4] to achieve this goal.

The non-anonymous verification equation of our RIC scheme

$$e\left(\prod_{j \in J} H(name||j)^{c_j} \cdot h^{\mu}, g_2\right) = \prod_{i=1}^{d} e\left(\Sigma_i, y_i\right)$$

can be expressed as

$$e\left(\prod_{j \in J} H(name||j)^{c_j}, g_2\right) = \prod_{i=1}^{d} e\left(\Sigma_i, y_i\right) \cdot e(h^{\mu}, g_2^{-1}) \ .$$

Similar to [4], we can hide h^{μ} as well as all the $\{\Sigma\}$ in the commitment to achieve both Anonymity and IND-Privacy. The equation is still in the form of

$$l(u \star \pi) = c \star k \ ,$$

where c and k will have extra components, and l, π need to be changed accordingly.

5.3   Data Dynamics

There is no ideal solution for supporting data dynamics at the moment. However, if the TPA is fixed, then we can make the TPA keep the index tables for the files to keep track of all the data dynamic operations as [15] did. The cloud users have to communicate with TPA after they update the files on cloud server.

Another solution for achieving data dynamic operations is to replace the index information i of a data block m in the computation of the authenticator, and use the Merkle Hash Tree (MHT) for the block sequence enforcement. This approach has been used in [14]. The authenticator will become $\sigma_j = (H(m_j) \cdot h^{m_j})^{1/x_s}$, and every time before auditing, the root stored on the cloud server and signed by the user will be verified first using some auxiliary information that allows reconstruction the MHT. The rest of our scheme remains unchanged.

6   Conclusion

In this paper, we introduced a new security notion – RIC Anonymity for RIC protocols. We also proposed a new RIC protocol that can preserve the identity privacy of the file owner when the TPA audits the files stored on the cloud server. We proved the soundness and the anonymity of the proposed protocol, and also showed that the protocol can support batch verifications of multiple RIC proofs, IND-Privacy, and data dynamic operations.

References

1. Ateniese, G., Burns, R., Curtmola, R., Herring, J., Kissner, L., Peterson, Z., Song, D.: Provable data possession at untrusted stores. In: ACM CCS, pp. 598–609 (2007)
2. Boneh, D., Gentry, C., Lynn, B., Shacham, H.: Aggregate and verifiably encrypted signatures from bilinear maps. In: EUROCRYPT, pp. 416–432 (2003)
3. Boneh, D., Lynn, B., Shacham, H.: Short signatures from the weil pairing. J. Cryptology **17**(4), 297–319 (2004)
4. Fan, X., Yang, G., Mu, Y., Yu, Y.: On indistinguishability in remote data integrity checking. The Computer Journal (2013)
5. Groth, J., Sahai, A.: Efficient Non-interactive Proof Systems for Bilinear Groups. In: Smart, N.P. (ed.) EUROCRYPT 2008. LNCS, vol. 4965, pp. 415–432. Springer, Heidelberg (2008)
6. Juels, A., Kaliski Jr., B.S.: Pors: proofs of retrievability for large files. In: ACM CCS, pp. 584–597 (2007)
7. Shacham, H., Waters, B.: Compact Proofs of Retrievability. In: Pieprzyk, J. (ed.) ASIACRYPT 2008. LNCS, vol. 5350, pp. 90–107. Springer, Heidelberg (2008)
8. Wang, B., Li, B., Li, H.: Knox: Privacy-Preserving Auditing for Shared Data with Large Groups in the Cloud. In: Bao, F., Samarati, P., Zhou, J. (eds.) ACNS 2012. LNCS, vol. 7341, pp. 507–525. Springer, Heidelberg (2012)

9. Wang, B., Li, B., Li, H.: Public auditing for shared data with efficient user revocation in the cloud. In: Joint Conference of the IEEE Computer and Communications Societies, pp. 2904–2912 (2013)
10. Wang, B., Li, B., Li, H.: Oruta: Privacy-preserving public auditing for shared data in the cloud. IEEE Transactions on Cloud Computing **2**(1), 43–56 (2014)
11. Wang, C., Chow, S.S.M., Wang, Q., Ren, K., Lou, W.: Privacy-preserving public auditing for secure cloud storage. IEEE Transaction on Computers 62(2), 362–375 (2013)
12. Wang, C., Wang, Q., Ren, K., Lou, W.: Privacy-preserving public auditing for data storage security in cloud computing. In: 2010 Proceedings IEEE INFOCOM, pp. 1–9, March 2010
13. Wang, Q., Wang, C., Li, J., Ren, K., Lou, W.: Enabling Public Verifiability and Data Dynamics for Storage Security in Cloud Computing. In: Backes, M., Ning, P. (eds.) ESORICS 2009. LNCS, vol. 5789, pp. 355–370. Springer, Heidelberg (2009)
14. Wang, Q., Wang, C., Ren, K., Lou, W., Li, J.: Enabling public auditability and data dynamics for storage security in cloud computing. IEEE Transactions on Parallel and Distributed System **22**(5), 847–859 (2011)
15. Yang, K., Jia, X.: An efficient and secure dynamic auditing protocol for data storage in cloud computing. IEEE Transactions on Parallel and Distributed Systems **24**(9), 1717–1726 (2013)

A   A Security Issue in Oruta

Recently, a new public auditing protocol was proposed by Wang et al. in [10] to achieve the desirable features like public auditing, group anonymity and data dynamics, which is described in the Literature Review. Nevertheless, we review the protocol in [10] and show that there is a security issue in the protocol: a dishonest cloud server can delete some data blocks in a file without being caught by the third-party auditor. The reason is that the cloud server maintains an index hash table in order to achieve data dynamics. During auditing process, the cloud server answers to the identifier query for challenged indices, which will be used in the verification, but the integrity of the identifier is not ensured.

A.1   Reviewing the Protocol

Similar to most of the protocols (e.g, [11,14,15], the protocol Oruta [10] is based on the homomorphic authenticators and spot-checking techniques. However, it uses a ring signature [2] as the authenticator to achieve anonymity for each block. As it is a variant of BLS signature [3], the ring signature still can be aggregated. Besides, it uses the index hash table to support data dynamic operations. We describe the five algorithms inside Oruta.

Setup. Let G_1, G_2 and G_T be three multiplicative cyclic groups of prime order p, and g_1 and g_2 be the generators of G_1 and G_2, respectively. Let $e : G_1 \times G_2 \rightarrow G_T$ be a bilinear map, and $\psi : G_2 \rightarrow G_1$ be a computable isomorphism with $\psi(g_2) = g_1$. Let $H_1 : \{0,1\}^* \rightarrow G_1, H_2 : \{0,1\}^* \rightarrow Z_q$, and $h : G_1 \rightarrow Z_p$

denote three cryptographic hash functions. The global system parameters are $(e, \psi, p, q, G_1, G_2, G_T, g_1, g_2, H_1, H_2, h)$.

An outsourced data file M is divided into n blocks, and each block m_j is divided into k elements in Z_p. Then, the data component M can be viewed as an $n \times k$ matrix. Also, let d denote the number of users in the group where the file is shared and they want to preserve identity privacy from TPA.

KeyGen. Each user u_i randomly chooses $x_i \in Z_p$ and computes $w_i = g_2^{x_i}$. Thus, the user u_i's public key is w_i, and the private key is x_i. Besides, the user who firstly creates the file should generate a public aggregate key $pak = \{\eta_1, ..., \eta_k\}$, where each η_l ($1 \leq l \leq k$) is a random elements of G_1.

SignGen. Given all members' public keys $\{w_1, ..., w_d\}$, a block $m_j = \{m_{j,1}, ..., m_{j,k}\}$, the identifier of the block id_j, a public aggregate key $pak = \{\eta_1, ..., \eta_k\}$ and the private key of the signer x_s, the user u_s generates a ring signature for this block as follows.

1. The signer first aggregates block m_j with the public aggregate key pak, and computes $\beta_j = H_1(id_j) \prod_{l=1}^{k} \eta_l^{m_{j,l}} \in G_1$.
2. Then the signer randomly chooses $a_{j,i} \in Z_p$ and sets $\sigma_{j,i} = g_1^{a_{j,i}}$ for all $i \neq s$. And for $i = s$, he/she computes $\sigma_{j,i} = (\frac{\beta_j}{\psi(\prod_{i \neq s} w_i^{a_{j,i}})})^{1/x_s}$. Therefore, the authenticator which is actually a ring signature of block m_j is $\sigma_j = \{\sigma_{j,1}, ..., \sigma_{j,d}\}$.

After the owner outsourced the file to the cloud server, any group members can send the auditing request to a third-party auditor (TPA). With the challenge and response process, the TPA checks the integrity of files without revealing the identity of the owner.

ProofGen. TPA generates the challenge in the following way:

1. The TPA picks c elements in set $[1, n]$, where n is the total number of blocks, to indicate the blocks that will be checked. Let J denote the indices of the chosen blocks.
2. For $j \in J$, the TPA randomly chooses $y_j \in Z_q$. Then the TPA sends $\{(j, y_j)\}_{j \in J}$ to the cloud server as a challenge message.

After receiving $\{(j, y_j)\}_{j \in J}$, the cloud server generates the proof as follows:

1. For $l \in [1, k]$, the cloud server randomly chooses $r_l \in Z_q$, and computes $\lambda_l = \eta_l^{r_l} \in G_1$, and $\mu_l = \sum_{j \in J} y_j m_{j,l} + r_l h(\lambda_l) \in Z_p$.
2. For $i \in [1, d]$, the cloud server computes $\phi_i = \prod_{j \in J} \sigma_{j,i}^{y_j}$.

Then the cloud server sends the proof $\{\{\lambda_l\}_{l \in [1,k]}, \{\mu_l\}_{l \in [1,k]}, \{\phi_i\}_{i \in [1,d]}, \{id_j\}_{j \in J}\}$ to TPA.

ProofVeriy. After receiving the proof, and given the public aggregate key $pak = \{\eta_1, ..., \eta_k\}$ and all the public keys $\{w_1, ..., w_d\}$ of the group members, the TPA verifies the proof by checking:

$$e(\prod_{j \in J} H_1(id_j)^{y_j} \cdot \prod_{l=1}^{k} \eta_l^{\mu_l}, g_2) \overset{?}{=} (\prod_{i=1}^{d} e(\phi_i, w_i)) \cdot e(\prod_{i=1}^{k} \lambda_l^{h(\lambda_l)}, g_2)$$

If this equation holds, the TPA sends a positive audit report back to the request user and vice versa.

Remarks. Instead of using the index of the block as its identifier (e.g. the index of block m_j is j), this scheme utilises index hash tables. An identifier from this table is described as $id_j = \{v_j, r_j\}$, where v_j is the virtual index of block m_j, and $r_j = H_2(m_j || v_j)$ is generated using a collision-resistance hash function $H_2 : \{0, 1\}^* \in Z_q$. Here q is a prime that is much smaller than p. If $v_i < v_j$, then block m_i is in front of m_j in the file. The initial virtual index of block m_j is set as $v_j = j \cdot \delta$, where δ indicates the number of data block that can be inserted into m_j and m_{j+1}. For example, if m'_j is inserted, then $v'_j = (v_{j-1} + v_j)/2, r'_j = H_2(m'_j || v'_j)$ is inserted into the index hash table; if m_j is deleted, then the corresponding entry is removed from the table. During the computation of the authenticators and the challenge/response process, the identifiers are used instead of the indices. However, the TPA does not know about this table, so the identifier needs to be returned by the cloud server.

A.2 On the Security of the Protocol

As the basic requirements of an auditing protocol, Yang and Jia [15] pointed out that three kinds of attack must be prevented: Replace, Forge and Replay. In the first attack, the adversary may choose another pair of uncorrupted data block and data tag to replace the challenged pair to generate a valid proof. In the second attack, the adversary may try to forge a data tag for a (modified) data block. Lastly, in the replay attack, the adversary may try to generate a valid proof based on previous proofs or other information without retrieving the data blocks and data tags honestly. Below we show that the Oruta scheme [10] is vulnerable to the first type of attack.

For simplicity, let's consider the case where the TPA challenges for only one block m_j, and sends (j, y_j) to the cloud. If m_j is deliberately deleted by the cloud server but not the user, the server can still use m_{j+1}, σ_{j+1} to generate a valid proof as follows.

1. For $l \in [1, k]$, the cloud server randomly chooses $r_l \in Z_q$, and computes $\lambda_l = \eta_l^{r_l} \in G_1$.
2. For $l \in [1, k]$, the cloud server also computes $\mu_l = y_j m_{j+1,l} + r_l h(\lambda_l) \in Z_p$.
3. For $i \in [1, d]$, the cloud server computes $\phi_i = \sigma_{j+1,i}^{y_j}$.
   Then the cloud server sends the proof $\{\{\lambda\}, \{\mu\}, \{\phi\}, \{id_{j+1}\}$ to the TPA.

The TPA verifies the proof by checking: $e(H_1(id_{j+1})^{y_j} \cdot \prod_{l=1}^{k} \eta_l^{\mu_l}, g_2) \overset{?}{=}$
$(\prod_{i=1}^{d} e(\phi_i, w_i)) \cdot e(\prod_{i=1}^{k} \lambda_l^{h(\lambda_l)}, g_2)$. Actually, this is still a valid proof as

$$RHS = (\prod_{i=1}^{d} e(\sigma_{j+1,i}^{y_j}, w_i) \cdot e(\prod_{l=1}^{k} \lambda_l^{h(\lambda_l)}, g_2)$$

$$= \left(\prod_{i=1}^{d} e(\sigma_{j+1,i}, w_i)\right)^{y_j} \cdot e(\prod_{l=1}^{k} \eta_l^{r_l h(\lambda_l)}, g_2)$$

$$= e(\beta_{j+1}, g_2)^{y_j} \cdot e(\prod_{l=1}^{k} \eta_l^{r_l h(\lambda_l)}, g_2)$$

$$= e((H_1(id_{j+1}) \prod_{l=1}^{k} \eta_l^{m_{j+1,l}})^{y_j}, g_2) \cdot e(\prod_{l=1}^{k} \eta_l^{r_l h(\lambda_l)}, g_2)$$

$$= e(H_1(id_{j+1})^{y_j} \cdot \prod_{l=1}^{k} \eta_l^{y_j m_{j+1,l} + r_l h(\lambda_l)}, g_2)$$

$$= e(H_1(id_{j+1})^{y_j} \cdot \prod_{l=1}^{k} \eta_l^{\mu_l}, g_2)$$

Back to the normal case, since the cloud server maintains the index hash table, it can always redirect the challenge on the corrupted blocks to uncorrupted blocks in order to pass the verification. The index hash table is used by Oruta to support data dynamic operations. However, our attack essentially shows that such a technique is not suitable since it makes the scheme vulnerable to the Replace attack.

In [10], the authors assumed that the cloud server will return the identifiers for challenged indices honestly in the soundness (Unforgeability of Response) model and proof. However, as is known, the cloud server is treated as a soundness adversary in Remote Integrity Check protocols. So the cloud server has the motivation not to return the correct identifiers.

A.3   Recommendation

Despite of many interesting features supported by this protocol, we showed that a dishonest cloud server can deliberately delete some data blocks in a file but still pass the verification. We also pointed out that the problem is caused by the technique used in "Oruta" for allowing data dynamic operations.

Based on Yang and Jia's scheme [15], we can let the TPA maintain the index hash table as the cloud server is treated as the soundness adversary of the RIC protocol. Nevertheless, the TPA becomes stateful if we adopt such an approach, and another verifier cannot perform the auditing without such a table. Another option to solve the problem is to use the Merkle Hash Tree (MHT) which has been used in [14]. It uses a tree structure to organise the file blocks, and the roots of the tree, which are derived from the file blocks, need to be verified in every operation.

B   Proof of Correctness

Correctness of the Non-anonymous Verification Equation:
$$e\left(\prod_{j\in J} H(name||j)^{c_j} \cdot h^{\mu}, g_2\right) = \prod_{i=1}^{d} e\left(\Sigma_i, y_i\right).$$

$$RHS = \prod_{i\neq s} e(\Sigma_i, y_i) \cdot e(\Sigma_s, y_s)$$

$$= \prod_{i\neq s} e\left(g_1^{a_i}, y_i\right) \cdot e\left(\left(\prod_{j\in J}\sigma_j^{c_j}\middle/\psi\left(\prod_{i\neq s} y_i^{a_i}\right)\right)^{1/x_s}, y_s\right)$$

$$= e\left(g_1, \prod_{i\neq s}^{n} y_i^{a_i}\right) \cdot e\left(1\middle/\psi\left(\prod_{i\neq s} y_i^{a_i}\right), g_2\right) \cdot e\left(\prod_{j\in J}\sigma_j^{c_j}, y_s\right)$$

$$= e\left(\psi\left(\prod_{i\neq s}^{n} y_i^{a_i}\right), g_2\right) \cdot e\left(1\middle/\psi\left(\prod_{i\neq s} y_i^{a_i}\right), g_2\right) \cdot e\left(\prod_{j\in J}\sigma_j^{c_j}, y_s\right)$$

$$= e\left(\prod_{j\in J}\sigma_j^{c_j}, y_s\right) = e\left(\prod_{j\in J}\left(H\left(name||j\right)\cdot h^{m_j}\right)^{c_j/x_s}, g_2^{x_s}\right)$$

$$= e\left(\prod_{j\in J} H\left(name||j\right)^{c_j} \cdot h^{\sum_{j\in J} c_j m_j}, g_2\right)$$

$$= e\left(\prod_{j\in J}\left(H\left(name||j\right)^{c_j} \cdot h^{\mu}, g_2\right)\right) = LHS$$

Correctness of the anonymous verification equation: $l(u \star \pi) = c \star k$.

$$LHS = l \; F(u_1, \pi_1)F(u_2, \pi_2)$$

$$= \begin{pmatrix} 1 & 1 \\ 1 & L \end{pmatrix}\begin{pmatrix} 1 & e(g_1, y_1^{r_{11}} y_2^{r_{21}} ... y_d^{r_{d1}}) \\ 1 & e(g_1^{\alpha}, y_1^{r_{11}} y_2^{r_{21}} ... y_d^{r_{d1}}) \end{pmatrix}$$

$$= \begin{pmatrix} 1 & e(g_1^{\tau}, y_1^{r_{12}} y_2^{r_{22}} ... y_d^{r_{d2}}) \\ 1 & e(g_1^{\tau\alpha}, y_1^{r_{12}} y_2^{r_{22}} ... y_d^{r_{d2}}) \end{pmatrix}$$

$$RHS = F(c_1, k_1)F(c_2, k_d)...F(c_d, k_d)$$

$$= \begin{pmatrix} 1 & e(g_1^{r_{11}+r_{12}\tau}, y_1) \\ 1 & e(g_1^{\alpha(r_{11}+r_{12}\tau)}\Sigma_1, y_1) \end{pmatrix}\begin{pmatrix} 1 & e(g_1^{r_{21}+r_{22}\tau}, y_2) \\ 1 & e(g_1^{\alpha(r_{21}+r_{22}\tau)}\Sigma_2, y_2) \end{pmatrix}\begin{pmatrix} 1 & e(g_1^{r_{d1}+r_{d2}\tau}, y_d) \\ 1 & e(g_1^{\alpha(r_{d1}+r_{d2}\tau)}\Sigma_d, y_d) \end{pmatrix}$$

Calculating Hadamard product:

$$e(g_1, y_1^{r_{11}} y_2^{r_{21}} ... y_d^{r_{d1}}) e(g_1^\tau, y_1^{r_{12}} y_2^{r_{22}} ... y_d^{r_{d2}})$$
$$= e(g_1, y_1^{r_{11}+r_{12}\tau}) e(g_1, y_2^{r_{21}+r_{22}\tau}) ... e(g_1, y_d^{r_{d1}+r_{d2}\tau})$$
$$= e(g_1^{r_{11}+r_{12}\tau}, y_1) e(g_1^{r_{21}+r_{22}\tau}, y_2) ... e(g_1^{r_{d1}+r_{d2}\tau}, y_d)$$

$$L \; e(g_1^\alpha, y_1^{r_{11}} y_2^{r_{21}} ... y_d^{r_{d1}}) e(g_1^{\tau\alpha}, y_1^{r_{12}} y_2^{r_{22}} ... y_d^{r_{d2}})$$
$$= L \; e(g_1^{\alpha(r_{11}+r_{12}\tau)}, y_1) e(g_1^{\alpha(r_{21}+r_{22}\tau)}, y_2) e(g_1^{\alpha(r_{d1}+r_{d2}\tau)}, y_d)$$
$$(\text{as } L \text{ can be viewed as } e(\Sigma_1, y_1) e(\Sigma_2, y_2) ... e(\Sigma_d, y_d))$$
$$= e(g_1^{\alpha(r_{11}+r_{12}\tau)} \Sigma_1, y_1) e(g_1^{\alpha(r_{21}+r_{22}\tau)} \Sigma_2, y_2) e(g_1^{\alpha(r_{d1}+r_{d2}\tau)} \Sigma_d, y_d)$$

C Proof of Anonymity (Theorem 1)

Proof. For the (unconditional) anonymity of the file tag, it directly follows that of the underlying ring signature (e.g., [2]). In the following we will focus on the anonymity of the responses returned from cloud server. Let $\mathcal{A}$ be the adversary who has a non-negligible advantage ϵ in winning the Anonymity game, we can construct a simulator $\mathcal{C}$ to solve the XDH problem.

Simulator $\mathcal{C}$ receives a challenge $gk, \psi, A = g_1^x, B = g_1^y, C = g_1^z$, where z is either xy or a random element ξ in Z_p. $\mathcal{C}$ simulates the game as follows.

Setup: Simulator $\mathcal{C}$ sets the commitment key to be $u_1 = (g_1, A)$, $u_2 = (B, C)$. $\mathcal{C}$ then uses the information in gk and ψ to generate all user public/private key pairs as described. Finally Simulator $\mathcal{C}$ randomly chooses a user $b \in [1, d]$ as the real owner of all the queried files.

Phase 1: Simulator $\mathcal{C}$ answers the tag queries honestly and stores the tokens, glue value and auxiliary information correctly.

Phase 2: To answer a proof query, $\mathcal{C}$ computes $\mu_b, \{\Sigma_b\}$ honestly. Then $\mathcal{C}$ uses $\{\Sigma_b\}$ to generate response as follows: Randomly choose $r_{11}, r_{12}, r_{21}, r_{22}...r_{d1}, r_{d2}$ from Z_p. Then compute the commitment $\mathbf{c}$: $c_{11} = g_1^{r_{11}} B^{r_{12}}$, $c_{12} = A^{r_{11}} C^{r_{12}} \Sigma_{b1}$, $c_{21} = g_1^{r_{21}} B^{r_{22}}$, $c_{22} = A^{r_{21}} C^{r_{22}} \Sigma_{b2}$, $... c_{d1} = g_1^{r_{d1}} B^{r_{d2}}$, $c_{d2} = A^{r_{d1}} C^{r_{d2}} \Sigma_{bd}$. Finally compute the proof $\boldsymbol{\pi} = (\pi_1, \pi_2)$ where $\pi_1 = (1, y_1^{r_{11}} y_2^{r_{21}} ... y_d^{r_{d1}})$ and $\pi_2 = (1, y_1^{r_{12}} y_2^{r_{22}} ... y_d^{r_{d2}})$.

Decision: Simulator $\mathcal{C}$ sends the response $(\mu, \mathbf{c}, \boldsymbol{\pi})$ to $\mathcal{A}$. $\mathcal{A}$ outputs b' as a guess of b. If $b' = b$, then simulator $\mathcal{C}$ outputs 1; otherwise $\mathcal{C}$ outputs 0 for the instance of the XDH problem.

Probability: Case 1: $z = xy$. In this case, the distribution of the response is identically to that of a real response, so we have $\Pr[b' = b] = 1/d + \epsilon$. **Case 2:** $z = \xi$. In this case, the commitment scheme is perfectly hiding and reveals no information about the value of b. Hence, under this case we have $\Pr[b' = b] = 1/d$. Combining both cases, $\mathcal{C}$ has advantage ϵ to solve the XDH problem.

D   Proof of Soundness (Theorem 2)

Proof. We will prove this by contradiction. If there exists an adversary $\mathcal{A}$ who can win the soundness game with non-negligible probability, then we can construct a simulator to solve the variant of the Co-CDH problem also with a non-negligible probability:

Setup: Simulator $\mathcal{C}$ sets up the system parameters and chooses $\alpha, \tau \in Z_p$ to generate the commitment key $u_1 = (g_1, g_1^\alpha)$ and $u_2 = (g_1^\tau, g_1^{\tau\alpha})$. $\mathcal{C}$ then sets $h = g_1^{ab}$ as the other generator in system parameter and constructs a table $< name, j, r_j, H(name||j) >$ for hash oracle. $\mathcal{C}$ also randomly chooses $x_i \in Z_p$ for each user and computes the public key $y_i = (g_2^a)^{x_i} = u^{x_i}$. (We can view the private key as ax_i.)

Phase 1: For simplicity, Simulator $\mathcal{C}$ chooses the first user as the signing user, and generates the file tag using the underlying ring signature scheme. $\mathcal{C}$ answers the token queries as follows:

- Hash Query: Simulator $\mathcal{C}$ randomly chooses $r_j \in Z_p$ and sets $H(name||j) = \psi(g_2^a)^{r_j}/h^{m_j}$. The entry $< name, j, r_j, H(name||j) >$ is stored into the table.
- Authenticator: $\sigma_j = (H(name||j) \cdot h^{m_j})^{1/ax_1} = \psi(g_2^a)^{r_j/ax_1} = g_1^{r_j/x_1}$

  Simulator $\mathcal{C}$ answers the glue queries as follows:

- For each user $i \neq 1$ in the ring, $\mathcal{C}$ chooses $a_i \in Z_p$, and computes auxiliary information. $b_i = g_1^{a_i}$
- $\mathcal{C}$ computes a glue value $\theta = \dfrac{1}{\psi\left(\prod_{i\neq 1}^d y_i^{a_i}\right)^{1/ax_1}} = \dfrac{1}{\psi\left(\prod_{i\neq 1}^n ((g_2^a)^{x_i})^{a_i}\right)^{1/ax_1}} = \dfrac{1}{g_1^{\left(\sum_{i\neq 1} a_i x_i\right)/x_1}}$.

Phase 2: Finally $\mathcal{A}$ outputs a proof $P' = (\mu', c, \pi)$ for $t', \{m'_j\}_{j\in J}$ and challenge $\{c_j\}_{j\in J}$, where at least one m'_j has been modified by the adversary.

  $\mathcal{C}$ uses the commitment secret key α to recover the $\Sigma'_i = c_{i2}/c_{i1}^\alpha$ and let $\mu = \sum_{j\in J} c_j m_j$, $\{\Sigma\}$ be the honestly generated component. Then we have the following equations: $e\left(\prod_{j\in J} H(name||j)^{c_j} \cdot h^{\mu'}, g_2\right) = \prod_{i=1}^n e(\Sigma'_i, y_i)$

then $e\left(\prod_{j\in J} H(name||j)^{c_j} \cdot h^\mu, g_2\right) = \prod_{i=1}^n e(\Sigma_i, y_i)$. Therefore, we can get $e(h^{\mu'-\mu}, g_2) = \prod_{i=1}^n e(\Sigma'_i/\Sigma_i, y_i)$ then $e(h^{\mu'-\mu}, g_2) = e\left(\prod_{i=1}^n (\Sigma'_i/\Sigma_i)^{x_i}, g_2^a\right)$. As $\mathcal{C}$ chooses the challenges c_j at random and $h = g_1^{ab}$, with overwhelming probability $1 - 1/p, \mu' = \sum_{j\in J} c_j m'_j \neq \mu = \sum_{j\in J} c_j m_j$, we can obtain

$$g_1^b = \left(\prod_{i=1}^n (\Sigma'_i/\Sigma_i)^{x_i}\right)^{1/(\mu'-\mu)}.$$

Efficient Dynamic Provable Data Possession with Public Verifiability and Data Privacy

Clémentine Gritti[✉], Willy Susilo, and Thomas Plantard

Centre for Computer and Information Security Research,
School of Computing and Information Technology,
University of Wollongong, Wollongong, Australia
cjpg967@uowmail.edu.au,
{wsusilo,thomaspl}@uow.edu.au

Abstract. We present a Dynamic Provable Data Possession (PDP) system with Public Verifiability and Data Privacy. Three entities are involved: a client who is the owner of the data to be stored, a server that stores the data and a Third Party Auditor (TPA) who may be required when the client wants to check the integrity of its data stored on the server. The system is publicly verifiable with the possible help of the TPA who acts on behalf of the client. The system exhibits data dynamicity at block level allowing data insertion, deletion and modification to be performed. Finally, the system is secure at the untrusted server and data private. We present a *practical* PDP system by adopting asymmetric pairings to gain efficiency and reduce the group exponentiation and pairing operations. In our scheme, no exponentiation and only three pairings are required during the proof of data possession check, which clearly outperforms all the existing schemes in the literature. Furthermore, our protocol supports proof of data possession on as many data blocks as possible at no extra cost.

Keywords: Provable Data Possession · Practicality · Data operations · Public verifiability · Data integrity · Data privacy

1 Introduction

One of the most essential issue in storing data at an untrusted server is the ability to check the integrity of the data. Data owner has to ensure that the server really possesses the claimed stored data. Numerous proof-of-storage solutions have been proposed such as Proofs of Retrievability systems [1,2] and Provable Data Possessions systems [3,4]. In the latter system, the client is able to check that a server has stored its data without retrieving them from the server and without letting the server to access the entire data file. Both systems should satisfy the main property of *efficiency* in terms of computational and communication complexities and the storage overhead on the server's side should be as

This work is partially supported by ARC Linkage Project LP12020052.

E. Foo and D. Stebila (Eds.): ACISP 2015, LNCS 9144, pp. 395–412, 2015.
DOI: 10.1007/978-3-319-19962-7_23

small as possible. The properties of unbounded uses on the number of proof-of-storage interactions and statelessness of the client are required to obtain systems with public verifiability, in which anyone can verify the integrity of the stored data [5,6]. More recently, an idea emerged as delegating the data integrity check to a Third Party Auditor (TPA) [7,8]. More precisely, the client retains its data on an untrusted server and asks a trusted TPA to verify the authenticity of the stored data. This concept can be seen as a particular case of public verifiability. At the same time, another idea arised as dynamically updating the stored data [9–11]. In other words, the client is able to insert, delete and modify its stored data blocks and the server should then update these blocks on its side.

It is widely acknowledged that a storage service is susceptible to attacks or failures and leads to possible non-retrievable losses of the client's stored data. A solution is to construct a system that offers an efficient, frequent and secure data integrity check process to the client. Nevertheless, the frequency of data integrity verification and the percentage of checked data are often limited because of the computational and communication costs on both server's and client's sides, although these two properties are really essential for storage service.

1.1 Our Contributions

In this work, we provide a Dynamic Provable Data Possession (PDP) system with Public Verifiability and Data Privacy. There are three entities in the system: a client who is the owner of the data to be stored, a server that stores the data (e.g. a cloud), and a semi-honest Third Party Auditor (TPA) who can be required when the client wants to check the integrity of its data stored on the server. The client gets a large amount of data that it wants to store on the server without retaining a local copy. The server gets an important storage space and computation resources and supplies services for the client. The system is public verifiable, meaning that anyone is enabled to check the integrity of the data, not only the TPA on behalf of the client or the client itself. However, the TPA can be requested to judge whether the data integrity is maintained by checking the proof of data possession. We stress that the client may be able to perform integrity checking by itself; however, it could be limited in resources and therefore it may be neceesary to ask to the TPA (such as when the client is a mobile phone). Since this often happens naturally in practice, we only consider the case of the TPA acting on behalf of the client.

The system is also data dynamic at the block level supporting three operations: data insertion, deletion and modification. Finally, the system is secure at the untrusted server, meaning that a server cannot successfully generate a correct proof of data possession without storing all the file blocks, and data private, meaning that the TPA learns nothing about the data of the client from all available information.

Our scheme outperforms the existing schemes in the literature in terms of practicality. The first refinement is a better efficiency due the use of asymmetric pairings. The second amelioration is a decrease of the number of group exponentiation and pairing computations. In particular, the TPA needs to compute no exponentiation and only three pairings in order to verify the proof of data possession generated by the server. This implies that the latter can be requested by the client through the TPA to create the proof on any percentage of the stored data, without any computational constraints. The result of these improvements is clear in terms of performance evaluation.

1.2 Related Work

Ateniese et al. [3] first defined the notion of Provable Data Possession (PDP), which allows a client to verify the integrity of its data stored at an untrusted server without retrieving the entire file. Their scheme is designed for static data and used public key-based homomorphic tags for auditing the data file. Nevertheless, the precomputation of the tags imposes heavy computation overhead that can be expensive for entire file. Subsequently, Ateniese et al. [4] constructed scalable and efficient schemes using symmetric keys in order to improve the efficiency of verification. This results in lower overhead than their previous scheme. The scheme partially supports dynamic data operations (block updates, deletions and appends to the stored file); however, it is not publicly verifiable and is limited in number of verification requests.

Thereafter, several works were done following the models given in [3,4]. Wang et al. [5] combined a BLS-based homomorphic authenticator with a Merkle hash tree to achieve a public auditing protocol with fully dynamic data. Hao et al. [6] designed a dynamic public auditing system based on RSA. However, they did not provide any proof of security. Their scheme is shown not to be secure in [12]. Erway et al. [9] proposed a fully dynamic PDP scheme based on rank-based authenticated dictionary. Unfortunately, their system is very inefficient. Zhu et al. [11] used index-hash tables to support fully dynamic data and constructed a zero-knowledge PDP. Zhu et al. [13] created a dynamic audit service based on fragment structure, random sampling and index-hash table that supports timely anomaly detection. Wang et al. [14] proposed a system to ensure the correctness of users' data stored on multiple servers by requiring homomorphic tokens and erasure codes in the auditing process. Le and Markopoulou [15] constructed an efficient dynamic remote data integrity checking scheme based on a homomorphic MAC scheme and CPA-secure encryption scheme and specifically designed for network coding based storage cloud. Wang et al. [16] gave a flexible distributed storage integrity auditing protocol utilizing the homomorphic token and the distributed erasure-coded data. Subsequently, Wang et al. [7] designed a privacy-preserving protocol, Oruta, that allows public auditing on shared data stored in the cloud. The scheme allows public auditing and identity privacy but fails to support large groups and traceability. In a parallel work, Wang et al. [8] presented a privacy-preserving auditing system, Knox, for data stored in the cloud and shared among a large number of users in the group. The scheme allows identity privacy, large users' number and traceability but is only for private auditing. Nevertheless, Yu et al. [17] demonstrated that the protocols in [7,8,16] are subject to active adversary attacks.

1.3 Paper Organization

In the next Section, we review the definitions and notations that will be used throughout this paper. Additionally, we also provide the definition of dynamic PDP scheme with public verifiability and data privacy, along with its security models. In Section 3, we present our scheme. In Section 4, we present the corresponding security proofs. In Section 5, we discuss about the computation and communication costs and we evaluate and compare the performance of our scheme with other existing ones. Finally, we conclude the paper in Section 6.

2 Definitions

We use the Homomorphic Verifiable Tags (HVT) [3] to build verification metadata linked to data blocks (defined in Appendix A). To construct our scheme, we use bilinear maps (defined in Appendix A for completness).

Throughout this paper, we write $i \in [a, b]$ to describe that i can take all the values in the interval of reals between a and b. Let $i \in]a, b]$ (resp. $[a, b[$) mean that i can take all the values in the interval of reals between a and b, but a excluded (resp. b excluded). Let $i = 1, \cdots, n$ mean that i can take all the values in $\mathbb{N} \cap [1, n]$, where $\mathbb{N}$ is the set of naturals $\{1, 2, \cdots\}$. $\mathbb{Z}$ denotes the set of the integers $\{\cdots, -2, -1, 0, 1, 2, \cdots\}$, $\mathbb{Z}_p$ denotes the set $\{0, \cdots, p-1\}$ and $\mathbb{Z}_p^*$ denotes the set of positive integers smaller than p and relatively prime with p. $\mathbb{Q}$ denotes the set of the rationals. We let $|I|$ denote the cardinality of the set I. Let $||$ denote the symbol of concatenation, e.g. $m = m_1 || m_2$ is the file made of the concatenation of the two blocks m_1 and m_2. We let $m = \perp$ mean that m does not take any value. Let $|m|$ denote the bit size of the element m.

2.1 DPDP Scheme

The following definition of the scheme follows the ones from [3] and [9]. A Dynamic Provable Data Possession scheme with Public Verifiability and Data Privacy $\Pi =$ (**KeyGen, Tag- Gen, PerfOp, CheckOp, Gen- Proof, CheckProof**) is as follows:

KeyGen$(\lambda) \rightarrow (pk, sk)$. The probabilistic key generation algorithm is run by the client to setup the scheme. It takes as input the security parameter λ, and outputs a pair of public and secret keys (pk, sk).

TagGen$(pk, sk, m) \rightarrow T_m$. The (possibly) probabilistic tag generation algorithm is run by the client to generate the verification metadata. It takes as inputs the public key pk, the secret key sk and a file block m, and outputs a verification metadata T_m. Then, the client stores all the file blocks m in an ordered collection $\mathbb{F}$ and the corresponding verification metadata T_m in an ordered collection $\mathbb{E}$. It forwards these two collections to the server and deletes them from its local storage.

PerfOp$(pk, \mathbb{F}, \mathbb{E}, info) \rightarrow (\mathbb{F}', \mathbb{E}', \nu')$. This algorithm is run by the server in response to a data operation requested by the client. It takes as inputs the public key pk, the previous collection $\mathbb{F}$ of all the file blocks, the previous collection $\mathbb{E}$ of all the verification metadata, and the data operation details $info$ given by the client. The element $info$ specifies the operation to be performed: it can be either insertion or deletion or modification, along with other information like the rank where the operation has to be performed, the file block and the corresponding metadata that are looked at. It outputs the updated verification metadata collection $\mathbb{F}'$, the updated verification metadata collection $\mathbb{E}'$, and the related updating proof ν'. The server sends ν' to the TPA. We give more information about the data operation process below.

$\mathbf{CheckOp}(pk, \nu') \rightarrow \{\text{"success"}, \text{"failure"}\}$. This algorithm is run by the TPA on behalf of the client to verify the server's behavior during the data operation (insertion, deletion or modification). It takes as inputs the public key pk and the updating proof ν' sent by the server. It outputs "success" if ν' is a correct updating proof; otherwise it outputs "failure". We assume that the answer is then forwarded to the client. We omit this part of the process.

$\mathbf{GenProof}(pk, F, chal, \Sigma) \rightarrow \nu$. This algorithm is run by the server in order to generate a proof of data possession. It takes as inputs the public key pk, an ordered collection $F \subset \mathbb{F}$ of blocks, a challenge $chal$ and an ordered collection $\Sigma \subset \mathbb{E}$ which are the verification metadata corresponding to the blocks in F. It outputs a proof of data possession ν for the blocks in F that are determined by the challenge $chal$.

We assume that a first challenge $chal_C$ is generated by the client and forwarded to the TPA. Then, the TPA generates a challenge $chal$ from $chal_C$ and sends it to the server. In particular, if the client wants to check the integrity of its data without the help of the TPA, then $chal_C = chal$. We omit the process done by the client at this point.

$\mathbf{CheckProof}(pk, chal, \nu) \rightarrow \{\text{"success"}, \text{"failure"}\}$. This algorithm is run by the TPA in order to validate the proof of data possession. It takes as inputs the public key pk, the challenge $chal$ and the proof of data possession ν. It outputs "success" if ν is a correct proof of data possession for the blocks determined by $chal$; otherwise it outputs "failure". We assume that the answer is then forwarded to the client. We omit this part of the process.

We require that a Dynamic Provable Data Possession scheme with Public Verifiability and Data Privacy Π is *correct* if for $(pk, sk) \leftarrow \mathbf{KeyGen}(\lambda)$, for $T_m \leftarrow \mathbf{TagGen}(pk, sk, m)$, for $(\mathbb{F}', \mathbb{E}', \nu') \leftarrow \mathbf{PerfOp}(pk, \mathbb{F}, \mathbb{E}, info)$, for $\nu \leftarrow \mathbf{GenProof}(pk, F, chal, \Sigma)$, then "success" $\leftarrow \mathbf{CheckOp}(pk, \nu')$ and "success" $\leftarrow \mathbf{CheckProof}(pk, chal, \nu)$. We now give more details about the data operations that can be performed.

$\mathbf{PerfOp}(pk, \mathbb{F}, \mathbb{E}, info = (\text{insertion}, \frac{2i+1}{2}, m_{\frac{2i+1}{2}}, T_{m_{\frac{2i+1}{2}}})) \rightarrow (\mathbb{F}', \mathbb{E}', \nu')$. This algorithm is run by the server in response to a data insertion requested by the client. It takes as inputs the public key pk, the previous collection $\mathbb{F}$ of all the file blocks, the previous collection $\mathbb{E}$ of all the verification metadata, the type "insertion" of the data operation to be performed, the index $\frac{2i+1}{2}$ denoting the rank where the data operation is performed (in the ordered collections $\mathbb{F}$ and $\mathbb{E}$), the file block $m_{\frac{2i+1}{2}}$ to be inserted, and the corresponding verification metadata

$T_{m_{\frac{2i+1}{2}}}$ to be inserted, for $i = 0, \cdots, n$. More precisely, $m_{\frac{2i+1}{2}}$ is inserted between the existing blocks m_i and m_{i+1} and $T_{m_{\frac{2i+1}{2}}}$ is inserted between the existing verification metadata T_{m_i} and $T_{m_{i+1}}$, for $i = 1, \cdots, n-1$. For $i = 0$, $m_{\frac{1}{2}}$ is appended before m_1 and $T_{m_{\frac{1}{2}}}$ is appended before T_{m_1}. For $i = n$, $m_{\frac{2n+1}{2}}$ is appended after m_n and $T_{m_{\frac{2n+1}{2}}}$ is appended after T_{m_n}. Finally, it outputs the updated file block collection $\mathbb{F}'$ containing $m_{\frac{2i+1}{2}}$, the updated verification metadata collection $\mathbb{E}'$ containing $T_{m_{\frac{2i+1}{2}}}$, and the related updating proof ν'. The server sends ν' to the TPA.

PerfOp$(pk, \mathbb{F}, \mathbb{E}, info = (\text{deletion}, i)) \to (\mathbb{F}', \mathbb{E}', \nu')$. This algorithm is run by the server in response to a data deletion requested by the client. It takes as inputs the public key pk, the previous collection $\mathbb{F}$ of all the file blocks, the previous collection $\mathbb{E}$ of all the verification metadata, the type "deletion" of the data operation to be performed, and the index i denoting the rank where the data operation is performed (in the ordered collections $\mathbb{F}$ and $\mathbb{E}$). The server deletes the existing file block m_i, and the corresponding verification metadata T_{m_i}, for $i = 1, \cdots, n$. More precisely, m_i is deleted, giving that m_{i-1} is followed by m_{i+1} and T_{m_i} is deleted, giving that $T_{m_{i-1}}$ is followed by $T_{m_{i+1}}$, for $i = 2, \cdots, n-1$. For $i = 1$, m_1 is removed, giving that the file now begins from m_2, and T_{m_1} is removed, giving that the collection of verification metadata now begins from T_{m_2}. For $i = n$, m_n is removed, giving that the file now ends at m_{n-1}, and T_{m_n} is removed, giving that the collection of verification metadata now ends at $T_{m_{n-1}}$. Finally, it outputs the updated file block collection $\mathbb{F}'$ that does not contain m_i anymore, the updated verification metadata collection $\mathbb{E}'$ that does not contain T_{m_i} anymore, and the related updating proof ν'. The server sends ν' to the TPA. The deletion operation stops when the number of blocks is equal to 0.

PerfOp$(pk, \mathbb{F}, \mathbb{E}, info = (\text{modification}, i, m_i', T_{m_i'})) \to (\mathbb{F}', \mathbb{E}', \nu')$. This algorithm is run by the server in response to a data modification requested by the client. It takes as inputs the public key pk, the previous collection $\mathbb{F}$ of all the file blocks, the previous collection $\mathbb{E}$ of all the verification metadata, the type "modification" of the data operation to be performed, the index i denoting the rank where the data operation is performed (in the ordered collections $\mathbb{F}$ and $\mathbb{E}$), the file block m_i' which replaces the existing block m_i, and the corresponding verification metadata $T_{m_i'}$ which replaces the existing verification metadata T_{m_i}, for $i = 1, \cdots, n$. We assume that the file block m_i' and the corresponding verification metadata $T_{m_i'}$ were provided by the client to the server, such that $T_{m_i'}$ was correctly computed by running the algorithm **TagGen**. It outputs the updated verification metadata collection $\mathbb{F}'$ replacing m_i by m_i', the updated verification metadata collection $\mathbb{E}'$ replacing T_{m_i} by $T_{m_i'}$, and the related updating proof ν'. The server sends ν' to the TPA. We allow the client to make full re-write updates, meaning that all the file blocks $m_1, \cdots, m_n$ are replaced by $m_1', \cdots, m_n'$ and all the verification metadata $T_{m_1}, \cdots, T_{m_n}$ are replaced by $T_{m_1'}, \cdots, T_{m_n'}$.

Remarks. About the proof of data possession: The set of data blocks (following a certain percentage of blocks; e.g. 90%) that are checked to be correctly stored are chosen by the TPA on behalf of the client. The server has to generate a proof of data possession based on this set. We notice that sometimes in the literature [6,12], the TPA just sends a challenge *chal* without specifying which blocks have to be checked, which leads to the fact that the server must generate a proof of data possession based on all the stored data blocks, at the cost of the communication overhead.

About the data operations: We assume that the frequency of checking the integrity of the data is much higher than the frequency of performing data operations. To generate an updating proof, no challenge is required, meaning that the updating proof is based only the recently updated file block and the corresponding verification metadata. Therefore, one can think that this proof is not strong enough, however we suppose that the TPA on behalf of the client regularly asks to the server to check the integrity of the data by generating a challenge that can include the file blocks recently updated. Moreover, when the server is generating the updating proof ν', it can include an element $info' \in \{\text{insertion, deletion, modification}\}$ in this proof to enable the TPA to know which operation was performed. A solution to check that the server has correctly updated the collection $\mathbb{F}'$ of the file blocks and the collection $\mathcal{E}'$ of the verification metadata after operation is to order the data into a Merkle hash tree [5] or rank-based authenticated skip lists [9].

2.2   Security Models

Security against the server. The below-mentioned definition of the scheme follows the ones from [3] and [9]. We consider a Dynamic Provable Data Possession scheme with Public Verifiability and Data Privacy $\Pi = (\textbf{KeyGen}, \textbf{TagGen}, \textbf{Perf- Op}, \textbf{CheckOp}, \textbf{GenProof}, \textbf{CheckProof})$. Let a data possession game between a challenger $\mathcal{C}$ and an adversary $\mathcal{A}$ be as follows:

KeyGen. $(pk, sk) \leftarrow \textbf{KeyGen}(\lambda)$ is run by $\mathcal{C}$. The element pk is given to $\mathcal{A}$.

Adaptive queries. $\mathcal{A}$ makes adaptive queries through the intermediary of two oracles. The adversary is given access to a tag generation oracle $\mathcal{O}_{TG}$ as follows. $\mathcal{A}$ chooses a first block m_1 and forwards it the challenger. $\mathcal{C}$ computes the corresponding verification metadata $T_{m_1} \leftarrow \textbf{TagGen}(pk, sk, m_1)$ and gives it to the adversary. The adversary keeps on the same queries process with $\mathcal{C}$ for the verification metadata $T_{m_2} \leftarrow \textbf{TagGen}(pk, sk, m_2), \cdots, T_{m_n} \leftarrow \textbf{TagGen}(pk, sk, m_n)$, where the blocks $m_2, \cdots, m_n$ are chosen by $\mathcal{A}$. Then, the adversary creates an ordered collection $\mathbb{F} = \{m_1, \cdots, m_n\}$ of file blocks along with an ordered collection $\mathbb{E} = \{T_{m_1}, \cdots, T_{m_n}\}$ of the corresponding verification metadata.

Thereafter, the adversary is given access to a data operation performance oracle $\mathcal{O}_{DOP}$ as follows. $\mathcal{A}$ submits to the challenger a block m_i, for $i = 1, \cdots, n$, and the corresponding value $info_i$ about the data operation that the adversary wants to perform. The adversary runs the algorithm **PerfOp** and outputs a new file blocks ordered collection $\mathbb{F}'$, a new metadata ordered collection $\mathbb{E}'$, and the corresponding updating proof ν'. $\mathcal{C}$ checks the value ν' by running the algorithm **CheckOp**(pk, ν') and gives back the resulting answer belonging to {"success", "failure"} to the adversary. If the answer is "failure", then the challenger aborts; otherwise, it proceeds. The above interaction between $\mathcal{A}$ and $\mathcal{C}$ can be repeated.

Setup. The adversary submits file blocks m_i^* along with the corresponding values $info_i^*$, for $i \in \mathcal{I} \subseteq]0, n+1[\cap\mathbb{Q}$. Adaptive queries are again generated by the adversary, such that the first $info_i^*$ specifies a full re-write update (this corresponds to the first time that the client sends a file to the server). The challenger verifies the data operations.

Challenge. The final version of the blocks $m_i \in \mathcal{I}$ is considered such that these blocks were created according to the data operations requested by the adversary, and verified and accepted by the challenger in the previous step. The challenger sets $\mathbb{F} = \{m_i\}_{i\in\mathcal{I}}$ of these file blocks and $\mathbb{E} = \{T_{m_i}\}_{i\in\mathcal{I}}$ of the corresponding verification metadata. $\mathcal{C}$ then takes an ordered collection $F = \{m_{i_1}, \cdots, m_{i_k}\} \subset \mathbb{F}$ and the corresponding verification metadata ordered collection $\Sigma = \{T_{m_{i_1}}, \cdots, T_{m_{i_k}}\} \subset \mathbb{E}$, for $i_j \in \mathcal{I}$, $j = 1, \cdots, k$. It generates a resulting challenge $chal$ for F and Σ and forwards it to $\mathcal{A}$.

Forge. The adversary generates a proof of data possession ν on $chal$. Then, the challenger runs **CheckProof**$(pk, chal, \nu)$ and gives the answer belonging to {"success", "failure"} to $\mathcal{A}$. If the answer is "success" then the adversary wins.

The Dynamic Provable Data Possession scheme with Public Verifiability and Data Privacy $\Pi = ($**KeyGen, TagGen, PerfOp, CheckOp, GenProof, Check- Proof**$)$ is said to be secure if for any probabilistic polynomial-time (PPT) adversary $\mathcal{A}$ who can win the above data possession game with non-negligible probability, then the challenger $\mathcal{C}$ can extract at least the challenged parts of the file by resetting and challenging the adversary polynomially many times by means of a knowledge extractor $\mathcal{E}$.

Privacy against the TPA. The below-mentioned definition of the scheme follows the one from [12]. We consider a Dynamic Provable Data Possession scheme with Public Verifiability and Data Privacy $\Pi = ($**KeyGen, TagGen, PerfOp, Check- Op, GenProof, CheckProof**$)$. Let a data privacy game between a challenger $\mathcal{C}$ and an adversary $\mathcal{A}$ be as follows:

KeyGen. $(pk, sk) \leftarrow$ **KeyGen**(λ) is run by $\mathcal{C}$. The element pk is given to $\mathcal{A}$.

Queries. $\mathcal{A}$ gives to the challenger two files $m_0 = m_{0,1}||\cdots||m_{0,n}$ and $m_1 = m_{1,1}||\cdots||m_{1,n}$ of equal length. $\mathcal{C}$ randomly selects a bit $b \in_R \{0,1\}$, computes $T_{m_{b,i}} \leftarrow$ **TagGen**$(pk, sk, m_{b,i})$ for $i = 1, \cdots, n$ and gives them to $\mathcal{A}$. Then, the adversary creates an ordered collection $\mathbb{F} = \{m_{b,1}, \cdots, m_{b,n}\}$ of file blocks along with an ordered collection $\mathbb{E} = \{T_{m_{b,1}}, \cdots, T_{m_{b,n}}\}$ of the corresponding verification metadata.

Challenge. The adversary forwards $chal$ to $\mathcal{C}$.

Generation of the Proof. The challenger outputs a proof of data possession $\nu^* \leftarrow$ **GenProof**$(pk, F, chal, \Sigma)$ for the blocks in F that are determined by the challenge $chal$, where $F = \{m_{b,i_1}, \cdots, m_{b,i_k}\} \subset \mathbb{F}$ is an ordered collection of blocks and $\Sigma = \{T_{m_{b,i_1}}, \cdots, T_{m_{b,i_k}}\} \subset \mathbb{E}$ is an ordered collectection of the verification metadata corresponding to the blocks in F, for $1 \le i_j \le n, 1 \le j \le k$ and $1 \le k \le n$.

Guess. The adversary returns a bit b'. $\mathcal{A}$ wins if $b' = b$.

The Dynamic Provable Data Possession scheme with Public Verifiability and Data Privacy $\Pi = $ (**KeyGen, TagGen, PerfOp, CheckOp, GenProof, Check-Proof**) is said to be data private if there is no probabilistic polynomial-time (PPT) adversary $\mathcal{A}$ who can win the above data privacy game with non-negligible advantage equal to $|Pr[b' = b] - \frac{1}{2}|$.

3   Our DPDP Construction

The file to be stored is split into n blocks, and each block is split into s sectors. We let each block and sector be elements of $\mathbb{Z}_p$ for some large prime p. For instance, let the file be b bits long. Then, the file is split into $n = \lceil b/s \cdot \log(p) \rceil$ blocks. The aforementioned intuition comes from [2]. Suppose that the blocks contain $s \ge 1$ elements of $\mathbb{Z}_p$. Therefore, a tradeoff exists between the storage overhead and the communtication overhead. More precisely, the communication complexity rises as $s + 1$ elements of $\mathbb{Z}_p$. Finally, a larger value of s yields less storage overhead at cost of a high communication. Moreover, p should be λ bits long, where λ is the security parameter such that $n >> \lambda$.

KeyGen$(\lambda) \to (pk, sk)$. Let **GroupGen**(λ) be an algorithm that, on input the security parameter λ, generates the cyclic groups $\mathbb{G}_1$, $\mathbb{G}_2$ and $\mathbb{G}_T$ of prime order $p = p(\lambda)$ with bilinear map $e : \mathbb{G}_1 \times \mathbb{G}_2 \to \mathbb{G}_T$. Let g_1 and g_2 be generators of $\mathbb{G}_1$ and $\mathbb{G}_2$ respectively. Then, the client randomly chooses s elements $h_1, \cdots, h_s \in_R \mathbb{G}_1$. Moreover, it selects at random $a \in_R \mathbb{Z}_p$ and sets its public key $pk = (p, \mathbb{G}_1, \mathbb{G}_2, e, g_1, g_2, h_1, \cdots, h_s, g_2^a)$ and its secret key $sk = a$.

TagGen$(pk, sk, m) \to T_m$. A file m is split into n blocks m_i, for $i = 1, \cdots, n$. Each block m_i is then split into s sectors $m_{i,j} \in \mathbb{Z}_p$, for $j = 1, \cdots, s$. We suppose that $|m| = b$ and $n = \lceil b/s \cdot \log(p) \rceil$. Therefore, the file m can be seen a $n \times s$ matrix with elements denoted as $m_{i,j}$. The client computes the verification metadata $T_{m_i} = (\prod_{j=1}^{s} h_j^{m_{i,j}})^{-sk} = (\prod_{j=1}^{s} h_j^{m_{i,j}})^{-a} = (\prod_{j=1}^{s} h_j^{-a \cdot m_{i,j}})$ for $i = 1, \cdots, n$. Then, it sets $T_m = (T_{m_1}, \cdots, T_{m_n}) \in \mathbb{G}_1^n$.

Then, the client stores all the file blocks m in an ordered collection $\mathbb{F}$ and the corresponding verification metadata T_m in an ordered collection $\mathbb{E}$. It forwards these two collections to the server and deletes them from its local storage.

PerfOp$(pk, \mathbb{F}, \mathbb{E}, info = (\text{insertion}, \frac{2i+1}{2}, m_{\frac{2i+1}{2}}, T_{m_{\frac{2i+1}{2}}})) \to (\mathbb{F}', \mathbb{E}', \nu')$.

After receiving the elements $\frac{2i+1}{2}$, $m_{\frac{2i+1}{2}}$ and $T_{m_{\frac{2i+1}{2}}}$ from the client, for $i = 0, \cdots, n$, the server prepares the updating proof as follows. It first selects at random $u_1, \cdots, u_s \in_R \mathbb{Z}_p$ and computes $U_1 = h_1^{u_1}, \cdots, U_s = h_s^{u_s}$. It also chooses at random $w_{\frac{2i+1}{2}} \in_R \mathbb{Z}_p$ and sets $c_j = m_{\frac{2i+1}{2}, j} \cdot w_{\frac{2i+1}{2}} + u_j \in \mathbb{Z}_p$ for $j = 1, \cdots, s$, then $C_j = h_j^{c_j}$ for $j = 1, \cdots, s$, and $d = T_{m_{\frac{2i+1}{2}}}^{w_{\frac{2i+1}{2}}}$. Finally, it returns $\nu' = (U_1, \cdots, U_s, C_1, \cdots, C_s, d) \in \mathbb{G}_1^{2s+1}$ to the TPA.

PerfOp$(pk, \mathbb{F}, \mathbb{E}, info = (\text{deletion}, i)) \to (\mathbb{F}', \mathbb{E}', \nu')$. After receiving an index $i = 1, \cdots, n$ from the client, the server prepares the updating proof as follows. It first selects at random $u_1, \cdots, u_s \in_R \mathbb{Z}_p$ and computes $U_1 = h_1^{u_1}, \cdots, U_s = h_s^{u_s}$. It also chooses at random $w_i \in_R \mathbb{Z}_p$ and sets $c_j = m_{i,j} \cdot w_i + u_j \in \mathbb{Z}_p$ for $j = 1, \cdots, s$, then $C_j = h_j^{c_j}$ for $j = 1, \cdots, s$, and $d = T_{m_i}^{w_i}$, where m_i and T_{m_i} are the existing file block and verification metadata to be deleted respectively. Finally, it returns $\nu' = (U_1, \cdots, U_s, C_1, \cdots, C_s, d) \in \mathbb{G}_1^{2s+1}$ to the TPA.

PerfOp$(pk, \mathbb{F}, \mathbb{E}, info = (\text{modification}, i, m_i', T_{m_i'})) \rightarrow (\mathbb{F}', \mathbb{E}', \nu')$. After receiving the elements i, m_i' and $T_{m_i'}$ from the client, the server prepares the updating proof as follows. It first selects at random $u_1, \cdots, u_s \in_R \mathbb{Z}_p$ and computes $U_1 = h_1^{u_1}, \cdots, U_s = h_s^{u_s}$. It also chooses at random $w_i \in_R \mathbb{Z}_p$ and sets $c_j = m_{i,j}' \cdot w_i + u_j \in \mathbb{Z}_p$ for $j = 1, \cdots, s$, then $C_j = h_j^{c_j}$ for $j = 1, \cdots, s$, and $d = T_{m_i'}^{w_i}$. Finally, it returns $\nu' = (U_1, \cdots, U_s, C_1, \cdots, C_s, d) \in \mathbb{G}_1^{2s+1}$ to the TPA.

CheckOp$(pk, \nu') \rightarrow \{\text{"success"}, \text{"failure"}\}$. The TPA has to check whether the following equation holds:

$$e(d, g_2^a) \cdot e(\prod_{j=1}^{s} U_j, g_2) \stackrel{?}{=} e(\prod_{j=1}^{s} C_j, g_2) \tag{1}$$

If Eq. 1 holds, then the TPA returns "success" to the client; otherwise. it returns "failure" to the client.

GenProof$(pk, F, chal, \Sigma) \rightarrow \nu$. After receiving a challenge $chal_C$ from the client, the TPA prepares a challenge $chal$ to send to the server as follows. First, it chooses a subset $I \subseteq]0, n+1[_\mathbb{Q}$, randomly chooses $|I|$ elements $v_i \in_R \mathbb{Z}_p$ and sets $chal = \{(i, v_i)\}_{i \in I}$. Second, after receiving the challenge $chal$ which indicates the specific blocks for which the client, through the TPA, wants a proof of data possession, the server sets the ordered collection $F = \{m_i\}_{i \in I} \subset \mathbb{F}$ of blocks and an ordered collection $\Sigma = \{T_{m_i}\}_{i \in I} \subset \mathbb{E}$ which are the verification metadata corresponding to the blocks in F. It then selects at random $r_1, \cdots, r_s \in_R \mathbb{Z}_p$ and computes $R_1 = h_1^{r_1}, \cdots, R_s = h_s^{r_s}$. It also sets $b_j = \sum_{(i,v_i) \in chal} m_{i,j} \cdot v_i + r_j \in \mathbb{Z}_p$ for $j = 1, \cdots, s$, then $B_j = h_j^{b_j}$ for $j = 1, \cdots, s$, and $c = \prod_{(i,v_i) \in chal} T_{m_i}^{v_i}$. Finally, it returns $\nu = (R_1, \cdots, R_s, B_1, \cdots, B_s, c) \in \mathbb{G}_1^{2s+1}$ to the TPA.

CheckProof$(pk, chal, \nu) \rightarrow \{\text{"success"}, \text{"failure"}\}$. The TPA has to check whether the following equation holds:

$$e(c, g_2^a) \cdot e(\prod_{j=1}^{s} R_j, g_2) \stackrel{?}{=} e(\prod_{j=1}^{s} B_j, g_2) \tag{2}$$

If Eq. 2 holds, then the TPA returns "success" to the client; otherwise. it returns "failure" to the client.

Correctness. If all the algorithms are correctly generated, then the above scheme is correct. For the updating proof, we have:

$$e(d, g_2^a) \cdot e(\prod_{j=1}^{s} U_j, g_2) = e(T_{m_i}^{w_i}, g_2^a) \cdot e(\prod_{j=1}^{s} h_j^{u_j}, g_2) = e(\prod_{j=1}^{s} h_j^{m_{i,j} \cdot w_i + u_j}, g_2)$$

$$= e(\prod_{j=1}^{s} h_j^{c_j}, g_2) = e(\prod_{j=1}^{s} C_j, g_2)$$

For the proof of data possession, we have:

$$e(c, g_2^a) \cdot e(\prod_{j=1}^{s} R_j, g_2) = e\left(\prod_{\substack{(i,v_i) \\ \in chal}} T_{m_i}^{v_i}, g_2^a\right) \cdot e(\prod_{j=1}^{s} h_j^{r_j}, g_2) = e(\prod_{j=1}^{s} h_j^{\sum_{\substack{(i,v_i) \\ \in chal}} m_{i,j} \cdot v_i + r_j}, g_2)$$

$$= e(\prod_{j=1}^{s} h_j^{b_j}, g_2) = e(\prod_{j=1}^{s} B_j, g_2)$$

Remarks. About the verification metadata: The size of the verification metadata T_m is small in comparison to the size of the data blocks m. Additionally, the verification metadata protect the integrity of the blocks. Indeed, the server generates the proofs of data possession that certify the verification metadata instead of the data blocks themselves.

About the proof of data possession: The element $b_j = \sum_{(i,v_i) \in chal} m_{i,j} \cdot v_i + r_j$, for $j = 1, \cdots, s$, has size approximately equal to the size of a single block.

4 Security Proofs

Discrete Logarithm (DL) Problem. Let $\mathbb{G}_1$ be a multiplicative cyclic group of prime order $p = p(\lambda)$ (where λ is the security parameter). The DL problem is as follows: for $a \in \mathbb{Z}_p$, given $g_1, g_1^a \in \mathbb{G}_1$, output a. The DL problem holds in $\mathbb{G}_1$ if no t-time algorithm has advantage at least ε in solving the DL problem in $\mathbb{G}_1$.

Security against the Server. For any probabilistic polynomial-time (PPT) adversary $\mathcal{A}$ who wins the game, there is a challenger $\mathcal{C}$ that interacts with the adversary $\mathcal{A}$ as follows.

KeyGen. $\mathcal{C}$ runs **GroupGen**$(\lambda) \rightarrow (p, \mathbb{G}_1, \mathbb{G}_2, \mathbb{G}_T, e)$ and selects two generators g_1 and g_2 of $\mathbb{G}_1$ and $\mathbb{G}_2$ respectively. Then, it randomly chooses s elements $h_1, \cdots, h_s \in_R \mathbb{G}_1$ and an element $a \in_R \mathbb{Z}_p$. It sets the public key $pk = (p, \mathbb{G}_1, \mathbb{G}_2, e, g_1, g_2, h_1, \cdots, h_s, g_2^a)$ and forwards it to $\mathcal{A}$. It sets the secret key $sk = a$ and keeps it.

Adaptive queries. $\mathcal{A}$ has access to the tag generation oracle $\mathcal{O}_{TG}$ as follows. It first adaptively selects blocks m_i, for $i = 1, \cdots, n$. $\mathcal{C}$ splits each block m_i, for $i = 1, \cdots, n$ into s sectors $m_{i,j}$. Then, it computes $T_{m_i} = (\prod_{j=1}^{s} h_j^{m_{i,j}})^{-sk} = (\prod_{j=1}^{s} h_j^{m_{i,j}})^{-a}$, for $i = 1, \cdots, n$, and gives them to $\mathcal{A}$. The adversary sets an ordered collection $\mathbb{F} = \{m_1, \cdots, m_n\}$ of blocks and an ordered collection $\mathbb{E} = \{T_{m_1}, \cdots, T_{m_n}\}$ which are the verification metadata corresponding to the blocks in $\mathbb{F}$. $\mathcal{A}$ has access to the data operation performance oracle $\mathcal{O}_{DOP}$ as follows. Repeatedly, the adversary selects a block m_l and the corresponding element $info_l$ and forwards them to the challenger. l denotes the rank where $\mathcal{A}$ wants the data operation to be performed; l is equal to $\frac{2i+1}{2}$ for an insertion and to i for a deletion or a modification. Moreover, $m_l = \perp$ in the case of a deletion, since only the rank is needed to perform this kind of operation. Then, $\mathcal{A}$ outputs a new file blocks ordered collection $\mathbb{F}'$ (containing the updated version of the block m_l), a new verification metadata ordered collection $\mathbb{E}'$ (containing the updated version of the verification metadata T_{m_l}) and a corresponding updating proof $\nu' = (U_1, \cdots, U_s, C_1, \cdots, C_s, d)$, such that w_l is randomly chosen from $\mathbb{Z}_p$, $d = T_{m_l}^{w_l}$, and for $j = 1, \cdots, s$, u_j is randomly chosen from $\mathbb{Z}_p$, $U_j = h_j^{r_j}$, $c_j = m_{l,j} \cdot w_l + u_j$ and $C_j = h_j^{c_j}$. $\mathcal{C}$ runs the algorithm **CheckOp** on the value ν' and sends the answer to $\mathcal{A}$. If the answer is "failure", then the challenger aborts; otherwise, it proceeds.

Setup. The adversary selects blocks m_i^* and the corresponding elements $info_i^*$, for $i \in \mathcal{I} \subseteq]0, n+1[\cap \mathbb{Q}$, and forwards them to the challenger who checks the data operations. In particular, the first $info_i^*$ indicates a full re-write.

Challenge. The challenger chooses a subset $I \subseteq \mathcal{I}$, randomly chooses $|I|$ elements $v_i \in_R \mathbb{Z}_p$ and sets $chal = \{(i, v_i)\}_{i \in I}$. It forwards $chal$ as a challenge to $\mathcal{A}$.

Forge. Upon receiving the challenge $chal$, the resulting proof of data possession on the correct stored file m should be $\nu = (R_1, \cdots, R_s, B_1, \cdots, B_s, c)$ and pass the Eq. 2. However, $\mathcal{A}$ generates a proof of data possession on an incorrect stored file $\tilde{m}$ as $\tilde{\nu} = (R_1, \cdots, R_s, \tilde{B}_1, \cdots, \tilde{B}_s, \tilde{c})$, such that r_j is randomly chosen from $\mathbb{Z}_p$, $R_j = h_j^{r_j}$, $\tilde{b}_j = \sum_{(i,v_i) \in chal} \tilde{m}_{i,j} \cdot v_i + r_j$ and $\tilde{B}_j = h_j^{\tilde{b}_j}$, for $j = 1, \cdots, s$. It also sets $\tilde{c} = \prod_{(i,v_i) \in chal} T_{\tilde{m}_i}^{v_i}$. Finally, it returns $\tilde{\nu} = (R_1, \cdots, R_s, \tilde{B}_1, \cdots, \tilde{B}_s, \tilde{c})$ to the challenger. If the proof of data possession still passes the verification, then $\mathcal{A}$ wins. Otherwise, it fails. We define $\Delta b_j = \tilde{b}_j - b_j$, for $j = 1, \cdots, s$. At least one element of $\{\Delta b_j\}_{j=1,\cdots,s}$ is non-zero.

Analysis: We provide the analysis of the above security proof in Appendix B.

Privacy against the TPA. For any probabilistic polynomial-time (PPT) adversary $\mathcal{A}$ who wins the game, there is a challenger $\mathcal{C}$ that interacts with the adversary $\mathcal{A}$ as follows.

KeyGen. $\mathcal{C}$ runs **GroupGen**$(\lambda) \to (p, \mathbb{G}_1, \mathbb{G}_2, \mathbb{G}_T, e)$ and selects two generators g_1 and g_2 of $\mathbb{G}_1$ and $\mathbb{G}_2$ respectively. Then, it randomly chooses s elements $h_1, \cdots, h_s \in_R \mathbb{G}_1$ and an element $a \in_R \mathbb{Z}_p$. It sets the public key $pk = (p, \mathbb{G}_1, \mathbb{G}_2, e, g_1, g_2, h_1, \cdots, h_s, g_2^a)$ and forwards it to $\mathcal{A}$. It sets the secret key $sk = a$ and keeps it.

Queries. $\mathcal{A}$ gives to the challenger two files $m_0 = m_{0,1} || \cdots || m_{0,n}$ and $m_1 = m_{1,1} || \cdots || m_{1,n}$ of equal length. $\mathcal{C}$ randomly selects a bit $b \in_R \{0,1\}$ and for $i = 1, \cdots, n$, splits each block $m_{b,i}$ into s sectors $m_{b,i,j}$. Then, it computes $T_{m_{b,i}} = (\prod_{j=1}^s h_j^{m_{b,i,j}})^{-sk} = (\prod_{j=1}^s h_j^{m_{b,i,j}})^{-a}$, for $i = 1, \cdots, n$, and gives them to $\mathcal{A}$.

Challenge. The adversary chooses a subset $I \subseteq \{1, \cdots, n\}$, randomly chooses $|I|$ elements $v_i \in_R \mathbb{Z}_p$ and sets $chal = \{(i, v_i)\}_{i \in I}$. It forwards $chal$ as a challenge to $\mathcal{C}$.

Generation of the Proof. Upon receiving the challenge $chal$, the challenger selects an ordered collection $F = \{m_i\}_{i \in I}$ of blocks and an ordered collection $\Sigma = \{T_{m_i}\}_{i \in I}$ which are the verification metadata corresponding to the blocks in F such that $T_{m_i} = (\prod_{j=1}^{s} h_j^{m_{i,j}})^{-sk} = (\prod_{j=1}^{s} h_j^{m_{i,j}})^{-a}$, for $i \in I$. It then randomly chooses $r_1, \cdots, r_s \in_R \mathbb{Z}_p$ and computes $R_1^* = h_1^{r_1}, \cdots, R_s^* = h_s^{r_s}$. It also randomly selects $b_1, \cdots, b_s \in \mathbb{Z}_p$ and computes $B_1^* = h_1^{b_1}, \cdots, B_s^* = h_s^{b_s}$. It sets $c^* = \prod_{(i,v_i) \in chal} T_{m_i}^{v_i}$ as well. Finally, the challenger returns $\nu^* = (R_1^*, \cdots, R_s^*, B_1^*, \cdots, B_s^*, c^*)$.

Guess. The adversary returns a bit b'.

Analysis: We provide the analysis of the above security proof in Appendix B.

5 Performance

5.1 Computational and Communication Costs

In Figure 1, we compare the computational cost of our scheme with the ones in [8,13]. We include the schemes from [8,13] for comparison since they are recent and the offer similar features to our scheme. In all the schemes, during the execution of the algorithm **KeyGen**, the number of exponentiations in $\mathbb{G}_1$ and

Sch.	Algorithm	Operation Total						P_	PV	D
[8]	**KeyGen**	-	-	$3E_{\mathbb{G}_1}$	$2E_{\mathbb{G}_2}$	-	-			
	TagGen	$1M_{\mathbb{Z}_p}$	$1M_{\mathbb{G}_1}$	$11E_{\mathbb{G}_1}$	-	$3E_{\mathbb{G}_T}$	3P	P_A	×	×
	GenPr.	$|I|M_{\mathbb{Z}_p}$	$(|I|-1)M_{\mathbb{G}_1}$	$|I|E_{\mathbb{G}_1}$	-	-	-			
	CheckPr.	$(s+|I|)M_{\mathbb{Z}_p}$	$(9|I|-6)M_{\mathbb{G}_1}$	$(8+8|I|)E_{\mathbb{G}_1}$	-	$|I|E_{\mathbb{G}_T}$	4P			
[13]	**KeyGen**	-	-	$2E_{\mathbb{G}_1}$	/	-	-			
	TagGen	-	$1M_{\mathbb{G}_1}$	$(s+2)E_{\mathbb{G}_1}$	/	-	-	P_S	✓	✓
	GenPr.	$|I|M_{\mathbb{Z}_p}$	$(s+|I|-2)M_{\mathbb{G}_1}$	$(s+|I|+1)E_{\mathbb{G}_1}$	/	-	1P			
	CheckPr.	-	$(s+|I|-2)M_{\mathbb{G}_1}$	$(s+|I|)E_{\mathbb{G}_1}$	/	-	3P			
Our PDP	**KeyGen**	-	-	-	$1E_{\mathbb{G}_2}$	-	-	P_A	✓	✓
	TagGen	-	$(s-1)M_{\mathbb{G}_1}$	$sE_{\mathbb{G}_1}$	-	-	-			
	GenPr.	$|I|M_{\mathbb{Z}_p}$	$(|I|-1)M_{\mathbb{G}_1}$	$(2s+|I|)E_{\mathbb{G}_1}$	-	-	-			
	CheckPr.	-	$(2s-2)M_{\mathbb{G}_1}$	-	-	-	3P			

Fig. 1. Group multiplication, group exponentiation and pairing benchmarks. $M_{\mathbb{Z}_p}$ and $M_{\mathbb{G}_1}$ denote multiplications in $\mathbb{Z}_p$ and $\mathbb{G}_1$ respectively. $E_{\mathbb{G}_1}$, $E_{\mathbb{G}_2}$ and $E_{\mathbb{G}_T}$ denote exponentiations in $\mathbb{G}_1$, $\mathbb{G}_2$ and $\mathbb{G}_T$ respectively. P, P_A and P_S denote pairings, asymmetric pairings and symmetric pairings respectively. Let "PV" denote "public verifiability" and "D" denote "dynamicity".; the expression "Let s be the number of sectors in one file block and $|I|$ be the cardinality of the set $I \subseteq]0, n+1[\cap \mathbb{Q}$ when setting the challenge $chal$. A blank means that there is no group operation performed. Let "/" point out symmetric pairings, i.e. $\mathbb{G}_1 = \mathbb{G}_2$ [13]. Let "-" mean that no operation is performed.

$\mathbb{G}_2$ is constant. The algorithm **TagGen** in [13] and ours requires $O(s)$ exponentiations in $\mathbb{G}_1$, where s is the number of sectors in each file block. In [8], **TagGen** needs only a constant number of exponentiations in $\mathbb{G}_1$, however there is an extra computation cost of generating the verification metadata, which is the cost of computing 3 exponentiations in $\mathbb{G}_T$ and 3 pairings. Moreover, the number of multiplications in $\mathbb{G}_1$ is constant in [8,13], whereas it is linear in s in our case. In [13] and our scheme, the generation of proof of prossession in **GenProof** needs the computation of $O(s + |I|)$ exponentiations in $\mathbb{G}_1$; whereas in [8], the generation of proof of prossession only involves the computation of $O(|I|)$ exponentiations in $\mathbb{G}_1$. In addition, the number of multiplications in $\mathbb{G}_1$ is linear in $|I|$ in our scheme and in [8], whereas it it linear in both $|I|$ and s in [13]. The computation cost of checking the proof in **CheckProof** differs in the three schemes. In [8], the algorithm **CheckProof** requires $O(|I|)$ exponentiations in $\mathbb{G}_1$ and $\mathbb{G}_T$ and 4 pairings. In [13], the algorithm **CheckProof** needs $O(s + |I|)$ exponentiations in $\mathbb{G}_1$ and a constant number of pairings equal to 3. Moreover, the number of multiplications in both $\mathbb{Z}_p$ and $\mathbb{G}_1$ varies between the three systems. In [8], $O(s + |I|)$ and $O(|I|)$ multiplications are required in $\mathbb{Z}_p$ and $\mathbb{G}_1$ respectively. In [13], $O(s + |I|)$ multiplications in $\mathbb{G}_1$ are computed, while $O(s)$ multiplications in $\mathbb{G}_1$ are needed in our case. Finally, in our scheme, the computation cost is lighter; more precisely it is only the cost of computing 3 pairings (no exponentiation is required).

The communication cost of our protocol is mostly due to two factors: the challenge and the proof of data possession. The communication cost of a challenge $chal = \{(i, v_i)\}_{i \in I}$ is $|I|(|n| + |p|)$ bits, where $|I|$ is the number of selected file blocks, $|n|$ is the length of an index and $|p|$ is the length of an element in $\mathbb{Z}_p$. The communication cost of a proof of data possession $\nu = (R_1, \cdots, R_s, B_1, \cdots, B_s, c)$ is $(2 \cdot s + 1)|p|$ bits, where s is the number of sectors in each block. An additional cost can be the communication cost of an updating proof $\nu' = (U_1, \cdots, U_s, C_1, \cdots, C_s, d)$, which is $(2 \cdot s + 1)|p|$ bits, where s is the number of sectors in each block. However, this happens only when the client wants to update its data. We assume that the frequency of checking the integrity of the data is much higher than the frequency of performing data operations. Therefore, we leave out this additional cost.

5.2 Evaluation and Comparison of the Performance

We evaluate the practicality of our scheme and compare it to the one of the scheme in [13]. We use results of cryptographic operation implementations (exponentiations and pairings) using the MIRACL library, provided by Certivox for the MIRACL Authentication Server Project Wiki. All the following experiments are based on Borland C/C++ Compiler/Assembler and tested on a processor 2.4 GHz Intel i5 520M. For symmetric pairing-based systems (e.g. the scheme in [13]), AES with a 80-bit key and a Super Singular curve over $\mathbb{GF}_p$, for a 512-bit modulus p and an embedding degree equal to 2, are used. For asymmetric pairing-based systems (e.g. our scheme), AES with a 80-bit key and a

	Expon. in $\mathbb{G}_1$	Expon. in $\mathbb{G}_2$	Expon. in $\mathbb{G}_T$	Pairings	Pairing Type
Time/computation	1.49	NA	0.36	3.34	Symmetric
	0.51	0.51	0.12	1.14	Asymmetric
[13] **KeyGen**	2.98	NA	-	-	
PDP **TagGen**	151.98	NA	-	-	Symmetric
GenProof	835.89	NA	-	3.34	
CheckProof	596	NA	-	10.02	
KeyGen	-	0.51	-	-	
Our **TagGen**	51	-	-	-	Asymmetric
PDP **GenProof**	255	-	-	-	
CheckProof	-	-	-	3.42	

Fig. 2. Timings for symmetric and asymmetric pairing types and pairing-based systems. Times are in milliseconds. Let "Expon." denote exponentations. Let "/" point out symmetric pairings, i.e. $\mathbb{G}_1 = \mathbb{G}_2$ [13]. Let "-" denote the results are equal to zero.

Cocks-Pinch curve over $\mathbb{GF}_p$, for a 512-bit modulus p and an embedding degree equal to 2, are used.

In Figure 2, we evaluate and compare the efficiency of our scheme. We assume that 2 GB data are stored. The file is split into one million blocks of size 2 KB, such that the size of the index is $|n| = 20$ bits. We assume that the number of sectors in each file block is $s = 100$ and the number of blocks determined in the challenge $chal$ is $|I| = 460$. The main difference of time between the two protocols is not due to the exponentiation and pairing number difference but rather to the use of symmetric or asymmetric pairings. The total time in the algorithm **KeyGen** is 2.98 milliseconds in [13], whereas it is only 0.51 milliseconds in our construction. In the algorithm **TagGen**, it takes 151.98 milliseconds to generate the verification metadata in [13], whereas it takes one third of this time in ours. Then, it requires a total time of 839.23 milliseconds in the algorithm **GenProof** of [13], whereas, in our case, it requires only one third of this time. The reason may be that there are two stages to generate the proof in [13] (called "commitment" and "response"), while we need only one stage. Finally, in the algorithm **CheckProof**, it takes 844.42 milliseconds to check the proof of data possession in [13], whereas the time in our case is negligible. Indeed, the cost for verifying the proof is constant in our protocol.

Remarks. The probability of detecting corrupted block is $1 - (1 - \frac{|X|}{n})^{|I|}$, where $|X|$ is the number of corrupted blocks. Given $1,000,000$ of blocks, the challenge requires 460 blocks to allow the detection of 1% fraction of incorrect data with 99% probability of detecting misbehavior [3]. In several papers [3,7,9,16], this observation is followed for the implementation and the experimentation of their protocol. Because the number of computations is constant in our verification process, we are able to check more than 460 blocks, nay all the one million of blocks. On the client's side, the computational cost remains the same during the algorithm **CheckProof** and slightly changes when creating the challenge: the client has to pick at random $|I|$ elements in $\mathbb{Z}_p$. If the number $|I|$ increases, then the client has to chooses more elements. However we consider that this cost is negligible. In addition, we assume that the server has huge storage space and computation stock: it is able to generate a proof of data possession on as many blocks as the client requests.

We note that the efficiency of the scheme in [13] and ours are dependent on the value of s. Thus, a bigger value s leads to a weaker efficiency for both of the systems. Nevertheless, our scheme still remains more practical than the one in [13] since the number of group exponentiations in the algorithms **TagGen** and **GenProof** is linear in s in both of the systems and the number of exponentiations in the algorithm **CheckProof** is also linear in s in [13] whereas there is no exponentation is required in our scheme.

6   Conclusion

We proposed an efficient Dynamic PDP with Public Verifiability and Data Privacy, which is more practical than the existing schemes in the literature. In particular, in order to check the proof of data possession generated by the server, the client is not required to compute any exponentiation but rather only a constant number of pairings.

References

1. Juels, A., Kaliski Jr., B.S.: Pors: proofs of retrievability for large files. In: Proc. of CCS 2007 (2007)
2. Shacham, H., Waters, B.: Compact proofs of retrievability. In: Pieprzyk, J. (ed.) ASIACRYPT 2008. LNCS, vol. 5350, pp. 90–107. Springer, Heidelberg (2008)
3. Ateniese, G., Burns, R., Curtmola, R., Herring, J., Kissner, L., Peterson, Z., Song, D.: Provable data possession at untrusted stores. In: Proc. of CCS 2007 (2007)
4. Ateniese, G., Di Pietro, R., Mancini, L.V., Tsudik, G.E.: Scalable and efficient provable data possession. In: Proc. of SecureComm 2008 (2008)
5. Wang, C., Wang, Q., Ren, K., Lou, W.: Privacy-preserving public auditing for data storage security in cloud computing. In: Proc. of INFOCOM 2010 (2010)
6. Hao, Z., Zhong, S., Yu, N.: A privacy-preserving remote data integrity checking protocol with data dynamics and public verifiability. IEEE TKDE **23**(9), 1432–1437 (2011)
7. Wang, B., Li, B., Li, H.: Oruta: privacy-preserving public auditing for shared data in the cloud. IEEE TCC **2**(1), 43–56 (2012)
8. Wang, B., Li, B., Li, H.: Knox: privacy-preserving auditing for shared data with large groups in the cloud. In: Bao, F., Samarati, P., Zhou, J. (eds.) ACNS 2012. LNCS, vol. 7341, pp. 507–525. Springer, Heidelberg (2012)
9. Erway, C., Küpçü, A., Papamanthou, C., Tamassia, R.: Dynamic provable data possession. In: Proc. of CCS 2009 (2009)
10. Wang, Q., Wang, C., Li, J., Ren, K., Lou, W.: Enabling public verifiability and data dynamics for storage security in cloud computing. In: Backes, M., Ning, P. (eds.) ESORICS 2009. LNCS, vol. 5789, pp. 355–370. Springer, Heidelberg (2009)
11. Zhu, Y., Wang, H., Hu, Z., Ahn, G.-J., Hu, H., Yau, S.S.: Dynamic audit services for integrity verification of outsourced storages in clouds. In: Proc. of SAC 2011 (2011)

12. Yu, Y., Au, M.H., Mu, Y., Tang, S., Ren, J., Susilo, W., Dong, L.: Enhanced privacy of a remote data integrity-checking protocol for secure cloud storage. IJIS, 1–12 (2014)
13. Zhu, Y., Ahn, G.-J., Hu, H., Yau, S.S., An, H.G., Hu, C.-J.: Dynamic audit services for outsourced storages in clouds. IEEE TSC **6**(2), 227–238 (2013)
14. Wang, C., Wang, Q., Ren, K., Lou, W.: Ensuring data storage security in cloud computing. In: Proc. of IWQoS 2009 (2009)
15. Le, A., Markopoulou, A.: Nc-audit: Auditing for network coding storage. CoRR, abs/1203.1730 (2012)
16. Wang, C., Wang, Q., Ren, K., Cao, N., Lou, W.: Toward secure and dependable storage services in cloud computing. IEEE TSC **5**(2), 220–232 (2012)
17. Yu, Y., Niu, L., Yang, G., Mu, Y., Susilo, W.: On the security of auditing mechanisms for secure cloud storage. GCS **30**(1), 127–132 (2014)

A   Definitions

Homomorphic Verifiable Tags (HVT). For each file block m, a HVT T_m is created. A HVT acts as a verification metadata for the file blocks and besides being unforgeable, it has the *blockless verification* property (the server constructs a proof of data possession allowing the client to verify if the server possesses certain file blocks even when the client does not have access to the actual file blocks along with the *homomorphic tags* property (given two verification metadata T_{m_i} and T_{m_j}, anyone can combine them into the verification metadata $T_{m_i+m_j}$ corresponding to the sum of the files $m_i + m_j$). The server stores the HVTs along with the file. The client should be able to check the HVTs on specific blocks, even though it does not possess any of these blocks, that is possible based on the blockless verification property of HVT.

Bilinear Maps. Let $\mathbb{G}_1$, $\mathbb{G}_2$ and $\mathbb{G}_T$ be three multiplicative cyclic groups of prime order $p = p(\lambda)$ (where λ is the security parameter). Let g_1 be a generator of $\mathbb{G}_1$, g_2 be a generator of $\mathbb{G}_2$ and $e : \mathbb{G}_1 \times \mathbb{G}_2 \to \mathbb{G}_T$ be a bilinear map with the *bilinearity* property ($\forall u \in \mathbb{G}_1, \forall v \in \mathbb{G}_2, \forall a, b \in \mathbb{Z}_p, e(u^a, v^b) = e(u,v)^{ab}$) along with the *non-degeneracy* property ($e(g_1, g_2) \neq 1_{\mathbb{G}_T}$). ($\mathbb{G}_1, \mathbb{G}_2$) is said to be a bilinear group if the group operation in ($\mathbb{G}_1, \mathbb{G}_2$) and the bilinear map e are both efficiently computable.

B   Analysis of the Security Proofs

Security against the Server. We prove that if the adversary can win the game, then a solution to the DL problem is found, which contradicts the assumption that the DL problem is hard in $\mathbb{G}_1$. Let assume that the server wins the game. Then, according to Eq. 2, we have $e(c, g_2^a) \cdot e(\prod_{j=1}^{s} R_j, g_2) = e(\prod_{j=1}^{s} \tilde{B}_j, g_2)$. Since the proof $\nu = (R_1, \cdots, R_s, B_1, \cdots, B_s, c)$ is a correct one, we also have $e(c, g_2^a) \cdot e(\prod_{j=1}^{s} R_j, g_2) = e(\prod_{j=1}^{s} B_j, g_2)$. Therefore, we get that $\prod_{j=1}^{s} \tilde{B}_j = \prod_{j=1}^{s} B_j$. We can re-write as $\prod_{j=1}^{s} h_j^{\tilde{b}_j} = \prod_{j=1}^{s} h_j^{b_j}$ or even as $\prod_{j=1}^{s} h_j^{\Delta b_j} = 1$.

For two elements $g, h \in \mathbb{G}_1$, there exists $x \in \mathbb{Z}_p$ such that $h = g^x$ since $\mathbb{G}_1$ is a cyclic group. Without loss of generality, given $g, h \in \mathbb{G}_1$, each h_j could randomly and correctly be generated by computing $h_j = g^{y_j} \cdot h^{z_j} \in \mathbb{G}_1$ such that y_j and z_j are random values of $\mathbb{Z}_p$. Then, we have $1 = \prod_{j=1}^{s} h_j^{\Delta b_j} = \prod_{j=1}^{s} (g^{y_j} \cdot h^{z_j})^{\Delta b_j} = g^{\sum_{j=1}^{s} y_j \cdot \Delta b_j} \cdot h^{\sum_{j=1}^{s} z_j \cdot \Delta b_j}$. Clearly, we can find a solution to the DL problem. More specifically, given $g, h = g^x \in \mathbb{G}_1$, we can compute $h = g^{\frac{\sum_{j=1}^{s} y_j \cdot \Delta b_j}{\sum_{j=1}^{s} z_j \cdot \Delta b_j}} = g^x$ unless the denominator is zero. However, as we defined in the game, at least one element of $\{\Delta b_j\}_{j=1,\cdots,s}$ is non-zero. Since z_j is a random element of $\mathbb{Z}_p$, the denominator is zero with probability equal to $1/p$, which is negligible. Thus, if the adversary wins the game, then a solution of the DL problem can be found with probability equal to $1 - \frac{1}{p}$, which contradicts the fact that the DL problem is assumed to be hard in $\mathbb{G}_1$. Therefore, for the adversary, it is computationally infeasible to win the game and generate an incorrect proof of data possession which can pass the verification.

Moreover, the simulation of the tag generation oracle $\mathcal{O}_{TG}$ is perfect. The simulation of the data operation performance oracle $\mathcal{O}_{DOP}$ is almost perfect except when the challenger aborts. This happens the data operation was not correclty performed. As previously, we can prove that if the adversary can pass the updating proof, then a solution to the DL problem is found. Following the above analysis and according to Eq. 1, if the adversary generates an incorrect updating proof which can pass the verification, then a solution of the DL problem can be found with probability equal to $1 - \frac{1}{p}$, which contradicts the fact that the DL problem is assumed to be hard in $\mathbb{G}_1$. Therefore, for the adversary, it is computationally infeasible to generate an incorrect updating proof which can pass the verification. The proof is completed.

Privacy against the TPA. The probability $Pr[b' = b]$ must be equal to $\frac{1}{2}$ since the verification metadata $T_{m_{b,i}}$, for $i = 1, \cdots, n$, and the proof ν^* are independent of the bit b. We now prove that the verification metadata and the proof of data possession given to the adversary are correctly distributed. The value $T_{m_{b,i}}$ is equal to $(\prod_{j=1}^{s} h_j^{m_{b,i,j}})^{-sk} = (\prod_{j=1}^{s} h_j^{m_{b,i,j}})^{-a}$. Since $sk = a$ is kept secret from $\mathcal{A}$, the above simulation is perfect. For a block file m_b, there exists $v_{b,i}$, for $(i, v_{b,i}) \in chal_b$, such that $b_{b,j} = \sum_{(i,v_{b,i}) \in chal_b} m_{b,i,j} \cdot v_{b,i} + r_{b,j}$. In addition, $R_{b,1}, \cdots, R_{b,s}, B_{b,1}, \cdots, B_{b,s}$ are statically indistinguishable with the actual outputs corresponding to m_0 or m_1. Thus, the answers given to the adversary are correctly distributed. The proof is completed.

Privately Computing Set-Union and Set-Intersection Cardinality via Bloom Filters

Rolf Egert, Marc Fischlin$^{(\boxtimes)}$, David Gens, Sven Jacob, Matthias Senker, and Jörn Tillmanns

Technische Universität Darmstadt, Darmstadt, Germany
marc.fischlin@cryptoplexity.de

Abstract. In this paper we propose a new approach to privately compute the set-union cardinality and the set-intersection cardinality among multiple honest-but-curious parties. Our approach is inspired by a proposal of Ashok and Mukkamala (DBSec'14) which deploys Bloom filters to approximate the size tightly. One advantage of their solution is that it avoids ample public-key cryptography. Unfortunately, we show here that their protocol is vulnerable to actual attacks. We therefore propose a new Bloom filter based protocol, also forgoing heavy cryptography, and prove its security.

1 Introduction

The set-union cardinality problem consists of n parties, each party holding a set X_i of data, and the task is to compute the size of the union of all sets, $s = |\bigcup X_i|$. Ideally, this should be done in a way such that only the final result s is revealed but nothing about the individual input sets. The problem is a close relative to other so-called privacy-preserving set operation problems, including the set-intersection cardinality problem where parties aim to compute $s = |\bigcap X_i|$ securely, and the more general set-union and set-intersection problems where the goal is to explicitly compute the union and the intersection, respectively, and not only their cardinality. There are also more relaxed versions of the problem, called disjointness and conjointness testing, where the parties only check whether the size of the intersection resp. union is 0 or not.

Protocols for privacy-preserving set operations have numerous applications, explaining the vast number of protocol proposals and publications (as discussed below). To name a few applications, De Cristofaro et al. [4] point out that such protocols can be used for anomaly detection in network monitoring or for identifying common friends in social networks. Kerschbaum [22] lists supply chain integrity protection as another application. De Cristofaro et al. [4] also discuss that the cardinality versions can be specifically used in the areas of genomic computations, location sharing, or affiliation-hiding authentication.

1.1 The Ashok-Mukkamala Protocol

Ashok and Mukkamala [1] recently proposed a fast multi-party protocol for the set union cardinality problem using Bloom filters. A Bloom filter [3] is an

© Springer International Publishing Switzerland 2015
E. Foo and D. Stebila (Eds.): ACISP 2015, LNCS 9144, pp. 413–430, 2015.
DOI: 10.1007/978-3-319-19962-7_24

array-based representation for sets where each inserted element induces a set of 1's in the array, based on the results of hashing the element with a set of public hash functions.[1] Verifying membership can be then carried out by re-hashing the element and checking for 1-entries in the array. As such, Bloom filters have a small but tolerable false-positive rate, since one may accidentally hit 1's caused by other elements. The size of a Bloom filter is usually proportional to the number of elements, independently of the size of the domain of the elements.

The idea of the Ashok and Mukkamala (AM) protocol is now to use the fact that unions of Bloom filters correspond to the bit-wise OR of the arrays, which facilitates the computation of the union of the underlying sets. The size of the union then corresponds, with exponentially high accuracy [27], to the number of 0's and 1's in the derived array. Unlike other solutions for the problem the AM protocol does not rely on expensive cryptographic operations and reduces the network communication overhead significantly.

Unfortunately, the authors of [1] only sketch some ideas why their protocol should indeed be secure, lacking a formal proof in the common simulation-based sense of secure multi-party computation. Our first result is to show that such a proof is elusive. We show how each party in the AM protocol can predict any other party's input set with very high precision, even if honestly following the protocol description, by inspecting the communication data afterwards. This clearly violates the notion of a secure protocol.

1.2 Secure Cardinality Protocols Based on Bloom Filters

We adopt the approach [1] to use Bloom filters to devise protocols for the cardinality problems. Our first protocol is for the set-union cardinality problem and for three (or more) parties. We assume that each party first locally computes the Bloom filter of its input set. In the protocol two dedicated parties act as accumulators, receiving random shares of each party's Bloom filter. The sharing will be such that it is compatible with the union operation for Bloom filters, enabling each accumulator to compute the union over their Bloom filter shares. Both accumulators agree on a random permutation and forward the permuted arrays of their shares to the third dedicated party, the evaluator. The evaluator then assembles the permuted filters of the accumulators, computes the size of the union from the number of 1's, and announces the result to the other parties (if required).

Our protocol computes the size of the union with very small error (due to the negligible error caused by the Bloom filter approach and some term related to the secret sharing of the filters). It withstands honest-but-curious adversaries, as long as the adversary can only inspect the data of one of the three dedicated parties, and it provably leaks only the size of the union of the input Bloom filters of all parties.[2] The protocol is perfectly secure and does not rely on any

---

[1] The hash functions do not need to be cryptographically secure, but can still be based on hash functions like SHA [29].

[2] Note that one can in principle compile protocols in the honest-but-curious case to thwart malicious attacks [13], albeit this comes with an observable slow down.

cryptographic assumption. It requires little interaction between parties and the bit communication of each party is proportional to the size m of the Bloom filter. The latter is based on the observation that, for the cardinality problem, we can use "small" error-prone Bloom filter shares, as we are still able to approximate the number of errors sufficiently well and to subtract them out of the final result. We actually determine parameters enabling varying levels of communication complexity and accuracy.

Next we briefly discuss how to extent our protocol if more than one party can be accessed by the adversary. Basically, to tolerate t accesses of *dedicated* parties (and an arbitrary number of further parties) we need $\Omega(t^2)$ parties in total, building different layers of accumulators. For example, for $t = 2$ we need at least 6 participants. The protocol remains perfectly secure in the honest-but-curious setting and still provides a linear communication complexity for each party (linear in the size m of the Bloom filter).

We conclude with a two-party protocol for the cardinality problem, still based on Bloom filters. The protocol is a slight modification of the protocol of Kiayias and Mitrofanova [24] for testing disjointness, adopted to the case of union cardinality and the Bloom filter setting. Here we however need to revert to cryptographic means like homomorphic encryption. Our protocol is based on the ElGamal encryption scheme and computes the set-union cardinality problem in the honest-but-curious model. As opposed to similar protocols for the general set-union problem we take advantage of the fact that we merely need to compute the size of the union. This allows us to outsource the major computational effort to compute m encryptions and thus modular exponentiations for the Bloom filter array of size m to one party, the server. The client side, on the other hand, only computes a single encryption and m modular multiplications. This protocol appears in Appendix A.

We finally discuss that all our protocols can be easily adapted to compute the set-intersection cardinality problem. Indeed, as pointed out in [4], solutions in the two-party case for the private set-union cardinality problem in principle also give rise to protocols for the intersection problem, noting that $|X_1 \cap X_2| = |X_1| + |X_2| - |X_1 \cup X_2|$. However, this requires that the sizes of the individual sets X_1, X_2 are public, or that incorporated privately into the computation. Also, the formula gets significantly more complicated for multiple parties.

Hence, we here instead use a direct approach for Bloom filters via De Morgan's law to adapt our protocols. This approach, surprisingly, went unnoticed in [1]. Given the Bloom filters each party first inverts its array bit-wise. Then they compute the cardinality of the union of these inverted filters with our protocol. This yields the bit-wise inverse of the AND of the original Bloom filters. The parties can thus derive the cardinality of the intersection by subtracting the cardinality of the obtained filter from the size of the Bloom filters.

1.3 Related Work

There are numerous works on privacy-preserving set operations, with various security and complexity properties. We list here only protocols specifically for set operation problems, neglecting general-purpose multi-party protocols. Still, we note that there are solutions which apply general methods like oblivious transfer to the set-operation setting. For a comprehensive overview about such approaches based on oblivious transfer, and their performance characteristics, see [28]. We also omit a comparison to assisted protocols in which (partially) trustworthy third parties support the evaluation; see [21] for an overview over these protocols.

The early proposals for set operation protocols by Freedman et al. [11] and by Kiayias and Mitrofanova [24] used polynomials to represent input sets and jointly evaluated the polynomials via homomorphic encryption. Several subsequent approaches [5,12,14,17,18,25] adopted this idea in order to improve over security guarantees, efficiency, or functionality. Compared to our protocols these works often aim at the more general problems of set intersection and set union, and start by designing versions withstanding honest-but-curious adversaries before adding (efficient) zero-knowledge proofs to achieve security against malicious adversaries. At the same time, the proposals are usually more costly, even in the honest-but-curious model, in the sense that they deploy public-key cryptographic operations, and they often focus on the two-party case. This is also true for other public-key based approaches like [4,6,7].

Besides the oblivious polynomial evaluation approach, intersections can also be computed via oblivious pseudorandom functions [10]. Basically, this allows one party to evaluate a pseudorandom function on selected values without knowledge of the key, such that intersections can be spotted by comparing function values. This approach has been refined in several works [16,19,20], including also proposals with trustworthy hardware tokens [9,15]. All these approaches are for two-parties only and, due to the current state of art of oblivious pseudorandom functions, based on public-key operations or additional hardware components.

Using Bloom filters for privacy-preserving set operations has been suggested before for example in [22,23]. The former work [22] describes a Bloom filter based two-party protocol using homomorphic encryption to allow membership verification of single elements. This comes at the cost of a high communication complexity and reveals the element to be checked. The latter paper [23] extends this idea and securely computes the set intersection via Bloom filters and homomorphic encryption, but adds extra computations on encrypted elements. Dong et al. [8] used so-called garbled Bloom filters to compute intersections based on oblivious transfer. Garbled Bloom filters basically store the bits of the underlying sets in a randomly shared way in a *single* filter. This is in contrast to our approach in which the original filter is split into many shares. In addition, the oblivious transfer step in their protocol is inherent, even in the honest-but-curious model.

There are also approaches for secure set-operation protocols which are built on top of very basic multi-party computation protocols. For example, using the SEPIA library with secure protocols for addition and multiplication of bits, Many et al. [26] propose to compute the union of Bloom filters via a bit-wise OR according to the formula $a \vee b = a + b - a \cdot b$. Especially the sub protocol for multiplication in this formula, however, adds a significant overhead. Similarly, Blanton and Aguiar [2] use basic comparison operations and oblivious sorting to implement set operations like the computation of the union in a modular way. Compared to our dedicated solution the overhead is again noticeable.

2   Preliminaries

2.1   Secure Multi-Party Computation

We briefly sketch here the prerequisites of secure multi-party computations as in, e.g., [13]. More details can be found in the full version.

The general multi-party computation model assumes n participants, sometimes also called sites here. The goal of the parties is to jointly compute a function f on their inputs, where we usually assume that one party derives this result and finally distributes it to all other parties. This computation takes places in the presence of an *honest-but-curious* adversary. This adversary may non-adaptively decide to inspect up to t views of the parties after protocol completion and is called *t-bounded*. The view of a party consists of the party's input, its randomness, and the incoming and outgoing communication in the execution.[3] To ensure that nothing about a party's input is leaked, we assume that there is a simulator which can generate the same distribution of the t views given only the inputs of the t inspected parties and the function value. In this case the protocol is said to provide *perfect privacy* or *perfect security*.

Here we sometimes relax the requirement on completeness in the sense that we allow for a small error in the protocol's output. For a real-valued function f as for our cardinality problems here we say that a protocol *securely ϵ-approximates* f if security holds as above, and the protocol yields with probability $99,9\%$ an output which is within the interval $v \pm \epsilon$ of the actual function value v.

2.2   Using Bloom Filters for Multi-Party Computations

In this work we use Bloom filters to represent the sets X_i. Bloom filters, introduced by Burton Howard Bloom in the 1970's [3], are data structures for membership checking on sets. Given a data set $X = \{x_1, x_2, \cdots, x_d\}$, a bit-array of size m, initialized with 0, and a set of public hash functions $H = \{h_1, h_2, \cdots, h_k\}$ with range $\{1, 2, \ldots, m\}$, one creates the Bloom filter BF for the set X as follows. For each pair $x_i \in X$ and $h_j \in H$ compute $h_j(x_i)$ and set the corresponding bit in the array to 1. To check if a given element a is in the set X one computes all values $h_j(a)$ for $j = 1, 2, \ldots, k$, looks up the corresponding entries in the previously generated array, and predicts membership of a in X if and only if all resulting array positions contain 1's. This can only result in false positives due to collisions, i.e., if the hash values $h_j(a)$ for some element $a \notin X$ all map to 1's which have been set by hashing other elements.

---

[3] We assume that all other network traffic is not available to the adversary, say, since it is encrypted with fast hybrid or symmetric encryption.

The error rate of Bloom filters directly corresponds to the size m of the bit array, the number k of hash functions and the size d of the data set. To get a good trade-off between size of the Bloom filter and error-rate, we choose the parameters such that the equation $k = \frac{m}{d} \ln 2$, taken from [29], holds. As usual, this assumes that the hash functions behave like independent random functions. With this the Bloom filter should be filled to approximately 50%.

When using Bloom filters for private set operations one usually starts with the representation of the input sets of the parties as Bloom filters for some agreed-upon hash functions. The protocol then usually computes the union or intersection (or their cardinality) of the Bloom filters BF_i, neglecting the small errors due to false-positive rate of the filters. In our case we thus compute the (parameterized) function $(X_1, \ldots, X_n) \mapsto |\bigvee_{i=1}^{n} BF_i|$ securely, where the hash functions are given as randomly chosen parameters (for the function and to the protocol participants, including the adversary) and are used to derive the Bloom filters BF_i. Note that computing $m - |\bigvee_{i=1}^{n} BF_i|$, as we actually do here, is equivalent.[4]

We remark that cryptographic protocols using Bloom filters implicitly assume an a-priori bound on the size of sets. The reason is that the common parameters for the Bloom filters are usually chosen to match these numbers. Else, if chosen independently of the data size, the error rate for functional correctness may increase significantly. We also make the assumption here, visualized by the fact that the k hash functions for the filter and the filters' size m are available to all parties in our protocol.

3   Attacks on the Ashok-Mukkamala Protocol

As mentioned before security of a protocol for the set-union cardinality problem should guarantee that participants cannot learn anything about other parties' inputs beyond the size of the union of all data. We now show that the scheme proposed in [1] violates this security property as an adversary can identify another party's input with high probability. This holds even if the adversary only inspects the communication data of a party after protocol completion.

3.1   The AM-Protocol in a Nutshell

Recall that the AM-Protocol is based on the approximation of the size of a set via the entries in a Bloom filter. That is, given k independent and agreed-upon hash functions $h_1, \ldots, h_k$ with range in $\{1, 2, \ldots, m\}$ —where we assume in the analysis that the functions are random— we build the Bloom filter of bit size m by hashing each element $x \in X$ via all functions $h_i(x)$ and setting the corresponding bit to 1. Then, given only the Bloom filter, we can approximate the size of X via the number z of zeros in the filter by:

---

[4] The protocol in [1] also seems to aim to compute this function securely, but this is not specified.

$$|X| = \frac{\ln(z/m)}{k \ln(1 - 1/m)}.$$

Furthermore, the approximation is quite tight [29].

The AM-Protocol exploits that the bitwise OR of partial Bloom filters for any r sets of hash function indices $K_1, K_2, \ldots, K_r \subseteq \{1, 2, \ldots, k\}$ yields a Bloom filter for the hash functions with indices in the union $K_1 \cup K_2 \cup \cdots \cup K_r$. More precisely, letting $\mathrm{BF}|_K$ denote the Bloom filter created by applying only hash functions with indices from $K \subseteq \{1, 2, \ldots, k\}$ to the set X, we have

$$\bigvee_{i=1}^{r} \mathrm{BF}|_{K_i} = \mathrm{BF}|_{\cup_{i=1}^{r} K_i}.$$

This enables each site S_i to split the entire Bloom filter for its input data into partial ones, one for each other party S_j, by picking random subsets $K_{S_i \rightarrow S_j} \subseteq \{1, 2, \ldots, k\}$ of all hash functions $h_1, \ldots, h_k$, and creating the partial Bloom filters $\mathrm{BF}_{S_i \rightarrow S_j} = \mathrm{BF}|_{K_{S_i \rightarrow S_j}}$. Each partial filter is then handed to the site S_j for further processing. This is called the decomposition phase in [1].

For correctness it is necessary to ensure that all hash keys are used in some Bloom filter $\mathrm{BF}_{S_i \rightarrow S_j}$ of party S_i. The AM-Protocol therefore first lets S_i pick a random number $r_{S_i \rightarrow S_j}$ in some range $[a, b]$ for each partial filter, and then lets S_i include $r_{S_i \rightarrow S_j}$ random keys in the subset $K_{S_i \rightarrow S_j}$. The exact figures and the roles of a, b remain unspecified; it seems to us that they should prevent trivial subsets. To ensure that each key appears in at least one filter, the AM-protocol once more lets S_i randomly assign each hash key to one of the n partial Bloom filters.

Once a party S_j has received the partial Bloom filters $\mathrm{BF}_{S_i \rightarrow S_j}$ from all sites S_i, the party S_j computes the union of all these Bloom filters to create a filter BF'_{S_j} and sends out this value to all other sites. This is called the reconstruction phase in [1]. In the final merger phase each site S_i computes the Bloom filter union over all values BF'_{S_j} received from the n sites S_j. The final step is now to approximate the size of the union of the input data via the number z of 0-entries in the final Bloom filter.

3.2   Attack #1: Computing a Candidate List

Note that the underlying security idea of the AM-Protocol is that in the decomposition phase each party S_j only obtains a partial Bloom filter $\mathrm{BF}_{S_i \rightarrow S_j}$ from any other party S_i. In fact, Ashok and Mukkamala [1] argue about the number $r_{S_i \rightarrow S_j}$ of used hash functions being well distributed, neglecting the question of how much information about the original data is still contained in a partial Bloom filter. This observation is the leverage for our first attack, which allows us to use the partial Bloom filters to verify, with high accuracy, if the other party's input contains some individual data x.

To illustrate our attack assume that $r_{S_i \rightarrow S_j}$ hash functions with indices $K_{S_i \rightarrow S_j}$ have been used to construct the partial Bloom filter $\mathrm{BF}_{S_i \rightarrow S_j}$. Both the number $r_{S_i \to S_j}$ and the actual set $K_{S_i \to S_j}$ are only known to party S_i. Party S_j now tries to check whether some data x is part of S_i's input or not. To do so, it first computes the fraction $p \in [0, 1]$ of 1-entries in the partial Bloom filter. Then S_j hashes x with *all* hash functions $h_1, \ldots, h_k$ and counts how often it hits 1's in the filter $\mathrm{BF}_{S_i \to S_j}$. If x is not part of S_i's input, the hash values will, on the average, hit kp times; if x on the other hand, is contained in the set, the process will generate $r_{S_i \to S_j}$ hits for the $r_{S_i \to S_j}$ actually chosen hash functions in $K_{S_i \to S_j}$, plus an expected $(k - r_{S_i \to S_j})p$ hits for the remaining, unused hashed functions. On the average these are about $kp + (1 - p)r_{S_i \to S_j}$ hits, which exceeds the amount in the other case significantly for reasonable parameter choices. Although this gap and the number of samples is presumably too small to apply the Chernoff-Hoeffding bounds for estimating the deviation of expectations, our experiments and threshold choice below show that this gap suffices for a good prediction. Hence, S_j can decide membership of x in S_i's input with high probability.

We have run simulations on how good we can actually predict membership of elements. For this we created two Bloom filters for sets X_i, X_j with a given overlap $|X_i \cap X_j|$ for the respective parameters m, $|X_i| = |X_j|$, and k. Since we work with the Bloom filters exclusively and the actual data are irrelevant, we emulated ideal hash functions by inserting 1's for each element at random positions to create the Bloom filters (but with consistent position choice for the common elements, of course). For the partial Bloom filters we picked a random subset $r_{S_i \to S_j} \in [a, b]$ of the hash functions, where we chose $a = 3$ and $b = k - 3$. For each parameter set we repeated the experiment 1,000 times, averaging the results.

Table 1. Simulation results for attack #1

$|X_i| = |X_j| = 10,000,$ $m = 1,000,000, k = 70$			$|X_i| = |X_j| = 10,000,$ $m = 2,000,000, k = 140$			$|X_i| = |X_j| = 25,000,$ $m = 1,000,000, k = 70$		
$|X_i \cap X_j|$	precision	recall	$|X_i \cap X_j|$	precision	recall	$|X_i \cap X_j|$	precision	recall
10	79.5 %	90.8 %	10	92.2 %	94.9 %	10	31.3 %	69.9 %
100	95.4 %	83.8 %	100	97.6 %	90.9 %	100	72.5 %	58.4 %
1000	99.2 %	71.7 %	1000	99.8 %	83.3 %	1000	93.9 %	45.3 %

To determine the candidate elements we first count the number of ones for each element. Then we compute the average and maximum count (AVG and MAX) over all elements. Finally we select all elements as candidates for which the count is equal or greater to the following bound:

$$\mathrm{AVG} + \max(0.6, p) \cdot (\mathrm{MAX} - \mathrm{AVG})$$

That is, if the hits exceeds the average number by about 60% of the gap to the maximum (or a p-fraction of the gap, where p is the ratio of 1's in the received

Bloom filter) then we consider the value to be in the set. Extensive simulations with different approaches to calculate the bound led us to the given formula.

Table 1 shows our simulation results. Here, *precision* (basically determining exactness) designates the percentage of correctly identified candidates out of all the chosen candidates. We mark the percentage of correctly identified candidates out of the actually shared elements as *recall* (basically determining completeness).

3.3   Attack #2: Reconstructing the Set of Hash Functions

For the second attack we use a candidate list of common elements which could have been generated, for example, by our first attack. The attack here takes advantage of the fact that, for common elements, we can check if one of the k hash functions coincides on these elements. That is, for each of the k hash functions we check how many of the elements in the list hit a 1 in the partial Bloom filter we have obtained. We can roughly expect that only the actually chosen r hash functions will produce hits for all candidates.

Once we have identified the used hash functions we can in principle use the partial Bloom filter to plot out the other party's elements, with an error which is higher than for the optimal choice for Bloom filter parameters, but still giving useful information to an attacker. We refrain from doing so here, though, as the importance to hide this choice has already been mentioned in [1].

We have again run experiments to verify the correctness of our idea. We have used the same parameters as for the first attack. We used the exact list of common elements as the candidate list. Our algorithm decided to include a hash function as chosen if the number of ones counted for that hash function is greater or equal to $(\text{AVG}_h + \text{MAX}_h)/2$ where AVG_h and MAX_h are the average and maximum number of ones for all hash functions. The results of our experiments are given in Table 2.

Table 2. Simulation results for attack #2

$|X_i| = |X_j| = 10,000,$ $m = 1,000,000, k = 70$		$|X_i| = |X_j| = 10,000,$ $m = 2,000,000, k = 140$		$|X_i| = |X_j| = 25,000,$ $m = 1,000,000, k = 70$	
$|X_i \cap X_j|$	success	$|X_i \cap X_j|$	success	$|X_i \cap X_j|$	success
10	99.2 %	10	97.3 %	10	65.2 %
100	100 %	100	100 %	100	100 %
1000	100 %	1000	100 %	1000	100 %

3.4   Combination of Attacks #1 and #2

As briefly mentioned before the attacks can also be combined. In the first step we use attack #1 to generate a list of candidates that, with high probability, are part of the other party's input. We subsequently use this candidate list as an input for attack #2 to reconstruct the hash function set. The results of the simulation of the combined attack are displayed in Table 3 where *success* denotes the likelihood of identifying the r chosen hash functions correctly. Note that we cannot expect to achieve the same success rate as in the case of the exact candidate list, but our experiments show that for sufficiently large intersections we still achieve overwhelming rates.

Table 3. Simulation results for combination of attacks #1 and #2

$|X_i| = |X_j| = 10,000,$
$m = 1,000,000, k = 70$

$|X_i \cap X_j|$	success
10	75.7 %
100	99.5 %
1000	99.9 %

$|X_i| = |X_j| = 10,000,$
$m = 2,000,000, k = 140$

$|X_i \cap X_j|$	success
10	90.1 %
100	99.9 %
1000	100 %

$|X_i| = |X_j| = 25,000,$
$m = 1,000,000, k = 70$

$|X_i \cap X_j|$	success
10	0.7 %
100	70.7 %
1000	99.7 %

4   Advanced Protocols for the Set-Union Cardinality Problem

In this section we present our new protocols. Although inspired by the general idea of using Bloom filters as in [1] our proposed solutions are substantially different in the way they deploy Bloom filters. We only describe here the set-union protocol; the set-intersection protocol can be derived by working over the inverted Bloom filters, as explained in the Introduction.

4.1   The Three-Party Case

We first discuss the most basic scenario of our protocol with an arbitrary number of regular participants and three core nodes A,B and C. Two of the core nodes will act as accumulators of intermediate results of other parties and forward their values to the third party, the evaluator, who will compute the final result (and possibly distribute it to all other parties). An overview over the proposed protocol is given in Figure 1. Each of the core nodes acts as a regular participant, too, but has to perform some additional work. The protocol consists of a general part which is executed by all members and a special part for the core nodes. For simplification we will refer to the core nodes as A, B and C for the rest of this section, where A and B are called accumulators and C is called the evaluator.

The idea of the first part of the protocol is that each party first locally computes its Bloom filter for its input. Then the party transforms the representation of its Bloom filter of 0's and 1's into b-bit values where

$$0 \mapsto 0 \bmod 2^b, \qquad 1 \mapsto \text{random element} \bmod 2^b.$$

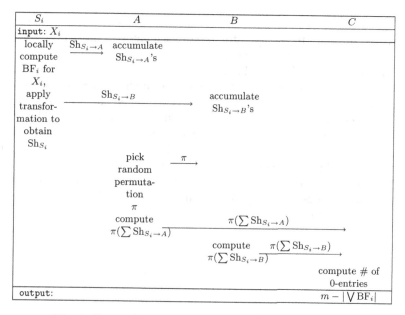

S_i		A		B		C
input: X_i						
locally compute BF_i for X_i,	$\xrightarrow{\mathrm{Sh}_{S_i \to A}}$	accumulate $\mathrm{Sh}_{S_i \to A}$'s				
apply transformation to obtain Sh_{S_i}	$\xrightarrow{\qquad \mathrm{Sh}_{S_i \to B} \qquad}$			accumulate $\mathrm{Sh}_{S_i \to B}$'s		
		pick random permutation π	$\xrightarrow{\pi}$			
		compute $\pi(\sum \mathrm{Sh}_{S_i \to A})$	$\xrightarrow{\qquad \pi(\sum \mathrm{Sh}_{S_i \to A}) \qquad}$			
				compute $\pi(\sum \mathrm{Sh}_{S_i \to B})$	$\xrightarrow{\qquad \pi(\sum \mathrm{Sh}_{S_i \to B}) \qquad}$	
						compute # of 0-entries
output:						$m - |\bigvee \mathrm{BF}_i|$

Fig. 1. Protocol steps in the case of three or more parties

Here $b = 4, 8$ or 16 may be appropriate choices, but even $b = 1$ is possible if one can tolerate slightly higher error rates. Subsequently the party splits its transformed Bloom filter representation into two equal-size shares $\mathrm{Sh}_{S_i \to A}$ and $\mathrm{Sh}_{S_i \to B}$ by mapping an entry $r \bmod 2^b$ to random $r_1, r_2 \bmod 2^b$ such that $r = r_1 + r_2 \bmod 2^b$ and placing r_1 in the first Bloom filter share and r_2 into the second one. Note that each of the two Bloom filter shares individually does not reveal any information about the original values. An example of this transformation process for $b = 8$ and thus $\mathbb{Z}_{256}$ is given in Figure 2.

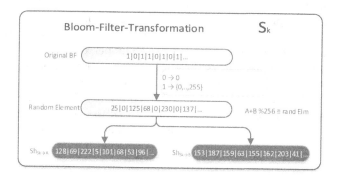

Fig. 2. Local share computation of a node's Bloom filter

The parties now all send their first Bloom filter share to the accumulator A, and their second share to accumulator B. For each entry in the arrays, the accumulator simply sums up the corresponding entries in all received filter shares. At this point neither A nor B individually possess any useful information about the Bloom filters of the other parties. Still they hold a shared version of the combined Bloom filter of all parties. Now they agree on a random permutation π over $\{1, 2, \ldots, m\}$ and permute the entries of their shares according to π. This step is necessary to ensure that the evaluator C cannot reconstruct information about individual data from the combined filter. Both A and B then send their permuted filters to C who adds the entries component-wise and finally counts the number of 0-entries in the derived filter. Eventually C can compute an approximation the size of the union set as in [1]. An example of the calculations performed by the accumulators and the evaluator is given in Figure 3.

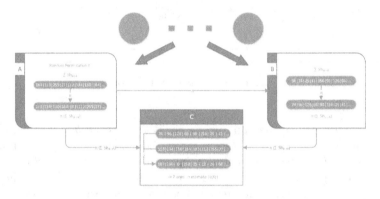

Fig. 3. Accumulation and evaluation of the transmitted Bloom filters by the core nodes

Note that the final result, independently of the inaccuracies due to the set-size approximation technique via the zeros, contains a small error. This error is introduced by the representation of 1's as random elements in $\mathbb{Z}_{2^b}$, potentially picking 0 mod 2^b for a 1-entry.[5] However, we can actually estimate these false elements quite accurately: Let z_0 denote the number of 0-entries in the final Bloom filter, and z_1 the number of (false) 0-representations of original 1-entries, such that $z = z_0 + z_1$ for the eventually derived number z of zeros. Note that the expected value (over the random representations of the parties) of z_1 is $2^{-b}(m - z_0)$ since each of the $m - z_0$ non-zero entries is misrepresented with probability 2^{-b}. It follows that the expected number E_{z_0} of z_0 is given by

$$E_{z_0} = \frac{z - 2^{-b}m}{1 - 2^{-b}}.$$

---

[5] Excluding 0-representations for 1's potentially enables an attacker to trace the original 0-entries with some small, yet noticeable probability, such that we rather accept an error on the side of correctness.

Hence, given z (and the parameters m, b) we can approximate the actual value of z_0 easily.

Furthermore, since z_1 is given by the sum of independent variables, the number of errors in our approximation follows a binomial distribution. Suppose we take for z_1 a confidence interval of 99.9%. Then we can calculate the error bounds for the estimation of z_0 and thus of the final result for different values of b and $|\bigcup X_i|$, the actual size of the union. Approximating the binomial distribution through the Gaussian distribution we obtain that with probability at least 99.9% the result of an honest execution of the protocol lies within an interval ± 3.29 times the standard deviation $\sigma := \sqrt{(m - z_0) \cdot 2^{-b}(1 - 2^{-b})}$ around the mean. In this case, using the formula for estimating z_0, our approximation is in the interval $(m - z_0) \pm 3.29\sigma/(1 - 2^{-b})$ for the standard deviation σ with probability 99.9%.

For a concrete example consider a densely filled Bloom filter of size $m = 1,000,000$, with only 10% of 0-entries, and let $b = 1$. Then with probability of 99.9% our guess will be within $\pm 1,561$ elements of the expected $450,000$ misrepresentations. Approximating z_0 as above with the same confidence we will output an estimation in the interval between $96,878$ and $103,122$ for the actual value $100,000$. For the same value of m, but 50% of the Bloom filter being filled, and now with $b = 8$, our approximation of the actual value of $500,000$ is within the range $498,854$ and $500,146$ with probability of at least 99.9%.

4.2   Proof of Security

We will now show security for our proposed protocol. Recall that the notion of ϵ-approximation means that, in terms of correctness, the output value (for a benign execution) is within an interval $\pm\epsilon$ of the actual function value with probability 99.9%.

Theorem 1. *Let $n \geq 3$ and consider the n-party protocol in Section 4.1. The protocol ϵ-approximates the function $f_{m, h_1, \ldots, h_k}(X_1, \ldots, X_n) = m - |\bigvee_{i=1}^{n} BF_i|$ perfectly secure in the honest-but-curious case against 1-bounded non-adaptive adversaries, where $\epsilon = 3.29 \cdot (1 - 2^{-b})^{-1} \cdot \sqrt{2^{-b} \cdot (1 - 2^{-b}) \cdot |\bigvee_{i=1}^{n} BF_i|}$.*

We stress again that the parameter b only influences the correctness of the computation. The bound for ϵ has already been derived in the previous section. Note that for large b, like $b = 128$, and reasonable filter size the approximation is correct with probability 99.9%.

Proof. First note that if the party inspected by the adversary is different from a core node then security is trivial, as such parties only send out information. Such a view is easy to simulate because the simulator receives the party's input. We can thus focus on the case of the adversary accessing one of the core nodes.

Consider first the case that an adversary inspects one of the accumulators A or B. We only consider the case of A here, as the case of B is analogous; the only difference is that A chooses the random permutation and transmits it. Because A

is an accumulator, the adversary in the actual protocol execution learns a single share of every Bloom filter of every participant of the protocol. The entries of these shares $\mathrm{Sh}_{S_i \to A}$, $i = 1, 2, \ldots, n$ are determined by the randomness of the corresponding participant S_i. Each share individually consists of m random elements from $\mathbb{Z}_{2^b}$.

We can devise a simulator for A as follows: The simulator receives as input A's input set and the output of the protocol $|\bigvee_{i=1}^{n} \mathrm{BF}_i|$ (if this value is eventually distributed to all participants by the evaluator C). It creates a view of A by faithfully computing the first outgoing messages of A as an ordinary participant via A's input data. Then it simulates each incoming share $\mathrm{Sh}_{S_i \to A}$ by picking m random elements from $\mathbb{Z}_{2^b}$. The simulator also places a random permutation π in A's view, and the aggregated and permuted filter shares as the message sent to C. It is easy to see that our simulator perfectly simulates the view of A in an actual protocol execution.

Finally consider the case that the adversary asks to see the view of the evaluating node C. The node C in the actual protocol execution receives as input two randomly permuted vectors sent by A and B. When put together, these vectors add up to $m - |\bigvee \mathrm{BF}_i|$ presentations of 0-entries plus a random set of false 0-presentations of 1-entries, i.e., where the shares add up to 0 mod 2^b. We can build a simulator as follows. The simulator, receiving $m - |\bigvee \mathrm{BF}_i|$ and C's data set, first creates the random filter shares C would send as an ordinary participant to A and B. It next prepares an empty Bloom filter and randomly distributes $|\bigvee \mathrm{BF}_i|$ random elements from $\mathbb{Z}_{2^b}$ and leaves the other entries as 0. It next splits all the entries of this filter randomly into two Bloom filters as the protocol participants, and puts these shares into the view of C. This again perfectly simulates the actual view of C in a genuine protocol execution, where C also receives randomly permuted entries of the same distribution.   □

4.3   Extensions to the Multi-Party Case

The basic three-party protocol which we described previously is only secure if at most one of the three core nodes is inspected by an adversary. For an adversary being able to access more core nodes we need to adapt the previous approach. The basic idea of our extension is to use additional layers of accumulators. The i-th layer (where we count the evaluator as layer 1 and the two accumulators of the basic case as layer 2) will consist of i accumulators. To withstand t-bounded adversaries we will use $t + 1$ of such layers where parties can only act as accumulators on one level. The set-up for $t = 2$ is given in Figure 4.

The execution starts by having each party compute its Bloom filter and splitting it up into $t + 1$ random shares over the group $\mathbb{Z}_{2^b}$ similar to the three-party case. i.e., 0-entries are random shares of 0, and 1-entries become random shares of random elements from $\mathbb{Z}_{2^b}$. Again all of the core nodes are also participating in the general Bloom filter distribution phase in the beginning, i.e., act both as accumulators as well as contributors. Then each party sends its $t + 1$ shares to the parties of the highest accumulator layer. The accumulators of a layer accumulate their shares and permute the accumulated Bloom filter shares randomly, where each layer picks a fresh permutation, e.g., chosen by one party and distributed to the accumulators of the same layer.

In the next step the accumulators forward their filters to the next lower layer. Here, allowing to reduce the communication overhead, it suffices that each lower-level accumulator receives at least two independent shares from the higher layer. In Figure 4 party B for example guarantees the two independent shares by splitting its share for the lower level, such that A and C can simply forward their share. When the evaluator eventually receives the shares it computes the output as before.

Security relies on the same observation as in the three-party case. First note that the adversary cannot obtain all individual shares of a participant sent to the $t + 1$ accumulators of the highest layer, as the adversary can only inspect up to t parties. The adversary could, potentially, inspect all t parties of the second highest layer, but then the data would correspond to randomly permuted shares of the overall result already. This is again easy to simulate, similar to the case of inspection of the evaluator C in the three party case.

If the adversary, on the other hand, inspects a party of the highest layer to learn the random permutation of that layer, then it must miss one of the t parties of the second highest layer and thus at least one of the shares. We can set this argument forth, noting that if the adversary misses the permutation of the Bloom filters (as the composition of all permutations of all t layers, except for layer 1) by not inspecting any party of some layer, then the t-bounded adversary cannot learn any information, besides inspecting the evaluator. But the t-bounded adversary can only learn the permutation if it inspects one accumulator for each layer. But then it misses the data of the evaluator and could only derive information about individual Bloom filters if it was able to access all shares of a layer. But by construction, since it inspects one party at each of the t layer levels, it must lack knowledge of a share on each level for every Bloom filter. It follows as in the three-party case that nothing is leaked except the function's output.

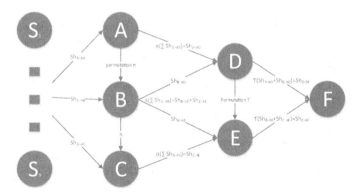

Fig. 4. Accumulation and evaluation by the core nodes in the multi-party case

5 Conclusion

Our protocols adopt the basic idea of the AM protocol to devise secure multi-party protocols which are provably secure, lightweight on the crypto operations, and low on network communication. It remains an interesting open question how one can enhance our protocol to withstand malicious adversaries, ideally forgoing expensive zero-knowledge proofs. Also, a worthwhile effort would be to devise errorless versions of our protocol.

Acknowledgments. Marc Fischlin is supported by the Heisenberg grant Fi 940/3-2 and SPP 1736 grant Fi 940/5-1 of the German Research Foundation (DFG).

References

1. Ashok, V.G., Mukkamala, R.: A scalable and efficient privacy preserving global itemset support approximation using bloom filters. In: Atluri, V., Pernul, G. (eds.) DBSec 2014. LNCS, vol. 8566, pp. 382–389. Springer, Heidelberg (2014)
2. Blanton, M., Aguiar, E.: Private and oblivious set and multiset operations. In: Youm, H.Y., Won, Y. (eds.) ASIACCS 2012, pp. 40–41. ACM Press, May 2012
3. Bloom, B.H.: Space/time trade-offs in hash coding with allowable errors. Communications of the ACM **13**(7), 422–426 (1970)
4. De Cristofaro, E., Gasti, P., Tsudik, G.: Fast and private computation of cardinality of set intersection and union. In: Pieprzyk, J., Sadeghi, A.-R., Manulis, M. (eds.) CANS 2012. LNCS, vol. 7712, pp. 218–231. Springer, Heidelberg (2012)
5. Dachman-Soled, D., Malkin, T., Raykova, M., Yung, M.: Efficient robust private set intersection. In: Abdalla, M., Pointcheval, D., Fouque, P.-A., Vergnaud, D. (eds.) ACNS 2009. LNCS, vol. 5536, pp. 125–142. Springer, Heidelberg (2009)
6. De Cristofaro, E., Kim, J., Tsudik, G.: Linear-complexity private set intersection protocols secure in malicious model. In: Abe, M. (ed.) ASIACRYPT 2010. LNCS, vol. 6477, pp. 213–231. Springer, Heidelberg (2010)
7. De Cristofaro, E., Tsudik, G.: Practical private set intersection protocols with linear complexity. In: Sion, R. (ed.) FC 2010. LNCS, vol. 6052, pp. 143–159. Springer, Heidelberg (2010)
8. Dong, C., Chen, L., Wen, Z.: When private set intersection meets big data: an efficient and scalable protocol. In: Sadeghi, A.R., Gligor, V.D., Yung, M. (eds.) ACM CCS 2013, pp. 789–800. ACM Press, November 2013
9. Fischlin, M., Pinkas, B., Sadeghi, A.-R., Schneider, T., Visconti, I.: Secure set intersection with untrusted hardware tokens. In: Kiayias, A. (ed.) CT-RSA 2011. LNCS, vol. 6558, pp. 1–16. Springer, Heidelberg (2011)
10. Freedman, M.J., Ishai, Y., Pinkas, B., Reingold, O.: Keyword search and oblivious pseudorandom functions. In: Kilian, J. (ed.) TCC 2005. LNCS, vol. 3378, pp. 303–324. Springer, Heidelberg (2005)
11. Freedman, M.J., Nissim, K., Pinkas, B.: Efficient private matching and set intersection. In: Cachin, C., Camenisch, J.L. (eds.) EUROCRYPT 2004. LNCS, vol. 3027, pp. 1–19. Springer, Heidelberg (2004)
12. Frikken, K.B.: Privacy-preserving set union. In: Katz, J., Yung, M. (eds.) ACNS 2007. LNCS, vol. 4521, pp. 237–252. Springer, Heidelberg (2007)
13. Goldreich, O.: The Foundations of Cryptography, vol. 2. Cambridge University Press (2004)

14. Hazay, C.: Oblivious polynomial evaluation and secure set-intersection from algebraic PRFs. In: Dodis, Y., Nielsen, J.B. (eds.) TCC 2015, Part II. LNCS, vol. 9015, pp. 90–120. Springer, Heidelberg (2015)
15. Hazay, C., Lindell, Y.: Constructions of truly practical secure protocols using standardsmartcards. In: Ning, P., Syverson, P.F., Jha, S. (eds.) ACM CCS 2008, pp. 491–500. ACM Press, October 2008
16. Hazay, C., Lindell, Y.: Efficient protocols for set intersection and pattern matching with security against malicious and covert adversaries. Journal of Cryptology **23**(3), 422–456 (2010)
17. Hazay, C., Nissim, K.: Efficient set operations in the presence of malicious adversaries. Journal of Cryptology **25**(3), 383–433 (2012)
18. Hohenberger, S., Weis, S.A.: Honest-verifier private disjointness testing without random oracles. In: Danezis, G., Golle, P. (eds.) PET 2006. LNCS, vol. 4258, pp. 277–294. Springer, Heidelberg (2006)
19. Jarecki, S., Liu, X.: Efficient oblivious pseudorandom function with applications to adaptive OT and secure computation of set intersection. In: Reingold, O. (ed.) TCC 2009. LNCS, vol. 5444, pp. 577–594. Springer, Heidelberg (2009)
20. Jarecki, S., Liu, X.: Fast secure computation of set intersection. In: Garay, J.A., De Prisco, R. (eds.) SCN 2010. LNCS, vol. 6280, pp. 418–435. Springer, Heidelberg (2010)
21. Kamara, S., Mohassel, P., Raykova, M., Sadeghian, S.: Scaling private set intersection to billion-element sets. In: Christin, N., Safavi-Naini, R. (eds.) FC 2014. LNCS, vol. 8437, pp. 195–215. Springer, Heidelberg (2014)
22. Kerschbaum, F.: Public-key encrypted bloom filters with applications to supply chain integrity. In: Li, Y. (ed.) Data and Applications Security and Privacy XXV. LNCS, vol. 6818, pp. 60–75. Springer, Heidelberg (2011)
23. Kerschbaum, F.: Outsourced private set intersection using homomorphic encryption. In: Youm, H.Y., Won, Y. (eds.) ASIACCS 2012, pp. 85–86. ACM Press, May 2012
24. Kiayias, A., Mitrofanova, A.: Testing disjointness of private datasets. In: S. Patrick, A., Yung, M. (eds.) FC 2005. LNCS, vol. 3570, pp. 109–124. Springer, Heidelberg (2005)
25. Kissner, L., Song, D.: Privacy-preserving set operations. In: Shoup, V. (ed.) CRYPTO 2005. LNCS, vol. 3621, pp. 241–257. Springer, Heidelberg (2005)
26. Many, D., Burkhart, M., Dimitropoulos, X.: Tech. Rep. TIK report no. 345, ETH Zurich, Switzerland (2012)
27. Papapetrou, O., Siberski, W., Nejdl, W.: Cardinality estimation and dynamic length adaptation for bloom filters. Distributed and Parallel Databases **28**(2–3), 119–156 (2010)
28. Pinkas, B., Schneider, T., Zohner, M.: Faster private set intersection based on OT extension. In: Proceedings of the 23rd USENIX Security Symposium, San Diego, CA, USA, August 20–22, pp. 797–812. USENIX Association (2014)
29. Tarkoma, S., Rothenberg, C.E., Lagerspetz, E.: Theory and practice of bloom filters for distributed systems. IEEE Communications Surveys and Tutorials **14**(1), 131–155 (2012)

A   The Two-Party Case

In the two-party case it seems inevitable to rely on public-key cryptography and computations on encrypted data. Our solution here utilizes the homomorphic property of the ElGamal encryption scheme. In the full version we discuss that it is computationally secure under the decisional Diffie-Hellman assumption. In contrast to the other protocols, the protocol here provides perfect correctness.

Our protocol has the interesting feature that the major part of computational complexity lies on one side, supporting typical client-server scenarios: While one party has to perform $2m$ exponentiations to create the m ElGamal encryptions of the m Bloom filter entries, the other party merely needs to compute two exponentiations and up to $2m + 2$ multiplications. In contrast to our previous protocols, the result of the protocol is perfectly correct.

The protocol in Figure 5 works as follows. First the parties will compute the intersection of the Bloom filters. For this party 1 encrypts the entries $\mathrm{BF}_1[i]$ of its Bloom filter bitwise as $g^{1-\mathrm{BF}_1[i]}$ to $(R_i, S_i) = (g^{r_i}, pk^{r_i} \cdot g^{1-\mathrm{BF}_1[i]})$ for random r_i. Among these m pairs, party 2 picks those for which its Bloom filter value $\mathrm{BF}_2[i]$ is 0, and multiplies them together (component-wise). To hide the choice of this subset, party 2 re-randomizes the result by multiplication with (g^s, pk^s). Note that, at this point, the obtained ciphertext (V, W) is an encryption of $g^{\sum_{i:\mathrm{BF}_2[i]=0}(1-\mathrm{BF}_1[i])}$, thus counting the number of entries i for which both filters are 0. Hence, if party 1 decrypts and determines this sum with at most m multiplications by comparing it to powers $g^0, g^1, g^2, \ldots g^m$, it obtains the size of the union of the filters by subtracting this sum from m.

Party 1	Party 2
input: Bloom filter BF_1 of size m	Bloom filter BF_2 of size m
pick (sk, pk) for ElGamal scheme over group $G = \langle g \rangle$ of prime order $q > m$	

for $i = 1$ **to** m **do:**
  pick $r_i \leftarrow \mathbb{Z}_q$
  set $(R_i, S_i) = (g^{r_i}, pk^{r_i} \cdot g^{1-\mathrm{BF}_1[i]})$	

$\xrightarrow{\quad pk, (R_i, S_i)_{i=1,2,\ldots,m} \quad}$	pick $s \leftarrow \mathbb{Z}_q$ compute $V = g^s \cdot \prod_{i:\mathrm{BF}_2[i]=0} R_i$ compute $W = pk^s \cdot \prod_{i:\mathrm{BF}_2[i]=0} S_i$
$\xleftarrow{\quad (V, W) \quad}$	
decrypt to $\Sigma = W \cdot V^{-sk}$ set $\sigma = 0$ //find σ with $\Sigma = g^\sigma$ **while** $\Sigma \neq 1$ and $\sigma \leq m$ **do** set $\Sigma \leftarrow \Sigma \cdot g^{-1}$ and $\sigma \leftarrow \sigma + 1$	
output: $m - \sigma$ //assume that party 1 sends the sum to party 2, too	

Fig. 5. Two-Party Protocol based on Bloom filters and the ElGamal encryption scheme

Symmetric Constructions

Generalizing PMAC Under Weaker Assumptions

Nilanjan Datta[1]($\boxtimes$) and Kan Yasuda[2]

[1] Indian Statistical Institute, Kolkata 203, B.T. Road, Kolkata 700108, India
nilanjan_isi_jrf@yahoo.com
[2] NTT Secure Platform Laboratories, 3-9-11 Midoricho Musashino-shi,
Tokyo 180-8585, Japan
yasuda.kan@lab.ntt.co.jp

Abstract. In this paper, we study the security of PMAC-type constructions generalizing the underlying primitive to keyed functions. We first consider the construction with two different primitives: one for intermediate calls and another for finalization. While the security of original PMAC was based on the assumption that the primitive (block ciphers) is a pseudo-random permutation (PRP), here we show that for MAC security of the construction, we just need MAC security of the internal primitives and privacy-preserving MAC (PP-MAC) security for the finalization primitive. As PP-MAC is strictly weaker than a pseudo-random function (PRF), this shows that *PRF assumption on underlying primitives is not a necessary condition to achieve MAC security* of PMAC type constructions. In the context, we also show that for PRF security of the construction, we only need the finalization primitive to be PRF secure. The requirement on the internal primitive reduces from PRF to just a secure MAC. Moreover, we show that for MAC security of the construction, PRF security of underlying primitive is not essential. We claim that, if we restrict to use only one primitive (as two keys are required, if two different primitives are used) then for MAC security, the primitive only needs to be PP-MAC secure. This essentially makes the construction single key PP-MAC domain extender, having the parallelizability advantage over iCBC-MAC. We also show that, if we want the construction to be PRF secure, then we need the underlying primitive to be PRF secure. This can be thought as an alternative proof of the original PMAC, not restricted to block-ciphers only but takes care any keyed functions.

Keywords: MAC · PMAC · Privacy preserving · Regular · Finalization

1 Introduction

Message Authenticated Codes. A message authentication code (MAC) is a symmetric-key algorithm that ensures the integrity of a message. A popular way of constructing a MAC scheme is to build it from a symmetric-key primitive,

---

Nilanjan Datta—The work of the paper was performed during the first author's internship at NTT.

E. Foo and D. Stebila (Eds.): ACISP 2015, LNCS 9144, pp. 433–450, 2015.
DOI: 10.1007/978-3-319-19962-7_25

such as a block cipher or a compression function. These "small" primitives take only fixed-length inputs, while a MAC scheme should be able to process variable-length messages. A straightforward approach to this problem is to iterate primitives in a certain orderly manner. For example, the NIST-standardized CMAC [8] iterates a block cipher in CBC mode, and the widely-deployed HMAC [2] iterates a compression function in the style of Merkle-Damgård construction.

PMAC. In this paper we focus on a construction called PMAC, which was developed by Black and Rogaway in 2002 [6]. PMAC improves upon the XOR MAC [1], which was parallelizable but not deterministic. We consider the efficiency of PMAC particularly advantageous. Indeed, PMAC iterates a block cipher in a fully parallelizable way, unlike CMAC or HMAC, both of which are structurally serial. Moreover, PMAC is rate-1, requiring just 1 block-cipher invocation per message block.

PMAC Variants and Security Proofs. PMAC is provided with proofs of security. In the original paper of PMAC [6] Black and Rogaway showed that PMAC is a variable-input-length pseudo-random function (PRF), and hence MAC-secure, assuming the underlying block cipher to be a pseudo-random permutation (PRP).

Subsequently, Rogaway introduced a new version of PMAC [11], where the mask update function, which had originally used Gray code, was replaced with "doubling" over a finite field. This new version of PMAC made it clear that the construction could be viewed as being based on a tweakable block cipher, and the security proof could be recast in the framework of a tweakable PRP. For this framework, it is crucial that the underlying block cipher E_K be a PRP. In particular, the proofs are based on the fact that the secret mask $L = E_K(0)$ is indistinguishable from a random value.

In addition, Sarkar presented a variant called iPMAC [12]. The iPMAC construction improves upon PMAC in the way of generating and updating secret masks. The security proof of iPMAC is also based on the assumption that the underlying primitive is a PRP/PRF.

Motivation Behind the Work. To summarize, we see that existing proofs of PMAC heavily rely on the PRP assumption about the block cipher and as a result prove that PMAC is not only MAC-secure but a PRF. However, we note that the notion of PRF is strictly stronger than a secure MAC. In fact, there are plenty of existing constructions [4,9,14] whose MAC security can be proven based on weaker-than-PRF assumptions about the underlying primitives. So let us pose the following basic question:

Q. Is the PRP/PRF assumption about the underlying primitive essential for the MAC security of PMAC-type constructions?

Table 1. Summary of our results

| PMAC - Type | Assumption on Primitive | | Achieved |
	(Internal)	(External)	
Two Key	MAC	PRF	PRF
//	MAC	PP-MAC	PP-MAC
One Key	PRF		PRF
//	PP-MAC		PP-MAC

This is our main motivation. In this paper we make attempts to identify the essential requirements on the underlying primitives in PMAC-type constructions. Our answer to the above question is negative. We obtain fairly subtle but significant results; we succeed in weakening the PRP/PRF assumption, but we do so only when slightly modifying the original PMAC construction.

Observations on Primitive Requirements. Before we state our results, let us explain why we considered that the answer to the above question was possibly negative. Our speculation was based on the following two observations:

- Finalization Specificity. We note a substantial difference between the security requirement on the internal primitive used for intermediate calls and that on the external primitive used for finalization. For example, the composition $G \circ \mathcal{F}$ is a PRF if G is a PRF and $\mathcal{F}$ a computationally almost universal function. Then the internal $\mathcal{F}$ can be constructed via universal hash functions or via differentially uniform functions. The former can be realized by, for example, multiplications over a finite field [13] and the latter by, for example, 4-round AES [10]. On the other hand, the external G needs to be a full-fledged primitive, such as the full, 10-round AES.

- Block-Cipher Specificity. A block cipher is a rather "disproportionate" primitive for constructing MACs. A block cipher is a keyed permutation, but generally its inverse does not get invoked for message authentication. Being a permutation often hinders our understanding of the exact requirements on the primitive; the fact that for a construction to be MAC secure, the block cipher needs to be a PRP does not automatically imply that a keyed function used instead must also be a PRF.

1.1   Our Contributions

Table 1 summarizes our results. We prove security of four constructions. The details are as follows:

1. Two-Key Generalized PMAC version. We generalize PMAC version by separating the intermediate calls from the finalization call. We do this by using two different keyed functions (compressed or), each having an independent key.

(a) In this setting we first show that, to achieve MAC security of the construction, PRF security of underlying primitives are *not necessary*. We show that, if the underlying external primitive is a privacy preserving MAC (PP-MAC), which is strictly weaker than PRF and the internal primitive is just MAC secure, then the construction is PP-MAC secure.

(b) Then we show that, in order to achieve PRF security of the construction, we need PRF security of the external primitive and MAC security of the internal primitives. As the block-cipher is one particular keyed function, the result shows that even for the original PMAC construction, we need the PRF security for the last block-cipher only. Just MAC-security of the internal block-ciphers is good enough to produce the PRF security of construction.

2. One-Key Generalized PMAC Version. Now, we consider the PMAC versions where only one key is being used meaning that we use only a single keyed function that acts both as internal as well as external primitive. For this scenario, we obtain the following results:

(a) We show that, if the underlying function is PP-MAC secure, then the construction is also a PP-MAC. Imporatance of this result is that, we can view this construction as the best known single-key domain extension of PP-MAC that has the following advantages over the construction iCBC-MAC [14]: (i) Unlike iCBC-MAC which is inherently sequential, this construction has the advantage of being fully parallelizable and (ii) One can use non-compressing functions as the underlying keyed function.

(b) Now, we show that if the underlying function is a PRF secure then the construction is PRF secure. This can be viewed as an alternative proof of the original PMAC which is not just restricted to block-ciphers, but also for generalized keyed functions.

Note that, for regular functions like block-cipher, the notion PP-MAC and PRF are equivalent. So, if we use block-cipher as underlying function, then for two key version, we need the finalize block-cipher to be PRF secure and for one key version, we need the underlying block-cipher to be PRF secure, even for the MAC security.

Practical Significance of Our Results. Using the result, potentially we might be able to construct a faster-than-PMAC mode of operation using a full round AES as external primitive and a reduced round AES as internal primitive assuming that round-shaved AES still is MAC-secure. To realize the construction by using a keyed function, one can use compression function of SHA-1 or SHA-2, making it keyed via IV. We note that the SHA instruction set will become soon available on Intel x86 platforms.

2 Preliminaries

2.1 Security Definitions

In this section we provide the definitions of cAU, MAC, PP-MAC and PRF security notions. Here we assume $\mathcal{A}$ to be a probabilistic adversary with it's random coin $r_{\mathcal{A}}$.

cAU (computationally Almost Universal). A keyed function F_K is sayed to have computationally almost universal if no adversary can find two messages (M, M') for which $F_K(M) = F_K(M')$ holds. The adversary doesn't have any oracle access of the function F_K. For formally, we define the *cAU advantage* of an adversary $\mathcal{A}$ against the scheme F_K as:

$$\mathbf{Adv}_F^{\mathrm{cAU}}(\mathcal{A}) \triangleq \Pr_{r_{\mathcal{A}}, K}[(M, M') \leftarrow \mathcal{A}, \ F_K(M) = F_K(M'), \ M \neq M']. \quad (1)$$

The keyed function F_K is called (t, ϵ)-cAU if for all collision adversaries $\mathcal{A}$ with complexity at most t has at most ϵ *cAU-advantage*.

MAC (Message Authentication Code). Message Authentication Code (MAC) is used to ensure the "integrity" of the message by sending a tag $T = F_K(M)$ along with the message M. The pair (M, T) is called a *valid pair*. The receiver verifies whether the obtained pair is valid or not. As far as security is concerned, a MAC needs to ensure that even if an adversary $\mathcal{A}$ possess some tagged messages (may be of adversary's own choice), it must not be able produce a valid tag corresponding to a new message, called *fresh* valid pair. More formally, we define the *MAC advantage* of a forgery adversary $\mathcal{A}$ against the scheme F as follows.

$$\mathbf{Adv}_F^{\mathrm{MAC}}(\mathcal{A}) \triangleq \Pr_{r_{\mathcal{A}}, K}[(M, T) \leftarrow \mathcal{A}^{F_K}, \ (M, T) \text{ is a fresh valid pair}]. \quad (2)$$

The algorithm F is called (t, q, ϵ)-mac if for any forgery adversary $\mathcal{A}$ making at most q queries with (time) complexity at most t has mac-advantage at most ϵ.

PP-MAC (Privacy-Preserving MAC). The notion of PP-MAC [4] is a combination of unforgeability and left or right indistinguishability. We already have the notion of MAC. Now we define the notion of privacy preservation. Let $G_K : X \to Y$ be a function family. The left oracle picks a key $K \leftarrow \mathcal{K}$ at the beginning of each experiment and replies $y = G_K(x)$ upon query (x, x'), whereas the right oracle replies $G_K(x')$ upon query (x, x'). The advantage of an adversary $\mathcal{A}$ to distinguish the left oracle to the right is given by,

$$\mathbf{Adv}_G^{\mathrm{PP}}(\mathcal{A}) \triangleq \Pr_{r_{\mathcal{A}}, K}[\mathcal{A}^{G_K(\mathsf{Left})} = 1] - \Pr_{r_{\mathcal{A}}, K}[\mathcal{A}^{G_K(\mathsf{Right})} = 1]. \quad (3)$$

Note that here we consider that the queries made by the adversary $\mathcal{A}$ are legitimate: $(x_i = x_j) \Leftrightarrow (x_i' = x_j')$. This means that the values $x_1, x_2, \ldots$ are all distinct, and so are $x_1', x_2', \ldots$, except when A repeats its queries.

PRF (Pseudo Random Function). The notion of PRF [7] is used for indistinguishability of a keyed function from a random function chosen at random. Let G_K be the keyed function. We define the distinguishing advantage of $\mathcal{A}$ distinguishing G_K from a function \$ chosen uniformly at random, as:

$$\mathbf{Adv}_G^{\mathrm{PRF}}(\mathcal{A}) \triangleq \mathrm{Pr}_{r_{\mathcal{A}},K}[\mathcal{A}^{G_K} = 1] - \mathrm{Pr}_{r_{\mathcal{A}},\$}[\mathcal{A}^{\$} = 1]. \tag{4}$$

We define the maximum prf-advantage $\mathbf{Adv}_G^{\mathrm{prf}}(q, \sigma, t) = \max_{\mathcal{A}} \mathbf{Adv}_G^{\mathrm{prf}}(\mathcal{A})$ where the maximum most q with the total number of blocks at most σ.

2.2   Known Implications Among PRF, PP-MAC, MAC and cAU

In this subsection, we briefly discuss the known implications among the above mentioned security definitions.

Relation between PP and MAC

(I) PP $\nRightarrow$ MAC: A constant function $G_K = 0$ is PP-secure but not MAC.
(II) MAC $\nRightarrow$ PP: Let G_K is secure MAC. Now the function $G'_K(x) = G_K(x)||lsb(x)$ is also a secure MAC but it's not PP.

Relation between PRF and PPMAC

(I) PRF $\Rightarrow$ PP-MAC: One can easily show that any (t, q, ϵ)-PRF G is $(t', q - 1, \epsilon - \frac{1}{2^n})$-MAC [5] and any (t, q, ϵ)-PRF G is $(t, q, \frac{\epsilon}{2})$-PP [4] for some $t' \approx t$.

(II) PP-MAC $\nRightarrow$ PRF: Consider the construction $G'_K(M) = G_K(M)||0$. It is easy to check that G'_K is a PP-MAC as G_K is PP-MAC but it is clearly not PRF as the last bit of G'_k is always 0.

(III) Regular + PP $\Rightarrow$ PRF: This can be shown from the following two known results:
(a) PP $\Rightarrow$ ROR: In [3], Bellare et al showed that PP and ROR are identical notions.
(b) Regular + ROR $\Rightarrow$ PRF: Let $G_K : D \rightarrow R$ be a regular function. This implies that if we choose r randomly from D and r' randomly from R; then $G_K(r)$ and r' are indistinguishable. Now by ROR property, we know that for any $M \in D$, $G_K(M)$ and $G_K(r)$ are indistinguishable. So these two imply $G_K(M)$ and r' are indistinguishable - implying the PRF security of G_K.

Relation between MAC and cAU

MAC $\Rightarrow$ cAU: It is easy to see that any $(t, 1, \epsilon)$-MAC G is (t, ϵ)-cAU as whenever an adversary against cAU finds a collision (M_1, M_2), the MAC adversary can query for M_1 to get a response T and forge for (M_2, T).

cAU $\nRightarrow$ MAC: It is easy to see that, the identity function $F_K(x) = x$ is cAU as no collision occurs but not MAC as the forger can easily forge even without making any queries.

Composition Results

(I) If g is a PP-MAC and H is a cAU then the composition $g \circ H$ is a PP-MAC.

(II) If g is a PRF and H is a cAU then their composition $g \circ H$ is a secure PRF.

Both of these composition results were given by Bellare in [4].

3 PMAC Based Generalized Constructions

Here we consider the generalized PMAC construction. It uses two primitives: internal primitive $F : \mathcal{K} \times \{0,1\}^m \to \{0,1\}^n$ and external primitive $G : \mathcal{K} \times \{0,1\}^m \to \{0,1\}^n$. For a message M, the tag T is generated as follows:

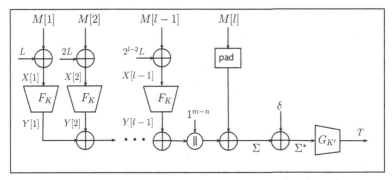

Fig. 1. Pictorial representation of the generalized PMAC

$$K, K' \xleftarrow{\$} \{0,1\}^{\mathcal{K}}$$
$$\Sigma^* \leftarrow H_{K,K'}(M)$$
$$T \leftarrow G_{K'}(\Sigma^*)$$

The description of $H_{K,K'}$ function on input M is given by the following equations:

$$L \leftarrow G_{K'}(0)||0^{m-n}$$
$$X[i] \leftarrow M[i] \oplus 2^{i-1}.L \quad \text{for } i = 1 \text{ to } (l-1)$$
$$Y[i] \leftarrow F_K(X[i]) \quad \text{for } i = 1 \text{ to } (l-1)$$
$$\Sigma \leftarrow ((Y[1] \oplus Y[2] \oplus \cdots \oplus Y[l-1])||1^{m-n}) \oplus \text{pad}(M[l])$$
$$\delta \leftarrow \begin{cases} 3.2^{l-2}.L & \text{if } |M[l]| = m \\ 5.2^{l-2}.L & \text{else} \end{cases}$$
$$\Sigma^* \leftarrow \Sigma \oplus \delta$$

We will consider the following two versions of PMAC type constructions which uses the above structure:

- PMAC$_{\text{TK}}[K, K']$ (PMAC Two-key version). Here we consider two different primitives: internal keyed function F_K and the external keyed function $G_{K'}$ where K and K' are two independent keys chosen uniformly at random from the key space.

- PMAC$_{\text{OK}}[K]$ (PMAC One-key version). Here we consider only one underlying keyed function F_K, which acts as both the internal and the external primitive. Again K has to be chosen uniformly at random from the key space.

4   Security of PMAC$_{\text{TK}}$ and PMAC$_{\text{OK}}$

In this section, we show the security of Generalized PMAC two key and one key version (PMAC$_{\text{TK}}$ and PMAC$_{\text{OK}}$ respectively) under different assumptions on the internal and external primitive. In fact we show the following:

- If F is MAC-secure and G is PP-MAC secure then PMAC$_{\text{TK}}$ is PP-MAC secure.
- If F is MAC-secure and G is PRF secure then PMAC$_{\text{TK}}$ is PRF secure.
- If F is PP-MAC secure then PMAC$_{\text{OK}}$ is PP-MAC secure.
- If F is PRF secure then PMAC$_{\text{OK}}$ is PRF secure.

More formally, the security of PMAC$_{\text{TK}}$ and PMAC$_{\text{OK}}$ are given by the following 4 theorems:

Theorem 1. *Any (t, q) oracle adversary, having an aggregate length of σ blocks, can break PP-MAC security of PMAC$_{\text{TK}}$ with only negligible probability:*

$$\mathbf{Adv}^{\text{MAC}}_{\text{PMAC}_{\text{TK}}[K,K']}(t, q) \leq \mathbf{Adv}^{\text{MAC}}_{G}(t, q) + \mathbf{Adv}^{\text{PP}}_{G}(t, q) + \epsilon_1 + \epsilon'_1$$
$$\mathbf{Adv}^{\text{PP}}_{\text{PMAC}_{\text{TK}}[K,K']}(t, q) \leq \mathbf{Adv}^{\text{PP}}_{G}(t, q) + \mathbf{Adv}^{\text{MAC}}_{G}(t, q) + \epsilon_1 + \epsilon'_1$$

where $\epsilon_1 = \binom{q}{2}.l.\mathbf{Adv}^{\text{MAC}}_{F}(t + O(l),\ 2l - 3) + \mathbf{Adv}^{\text{MAC}}_{G}(t, 0)$ and $\epsilon'_1 = \binom{\sigma-q}{2}.\mathbf{Adv}^{\text{MAC}}_{G}(t, 0) + q.\mathbf{Adv}^{\text{MAC}}_{F}(t + O(l),\ l - 2)$.

Theorem 2. *Any (t, q) oracle adversary, having an aggregate length of σ blocks, to distinguish PMAC$_{\text{TK}}$ from a random function has negligible prf advantage:*

$$\mathbf{Adv}^{\text{PRF}}_{\text{PMAC}_{\text{TK}}[K,K']}(t, q) \leq \mathbf{Adv}^{\text{PRF}}_{G}(t + O(\sigma), \sigma) + \epsilon_2 + \epsilon'_2$$

where $\epsilon_2 = \binom{q}{2}.l.\mathbf{Adv}^{\text{MAC}}_{F}(t + O(l),\ 2l - 3) + \frac{1}{2^n}$ and $\epsilon'_2 = \frac{\binom{\sigma-q}{2}}{2^n} + q.\mathbf{Adv}^{\text{MAC}}_{F}(t + O(l),\ l - 2)$.

Theorem 3. *Any (t, q) oracle adversary, having an aggregate length of σ blocks, can break PP-MAC security of PMAC$_{\text{OK}}$ with only negligible probability:*

$$\mathbf{Adv}^{\text{MAC}}_{\text{PMAC}_{\text{OK}}[K]}(t, q) \leq \mathbf{Adv}^{\text{MAC}}_{F}(t + O(\sigma), \sigma + l) + \mathbf{Adv}^{\text{PP}}_{F}(t + O(\sigma), \sigma)$$
$$+ 2(\sigma + \sigma^2).\mathbf{Adv}^{\text{MAC}}_{F}(t + O(l), 2l)$$
$$\mathbf{Adv}^{\text{PP}}_{\text{PMAC}_{\text{OK}}[K]}(t, q) \leq 3.\mathbf{Adv}^{\text{PP}}_{F}(t + O(\sigma), 2.\sigma) + 4(\sigma + \sigma^2).\mathbf{Adv}^{\text{MAC}}_{F}(t + O(l), 2l)$$

Theorem 4. *Any (t, q) oracle adversary, having an aggregate length of σ blocks, to distinguish $\mathrm{PMAC_{OK}}$ from a random function has negligible prf advantage:*

$$\mathbf{Adv}^{\mathrm{PRF}}_{\mathrm{PMAC_{OK}}[K]}(t, q) \leq \mathbf{Adv}^{\mathrm{PRF}}_{F}(t + O(\sigma), \sigma) + \frac{2(\sigma + \sigma^2)}{2^n}$$

Note that, by (t, q) oracle adversary we mean an adversary that can make at most q many queries to the oracle and has time complexity at most t and l denotes the maximum block length of an adversarial query.

High-level proof idea of these theorems:

- The main idea is that, we can show the function $H(\cdot)$ is computationally Almost Universal (cAU) function i.e. there will be no collision in the value Σ^* for any 2 of the q messages. Infact, we will show that, if there is a collision in Σ^* for any two distinct messages, then using that information an adversary can break the MAC or PRF security of the underlying primitives, with very high probability, which violates our assumptions.

- Now, using the fact that the composition of a PP-MAC with a cAU is indeed a PP-MAC [4]; we prove theorem 1. For theorem 2, we use the fact that the composition of cAU with a PRF is indeed a PRF [4]. Theorem 3 and 4 are basically careful extensions of Theorem 1 and 2 which incorporating only one-key using a technique similar to the one, used in the proof of iCBC-MAC [14].

4.1   Security of Generalized PMAC (Two Key) Version

Consider a (t, q)-adversary which runs in $O(t)$ time and can make at most q distinct queries say $M_1, \ldots, M_q$. Let $l_i := |M_i|$ denote the length of message M_i in blocks where a block consists of n bits. By $M_i[j]$, we denotes the jth block of message M_i. We similarly define $X_i[j], Y_i[j], \Sigma_i$. By our assumption $\sigma = \sum_{i=1}^{q} l_i$. We denote $\overline{E}$ as the complement of the event E and $\overline{E}_{1..j}$ as the event $\wedge_{i=1}^{j} \overline{E}_i$. We call two message $M_j[1..l_j]$ and $M_k[1..l_k]$ to be *identical*, if one of them has full final block and the other has an incomplete final block and $l_j = l_k$, $\forall i < l_j$, $M_j[i] = M_k[i]$, $pad(M_j[l_j]) = pad(M_k[l_j])$. Now we define the following events:

COLL_j: It is event that there is a collision for the jth message with one of it's previous message. More formally, we can write it as the event $\{\Sigma_j^* = \Sigma_i^*$, for some $i < j\}$.

BAD_j: It is the event that a non-trivial collision occurs in the inputs of the internal primitive or the external primitive while processing the jth message. For the two key versions, it means a non-trivial collision in some X variables (internal primitive F) or a non-trivial collision in Σ and 0 in the external primitive G.

Now we state and prove a very important lemma on how to bound the collision probability for generalized PMAC based constructions:

Lemma 1. *If* $\forall j \leq q$, *(i)* $\Pr[COLL_j \mid \overline{COLL}_{1..(j-1)} \wedge \overline{BAD}_j] \leq \epsilon_{j1}$ *and* *(ii)* $\Pr[BAD_j \mid \overline{COLL}_{1..(j-1)}] \leq \epsilon_{j2}$, *then* $\Pr[COLL] \leq \sum_{j=1}^{q}(\epsilon_{j1} + \epsilon_{j2})$.

Proof. The proof of lemma is provided through the following set of equalities:

$$\Pr[COLL] \leq \Pr[\vee_{j=1}^{q}(COLL_j \wedge \overline{COLL}_{1..(j-1)})]$$

$$\leq \sum_{j=1}^{q}\Pr[(COLL_j \wedge \overline{COLL}_{1..(j-1)})]$$

$$\leq \sum_{j=1}^{q}\Pr[COLL_j \wedge \overline{COLL}_{1..(j-1)} \wedge \overline{BAD}_j] + \sum_{j=1}^{q}\Pr[COLL_j \wedge \overline{COLL}_{1..(j-1)} \wedge BAD_j]$$

$$\leq \sum_{j=1}^{q}\Pr[COLL_j \mid \overline{COLL}_{1..(j-1)} \wedge \overline{BAD}_j] + \sum_{j=1}^{q}\Pr[BAD_j \mid \overline{COLL}_{1..(j-1)}]$$

$$\leq \sum_{j=1}^{q}\epsilon_{j1} + \epsilon_{j2}$$

(I) If F is MAC-secure and G is PP-MAC secure then the generalized PMAC is PP-MAC secure.

In this subsection, we prove that MAC security of F and PP-MAC security of G is good enough to make the construction PP-MAC security of G-PMAC. More formally, we will prove theorem 1. For that, we first bound ϵ_{j1} and ϵ_{j2} for MAC secure F and PP-MAC secure G and then apply those results in lemma 1 to obtain our result. First we state and prove the two lemmas:

Lemma 2. *If F is a MAC and G is a PP-MAC, then for* $PMAC_{TK}$,

$$\epsilon_{j1} \leq (j-1).(l-1).\mathbf{Adv}_F^{MAC}(t + O(l), 2l - 3) + \mathbf{Adv}_G^{MAC}(t, 0).$$

Proof. Suppose the event $COLL_j$ occurs. Then one of the following two cases occur:

- **Case 1.** Collision occur in M_j with a message which are not identical: This case yields a non-trivial equation of $Y := F_K(X)$ variables, which can be used by adversary $\mathcal{A}_1$ (runs in time $t + O(l)$) which uses the collision of two non-identical messages to break the MAC security of F_K with probability $\frac{1}{(l-1).(j-1)}$, making at most $(2l-3)$-many queries. This ensures that the probability of occuring this case can be bounded by $(l-1).(j-1).Adv_F^{MAC}(t + O(l), 2l-3)$.

- **Case 2.** Collision occurs in M_j with an identical message. In this case, we obtain the non-trivial equation $L := G_{K'}(0) = 0$, which can be used by an adversary to forge with $(0,0)$ against the external primitive $G_{K'}$. So, the probability of occuring this case can be bounded by $\mathbf{Adv}_G^{MAC}(t, 0)$.

The lemma follows from the two cases.

Lemma 3. *If F is a MAC and G is a PP-MAC, then for* $PMAC_{TK}$,

---

Adversary $\mathcal{A}_1$

1 $K' \leftarrow_\$ \{0,1\}^n$; $L \leftarrow G_{K'}(0)||0^{m-n}$; choose $k \leftarrow_\$ [1..(j-1)]$

2 For $i = 1..(l_j - 1)$ and $i' = 1..(l_k - 1)$

3    $X_j[i] \leftarrow M_j[i] \oplus 2^{i-1}L$; $X_k[i'] \leftarrow M_k[i'] \oplus 2^{i'-1}L$

4 Choose $c \leftarrow_\$ [1..(l_j - 1)]$

5 For $i = 1..(l_j - 1)$ except $i = c$,

6    $Y_j[i] = F_K(X_j[i])$

7 For $i = 1..(l_k - 1)$

8    $Y_k[i] = F_K(X_k[i])$

9 $Y_j[c] \leftarrow ((\sum_{i \neq c} Y_j[i] + \sum_i Y_j[i])||1^{m-n}) + \delta_{M_j} + \delta_{M_k} + pad(M_k[l_k]) + pad(M_j[l_j])$

10 Forge F_K with $(X_j[c], Y_j[c])$

Algorithm 1: From COLL to Forge.

$$\epsilon_{j2} \leq [\binom{l_j - 1}{2} + (l_j - 1).(\sum_{i=1}^{j-1}(l_i - 1))].\mathbf{Adv}_G^{MAC}(t, 0) + \mathbf{Adv}_F^{MAC}(t + O(l), l - 2)$$

Proof. Here we show, how to bound the probabilities of the BAD events i.e non-trivial collisions in the internal primitive F_K or the external primitive $G_{K'}$. Note that, the event BAD_j (BAD event while processing j^{th} message) occurs, if one of these three events occurs:

- Event E_1 ($\exists k \neq k'$, $X_j[k] = X_j[k']$): This is a collision in internal primitive F_K occurs in two different X blocks of jth Message. Now, one can claim that, $\Pr[E_1|\overline{COLL}_{1..(j-1)}] \leq \binom{l_j}{2}.\mathbf{Adv}_G^{MAC}(t, 0)$. Note that, for any pair (k, k'), $X_j[k] = X_j[k']$ gives rise to the non-trivial equation $L := G_{K'}(0) = (\frac{M_j[k] + M_j[k']}{2^{k-1} + 2^{k'-1}})_n$, which can be used to forge against G with $(0, L)$. The result follows as there can be atmost $\binom{l_j - 1}{2}$ many (k, k') pairs.

- Event E_2 ($\exists j' < j$, $k \neq k'$, $X_j[k] = X_{j'}[k']$): This is a collision in internal primitive F_K occurs in a X block of jth Message with another X block in j'^{th} Message. Using the similar idea as used for event E_1, one can easily show that, $\Pr[E_2|\overline{COLL}_{1..(j-1)}] \leq (l_j - 1).(\sum_{i=1}^{j-1}(l_i - 1)).\mathbf{Adv}_G^{MAC}(t, 0)$.

- Event E_3 ($\Sigma_j^* = 0$): If $\Sigma_j^* = 0$, then we have a non-trivial equation of F_K of X variables: $\sum_{i=1}^{l_j - 1} F_K(X_j[i]) = M_j[l_j] + \delta_{M_j}$, which can be used by an adversary (making at most $l - 2$ many queries) to forge the MAC security of F. More formally, one can show that, $\Pr[E_3|\overline{COLL}_{1..(j-1)}] \leq \mathbf{Adv}_F^{MAC}(t + O(l), l - 2)$.

Adding the probability of all these above mentioned Bad events, we obtain lemma 3. □

Proof of Theorem 1. To prove theorem 1, we apply lemma 2 and lemma 3 in lemma 1 and obtain the following relation:

$$\Pr[\mathsf{COLL}] \leq \sum_{j=1}^{q}(\epsilon_{j1} + \epsilon_{j2})$$

$$\leq \binom{q}{2}l.\mathbf{Adv}_F^{\mathrm{MAC}}(t + O(l),\ 2l - 3) + \mathbf{Adv}_G^{\mathrm{MAC}}(t, 0)$$

$$+\ [\ \binom{\sigma - q}{2}.\mathbf{Adv}_G^{\mathrm{MAC}}(t, 0) + q.\mathbf{Adv}_F^{\mathrm{MAC}}(t + O(l),\ l - 2)\ ]$$

The theorem follows as we put the value of $\Pr[\mathsf{COLL}]$ in the following equations:

$$\mathbf{Adv}_{\mathrm{PMAC}_{\mathrm{TK}}[K,K]}^{\mathrm{MAC}}(t, q) \leq \mathbf{Adv}_G^{\mathrm{MAC}}(t, q) + \mathbf{Adv}_G^{\mathrm{PP}}(t, q) + \Pr[\mathsf{COLL}]$$
$$\mathbf{Adv}_{\mathrm{PMAC}_{\mathrm{TK}}[K,K']}^{\mathrm{PP}}(t, q) \leq \mathbf{Adv}_G^{\mathrm{PP}}(t, q) + \mathbf{Adv}_G^{\mathrm{MAC}}(t, q) + \Pr[\mathsf{COLL}]$$

$\square$

Remark 1. This shows that, if we can use different internal and external primitives (which requires two different keys chosen uniformly at random), then to obtain MAC security, we only need PP-MAC security of the external primitive and MAC security of the internal primitives implying PRF security of primitives are not necessary.

(II) If F is MAC-secure and G is PRF Secure then PMAC$_{\mathrm{TK}}$ is PRF Secure.
Now, we look at the security of the construction when the finalizing function $G_{K'}$ is a PRF and prove the construction as PRF. The proof is identical to the previous proof. So, instead of providing the details once again, we just mention the places where it differs.

Lemma 4. *If F is a MAC and G is a PRF, then for* PMAC$_{\mathrm{TK}}$,

$$\epsilon_{j1} \leq (j - 1).(l - 1).\mathbf{Adv}_F^{\mathrm{MAC}}(t + O(l), 2l - 3) + \tfrac{1}{2^n}.$$

Proof. The proof is identical to Lemma 2 except that the probability of occuring case 2 is bounded by $\frac{1}{2^n}$ as G is considered as a PRF. As the forging probability of F is atleast $\frac{1}{2^n}$, the result follows. $\square$

Lemma 5. *If F is a MAC and G is a PRF, then for* PMAC$_{\mathrm{TK}}$,

$$\epsilon_{j2} \leq [\binom{l_j - 1}{2} + (l_j - 1).(\textstyle\sum_{i=1}^{j-1}(l_i - 1))].\tfrac{1}{2^n} + \mathbf{Adv}_F^{\mathrm{MAC}}(t + O(l),\ l - 2)$$

Proof. This proof is identical to Lemma 3 except that the probability of occuring case 1 and 2 is bounded by $\frac{1}{2^n}$ as G is considered as a PRF. $\square$

Proof of Theorem 2. To prove theorem 2, we apply lemma 4 and lemma 5 in lemma 1 and obtain the following relation:

$$
\Pr[\mathsf{COLL}] \leq \sum_{j=1}^{q} (\epsilon_{j1} + \epsilon_{j2})
$$

$$
\leq \binom{q}{2} . l. \mathbf{Adv}_F^{\mathrm{MAC}}(t + O(l), \ 2l - 3) + \frac{1}{2^n}
$$

$$
+ \ [\ \binom{\sigma - q}{2} . \frac{1}{2^n} + q. \mathbf{Adv}_F^{\mathrm{MAC}}(t + O(l), \ l - 2) \ ]
$$

The theorem follows as we put the value of $\Pr[\mathsf{COLL}]$ in the following equation:

$$
\mathbf{Adv}_{\mathrm{PMAC_{TK}}[K,K']}^{\mathrm{PRF}}(t,q) \ \leq \ \mathbf{Adv}_G^{\mathrm{PRF}}(t + O(\sigma), \sigma) + \Pr[\mathsf{COLL}]
$$

$\square$

Remark 2. If we consider only block-ciphers (of n bits) as the primitives, then also the above theorem holds as it is just a subcase of the General PMAC version. This shows that for PRF security of the original PMAC, we need PRF security only for external block-cipher and MAC security for the internal primitives.

4.2 Security of Generalized PMAC (One Key) Version

Now, we look at the security of the relaxed version of the generalized PMAC construction when we use only one key K and the function F_K is used both internal as well as external primitive. The proof idea is similar to the proof of iCBC-MAC, presented by Yasuda.

First we recall the definition of Higher-Order AU (hoau), introduced by Yasuda in [14]. The notion is as follows: A hoau-adversary A, given access to its oracle $F_K(\cdot)$, outputs a pair of distinct messages $M, M' \in \{0,1\}^*$. A's goal is to come up with such a pair as $H_K(M) = H_K(M')$, where H is defined in the definition of generalized PMAC. In order for A to succeed, the criteria is that M and M' needs to be fresh, meaning that, during the computation of $H_K(M)$ and $H_K(M')$, all the input values to F should be new, i.e., none of the input values to F has been queried by A to its oracle $F_K(\cdot)$. More formally,

$$
\mathbf{Adv}_F^{\mathrm{hoau}}(A) = \Pr[M, M' \text{ are fresh}, M \neq M', H_K(M) = H_K(M') | (M, M') \leftarrow A^{F_K(\cdot)}]
$$

Now we prove the important lemma which says that If F_K is a secure MAC then it is hoau:

Lemma 6. $\mathbf{Adv}_F^{\mathrm{hoau}}(t,q,l) \leq 4.l^2.Adv_F^{\mathrm{MAC}}(t + 2l - 1, q + 2l + 1)$

Proof. Here we provide a brief sketch of the proof. Detailed proof can be found in the full version. Let A be an adversary that runs in time at most t, makes q many queries to F_K oracle and outputs a pair of message (M, M') in order to attack the Hoau property of F. Now consider the following cases:

Case 1. Internal Input Collision: In this case there exists $i \neq j$ such that $X[i] = X'[j]$ or $X[i] = X[j]$ or $X'[i] = X'[j]$ occurs. Let the event be denoted as InColl. One can show that,

$$Pr[\text{InColl}] \leq (2l^2 - l).\mathbf{Adv}_F^{\text{MAC}}(t + O(1), 0)$$

Case 2. Internal Output Collision: In this case there exists i, j such that (i) $X[i] \neq X'[j]$ but $Y[i] = Y'[j]$ or (ii) $X[i] \neq X[j]$ but $Y[i] = Y[j]$ or (iii) $Y'[i] = Y'[j]$ occurs. Let the event be denoted as OutColl. One can show that,

$$Pr[\text{OutColl}] \leq (2l^2 - l).\mathbf{Adv}_F^{\text{MAC}}(t + O(1), 0)$$

Case 3. Final Output Collision: In this case no internal and external collision occurs we have $H_K(M) = H_K(M')$. Let the event be denoted as FinalColl. For this case, one can show that,

$$Pr[\text{FinalColl}] \leq l.\mathbf{Adv}_F^{\text{MAC}}(t + O(2l), 2l)$$

It is easy to see that whenever A succeeds, one of the following cases occur and hence we have the following hoau advantage

$$\begin{aligned}
\mathbf{Adv}_F^{\text{hoau}} &\leq Pr[\text{InColl} \wedge \text{OutColl} \wedge \text{FinalColl}] \\
&\leq Pr[\text{InColl}] + Pr[\text{OutColl}] + Pr[\text{FinalColl}] \\
&\leq 4l^2.\mathbf{Adv}_F^{\text{MAC}}(t + O(2l), 2l) \qquad \qquad \qquad \qquad \square
\end{aligned}$$

(I) If F is PP-MAC Secure then PMAC_{OK} is PP-MAC Secure. We'll prove it in two parts: first we prove the MAC part i.e. if F is PP-MAC secure then PMAC_{OK} is MAC secure and then we show the PP part i.e. if F is PP-MAC secure then PMAC_{OK} is PP secure.

Proof of Theorem 3. Suppose A be an adversary that runs at time at most t and makes exactly q distinct queries in order to attack the MAC security of the construction PMAC_{OK}. At the end A outputs (M', T') as the forgery. Now consider the two games G_1 and G_2:

Now observe that, if adversary $\mathcal{A}$ succeeds in forgery, then at least one of the events Forge, Zero or Coll occurs in game G_1. Note that, according to the game definition, these three events are disjoint. Hence we obtain,

$$\begin{aligned}
\mathbf{Adv}_F^{\text{MAC}}(A) &\leq Pr[G_1(A) \text{ sets Forge, Zero or Coll}] \\
&= Pr[G_1(A) \text{ sets Forge}] + Pr[G_1(A) \text{ sets Zero or Coll}] \\
&\quad - Pr[G_2(A) \text{ sets Zero or Coll}] + Pr[G_2(A) \text{ sets Zero or Coll}] \\
&= Pr[\text{Forge}] + (Pr[G_1(A) = 1] - Pr[G_2(A) = 1]) \\
&\quad + Pr[G_2(A) \text{ sets Zero}] + Pr[G_2(A) \text{ sets Coll}] \qquad (5)
\end{aligned}$$

Now consider the following cases:

Case 1. One can construct a forger $\mathcal{F}$, which makes at most $\sigma + l$ queries and

$\boxed{Game\ G_1(A)}$ Game $G_2(A)$

1 $K \leftarrow_\$ \{0,1\}^n;\ L \leftarrow F_K(0)||0; Y \leftarrow \phi$
2 $(M', T') \leftarrow A^{(\cdot)}$ where upon A's i-th query M do
3   For $j = 1, \ldots, (l-1)$
4          $X[j] = M[j] + 2^{j-1}.L;$ If $X[j] = 0$ set $Zero_1 \leftarrow 1$ Return 1
5          $Y[j] = F_K(X[j])$
6      $\Sigma^* = (Y[1] + \cdots + Y[l-1]||1) + pad(M[l]) + \delta_M$
7   If $\Sigma \in Y$ then $Coll \leftarrow 1;$ Return 1; If $\Sigma = 0$ then $Zero_2 \leftarrow 1;$ Return 1
8      $Y \leftarrow Y \cup \Sigma_i;\ \boxed{\Sigma_i \leftarrow <i>_m}$
9      $T \leftarrow F_K(\Sigma_i);$ Return T to A
10 For $j = 1, \ldots, (l'-1)$
11     $X'[j] = M'[j] + 2^{j-1}.L$
12   If $X'[j] = 0$ set $Zero_1 \leftarrow 1$ Return 1
13     $Y'[j] = F_K(X'[j])$
14 $(\Sigma')^* = (Y'[1] + \cdots + Y'[l-1]||1) + M'[l'] + \delta_{M'}$
15 If $(\Sigma')^* \in Y$ then $Coll \leftarrow 1;$ Return 1; If $(\Sigma')^* = 0$ then $Zero_2 \leftarrow 1;$ Return 1
16 $\boxed{\text{If } F_K((\Sigma')^*) = T' \text{ then Forge} \leftarrow 1}$ Return 0.

Algorithm 2: Game $G_1(A)$ and $G_2(A)$: Boxed statements are only for Game $G_1(A)$

succeeds in producing a forgery whenever the Forge event occurs. Hence, we obtain

$$Pr[\text{ Forge}] \leq \mathbf{Adv}_F^{MAC}(\mathcal{F})$$
$$\leq \mathbf{Adv}_F^{MAC}(t + O(\sigma), \sigma + l) \qquad (6)$$

Details of this forger can be found in the full version.

$\boxed{\text{Case 2}}$. One can construct a PP-adversary $\mathcal{D}$, which behaves as follows: if the oracle $\mathcal{O}$ with which $\mathcal{D}$ interacts is the Left F_K oracle, then running $\mathcal{D}^\mathcal{O}$ coincides with $G_1(A)$ and if oracle $\mathcal{O}$ is the Right F_K oracle, then $\mathcal{D}^\mathcal{O}$ coincides with $G_2(A)$. Details of $\mathcal{D}$ can be found in the full version. Using that distinguisher $\mathcal{D}$, one can show that,

$$Pr[G_1(A) = 1] - Pr[G_2(A) = 1] = Pr[\mathcal{D}^{\text{Left}} = 1] - Pr[\mathcal{D}^{\text{Right}} = 1]$$
$$= \mathbf{Adv}_F^{PP}(\mathcal{D}) \leq \mathbf{Adv}_F^{PP}(t + O(\sigma), \sigma + l)\,(7)$$

$\boxed{\text{Case 3.}}$ One can construct two adversaries $\mathcal{Z}_1$ and $\mathcal{Z}_2$ which makes at most l-many queries such that, whenever $Zero_1$ occurs in $G_2(A)$ then adversary $\mathcal{Z}_1$ breaks mac security of F with probability $\frac{1}{(q+1).(l-1)}$ and whenever $Zero_2$ occurs adversary $\mathcal{Z}_2$ breaks mac security of F with probability $\frac{1}{q+1}$. So, we have,

$$Pr[G_2(A) \text{ sets Zero}] = Pr[G_2(A) \text{ sets Zero}_1] + Pr[G_2(A) \text{ sets Zero}_2]$$
$$\leq (\sigma + l).\mathbf{Adv}_F^{MAC}(t + O(l), l) \qquad (8)$$

Case 4. Consider the adversary $\mathcal{C}$ which chooses α, β uniformly from $[1, q+1]$ and return $(M = M_\alpha, M' = M_\beta)$.

Given two integers $i, j : 1 \le i < j \le (q+1)$, let $\mathrm{Coll}_{i,j}$ denotes the event that the flag Coll in game G_2 gets set at A's j-th query in such a way as $\Sigma_i^* = \Sigma_j^*$. Note that the events $\mathrm{Coll}_{i,j}$ are disjoint. Now observe that adversary $\mathcal{C}$ wins in the hoau sense if the guessed values α, β coincide with i, j, because the message pair (M, M') is guaranteed to be fresh owing to the fact that Coll and Zero are disjoint in game G_2 by definition. Therefore, we have, $\mathbf{Adv}_F^{\mathrm{hoau}}(\mathcal{C}) \ge Pr[\vee_{i,j}(\mathrm{Coll}_{i,j} \wedge ?(i,j) = (\alpha, \beta))] = \sum_{i,j} Pr[\mathrm{Coll}_{i,j}].Pr[(i,j) = (\alpha, \beta)] = \frac{1}{\binom{q+1}{2}} Pr[G_2(A) \text{ sets Coll}]$ which imply,

$$Pr[G_2(A) \text{ sets Coll}] \le \binom{q+1}{2}.\mathbf{Adv}_F^{\mathrm{hoau}}(t, q)$$

$$\le \frac{4.\sigma^2}{2}.\mathbf{Adv}_F^{\mathrm{MAC}}(t + O(l), 2l) \qquad (9)$$

The first part of theorem 3, is obtained from the equation (5) to (9). Using similar idea, one can proof the PP part also. We skip the proof due to page limitation and can be found in the full version. □

Remark 3. This shows that, for single key generalized PMAC version, to obtain MAC security, we need only PP-MAC security of the underlying primitive, which is strictly weaker than PRF assumption. This beats the existing PP-MAC domain extender iCBC-MAC as this construction is parallel and there is no restriction in the domain and range size of the function.

(II) If F is PRF Secure then PMAC$_{\mathrm{OK}}$ is PRF Secure. Suppose A be a prf-adversary that runs at time at most t and makes exactly q distinct queries in order to attack PRF-security of the construction PMAC$_{\mathrm{OK}}$.

Proof of Theorem 4. Let $f : \{0,1\}^m \to \{0,1\}^n$ be a function chosen uniformly random. Consider the algorithm PMAC$_f : \{0,1\}^* \to \{0,1\}^n$ which is identical to PMAC$_{\mathrm{OK}}$ except that instead of F_K, it uses f. Suppose $\$: \{0,1\}^* \to \{0,1\}^n$ is a function chosen uniformly at random. Now, it is easy to check that

$$\mathbf{Adv}_F^{\mathrm{PRF}}(A) = Pr[A^{\mathrm{PMAC}_{\mathrm{OK}}} = 1] - Pr[A^\$ = 1]$$
$$= Pr[A^{\mathrm{PMAC}_{\mathrm{OK}}}] - Pr[A^{\mathrm{PMAC}_f}] + Pr[A^{\mathrm{PMAC}_f}] - Pr[A^\$ = 1]$$
$$\le \mathbf{Adv}_F^{\mathrm{PRF}}(t + O(\sigma), \sigma) + Pr[A^{\mathrm{PMAC}_f}] - Pr[A^\$ = 1] \qquad (10)$$

Now consider the game G_3 defined in algorithm 3.

Observe that, PMAC$_f$ behaves just like a true random function unless Zero or

---

Game $G_3(A)$

1 $K \leftarrow_\$ \{0,1\}^n; L \leftarrow F_K(0)\|0; Y \leftarrow \phi$

2 $b \leftarrow A^{(\cdot)}$ where on A's i-th query M do

3   For $j = 1, \ldots, (l-1)$

4          $X[j] = M[j] + 2^{j-1}.L$; If $X[j] = 0$ set Zero $\leftarrow 1$ Return 1

5          $Y[j] = f(X[j])$

6      $\Sigma^* = (Y[1] + \cdots + Y[l-1]\|1) + pad(M[l]) + \delta_M$

7   If $\Sigma^* \in Y$ then Coll $\leftarrow 1$; Return 1 ; Else $Y \leftarrow Y \cup \Sigma^*$

8      $T \leftarrow f(\Sigma^*)$; Return T to A

9 Return b

Algorithm 3: Description of Game $G_3(A)$

Coll occurs. Hence,

$$Pr[A^{\mathrm{PMAC}_f}] - Pr[A^\$ = 1] \leq Pr[A^{\mathrm{PMAC}_f} \text{ sets Zero or Coll}]$$

$$\leq \frac{q.l}{2^n} + 4l^2 . \binom{q}{2} . \frac{1}{2^n}$$

$$\leq \frac{\sigma + 2.\sigma^2}{2^n} \qquad (11)$$

Theorem 4 obtained from the equation (10) and (11).   □

Remark 4. If we consider only block-ciphers (of n bits) as primitive, then this can thought as an alternative security proof of the original PMAC.

5   Conclusions

In this paper we have shown that the underlying primitives used in PMAC-type constructions need not necessarily be PRF(PRP) in general. Specifically, we have proven that it suffices for the primitives to be PP-MAC, and under such conditions PMAC-type constructions are ensured to be secure MACs. An interesting case is when the primitive is a regular function, including the case of a permutation (block cipher). In such a case the requirement of PP-MAC becomes equivalent to that of PRF(PRP). In this paper we have also explored the case where two different primitives are used, one for intermediate calls and another for finalization. In this case, while the finalizing primitive still needs to be a PP-MAC, the internal primitive only needs to be a secure MAC. Therefore, when applied to a PMAC based on block ciphers using two independent keys, our result implies that it might be possible to use a faster, MAC-secure block cipher for the intermediate calls.

References

1. Bellare, M., Guérin, R., Rogaway, P.: XOR MACs: new methods for message authentication using finite pseudorandom functions. In: Coppersmith, D. (ed.) CRYPTO 1995. LNCS, vol. 963, pp. 15–28. Springer, Heidelberg (1995). §1
2. Bellare, M., Canetti, R., Krawczyk, H.: Keying hash functions for message authentication. In: Koblitz, N. (ed.) CRYPTO 1996. LNCS, vol. 1109, pp. 1–15. Springer, Heidelberg (1996). §1
3. Bellare, M., Desai, A., Jokipii, E., Rogaway, P.: A concrete security treatment of symmetric encryption. In: Proceedings of the 38th Annual Symposium on Foundations of Computer science, FOCS, vol. 394 (1997). §2.2
4. Bellare, M.: New proofs for NMAC and HMAC: security without collision-resistance. In: Dwork, C. (ed.) CRYPTO 2006. LNCS, vol. 4117, pp. 602–619. Springer, Heidelberg (2006). §2.1, §2.2, §2.2, §4, §4
5. Bellare, M., Goldrich, O., Mityagin, A.: The power of verification queries in message authentication and authenticated encryption. Cryptology ePrint Archive: Report 2004/309 (2004). §2.2
6. Black, J.A., Rogaway, P.: A block-cipher mode of operation for parallelizable message authentication. In: Knudsen, L.R. (ed.) EUROCRYPT 2002. LNCS, vol. 2332, pp. 384–397. Springer, Heidelberg (2002)
7. Goldreich, O., Goldwasser, S., Micali, S.: How to construct random functions. In: JACM 1986, pp. 792–807 (1986). §2.1
8. Iwata, T., Kurosawa, K.: OMAC: one-key CBC MAC. In: Johansson, T. (ed.) FSE 2003. LNCS, vol. 2887, pp. 129–153. Springer, Heidelberg (2003). §1
9. Maurer, U.M., Sjödin, J.: Single-key AIL-MACs from any FIL-MAC. In: Caires, L., Italiano, G.F., Monteiro, L., Palamidessi, C., Yung, M. (eds.) ICALP 2005. LNCS, vol. 3580, pp. 472–484. Springer, Heidelberg (2005)
10. Minematsu, K., Tsunoo, Y.: Provably secure MACs from differentially-uniform permutations and AES-based implementations. In: Robshaw, M. (ed.) FSE 2006. LNCS, vol. 4047, pp. 226–241. Springer, Heidelberg (2006). §1
11. Rogaway, P.: Efficient instantiations of tweakable blockciphers and refinements to modes OCB and PMAC. In: Lee, P.J. (ed.) ASIACRYPT 2004. LNCS, vol. 3329, pp. 16–31. Springer, Heidelberg (2004). §1
12. Sarkar, P.: Pesudo-Random functions and parallelizable modes of operations of a block cipher. IEEE Transaction on Information Theory **56**, 4025–4037 (2010). §1
13. Shoup, V.: On fast and provably secure message authentication based on universal hashing. In: Koblitz, N. (ed.) CRYPTO 1996. LNCS, vol. 1109, pp. 313–328. Springer, Heidelberg (1996). §1
14. Yasuda, K.: A single-key domain extender for privacy-preserving MACs and PRFs. In: Lee, P.J., Cheon, J.H. (eds.) ICISC 2008. LNCS, vol. 5461, pp. 268–285. Springer, Heidelberg (2009). §2a, §4, §4.2

sp-AELM: Sponge Based Authenticated Encryption Scheme for Memory Constrained Devices

Megha Agrawal$^{(\boxtimes)}$, Donghoon Chang, and Somitra Sanadhya

Indraprastha Institute of Information Technology, Delhi (IIIT-D), India
{meghaa,donghoon,somitra}@iiitd.ac.in

Abstract. In authenticated encryption schemes, there are two techniques for handling long ciphertexts while working within the constraints of a low buffer size: Releasing unverified plaintext (RUP) or Producing intermediate tags (PIT). In this paper, in addition to these two techniques, we propose another way to handle a long ciphertext with a low buffer size by storing and releasing only one (generally, or only few) intermediate state, without releasing or storing any part of an unverified plaintext and without need of generating any intermediate tag. In this paper we explain this generalized technique using our new construction sp-AELM. sp-AELM is a sponge based authenticated encryption scheme that provides support for limited memory devices. We also provide its security proof for privacy and authenticity in an ideal permutation model, using a code based game playing framework. Furthermore, we also present two more variants of sp-AELM that serve the same purpose and are more efficient than sp-AELM.

The ongoing CAESAR competition has 9 submissions which are based on the Sponge construction. We apply our generalized technique of storing single intermediate state to all these submissions, to determine their suitability with a devices having limited memory. Our findings show that only ASCON and one of the PRIMATE's mode(namely GIBBON) satisify the limited memory constraint using this technique, while the remaining 8 schemes (namely, Artemia, ICEPOLE, Ketje, Keyak, NORX, Π-cipher, STRIBOB and two of the PRIMATEs mode: APE & HANUMAN) are not suitable for this scenario directly.

Keywords: Authenticated encryption · CAESAR · Cryptographic module · Remote key authenticated encryption · Decrypt-then-mask protocol · Privacy · Authenticity

1 Introduction

Authenticated encryption (AE), formalized in [4,5], is a technique that combines encryption and authentication to provide both privacy and authenticity of the data by means of a single construction, usually with a single key. The formal definition of privacy and authenticity are provided in [5], where AE is introduced

© Springer International Publishing Switzerland 2015
E. Foo and D. Stebila (Eds.): ACISP 2015, LNCS 9144, pp. 451–468, 2015.
DOI: 10.1007/978-3-319-19962-7_26

as a block cipher mode of operation with the same block cipher performing both encryption and authentication. Informally, an AE scheme receives a message and a secret key as inputs and generates a ciphertext and a tag during encryption process. On the receiver side, the ciphertext and tag pair is verified, and the corresponding plaintext after decryption is returned only if the AE scheme verifies the supplied tag.

There exist a wide variety of AE modes. Some of the popular AE modes are GCM [27], OCB [29], EAX [7], CCM [15] and CWC [23]. In these "offline" AE modes, the device needs to store the complete plaintext, in the encryption mode, to produce the tag. Not all devices possess large memory to completely store a message and hence the modes mentioned earlier can't be directly used in the case of a long message. Consequently, the concept of online authenticated encryption was proposed in [18], in which encryption can be done on the fly. If the message (resp. ciphertext) blocks are denoted by $M_1, M_2, \ldots$ (resp. $C_1, C_2, \ldots$), then the requirement of online AE means that the ciphertext block C_i can be computed without the knowledge of plaintext block M_j for any $j > i$. Most of the block-cipher based authenticated encryption schemes can be used in online encryption mode. Many authenticated encryption schemes that support online encryption have been submitted to the currently on going CAESAR competition [1]. Some of these are APE [3], NORX [22], AEGIS [30] etc.

However, decryption in an AE scheme can never be online due to the fact that the ciphertext needs to be verified before producing the plaintext. If this was not the case then an attacker could simply ask for the decryption of a ciphertext of his choice, while associating any arbitrary tag with the ciphertext. The requirement of verifying the tag before producing the decrypted text can be solved in two different ways. In one case, the system implementing the decryption process could store the complete plaintext and produce it only if the tag verifies. In the other case, the system first applies the tag verification algorithm and then produces the plaintext, block by block, only if the tag verifies. It may be possible to achieve the implementation of the first method in a single pass over the ciphertext, whereas the second method can't be implemented in less than 2 passes over the ciphertext. However, the first method requires potentially large memory on the device while the second method could be implemented even on low memory devices. In fact, with the increasing usage of low cost RFID devices, sensors and trusted platform modules (TPM), the need for an AE scheme which can supports both the encryption and decryption functions in an online form is increasing day by day. None of the schemes submitted in the CAESAR competition consider this limited memory constraint explicitly.

Related Work: At FSE 1996, Blaze [10] proposed a new paradigm for secret-key block ciphers: Remotely keyed encryption (RKE). RKE is concerned with the problem of "high-bandwidth encryption with low bandwidth smartcards". A scheme to achieve the same was proposed in this work, but some limitations of the scheme were also mentioned in the same work. Later, Lucks [24] provided the first formal model for RKE and chose to interpret the question as that of implementing a remotely key pseudorandom permutation (RKPRP). The work [24] was further improved, both in terms of formal modelling and the actual construction, by an influential work of Blaze et al. [11]. It was observed in this later work that the PRP's length preserving property implies that it can not be semantically secure when viewed as encryption function alone. Thus, in addition to the RKPRP which was termed "length preserving RKE", the work [11] also introduced the notion of "length increasing RKE" which was also referred to as "remote key authenticated encryption" (RKAE). While the definition given in [11] was important and the first step towards formalizing this new notion, it turns out to be quite nonstandard (it involves an "arbiter" who can fool any adversary). The notion of such an arbiter looks quite artificial. Later, Dodis et al. [14] provided the formal definition of a remote key authenticated encryption. The RKAE scheme solves the problem where one wishes to split the task of high bandwidth authenticated encryption between a secure client (but limited bandwidth or computationally limited device) and an insecure (but computationally powerful) host. Though RKAE *is efficient, but the Crypto device (e.g. a card) that performs encryption and decryption doesn't know the actual value of plaintext and ciphertext* (Refer Table 1). *Rather, it trusts the insecure host to provide these values, making it unsuitable for real world applications.* Further, the security of this scheme is proved in a setting where the adversary has oracle access only to the combined functionality of the host and the card. However, the host is assumed to be insecure (subject to break-in by an adversary) in this scheme, i.e., the adversary can have access to the internal state of an encryption algorithm executed on the host side. So, the underlying assumption of having oracle access to combined functionality is not justified for defining security of the scheme.

Later, Fouque et al. at SAC 2003 proposed a decryption protocol named Decrypt-Then-Mask (DTM) [18]. The main idea behind this protocol is to blind the plaintext blocks obtained after decryption by XORing them with a pseudorandom sequence of bits and return it to the sender. These blocks do not "look" meaningful to the attacker until "unmasking" is applied. Once a tag gets verified at the receiver end, the seed of the pseudorandom number generator(PRNG) used to mask the plaintext blocks is returned to the sender. This allows the sender to run the same PRNG and un-mask the plaintext blocks. However this protocol has a drawback. *The DTM requires two additional passes excluding no. of passes required for underlying AE during decryption, which makes it computationally expensive, specially in the case of long messages.* These two extra passes (one at the crypto module and another one at the user side) in DTM are due to the use of PRNG, which creates extra overhead particularly in case of long message. The scenarios mentioned above point towards the need of an authenticated encryption scheme which remains efficiently implementable with low memory crypto module even while handling long messages.

Recently, Andreeva et al. in ASIACRYPT 2014 [16] provides definitions to formalize an AE scheme's security against release of unverified plaintexts. Even though these settings provide support for the devices with limited memory constraint but from the security point of view, it is essential to have a tag verification before releasing the plaintext.

454   M. Agrawal et al.

The issue of releasing unverified plaintext has also been discussed in on going CAESAR competition [1]. Its feature page explicitly states: *"Beware that security questions are raised by any authenticated cipher that handles a long ciphertext in one pass without using a large buffer: releasing unverified plaintext to applications often means releasing it to attackers and also requires an analysis of how the applications will react"*. However releasing unverified plaintext is not the only solution to handle large ciphertexts in memory constrained environment. In this work, we present a new solution that serves the same purpose, even though, it requires two passes, among them only one pass is effective as another pass takes place on user side and we usually assume that the user has enough memory on their side.

Another requirement regarding intermediate tags mentioned in CAESAR [1] feature page states: *"If a long plaintext is split into separate packets, each of which is separately authenticated (and encrypted), then a long forgery need not be buffered before it is rejected. Applying this split to any MAC (or authenticated cipher) produces a new MAC (or authenticated cipher) with different performance properties; perhaps the same type of fast rejection can be better achieved in another way"*. These settings still require significant memory to store the decrypted text and tags for every packet, which may not be available for the devices with the limited memory constraint. However the scheme proposed in this paper can support intermediate tag even for devices with the limited memory as we only need to store one intermediate state for all the packets and can also support fast rejection by checking those intermediate tags. For more details one can refer to full version of this paper [2].

Our Contribution: In this paper, we introduced a new generalized technique for authenticated encryption which store only one intermediate state instead of entire plaintext during tag verification. And then this intermediate state is used by the user on their side to decrypt ciphertext. Without releasing unverified plaintext this technique allow us to do a tag verification for a long message on the devices with limited memory settings. We explained this generalized technique using our new construction sp-AELM and its variants. This new construction and its two more variants support both online encryption as well as tag verification in constrained memory setting for long messages, which makes it suitable for implementation on devices that have limited memory. The Sponge construction supports arbitrarily long input and output sizes, and hence allows building various cryptographic primitives such as a hash function or a stream cipher [9]. More recently, use of Sponge based hash functions as an authenticated encryption primitive has been proposed in [8]. Keccak, the winner of the SHA-3 competition, is also built on the Sponge construction. Considering the acceptability and future adaptability of the Sponge construnction in Cryptographic software/hardware, we choose the Sponge function as a basic primitive for the construction of our authenticated encryption scheme sp-ALEM.

In sp-AELM, instead of returning all the plaintext blocks, we provide only one internal state to the user, using which plaintext can be computed easily at his side. Our scheme requires a total of three passes, one for encryption and two for decryption. This compares favourably with the DTM scheme, which requires overall more number of passes (discussed in Table 1), making our scheme more efficient. In sp-AELM, all computations are proposed to be done inside a cryptographic module, where the actual plaintext and ciphertext values are securely known, as opposed to the RKAE scheme [14]. More details about sp-AELM are given in Section 4. In addition to this, we also present two more efficient variants of sp-AELM. More details about these variants are given in Section 6.

Table 1 Description: This table shows the comparison of RKAE, DTM, the proposed scheme sp-AELM and sp-AELM variants. Our proposed scheme and its variants support online encryption. However, in the case of RKAE and DTM, it depends on the underlying AE scheme that is used. All these three schemes support low memory verification, i.e., there is no need to store message blocks on a cryptographic module during decryption. Next we compare these schemes on the basis of number of passes required for encryption and decryption. For a given message M of n blocks, we use the usual notion of a "pass" as the processing of all n blocks of M once. The RKAE scheme requires two passes[1] for encryption during execution of Conceal algorithm (one pass for encrypting n block message and another pass for computing the hash value on the output of the first pass, explained in Fig. 1(a)), while the number of passes required for DTM depends on the underlying AE scheme. sp-AELM and its variants require only one pass for encryption i.e. it visits the n block message exactly once. For decryption and verification, RKAE requires two passes[1] as shown in Fig. 1(b) (one pass for computing the hash value and another one for decryption). DTM uses two additional passes for pseudo random number generator (one pass for masking the n block message and another for unmasking the n blocks) apart from the number of passes for the underlying authenticated decryption algorithm. sp-AELM and its variants require only two passes (one at the receiver side and another one at the sender side as shown in Fig. 4(b)) for the decryption and verification. We have also used communication overhead between the host and the Crypto module as a comparison parameter in terms of number of message blocks n. RKAE require only 2 communications(shown in Fig. 1b), DTM require $2n + 2$ communications(shown in Fig. 2(b)) whereas sp-AELM and its variants require $n + 2$ communications(shown in Fig. 4(b)).

   In addition to this, we also applied the same technique used in sp-AELM on all Sponge based authenticated encryption schemes submitted to the CAESAR competition, to evaluate their suitability for supporting low memory constraint. Currently there are nine Sponge based AE schemes in the CAESAR competition. We addressed all these nine schemes using the same technique that we used in sp-AELM, i.e., during verification and decryption, storing only one intermediate state instead of storing all decrypted text and returning this intermediate state only when tag gets verified. Detailed analysis of the individual scheme is provided in Section 7. Our findings are briefly summarized in Table 2.

---

[1] For RKAE encryption/decryption we neglect the computations carried out at the Crypto module, as it is processed on a small data.

Table 1. Comparison of RKAE, DTM, sp-AELM and sp-AELM variants:(a) One pass is defined as processing of n blocks of a message once.(b)The communication overhead is given in terms of number of blocks n for a message M.

Parameters	RKAE [14]	DTM [18]	sp-AELM [This paper]	sp-AELM variants [This paper]
Online Encryption	Depends on underlying AE	Depends on underlying AE	Yes	Yes
Support for low memory verification	Yes	Yes	Yes	Yes
No. of Passes required for Encryption and tag generation	Two	Depends on underlying AE	One	One
No. of Passes required for Decryption and Verification	Two	2 + Depends on underlying AE	Two	Two
Communications overhead b/w Host and Crypto module during verification and decryption	2	$2n + 2$	$n + 2$	$n + 2$
Knowledge of Plaintext and Ciphertext to Crypto module	No	Yes	Yes	Yes

Table 2. Analysis of CAESAR schemes showing their suitability for supporting limited memory constraint.

Sponge based AE Schemes submitted in CAESAR	Support for limited memory devices (shown in Section 7)
Artemia [21], ICEPOLE [28], Ketje [19], Keyak [20], NORX [22], PRIMATEs(APE, HANUMAN) [17], Π-Cipher [13], STRIBOB [26]	No
Ascon [12], PRIMATEs(GIBBON) [17]	Yes

Roadmap : The rest of this paper is organized as follows: Section 2 gives the brief description of Remote Key Authenticated Encryption [14] and the protocol defined in [18]. Section 3 defines some preliminaries followed by Section 4 that defines the construction of the proposed AE scheme (sp-AELM). We provide the security proof of the proposed scheme in Section 5. In Section 6, we present two more efficient variants of sp-AELM. Section 7 presents the brief analysis of all Sponge base AE schemes submitted to the CAESAR competition. Finally, we conclude this paper with Section 8.

2 Previous Work

2.1 Remotely Keyed Authenticated Encryption

In [14] Dodis et al. proposed a formalized solution to the problem of remotely keyed authenticated encryption (RKAE). One round of the proposed scheme consists of seven different algorithms that run between two parties called the host and the cryptographic module: (RKG, StartAE, CardAE, FinishAE, StartAD, CardAD, FinishAD). In this scheme, the authors used the smart card as the Crypto module. The host is assumed to be powerful but insecure, and the Crypto module is assumed to have low bandwidth and limited memory but taken to be secure. For a given authenticated encryption scheme AE, we explain the RKAE using an example in Fig. 1. The process of encryption and decryption is individually shown in Fig. 1(a) and Fig. 1(b) respectively.

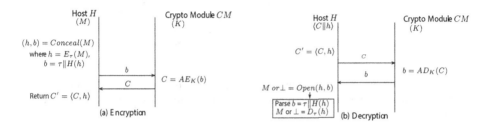

Fig. 1. Remote Key Authenticated Encyprion

2.2 Decrypt-Then-Mask Protocol

In [18], Fouque et al. proposed a generic construction called Decrypt-then-mask. Their construction doesn't affect encryption, only the decryption part is modified. They use a pseudorandom number generator to mask the plaintext blocks, to eliminate the need of storing plaintext blocks. Once the tag gets verified, the scheme returns the seed of the PRNG that has been used to mask the plaintext blocks. We use CM to denote cryptographic module and U to represent user of this device in further description of the scheme. For a given authenticated encryption scheme AE, the encryption and decryption component work as shown in Fig. 2.

3 Preliminaries

Definition 1 (Ideal Online Function). *Let $func(A, B)$ be defined as set of all functions from set A to set B. Now, we define ideal online function $\$_{pad}$ as:*

$$\$_{pad}(N, A, M, flag) \rightarrow \begin{cases} (C, T) & \text{if } flag \text{ is } 1, \\ C & \text{if } flag \text{ is } 0, \end{cases}$$

where,

$pad(X) = X \| 10^t$ *where t is a non-negative integer s.t $|X\|10^t| = pr$ for $p > 0$ and some fixed r.*

$N =$ *nonce of r bit,*

$A =$ *Associated data, where $|A| < r$ and $A' = pad(A)$,*

$M =$ *input message that can be partial or complete depending on the flag value,*

$$flag = \begin{cases} 0 \text{ ; } & \text{if user has queried partial message } M, \\ 1 \text{ ; } & \text{if user has queried complete message } M. \end{cases}$$

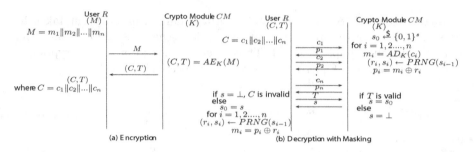

Fig. 2. Encryption and Decryption using Decrypt-Then-Mask Protocol: In (b)decryption, to represent it diagrammatically we assume $AD_K(c_i)$ returns the intermediate value m_i

In case $flag = 0$, we are assuming user has supplied incomplete message and wlog length of supplied message $(|M|)$ is multiple of r.

$$M' = \begin{cases} m_0\| \dots \|m_{n-1} = M, where\ n = |M|/r\ and\ |m_i| = r & ;\ if\ flag{=}0\ , \\ m_0\| \dots \|m_{n-1} = pad(M)\ s.t.\ |m_i| = r\ for\ 0 \le i \le n-1\ ;\ if\ flag{=}1 \ . \end{cases}$$
$C = c_0\|c_1\| \dots \|c_{n-1}$ where $c_j = g(N, A', m_0\| \dots \|m_j)$ for $j = 0, \dots, n-1$,
and
$$g \xleftarrow{\$} func(\{0,1\}^r \times \{0,1\}^r \times (\{0,1\}^r)^+, \{0,1\}^r),$$
$$T = g'(N, A', M'), where\ g' \xleftarrow{\$} func(\{0,1\}^r \times \{0,1\}^r \times (\{0,1\}^r)^+, \{0,1\}^t).$$

Notice that above function is online: here prefixes of outputs remain the same if prefixes of the inputs remain constant. Furthermore, if we consider that nonce and associated data are unique for each function invocation in the ideal online function, then we acheive full privacy. This is because the inputs to g and g' will then be unique for each invocations, and since g and g' are functions randomly chosen from func, we get outputs that are independent and uniformly distributed.

Definition 2 (Privacy). *For a given authenticated encryption scheme $\mathcal{AE} = (\mathcal{K}, \mathcal{E}, \mathcal{D})$, we define privacy in terms of the ability of an adversary A to distinguish between the output of an encryption oracle $\mathcal{E}$ from the output of an ideal online function $\$_{pad}$. We define*

$$Adv_{\mathcal{AE}}^{priv}(A) = Pr[K \xleftarrow{\$} \mathcal{K} : A^{\mathcal{E}_K(\cdot,\cdot,\cdot,\cdot)} \Rightarrow 1] - Pr[A^{\$_{pad}(\cdot,\cdot,\cdot,\cdot)} \Rightarrow 1]$$

The oracle $\mathcal{E}_K$ on input $(N, A, M, flag)$, returns the C or (C,T) depending on the flag value whereas the oracle $\$_{pad}$ on input $(N, A, M, flag)$, works as defined in Def. 1. Here the advantage of an adversary A will be its ability to distinguish between the ciphertext outputs from the $\mathcal{E}_K$ and $\$_{pad}$.

Definition 3 (Authenticity). *Here we give a notion of authenticity of the ciphertext tag pair of an authenticated encryption scheme. For a given authenticted encryption scheme $\mathcal{AE} = (\mathcal{K}, \mathcal{E}, \mathcal{D})$, let A be an adversary having an* encryption oracle $\mathcal{E}_K$. We say that A forges if it outputs a (N, A, C, T) tuple where $\mathcal{D}_K(N, A, C, T) \neq INVALID$ and adversary A didn't ask a query $\mathcal{E}_K(N, A, M, flag)$ that resulted in response (C, T).

Let $Exp_{\Pi}^{Auth}(A)$ be the forging experiment for a given $\mathcal{AE}$. Then the forging experiment is defined as follows:

1. Adversary A can query encryption oracle $\mathcal{E}$, decryption oracle $\mathcal{D}$ atmost q_{enc}, q_{dec} times respectively.
2. All the query responses of encryption oracle $\mathcal{E}$, are stored in a set, say R. This R set contain (N, A, C, T) tuple.
3. If adversary A is able to generate a (N, A, C, T) tuple $\notin R$ that produces valid message M, then he wins and output is 1 otherwise output is 0, after trying q_{dec} number of queries.

We say adversary wins i.e. he succeed in creating forgery if $Exp_{AE}^{Auth}(A) = 1$. So, the advantage of adversary in forging the scheme is defined as:

$$Adv_{AE}^{Auth}(A) = Pr[Exp_{AE}^{Auth}(A) = 1]$$

4   Our Construction: sp-AELM

A cryptographic module should not reveal any information about the plaintext until ciphertext-tag pair gets verified. Once the ciphertext gets verified, then crypto device is allowed to reveal the plaintext. However, a cryptographic module is likely to have some storage restriction. Therefore, it can not store a large plaintext M, verify the tag and output M only when M is valid. Traditional authenticated encryption schemes do not satisfy this usage scenario. We propose a new sponge based authenticated encryption scheme sp-AELM that considers this situation. sp-AELM uses a permutation as the underlying cryptographic primitive. Section 4.1 gives detail of the proposed scheme.

4.1   Description of sp-AELM

We now describe the new authenticated encryption scheme sp-AELM that addresses the low memory issue mentioned earlier. Schematic structure of sp-AELM is shown in Fig. 3. Our authenticated encryption scheme takes key K, nonce N, associated data A, plaintext M and $flag$ as inputs and returns C or (C, T) depending on the value of the $flag$, where C represents the ciphertext and T denotes tag or message authentication code (MAC). We denote cryptographic module by CM and the user of this module by U. The user U uses the crypto module CM for encryption, decryption and verification.

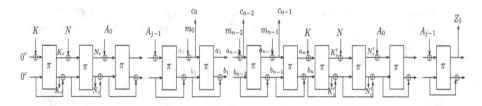

Fig. 3. sp-AELM Construction

Algorithm 1. Encryption $\mathcal{E}_K(N, A, M, flag)$

1 Initialization: $IV_1 = 0^r$, $IV_2 = 0^c$,
   $K_r \| K_c \xleftarrow{\$} \{0, 1\}^b$,
   $I_\pi = \{((IV_1 \oplus K) \| IV_2, K_r \| K_c)\}$
2 **if** $(flag = 1)$ **then**
3      $M = m_0 \| m_1 \| \ldots \| m_{n-1}$, Where $|m_i| = r$ and $0 \leq i < (n - 1)$
4      $Pad(M) =$
5 **else**
       $m_0 \| m_1 \| \ldots \| (m_{n-1} \| 10^{r-(|m_{n-1}|+1)})$
6      $M = m_0 \| m_1 \| \ldots \| m_{n-1}$, Where $|m_i| = r$
7   **if** $|m_{n-1}| < r$ **then** {return Invalid;}
8 $Pad(A) = A_0 \| A_1 \ldots \| A_{j-1}$ s.t. $|A_i| = r$ and $0 \leq i < (j - 1)$
9 $x = K_r \oplus N$, $w = K_c$
10 $N_r \| N_c = \pi(x \| w)$
11 $x = N_r$, $w = N_c \oplus w$
12 **for** $i = 0 \rightarrow j - 1$ **do**
13     $x' \| w' = \pi(x \oplus A_i \| w)$
14     $w = w' \oplus w$, $x = x'$
15 $a_0 = x'$, $b_0 = w'$
16 $c_0 = a_0 \oplus m_0$
17 **for** $i = 1 \rightarrow n - 1$ **do**
18     $x' \| w' = \pi(c_{i-1} \| b_{i-1})$
19     $b_i = b_{i-1} \oplus w'$
20     $a_i = x'$
21     $c_i = a_i \oplus m_i$
22 $C = c_0 \| c_1 \| \ldots \| c_{n-1}$
23 **if** $(flag = 0)$ **then**
24   Return C; Exit
25 $a_n \| b_n = \pi(c_{n-1} \| b_{n-1})$
26 $x = a_n$, $w = b_n$
27 $x = x \oplus K$
28 $K_r' \| K_c' = \pi(x \| w)$
29 $x = K_r' \oplus N$, $w = K_c' \oplus w$
30 $N_r' \| N_c' = \pi(x \| w)$
31 $x = N_r'$, $w = N_c' \oplus w$
32 **for** $i = 0 \rightarrow j - 1$ **do**
33     $x' \| w' = \pi(x \oplus A_i \| w)$
34     $w = w' \oplus w$, $x = x'$
35 $T = Z_0 = x$
36 Return (C, T)

Algorithm 2. Decryption $\mathcal{D}_K$ (N, A, C, T)

1 Initialization: $IV_1 = 0^r$, $IV_2 = 0^c$,
   $K_r \| K_c \xleftarrow{\$} \{0, 1\}^b$,
   $I_\pi = \{((IV_1 \oplus K) \| IV_2, K_r \| K_c)\}$
2 $|Pad(A)| = r$
3 $x = K_r \oplus N$, $w = K_c$
4 $N_r \| N_c = \pi(x \| w)$
5 $x = N_r$, $w = N_c \oplus w$
6 **for** $i = 0 \rightarrow j - 1$ **do**
7      $x' \| w' = \pi(x \oplus A_i \| w)$
8      $w = w' \oplus w$, $x = x'$
9 $a_0 = x$, $b_0 = w$
10 $m_0 = a_0 \oplus c_0$
11 **for** $i = 1 \rightarrow n - 1$ **do**
12     $x' \| w' = \pi(c_{i-1} \| b_{i-1})$
13     $b_i = b_{i-1} \oplus w'$
14     $a_i = x'$
15     $m_i = a_i \oplus c_i$
16 $M = m_0 \| m_1 \| \ldots \| m_{n-1}$
17 $x = a_n$, $w = b_n$
18 $x = x \oplus K$
19 $K_r' \| K_c' = \pi(x \| w)$
20 $x = K_r' \oplus N$, $w = K_c' \oplus w$
21 $N_r' \| N_c' = \pi(x \| w)$
22 $x = N_r'$, $w = N_c' \oplus w$
23 **for** $i = 0 \rightarrow j - 1$ **do**
24     $x' \| w' = \pi(x \oplus A_i \| w)$
25     $w = w' \oplus w$, $x = x'$
26 $Z_0 = x$
27 **if** $(Z_0 == T)$ **then**
28   Return (a_0, b_0)
29 **else**
30   Return $\perp$

4.1.1 Encryption.

The algorithm for encryption, $\mathcal{E}_K(., ., ., .)$ is explained in Algorithm 1. It takes an input, the secret key K of r bits, nonce N of r bits and associated data A, plaintext M and a $flag$ value. This flag value can be 0 or 1, where 0 represents continue i.e. partial M is provided as an input and 1 represents stop i.e., M is complete, we can do the tag computation. Associatd data A is partitioned into r bit blocks($A_0\|\ldots A_{j-1}$) and 10* padding is used for last block if required. We use two initialization vectors IV_1 and IV_2 of size r and c respectively, each of which is initialized to zero. Further, flag value is checked, if it is 1, then the message M is padded using $Pad(M)$ and divided into n blocks ($M = m_0\|m_1\|\ldots m_{n-1}$), each block is of r bit (i.e. $|M|/r = n$). Otherwise it is just processed into r bit blocks. Algorithm iterates a fixed permutation $\pi : A \times B \to A \times B$, where $|A| = r$ and $|B| = c$. First $(IV_1 \oplus K)\|IV_2$ is given input to π and the output is $K_r\|K_c$. Then IV_2 is XORed with K_c(say this value X). The next input to π is $(K_r \oplus N)\|X$ and the corresponding output is $N_r\|N_c$. Then this N_c valus is XORed with X. Similarly associated data A is processed. After that message block $m_i's$ for $i = 0, 2, ..(n-1)$ get processed. Note that encryption is online here, we don't need to know message blocks in advance i.e., c_i can be calculated without prior knowledge of m_j for any $j > i$. Once all the message blocks are processed and $flag$ is 0, then $C = c_0\|c_1\|....\|c_{n-1}$ is return to the user and algorithm terminates. Otherwise K, N, A are processed again in a order followed by tag generation. Tag T is generated from Z_0 value in Fig. 3. Finally (C,T) pair is returned to the user, where $C = c_0\|c_1\|....\|c_{n-1}$.

4.1.2   Decryption and Verification.

The algorithm for decryption $\mathcal{D}_K(.,.,.,.)$ is given in Algorithm 2. The decryption process is similar to encryption. All the steps are same except for XORing with the message. The only difference is rather than XORing with m_i, we XOR with c_i. Once the message block m_i is evaluated we use that as input just like encryption. Here in this decryption algorithm, we just store (a_0, b_0) value, all $m_i's$ block not get stored anywhere. Finally tag Z_0 is calculated. Once the tag becomes available , the given tag T is compared with Z_0. If tag gets verified, i.e., $Z_0 = T$, then algorithm returns (a_0, b_0) value. Once the user get this value, he can easily recover plaintext M from C as $m_0 = c_0 \oplus a_0$, $m_1 = c_1 \oplus \pi(c_0, b_0)$[initial r bit] and so on (explained in Algorithm 2). If tag doesn't get verified, then it returns invalid operator, i.e., plaintext cannot be calculated in this case. Fig. 4(b) shows the decryption protocol used in this new scheme.

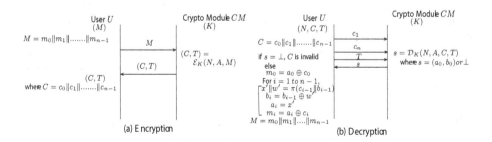

(a) Encryption   (b) Decryption

Fig. 4. Encryption and Decryption protocol for sp-AELM

5   Security Proof

In this section, we state theorems for the privacy and authenticity proof of sp-AELM. For the detailed proof of these theorems, one can refer to full version [2]. We have used recently evolved game playing technique proposed by Bellare and Rogaway in [6]. We prove security of sp-AELM in the ideal permutation model, where the underlying permutation is assumed to behave perfectly random. We also restrict our proof to the assumption that nonce N will always be generated different and randomly by the attacker. As it is not practically feasible by the algorithm to generate it randomly and differently everytime.

5.1   Privacy

We obtain an upper bound for the advatnage of the adversary who can distinguish the output of the proposed scheme with a random oracle in the ideal permutation model.

Theorem 1. *Let* $\Pi = (\mathcal{K}, \mathcal{E}, \mathcal{D})$ *denote the proposed Authenticated Encryption scheme with defined padding rule and an permutation* π*, which operates on b bits. The adversary A has given access to* π, π^{-1}*. Then the advantage of A relative to* $\mathcal{E}$ *is given by*

$$Adv_{\Pi}^{priv}(A) = Pr[K \xleftarrow{\$} \mathcal{K} : A^{\mathcal{E}_K(), \pi, \pi^{-1}} = 1] - Pr[K \xleftarrow{\$} \mathcal{K} : A^{\$_{pad}(), \pi, \pi^{-1}} = 1] \ .$$

$$Adv_{\Pi}^{priv}(A) \leq \frac{\sigma(\sigma - 1)}{2^b + 1} + \frac{\sigma(\sigma - 1)}{2^c + 1} + \frac{(q_\pi + q_{\pi-1}).q_{enc}}{2^r} + \frac{2(q_\pi + q_{\pi-1})\sigma}{2^c - \sigma} + \frac{q_\pi}{2^r} \ .$$

where $\$_{pad}$ *is defined in Def. 1,* σ *is the maximum number of block calls to* π, π^{-1} *by encryption* $\mathcal{E}$ *and decryption* $\mathcal{D}$ *algorithm .* q_{enc}, q_π *and* $q_{\pi-1}$ *are the maximum number of queries to encryption oracle Enc,* π *and* π^{-1} *oracle respectively by adversary A.* $b(= r + c)$ *is the size on which* π *permutation operates.*

Proof. Refer to full version [2].

5.2   Authenticity

In this section, we analyze the security of authenticity of the tag produced in our scheme. The forgery of an AE scheme is defined as the ability of an adversary A to generate a valid (N, A, C, T) tuple, without directly querying it to the encryption oracle. The adversary is allowed to make limited number of queries to encryption, decryption, π and π^{-1} oracles. For an AE scheme, we say the adversary A is successful in forging if it outputs a (N, A, C, T) tuple where $\mathcal{D}_K(N, A, C, T) \neq INVALID$ and adversary A didn't ask a query $\mathcal{E}_K(N, A, M, flag)$ that resulted in response (C, T) .

Theorem 2. *Let* $\Pi = (\mathcal{K}, \mathcal{E}, \mathcal{D})$ *be the proposed authenticated encryption scheme with defined padding rule (pad) and ideal permutation* (π) *which operate on* $b(= r + c)$ *bits. The adversary A is given access to Encryption oracle* $\mathcal{E}$*, Decryption oracle* $\mathcal{D}$*,* π *and* π^{-1} *oracle. Then* $\Pi = (\mathcal{K}, \mathcal{E}, \mathcal{D})$ *is forgeable with the probability*

$$Pr[Exp_{\Pi}^{Auth}(A) = 1] \leq \frac{\sigma(\sigma - 1)}{2^{b+1}} + \frac{\sigma(\sigma - 1)}{2^c + 1} + \frac{q_{dec}}{2^{|T|}} + \frac{q_\pi}{2^r}.$$

where σ is maximum number of blocks to π, π^{-1} by encryption oracle $\mathcal{E}$, and decryption oracle $\mathcal{D}$, q_{dec} is the number of queries to decryption oracle, q_π is the number of queries to π oracle and $|T|$ is the tag length.

Proof. Refer to full version [2].

6   More Variants of sp-AELM

This section presents two more variants of sp-AELM. The advantage of these variants over actual construction is that it doesn't require feed forward operation. Schematically construction of sp-AELM variants are shown in Fig. 5 and Fig. 6. These variants support the low memory constraint in a same way as in sp-AELM by storing only one intermediate state(shown using red line in Fig. 5) instead of storing complete text. Security proof for these constructions are not provided here due to space restrictions, although, it can be proved in same manner as sp-AELM. Intuitively, we can say these are secure as releasing intermediate state will not result for the adversary to gain any information about key. One can choose these variants over sp-AELM, when there is very limited amount of memory, which is not even capable of storing states required for feed-forward operation.

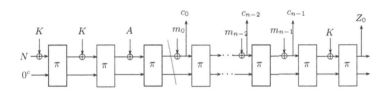

Fig. 5. sp-AELM variant 1

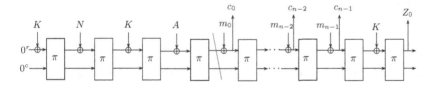

Fig. 6. sp-AELM variant 2

7   Analysis of Sponge Based AE Schemes Submitted in CAESAR

In this section, we apply our newly proposed generalized technique, which stores only one intermediate state instead of entire plaintext during tag verification, on various sponge based schemes submitted to the CAESAR competition to determine their suitability for supporting devices having limited memory constraint. There are ten sponge based AE schemes submitted to CAESAR for the first round, out of which one scheme (CBEAM [25]) has been withdrawn. Currently there are nine sponge based *AE* schemes competing for the next round. In the following subsections we present the brief analysis of some of the schemes ARTEMIA, ASCON, PRIMATE and Π-cipher, after applying the same technique used in sp-AELM. Rest of the schemes(ICEPOLE [28], STRIBOB [26], NORX [22], Ketje [19] and Keyak [20])can be analyzed in a similar way.

7.1   ARTEMIA [21]

Artemia is family of dedicated authenticated encryption scheme. It is based on JHAE mode as shown in Fig. 7.

While analyzing this mode, we find that it can not support low memory device constraint. Our analysis is based on the same technique proposed in sp-AELM i.e., storing only one intermediate state(shown using red line in Fig. 7) instead of storing whole message during decryption. This technique can not be applied here. As releasing this intermediate state will result in attacker to find the value of key. Since he already knows the value of T and can do the forward computation using C_i^s to get the state value after last π block, XORing this value with T will result in value of K.

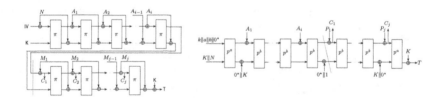

Fig. 7. JHAE Mode   **Fig. 8.** ASCON

7.2   ASCON [12]

ASCON is a family of authenticated encryption designs $ASCON_{a,b} - k$. The family members are parameterized by the key length $k \leq 128$ and internal round numbers a and b. Each design specifies an authenticated encryption algorithm $\mathcal{E}_{k,a,b}$ and decryption algorithm $\mathcal{D}_{k,a,b}$.

On analyzing this scheme, we find out that it can support low memory devices by storing only one intermediate value(shown using red line in Fig. 8) instead of storing all decrypted blocks during decryption, without breaking the security of construction. Further, this intermediate value can be used to decrypt the message at user side. This is due to the use of key at the end, which also prevents attcacker from doing forgery.

ARTEMIA [21], ICEPOLE [28], STRIBOB [26], NORX [22], Ketje [19] and Keyak [20] are analyzed in similar way as ASCON and the results predict that these schemes can not support the limited memory constraint using this technique. For more details refer to full version [2].

7.3 Π-Cipher [13]

Π-Cipher is parallel, incremental, nonce based, tag second-preimage resistant, authenticated encryption cipher with associated data. Its construction is shown in Fig. 9.

This AE scheme can not support limited memory constraint. Suppose if we store CIS'' and $ctr + i + 2$ values instead of storing all decrypted text blocks. Now using these intermediate values and known ciphertext values attacker can calculate the plaintext and Tag T''. However using this T'' he can not get the key due to the unavailability of Secret message number(SMN). Though it is secure against key recovery attack but forgery is possible here. As using T'', it is easy to generate a new ciphertext C and its corresponding valid tag T using a repeated nonce(SMN). This is due to the reason that T'' value will be same for a given key K and secret message number SMN.

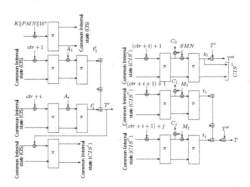

Fig. 9. Π Cipher

7.4 PRIMATE [17]

The authenticated encryption family PRIMATEs is defined by two parameters: the security level $s \in \{10, 15\}$ and mode of operation scheme $\in \{$GIBBON, HANUMAN, APE$\}$. These modes are shown in Fig. 10, 11, 12. Out of these three modes of operation of PRIMATE authenticated encryption family, only GIBBON can support limited memory constraint by storing only one intermediate state(shown using red line in Fig. 10), without revealing key to the attacker. Also, attacker will not be able to create forgery due to the use of key at the end. HANUMAN and APE can be easily broken to get the key, when storing only intermediate state. For more explaination refer full version [2].

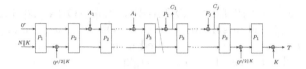

Fig. 10. GIBBON

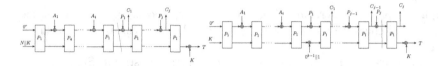

Fig. 11. HANUMAN   **Fig. 12.** APE

8 Conclusion

In this paper, we proposed a new generalized technique for AE schmes to support devices with limited memory. This new technique has been explained in this paper through a new sponge based AE scheme sp-AELM. sp-AELM can be used to support cryptographic modules having limited storage capabilities. We provided its security proof in an ideal permutation model using code based game playing framework for both privacy and authenticity. In addition to this, we also present two more variants of sp-AELM that serve the same purpose and are more efficient than sp-AELM. Further, we applied this newly introduced technique to all Sponge based AE schemes submitted to the CAESAR competition for determining their suitability to support devices with memory constraint. Our analysis shows that ASCON and one of the PRIMATEs instance namely GIBBON, can support limited memory constraint using this technique, while remaining schemes are not directly suitable for this scenario.

Acknowledgments. We thank our crypto group at IIIT Delhi and the ACISP 2015 PC members for their valuable comments.

References

1. CAESAR: Competition for authenticated encryption: Security, applicability, and robustness (2014). http://competitions.cr.yp.to/caesar.html
2. Agrawal, M., Chang, D., Sanadhya, S.: A new authenticated encryption technique for handling long ciphertexts in memory constrained devices. Cryptology ePrint Archive, Report 2015/331 (2015). http://eprint.iacr.org/
3. Andreeva, E., Bilgin, B., Bogdanov, A., Luykx, A., Mennink, B., Mouha, N., Yasuda, K.: APE: Authenticated permutation-based encryption for lightweight cryptography. IACR Cryptology ePrint Archive **2013**, 791 (2013)

4. Bellare, M., Namprempre, C.: Authenticated Encryption: Relations Among Notions and Analysis of the Generic Composition Paradigm. J. Cryptol. **21**(4), 469–491 (2008)
5. Bellare, M., Rogaway, P.: Encode-then-encipher encryption: how to exploit nonces or redundancy in plaintexts for efficient cryptography. In: Okamoto, T. (ed.) ASIACRYPT 2000. LNCS, vol. 1976, pp. 317–330. Springer, Heidelberg (2000)
6. Bellare, M., Rogaway, P.: Code-Based Game-Playing Proofs and the Security of Triple Encryption. IACR Cryptology ePrint Archive **2004**, 331 (2004)
7. Bellare, M., Rogaway, P., Wagner, D.: EAX: A Conventional Authenticated-Encryption Mode. IACR Cryptology ePrint Archive **2003**, 69 (2003)
8. Bertoni, G., Daemen, J., Peeters, M., Van Assche, G.: Duplexing the sponge: single-pass authenticated encryption and other applications. In: Miri, A., Vaudenay, S. (eds.) SAC 2011. LNCS, vol. 7118, pp. 320–337. Springer, Heidelberg (2012)
9. Bertoni, G., Daemen, J., Peeters, M., Van Assche, G.: Cryptographic sponge functions (2011). http://sponge.noekeon.org/
10. Blaze, M.: High-bandwidth encryption with low-bandwidth smartcards. In: Gollmann, G. (ed.) Fast Software Encryption. Lecture Notes in Computer Science, vol. 1039, pp. 33–40. Springer, Heidelberg (1996)
11. Blaze, M., Feigenbaum, J., Naor, M.: A formal treatment of remotely keyed encryption. In: Nyberg, K. (ed.) EUROCRYPT 1998. LNCS, vol. 1403, pp. 251–265. Springer, Heidelberg (1998)
12. Dobraunig, C., Eichlseder, M., Mendel, F., Schlaffer, M.: Ascon v1. http://competitions.cr.yp.to/round1/asconv1.pdf
13. Gligoroski, D., Mihajloska, H., Samardjiska, S., Jacobsen, H., El-Hadedy, M., Jensen, R.E.: PiCipher v1. http://competitions.cr.yp.to/round1/picipherv1.pdf
14. Dodis, Y.: Concealment and Its Applications to Authenticated Encryption. In: Dent, A.W., Zheng, Y. (eds.) Practical Signcryption. Information Security and Cryptography, pp. 149–173. Springer, Heidelberg (2010)
15. Dworkin, M.J.: Sp 800–38c. recommendation for block cipher modes of operation: The CCM mode for authentication and confidentiality. Technical report, Gaithersburg, MD, United States (2004)
16. Andreeva, E., Bogdanov, A., Luykx, A., Mennink, B., Mouha, N., Yasuda, K.: How to securely release unverified plaintext in authenticated encryption. In: Sarkar, P., Iwata, T. (eds.) ASIACRYPT 2014. LNCS, vol. 8873, pp. 105–125. Springer, Heidelberg (2014)
17. Andreeva, E., Bilgin, B., Bogdanov, A., Luykx, A., Mendel, F., Mennink, B., Mouha, N., Wang, Q., Yasuda, K.: PRIMATEs v1. http://competitions.cr.yp.to/round1/primatesv1.pdf
18. Fouque, P.-A., Joux, A., Martinet, G., Valette, F.: Authenticated On-Line Encryption. In: Matsui, M., Zuccherato, R.J. (eds.) Selected Areas in Cryptography. Lecture Notes in Computer Science, vol. 3006, pp. 145–159. Springer, Heidelberg (2003)
19. Bertoni, G., Daemen, J., Peeters, M., Van Assche, G., Van Keer, R.: Ketje v1. http://competitions.cr.yp.to/round1/ketjev11.pdf
20. Bertoni, G., Daemen, J., Peeters, M., Van Assche, G., Van Keer, R.: Ketje v1. http://keyak.noekeon.org/Keyak-1.2.pdf
21. Alizadeh, J., Aref, M.R., Bagheri, N.: Artemia v1. http://competitions.cr.yp.to/round1/artemiav1.pdf
22. Neves, S., Aumasson, J.-P., Jovanovic, P.: NORX: Parallel and Scalable AEAD (2014). https://norx.io/

23. Kohno, T., Viega, J., Whiting, D.: CWC: a high-performance conventional authenticated encryption mode. In: Roy, B., Meier, W. (eds.) FSE 2004. LNCS, vol. 3017, pp. 408–426. Springer, Heidelberg (2004)

24. Lucks, S.: On the security of remotely keyed encryption. In: Biham, E. (ed.) FSE 1997. LNCS, vol. 1267, pp. 219–229. Springer, Heidelberg (1997)

25. Saarinen, M.-J.O.: The CBEAMr1 Authenticated Encryption Algorithm. http:// competitions.cr.yp.to/round1/cbeamr1.pdf

26. Saarinen, M.-J.O.: The STRIBOBr 1 Authenticated Encryption Algorithm. http:// competitions.cr.yp.to/round1/stribobr1.pdf

27. McGrew, D.A., Viega, J.: The security and performance of the galois/counter mode (GCM) of operation. In: Canteaut, A., Viswanathan, K. (eds.) INDOCRYPT 2004. LNCS, vol. 3348, pp. 343–355. Springer, Heidelberg (2004)

28. Morawiecki, P., Gaj, K., Homsirikamol, E., Matusiewicz, K., Pieprzyk, J., Rogawski, M., Srebrny, M., Wojcik, M.: ICEPOLE v1. http://competitions.cr.yp. to/round1/icepolev1.pdf

29. Rogaway, P., Bellare, M., Black, J.: OCB: A block-cipher mode of operation for efficient authenticated encryption. ACM Trans. Inf. Syst. Secur. 6(3), 365–403 (2003)

30. Wu, H., Preneel, B.: AEGIS: A Fast Authenticated Encryption Algorithm. In: Lange, T., Lauter, K., Lisoněk, P. (eds.) SAC 2013. LNCS, vol. 8282, pp. 185–202. Springer, Heidelberg (2014)

Homomorphic Encryption
and Obfuscation

Secure Statistical Analysis Using RLWE-Based Homomorphic Encryption

Masaya Yasuda[1]([✉]), Takeshi Shimoyama[2], Jun Kogure[2],
Kazuhiro Yokoyama[3], and Takeshi Koshiba[4]

[1] Institute of Mathematics for Industry, Kyushu University,
744 Motooka Nishi-ku, Fukuoka 819-0395, Japan
yasuda@imi.kyushu-u.ac.jp
[2] FUJITSU LABORATORIES LTD., 1-1, Kamikodanaka 4-chome,
Nakahara-ku, Kawasaki 211-8588, Japan
[3] Department of Mathematics, Rikkyo University, Nishi-Ikebukuro,
Tokyo 171-8501, Japan
[4] Division of Mathematics, Electronics and Informatics,
Graduate School of Science and Engineering, Saitama University,
255 Shimo-Okubo, Sakura, Saitama 338-8570, Japan

Abstract. Homomorphic encryption enables various calculations while preserving the data confidentiality. Here we apply the homomorphic encryption scheme proposed by Brakerski and Vaikuntanathan (CRYPTO 2011) to secure statistical analysis between two variables. For reduction of ciphertext size and practical performance, we propose a method to pack multiple integers into a few ciphertexts so that it enables efficient computation over the packed ciphertexts. Our packing method is based on Yasuda et al.'s one (DPM 2013). While their method gives efficient secure computation only for small integers, our modification is effective for larger integers. Our implementation shows that our method is faster than the state-of-the-art work. Specifically, for one million integers of 16 bits (resp. 128 bits), it takes about 20 minutes (resp. 3.6 hours) for secure covariance and correlation on an Intel Core i7-3770 3.40 GHz CPU.

Keywords: Homomorphic encryption · Ring-LWE assumption · Packing methods · Secure covariance and correlation

1 Introduction

The recent development of cloud computing easily allows clients to outsource their data to cloud services. However, security and privacy issues have risen at the same time (e.g., see [8] for such issues). Homomorphic encryption is encryption with the additional property that it can support operations on encrypted data

---

A part of this research was done when the first author belonged to Fujitsu Laboratories Ltd.

E. Foo and D. Stebila (Eds.): ACISP 2015, LNCS 9144, pp. 471–487, 2015.
DOI: 10.1007/978-3-319-19962-7_27

(without decryption). If clients send their data in homomorphically encrypted format, the cloud can still perform calculation on encrypted data. Since all data in the cloud are encrypted, the confidentiality of clients' data can be preserved irrespective of any actions in the cloud. Therefore this technology gives a powerful tool to break several barriers for adoption of various cloud services. Here we focus on application of homomorphic encryption to secure statistical analysis. Among privacy-preserving data mining techniques [1], the randomization method is useful for such statistical analysis, in which sufficiently large noises are added to raw values so that individual values cannot be recovered but only the entire statistics can be approximately obtained. The randomization method is simple and effective, but it can only recover *rough* statistical information. In contrast, the homomorphic encryption technology enables to output *accurate* results and hence it is expected to be applied to various areas such as health care, chemical analysis and marketing analysis.

Depending on possible operations, we classify homomorphic encryption schemes into the following types:

- *Additive or multiplicative schemes (e.g., the Paillier scheme [19] is additive) can support only additions or multiplications on encrypted data (electronic voting is a possible application of an additive scheme).*
- *Fully homomorphic encryption (FHE) schemes* can support "arbitrary" operations. After Gentry's breakthrough [11], a number of new FHE schemes and implementations have been proposed (e.g., [3,5,6,9,12]), but current FHE schemes are impractical (recently, Ducas and Micciancio [10] gave a new method to make FHE schemes efficient).
- *Somewhat homomorphic encryption (SHE) schemes* can support a limited number of both additions and multiplications. The construction of almost all FHE schemes starts from an SHE scheme. The associated SHE schemes are much more practical than FHE, and they are applicable to various applications (note that SHE schemes are faster than [10]).

1.1   Related Work

Several work for statistical analysis have been proposed so far. In 2011, Lauter, Naehrig and Vaikuntanathan [16] utilized the SHE scheme of [5] for secure standard deviation and logistical regression computations. They also proposed a method to pack a large integer (e.g., 128 bits) into a single ciphertext for efficient secure sums and products over integers. In 2013, Yasuda et al. [23] extended Lauter et al.'s method to pack *multiple* integers, and their extension enables efficient secure inner product computation. Unlike [16,23], Wu and Haven [14] in 2012 used the leveled FHE scheme of [3] for large-scale analysis such as covariance and linear regression computations. Moreover, they used the CRT (Chinese Remainder Theorem) packing method proposed by Smart and Vercauteren [21] to operate multiple integers simultaneously. Recently, Lauter, López-Alt and Naehrig [15] applied a ring-based scheme for computing on encrypted genomic data. Different from the above packing methods, they focus on the structure of data and show how to encode two types of genomic data for genomic algorithms.

1.2   Our Contributions

As in [16, 23], we use the SHE scheme proposed by Brakerski and Vaikuntanathan [5]. The security of the scheme relies on the hardness of the ring learning with errors (RLWE) problem. Denote $R = \mathbb{Z}[x]/(x^n + 1)$ for n a power of 2. The packing method of [23] first transforms multiple integers a_i's into a polynomial $f(x) \in R$ with coefficients given by the a_i's, and then encrypts the polynomial. The homomorphic correctness over R enables to operate on multiple integers over packed ciphertexts. The method is effective for small integers of size 1 or 2 bits (in fact, it is implemented in [23] for secure distance computation between "binary" vectors). However, the method becomes much less efficient for larger integers since larger coefficients of $f(x)$ requires larger plaintext space and then it causes slower performance (see also [16, Section 4.1] for the same obstacle).

1. Our main contribution is to modify the packing method of [23] for integers of practical bit-size p (e.g., $p = 16$ or 32). The basic idea is to use binary representation of an integer for polynomial transformation in order to make the coefficients of $f(x)$ always small. Our main trick involves an array of coefficients of $f(x)$ consisting of multiple integers, which enables efficient computation of secure inner product for integers of p bits as in [23].
2. We implemented the SHE scheme with our modified packing method for secure statistical analysis for $p = 16 \sim 128$. Our experiments show that our method gives faster performance than [14] for secure covariance of integers of 128 bits. Specifically, for one million integers of 16 bits (resp. 128 bits), our method takes about 20 minutes (resp. 3.6 hours) for secure covariance and correlation on an Intel Core i7-3770 3.40 GHz CPU.

NOTATION The symbols $\mathbb{Z}$ and $\mathbb{Q}$ denote the ring of integers and the field of rational numbers, respectively. For a prime number p, the finite field with p elements is denoted by $\mathbb{F}_p$. For two integers z and d, let $[z]_d$ denote the reduction of z modulo d included in the interval $[-d/2, d/2)$ (the reduction of z modulo d included in the interval $[0, d)$ is denoted by "$z \bmod d$"). For $A = (a_0, a_1, \ldots, a_{k-1})$, let $||A||_\infty$ denote the ∞-norm defined by $\max_i |a_i|$. We also let $\langle A, B \rangle$ denote the inner product of two vectors A and B of same length. Finally, let $\lg(q)$ denote the logarithm value of an integer q with base 2.

2   RLWE-Based Somewhat Homomorphic Encryption

In this section, we briefly review the construction and the homomorphic correctness of the SHE scheme proposed by Brakerski and Vaikuntanathan [5]. For the construction, it requires the following four parameters:

n: a 2-power integer defining the base ring $R = \mathbb{Z}[x]/(x^n + 1)$ for the scheme. The degree n is sometimes called the *lattice dimension*.

q: a prime number with $q \equiv 1 \bmod 2n$, defining the ring $R_q = \mathbb{F}_q[x]/(x^n + 1)$, which is the ciphertext space. Note that according to [4], the condition $q \equiv 1 \bmod 2n$ is not necessary for the construction and the security (but the setting $q \equiv 1 \bmod 2n$ is selected in numerous papers for efficiency).

t: an integer with $t < q$ to determine a plaintext space $R_t = (\mathbb{Z}/t\mathbb{Z})[x]/(f(x))$.
σ: the parameter defining a discrete Gaussian error distribution $\chi = D_{\mathbb{Z}^n,\sigma}$.

The security of the scheme (constructed in Section 2.1 below) relies on the following assumption, which is a simplified version of the RLWE assumption of Lyubashevsky, Peikert and Regev [18] (the following assumption is independent of the parameter t, see [5, Proposition 1] for details):

Definition 1 (RLWE). *Given parameters* (n, q, t, σ), *the assumption* RLWE$_{n,q,\chi}$ *is that it is infeasible to distinguish the following two distributions:*

1. *One samples* (a_i, b_i) *uniformly from* $(R_q)^2$.
2. *One first draws* $s \leftarrow \chi = D_{\mathbb{Z}^n,\sigma}$ *uniformly and then samples* $(a_i, b_i) \in (R_q)^2$ *by sampling* $a_i \leftarrow R_q$ *uniformly,* $e_i \leftarrow \chi$ *and setting* $b_i = a_i s + e_i$.

2.1 Construction of SHE Scheme

Here we give only the construction of the public-key variant scheme (specifically, the following construction is the slight variant of [16, Section 3.2]).

- **Key Generation** We choose an element $R \ni s \leftarrow \chi$. We then sample a uniformly random element $p_1 \in R_q$ and an error $R \ni e \leftarrow \chi$. Set pk $= (p_0, p_1)$ with $p_0 = -(p_1 s + te)$ as the public key and sk $= s$ as the secret key.
- **Encryption** For a plaintext $m \in R_t$ and the public key pk $= (p_0, p_1)$, the encryption samples $R \ni u, f, g \leftarrow \chi$ and compute the "fresh" ciphertext by

$$\mathsf{Enc}(m, \mathsf{pk}) = (c_0, c_1) = (p_0 u + tg + m, p_1 u + tf), \tag{1}$$

  where the plaintext $m \in R_t$ is regarded as an element of R_q in the natural way due to the condition $t < q$.
- **Homomorphic Operations** Given two ciphertexts $\mathsf{ct} = (c_0, \ldots, c_\xi)$ and $\mathsf{ct}' = (c_0', \ldots, c_\eta')$, the homomorphic addition "$\dotplus$" is computed by component-wise addition $\mathsf{ct} \dotplus \mathsf{ct}' = (c_0 + c_0', \ldots, c_{\max(\xi,\eta)} + c_{\max(\xi,\eta)}')$ (by padding with zeros if necessary). Similarly, the homomorphic subtraction is given by component-wise subtraction. The homomorphic multiplication "$*$" is computed by $\mathsf{ct} * \mathsf{ct}' = (\hat{c}_0, \ldots, \hat{c}_{\xi+\eta})$, with ($z$ denotes a symbolic variable)

$$\sum_{i=0}^{\xi+\eta} \hat{c}_i z^i = \left(\sum_{i=0}^{\xi} c_i z^i \right) \cdot \left(\sum_{j=0}^{\eta} c_j' z^j \right).$$

- **Decryption** For a (fresh or homomorphically operated) ciphertext $\mathsf{ct} = (c_0, \ldots, c_\xi)$, the decryption with the secret key sk $= s$ is computed by

$$\mathsf{Dec}(\mathsf{ct}, \mathsf{sk}) = [\tilde{m}]_q \bmod t \in R_t, \tag{2}$$

where $\tilde{m} = \sum_{i=0}^{\xi} c_i s^i \in R_q$. For the secret key vector $\boldsymbol{s} = (1, s, s^2, \ldots)$, we can simply rewrite $\mathsf{Dec}(\mathsf{ct}, \mathsf{sk}) = [\langle \mathsf{ct}, \boldsymbol{s} \rangle]_q \bmod t$.

Remark 1. Given a fresh ciphertext $\mathsf{ct} = (c_0, c_1)$ generated by (1), we have

$$\langle \mathsf{ct}, s \rangle = (p_0 u + tg + m) + s \cdot (p_1 u + tf) = m + t \cdot (g + sf - ue) \qquad (3)$$

in the ring R_q since $p_0 + p_1 s = -te$. If the value $m + t \cdot (g + sf - ue)$ does not wrap around mod q (all errors $e, f, g, u \leftarrow \chi$ must be sufficiently small), we have $[\langle \mathsf{ct}, s \rangle]_q = m + t \cdot (g + sf - ue)$ in "the base ring R" (see also Lemma 1 below for details). In this case, we can recover the correct plaintext m by mod t-operation, which shows the decryption mechanism for any *fresh* ciphertexts. For two fresh ciphertexts $\mathsf{ct}_1, \mathsf{ct}_2$, we clearly have

$$\begin{cases} \langle \mathsf{ct}_1 \dotplus \mathsf{ct}_2, s \rangle = \langle \mathsf{ct}_1, s \rangle + \langle \mathsf{ct}_2, s \rangle \\ \langle \mathsf{ct}_1 * \mathsf{ct}_2, s \rangle = \langle \mathsf{ct}_1, s \rangle \cdot \langle \mathsf{ct}_2, s \rangle \end{cases} \qquad (4)$$

by the construction of homomorphic operations. These two equations imply that the homomorphic correctness of the encryption scheme holds (see also (5) below).

2.2   Homomorphic Correctness

The "homomorphic correctness" means that the decryption procedure can recover the operated result over plaintexts after performing several homomorphic operations over ciphertexts. It follows from the proof of [16, Lemma 3.3] that homomorphic operations over ciphertexts correspond to the ring structure of the plaintext space R_t (here we say that the scheme has the homomorphic correctness over R_t). Specifically, we have

$$\begin{cases} \mathsf{Dec}(\mathsf{ct} \dotplus \mathsf{ct}', \mathsf{sk}) = m + m' \in R_t \\ \mathsf{Dec}(\mathsf{ct} * \mathsf{ct}', \mathsf{sk}) = m \times m' \in R_t \end{cases} \qquad (5)$$

for ciphertexts $\mathsf{ct}, \mathsf{ct}'$ corresponding to plaintexts m, m', respectively. However, the scheme merely gives an SHE scheme (not an FHE scheme), and its correctness holds under the following condition (the below lemma is very important for choosing suitable parameters (n, q, t, σ) in order to avoid decryption failure):

Lemma 1 (Condition for successful decryption). *For a ciphertext* ct*, the decryption* $\mathsf{Dec}(\mathsf{ct}, \mathsf{sk})$ *recovers the correct result if it satisfies the condition*

$$\|\langle \mathsf{ct}, s \rangle\|_\infty < q/2.$$

In the inequality, we regard $\langle \mathsf{ct}, s \rangle$ *as the element of R calculated by the right hand side of (3) and (4), and for $a = \sum_{i=0}^{n-1} a_i x^i \in R$, let $\|a\|_\infty = \max |a_i|$ denote the ∞-norm of its coefficient representation. Specifically, for a fresh ciphertext* ct*, the ∞-norm $\|\langle \mathsf{ct}, s \rangle\|_\infty$ is given by $\|m + t(g + sf - ue)\|_\infty$ with $t \in \mathbb{Z}, m \in R_t \subset R$ and $e, f, g, u, s \leftarrow \chi = D_{\mathbb{Z}^n, \sigma}$ (i.e., we here regard $\langle \mathsf{ct}, s \rangle \in R$ for evaluation). Furthermore, for a homomorphically operated ciphertext, the ∞-norm can be calculated by (4).*

3   Packing Method for Secure Statistical Computations

A certain special packing method enables us to efficiently perform several secure computations, using the RLWE-based homomorphic encryption scheme constructed in Section 2.1. Before presenting our packing method, let us first review previous methods.

3.1   Review of Previous Packing Methods

Packing Method by [16]. Lauter et al. [16, Section 4.1] introduce a message encoding technique for secure statistics over *large* integers such as 128 bits. Their technique can pack a large integer into a single ciphertext, and it also enables efficient computation of sums and products over packed ciphertexts. Specifically, for the degree parameter n of Section 2.1, their technique breaks an integer M of up to n bits into a binary vector $(m_0, \ldots, m_{n-1})$, creates a polynomial by

$$\mathsf{pm}(M) = \sum_{i=0}^{n-1} m_i x^i,$$

and finally encrypts M as $\mathsf{ct}_{\mathrm{pack}}(M) := \mathsf{Enc}\,(\mathsf{pm}(M), \mathsf{pk})$, where $\mathsf{pm}(M)$ is regarded as an element of R_t for taking sufficiently large t. We have $\mathsf{pm}(M)|_{x=2} = M$, where $f(x)|_{x=a} = f(a)$ for a polynomial $f(x)$ and an integer a. For two integers M, M', the homomorphic addition $\mathsf{ct}_{\mathrm{pack}}(M) + \mathsf{ct}_{\mathrm{pack}}(M')$ gives the polynomial addition $\mathsf{pm}(M) + \mathsf{pm}(M')$ on encrypted data by the homomorphic correctness (5), and it also gives the integer addition $\mathsf{pm}(M) + \mathsf{pm}(M')|_{x=2} = M + M'$. However, the integer multiplication causes a obstacle since the polynomial multiplication $\mathsf{pm}(M) \cdot \mathsf{pm}(M')$ has degree larger than n in general. Their solution is to encode integers of at most (n/d) bits when it requires d homomorphic multiplications. Their technique is effective in computing low degree multiplications such as the standard deviation.

Extension by [23]. Yasuda et al. [23] extends the packing method of Lauter et al., by taking *two types* of packed ciphertexts as follows; For an integral vector $A = (a_0, \ldots, a_{n-1})$ of length n, set

$$\mathsf{pm}^{(1)}(A) = \sum_{i=0}^{n-1} a_i x^i \ \text{and} \ \mathsf{pm}^{(2)}(A) = -\sum_{i=0}^{n-1} a_i x^{n-i}, \qquad (6)$$

and then packed ciphertexts are defined as $\mathsf{ct}_{\mathrm{pack}}^{(i)}(A) := \mathsf{Enc}\,(\mathsf{pm}^{(i)}(A), \mathsf{pk})$ for $i = 1, 2$ as in [16]. The first type is same as Lauter et al.'s technique, but the second one enables efficient computation of secure inner product. Specifically, for two vectors A and B of length n, only one homomorphic multiplication over $\mathsf{ct}_{\mathrm{pack}}^{(1)}(A)$ and $\mathsf{ct}_{\mathrm{pack}}^{(2)}(B)$ can give the inner product $\langle A, B \rangle$ on encrypted data [23, Proposition1]. This inner product computation is effective for secure distance computations such as the Euclidean and the Hamming distances, rather than secure statistical analysis (see [23, Section 4] for the application of secure Hamming distance to privacy-preserving biometrics).

3.2   Our Modified Packing Method

When we handle integers of very small size (e.g., 1 or 2 bits), the packing method of [23] is effective and sufficient for secure statistics. However, for integers of practical bit-size (e.g., even for 16 or 32 bits), the packing method enforces to set the size parameter t of the plaintext space R_t to be considerably large, and then such parameter setting would cause slow performance (see also [16, Section 4.1] for their description on the same problem). Specifically, let $A = (a_0, \ldots, a_{n-1})$ and $B = (b_0, \ldots, b_{n-1})$ be two integral vectors of length n with entries a_i, b_i of p bits. For obtaining secure inner product, we should take the parameter t larger than the value $\langle A, B \rangle = \sum_{i=0}^{n-1} a_i b_i$ so that the decryption result can not wrap around by modulo t-operation (see the decryption procedure (2)). Since $a_i b_i$ is of $2p$ bits, we should set

$$t \geq n \cdot 2^{2p},$$

which is too large to have practical performance. More specifically, when we use such a huge parameter t, the encryption (1) generates a fresh ciphertext with huge noises tg and tf where $f, g \leftarrow \chi$. In this case, Lemma 1 requires huge q in order to avoid decryption failure, and it also requires huge n for sufficient security (e.g., see Appendix A for selection of parameters). As a result, such parameter setting makes the size of ciphertexts huge (the size of a fresh ciphertext is given by $2n \cdot \lg(q)$), and then it causes impractical performance of the encryption scheme. Then, in the below, we shall modify the packing method of [23] for secure statistics over integers of practical bit-size.

Polynomial Transformation Modification. Given an integer m, let $A = (a_0, a_1, \ldots, a_{m-1})$ be a vector of length m with entries a_i of less than p bits (e.g., consider $p = 16$ or 32). For a chosen integer $r > 0$ (typically set $r = 2$), write each integral entry a_i in the base-r representation, namely, we have

$$a_i = \sum_{u=0}^{d-1} a_{i,u} r^u \quad \text{with } \exists a_{i,u} \in \{0, 1, \ldots, r-1\}, \tag{7}$$

where $d = \lceil \log_r 2^p \rceil$. Unlike the packing method of [23], we consider the following two types of polynomials in the base ring $R = \mathbb{Z}[x]/(x^n + 1)$:

Definition 2 (Modified Packing Method). *Assume $n \geq 2md$. Two types of our modified polynomial transformation in the ring R are defined by (cf. (6))*

$$\begin{cases} \mathsf{pm}_{m,p,r}^{(1)}(A) = \displaystyle\sum_{i=0}^{m-1} \left(\sum_{u=0}^{d-1} a_{i,u} x^u \right) x^{2id} \quad and \\[2em] \mathsf{pm}_{m,p,r}^{(2)}(A) = - \displaystyle\sum_{i=0}^{m-1} \left(\sum_{u=0}^{d-1} a_{i,u} x^u \right) x^{n-2id}. \end{cases} \tag{8}$$

Then, as in [16,23], two types of our packed ciphertexts are given by $\mathsf{ct}_{m,p,r}^{(i)}(A) := \mathsf{Enc}(\mathsf{pm}_{m,p,r}^{(i)}(A), \mathsf{pk})$ for $i = 1, 2$. In the typical case where $r = 2$, we omit "r" like $\mathsf{pm}_{m,p}^{(i)}(A)$ and $\mathsf{ct}_{m,p}^{(i)}(A)$ for $i = 1, 2$.

By (7), the value substituted $x = r$ for the polynomial $\sum_{u=0}^{d-1} a_{i,u} x^u$ is clearly equal to the integer a_i for any i (the idea is derived from Lauter et al.'s method). Hence the two polynomials (8) correspond to $\sum_{i=0}^{m-1} a_i x^{2id}$ and $-\sum_{i=0}^{m-1} a_i x^{n-2id}$, respectively. These polynomial transformations are similar to the ones (6) introduced in [23]. Therefore our modification can be considered as a combination of [16] and [23], but our trick is the "2d-th power of x" in the above polynomials (see the next discussion for this trick).

Secure Inner Product Using Our Modification. Given $A = (a_0, \dots, a_{m-1})$ and $B = (b_0, \dots, b_{m-1})$ of same length m with entries a_i, b_i of less than p bits, we assume $n \geq 2md$ as in Definition 2. From a similar argument of the proof of [23, Proposition 1], the fact $x^n = -1$ in the base ring R tells that the polynomial multiplication $\mathrm{pm}_{m,p,r}^{(1)}(A) \times \mathrm{pm}_{m,p,r}^{(2)}(B)$ in the base ring R is equal to

$$
\left(\sum_{i=0}^{m-1} A_i(x) \cdot x^{2id} \right) \times \left(- \sum_{j=0}^{m-1} B_j(x) \cdot x^{n-2jd} \right)
$$

$$
= - \sum_{i=0}^{m-1} A_i(x) B_i(x) x^n + \cdots = \sum_{i=0}^{m-1} A_i(x) B_i(x) + \text{terms of deg} \geq 2d \quad (9)
$$

where we set

$$
A_i(x) = \sum_{u=0}^{d-1} a_{i,u} x^u \text{ and } B_i(x) = \sum_{v=0}^{d-1} b_{i,v} x^v.
$$

Note that $a_{i,u}, b_{i,v}$ are obtained by the base-r representation (7) for integers a_i, b_i. Since $\sum_{i=0}^{m-1} A_i(x) B_i(x)$ has degree smaller than $2d$, we can pick up the subpolynomial from the expression (9) since the other terms have degree larger than $2d$, due to our trick of taking the $2d$-th power of x in our modified polynomials (8). Moreover, the value substituted $x = r$ for $\sum_{i=0}^{m-1} A_i(x) B_i(x)$ is equal to

$$
\sum_{i=0}^{m-1} A_i(r) B_i(r) = \sum_{i=0}^{m-1} \left(\sum_{u=0}^{d-1} a_{i,u} r^u \right) \left(\sum_{v=0}^{d-1} b_{i,v} r^v \right) = \sum_{i=0}^{m-1} a_i b_i = \langle A, B \rangle
$$

by the base-r representation (7) for integers a_i's and b_i's (note that this idea is similar to the multiplication $\mathrm{pm}(M) \cdot \mathrm{pm}(M')$ in the packing method of [16] for obtaining integer multiplication $M \cdot M'$). Then the homomorphic correctness (5) of the encryption scheme gives the following result (cf. [23, Proposition 1]):

Theorem 1. Let $A = (a_0, \dots, a_{m-1})$ and $B = (b_0, \dots, b_{m-1})$ be two integral vector of same length m with entries a_i, b_i of less than p bits. Assume $n \geq 2md$ as in Definition 2, where $d = \lceil \log_r 2^p \rceil$ for a fixed positive integer r. Let

$$
\mathrm{ct} = \mathrm{ct}_{m,p,r}^{(1)}(A) * \mathrm{ct}_{m,p,r}^{(2)}(B),
$$

and let $\text{Dec}(\text{ct}, \text{sk}) = \sum_{i=0}^{n-1} m_i x^i \in R_t$ denote its decryption result. Then, under the condition of Lemma 1 for the ciphertext ct, the sum $\sum_{i=0}^{2d-1} m_i r^i \in \mathbb{Z}$ gives the inner product $\langle \boldsymbol{A}, \boldsymbol{B} \rangle$ modulo t.

For longer vectors, we must divide the vectors into sub-vectors of length m; Given two vectors $\boldsymbol{A}$ and $\boldsymbol{B}$ of same length $N > m$, let $\boldsymbol{A}_i$ and $\boldsymbol{B}_i$ be the i-th sub-vector of length m such that $\boldsymbol{A} = (\boldsymbol{A}_1 \mid \ldots \mid \boldsymbol{A}_k)$ and $\boldsymbol{B} = (\boldsymbol{B}_1 \mid \ldots \mid \boldsymbol{B}_k)$ for $k = \lceil N/m \rceil$ (by padding with zeros if necessary). For encryption of the vector $\boldsymbol{A}$ (resp. $\boldsymbol{B}$), consider k ciphertexts $\text{ct}_{m,p,r}^{(1)}(\boldsymbol{A}_i)$ (resp. $\text{ct}_{m,p,r}^{(2)}(\boldsymbol{B}_i)$) for $i = 1, \ldots, k$. Then, by Theorem 1 and the homomorphic correctness (5), the combination of k homomorphic additions and k homomorphic multiplications

$$\text{ct} := \sum_{i=1}^{k} \text{ct}_{m,p,r}^{(1)}(\boldsymbol{A}_i) * \text{ct}_{m,p,r}^{(2)}(\boldsymbol{B}_i) \tag{10}$$

gives the inner product $\langle \boldsymbol{A}, \boldsymbol{B} \rangle$ modulo t on encrypted data. Specifically, let $\sum_{i=0}^{n-1} m_i x^i \in R_t$ denote the decryption result $\text{Dec}(\text{ct}, \text{sk})$ as in Theorem 1, and then the sum $\sum_{i=0}^{2d-1} m_i r^i \in \mathbb{Z}$ equals to $\langle \boldsymbol{A}, \boldsymbol{B} \rangle$ modulo t. In order to obtain the correct inner product, we should take the parameter t so that the inner product does not wrap around by modulo t-operation. Note that we clearly have

$$\sum_{i=0}^{n-1} m_i x^i \equiv \sum_{j=1}^{k} \text{pm}_{m,p,r}^{(1)}(\boldsymbol{A}_j) \times \text{pm}_{m,p,r}^{(2)}(\boldsymbol{B}_j) \pmod{t} \tag{11}$$

in the plaintext ring R_t, and each coefficient of $\text{pm}_{m,p,r}^{(1)}(\boldsymbol{A}_j)$ and $\text{pm}_{m,p,r}^{(2)}(\boldsymbol{B}_j)$ is up to $(r-1)$ by the base-r representation (7). Then, due to our trick of the $2d$-th power of x in Definition 2, the equation on the right side of (11) has coefficients up to $N(r-1)^2 d$ (since $\text{pm}_{m,p,r}^{(1)}(\boldsymbol{A}_j) \times \text{pm}_{m,p,r}^{(2)}(\boldsymbol{B}_j)$ has coefficients up to $m(r-1)^2 d$ by the equation (9)), and hence it requires $t \geq N(r-1)^2 d$ to obtain the correct inner product. In particular, in the case $r = 2$, it requires

$$t \geq N \cdot p \tag{12}$$

since $d = p$ (cf. the packing method of [23] requires $t \geq N \cdot 2^{2p}$ for secure inner product between two vectors of length N, as described in the first paragraph of Section 3.2). The inequality (12) helps us to take practical parameters (n, q, t, σ) of the encryption scheme for secure statistics (see Appendix A for details).

Features of Our Modification. Set $r = 2$. Given p and n (then $d = p$), our method can pack at most $\lfloor n/2p \rfloor$ integers of less than p bits into a single ciphertext. By Theorem 1, our method further enables to perform secure inner product between two vectors of length $\lfloor n/2p \rfloor$, by only one homomorphic multiplication. Moreover, our method gives a generalization of the two packing methods of [16] and [23]; Actually, in the case $p = n$, the first type of our packing method is same as in [16], and it can pack an integer of at most n bits. In contrast, in the case $p = 1$, our method is almost same as in [23] (the main difference is the $2d$-th power of x in Definition 2), and our method can give efficient secure inner product between two *binary* vectors. This shows that for fixed n the parameter p gives a trade-off between the length $\lfloor n/2p \rfloor$ of a vector which we can pack and the bit-size p of entries which we can handle. In particular, for practical bit-size p (e.g., $p = 16$ or 32), while the method of [16] can handle only one integer, our method can handle *multiple* integers of simultaneously (specifically, our method is about m times faster than [16] for a secure inner product).

Remark 2. Our method does not change the encryption algorithm of the RLWE-based scheme of [5] (our technique is transformation from a vector to an element of R before encryption). Therefore, as well as [16,23], our method does not change the provable security of the original scheme.

Comparison to Other Packing Methods. Smart and Vercauteren [21] propose the polynomial-CRT packing method, applicable for lattices based homomorphic encryption. The CRT packing method is useful to perform SIMD (Single Instruction - Multiple Data) operations on encrypted data, and the basic strategy in the RLWE-based scheme of Section 2.1 is as follows; If $f(x) = x^n + 1$ factorizes into r-factors modulo t such as $f(x) \equiv \prod_{i=1}^{r} f_i(x) \bmod t$, then the plaintext space ring $R_t = (\mathbb{Z}/t\mathbb{Z})[x]/(f(x))$ can split into the direct product

$$R_t \simeq \prod_{i=1}^{r} \mathbb{F}_t[x]/(f_i(x)).$$

In particular, if t satisfies $t \equiv 1 \bmod 2n$, then the base ring R completely splits modulo t, namely, we have $R_t \simeq (\mathbb{Z}/t\mathbb{Z})^n$. This property enables us to operate multiple elements of $\mathbb{Z}/t\mathbb{Z}$ in parallel. Specifically, given n elements $m_1, \ldots, m_n \in \mathbb{F}_t$, we first transform the n-fold vector $(m_1, \ldots, m_n)$ to the element $m \in R_t$, and then encrypt it. Then the generated ciphertext is a packed one of the m_i's. Based on the work of [13] for homomorphic evaluation of the AES circuit, Wu and Haven [14] use the CRT packing method in the leveled fully homomorphic encryption scheme of [3] for secure statistical analysis. As in our work, they in [14, Section 4.2] introduce an efficient computation of secure inner product; Given two vectors $u = (u_1, \ldots, u_n), v = (v_1, \ldots, v_n) \in \mathbb{Z}^n$, let $\mathsf{ct}(u)$ and $\mathsf{ct}(v)$ denote two CRT-packed ciphertexts, respectively. One homomorphic multiplication $\mathsf{ct}(u) * \mathsf{ct}(v)$ gives all n products $u_i v_i$'s separately, but the CRT packing method requires additional procedure (e.g., several homomorphic additions and rotations) to obtain the inner product $\sum u_i v_i$. In contrast, our packing method does not require such the additional procedure.

3.3 Secure Statistical Computations

Basic Statistical Analysis. Let $(X, Y) = (x_0, y_0), \ldots, (x_{N-1}, y_{N-1})$ be a pair of two variables with N independent integer sample pairs (x_i, y_i). In particular, covariance and correlation defined below can describe how two random variables X and Y are related (in this paper, we focus on covariance and correlation, which are more complex than fundamental statistics such as mean and variance).

Mean, Variance, and Standard Deviation The mean is the average of a set of numbers. In contrast, the variance is a measure of the dispersion around the mean. For a variable X, the variance is denoted by s_X^2 (s_X denotes the standard deviation), and it is defined $s_X^2 = \dfrac{\sum_{i=0}^{N-1}(x_i - m_X)^2}{N}$, where m_X denotes the mean of the variable. It can be rewritten as $s_X^2 = \left(\dfrac{1}{N}\displaystyle\sum_{i=0}^{N-1} x_i^2\right) - m_X^2$.

Covariance and Correlation The covariance can measure the linear relationship between two variables X and Y, and the formula is given as $\mathrm{cov}(X,Y) = \dfrac{1}{N-1}\displaystyle\sum_{i=0}^{N-1}(x_i - m_X)(y_i - m_Y)$. Its alternative expression is given as $\mathrm{cov}(X,Y) = \dfrac{1}{N-1}\left(\displaystyle\sum_{i=0}^{N-1} x_i y_i - N m_X m_Y\right)$. In contrast, the correlation examines the relationship between two variables in a symmetric manner. Its formula is written as $r(X,Y) = \dfrac{\mathrm{cov}(X,Y)}{s_X s_Y}$.

Computations over Our Packed Ciphertexts. As we can easily see, it suffices to compute five values

$$\sum_{i=0}^{N-1} x_i, \quad \sum_{i=0}^{N-1} y_i, \quad \sum_{i=0}^{N-1} x_i^2, \quad \sum_{i=0}^{N-1} y_i^2, \quad \text{and} \quad \sum_{i=0}^{N-1} x_i y_i \tag{13}$$

for the covariance $\mathrm{cor}(X,Y)$ and the correlation $r(X,Y)$. Here we shall give efficient computation of (13) on encrypted data, by using our packing method of Definition 2. After decryption to obtain the five values (13), we need to perform additional procedures over plaintexts for the covariance and the correlation, but the procedures are tiny (note that we cannot actually compute the standard deviation s_X or s_Y since the square root computation has to be done after decryption). Given two parameters m and p, assume that all integers x_i's and y_i's are of less than p bits and the degree parameter n satisfies $n \geq 2mp$ (after this subsection, we always set $r = 2$, and then $d = \lceil \log_r 2^p \rceil = p$). For encryption of X and Y, we first construct vectors $\boldsymbol{X}_i = (x_{m(i-1)}, \ldots, x_{mi-1})$ and $\boldsymbol{Y}_i = (y_{m(i-1)}, \ldots, y_{mi-1})$ of length m for $i = 1, \ldots, k$ with $k = \lceil N/m \rceil$ (by padding with zeros if necessary), and then generate $4k$ packed ciphertexts

$$\left\{\left(\mathrm{ct}_{m,p}^{(1)}(\boldsymbol{X}_i),\ \mathrm{ct}_{m,p}^{(2)}(\boldsymbol{X}_i)\right)\right\}_{i=1}^{k} \quad \text{and} \quad \left\{\left(\mathrm{ct}_{m,p}^{(1)}(\boldsymbol{Y}_i),\ \mathrm{ct}_{m,p}^{(2)}(\boldsymbol{Y}_i)\right)\right\}_{i=1}^{k}. \tag{14}$$

For two sums $\sum x_i$ and $\sum y_i$ over packed ciphertexts, we set $C = \sum\limits_{i=0}^{m-1} x^{2pi}$, which clearly equals to $\mathsf{pm}_{m,p}^{(1)}(\boldsymbol{T})$ where set $\boldsymbol{T} = (1,\dots,1)$ of length m. By a similar argument on Theorem 1, the homomorphic operations

$$\mathsf{ct_S}(X) := \sum_{i=1}^{k} C * \mathsf{ct}_{m,p}^{(2)}(\boldsymbol{X}_i) \text{ and } \mathsf{ct_S}(Y) := \sum_{i=1}^{k} C * \mathsf{ct}_{m,p}^{(2)}(\boldsymbol{Y}_i)$$

give two sums $\sum x_i$ and $\sum y_i$ on encrypted data, respectively, where the homomorphic multiplication between the constant C and any ciphertext is defined as in Section 2.1 (e.g., the homomorphic multiplication $C * \mathsf{ct}_{m,p}^{(2)}(\boldsymbol{X}_i)$ corresponds to the polynomial multiplication $C \times \mathsf{pm}_{m,p}^{(2)}(\boldsymbol{X}_i)$, which can give the sum of entries of $\boldsymbol{X}_i$ as in Theorem 1). Moreover, the result of Theorem 1 shows that

$$\mathsf{ct_{SS}}(X) := \sum_{i=1}^{k} \mathsf{ct}_{m,p}^{(1)}(\boldsymbol{X}_i) * \mathsf{ct}_{m,p}^{(2)}(\boldsymbol{X}_i) \text{ and } \mathsf{ct_{SS}}(Y) := \sum_{i=1}^{k} \mathsf{ct}_{m,p}^{(1)}(\boldsymbol{Y}_i) * \mathsf{ct}_{m,p}^{(2)}(\boldsymbol{Y}_i)$$

give two sums of squares of x_i's and y_i's, respectively, and

$$\mathsf{ct_{IP}}(X,Y) := \sum_{i=1}^{k} \mathsf{ct}_{m,p}^{(1)}(\boldsymbol{X}_i) * \mathsf{ct}_{m,p}^{(2)}(\boldsymbol{Y}_i) \left(\text{or } \sum_{i=1}^{k} \mathsf{ct}_{m,p}^{(2)}(\boldsymbol{X}_i) * \mathsf{ct}_{m,p}^{(1)}(\boldsymbol{Y}_i) \right)$$

gives the inner product $\sum x_i y_i$. As a summary, five homomorphic operations

$$\mathsf{ct_S}(X), \ \mathsf{ct_S}(Y), \ \mathsf{ct_{SS}}(X), \ \mathsf{ct_{SS}}(Y), \text{ and } \mathsf{ct_{IP}}(X,Y) \tag{15}$$

enable us to perform our desired values (13) over the packed ciphertexts (14).

Remark 3. Linear regression is one of the statistical estimation problems; Given a dataset $\{(\boldsymbol{x}_i, y_i)\}_{i=1}^{N}$ with input variables $\boldsymbol{x}_i \in \mathbb{Z}^p$ and output variables $y_i \in \mathbb{Z}$. The aim of linear regression is to approximate $\boldsymbol{y} = (y_1,\dots,y_N)^T$ as a linear function $h(\boldsymbol{x}) = \boldsymbol{\theta}^T \boldsymbol{x}$ with certain $\boldsymbol{\theta} \in \mathbb{Q}^p$. Then we need to take $\boldsymbol{\theta}$ in order to minimize the least-squares regression error. It requires to compute $\widehat{\boldsymbol{\theta}} = (\mathbf{X}^T\mathbf{X})^{-1}\mathbf{X}^T\boldsymbol{y}$, where $\mathbf{X} = (\boldsymbol{x}_1,\dots,\boldsymbol{x}_N)^T$. For such matrix-matrix and matrix-vector products, we can apply our secure inner products computation. But we have to separately compute the numerator and denominator of $\widehat{\theta}$ (specifically, the denominator of $\widehat{\theta}$ is given by the determinant of $\mathbf{X}^T\mathbf{X}$). On the other hand, it is difficult to evaluate computations such as the median and the 1-norm since we cannot compare two values without secret keys.

Remark 4. With the five values (13), a decryptor can compute basic statistical analysis such as the covariance and the correlation. The values reveal *more information* than the covariance and the correlation. Actually the values reveal means m_X, m_Y, standard deviations s_X, s_Y, and the covariance $\mathrm{cov}(X,Y)$. However, even though they do reveal more information than the covariance and the correlation, this is reasonable to assume that it is not a problem in most cases. If we compute the covariance directly, we need to have ciphertexts of $\sum x_i$ and $\sum y_i$. Namely, with the additional ciphertexts, we can compute $N(N-1)\mathrm{cov}(X,Y)$ directly on encrypted data (we assume that N is public). On the other hand, for the correlation $r(X,Y) = \frac{\mathrm{cov}(X,Y)}{s_X s_Y}$, we cannot compute $s_X s_Y$ directly from our packed ciphertexts. Therefore, for the value $s_X s_Y$, we need to have ciphertexts of s_X and s_Y additionally (in other words, each client computes s_X or s_Y on plaintexts and sends it in encrypted format). Then the decryptor only knows the numerator and the denominator of $r(X,Y)$.

Remark 5 (Additional Procedure for Privacy Enhancing). Let ct be one of the ciphertexts in (15). By Theorem 1, our packing method uses the x^k-coefficient of the decryption result $\mathsf{Dec}(\mathsf{ct},\mathsf{sk}) \in R_t$ with only $0 \leq k \leq 2d-1$ ($d = p$ in the case $r = 2$). In other words, our packed ciphertexts may include extra information in x^k-coefficients with $2d \leq k \leq n-1$. In order not to give a decryptor such extra information, we here introduce a method to add random noises to the ciphertext ct. For example, given $\mathsf{ct} = \mathsf{ct}_{\mathrm{IP}}(X,Y)$ consisting of three elements $(c_0, c_1, c_2) \in (R_q)^2$ by homomorphic operations, we first generate a random polynomial

$$ r = r_d x^d + r_{d+1} x^{d+1} + \cdots + r_{n-1} x^{n-1} \in R $$

and then computes a ciphertext given by one homomorphic addition $\mathsf{ct} \dot{+} r = (c_0 + r, c_1, c_2)$. Then the decryption of the ciphertext $\mathsf{ct} \dot{+} r$ includes our desired values in the first $2d$ coefficients, but the other coefficients are masked by random information r_i's. Therefore this procedure can make a decryptor not to obtain extra information other than necessary information for statistical analysis.

4   Experimental Evaluation

In this section, we give implementation results of our packing method for secure statistical computations (15). Before reporting our implementation results, let us describe our method to choose suitable parameters (n, q, t, σ) of the RLWE-based encryption scheme.

4.1   Selection of Parameters

Here we describe how to choose suitable parameters (n, q, t, σ) for our implementation (here we focus on taking suitable parameters for the case $p = 16$ and $N = 10^4$). By Lemma 1, we need to evaluate the ∞-norm size of $\langle \mathsf{ct}, s \rangle$ for each ciphertext ct in (15) to avoid decryption failure, where s denote the secret key vector defined in Section 2.1. It is sufficient to consider only the ciphertext $\mathsf{ct}_{\mathrm{IP}} := \mathsf{ct}_{\mathrm{IP}}(X,Y)$, which has the largest size among five ciphertexts in (15) (actually, $\mathsf{ct}_{\mathrm{SS}}(X)$, $\mathsf{ct}_{\mathrm{SS}}(Y)$, and $\mathsf{ct}_{\mathrm{IP}}(X,Y)$ have almost same norm size). We clearly have

$$ \langle \mathsf{ct}_{\mathrm{IP}}, s \rangle = \sum_{i=1}^{k} \left\langle \mathsf{ct}_{m,p}^{(1)}(X_i), s \right\rangle \cdot \left\langle \mathsf{ct}_{m,p}^{(2)}(Y_i), s \right\rangle \tag{16} $$

in the base ring R_q of the ciphertext space. Let U denote an upper bound of the ∞-norm size $\|\langle \text{ct}, \boldsymbol{s} \rangle\|_\infty$ for any *fresh* ciphertext ct. Since $\text{ct}^{(1)}_{m,p}(\boldsymbol{X}_i)$ and $\text{ct}^{(2)}_{m,p}(\boldsymbol{Y}_i)$ are fresh ciphertexts by our construction, all these ciphertexts have ∞-norm size at most U. By the well-known fact (e.g., see [16, Lemma 3.2]) that

$$\|a + b\|_\infty \le \|a\|_\infty + \|b\|_\infty \text{ and } \|a \cdot b\|_\infty \le n \cdot \|a\|_\infty \cdot \|b\|_\infty \qquad (17)$$

for any two elements $a, b \in R_q$, we have $\|\langle \text{ct}_{\text{IP}}, \boldsymbol{s} \rangle\|_\infty \le knU^2$ by the equation (16). With respect to the upper bound U, let ct denote a fresh ciphertext given by (1). Note that $\|\langle \text{ct}, \boldsymbol{s} \rangle\|_\infty \approx t \cdot \|g + sf - ue\|_\infty$ with $e, f, g, u, s \leftarrow \chi$ (see also Remark 1). By [16, Lemma 3.1], any element drawn from $\chi = D_{\mathbb{Z}^n, \sigma}$ has magnitude at most $\sigma\sqrt{n}$ with probability $1 - 2^{-n+1}$. Then we can estimate $\|\langle \text{ct}, \boldsymbol{s} \rangle\|_\infty \le 2t \cdot (\sigma\sqrt{n})^2$ with overwhelmingly probability (a theoretical upper bound is given as $2t \cdot (\sigma\sqrt{n})^2 \cdot n$ by the property (17), but it seems too large in practice). Then we set $U = 2t\sigma^2 n$. By using this estimate for U, we have $\|\langle \text{ct}_{\text{IP}}, \boldsymbol{s} \rangle\|_\infty \le knU^2 = 4kn^3t^2\sigma^4$, and hence Lemma 1 requires

$$q > 8kn^3t^2\sigma^4 \qquad (18)$$

for our targeted ciphertext ct_{IP} (then it also enables to avoid decryption failure for all the five ciphertexts in (15)).

Here we give concrete parameters (n, q, t, σ) of the RLWE-based scheme of Section 2.1 for secure statistic computation (15) of N integers of bit-size $p = 16 \sim 128$. For parameter setting, we always set $\sigma = 8$ as in [16], and we here consider to pack $m = 100$ integers into a single ciphertext by using our packing method of Definition 2. In Table 1, given the maximum bit-size p and the number N of integers (i.e., the number of records), we give our chosen parameters (n, q). For example, given $p = 16$ and $N = 10^4$, we describe how to choose suitable parameters (n, q); At first, our packing method requires $n \ge 2mp = 3200$ and then we set $n = 4096 = 2^{12}$, the minimum 2-power integer larger than 3200. Furthermore, we set $t = N \cdot p = 16,000 < 2^{14}$ by the condition (12). Finally, we make use of the inequality (18) to find a suitable prime q. Specifically, since $k = \lceil N/m \rceil = 100 < 2^7$, the inequality (18) requires

$$q > 2^{3+7+36+28+12} = 2^{85}.$$

Then we set the bit-size of q to be 85 for these p and N.

Security Level of Our Chosen Parameters. The computational hardness of lattice problems, including the RLWE assumption $\text{RLWE}_{n,q,\chi}$ of Definition 1 (which assures the security of the scheme of Section 2.1), can be measured by the *root Hermite factor*. According to [17], given parameters (n, q, t, σ), the root Hermite factor δ of $\text{RLWE}_{n,q,\chi}$ can be calculated by (the factor δ does not depends on t)

$$c \cdot q/\sigma = 2^{2\sqrt{n \cdot \lg(q) \cdot \lg(\delta)}},$$

where c is the constant determined by attack advantage ε $(c \approx \sqrt{\lg(1/\varepsilon)/\pi})$, and we here take $c = 2.657$ corresponding to $\varepsilon = 2^{-32}$ as in [16]. For our chosen parameters, we calculate the corresponding factor δ and give it in Table 1 below. According to the state-of-the-art security analysis of [7] for lattice problems, a root Hermite factor smaller than 1.0050 is estimated to have 80-bit security level with an enough margin (as the factor δ is smaller, the security level becomes higher). Since our chosen parameters always satisfy $\delta < 1.0050$, we estimate that all our chosen parameters have (much) more than 80-bit security.

4.2   Implementation Results

For our chosen parameters (see values of $(n, \lg(q))$ in Table 1), we implemented the RLWE-based homomorphic encryption scheme using our packing method for secure statistical analysis. Note that all our chosen parameters are estimated to give 80-bit security level for the encryption scheme with enough margins (see the previous subsection for details). Our experiments ran on an Intel Core i7-3770 CPU with 3.40 GHz and 16.0 GB RAM, using PARI C library [22] (version 2.5.5) for arithmetic of large integers (we also use gcc 4.6.0 with -O3 compiler option). In Table 1, we give our informative implementation results; For example, for $N = 10^4$ sample pairs $(X, Y) = \{(x_i, y_i)\}_{i=1}^N$ of integers of less than $p = 16$ bits, we fixed parameters $(n, \lg(q)) = (4096, 85)$. In this parameter setting, Table 1 shows that it took 2.82 seconds to generate $2k$ packed ciphertexts

Table 1. Performance and ciphertext sizes of secure computations (15) for covariance and correlation between two variables X and Y with N sample pairs $(X, Y) = \{(x_i, y_i)\}_{i=1}^N$ of integers of less than p bits (we always pack $m = 100$ integers into a single ciphertext by using our packing method of Definition 2)

Parameters			Performance (seconds)			Size of packed
p	N	$(n, \lg(q), \delta)$	Packed Enc.[†]	Secure comp.	Dec.	ciphertexts[‡]
16	10^4	$(4096, 85, 1.0036)$	2.82	8.74	0.05	34.8 MB
	10^5	$(4096, 97, 1.0040)$	28.4	113.2	0.05	397 MB
	10^6	$(4096, 107, 1.0044)$	282	1140	0.05	4.38 GB
32	10^4	$(8192, 88, 1.0018)$	6.21	19.73	0.09	72.1 MB
	10^5	$(8192, 100, 1.0021)$	61.9	262.1	0.09	819 MB
	10^6	$(8192, 110, 1.0023)$	739	2616	0.09	9.01 GB
64	10^4	$(16384, 91, 1.0009)$	11.25	57.78	0.25	149 MB
	10^5	$(16384, 103, 1.0011)$	137.4	579.4	0.25	1.69 GB
	10^6	$(16384, 113, 1.0012)$	1395*	6083*	0.25	18.5 GB
128	10^4	$(32768, 94, 1.0005)$	23.06	122.56	0.55	308 MB
	10^5	$(32768, 106, 1.0005)$	256.1	1231.4	0.55	3.47 GB
	10^6	$(32768, 116, 1.0006)$	2992*	13014*	0.55	38.0 GB

[†]Time to generate $2k$ packed ciphertexts $\{(\mathsf{ct}_{m,p}^{(1)}(\boldsymbol{X}_i), \mathsf{ct}_{m,p}^{(2)}(\boldsymbol{X}_i))\}_{i=1}^k$ with $k = \lceil N/m \rceil$ for the variable X with N samples x_j's, [‡]Size of $4k$ packed ciphertexts (14) for two variables X and Y (one packed ciphertext has size of $2n \cdot \lg(q)$-bit)
*Estimated times (due to memory constraints, we cannot perform actual experiments)

$\{(\mathrm{ct}_{m,p}^{(1)}(\boldsymbol{X}_i), \mathrm{ct}_{m,p}^{(2)}(\boldsymbol{X}_i))\}_{i=1}^k$ (the size of each ciphertext is $2n \cdot \lg(q) \approx 87$ KByte, and hence $4k = 400$ packed ciphertexts have size about 400×87 KByte $= 34.8$ MByte). It also took 8.74 seconds to perform secure computations (15), and finally five decryption procedures took 0.05 seconds to obtain five values (13).

Performance Comparison to Related Work. As introduced in Section 3.2, Wu and Haven [14] implemented the leveled FHE scheme of [3] using the CRT packing method for large-scale analysis. According to their implementation results of [14, Table 5], it costs 1.89 minutes (i.e., about 113 seconds) to compute mean and covariance on encrypted data for 4096 integers of 128 bits (their experiments ran on a 24-core AMD Opteron processor with 2.1 GHz, 512 KB of cache and 96 GB of available memory using NTL C++ library). In contrast, Table 1 shows that ours costs 122.56 seconds for 10^4 integers of 128 bits, and hence it is estimated to cost only about 50 seconds for 4096 integers. When we ignore the slight difference of PC environments and implementation levels, ours is estimated to be *about* $\frac{113}{50} = 2.26$ *times faster* than [14] (note again that it costs about 113 seconds in [14]). Furthermore, we note that our parameter setting is not optimal for $p = 128$-bit but for 16-bit integers, and hence ours would be even faster if we take optimal parameters for 128 bits.

5   Conclusion

For secure statistical analysis over integers of practical bit-size, we modified the packing method of [23] over RLWE-based homomorphic encryption schemes. The main part of our modification is the polynomial transformations (8), and it gives a generalization of [16] and [23]. We also implemented our method for secure covariance and correlation between two variables with N sample pairs of integers of less than p bits for $N = 10^4 \sim 10^6$ and $p = 16 \sim 128$ (see Table 1 for details). Our method took about 2 minutes for $N = 10^4$ integers of $p = 128$ bits, which is at least twice faster than [14].

Acknowledgments. The authors thank Arnab Roy and Avradip Mandal, research members of Fujitsu Laboratories of America (FLA), for reviewing a draft paper and giving useful comments.

References

1. Aggrawal, C.C., Philip, S.Y.: A general survey of privacy-preserving data mining models and algorithms. Springer (2008)
2. Brakerski, Z., Gentry, C., Halevi, S.: Packed ciphertexts in LWE-based homomorphic Encryption. In: Kurosawa, K., Hanaoka, G. (eds.) PKC 2013. LNCS, vol. 7778, pp. 1–13. Springer, Heidelberg (2013)
3. Brakerski, Z., Gentry, C., Vaikuntanathan, V.: (Leveled) fully homomorphic encryption without bootstrapping. In: Innovations in Theoretical Computer Science-ITCS 2012, pp. 309–325. ACM (2012)
4. Brakerski, Z., Langlois, A., Peikert, C., Regev, O., Stehlé, D.: Classical hardness of learning with errors. In: Symposium on Theory of Computing-STOC 2013, PP. 575–584. ACM (2013)

5. Brakerski, Z., Vaikuntanathan, V.: Fully homomorphic encryption from ring-LWE and security for key dependent messages. In: Rogaway, P. (ed.) CRYPTO 2011. LNCS, vol. 6841, pp. 505–524. Springer, Heidelberg (2011)
6. Brakerski, Z., Vaikuntanathan, V.: Efficient fully homomorphic encryption from (standard) LWE. In: Foundations of Computer Science-FOCS 2011, 97–106. IEEE (2011)
7. Chen, Y., Nguyen, P.Q.: BKZ 2.0: better lattice security estimates. In: Lee, D.H., Wang, X. (eds.) ASIACRYPT 2011. LNCS, vol. 7073, pp. 1–20. Springer, Heidelberg (2011)
8. Cloud Security Alliance (CSA), Security guidance for critical areas of focus in cloud computing, December 2009. https://cloudsecurityalliance.org/csaguide.pdf
9. van Dijk, M., Gentry, C., Halevi, S., Vaikuntanathan, V.: Fully homomorphic encryption over the integers. In: Gilbert, H. (ed.) EUROCRYPT 2010. LNCS, vol. 6110, pp. 24–43. Springer, Heidelberg (2010)
10. Ducas, L., Micciancio, D.: FHEW: Bootstrapping homomorphic encryption in less than a second. Cryptology ePrint Archive: report 2014/816 (2014)
11. Gentry, C.: Fully homomorphic encryption using ideal lattices. In: Symposium on Theory of Computing-STOC 2009, pp. 169–178. ACM (2009)
12. Gentry, C., Halevi, S.: Implementing gentry's fully-homomorphic encryption scheme. In: Paterson, K.G. (ed.) EUROCRYPT 2011. LNCS, vol. 6632, pp. 129–148. Springer, Heidelberg (2011)
13. Gentry, C., Halevi, S., Smart, N.P.: Homomorphic evaluation of the AES circuit. In: Safavi-Naini, R., Canetti, R. (eds.) CRYPTO 2012. LNCS, vol. 7417, pp. 850–867. Springer, Heidelberg (2012)
14. Wuhan, D., Haven, J.: Using homomorphic encryption for large scale statistical analysis (2012). http://cs.stanford.edu/people/dwu4//FHE-SI_Report.pdf
15. Lauter, K., López-Alt, A., Naehrig, M.: Private computation on encrypted genomic data. In: Aranha, D.F., Menezes, A. (eds.) LATINCRYPT 2014. LNCS, vol. 8895, pp. 3–27. Springer, Heidelberg (2015)
16. Lauter, K., Naehrig, M., Vaikuntanathan, V.: Can homomorphic encryption be practical?. In: ACM workshop on Cloud computing security workshop-CCSW 2011, pp. 113–124. ACM (2011)
17. Lindner, R., Peikert, C.: Better key sizes (and Attacks) for LWE-based encryption. In: Kiayias, A. (ed.) CT-RSA 2011. LNCS, vol. 6558, pp. 319–339. Springer, Heidelberg (2011)
18. Lyubashevsky, V., Peikert, C., Regev, O.: On ideal lattices and learning with errors over rings. In: Gilbert, H. (ed.) EUROCRYPT 2010. LNCS, vol. 6110, pp. 1–23. Springer, Heidelberg (2010)
19. Paillier, P.: Public-key cryptosystems based on composite degree residuosity classes. In: Stern, J. (ed.) EUROCRYPT 1999. LNCS, vol. 1592, pp. 223–238. Springer, Heidelberg (1999)
20. Peikert, C., Vaikuntanathan, V., Waters, B.: A framework for efficient and composable oblivious transfer. In: Wagner, D. (ed.) CRYPTO 2008. LNCS, vol. 5157, pp. 554–571. Springer, Heidelberg (2008)
21. Smart, N.P., Vercauteren, F.: Fully homomorphic SIMD operations. Designs, Codes and Cryptography **71**(1), 57–81 (2014)
22. The PARI Group, Bordeaux, PARI/GP. http://pari.math.u-bordeaux.fr/doc.html
23. Yasuda, M., Shimoyama, T., Kogure, J., Yokoyama, K., Koshiba, T.: Practical packing method in somewhat homomorphic encryption. In: Garcia-Alfaro, J., Lioudakis, G., Cuppens-Boulahia, N., Foley, S., Fitzgerald, W.M. (eds.) DPM 2013 and SETOP 2013. LNCS, vol. 8247, pp. 34–50. Springer, Heidelberg (2014)

Bad Directions in Cryptographic Hash Functions

Daniel J. Bernstein[1,2](✉), Andreas Hülsing[2](✉), Tanja Lange[2](✉),
and Ruben Niederhagen[2](✉)

[1] Department of Computer Science, University of Illinois at Chicago,
Chicago, IL 60607–7045, USA
djb@cr.yp.to
[2] Department of Mathematics and Computer Science, Technische Universiteit
Eindhoven, P.O. Box 513, 5600 MB Eindhoven, The Netherlands
andreas.huelsing@googlemail.com, tanja@hyperelliptic.org,
ruben@polycephaly.org

Abstract. A 25-gigabyte "point obfuscation" challenge "using security
parameter 60" was announced at the Crypto 2014 rump session; "point
obfuscation" is another name for password hashing. This paper shows
that the particular matrix-multiplication hash function used in the challenge is much less secure than previous password-hashing functions are
believed to be. This paper's attack algorithm broke the challenge in just
19 minutes using a cluster of 21 PCs.

Keywords: Symmetric cryptography · Hash functions · Password hashing · Point obfuscation · Matrix multiplication · Meet-in-the-middle
attacks · Meet-in-many-middles attacks

1 Introduction

*Under normal circumstances, the system protected the passwords so that
they could be accessed only by privileged users and operating system
utilities. But through accident, programming error, or deliberate act,
the contents of the password file could occasionally become available to
unprivileged users. ... For example, if the password file is saved on
backup tapes, then those backups must be kept in a physically secure
place. If a backup tape is stolen, then everybody's password needs to be
changed. Unix avoids this problem by not keeping actual passwords anywhere on the system.* —"Practical UNIX & Internet Security" [24,
p. 84], 2003

The full version of this paper is available on IACR eprint [13]. The numbering
between both versions is synchronized for easy reference. This work was supported by
the National Science Foundation under grant 1018836, by the Netherlands Organisation for Scientific Research (NWO) under grant 639.073.005, and by the European
Commission through the ICT program under contract INFSO-ICT-284833 (PUF-
FIN). Permanent ID of this document: 7c4f480d7f090d69c58b96437b6011b1. Date:
2015.04.22.

© Springer International Publishing Switzerland 2015
E. Foo and D. Stebila (Eds.): ACISP 2015, LNCS 9144, pp. 488–508, 2015.
DOI: 10.1007/978-3-319-19962-7_28

Consider a server that knows a secret password 11000101100100. The server could check an input password against this secret password using the following checkpassword algorithm (expressed in the Python language):

```python
def checkpassword(input):
    return int(input == "11000101100100")
```

But it is much better for the server to use the following checkpassword_hashed algorithm (see the full version [13] for the definition of sha256hex):

```python
def checkpassword_hashed(input):
    return int(sha256hex(input) == (
        "ba0ab099c882de48c4156fc19c55762e"
        "83119f44b1d8401dba3745946a403a4f"
    ))
```

It is easy for the server to write down this checkpassword_hashed algorithm in the first place: apply SHA-256 to the secret password to obtain the string ba0...a4f, and then insert that string into a checkpassword_hashed template. There is no reason to believe that these two algorithms compute identical functions. Presumably SHA-256 has a second (and third and so on) preimage of SHA-256(11000101100100), i.e., a string for which checkpassword_hashed returns 1 while checkpassword returns 0. However, finding any such string would be a huge advance in SHA-256 cryptanalysis. The checkpassword_hashed algorithm outputs 1 for input 11000101100100, just like checkpassword, and outputs 0 for all other inputs that have been tried, just like checkpassword.

The core advantage of checkpassword_hashed over checkpassword is that it is **obfuscated**. If the checkpassword algorithm is leaked to an attacker then the attacker immediately sees the secret password and seizes control of all resources protected by that password. If checkpassword_hashed is leaked, the attacker does not see the secret password without solving a SHA-256 preimage problem: the loss of confidentiality does not immediately create a loss of integrity.

Obfuscation is a broad concept. There are many aspects of programs that one might wish to obfuscate and that are not obfuscated in checkpassword_hashed: for example, one can immediately see that the program is carrying out a SHA-256 computation, and that (unless SHA-256 is weak) there are very few short inputs for which the program prints 1. In the terminology of some recent papers (see Section 2), what is obfuscated here is the key in a particular family of "keyed functions", but not the choice of family. Further comments on general obfuscation appear below. We emphasize password obfuscation (also known as "password hashing" or "point obfuscation") because it is an important special case: a widely deployed application using widely studied symmetric techniques.

1.1. State-of-the-art Password Hashing. See full version of this paper [13].

1.2. Matrix-Multiplication Password Hashing: the "Point Obfuscation" Challenge. A "point obfuscation" challenge was announced by Apon,

Huang, Katz, and Malozemoff [7] at the Crypto 2014 rump session. "Point obfus-cation" is the same concept as password hashing: see, e.g., [34] (a hashed pass-word is a "provably secure obfuscation of a 'point function' under the random oracle model").

The challenge consists of "an obfuscated 14-bit point function on Dropbox": a 25-gigabyte program with the promise that the program returns 1 for one secret 14-bit input and 0 for all other 14-bit inputs. The goal of the challenge is to deter-mine the secret 14-bit input: "learn the point and you win!" An accompanying October 2014 paper [5] described the challenge as having "security parameter 60", where "security parameter λ is designed to bound the probability of suc-cessful attacks by $2^{-\lambda}$".

We tried the 25-gigabyte program on a PC with the following relevant resources: an 8-core 125-watt AMD FX-8350 "Piledriver" CPU (about \$200), 32 gigabytes of RAM (about \$400), and a 2-terabyte hard drive (about \$100). The program took slightly over 4 hours for a single input. A brute-force attack using this program would obviously have been feasible but would have taken over 65536 hours worst-case and over 32768 hours on average, i.e., an average of nearly 4 years on the same PC, consuming 500 watt-years of electricity.

1.3. Attacking Matrix-Multiplication Password Hashing. In this paper we explain how we solved the same challenge in just 19 minutes using a cluster of 21 such PCs. The solution is 11000101100100; we reused this string above as our example of a secret password. Of course, knowing this solution allowed us to compress the original program to a much faster checkpassword algorithm.

The time for our attack algorithm against a worst-case input point would have been just 34 minutes, about 5000 times faster than the original brute-force attack, using under 0.2 watt-years of electricity. Our current software is slightly faster: it uses just 29.5 minutes on 22 PCs, or 35.7 minutes on 16 PCs.

More generally, for an n-bit point function obfuscated in the same way, our attack algorithm is asymptotically $n^4/2$ times faster than a brute-force search using the original program. This quartic speedup combines four linear speedups explained in this paper, taking advantage of the matrix-multiplication structure of the obfuscated program. Two of the four speedups (Section 3) are applicable to individual inputs, and could have been integrated into the original program, preserving the ratio between attack time and evaluation time; but the other two speedups (Section 4) share work between separate inputs, making the attack much faster than a simple brute-force attack.

See Section 1.6 for generalizations to more functions.

1.4. Matrix-Multiplication Password Hashing vs. State-of-the-art Password Hashing. It is well known that a 2^n-guess preimage attack against a hash function, cipher, etc. does not cost *exactly* 2^n times as much as a single function evaluation: there are always ways to merge small amounts of initial work across multiple inputs, and to skip small amounts of final work. See, for exam-ple, [35] ("Reduce the DES encryption from 16 rounds to the equivalent of ≈9.5 rounds, by shortcircuit evaluation and early aborts"), [30] ("biclique" attacks against various hash functions), and [14] ("biclique" attacks against AES).

However, one expects these speedups to become less and less noticeable for functions that have more and more rounds. For any state-of-the-art cost-C password-hashing function, the cost of a 2^n-guess preimage attack is very close to $2^n C$. The matrix-multiplication function is much weaker: the cost of our attacks is far below 2^n times the cost of the best method known to evaluate the function.

Even worse, the matrix-multiplication approach has severe performance problems that end up limiting the number n of input bits. The "obfuscated point function" includes $2n$ matrices, each matrix having $n+2$ rows and $n+2$ columns, each entry having approximately $4((\lambda + 1)(n + 4) + 2)^2 \log_2 \lambda$ bits; recall that λ is the target "security parameter". If λ is just 60 and n is above 36 then a single obfuscated password does not fit on a 2-terabyte hard drive, never mind the time and memory required to print and evaluate the function.

Earlier password-hashing functions handle a practically unlimited number of input bits with negligible slowdowns; fit obfuscated passwords into far fewer bits (a small constant times the target security level); allow the user far more flexibility to select the amount of time and memory used to check a password; and do not have the worrisome matrix structure exploited by our attacks.

1.5. Context: Obfuscating other Functions. Why, given the extensive hashing literature, would anyone introduce a new password-obfuscation method with unnecessary mathematical structure, obvious performance problems, and no obvious advantages? To answer this question, we now explain the context of the Apon–Huang–Katz–Malozemoff point-obfuscation challenge; we start by emphasizing that their goal was *not* to introduce a new point-obfuscation method.

Point functions are not the only functions that cryptographers obfuscate. Consider, for example, the following fast algorithm to compute the pqth power of an input mod pq, where p and q are particular prime numbers shown in the algorithm:

```
def rsa_encrypt_unobfuscated(x):
    p = 3797522793694367392280887275544562785456553638199
    q = 4009469095092088103068373529276146838921489972406 1
    pinv = 236369491094945993605686675623685455559934804514793
    qinv = 155877619438586464845346229355008040866846082271 53
    return (qinv*q*pow(x,q,p) + pinv*p*pow(x,p,q)) % (p*q)
```

The following algorithm is not as fast but uses only the product pq:

```
def rsa_encrypt(x):
    pq = int("15226050279225333605356183781326374297180681149613"
             "8068865790849458012296325895289765400035069 2006139")
    return pow(x,pq,pq)
```

These algorithms compute exactly the same function $x \mapsto x^{pq} \bmod pq$, but the primes p and q are exposed in `rsa_encrypt_unobfuscated` while they are obfuscated in `rsa_encrypt`. This obfuscation is exactly the reason that `rsa_encrypt` is safe to publish. In other words, RSA public-key encryption is an obfuscation of a secret-key encryption scheme.

(Note that this size of pq is too small for serious security. The particular pq shown here was introduced many years ago as the "RSA-100" challenge and was factored in 1991. One should take larger primes p and q.)

In a FOCS 2013 paper [26], Garg, Gentry, Halevi, Raykova, Sahai, and Waters proposed an obfuscation method that takes *any* fast algorithm A as input and "efficiently" produces an obfuscated algorithm Obf(A). The security goal for Obf is to be an "indistinguishability obfuscator": this means that Obf(A) is indistinguishable from Obf(A') if A and A' are fast algorithms computing the *same* function.

For example, if Obf is an indistinguishability obfuscator, and if an attacker can extract p and q from Obf(rsa_encrypt_unobfuscated), then the attacker can also extract p and q from Obf(rsa_encrypt), since the two obfuscations are indistinguishable; so the attacker can "efficiently" extract p and q from pq, by first computing Obf(rsa_encrypt). Contrapositive: if Obf is an indistinguishability obfuscator and the attacker *cannot* "efficiently" extract p and q from pq, then the attacker cannot extract p and q from Obf(rsa_encrypt_unobfuscated); i.e., Obf(rsa_encrypt_unobfuscated) hides p and q at least as effectively as rsa_encrypt does.

Another example, returning to symmetric cryptography: It is reasonable to assume that checkpassword and checkpassword_hashed compute the same function if the input length is restricted to, e.g., 200 bits. This assumption, together with the assumption that Obf is an indistinguishability obfuscator, implies that Obf(checkpassword) hides a $\leq$200-bit secret password at least as effectively as checkpassword_hashed does.

These examples illustrate the generality of indistinguishability obfuscation. In the words of Goldwasser and Rothblum [28], efficient indistinguishability obfuscation is "best-possible obfuscation", hiding everything that ad-hoc techniques would be able to hide.

There are, however, two critical caveats. First, it is not at all clear that the Obf proposal from [26] (or any newer proposal) will survive cryptanalysis. There are actually two alternative proposals in [26]: the first relies on multilinear maps [25] from Garg, Gentry, and Halevi, and the second relies on multilinear maps [23] from Coron, Lepoint, and Tibouchi. In a paper [20] posted early November 2014 (a week after we announced our solution to the "point obfuscation" challenge), Cheon, Han, Lee, Ryu, and Stehlé announced a complete break of the main security assumption in [23], undermining a remarkable number of papers built on top of [23]. The attack from [20] does not seem to break the application of [23] to point obfuscation (since "encodings of zero" are not provided in this context), but it illustrates the importance of leaving adequate time for cryptanalysis. A followup work by Gentry, Halevi, Maji, and Sahai [27] extends the attack from [20] to some settings where no "encodings of zero" below the "maximal level" are available, although the authors of [27] state that "so far we do not have a working attack on current obfuscation candidates".

Second, the literature already contains much simpler, much faster, much more thoroughly studied techniques for important examples of obfuscation, such as password hashing and public-key encryption. Even if the new proposals in fact provide indistinguishability obfuscation for more general functions, there is no reason to believe that they can provide competitive security and performance for functions where the previous techniques apply. We would expect the generality of these proposals to damage the security-performance curve in a broad range of real applications covered by the previous techniques, implying that these proposals should be used only for applications outside that range.

The goal of Apon, Huang, Katz, and Malozemoff was to investigate "the practicality of cryptographic program obfuscation". Their obfuscator is not limited to point functions; it takes more general circuits as input. However, after performance evaluation, they concluded that "program obfuscation is still far from being deployable, with the most complex functionality we are able to obfuscate being a 16-bit point function"; see [5, page 2]. They chose a 14-bit point function as a challenge.

1.6. Attacking Matrix-Multiplication-Based Obfuscation of any Function. The real-world importance of password hashing justifies focusing on point functions, but we have also adapted our attack algorithm to arbitrary n-bit-to-1-bit functions. Specifically, we have considered the method explained in [5] to obfuscate an arbitrary n-bit-to-1-bit function, and adapted our attack algorithm to this level of generality. For the general case, with u pairs of $w \times w$ matrices using n input bits, we save a factor of roughly $uw/2$ in evaluating each input, and a further factor of approximately $n/\log_2 w$ in evaluating all inputs. The $n/\log_2 w$ increases to $n/2$ for the standard input-bit order described in [5], but for an arbitrary input-bit order our attack is still considerably faster than a simple brute-force attack. See Section 8.

We comment that standard cryptographic hashing can be used to obfuscate general functions. We suggest the following trivial obfuscation technique as a baseline for future obfuscation challenges: precompute a table of hashes of the inputs that produce 1; add fake random hashes to pad the table to size 2^n (or a smaller size T, if it is acceptable to reveal that at most T inputs produce 1); and sort the table for fast lookups. This does not take polynomial time as $n \to \infty$ (for $T = 2^n$), but it nevertheless appears to be smaller, faster, and stronger than all of the recently proposed matrix-multiplication-based obfuscation techniques for every feasible value of n.

2   Review of the Obfuscation Scheme

Since the initial Obf proposal by Garg, Gentry, Halevi, Raykova, Sahai, and Waters [26] a lot of research was spent on finding applications and improving the proposed scheme. The challenge from [5] which we broke uses the relaxed-matrix-branching-program method by Ananth, Gupta, Ishai, and Sahai [4] to generate a size-reduced obfuscated program and combines it with the integer-based multilinear map (CLT) due to Coron, Lepoint, and Tibouchi [23]. As mentioned in

Section 1, the recent CLT attack by Cheon, Han, Lee, Ryu, and Stehlé [20] relies on "encodings of zero" and therefore does not apply to this point-obfuscation scheme. Our attack will also work for other matrix-multiplication-type obfuscation schemes with a similar structure, and in particular we see no obstacle to applying the same attack strategy with the Garg–Gentry–Halevi [25] multilinear map in place of CLT.

Most of the Obf literature does not state concrete parameters and does not present computer-verified examples. The first implementations, first examples, and first challenge were from Apon, Huang, Katz, and Malozemoff in [5], [6], and [7], providing an important foundation for quantifying and verifying attack performance.

The challenge given in [5] is an obfuscation of a point function, so we first give a self-contained description of these obfuscated point-function programs from the attacker's perspective; we then comment briefly on more general functions. For details on how the matrices below are constructed, we refer the reader to [4], [23], and of course [5]; but these details are not relevant to our attack.

2.1. Obfuscated Point Functions. A point function is a function on $\{0,1\}^n$ that returns 1 for exactly one secret vector of length n and 0 otherwise. The obfuscation scheme starts with this secret vector and an additional security parameter λ related to the security of the multilinear map.

The obfuscated version of the point function is given by a list of $2n$ public $(n+2) \times (n+2)$ matrices $B_{b,k}$ for $1 \le b \le n$ and $k \in \{0,1\}$ with integer entries; a row vector s of length $n+2$ with integer entries; a column vector t of length $n+2$ with integer entries; an integer p_{zt} (a "zero test" value, not to be confused with an "encoding of zero"); and a positive integer q. All of the entries and p_{zt} are between 0 and $q-1$ and appear random. The number of bits of q has an essentially linear impact upon our attack cost; [5] chooses the number of bits of q to be approximately $4((\lambda+1)(n+4)+2)^2 \log_2 \lambda$ for multilinear-map security reasons.

The obfuscated program works as follows:

- Take as input an n-bit vector $x = (x[1], x[2], \ldots, x[n])$.
- Compute the integer matrix $A = B_{1,x[1]}B_{2,x[2]} \cdots B_{n,x[n]}$ by successive matrix multiplications.
- Compute the integer $y(x) = sAt$ by a vector-matrix multiplication and a dot product.
- Compute $y(x)p_{zt}$ and reduce mod q to the range $[-(q-1)/2, (q-1)/2]$.
- Multiply the remainder by $2^{2\lambda+11}$, divide by q, and round to the nearest integer. This result is by definition the matrix-multiplication hash of x.
- Output 0 if this hash is 0; output 1 otherwise.

We have confirmed these steps against the software in [6].

The matrix-multiplication hash here is reminiscent of "Fast VSH" from [21]. Fast VSH hashes a block of input as follows: use input bits to select precomputed primes from a table, multiply those primes, and reduce mod something. The matrix-multiplication hash hashes a block of input as follows: use input bits to select precomputed matrices from a table, multiply those matrices, and reduce mod something. The matrices are secretly chosen with additional structure, but we do not use that structure in our attack.

2.2. Initial Security Analysis. A straightforward brute-force attack determines the secret vector by computing the matrix-multiplication hash of all 2^n vectors x. Of course, the computation stops once a correct hash is found.

Unfortunately [5] and [7] do not include timings for $\lambda = 60$ and $n = 14$, so we timed the software from [6] on one of our PCs and saw that each evaluation took 245 minutes, i.e., $2^{45.74}$ cycles at 4GHz. As the code automatically used all 8 cores of the CPU, this leads to a total of $2^{48.74}$ cycles per evaluation. A brute-force computation using this software would take $2^{14} \cdot 2^{48.74} = 2^{62.74}$ cycles worst-case, and would take more than 2^{60} cycles for 85% of all inputs. For comparison, recall that the CLT parameters were designed to just barely provide $2^{\lambda} = 2^{60}$ security, although the time scale for the 2^{60} here is not clear. If the time scale of the security parameter is close to one cycle then the cost of these two attacks is balanced.

In their Crypto 2014 rump-session announcement [8], the authors declared this brute-force attack to be infeasible: "The great part is, it's only 14 bits, so you think you can try all 2 to the 14 points, but it takes so long to evaluate that it's not feasible." The authors concluded in [5, Section 5] that they were "able to obfuscate some 'meaningful' programs" and that "it is important to note that the fact that we can produce *any* 'useful' obfuscations at all is surprising".

We agree that a 500-watt-year computation is a nonnegligible investment of computer time (although we would not characterize it as "infeasible"). However, in Section 3 we show how to make evaluation two orders of magnitude faster, bringing a brute-force attack within reach of a small computer cluster in a matter of days. Furthermore, in Section 4 we present a meet-in-the-middle attack that is another two orders of magnitude faster.

2.3. Obfuscation of General Functions and Keyed Functions. The obfuscation scheme in [4] transforms any function into a sequence of matrix multiplications. At every multiplication the matrix is selected based on a bit of the input x but usually the bits of x are used multiple times. For general circuits of length ℓ the paper constructs an oblivious relaxed matrix branching program of length $n\ell$ which cycles ℓ times through the n entries of x in sequence to select from $2n\ell$ matrices. In that case most of the matrices are obfuscated identity matrices but the regular access pattern stops the attacker from learning anything about the function.

Sometimes (as in the password-hashing example) the structure of the circuit is already public, and all that one wants to obfuscate is a secret key. In other words, the circuit computes $f_z(x) = \phi(z, x)$ for some secret key z, where ϕ is a publicly known branching program; the obfuscation needs to protect only the secret key z, and does not need to hide the function ϕ. This is called "obfuscation of keyed functions" in [4]. For this class of functions the length of the obfuscated program equals the length of the circuit for ϕ; the bits of x are used (and reused as often as necessary) in a public order determined by ϕ.

The designer can drive up the cost of brute-force attacks by including additional matrices as in the general case, but this also increases the obfuscation time, obfuscated-program size, and evaluation time.

3   Faster Algorithms for One Input

This section describes two speedups to the obfuscated programs described in Section 2. These speedups are important for constructive as well as destructive applications.

Combining these two ideas reduced our time to evaluate the obfuscated point function for a single input from 245 minutes to under 5 minutes (4 minutes 51 seconds), both measured on the same 8-core CPU. The authors of [6] have recently included these speedups in their software, with credit to us.

3.1. Cost Analysis for the Original Algorithm. Schoolbook multiplication of the two $(n+2) \times (n+2)$ matrices $B_{1,x[1]}$ and $B_{2,x[2]}$ uses $(n+2)^3$ multiplications of matrix entries. Similar comments apply to all $n-1$ matrix multiplications, for a total of $(n-1)(n+2)^3$ multiplications of matrix entries.

This quartic operation count understates the asymptotic complexity of the algorithm for two reasons, even when the security parameter λ is treated as a constant. The first reason is that the number of bits of q grows quadratically with n. The second reason is that the entries in $B_{1,x[1]}B_{2,x[2]}$ have about twice as many bits as the entries in the original matrices, the entries in $B_{1,x[1]}B_{2,x[2]}B_{3,x[3]}$ have about three times as many bits, etc. The paper [5] reports timings for point functions with $n \in \{8, 12, 16\}$ for security parameter 52, and in particular reports microbenchmarks of the time taken for each of the matrix products, starting with the first; these microbenchmarks clearly show the slowdown from one product to the next, and the paper explains that "each multiplication increases the multilinearity level of the underlying graded encoding scheme and thus the size of the resulting encoding".

We now account for the size of the matrix entries. Recall that state-of-the-art multiplication techniques (see, e.g., [11]) take time essentially linear in b, i.e., $b^{1+o(1)}$, to multiply b-bit integers. The original entries have size quadratic in n, and the products quickly grow to size cubic in n. More precisely, the final product $A = B_{1,x[1]} \cdots B_{n,x[n]}$ has entries bounded by $(n+2)^{n-1}(q-1)^n$ and typically larger than $(q-1)^n$; similar bounds apply to intermediate products. More than $n/2$ of the products have typical entries above $(q-1)^{n/2}$, so the multiplication time is dominated by integers having size cubic in n.

The total time to compute A is $n^{7+o(1)}$ for constant λ, equivalent to $n^{5+o(1)}$ multiplications of integers on the scale of q. This time dominates the total time for the algorithm.

3.2. Intermediate Reductions Mod q. We do better by limiting the growth of the elements in the computation. The final result $y(x)p_{zt}$ is in $\mathbf{Z}/q$, the ring of integers mod q, and is obtained by a sequence of multiplications and additions, so we are free to reduce mod q at any moment in the computation. Any of the initial integer multiplications has inputs at most $q - 1$; we allow the temporary values to grow to at most $(n + 2)(q - 1)^2$ by computing the sum of the products for one entry and then reduce mod q. Thus any future multiplication also has its inputs at most $q - 1$.

State-of-the-art division techniques take time within a constant factor of state-of-the-art multiplication techniques, so $(n + 2)^2$ reductions mod q take asymptotically negligible time compared to $(n+2)^3$ multiplications. The number of bits in each intermediate integer drops from cubic in n to quadratic in n.

More precisely, the asymptotic speedup factor is $n/2$, since the original multiplication inputs had on average about $n/2$ times as many bits as q. We observe a smaller speedup factor for concrete values of n, mainly because of the overhead for the extra divisions.

The total time to compute $A \bmod q$ is $n^{6+o(1)}$ for constant λ, dominated by $(n - 1)(n + 2)^3 = n^4 + 5n^3 + 6n^2 - 4n - 8$ multiplications of integers bounded by q, inside $(n - 1)(n + 2)^2 = n^3 + 3n^2 - 4$ dot products mod q.

3.3. Matrix-Vector Multiplications. We further improve the computation by reordering the operations used to compute $y(x)$: specifically, instead of computing A, we compute $y(x) = \left(\cdots \left((sB_{1,x[1]})B_{2,x[2]} \right) \cdots B_{n,x[n]} \right) t$. This sequence of operations requires n vector-matrix products and a final vector-vector multiplication.

This combines straightforwardly with intermediate reductions mod q as above. The total time to compute $y(x) \bmod q$ is $n^{5+o(1)}$, dominated by $n(n + 2) + 1 = (n + 1)^2$ dot products mod q.

4   Faster Algorithms for Many Inputs

A brute-force attack iterates through the whole input range and computes the evaluation for each possible input until the result of the evaluation is 1 and thus the correct input has been found. In terms of complexity our improvements from Section 3 reduced the cost of brute-forcing an n-bit point function from time $n^{7+o(1)}2^n$ to time $n^{5+o(1)}2^n$ for constant λ, dominated by $(n + 1)^2 2^n$ dot products mod q. This algorithm is displayed in Figure 4.1 of [13].

This section presents further reductions to the complexity of the attack. These share computations between evaluations of many inputs and have no matching speedups on the constructive side (which usually only evaluates at a single point at once and in any case cannot be expected to have related inputs).

4.2. Reusing Intermediate Products. Recall that Section 3 computes $y(x) = sB_{1,x[1]} \cdots B_{n,x[n]}t \bmod q$ by multiplying from left to right: the last two steps are to multiply the vector $sB_{1,x[1]} \cdots B_{n-1,x[n-1]}$ by $B_{n,x[n]}$ and then by t.

Notice that this vector does not depend on the choice of $x[n]$. By computing this vector, multiplying the vector by $B_{n,0}$ and then by t, and multiplying the same vector by $B_{n,1}$ and then by t, we obtain both $y(x[1], \ldots, x[n - 1], 0)$ and $y(x[1], \ldots, x[n - 1], 1)$. This saves almost half of the cost of the computation.

Similarly, we need only two computations of $sB_{1,x[1]}$ for the two choices of $x[1]$; four computations of $sB_{1,x[1]}B_{2,x[2]}$ for the four choices of $(x[1], x[2])$; etc.

Overall there are $2 + 4 + 8 + \cdots + 2^n = 2^{n+1} - 2$ vector-matrix multiplications here, plus 2^n final multiplications by t, for a total of $(n + 2)(2^{n+1} - 2) + 2^n = (2n + 5)2^n - 2(n + 2)$ dot products mod q.

To minimize memory requirements, we enumerate x in lexicographic order, maintaining a stack of intermediate products. We reuse products on the stack to the extent allowed by the common prefix between x and the previous x. In most cases this common prefix is almost the entire stack. On average slightly fewer than two matrix-vector products need to be recomputed for each x. See Figure 4.3 of [13] for a recursive version of this algorithm.

4.4. A Meet-in-the-middle Attack. To do better we change the order of matrix multiplication yet again, separating ℓ "left" bits from $n - \ell$ "right" bits:

$$y(x) = (sB_{1,x[1]} \cdots B_{\ell,x[\ell]})(B_{\ell+1,x[\ell+1]} \cdots B_{n,x[n]}t).$$

We exploit this separation to store and reuse some computations. Specifically, we precompute a table of "left" products

$$L[x[1], \ldots, x[\ell]] = sB_{1,x[1]} \cdots B_{\ell,x[\ell]}$$

for all 2^ℓ choices of $(x[1], \ldots, x[\ell])$. The main computation of all $y(x)$ works as follows: for each choice of $(x[\ell + 1], \ldots, x[n])$, compute the "right" product

$$R[x[\ell + 1], \ldots, x[n]] = B_{\ell+1,x[\ell+1]} \cdots B_{n,x[n]}t,$$

and then multiply each element of the L table by this vector.

Computing a single left product $sB_{1,x[1]} \cdots B_{\ell,x[\ell]}$ from left to right, as in Section 3, takes ℓ vector-matrix products, i.e., $\ell(n + 2)$ dot products mod q. Overall the precomputation uses $\ell(n + 2)2^\ell$ dot products mod q.

Computing a single right product $B_{\ell+1,x[\ell+1]} \cdots B_{n,x[n]}t$ from right to left (starting from t) takes $n - \ell$ matrix-vector products, for a total of $(n - \ell)(n + 2)$ dot products mod q. The outer loop in the main computation therefore uses $(n - \ell)(n + 2)2^{n-\ell}$ dot products mod q in the worst case. The inner loop in the main computation, computing all $y(x)$, uses just 2^n dot products mod q in total in the worst case.

The total number of dot products mod q in this algorithm, including precomputation, is $\ell(n+2)2^\ell + (n-\ell)(n+2)2^{n-\ell} + 2^n$. In particular, for $\ell = n/2$ (assuming n is even), the number of dot products mod q simplifies to $n(n + 2)2^{n/2} + 2^n$.

For a traditional meet-in-the-middle attack, the outer loop of the main computation simply looks up each result in a precomputed sorted table. Our notion of "meet" is more complicated, and requires inspecting each element of the table, but this is still a considerable speedup: each inspection is simply a dot product, much faster than the vector-matrix multiplications used before.

We comment that taking ℓ logarithmic in n produces almost the same speedup with polynomial memory consumption. More precisely, taking ℓ close to $2\log_2 n$ means that $2^{n-\ell}$ is smaller than 2^n by a factor roughly n^2, so the term $(n - \ell)(n + 2)2^{n-\ell}$ is on the same scale as 2^n. The table then contains roughly n^2 vectors, similar size to the original $2n$ matrices. Taking slightly larger

ℓ reduces the term $(n - \ell)(n + 2)2^{n-\ell}$ to a smaller scale. A similar choice of ℓ becomes important for speed in our attack on obfuscations of general functions in Section 8.2.

4.5. Combining the Ideas. One can easily reuse intermediate products in the meet-in-the-middle attack. See Figure 4.6 of [13]. This reduces the precomputation to $2^{\ell+1} - 2$ vector-matrix multiplications, i.e., $(n + 2)(2^{\ell+1} - 2)$ dot products mod q. It similarly reduces the outer loop of the main computation to $(n + 2)(2^{n-\ell+1} - 2)$ dot products mod q.

The total number of dot products mod q in the entire algorithm is now $(n + 2)(2^{\ell+1} + 2^{n-\ell+1} - 4) + 2^n$. For example, for $\ell = n/2$, the number of dot products mod q simplifies to $4(n + 2)(2^{n/2} - 1) + 2^n$.

This is not much smaller than the meet-in-the-middle attack without reuse: the dominant term is the same 2^n. However, as above one can take much smaller ℓ to reduce memory consumption. The reuse now allows ℓ to be taken almost as small as $\log_2 n$ without significantly compromising speed, so the precomputed table is now much smaller than the original $2n$ matrices.

If memory consumption is not a concern then one should compute both an L table and an R table, interleaving the computations of the tables and obtaining each LR product as soon as both L and R are known. For equal-size tables this means computing L_0, R_0, L_0R_0, L_1, L_1R_0, R_1, L_0R_1, L_1R_1, etc. This order of operations does not improve worst-case performance, but it does improve average-case performance. The same improvement has been previously applied to other meet-in-the-middle attacks: for example, Pollard applied this improvement to Shanks's "baby-step giant-step" discrete-logarithm method. Compare [38, pages 419–420] to [36, page 439, top].

5 Parallelization

We implemented our attack for shared-memory systems using OpenMP and for cluster systems using MPI. In general, brute-force attacks are embarrassingly parallel, i.e., the search space can be distributed over the computing nodes without any need for communication, resulting in a perfectly scalable parallelization. However, for this attack, some computations are shared between consecutive iterations. Therefore, some cooperation and communication are required between computing nodes.

5.1. Precomputation. Recall that the precomputation step computes all 2^ℓ possible cases for the "left" ℓ bits of the whole input space. A non-parallel implementation first computes ℓ vector-matrix multiplications for $sB_{1,0} \cdots B_{\ell,0}$ and stores the first $\ell - 1$ intermediate products on a stack. As many intermediate products as possible are reused for each subsequent case.

For a shared-memory system, all data can be shared between the threads. Furthermore, the vector-matrix multiplications expose a sufficient amount of parallelism such that the threads can cooperate on the computation of each multiplication. There is some loss in parallel efficiency due to the need for synchronization and work-share imbalance.

For a cluster system, communication and synchronization of such a workload distribution would be too expensive. Therefore, we split the input range for the precomputation between the cluster nodes, compute each section of the precomputed table independently, and finally broadcast the table entries to all cluster nodes. For simplicity, we split the input range evenly which results in some workload imbalance. (On each node, the workload is distributed as described above over several threads to use all CPU cores on each node.) This procedure has some loss in parallel efficiency due to the fact that each cluster node separately performs k vector-matrix multiplications for the first precomputation in its range, due to some workload imbalance, and due to the final all-to-all communication.

5.2. Main Computation. For simplicity, we start the main computation once the whole precomputed table L is available. Recall that a non-parallel implementation of the main computation first computes the vector $R[0, \ldots, 0] = B_{\ell+1,0} \cdots B_{n,0} t$ using $n - \ell$ matrix-vector multiplications, and multiplies this vector by all 2^ℓ table entries. It then moves to other possibilities for the "right" $n - \ell$ bits, reusing intermediate products in a similar way to the precomputation and multiplying each resulting vector $R[\ldots]$ by all 2^ℓ table entries.

For a shared-memory system, the computations of $R[\ldots]$ are distributed between the threads the same way as for the precomputation. However, vector-vector multiplication does not expose as much parallelism as vector-matrix multiplication. Therefore, we distribute over the threads the 2^ℓ independent vector-vector multiplications of each of the 2^ℓ table entries with $R[0, \ldots, 0]$. As in the parallelization of precomputation, there is some loss of parallel efficiency due to synchronization and work-share imbalance for the vector-matrix multiplications and some loss due to work-share imbalance for the vector-vector multiplications.

For a cluster system we again cannot efficiently distribute the workload of one vector-matrix multiplication over several cluster nodes. Therefore, we distribute the search space evenly over the cluster nodes and let each cluster node compute its share of the workload independently. This approach creates some redundant work because each cluster node computes its own initial $R[\ldots]$ using $n-\ell$ matrix-vector multiplications.

6   Performance Measurements

We used 22 PCs in the Saber cluster [12] for the attack. Each PC is of the type described earlier, including an 8-core CPU. The PCs are connected by a gigabit Ethernet network. Each PC also has two GK110 GPUs but we did not use these GPUs.

6.1. First Break of the Challenge. We implemented the single-input optimizations described in Section 3 and used 20 PCs to compute 2^{14} point evaluations for all possible inputs. This revealed the secret point 11000101100100 after about 23 hours. The worst-case runtime for this approach on these 20 PCs is about 52 hours for checking all 2^{14} possible input points. On 18 October 2014

Table 6.4. Measurements of real time actually consumed by various components of complete attack, starting from announcement of challenge

Attack component	Real time
Initial procrastination	a few days
First attempt to download challenge (failed)	82 minutes
Subsequent procrastination	40 days and 40 nights
Fourth attempt to download challenge (succeeded)	about an hour
Original program [6] evaluating one input	245 minutes
Original program evaluating all inputs on one computer	(extrapolated) 7.6 years
Copying challenge to cluster (without UDP broadcasts)	about an hour
Reading challenge from disk into RAM	2.5 minutes
Our faster program evaluating one input	4.85 minutes
First successful break of challenge on 20 PCs	23 hours
Further procrastination ("this is fast enough")	about half a week
Our faster program evaluating all inputs on 21 PCs	34 minutes
Second successful break of challenge on 21 PCs	19 minutes
Our current program evaluating all inputs on 1 PC	444.2 minutes
Our current program evaluating all inputs on 22 PCs	29.5 minutes
Time for an average input point on 22 PCs	19.9 minutes
Successful break of challenge on 22 PCs	17.5 minutes

we sent the authors of [5] the solution to the challenge, and a few hours later they confirmed that the solution was correct.

6.2. Second Break of the Challenge. We implemented the multiple-input optimizations described in Section 4 and the parallelization described in Section 5. Our optimized attack implementation found the input point in under 19 minutes on 21 PCs; this includes the time to precompute a table L of size 2^7. The worst-case runtime of the attack for checking all 2^{14} possible input points is under 34 minutes on 21 PCs.

6.3. Additional Latency. Obviously "19 minutes" understates the real time that elapsed between the announcement of the challenge (19 August 2014) and our solution of the challenge with our second program (25 October 2014). See Table 6.4 for a broader perspective.

The largest deterrent was the difficulty of downloading 25 gigabytes. Whenever a connection broke, the server would insist on starting from the beginning ("HTTP server doesn't seem to support byte ranges"), presumably because the server stores all files in a compressed format that does not support random access. The same restriction also meant that we could not download different portions of the file in parallel.

To truly minimize latency we would have had to overlap the download of the challenge, the broadcast of the challenge to the cluster, and the computation, and of course our optimizations and software would have had to be ready first. In this context, the precompute-L-table algorithm in Section 4 has a latency advantage compared to a bit-reversed algorithm that precomputes an R table instead of an L table: the portion of the input relevant to L is available sooner than the portion of the input relevant to R.

6.5. Timings of Various Software Components. We have put the latest version of our software online at http://obviouscation.cr.yp.to. We applied this software to the same challenge on 22 PCs. We have applied the latest version of our software to the same challenge on 22 PCs. The software took a total time of 1769 seconds (29.5 minutes) to check all 2^{14} input points. An average input point was checked within 1191 seconds (19.9 minutes). The secret challenge point was found within 1048 seconds (17.5 minutes).

The rest of this section describes the time taken by various components of this computation.

Each vector-matrix multiplication took 15.577 s on average (15.091 minimum, 16.421 maximum), using all eight cores jointly. For comparison, on a single core, a vector-matrix multiplication requires about 115 s. Therefore, we achieve a parallel efficiency of $\frac{115s/8}{15.577s} \approx 92\%$ for parallel vector-matrix multiplication.

Each y computation took 8.986 s on average (7.975 minimum, 9.820 maximum), using a single core. Each y computation consists of one vector-vector multiplication, one multiplication by p_{zt} (which we could absorb into the precomputed table, producing a small speedup), and one reduction mod q.

On a single machine (no MPI parallelization), after a reboot to flush the challenge from RAM, the timing breaks down as follows:

1. Loading the matrices for "left" bit positions: 83.999 s.
2. Total precomputation of $2^7 = 128$ table entries: 4055.408 s.
   (a) Computing the first $\ell = 7$ vector-matrix products: 107.623 s.
4. Loading the matrices for "right" bit positions: 78.490 s.
5. Total computation of all 2^{14} evaluations: 22518.900 s.
   (a) Computing the first $n - \ell = 7$ matrix-vector products: 109.731 s.

Overall total runtime: 26654 s (444.2 minutes). From these computations, steps 1, 2a, 4, and 5a are not parallelized for cluster computation. The total timing breakdown on 22 PCs, after a reboot of all PCs, is as follows:

1. Loading the matrices for "left" bit positions: 89.449 s average (75.786 on the fastest node, 104.696 on the slowest node). With more effort we could have overlapped most of this loading (and the subsequent loading) with computation, or skipped all disk copies by keeping the matrices in RAM.
2. Total precomputation of $2^7 = 128$ table entries: 253.346 s average (217.893 minimum, 295.999 maximum).
   (a) Computing the first $\ell = 7$ vector-matrix products: 107.951 s average (107.173 minimum, 109.297 maximum).
3. All-to-all communication: 153.591 s average (100.848 minimum, 199.200 maximum); i.e., about 53 s average idle time for the busier nodes to catch up, followed by about 101 s of communication. With more effort we could have overlapped most of this communication with computation.

4. Loading the matrices for "right" bit positions: 85.412 s average (73.710 minimum, 97.526 maximum).
5. Total computation of all 2^{14} evaluations: 1097.680 s average (942.981 minimum, 1169.520 maximum).
   (a) Computing the first $n - \ell = 7$ matrix-vector products: 108.878 s average (107.713 minimum, 110.001 maximum).
6. Final idle time waiting for all other nodes to finish computation: 80.277 s average (0.076 minimum, 80.277 maximum).

Overall total runtime, including MPI startup overhead: 1769 s (29.5 minutes). The overall parallel efficiency of the cluster parallelization thus is $\frac{26654\,\mathrm{s}/22}{1769\,\mathrm{s}} \approx$ 68%. Steps 1, 2a, 3, 4, and 5a, totaling 545.281 s, are those parts of the computation that contain parallelization overhead (in particular the communication time in step 3 is added compared to the single-machine case). Removing these steps from the efficiency calculation results in a parallel efficiency of $\frac{(26654\,\mathrm{s} - 380\,\mathrm{s})/22}{1769\,\mathrm{s} - 545\,\mathrm{s}} \approx 98\%$, which shows that those steps are responsible for almost all of the loss in parallel efficiency.

7 Further Speedups — see [13]

8 Generalizing the Attack Beyond Point Functions

This section looks beyond point functions: it considers the general obfuscation method explained in [5] for any program. Recall from Section 2 that for general programs the number of pairs of matrices, say u, is no longer tied to the number n of input bits: usually each input bit is used multiple times. Furthermore, each matrix is $w \times w$ and each vector has length w for some $w > n$, where the choice of w depends on the function and is no longer required to be $n + 2$.

The speedups from Section 3 rely only on the general matrix-multiplication structure, not on the pattern of accessing input bits. Reducing intermediate results mod q saves a factor approximately $u/2$. Using vector-matrix multiplication rather than matrix-matrix multiplication saves a factor w.

However, the attacks from Section 4 rely on having each input bit used exactly once. We cannot simply reorder the matrices to bring together the uses of an input bit: matrix multiplication is not commutative. Usually many of the matrices are obfuscated identity matrices, but the way the matrices are randomized prevents these matrices from being removed or reordered; see [5] for details.

This section explains two attacks that apply in more generality. The first attack allows cycling through the input bits any number of times, and saves a factor approximately $n/2$ compared to brute force. The second attack allows using and reusing input bits any number of times in any pattern, and saves a factor approximately $n/(2\log_2 w)$ compared to brute force. The first attack is what one might call a "meet-in-many-middles" attack; the second attack does not involve precomputations. Both attacks exploit the idea of reusing intermediate products, sharing computations between adjacent inputs; both attacks can be parallelized by ideas similar to Section 5.

8.1. Speedup $n/2$ for Cycling Through Input Bits. Our first attack applies to any circuit obfuscated as explained in [5, Section 2.2.1]. The obfuscated circuit is constructed to "cycle through each of the input bits $x_1, x_2, \ldots, x_n$ in order, m times", using $u = mn$ pairs of matrices. In other words, $y(x)$ is defined as

$$s(B_{1,x[1]} \cdots B_{n,x[n]})(B_{n+1,x[1]} \cdots B_{2n,x[n]}) \cdots (B_{(m-1)n+1,x[1]} \cdots B_{mn,x[n]})t.$$

Evaluating $y(x)$ for one x from left to right takes mn vector-matrix multiplications and 1 vector-vector multiplication, i.e., $uw + 1$ dot products mod q. A straightforward brute-force attack thus takes $(uw + 1)2^n$ dot products mod q.

One can split the sequence of mn matrices at some position ℓ, and carry out a meet-in-the-middle attack as in Section 4. However, this produces at most a constant-factor speedup once $m \geq 2$: either the precomputation has to compute products at most of the positions for all 2^n inputs, or the main computation has to compute products at most of the positions for all 2^n inputs, or both, depending on ℓ.

We do better by splitting the sequence of *input bits* at some position ℓ. This means grouping the matrix positions into two disjoint "left" and "right" sets as follows, splitting each input cycle:

$$y(x) = \big(sB_{1,x[1]} \cdots B_{\ell,x[\ell]}\big)\big(B_{\ell+1,x[\ell+1]} \cdots B_{n,x[n]}\big)$$
$$\big(B_{n+1,x[1]} \cdots B_{n+\ell,x[\ell]}\big)\big(B_{n+\ell+1,x[\ell+1]} \cdots B_{2n,x[n]}\big)$$
$$\vdots$$
$$\big(B_{(m-1)n+1,x[1]} \cdots B_{(m-1)n+\ell,x[\ell]}\big)\big(B_{(m-1)n+\ell+1,x[\ell+1]} \cdots B_{mn,x[n]}t\big)$$
$$= L_1[x[1], \ldots, x[\ell]]R_1[x[\ell+1], \ldots, x[n]]$$
$$L_2[x[1], \ldots, x[\ell]]R_2[x[\ell+1], \ldots, x[n]]$$
$$\vdots$$
$$L_m[x[1], \ldots, x[\ell]]R_m[x[\ell+1], \ldots, x[n]],$$

where

$$L_1[x[1], \ldots, x[\ell]] = sB_{1,x[1]} \cdots B_{\ell,x[\ell]},$$
$$L_i[x[1], \ldots, x[\ell]] = B_{(i-1)n+1,x[1]} \cdots B_{(i-1)n+\ell,x[\ell]} \qquad \text{for } 2 \leq i \leq m,$$
$$R_i[x[\ell+1], \ldots, x[n]] = B_{(i-1)n+\ell+1,x[\ell+1]} \cdots B_{in,x[n]} \qquad \text{for } 1 \leq i \leq m-1,$$
$$R_m[x[\ell+1], \ldots, x[n]] = B_{(m-1)n+\ell+1,x[\ell+1]} \cdots B_{mn,x[n]}t.$$

We exploit this grouping as follows. We use $2^{\ell+1} - 2$ vector-matrix multiplications to precompute a table of the vectors $L_1[x[1], \ldots, x[\ell]]$ for all 2^ℓ choices of $x[1], \ldots, x[\ell]$, as in Section 4. Similarly, for each $i \in \{2, \ldots, m\}$, we use $2^{\ell+1} - 4$ matrix-matrix multiplications to precompute a table of the matrices $L_i[x[1], \ldots, x[\ell]]$ for all 2^ℓ choices of $x[1], \ldots, x[\ell]$. The tables use space for $(w + (m-1)w^2)2^\ell$ integers mod q.

After this precomputation, the outer loop of the main computation runs through each choice of $x[\ell+1], \ldots, x[n]$, computing the corresponding matrices

$R_1[\ldots], \ldots, R_{m-1}[\ldots]$ and vector $R_m[\ldots]$. The inner loop runs through each choice of $x[1], \ldots, x[\ell]$, computing each $y(x)$ by multiplying $L_1, R_1, \ldots, L_m, R_m$; each x here takes $2m - 2$ vector-matrix multiplications and 1 vector-vector multiplication.

Overall the precomputation costs $((m - 1)w^2 + w)(2^{\ell+1} - 2) - 2(m - 1)w^2$ dot products mod q; the outer loop of the main computation costs $((m-1)w^2 + w)(2^{n-\ell+1} - 2) - 2(m - 1)w^2$ dot products mod q; and the inner loop costs $((2m - 2)w + 1)2^n$ dot products mod q.

In particular, taking $\ell = n/2$ (assuming as before that n is even) simplifies the total cost to $4w(2^{n/2} - 1) + 2^n$ for $m = 1$, exactly as in Section 4, and $4w((m - 1)w + 1)(2^{n/2} - 1) + ((2m - 2)w + 1)2^n - 4(m - 1)w^2$ for general m. Recall that brute force costs $(uw+1)2^n = (mnw+1)2^n$. For large n, large w, and $m \geq 2$, the asymptotically dominant term has dropped from $mnw2^n$ to $2mw2^n$, saving a factor of $n/2$.

The same asymptotic savings appears with much smaller ℓ, almost as small as $\log_2 w$. Beware that this does not make the tables asymptotically smaller than the original $2mn$ matrices for $m \geq 2$: most of the table space here is consumed by matrices rather than vectors.

8.2. Speedup $n/\log_2 w$ for any Order of Input Bits.
One can try to spoil the above attack by changing the order of input bits. A slightly different order of input bits, rotating positions in each round, is already stated in [4, Section 3, Claim 2, final formula], but it is easy to adapt the attack to this order. It is more difficult to adapt the attack to an order chosen randomly, or an order that combinatorially avoids keeping bits together. Varying the input order is not a new idea: see, e.g., the compression functions inside MD5 [37] and BLAKE [10]. Many other orders of input bits also arise naturally in "keyed" functions; see Section 2.

The general picture is that $y(x)$ is defined by the formula

$$y(x) = sB_{1,x[\text{inp}(1)]}B_{2,x[\text{inp}(2)]} \cdots B_{u,x[\text{inp}(u)]}t$$

for some constants $\text{inp}(1), \text{inp}(2), \ldots, \text{inp}(u) \in \{1, 2, \ldots, n\}$. As a first unification we multiply s into $B_{1,0}$ and into $B_{1,1}$, and then multiply t into $B_{u,0}$ and into $B_{u,1}$. Now $B_{1,0}, B_{1,1}, B_{u,0}, B_{u,1}$ are vectors, except that they are integers if $u = 1$; and $y(x)$ is defined by

$$y(x) = B_{1,x[\text{inp}(1)]}B_{2,x[\text{inp}(2)]} \cdots B_{u,x[\text{inp}(u)]}.$$

We now explain a general recursive strategy to evaluate this formula for all inputs without exploiting any particular pattern in $\text{inp}(1), \text{inp}(2), \ldots, \text{inp}(u)$. The strategy is reducing the number of variable bits in x by one in each iteration.

Assume that not all of $\text{inp}(1), \text{inp}(2), \ldots, \text{inp}(u)$ are equal to n. Substitute $x[n] = 0$ into the formula for $y(x)$. This means, for each i with $\text{inp}(i) = n$ in turn, eliminating the expression "$B_{i,x[n]}$" as follows:

- multiply $B_{i,0}$ into $B_{i+1,0}$ and into $B_{i+1,1}$ if $i < u$;
- multiply $B_{i,0}$ into $B_{i-1,0}$ and into $B_{i-1,1}$ if $i = u$;

- set $B_i \leftarrow B_{i+1}$, then $B_{i+1} \leftarrow B_{i+2}, \ldots$, then $B_{u-1} \leftarrow B_u$;
- reduce u to $u - 1$.

Recursively evaluate the resulting formula for all choices of $x[1], \ldots, x[n-1]$. Then do all the same steps again with $x[n] = 1$ instead of $x[n] = 0$.

More generally, one can recurse on the two choices of $x[b]$ for any b. It is most efficient to recurse on the most frequently used index b (or one of the most frequent indices b if there are several), since this minimizes the length of the formula to handle recursively. This is equivalent to first relabeling the indices so that they are in nondecreasing order of frequency, and then always recursing on the last bit.

Once n is sufficiently small (see below), stop the recursion. This means separately enumerating all possibilities for $(x[1], \ldots, x[n])$ and, for each possibility, evaluating the given formula

$$y(x) = B_{1,x[\mathrm{inp}(1)]} B_{2,x[\mathrm{inp}(2)]} \cdots B_{u,x[\mathrm{inp}(u)]}$$

by multiplication from left to right. Recall that $B_{1,x[\mathrm{inp}(1)]}$ is actually a vector (or an integer if $u = 1$). Each computation takes $u - 1$ vector-matrix multiplications, i.e., $(u - 1)w$ dot products mod q. (Here we ignore the extra speed of the final vector-vector multiplication.) The total across all inputs is $(u - 1)w2^n$ dot products mod q.

To see that the recursion reduces this complexity, consider the impact of using exactly one level of recursion, from n down to $n - 1$. If index n is used u_n times then eliminating each $B_{i,x[n]}$ costs $2u_n$ matrix multiplications, and produces a formula of length $u - u_n$ instead of u, so each recursive call uses $(u - u_n - 1)w2^{n-1}$ dot products mod q. The bound on the total number of dot products mod q drops from $(u - 1)w2^n$ to $4u_n w^2 + (u - u_n - 1)w2^n$, saving $u_n w2^n - 4u_n w^2$. This analysis suggests stopping the recursion when 2^n drops below $4w$, i.e., at $n = \lceil \log_2 w \rceil + 1$.

More generally, the algorithm costs a total of $4u_n w^2 + 8u_{n-1}w^2 + 16u_{n-2}w^2 + \cdots + 2^{n-\ell+1}u_{\ell+1}w^2 + 2^n(u_\ell + \cdots + u_1 - 1)w$ dot products mod q if the recursion stops at level ℓ. We relabel as explained above so that $u_n \geq u_{n-1} \geq \cdots \geq u_1$, and assume $n > \ell$. The sum $u_\ell + \cdots + u_1$ is at most $\ell u/n$, and the sum $u_n + 2u_{n-1} + 4u_{n-2} + \cdots + 2^{n-\ell-1}u_{\ell+1}$ is at most $2^{n-\ell}u/(n - \ell)$, for a total of less than $(4w2^{-\ell}/(n - \ell) + \ell/n)uw2^n$. Taking $\ell = \lceil \log_2 w \rceil + 1$ reduces this total to at most $(4/(n - \lceil \log_2 w \rceil - 1) + (\lceil \log_2 w \rceil + 1)/n)uw2^n$.

For comparison, a brute-force attack against the original problem (separately evaluating $y(x)$ for each x) costs $(u - 1)w2^n$. We have thus saved a factor of approximately $n/\log_2 w$.

References

[4] Ananth, P., Gupta, D., Ishai, Y., Sahai, A.: Optimizing obfuscation: avoiding Barrington's theorem. In: ACM-CCS 2014 (2014). https://eprint.iacr.org/2014/222

[5] Apon, D., Huang, Y., Katz, J., Malozemoff, A.J.: Implementing cryptographic program obfuscation, version 20141005 (2014). https://eprint.iacr.org/2014/779

[6] Apon, D., Huang, Y., Katz, J., Malozemoff, A.J.: Implementing cryptographic program obfuscation (software) (2014). https://github.com/amaloz/obfuscation

[7] Apon, D., Huang, Y., Katz, J., Malozemoff, A.J.: Implementing cryptographic program obfuscation (slides). In: Crypto 2014 Rump Session (2014). http://crypto.2014.rump.cr.yp.to/bca480a4e7fcdaf5bfa9dec75ff890c8.pdf

[8] Apon, D., Huang, Y., Katz, J., Malozemoff, A.J.: Implementing cryptographic program obfuscation (video). In: Crypto 2014 Rump Session, starting at 3:56:25 (2014). https://gauchocast.ucsb.edu/Panopto/Pages/Viewer.aspx?id=d34af80d-bdb5-464b-a8ac-2c3adefc5194

[10] Aumasson, J.-P., Henzen, L., Meier, W., Phan, R.C.-W.: SHA-3 proposal BLAKE (version 1.3) (2010). https://www.131002.net/blake/blake.pdf

[11] Bernstein, D.J.: Fast multiplication and its applications, in Surveys in algorithmic number theory, pp. 325–384. Cambridge University Press (2008)

[12] Bernstein, D.J.: The Saber cluster (2014). http://blog.cr.yp.to/20140602-saber.html

[13] Bernstein, D.J., Hülsing, A., Lange, T., Niederhagen, R.: Bad directions in cryptographic hash functions (2015). https://eprint.iacr.org/2015/151

[14] Bogdanov, A., Khovratovich, D., Rechberger, C.: Biclique cryptanalysis of the full AES. In: Lee, D.H., Wang, X. (eds.) ASIACRYPT 2011. LNCS, vol. 7073, pp. 344–371. Springer, Heidelberg (2011)

[20] Cheon, J.H., Han, K., Lee, C., Ryu, H., Stehlé, D.: Cryptanalysis of the multilinear map over the integers. In: Oswald, E., Fischlin, M. (eds.) EURO-CRYPT 2015. LNCS, vol. 9056, pp. 3–12. Springer, Heidelberg (2015). https://eprint.iacr.org/2014/906

[21] Contini, S., Lenstra, A.K., Steinfeld, R.: VSH, an efficient and provable collision-resistant hash function. In: Vaudenay, S. (ed.) EUROCRYPT 2006. LNCS, vol. 4004, pp. 165–182. Springer, Heidelberg (2006)

[23] Coron, J.-S., Lepoint, T., Tibouchi, M.: Practical multilinear maps over the integers. In: Canetti, R., Garay, J.A. (eds.) CRYPTO 2013, Part I. LNCS, vol. 8042, pp. 476–493. Springer, Heidelberg (2013)

[24] Garfinkel, S., Spafford, G., Schwartz, A.: Practical UNIX & Internet security, 3rd edn. O'Reilly (2003)

[25] Garg, S., Gentry, C., Halevi, S.: Candidate multilinear maps from ideal lattices. In: Johansson, T., Nguyen, P.Q. (eds.) EUROCRYPT 2013. LNCS, vol. 7881, pp. 1–17. Springer, Heidelberg (2013)

[26] Garg, S., Gentry, C., Halevi, S., Raykova, M., Sahai, A., Waters, B.: Candidate indistinguishability obfuscation and functional encryption for all circuits. In: FOCS 2013, pp. 40–49 (2013)

[27] Gentry, C., Halevi, S., Maji, H.K., Sahai, A.: Zeroizing without zeroes: Cryptanalyzing multilinear maps without encodings of zero (2014). https://eprint.iacr.org/2014/929

[28] Goldwasser, S., Rothblum, G.N.: On best-possible obfuscation. Journal of Cryptology **27**, 480–505 (2014)

[30] Khovratovich, D., Rechberger, C., Savelieva, A.: Bicliques for preimages: attacks on Skein-512 and the SHA-2 family. In: Canteaut, A. (ed.) FSE 2012. LNCS, vol. 7549, pp. 244–263. Springer, Heidelberg (2012)

[34] Lynn, B.Y.S., Prabhakaran, M., Sahai, A.: Positive Results and Techniques for Obfuscation. In: Cachin, C., Camenisch, J.L. (eds.) EUROCRYPT 2004. LNCS, vol. 3027, pp. 20–39. Springer, Heidelberg (2004)

[35] Osvik, D.A., Tromer, E.: Cryptologic applications of the PlayStation 3: Cell SPEED, SPEED (2007). https://hyperelliptic.org/SPEED/slides/Osvik_cell-speed.pdf

[36] Pollard, J.M.: Kangaroos, Monopoly and discrete logarithms. Journal of Cryptology **13**, 437–447 (2000)

[37] Rivest, R.L.: The MD5 message-digest algorithm. RFC 1321 (1992). https://tools.ietf.org/html/rfc1321

[38] Shanks, D.: Class number, a theory of factorization, and genera. In: Proceedings of Symposia in Pure Mathematics, vol. 20, pp. 415–440. AMS (1971)

Author Index

Printed in the United States
By Bookmasters